AN EXEGETICAL SUMMARY OF
1 CORINTHIANS 10–16

AN EXEGETICAL SUMMARY OF
1 CORINTHIANS 10–16

Second Edition

Ronald L. Trail

SIL International

Second Edition
© 2001, 2008 by SIL International

Library of Congress Catalog Card Number: 2008923531
ISBN: 978-155671-205-0

Printed in the United States of America

All Rights Reserved
No part of this publication may be reproduced, stored in a retrieval system, or transmitted in any form or by any means without the express permission of SIL International. However, brief excerpts, generally understood to be within the limits of fair use, may be quoted without written permission.

Copies of this and other publications
of SIL International may be obtained from

International Academic Bookstore
SIL International
7500 West Camp Wisdom Road
Dallas, TX 75236-5699, USA

Voice: 972-708-7404
Fax: 972-708-7363
academic_books@sil.org
www.ethnologue.com

PREFACE

Exegesis is concerned with the interpretation of a text. Exegesis of the New Testament involves determining the meaning of the Greek text. Translators must be especially careful and thorough in their exegesis of the New Testament in order to accurately communicate its message in the vocabulary, grammar, and literary devices of another language. Questions occurring to translators as they study the Greek text are answered by summarizing how scholars have interpreted the text. This is information that should be considered by translators as they make their own exegetical decisions regarding the message they will communicate in their translations.

The Semi-Literal Translation

As a basis for discussion, a semi-literal translation of the Greek text is given so that the reasons for different interpretations can best be seen. When one Greek word is translated into English by several words, these words are joined by hyphens. There are a few times when clarity requires that a string of words joined by hyphens have a separate word, such as "not" (μή), inserted in their midst. In this case, the separate word is surrounded by spaces between the hyphens. When alternate translations of a Greek word are given, these are separated by slashes.

The Text

Variations in the Greek text are noted under the heading TEXT. The base text for the summary is the text of the fourth revised edition of *The Greek New Testament,* published by the United Bible Societies, which has the same text as the twenty-sixth edition of the *Novum Testamentum Graece* (Nestle-Aland). Dr. J. Harold Greenlee researched the variants and has written the notes for this part of the summary. The versions that follow different variations are listed without evaluating their choices.

The Lexicon

The meaning of a key word in context is the first question to be answered. Words marked with a raised letter in the semi-literal translation are treated separately under the heading LEXICON. First, the lexicon form of the Greek word is given. Within the parentheses following the Greek word is the location number where, in the author's judgment, this word is defined in the *Greek-English Lexicon of the New Testament Based on Semantic Domains* (Louw and Nida 1988). When a semantic domain includes a translation of the particular verse being treated, **LN** in bold type indicates that specific translation. If the specific reference for the verse is listed in *A Greek-English Lexicon of the New Testament and Other Early Christian Literature* (Bauer, Arndt, Gingrich, and Danker 1979), the outline location and page number is given. Then English equivalents of the Greek word are given to show how it is translated by commentators who offer their own translations of the whole text and, after a semicolon, all the versions in the list of abbreviations for translations. When reference is made to "all versions," it refers to only the versions in the list of translations. Sometimes further comments are made about the meaning of the word or the significance of a verb's tense, voice, or mood.

The Questions

Under the heading QUESTION, a question is asked that comes from examining the Greek text under consideration. Typical questions concern the identity of an implied actor or object of an event word, the antecedent of a pronominal reference, the connection indicated by a relational word, the meaning of a genitive construction, the meaning of figurative language, the function of a rhetorical question, the identification of an ambiguity, and the presence of implied information that is needed to understand the passage correctly. Background information is also considered for a proper understanding of a passage. Although not all implied information and background information is made explicit in a translation, it is important to consider it so that the translation will not be stated in such a way that prevents a reader from arriving at the proper interpretation. The question is answered with a summary of what commentators have said. If there are contrasting differences of opinion, the different interpretations are numbered and the commentaries that support each are listed. Differences that are not treated by many of the commentaries often are not numbered, but are introduced with a contrastive 'Or' at the beginning of the sentence. No attempt has been made to select which interpretation is best.

In listing support for various statements of interpretation, the author is often faced with the difficult task of matching the different terminologies used in commentaries with the terminology he has adopted. Sometimes he can only infer the position of a commentary from incidental remarks. This book, then, includes the author's interpretation of the views taken in the various commentaries. General statements are followed by specific statements, which indicate the author's understanding of the pertinent relationships, actors, events, and objects implied by that interpretation.

The Use of This Book

This book does not replace the commentaries that it summarizes. Commentaries contain much more information about the meaning of words and passages. They often contain arguments for the interpretations that are taken and they may have important discussions about the discourse features of the text. In addition, they have information about the historical, geographical, and cultural setting. Translators will want to refer to at least four commentaries as they exegete a passage. However, since no one commentary contains all the answers translators need, this book will be a valuable supplement. It makes more sources of exegetical help available than most translators have access to. Even if they had all the books available, few would have the time to search through all of them for the answers.

When many commentaries are studied, it soon becomes apparent that they frequently disagree in their interpretations. That is the reason why so many answers in this book are divided into two or more interpretations. The reader's initial reaction may be that all of these different interpretations complicate exegesis rather than help it. However, before translating a passage, a translator needs to know exactly where there is a problem of interpretation and what the exegetical options are.

Acknowledgments

This summary was a team effort. First of all, much of the initial research was already done by Richard Blight who prepared the original *Exegetical Helps on 1 Corinthians* up to 14:25. It was from this version that the present volume was prepared. Then Dr. Harold Greenlee prepared all the Louw and Nida and Arndt and Gingrich lexicon readings and completed the renderings from the 12 versions that Daniel Hallberg had begun. My wife, Gail, proofread and checked formatting, consistency, and other details. Finally Richard Blight edited the final copy for its content and its presentation prior to publication. The author would like to express his sincere thanks to each one of these.

ABBREVIATIONS
COMMENTARIES AND REFERENCE BOOKS

AB   Orr, William F., and James Arthur Walther. *1 Corinthians.* The Anchor Bible, edited by W. F. Albright and D. N. Freedman. Garden City, N.Y.: Doubleday, 1976.

Alf   Alford, Henry. *The Greek Testament.* Vol. 2. 1865. Revised by Everett F. Harrison. Chicago: Moody, 1968.

BAGD   Bauer, Walter. *A Greek-English Lexicon of the New Testament and Other Early Christian Literature.* Translated and adapted from the 5th ed., 1958 by William F. Arndt and F. Wilbur Gingrich. 2d English ed. revised and augmented by F. Wilbur Gingrich and Frederick W. Danker. Chicago: University of Chicago Press, 1979.

Ed   Edwards, Thomas Charles. *A Commentary on the First Epistle to the Corinthians.* 1885. Reprint. Minneapolis: Klock and Klock, 1979.

EGT   Findlay, G. G. St. *Paul's First Epistle to the Corinthians.* In the Expositor's Greek Testament, edited by W. Robertson Nicoll. Vol. 2. 1900. Reprint. Grand Rapids: Eerdmans, 1970.

Gdt   Godet, F. L. *The First Epistle to the Corinthians.* Translated by A. Cusin. 1886. Reprint. Grand Rapids: Zondervan, 1971.

Herm   Conzelmann, Hans. *1 Corinthians.* Hermeneia—A Critical and Historical Commentary on the Bible. 1969. Translated by James W. Leitch. Philadelphia: Fortress Press, 1975.

HNTC   Barrett, C. K. *A Commentary on the First Epistle to the Corinthians.* Harper's New Testament Commentaries, edited by Henry Chadwick. New York: Harper & Row, 1968.

Ho   Hodge, Charles. *An Exposition of the First Epistle to the Corinthians.* Thornapple Commentaries. 1857. Reprint. Grand Rapids: Baker, 1980.

ICC   Robertson, Archibald, and Alford Plummer. *A Critical and Exegetical Commentary on the First Epistle of St Paul to the Corinthians.* 2d ed. The International Critical Commentary, ed. S. R. Driver, A. Plummer, and C. A. Briggs. 1914. Reprint. Edinburgh: T. & T. Clark, 1971.

LN   Louw, Johannes P., and Eugene A. Nida. *Greek-English Lexicon of the New Testament Based on Semantic Domains.* New York: United Bible Societies, 1988.

Lns   Lenski, R. C. H. *The Interpretation of St. Paul's First and Second Epistles to the Corinthians.* Minneapolis: Augsburg, 1963.

MNTC   MacArthur, John. *1 Corinthians.* MacArthur New Testament Commentary. Chicago: Moody, 1984.

My	Meyer, Heinrich August Wilhelm. *Critical and Exegetical Handbook to the Epistles to the Corinthians*. Translated from the 5th ed. by D. Douglas Bannerman. Edited by William P. Dickson. Meyer's Commentary on the New Testament. New York: Funk & Wagnalls, 1890.
NCBC	Bruce, F. F. *1 and 2 Corinthians*. New Century Bible Commentary, edited by M. Black. Grand Rapids: Eerdmans, 1971.
NIC	Grosheide, F. W. *Commentary on the First Epistle to the Corinthians*. The New International Commentary on the New Testament, edited by F. F. Bruce. Grand Rapids: Eerdmans, 1953.
NIC2	Fee, Gordon D. *The First Epistle to the Corinthians*. The New International Commentary on the New Testament, edited by F. F. Bruce. Grand Rapids: Eerdmans, 1987.
NIGTC	Thiselton, Anthony C. *The First Epistle to the Corinthians*. The New International Greek Testament Commentary. Grand Rapids: Eerdmans, 2000.
NTC	Kistemaker, Simon J. *Exposition of the First Epistle to the Corinthians*. New Testament Commentary. Grand Rapids: Baker, 1986.
Rb	Robertson, Archibald Thomas. *The Epistles of Paul*. Word Pictures in the New Testament. Vol. 4. Nashville, Tenn.: Broadman, 1931.
TG	Bratcher, Robert G. *A Translator's Guide to Paul's First Letter to the Corinthians*. Helps for Translators. London: United Bible Societies, 1982.
TH	Ellingworth, Paul, and Howard A. Hatton. *A Handbook on Paul's First Letter to the Corinthians*. 2nd ed. New York: United Bible Societies, 1994.
TNTC	Morris, Leon. *The First Epistle of Paul to the Corinthians*. 2d ed. The Tyndale New Testament Commentaries. Grand Rapids: Eerdmans, 1985.
Vn	Vine, W. E. *1 Corinthians*. N.d. Reprint. Grand Rapids: Zondervan, 1951.

GREEK TEXT AND TRANSLATIONS

GNT	The Greek New Testament. Edited by B. Aland, K Aland, J. Karavidopoulos, C. Martini, and B. Metzger. 4th ed. London, New York: United Bible Societies, 1993.
CEV	The Holy Bible, Contemporary English Version. New York: American Bible Society, 1995.
ISV	The Holy Bible, New Testament, International Standard Version. Yorba Linda, Calif.: Davidson Press, 1998.
KJV	The Holy Bible. Authorized (or King James) Version. 1611.
NAB	The New American Bible. Camden, New Jersey: Thomas Nelson, 1971.

NET	The Net Bible, New English Translation, New Testament, Version 9.206. WWW.NETBIBLE.COM: Biblical Studies Press, 1999
NIV	The Holy Bible, New International Version. Grand Rapids: Zondervan, 1984.
NJB	The New Jerusalem Bible. Garden City, New York: Doubleday, 1985.
NLT	The Holy Bible, New Living Translation. Wheaton, Ill.: Tyndale House Publishers, 1996.
NRSV	The Holy Bible: New Revised Standard Version. New York: Oxford University Press, 1989.
REB	The Revised English Bible. Oxford: Oxford University Press and Cambridge University Press, 1989.
TEV	Good News Bible, Today's English Version. 2d ed. New York: American Bible Society, 1992.
TNT	The Translator's New Testament. London: British and Foreign Bible Society, 1973.

GRAMMATICAL TERMS

act.	active
fut.	future
impera.	imperative
indic.	indicative
infin.	infinitive
mid.	middle
opt.	optative
pass.	passive
perf.	perfect
pres.	present
subj.	subjunctive\

EXEGETICAL SUMMARY OF 1 CORINTHIANS

DISCOURSE UNIT: 10:1–11:1 [ICC, My, NCBC, NIGTC, NTC, TG; NLT, TEV]. The topic is idolatry [TG], warnings and freedom [NTC], warnings against idolatry [NLT, TEV], principles concerning food offered to idols applied [ICC], third part of response to questions about meat [NIGTC].

DISCOURSE UNIT: 10:1–13 [NIGTC; NET]. The topic is learning from Israel's failures [NET], warning about craving and idolatry [NIGTC].

10:1 For[a] not I-wish you to-be-ignorant,[b] brothers,[c]

LEXICON—a. γάρ (LN 89.23) (BAGD p. 151): 'for' [Herm, Lns, NIGTC, NTC; ISV, NASB, NET, NIV], not explicit [all other versions except KJV], 'moreover' [KJV (which translates the alternative reading δέ)].
  b. pres. act. infin. of ἀγνοέω (LN 28.13, 32.7) (BAGD 1. p. 11): 'to be ignorant' [AB, HNTC, LN (28.13), Lns, NTC; ISV, KJV, NIV], 'to have (someone) ignorant' [Herm], 'to be unaware' [LN (28.13); NET, NRSV], 'to forget' [NLT], 'to not know' [LN (28.13)], 'not to understand, to fail to understand' [LN (32.7)] 'to fail to recognize' [NIGTC]. The phrase οὐ θέλω ὑμᾶς ἀγνοεῖν 'I do not wish you to be ignorant' is translated 'I want you to know' [BAGD], 'I want you to understand' [TNT], 'I want you to be quite certain' [NJB], 'I want you to remember' [NAB, TEV], 'I want to remind you' [CEV], 'let me remind you' [REB].
  c. ἀδελφός (LN 10.49, 11.23) (BAGD p. 16): 'brother' [AB, Herm, HNTC, LN (10.49), Lns, NTC; ISV, KJV, NAB, NIV, NJB, TNT], 'friend' [CEV, REB, TEV], 'Christian brother' [LN (11.23)], 'fellow believer' [LN (11.23), TG, TH], 'fellow Christian' [TG, TH], 'dear fellow Christians' [NIGTC]. The plural of this word is translated 'brothers and sisters' [TG; NET, NRSV], 'dear brothers and sisters' [NLT].

QUESTION—What relationship is indicated by γάρ 'for'?
  It indicates the reason for Paul's self-discipline and his fear of being disqualified [Alf, Ed, EGT, Gdt, Ho, ICC, Lns, My, NIC, NIC2, Rb, TNTC]: I discipline myself in order that I not be disqualified *because* the ancient Israelis did not discipline themselves and God punished them. What happened to the Israelites shows that there is a real danger of being disqualified (9:27) [TNTC].

QUESTION—What is the significance of the double negative in the clause οὐ θέλω ὑμᾶς ἀγνοεῖν '*not* want you to *be ignorant*'?
  It is a literary device that indicates a positive meaning, 'I want you to know' [BAGD, Lns; CEV, NAB, NJB, REB, TEV, TNT]. It functions to introduce something important [AB, Lns, NIC2, TH, TNTC]: I want you to know this important information.

QUESTION—Did Paul want them to know new information or to remind them of what they already knew?
1. He wanted to remind them of what they already knew [AB, Gdt, HNTC, MNTC, TG, TH; CEV, NAB, NLT, REB, TEV].
2. He was introducing new information [Ed, EGT, TNTC].

that our fathers[a] were all under[b] the cloud
LEXICON—a. πατήρ (LN 10.20) (BAGD 2.e. p. 635): 'father' [BAGD, HNTC, Lns, NTC; KJV, NAB, NET, TNT], 'forefather' [AB, LN; NIV], 'ancestor' [Herm, ICC, LN; CEV, ISV, NJB, NLT, NRSV, REB, TEV], 'spiritual ancestor' [NIGTC], 'the great religious heroes of the OT' [BAGD]. The phrase 'that our fathers' is translated 'what happened to our fathers' [TNT], 'what happened to our ancestors in the wilderness long ago' [NLT].
b. ὑπό with accusative object (LN 83.51) (BAGD 2.a.β. p. 843): 'under' [AB, BAGD, Herm, HNTC, LN, Lns, NIGTC, NTC; CEV, ISV, KJV, NAB, NET, NIV, NRSV, REB], 'under the protection of' [TEV]. The phrase ὑπὸ τὴν νεφέλην ἦσαν 'were under the cloud' is translated 'were...protected by the cloud' [ICC], 'they were all...guided by the cloud' [TNT], 'had the cloud over them' [NJB], 'God guided them by sending a cloud that moved along ahead of them' [NLT].

QUESTION—To whom does ἡμῶν 'our' refer?
1. It refers to all Christians, both Jews and Gentiles [AB, Alf, BAGD, Ed, EGT, Gdt, Herm, HNTC, ICC, Lns, MNTC, NIC, NIC2, NTC, TG, TH, TNTC]: the fathers of us believers, both Jews and Gentiles. Gentiles are included on the basis that they are considered to be spiritual descendants of Israel [AB, Alf, EGT, Gdt, HNTC, ICC, MNTC, NIC, NIC2, TG, TNTC]. The church at Corinth was largely made up of Gentiles [HNTC, NIC, NIC2, NTC, TNTC]
2. It refers only to Jews, excluding Gentile believers [Ho, My]: the fathers of us Jews.

QUESTION—What is the significance of the five repetitions of the word πάντες 'all' in 10:1–4?
It serves to emphasize the correlation between the all inclusive number of those that participated in these events and the large percent of those that failed to benefit by having done so [Alf, EGT, Gdt, ICC, TNTC]. It serves to emphasize the greatness of their failure to gain God's pleasure [NIC2].

QUESTION—To what is Paul comparing the cloud, sea, food, and drink?
He is comparing them to Christian baptism and communion [AB, Alf, Gdt, Ho, Lns, NIC2, TNTC]. Paul is suggesting baptism and communion because the Corinthians were thinking that participation in these guaranteed their favorable acceptance by God [HNTC, NIC, NIC2].

QUESTION—In what sense were the fathers ὑπὸ τήν νεφέλην 'under the cloud'?
1. They were under the cloud in the sense that the cloud was physically above them [Ho, My, Rb, TG, TNTC; TNT]: the cloud was over their heads. The cloud above them was their means of guidance [Ho, TG, TNTC; TNT].
2. They were under the cloud in the sense that they were under the protection of the cloud [Alf, Lns, TG, TH; TEV]: the cloud protected them.
3. They were under the cloud in both of these senses [EGT, Gdt, ICC]: the cloud was over their heads and protected them.

and all went-through^a through the sea
LEXICON—a. διέρχομαι (LN 15.31) (BAGD 1.b.α. p. 194): 'to go through' [BAGD], 'to cross over, to go over' [LN]. The phrase διά…διῆλθον 'through…went-through' is translated 'to pass safely through' [ICC; TEV], 'to go safely through' [TNT], 'to go through' [Lns; CEV, ISV], 'to pass through' [AB, Herm, HNTC, NIGTC, NTC; KJV, NAB, NET, NIV, NJB, NRSV, REB]. This entire clause is translated 'he brought them all safely through the waters of the sea on dry ground' [NLT].
QUESTION—To which sea does the word θάλασσα refer?
It refers to the Red Sea [BAGD, Lns, NTC; REB, TEV, TNT].

10:2 and all were-baptized^a into^b Moses in^c the cloud and in^c the sea
LEXICON—a. aorist pass. indic. of βαπτίζω (LN 53.41) (BAGD 3.a. p. 132): 'to be baptized' [Herm, Lns, NTC; all versions except CEV, REB], 'to receive baptism' [REB], 'to undergo baptism' [AB], 'to accept baptism' [HNTC], 'to have oneself baptized' [NIGTC], 'to be dipped (in figurative sense, typologically of Israel's passage through the Red Sea)' [BAGD]. The entire clause is translated 'this was like being baptized and becoming followers of Moses' [CEV], 'and all pledged themselves to trust in Moses by virtue of their trustful following of the cloud and their trustful march in the sea' [ICC]. Βαπτίζω means to employ water in a religious ceremony designed to symbolize purification and initiation on the basis of repentance. It also indicates initiation into a religious community [LN].
b. εἰς with accusative object (LN 84.22): 'into' [AB, Herm, HNTC, LN, NIGTC, NTC; ISV, NAB, NET, NIV, NJB, NRSV], 'into the fellowship of' [REB, TNT], 'as followers of' [TEV], 'unto' [KJV], 'to' [Lns], not explicit [ICC; CEV, NLT].
c. ἐν with dative object (LN 83.13): 'in' [AB, Herm, HNTC, ICC, LN, Lns, NIGTC, NTC; all versions except CEV, NAB], 'by' [NAB], 'following of (the cloud)…(march) in (the sea)' [ICC], not explicit [CEV].
QUESTION—What is meant by baptism *into* a person?
1. It means becoming a follower or disciple of that person [Ho, MNTC, My, NCBC, NIC, TNTC; CEV, NLT, TEV]: they all became followers of Moses.

2. It means becoming united with that person [Gdt, ICC, Lns, TG, TH]: they all became united with Moses. It means that they became his people [Gdt]. They were united with Moses as they experienced the exodus with him [TH]. Union also signifies fellowship with [TG, TH; REB, TNT].
3. It means being delivered by that person [NIC2, NTC]: they all were delivered by Moses.

QUESTION—In what sense did being in the cloud and in the sea constitute baptism?

The cloud was above them and the waters were on either side putting them in the midst of water as in baptism [My, Rb, Vn]. Both the cloud and the sea separated the Israelites from the Egyptians just as baptism separates Christians from the world [Lns].

QUESTION—What relationship is indicated by ἐν 'in'?
1. It indicates a local relationship [ICC, My, NIC2; all versions except NAB]: they were baptized in the cloud and the sea.
2. It indicates an instrumental relationship [Gdt; NAB]: they were baptized by the cloud and the sea.

10:3 and all ate the same spiritual[a] food[b]

LEXICON—a. πνευματικός (LN 26.10, 79.3, 79.6) (BAGD 2.a.β. p. 679): 'spiritual' [AB, BAGD, Herm, HNTC, LN (26.10, 79.3, 79.6), Lns, NIGTC, NTC; all versions except NLT, REB, TNT], 'supernatural' [ICC, LN (79.6); REB, TNT], 'not physical, not material' [LN (79.3)], 'miraculous' [NLT]. Πνευματικός refers to a quality that belongs to the supernatural realm [BAGD].

b. βρῶμα (LN 5.1, 5.7) (BAGD 1. p. 148): 'food' [AB, BAGD, Herm, HNTC, ICC, LN (5.1), Lns, NIGTC, NTC; all versions except KJV, TEV], 'solid food, flesh' [LN (5.7)], 'bread' [TEV], 'meat' [LN (5.7); KJV].

QUESTION—What is the significance of τὸ αὐτὸ 'the same'?

It signifies that the fathers ate the same food and drank the same drink as each other [Gdt, Ho, Lns, NIC2, TH].

QUESTION—What is the significance of πνευματικός 'spiritual'?

It signifies that the food and drink were miraculously or supernaturally produced [Gdt, Ho, ICC, MNTC, NIC, NTC, TG, TH, TNTC; NLT, REB, TNT]. 'Spiritual' implies something given or provided by the Spirit [Ho]. It signifies that the ultimate source was God [BAGD, LN]. It means something that has importance as a type [AB, HNTC]. It signifies a quality that conveys spiritual sustenance to those who consumed it [EGT, HNTC, ICC, Lns].

QUESTION—To what does βπῶμα 'food' refer?

It refers to the manna which the Israelites ate in the desert [AB, Alf, EGT, HNTC, Ho, Lns, MNTC, My, NIC, NTC, Rb, TG, TNTC, Vn].

10:4 and all drank the same spiritual[a] drink;[b]

LEXICON—a. πνευματικός (LN 79.6): 'spiritual' [AB, BAGD, Herm, HNTC, **LN,** Lns, NIGTC, NTC; all versions except NLT, REB, TNT],

'supernatural' [ICC, LN; REB, TNT], 'miraculous' [NLT]. The meaning of 'spiritual' can also be expressed as 'which comes from God, provided by God' [LN]. See this word also at 10:3.
  b. πόμα (LN 5.6) (BAGD 2. p. 690): 'drink' [AB, BAGD, Herm, HNTC, ICC, LN, Lns, NIGTC, NTC; all versions except NLT], 'water' [NLT].
QUESTION—To what specific incidents does this refer?
  It refers to the two times that the Israelites drank water from the rock: once at Rephidim (Exodus 17:6), and once at Kadesh (Numbers 20:11) [TG].

for they-were-drinking from[a] the spiritual following[b] rock,
LEXICON—a. ἐκ with genitive object (LN 90.16) (BAGD 1.a. p. 234): 'from' [AB, BAGD, Herm, HNTC, ICC, LN, NIGTC, NTC; all versions except CEV, KJV], 'out of' [Lns], 'of' [KJV], 'which flowed from' [CEV].
  b. pres. act. participle of ἀκολουθέω (LN 15.144) (BAGD 1. p. 31): 'to follow' [AB, BAGD, Herm, LN, NTC; CEV, KJV, NAB, NET, NJB, NRSV, TNT], 'to accompany' [HNTC, Lns, My; NIV], 'to accompany (their) travels' [REB], 'to go with' [NIGTC; ISV, TEV], 'to travel with' [NLT], 'to come after' [BAGD], 'to come behind, to go behind' [LN], 'to attend' [ICC].
QUESTION—What relationship is indicated by γάρ 'for'.
  It indicates the grounds for making the previous statement [EGT, Lns, NIC2]: they all drank the same spiritual drink *because* they were drinking from the spiritual rock that followed them. Paul was giving the reason for saying that they drank a spiritual drink—they had a spiritual provider [EGT, Lns]. It has no special significance here and may be omitted [TH].
QUESTION—What is the significance of the imperfect tense ἔπινον 'they were drinking'?
  It signifies an action that was taking place in the past over a period of time [Gdt, ICC, NIC2, Rb, Vn].
QUESTION—What is the significance of πνευματικός 'spiritual'?
  It signifies the nature of the rock, that it was supernatural [Ho].
QUESTION—In what sense was the rock following the Israelites?
  It was following in the sense that Christ accompanied the Israelites through the desert [Alf, EGT, Gdt, HNTC, Ho, ICC, Lns, MNTC, NIC, NIC2, NTC]. This is to be taken figuratively since 'spiritual' does not describe the material rock in Exodus 17 but the spiritual rock, Christ, who followed them everywhere and was the source of all their blessings which are described in terms of water flowing from the rock [NIC]. Christ, the spiritual rock, provided the water that came out of the two natural rocks and also the water they drank all through the journey [Lns]. Christ was a fountain of living water to them, he was their support during their journey through the wilderness [Ho].

and the rock was Christ.
QUESTION—In what sense was the rock Christ?
> The rock was Christ in a figurative sense [Ho, ICC]. It means that Christ was the source of spiritual water [Ho, ICC, NIC, NIC2]. Paul transfers to Christ the title of Rock that is used of Yahweh in the OT [Alf, TNTC].

QUESTION—What is the significance of this clause?
> It emphasizes who the rock was [TH; TEV, TNT]: the rock was Christ himself.

DISCOURSE UNIT: 10:5–10 [AB, MNTC]. The topic is their idolatry in the desert [AB], the abuse of liberty [MNTC].

10:5 But^a God (was) not pleased^b with^c the most^d of-them,

LEXICON—a. ἀλλά (LN 89.125) (BAGD p. 38): 'but' [Herm, LN (89.125), Lns; CEV, ISV, KJV, NET], 'yet' [AB, LN (91.2); REB, TNT], 'yet after all this' (NLT), 'yet we know' [NAB], 'yet in spite of these amazing advantages' [ICC], 'in spite of this' (NJB), 'but even then' (TEV), 'nevertheless' (HNTC, NIGTC; NIV, NRSV), 'however' (NTC), 'on the contrary, instead' [LN (89.125)], 'even after all this' [TH]. Ἀλλά is an emphatic negative [EGT, ICC, NIC2, TG, TH, TNTC; NLT, TEV].

  b. aorist act. indic. of εὐδοκέω (LN 25.87) (BAGD 2.a. p. 319): 'to be pleased' [AB, HNTC, LN, NTC; ISV, NAB, NET, NIV, NJB, NLT, NRSV, TEV], 'to be well-pleased' [BAGD, Herm, Lns; KJV]. This expression is also translated '(the vast majority of them) frustrated (the good purpose of God)' (ICC), '(most of them) did not please (God)' [CEV], '(most of them) were not accepted by (God)' [REB], '(most of them) incurred (God's) displeasure' [TNT], '(on the far greater part of their number God) visited his displeasure' [NIGTC].

  c. ἐν with dative object (LN 89.5): 'with' [AB, Herm, HNTC, Lns, NTC; all versions except CEV, REB, TNT], 'in, with regard to, in the case of, about' [LN], not explicit [ICC, NIGTC; CEV, REB, TNT].

  d. πλείων (LN 59.1) (BAGD II.2.a.α. p. 689): 'most' [AB, BAGD, Herm, Lns, NTC; all versions except KJV], 'a great deal of, a great number of' [LN], 'the majority' [BAGD, HNTC], 'the vast majority' [ICC], 'many' [LN; KJV]. The phrase οὐκ ἐν τοῖς πλείοσιν αὐτῶν 'not in the most of them' is translated 'the far greater part of their number' [NIGTC], 'with only a few of them' [BAGD].

QUESTION—What relationship is indicated by ἀλλά 'but'?
> It contrasts this verse with 1b-4 [TH]: in spite of all that God did for them, *yet* he was angry with them to the extent that they were struck down. It contrasts this verse with the positives that have just been stated [EGT].

QUESTION—What is the significance of πλείοσιν αὐτῶν 'most of them'?
> It is an understatement since all but two, Caleb and Joshua, died [EGT, ICC, Lns, TNTC].

1 CORINTHIANS 10:5

QUESTION—What is the significance of the phrase 'God was not pleased'?
It is a litotes and emphatically affirms that God was angry with them by denying its opposite [Lns, My, TH; TNT]: God was angry with them.

for they-were-struck-down[a] in[b] the wilderness.[c]
LEXICON—a. aorist pass. indic. of καταστρώννυμι (LN **20.63**) (BAGD 1. p. 419): 'to be struck down' [Lns; ISV, NAB, NRSV], 'to be cut down' [NET], 'to be laid low' [AB, BAGD, Herm, HNTC], 'to be overthrown' [ICC; KJV], 'to be scattered' [NIC2, NTC; NIV, NJB], 'to be killed' [BAGD, **LN**], '(figurative…meaning of 'to spread out') to be strewn' [LN]. This passive verb is also translated actively: 'he destroyed them' [NLT], 'they died' [CEV]. This entire clause is translated 'for the wilderness was strewn with their corpses' [REB], 'and so their dead bodies were scattered over the desert' [TEV], 'for their corpses were strewn over the wilderness' [NIGTC], 'for the desert was littered with their dead bodies' [TNT].
   b. ἐν with dative object (LN 83.13): 'in' [AB, Herm, HNTC, ICC, LN, Lns; ISV, KJV, NAB, NET, NLT, NRSV], 'over' [NIGTC, NTC; NIV, NJB, TEV], 'all over' [CEV], not explicit [REB, TNT].
   c. ἔρημος (LN 1.86)(BAGD 2. p. 309): 'wilderness' [BAGD, Herm, ICC, LN, Lns, NIGTC; ISV, KJV, NLT, NRSV, REB], 'desert' [AB, BAGD, HNTC, LN, NTC; CEV, NAB, NET, NIV, NJB, TEV, TNT], 'lonely place' [LN].
QUESTION—What relationship is indicated by γάρ 'for'?
It indicates the grounds for saying that God was not pleased [EGT, HNTC, Ho, ICC, Lns, NIC2, TH]: it is true that God was not pleased *since* they were all overthrown in the desert. It also indicates the result of God's displeasure [TH].
QUESTION—Who is the actor of κατεστρώθησαν 'they were killed'?
God is the actor [ICC, Lns, TH; NLT]: God struck them down. Their deaths were not natural but were the result of the judgment of God [ICC, TNTC].

DISCOURSE UNIT: 10:6–14 [EGT]. The topic is the moral contagion of idolatry.

10:6 Now these-things became examples[a] for-us,
LEXICON—a. τύπος (LN **58.59**) (BAGD 6. p. 830): 'example' [AB, Herm, HNTC, **LN**, Lns, NTC; ISV, KJV, NAB, NET, NIV, NJB, NRSV, TEV, TNT], 'model' [LN], 'formative model' [NIGTC], 'type' [BAGD], 'warning' [CEV, NLT, REB], 'examples which we possess for our guidance' [ICC].
QUESTION—What relationship is indicated by δέ 'now'?
It indicates a transition [Alf, NTC, TH]. It indicates a transition from the events to their application [Alf]. It indicates a move to a new point but is related to what has preceded [TH]. It serves to introduce a summary that relates to the preceding [NTC].

QUESTION—To what does ταῦτα 'these things' refer?
It refers to the events that happened in the times of the fathers, not in the time of the Corinthians [NIC, NIC2, TH; CEV]: what happened long ago are examples to us. It refers to the events mentioned in the preceding verse [ICC, NIC] and could also be taken for the whole history of Israel [Ho, NIC]. It refers specifically to God's rejection after such blessings [Gdt].

QUESTION—To whom does ἡμῶν 'for us' refer?
It includes Paul and refers to Christians in general [Alf, HNTC, NTC, TG].

So-that[a] we might not be ones-who-greatly-desire[b] evil-things,

LEXICON—a. εἰς with accusative object (LN 89.57): 'so that' [AB, NTC; ISV, NET, NLT, NRSV], 'in order that' [Herm], 'to the intent' [KJV], 'to the intent that' [Lns], 'for the purpose of, in order to' [LN], 'with a view to' [NIGTC], 'to (warn us)' [HNTC, ICC; TEV], 'to (keep us)' [CEV, NAB, NIV, TNT], not explicit [REB]. This is God's purpose [Alf].

b. ἐπιθυμητής (LN **25.13**) (BAGD p. 293): 'one who greatly desires' [LN], 'one who desires (also in a bad sense 'desirous of evil')' [BAGD], 'men lusting (after)' [HNTC], 'persons lusting' [Lns]. This noun is derived from the verb ἐπιθυμέω 'to desire very much' [LN] and is more frequently translated as a verb: 'to desire' [**LN**; NRSV, TEV, TNT], 'to be desirous' [AB], 'to set (one's) heart on' [ISV, NIV, NJB], 'to set (one's) desires on' [REB], 'to have a craving for' [Herm], 'to crave' [TH; NET, NLT], 'to want' [CEV], 'to lust' [NIC2], 'to lust after' [KJV, ICC], 'to long for' [NTC]. The clause εἰς τὸ μὴ εἶναι ἡμᾶς ἐπιθυμητάς 'in order that we might not be ones who greatly desire' is translated 'to keep us from wicked desires' [NAB], 'with a view to our not craving for evil things' [NIGTC].

QUESTION—What is meant by κακῶν 'evil things'?
Paul leaves this general [TG]. The aorist tense in the following clause indicates the lustful conduct of the Israelites [Lns]. It includes all of the sins listed in the following verses [Alf, Gdt, HNTC], especially idolatry and fornication [ICC].

just-as[a] those-people-also greatly-desired.[b]

LEXICON—a. καθώς (LN 64.14) (BAGD 1. p. 391): 'just as' [BAGD, ICC, LN, NTC], 'the same way as' [LN], 'as' [BAGD, Herm, HNTC; ISV, KJV, NET, NIV, NJB, NLT, NRSV, REB, TEV, TNT], 'even as' [AB, Lns, NIGTC], 'such as' [NAB]. This word is also translated as an adjective: 'the same (evil things)' [CEV].

b. aorist act. indic. of ἐπιθυμέω (LN 25.12) (BAGD p. 293): 'to desire very much' [LN], 'to desire' [AB, BAGD], 'to long for' [BAGD, LN], 'to lust' [Lns; KJV], 'to crave' [Herm, NIGTC], not explicit [CEV]. This clause is translated 'as they did' [ICC, NTC; ISV, NET, NIV, NJB, NLT, NRSV, REB, TNT], 'as some of them did' [TEV], 'such as theirs' [NAB], 'as they were' [HNTC]. This is the verb form of the noun ἐπιθυμητής 'one who greatly desires' in the previous clause [LN].

QUESTION—What is the significance of the placement of κακεῖνοι 'those people also' before the verb?

It serves to emphasize 'those people' [TH]: as those people themselves also greatly desired.

10:7 And-(do)-not[a] become idolaters,[b] just-as some of-them,

LEXICON—a. μηδέ (LN 69.7): 'do not' [AB, Herm, NIGTC, NTC; CEV, NAB, NIV, NRSV, REB, TNT], 'and not' [LN], 'nor' [LN; NJB, TEV], 'or' [NLT], 'neither' [LN, Lns; KJV], 'stop (being idolaters)' [ISV], 'and so (you) must not' [ICC], 'so do not' [NET], 'again do not' [HNTC].

b. εἰδωλολάτρης (LN **53.64**) (BAGD p.221): 'idolater' [AB, Herm, HNTC, LN, Lns, NTC; ISV, KJV, NAB, NET, NIV, NRSV, REB, TNT], 'worshiper of idols' [**LN**]. The phrase εἰδωλολάτραι γίνεσθε 'become idol-worshipers' is translated 'take part in idol-worship' [BAGD, NIGTC], 'worship idols' [CEV, NLT, TEV], 'worship false gods' [NJB], 'to fall into idolatry' [ICC].

QUESTION—What is the significance of μηδέ 'and not'?

1. It serves to introduce a series of specific prohibitions of which κακῶν 'evil things' of 10:6 is the generic [Alf, Gdt, Lns].
2. The word δέ, of μηδέ is logical and indicates a conclusion [ICC; NET]: so, do not...

QUESTION—What is the significance of the present tense in εἰδωλολάτραι γίνεσθε 'become idolaters'?

It signifies that one should stop doing something already in progress [Rb; ISV]: Stop being idolaters!

as it-is-written, "The people sat-down to-eat and to-drink and rose-up to-play."[a]

LEXICON—a. pres. act. infin. of παίζω (LN **50.8**) (BAGD p. 604): 'to play' [BAGD, Herm, **LN**, Lns, NTC; ISV, KJV, NET, NRSV], 'to play around' [AB], 'to take (one's) pleasure' [NAB], 'to amuse (oneself)' [BAGD; NJB], 'to dance' [BAGD; TNT], 'to dance around' [CEV], 'to revel' [REB], 'to indulge in pagan revelry' [NIV], 'to sport' [ICC]. This verb is also translated as a noun: 'for sport' [HNTC]. The phrase ἀνέστησαν παίζειν 'rose up to play' is translated 'they indulged themselves in pagan revelry' [NLT], 'rose up to virtual orgy' [NIGTC]. The quotation is translated 'the people sat down to a feast which turned into an orgy of drinking and sex' [TEV]. This word probably refers here specifically to 'dancing' [EGT, Gdt, Herm, Ho, ICC, LN, Lns, TH]. It includes singing and dancing [EGT]. It carries the connotation of 'sexual play' [HNTC, MNTC, NIC2, NTC, TG].

QUESTION—What Scripture is being referred to?

The Scripture referred to is Exodus 32:6 [ICC, Lns, NIC2, NTC, TH].

QUESTION—To what 'people' does ὁ λαός 'the people' refer?

It refers to the Israelites [Lns].

QUESTION—Why does Paul join idolatry with eating and drinking?

He does this because it was about eating food offered to idols that the Corinthians were asking. Feasting before an idol was a precursor to idolatry, and if the Corinthians joined in the idol feasts they were in danger of being drawn into idolatry [ICC, NIC2].

10:8 Neither let-us-commit-sexual-immorality,[a] just-as some of-them committed-immorality

LEXICON—a. pres. act. subj. of πορνεύω (LN 88.271) (BAGD 1. p. 693): 'to commit sexual immorality' [AB, LN, NIGTC; NIV], 'to practice sexual immorality' [BAGD, Herm, NTC], 'to engage in sexual immorality' [NLT], 'to indulge in sexual immorality' [NRSV], 'to fall into sexual immorality' [NJB], 'to be guilty of sexual immorality' [TEV], 'to be immoral' [NET], 'to sin sexually' [ISV], 'to practice sexual vice' [TNT], 'to commit fornication' [HNTC, ICC, LN, Lns; KJV, REB], 'to indulge in lewdness' [NAB], 'to do shameful things' [CEV], 'to commit immorality, to engage in illicit sex, to commit prostitution' [LN].

QUESTION—Why does Paul use the first person plural in this warning?

It functions to soften the tone of the command [NIC].

QUESTION—What is the significance of the present tense in this warning?

It signifies that the action was already going on [Rb; ISV]: let us stop committing immorality.

and fell[a] in-one day twenty-three thousand.

LEXICON—a. aorist act. indic. of πίπτω (LN 15.118, **23.105**) (BAGD 1.b.α. p. 659): 'to fall' [AB, Herm, HNTC, LN (15.118), Lns, NIGTC; KJV, NRSV, TNT], 'to meet (one's) downfall' [NJB], 'to fall dead' [BAGD, NTC; ISV, TEV], 'to die' [ICC, **LN** (23.105); CEV, NET, NIV, NLT, REB], 'to perish' [NAB]. This is a euphemistic expression of a violent death [LN (23.105)].

QUESTION—What relationship is indicated by καί 'and'?

It indicates the result of committing immorality [HNTC, TH; NLT]: some committed sexual immorality *with the result that* twenty-three thousand fell in one day.

QUESTION—To what specific reference does this event refer?

It refers to Numbers 25:1–9 where twenty-four thousand died by plague [NIC2]. Both twenty-three thousand and twenty-four thousand are rounded numbers, the exact number being unimportant [Alf, Ed, Gdt, Ho, ICC]. Perhaps Paul is not including those killed by the judges (Num. 25:4) [TNTC].

10:9 Neither let-us-put-to-the-test[a] Christ,

TEXT—Instead of Χριστόν 'Christ' some manuscripts have κύριον 'Lord' and other manuscripts read θεόν 'God'. GNT selects the reading Χριστόν 'Christ' with a B decision, indicating that the text is almost certain. The reading Χριστόν 'Christ' is read by AB, Herm, Ho, NIC2, NIGTC, NTC,

TG; CEV, KJV, NET, NLT, NRSV. The reading Κύριον 'Lord' is read by HNTC, ICC, Lns; ISV, NAB, NIV, NJB, REB, TEV, TNT. The reading θεόν 'God' is read by no version.

LEXICON—a. pres. act. subj. of ἐκπειράζω (LN 27.31) (BAGD p. 243): 'to put to the test' [AB, BAGD, NIGTC; ISV, NET, NJB, NLT, NRSV, REB, TEV, TNT], 'to test' [CEV, NAB, NIV], 'to try' [BAGD, HNTC], 'to tempt' [BAGD, Herm, LN (88.308) Lns; KJV], 'to strain beyond all bounds one's forbearance' [ICC], 'to try to trap, to attempt to catch in a mistake' [LN].

QUESTION—What is meant by ἐκπειράζω 'to put to the test'?

It has the meaning of seeing how far one can go and get away with it without getting punished [Lns, TH, TNTC]. It signifies testing with the intention of the person failing the test [TNTC]. It signifies doing evil in order to discover what God's reaction will be [NIC]. It describes their murmuring against God (Num. 21:5) [Gdt, Herm, Lns, NIC, TG]. It is a refusal to accept God's directions [HNTC].

QUESTION—What is the significance of the present tense in this warning?

It signifies that the action was already going on [ISV]: let us stop putting Christ to the test.

just-as some of-them put-(him)-to-the-test[a]

LEXICON—a. aorist act. indic. of πειράζω (LN 27.31, 88.308) (BAGD 2.e. p. 640): 'to put to the test' [BAGD; NJB], 'to test' [AB, NIGTC, NTC], 'to tempt' [LN (88.308), Lns; KJV], 'to make trial of, to try' [BAGD], 'to try to trap' [LN (27.31)], 'to trap' [LN (88.308)]. All other versions render this verb with a form of 'to do' or 'to strain'.

QUESTION—What particular event is referred to here?

It refers to Numbers 21:5 when Israel murmured against God [Gdt, Herm, Lns, MNTC, NIC, NIC2, TG, TH].

QUESTION—How were the Corinthians similar to the Israelites in this connection?

The Israelites were discontent because they were denied the pleasures of Egypt. The Corinthians were discontent because they were denied the pleasures of eating in the idol feasts [Gdt, Lns].

QUESTION—Who is the direct object of ἐπείρασαν 'they put to the test'?

It refers to Christ [Ho, NIC2, NTC]: they put Christ to the test.

and were-being-destroyed[a] **by**[b] **the snakes.**

LEXICON—a. imperf. pass. indic. of ἀπόλλυμι (LN 20.31, 23.106) (BAGD 2.a.α. p. 95): 'to be destroyed' [Herm, HNTC, ICC, LN (20.31), NTC; ISV, KJV, NAB, NET, NRSV, REB, TNT], 'to be killed' [BAGD; NIV, NJB, TEV], 'to suffer the process of destruction' [NIGTC], 'to be bitten' [CEV], 'to be ruined' [LN (20.31)], 'to perish' [AB, LN (23.106), Lns], 'to die' [LN (23.106)], 'to die (from snakebite)' [NLT]. See this word also at 1:18.

b. ὑπό with genitive object (LN 90.1) (BAGD 1.b. p. 843): 'by' [BAGD, Herm, LN, NIGTC; all versions except KJV, NLT], 'of' [KJV], 'from' [NLT].

QUESTION—What relationship is indicated by καί 'and'?

It indicates the result of putting Christ to the test [HNTC, TH]: they put him to the test *with the result that* they were being destroyed by the snakes.

QUESTION—What is the significance of the imperfect tense, 'were being destroyed'?

It signifies that the judgment took place over a period of time, that is, they didn't all die at once [AB, ICC, Lns, NIC2, Rb]. The imperfect may refer to the fact that this judgment was stopped after some time [AB].

10:10 Neither grumble,[a] as[b] some of-them grumbled,

LEXICON—a. pres. act. impera. of γογγύζω (LN 33.382) (BAGD 1. p. 164): 'to grumble' [AB, BAGD, Herm, LN, NTC; CEV, NAB, NIV, NLT, REB, TNT], 'to complain' [HNTC, LN; ISV, NET, NJB, NRSV, TEV], 'to murmur' [BAGD, ICC, Lns; KJV], 'to stop one's querulous moaning' [NIGTC]. Γογγύζω signifies the act of expressing unjustifiable dissatisfaction, complaining [Ho]. The present tense signifies that the action was already going on [AB, NIGTC; ISV]: stop grumbling.

b. καθάπερ (LN **64.15**): 'as' [Herm, **LN**; all versions except NJB], 'even as' [Lns], 'which is just what' [ICC], 'just as' [LN, NIGTC], not explicit [NJB]. Καθάπερ signifies an intensive or emphatic form of 'as' [LN, NTC]: 'just as'.

QUESTION—What particular event is referred to here?

It refers to the events in Numbers 16, detailing the rebellion of Korah and the murmuring of the Israelites [Alf, EGT, Gdt, Ho, ICC, Lns, MNTC, My, NTC, Rb, TG, TH, TNTC, Vn]. It may refer to the event detailed in Numbers 14:2 [Alf, Ho, NIC2]. It refers to Numbers 17:6 [HNTC].

and were destroyed[a] by the destroyer.[b]

LEXICON—a. aorist mid. indic. of ἀπόλλυμι (See this word at 10:9): 'to be destroyed' [HNTC, ICC, NTC; ISV, KJV, NRSV, REB, TEV, TNT], 'to suffer destruction' [NIGTC], 'to be killed' [CEV, NAB, NET, NIV, NJB], 'to perish' [AB, Herm, Lns]. This entire clause is translated actively: 'for that is why God sent his angel of death to destroy them' [NLT].

b. ὀλοθρευτής (LN **20.36**) (BAGD p. 564): 'destroyer' [AB, BAGD, Herm, **LN**, Lns; KJV, NET, NRSV], 'the Agent of Destruction' [HNTC], 'the Destroyer' [NIGTC; NJB, REB], 'destroying angel' [ICC; CEV, ISV, NAB, NIV], 'the Destroying Angel' [TNT], 'angel that destroys' [NTC], 'angel of death' [NLT], 'the Angel of Death' [TEV]. The word ὀλοθρευτής may serve as a title referring to a destroying angel or even to Satan [LN].

QUESTION—What relationship is indicated by καί 'and'?

It indicates the result of grumbling [HNTC, TH]: some of them grumbled *and as a result* were destroyed.

QUESTION—To whom does ὑπὸ τοῦ ὀλοθρευτοῦ 'by the destroyer' refer?
It refers to an angel sent by God to carry out his judgment [Alf, EGT, Gdt, Lns, MNTC, My, NIC, NIC2, NTC, Rb, TH, Vn].

DISCOURSE UNIT: 10:11-15 [AB]. The topic is the warning afforded and God's escape provided.

10:11 Now[a] these-things were-happening to-those (persons) as-examples,[b]
TEXT—Some manuscripts include πάντα 'all' before or after ταῦτα 'these things'. It is omitted by GNT with a B rating, indicating that the text is almost certain. It is also omitted by AB, Herm, HNTC, Lns, NIGTC, NTC; CEV, ISV, NAB, NET, NIV, NRSV. It is included by ICC; KJV, NJB, NLT, REB, TEV, and TNT.
LEXICON—a. δέ (LN 89.94): 'now' [AB, ICC, Lns, NTC; KJV, NJB], 'and' [LN], not explicit [HNTC, NIGTC; all other versions].
  b. τυπικῶς (LN **58.60**) (BAGD p. 829): 'as an example' [AB, BAGD, LN; NAB, NET, NIV, NLT], 'as an example for others' [TEV], 'by way of example' [Herm, HNTC, Lns; NJB, TNT], 'for an ensample' [KJV], 'were symbolic' [REB], 'as a warning' [NTC; CEV], 'to serve as an example' [ISV, NRSV], 'formative models of broader patterns' [NIGTC], 'typologically, as a warning' [BAGD].
QUESTION—What relationship is indicated by δέ 'now'?
It sums up what has gone before [Gdt, TNTC]. It marks an end of the warnings and a beginning to an explanation of their significance [HNTC]. Paul returns to the admonition he gave in 10:6 [Lns, TG].
QUESTION—To whom does ἐκείνοις 'to those persons' refer?
It refers to the Israelites who have been mentioned in the previous verses of this chapter [NTC, TH].
QUESTION—What is the significance of the imperfect tense of συνέβαινεν 'they were happening'?
It signifies that these events were occurring in the past one after another over a period of time [ICC, Lns, NIC2, NTC].
QUESTION—For whom were these events to function as examples?
They were to function as examples for Paul and the Corinthians [NIC2]. The punishments they received were examples not only to their fellow Hebrews, but also to all believers since then [MNTC, TH].

and they-were-written for[a] our warning,[b]
LEXICON—a. πρός with accusative object (LN 89.60) (BAGD III.3.a. p. 710): 'for' [BAGD, Lns, NTC; KJV, NET], 'for the purpose of' [BAGD, LN], 'in order to, for the sake of' [LN], 'as' [AB, HNTC; ISV, NAB, NIV, REB, TEV, TNT], 'to be (a lesson/warning)' [Herm; NJB], 'to' [CEV, NLT, NRSV], 'with a view to' [ICC], 'to serve as' [NIGTC].
  b. νουθεσία (LN 33.231, **33.424**) (BAGD p. 544): 'warning' [Herm, HNTC, **LN**, NIGTC; ISV, NAB, REB, TEV, TNT], 'admonition' [AB, Lns, NTC; KJV], 'instruction' [BAGD, LN (33.231); NET], 'teaching' [LN

(33.231)], 'lesson' [NJB]. This singular noun is translated as a plural: 'warnings' [NIV], and as a participle: 'admonishing' [ICC]. The phrase πρὸς νουθεσίαν ἡμῶν 'for our warning' is translated 'to instruct us' [NRSV], 'to teach us' [CEV], 'to warn us' [NLT].

QUESTION—Who is included in the word ἡμῶν, 'our'?

It is inclusive of all Christians [MNTC, TG].

on[a] whom the ends[b] of-the ages[c] have-come.[d]

LEXICON—a. εἰς with accusative object (LN 90.23): 'on' [NET, NIV, NRSV], 'in' [LN; ISV], 'upon' [Herm, Lns, NIGTC, NTC; KJV, NAB, REB], 'to' [AB; NJB], 'unto' [ICC], 'with reference to, with respect to, concerning, about' [LN], not explicit [HNTC; CEV, NLT, TEV]. The phrase εἰς οὕς 'on whom' is translated 'in whose days' [TNT].

  b. τέλος (LN 67.66) (BAGD 1.b. p. 811): 'end' [Herm, ICC, LN, Lns, NIGTC, NTC; KJV, NAB, NET, NRSV], 'last days' [NJB], 'last part, close, conclusion' [BAGD], 'climax' [ISV], 'fulfillment' [NIV, TNT]. This plural noun is translated as a singular noun: 'end' [AB; REB, TEV]. It is also translated as an adjective: 'past' [HNTC]. This entire clause is translated 'who live in these last days' [CEV], 'who live at the time when this age is drawing to a close' [NLT], 'we live at a time when the end is about to come' [TEV], 'who are confronted by these past ages of history' [HNTC].

  c. αἰών (LN 67.143) (BAGD 2.b. p. 28): 'age' [BAGD, Herm, ICC, LN, Lns, NIGTC, NTC; all versions except CEV, KJV, NLT], 'age of history' [HNTC], 'era' [LN], 'world' [KJV], not explicit [CEV]. This plural noun is also translated as a singular noun: 'age' [AB; NLT].

  d. perf. act. indic. of καταντάω (LN **13.121**) (BAGD 2.b. p. 415): 'to come on' [**LN**; NET, NIV, NRSV], 'to come upon' [LN, Lns, NTC; KJV, NAB, REB], 'to come to' [BAGD], 'to come' [Herm, NIGTC; TEV, TNT], 'to come down with a weight of authority' [ICC], 'to be realized' [ISV], 'to draw near' [AB], 'it has fallen to live in' [NJB], not explicit [CEV, NLT]. This active verb is also translated passively: 'to be confronted' [HNTC].

QUESTION—What is meant by αἰών 'age'?

It means a period of time such as the time of the Jews before the coming of Christ [Ho]. The plural may refer to the time of the Jews and the time of the Gentiles or pagans, both occurring concurrently and being terminated at the coming of Christ [EGT].

QUESTION—What is the meaning of the phrase εἰς οὕς τὰ τέλη τῶν αἰώνων κατήντηκεν 'on whom the ends of the ages have come'?

It means that the Christian era—the time in which the Corinthians were living—is the era that marks the end of time [Ho, ICC, MNTC, NIC2, NTC, TG, TH]. It means that the Christian era inherits the spiritual benefits of the eras that have gone before [EGT, ICC, Lns]. It means that the climax of past ages has arrived [NTC, TNTC].

DISCOURSE UNIT: 10:12–22 [Gdt]. The topic is the application of these examples to the church of Corinth.

10:12 Therefore[a] the-(one) thinking he-stands[b] let-him-be-careful[c] lest[d] he-fall.[e]

LEXICON—a. ὥστε (LN 89.52) (BAGD p. 899): 'therefore' [AB, BAGD, Herm, ICC, LN; ISV], 'wherefore' [Lns; KJV], 'so' [BAGD, NTC; NET, NIV, NRSV, TNT], 'for all these reasons' [NAB], 'the moral is' [HNTC], 'so then' [LN, NIC2, NIGTC], 'for this reason' [BAGD], '(so) accordingly, as a result, so that, and so' [LN], not explicit [CEV, NJB, NLT, REB, TEV]. This word is strongly inferential [NIC2].

b. perf. act. infin. of ἵστημι (LN 13.29, 17.1) (BAGD II.2.c.α. p. 382): 'to stand' [Herm, LN (17.1), Lns, NTC; KJV, NET, NJB, NRSV], 'to stand secure' [TNT], 'to stand securely' [ICC; ISV], 'to stand firm' [BAGD; NIV, REB, TEV], 'to stand firmly' [AB], 'to stand strong' [NLT], 'to stand upright' [NAB], 'to stand fast' [HNTC, NIGTC], 'to stand up to temptation' [CEV], 'to firmly remain, to continue steadfastly' [LN (13.29)]. This word is used here in a spiritual sense [NIC, TG]. This word denotes remaining firmly or well-established in a particular state [LN (13.29)].

c. pres. act. impera. of βλέπω (LN 27.58) (BAGD 6. p. 143): 'to be careful' [NTC; CEV, NET, NIV, NJB, NLT, TEV], 'to take care' [BAGD; REB, TNT], 'to take heed' [Lns; KJV], 'to watch out' [NIGTC; ISV, NAB, NRSV], 'to beware' [Herm, HNTC, ICC], 'to look out' [AB], 'to watch out for, to beware of, to pay attention to' [LN], 'to see to it' [BAGD].

d. μή (LN 89.62) (BAGD B.1.b. p. 517): 'lest' [AB, BAGD, Herm, HNTC, ICC, LN, Lns, NIGTC; KJV, NAB], 'that...not' [BAGD; ISV, NIV, NRSV, TEV, TNT], 'not' [NTC; CEV, NET, NJB], 'in order that...not, so that...not' [LN]. The phrase μὴ πέσῃ 'lest he fall' is translated 'or you may fall' [REB], 'for you, too, may fall into the same sin' [NLT].

e. aorist act. subj. of πίπτω (LN 13.59) (BAGD 2.a.β. p. 660): 'to fall' [AB, Herm, HNTC, Lns, NIGTC, NTC; all versions], 'to go astray morally' [BAGD], 'to fall from, to worsen' [LN]. This indicates falling in a moral or spiritual sense [BAGD, EGT, Lns, My, NIC]: 'be completely ruined' [BAGD]. This implies falling from a secure position and becoming disqualified as Paul mentions in 9:27 [ICC, Vn]. It implies falling so as to be destroyed [TH].

QUESTION—What relationship is indicated by ὥστε 'therefore'?

It indicates a warning based on the preceding verse [Gdt, HNTC, Ho, My, NIC, NIC2; NAB]: For these reasons (the preceding examples of the Israelites who did fall), let the one who thinks he stands, be careful that he not fall.

QUESTION—What does ἵστημι 'to stand' represent?
It represents a state of immovability in regards to ever giving in to temptation [Gdt, Ho]. It represents a state of security in regards to ever losing one's salvation [Alf, Lns, NIC, NIC2].

QUESTION—To what particular temptation does the context refer?
It refers to the temptation to think oneself free from danger while attending the idol feasts [ICC, NIC2, NTC].

10:13 No temptation[a] has-overtaken[b] you except what-is-common-to-man;[c]

LEXICON—a. πειρασμός (LN 27.46, 88.308) (BAGD 2.b. p. 641): 'temptation' [AB, BAGD, Herm, ICC, LN (88.308), Lns, NIGTC, NTC; ISV, KJV, NIV, NLT], 'testing' [HNTC, LN (27.46); NRSV], 'test' [NAB, TEV], 'trial' [NET, NJB, REB, TNT], 'examination' [LN (27.46)]. This noun is also translated as a verb: 'to be tempted' [CEV].
  b. perf. act. indic. of λαμβάνω (LN 18.1) (BAGD 1.c. p. 464): 'to overtake' [AB, Lns, NTC; ISV, NET, NRSV], 'to take' [ICC; KJV], 'to seize' [BAGD; NIV], 'to fasten upon' [NIGTC], 'to come upon' [NJB], 'to come into (one's) life' [NLT], 'to fall upon' [HNTC], 'to take hold of, to grasp, to grab' [LN]. This active verb is translated as a passive: 'to be overtaken' [Herm], 'to be sent' [NAB]. It is also translated reciprocally: 'to face' [REB], 'to experience' [TEV], 'to be involved in' [TNT]. The phrase πειρασμὸς ὑμᾶς οὐκ εἴληθεν 'temptation has not taken you' is translated positively: 'you are tempted (in the same way that everyone else is tempted)' [CEV].
  c. ἀνθρώπινος (LN 9.6) (BAGD 1. p. 67): 'what is common to man' [NIV], 'that which is common to everyone' [NTC], 'what is the common lot of men' [HNTC], 'such as is common to man' [KJV], 'that of a common human kind' [AB], 'what is part and parcel of being human' [NIGTC], 'common to man' [BAGD], 'what is human' [Herm], 'human, of people' [LN]. The phrase εἰ μὴ ἀνθρώπινος 'except what is common to man' is translated 'that is not faced by others' [NET], 'that is unusual for human beings' [ISV], 'that is not common to everyone' [NRSV], 'that does not come to all men' [NAB], 'that is not common to all men' [TNT], 'no different from what others experience' [NLT], 'other than a man can withstand' [ICC], 'beyond human endurance' [REB], 'more than a human being can stand' [NJB].

QUESTION—Does πειρασμός 'temptation' denote a 'trial' or a 'temptation to sin'?

1. It denotes a 'trial' or the 'testing' of a person's character [Gdt, HNTC, NIC2, TG]. Such a trial could be a trouble which could cause a person to lose his faith [TG].
2. It denotes an endeavor to tempt someone to sin [AB, Alf, My]. The context does not justify the sense of 'trial' in that neither suffering nor persecution have been mentioned [My].

3. It includes both [Gdt, Ho, Lns, MNTC, NIC, NTC, TH, TNTC]. It includes moral temptations and such trials as persecutions [TH].

QUESTION—To some this verse seems to be out of place in a context of warning. The question is, did Paul intend this verse to be a warning or an encouragement to the Corinthians?

1. It should be taken as a warning [Gdt, HNTC]. This is a continuation of the warning of the preceding verse and the trials that the Corinthians have so far faced have been relatively easy and to fail in them would be not excusable. In the future, more severe trials might come [Gdt, HNTC].
2. It should be taken as an encouragement [AB, Alf, EGT, Ho, ICC, Lns, My, NIC, NIC2, NTC, TNTC]. Although falling was a possibility, it was not a foregone conclusion. Trials or temptations were not beyond their strength and God would enable them to endure [NIC2].

QUESTION—What is meant by ἀνθρώπινος 'common to man'?

It means that all temptations are encountered by mankind in general and are not exceptional [AB, HNTC, Ho, MNTC, NIC, NIC2, NTC, TG, Vn]. It implies that they are endurable [EGT, Gdt, ICC, Lns; REB].

but/and^a God (is) faithful,^b

LEXICON—a. δέ (LN 89.124, 89.87): 'but' [Herm, HNTC, Lns, NTC; CEV, ISV, KJV, TEV], 'and' [AB; NET, NIV, NLT], 'now' [NIGTC], 'besides' [NAB], 'Yes' [ICC], not explicit [all other versions].

b. πιστός (LN 31.87) (BAGD 1.a.β. p. 664): 'faithful' [AB, BAGD, Herm, LN, Lns, NIGTC, NTC; ISV, KJV, NET, NIV, NLT, NRSV, TNT], 'dependable' [BAGD, LN], 'reliable' [LN], 'trustworthy' [BAGD, LN]. This adjective is translated as a verb phrase: 'to be able to be trusted' [HNTC; CEV], 'to keep faith' [REB], 'to keep (his) promise' [NAB, TEV]. This clause is translated 'you can trust God' [NJB], 'you may trust God' [ICC]. See this word also at 1:9.

QUESTION—What relationship is indicated by δέ 'but/and'?

1. It indicates a contrastive relationship [EGT, HNTC, Lns, NTC; CEV, ISV, KJV, TEV]: no temptation has overtaken you except what is common to man, *but* God is faithful. It contrasts the human trial and the divine promise of aid [EGT].
2. It indicates a conjoining relationship [AB, ICC; NAB, NET, NIV, NLT]: no temptation has overtaken you except what is common to man, *and furthermore* God is faithful. This continues and strengthens the encouragement [ICC].

who (will) not let^a you be-tempted^b beyond^c that-which you-are-able^d

LEXICON—a. fut. act. indic. of ἐάω (LN 13.138) (BAGD 1. p. 212): 'to let' [BAGD, ICC, LN; CEV, NAB, NET, NIV, NJB, NRSV, REB], 'to allow' [Herm, HNTC, LN, NIGTC, NTC; ISV, TEV, TNT], 'to permit' [AB, BAGD, LN, Lns], 'to suffer' [KJV]. This entire clause is translated 'he will keep the temptation from becoming so strong that you can't stand up against it' [NLT].

b. aorist pass. infin. of πειράζω (LN 27.46, 88.308) (BAGD 2.b. p. 640): 'to be tempted' [AB, Herm, ICC, LN (88.308), Lns, NIGTC, NTC; CEV, ISV, KJV, NIV], 'to be tried' [BAGD; NET, TNT], 'to be put to the test' [BAGD, LN (27.46); NJB], 'to be tested' [HNTC, LN (27.46); NAB, NRSV, REB, TEV], 'to be examined' [LN (27.46)], 'to be led into temptation' [LN (88.308)]. This verb is also translated as a noun: 'temptation' [NLT].

c. ὑπέρ with accusative object (LN **78.29**) (BAGD 2. p. 839): 'beyond' [AB, BAGD, Herm, HNTC, ICC, **LN**, NIGTC, NTC; ISV, NAB, NIV, NJB, NRSV, REB, TEV, TNT], 'too much' [CEV, NET], 'above' [Lns; KJV], 'more than' [BAGD, LN], 'to a greater degree than' [LN]. The phrase ὑπὲρ ὃ δύνασθε 'above that which you are able' is translated 'so strong that you can't stand up against it' [NLT].

d. pres. mid. (deponent = act.) indic. of δύναμαι (LN 74.5) (BAGD 2. p. 207): 'to be able' [LN; KJV, NIV, TNT], 'to be able to resist' [AB], 'to be able to bear' [NTC], 'to be able to stand up against' [NLT]. This infinitive is also translated as a finite verb: 'can' [LN], and as a noun: '(beyond your) power(s)' [Herm, HNTC, NIGTC; REB], '(above your) ability' [Lns], '(beyond your) strength' [BAGD, ICC; ISV, NAB, NJB, NRSV], 'power (to remain firm)' [TEV], not explicit [CEV, NET].

QUESTION—In what ways is God dependable?

He can be depended on both to control the strength of the test and to supply a way to pass the test successfully [NIC2].

but also will-provide^a with^b the temptation the way-out^c

LEXICON—a. fut. act. indic. of ποιέω (LN 13.9) (BAGD I.1.b.γ. p. 681): 'to provide' [AB, BAGD, Herm, HNTC, NTC; ISV, NET, NIV, NJB, NRSV, REB, TEV, TNT], 'to make' [LN, Lns, NIGTC; KJV], 'to cause to be' [LN], 'to give' [NAB], 'to show' [NLT], 'to arrange' [ICC]. This entire clause is translated 'and he will show you how to escape from your temptations' [CEV].

b. σύν with dative object (LN **89.105**, 89.107) (BAGD 4.a. p. 782): 'with' [AB, BAGD, Herm, LN (89.105, 89.107), NTC; KJV, NET, NJB, NRSV, TNT], 'along with' [HNTC; ISV, NAB], 'alongside' [NIGTC], 'together with' [**LN** (89.105), Lns]. The phrase σὺν τῷ πειρασμῷ 'with the temptation' is translated 'when you are tempted' [NIV, NLT], 'when the test comes' [REB], 'at the time you are put to the test' [TEV], not explicit [ICC; CEV].

c. ἔκβασις (LN **21.16**) (BAGD p. 237): 'way out' [AB, BAGD, Herm, HNTC, Lns; all versions except CEV, KJV, NET], 'way through (it)' [NET], 'way of escape' [ICC, LN, NTC], 'way to escape' [KJV], 'how to escape' [CEV], 'means of escape' [**LN**], 'exit path' [NIGTC].

QUESTION—The text can either mean that God provides both the temptation and the way of escape or that when the temptation comes He provides the way of escape. Does God provide both the temptation and the way out or only the way out?

1. God provides both the temptation and the way of escape [Alf, Ho, ICC, LN, My]. This meaning rests on the word σύν 'with': God provides, together with the temptation, also the way to escape [Ho]. The articles before the words 'temptation' and 'way of escape', plus the word σύν 'with', show that the two go together as a pair, both arranged by God: 'While He arranges the temptation to brace your character, He will also arrange the necessary way of escape' [ICC].
2. God provides only the way of escape [EGT, Gdt, Lns, NIC2; NIV, NLT, REB, TEV]. The verse says that God limits the temptation, not provides it. The σύν 'with' simply states that He provides the way of escape when the temptation comes [EGT].

QUESTION—What is the significance of the definite article in the phrase τὴν ἔκβασιν 'the way of escape'?

It signifies that '*the* way of escape' is specific to '*the* temptation' [EGT, ICC, NTC]. It signifies that there is only one way out, and it is by passing through the temptation [MNTC].

in-order-that/namely that (you) may-be-able to-endure.[a]

LEXICON—a. pres. mid. (deponent = act.) infin. of δύναμαι (LN 74.5) (BAGD 2. p. 207): 'to be able' [AB, BAGD, HNTC, LN, NTC; KJV, NAB, NET, NRSV, TNT], 'to enable' [NJB, REB], 'to give strength' [TEV], not explicit [CEV]. This infinitive is translated as a finite verb: 'can' [Herm, LN; ISV, NIV]. It is also translated as a noun: 'ability (to bear)' [Lns], 'strength (to endure)' [ICC]. The entire phrase is translated 'so that you will not give in to it' [NLT], 'his purpose in this is for you to bear up under it' [NIGTC].

QUESTION—What is the function of τοῦ δύνασθαι ὑπενεγκεῖν 'of the to be able to endure'?

1. It indicates the purpose of the way of escape [AB, Alf, EGT, HNTC, Ho, ICC, My, NIGTC, NTC; ISV, KJV, NAB, NET, NIV, NLT, NRSV, TNT]: he will provide the way out so that you will be able to endure it.
2. It indicates the definition of the way of escape [Lns, MNTC, NIC, TG; NJB, REB, TEV]: he will provide the way out, namely, that you will be able to endure it.

DISCOURSE UNIT: 10:14–22 [Herm, HNTC, Ho, ICC, MNTC, NCBC, NIC2, NIGTC, NTC, TG, TH, TNTC; NAB, NET, NIV, NJB]. The topic is the prohibition and its basis [NIC2], the truth about idolatry [MNTC], the incompatibility of Christian and idol feasts [TNTC], problems of Corinthian believers [TG], the Lord's Supper as criterion [Herm], Christianity inconsistent with idolatry [HNTC], the Eucharist versus pagan sacrifices [NAB], avoiding idol feasts [NET], idol feasts and the Lord's Supper [NIV], sacrificial feasts—no compromise with idolatry [NJB], exclusive loyalty to God [NIGTC], warnings against idolatry [NTC].

10:14 Therefore,[a] my dearly-beloved,[b] flee[c] from idolatry.[d]

LEXICON—a. διόπερ (LN **89.47**) (BAGD p. 199): 'therefore' [BAGD, Herm, LN, Lns, NTC; NIV, NRSV, TNT], 'wherefore' [AB; KJV], 'so' [NLT], 'so then' [**LN**, NIGTC; NET, REB, TEV], 'for that reason' [NJB], 'and so' [ICC; ISV], 'the conclusion of this…is' [HNTC], 'for this reason' [LN], 'for this very reason' [BAGD, LN], not explicit [CEV, NAB]. This word is strongly inferential [NIC2, TNTC].

b. ἀγαπητός (LN 25.45) (BAGD 2. p. 6): 'dearly beloved' [KJV], 'dear friend' [Herm, HNTC, NTC; all versions except CEV, KJV, NAB], 'very dear friend' [NIGTC], 'friend' [CEV], '(one) whom (one) loves' [NAB], 'beloved ones' [AB], 'beloved' [BAGD, LN], 'dear' [BAGD, LN], '(my) affection for (you)' [ICC].

c. pres. act. impera. of φεύγω (LN 15.61) (BAGD 3. p. 856): 'to flee' [BAGD, HNTC, LN, NIGTC, NTC; KJV, NET, NIV, NLT, NRSV], 'continue to flee' [Lns], 'to shun' [AB, BAGD, Herm; NAB, TNT], 'to have nothing to do with' [NJB, REB], 'to keep away from' [CEV, TEV], 'to run away' [LN; ISV], 'to escape…to avoid all contact with' [ICC], 'to avoid' [BAGD].

d. εἰδωλολατρία (LN **53.63**) (BAGD p. 221): 'idolatry' [AB, BAGD, Herm, HNTC, LN, Lns, NIGTC, NTC; ISV, KJV, NET, NIV, REB, TNT], 'temptation to idolatry' [ICC], 'worship of idols' [**LN**; NAB, NLT, NRSV, TEV], 'worship of false gods' [NJB], 'idols' [CEV].

QUESTION—What relationship is indicated by διόπερ 'therefore'?

It indicates a command based on the preceding argument [Ed, EGT, Gdt, Ho, ICC, My, NIC2, NTC]. They should flee from idolatry because that would cut them off from God's help in temptation [My]. They should flee from idolatry because God would be their strength to do so [EGT, Gdt, ICC]. They should flee from idolatry because of the danger of its bringing on them the same judgment that it brought on Israel [EGT, Ho, NTC]. They should flee from idolatry because it, being of their own making and unlike an ordinary trial, did not qualify for God's help [Gdt, NIC2].

QUESTION—What is the significance of the present tense in φεύγετε 'Flee!'?

It signifies that the action should be carried on habitually or continually [Lns, NIC, NIC2, TNTC]: Keep on fleeing from idolatry! It does not imply that they were guilty of idolatry, but that they were in danger of it [Lns].

DISCOURSE UNIT: 10:15–22 [Alf, EGT, My]. The topic is the communion of the Lord and of demons.

10:15 I-speak as[a] to-sensible-people;[b]

LEXICON—a. ὡς (LN 64.12) (BAGD III.1.a. p. 898): 'as' [AB, BAGD, Herm, HNTC, LN, Lns, NTC; CEV, KJV, NAB, NJB, NRSV, REB, TEV, TNT], 'like' [LN], not explicit [ICC, NIGTC; ISV, NET, NIV, NLT].

b. φρόνιμος (LN 32.31) (BAGD p. 866): 'sensible people' [ISV, NAB, NIV, NJB, NRSV, REB, TEV], 'sensible men' [HNTC, Lns], 'reasonable people' [NLT], 'intelligent people' [AB, Herm], 'thoughtful people'

[NET], 'the wise' [NTC], 'wise men' [KJV], 'men of prudence' [TNT], '(your) good sense' [ICC]. The clause is translated 'I am speaking to you as people who have enough sense' [CEV], 'I appeal to your common sense' [NIGTC]. The adjective has the meaning of 'wise' [BAGD, LN], 'sensible, thoughtful, prudent' [BAGD], 'with understanding, with insight' [LN]. This word carries the idea of being capable of understanding the force of an argument [Ho].

QUESTION—Is Paul sincere here, or does he speak ironically?

Paul is sincere [Alf, ICC, My, NIC, NIC2, TH; other commentaries support sincerity by giving the adjective its primary meaning]. Paul assumes that they are capable of seeing the force of his argument [Ho]. The 'as' does not indicate a hypothetical quality of sensibleness, but assumes its reality [NIC2]. There is a touch of irony in Paul's compliment since it seems that the Corinthians boasted of their special knowledge [HNTC].

you judge^a what I-say.^b

LEXICON—a. aorist act. impera. of κρίνω (LN **30.108**) (BAGD 2. p. 451): 'to judge' [AB, HNTC, **LN**, Lns, NIGTC, NTC; KJV, NAB, NIV, NRSV, TEV, TNT], 'to be capable of judging' [ICC], 'to form (one's own) judgment on' [REB], 'to consider' [NET], 'to decide' [ISV, NLT], 'to weigh up' [NJB], 'to know' [CEV], 'to judge (for oneself)' [Herm], 'to pass (one's own) judgment on' [BAGD], 'to evaluate' [LN].

b. pres. indic. act. of φημί 'to say' (LN 33.69, 33.140) (BAGD 2. p. 856): 'to say' [AB, Herm, HNTC, LN (33.69), NTC; ISV, KJV, NAB, NET, NIV, NRSV, REB, TEV, TNT], 'to be about to say' [NLT], 'to have to say' [NJB], 'to claim' [Lns], 'to mean' [BAGD, LN (33.140); NJB], 'to imply' [ICC, LN (33.140)], 'to talk about' [CEV], 'to tell, to talk, to speak' [LN (33.69)], 'to declare' [NIGTC]. This verb is also translated as a noun: '(my) arguments' [ICC]. This word either means to say something in order to explain more fully the implications or intent of what has been said [LN (33.140)], or it means to speak with apparent focus upon the content of what is said [LN (33.69)]. See this word also at 7:29.

QUESTION—What is the significance of the presence of the pronoun ὑμεῖς 'you'?

It signifies that it is emphatic [AB, Alf, HNTC, ICC, Lns, My, NTC, TH, TNTC, Vn]: you yourselves judge what I say.

QUESTION—Does φημί 'I say' refer to what Paul had said or is about to say?

It refers to what he is about to say [Alf, Ed, Gdt, My, NIC2, TH].

DISCOURSE UNIT: 10:16–22 [AB]. The topic is the Lord's supper and food offered to idols.

10:16 The cup[a] of-the blessing[b] which we-give-thanks-for,[c] is-it not[d] a-sharing[e] of-the blood of Christ?

LEXICON—a. ποτήριον (LN 6.121) (BAGD 1. p. 695): 'cup' [AB, BAGD, Herm, HNTC, ICC, LN, Lns, NIGTC, NTC; all versions], 'drinking vessel' [BAGD].
  b. εὐλογία (LN 33.470) (BAGD 4. p. 323): 'blessing' [AB, BAGD, Herm, HNTC, ICC, LN, Lns, NIGTC, NTC; ISV, KJV, NAB, NET, NJB, NRSV, REB, TNT], 'thanksgiving' [NIV]. This noun is also translated as an adjective: 'consecrated (cup)' [BAGD]. It is also translated as a phrase: '(the cup) at the Lord's Table' [NLT], '(the cup) we use in the Lord's Supper' [TEV]. The phrase τῆς εὐλογία ὃ εὐλογοῦμεν 'of the blessing which we give thanks for' is translated 'that we ask God to bless' [CEV].
  c. pres. act. indic. of εὐλογέω (LN 33.470, 33.356) (BAGD 2.b. p. 322): 'to give thanks for' [NTC; NIV], 'to give thanks to God for' [TEV], 'to bless' [AB, BAGD, Herm, LN (33.470), Lns; CEV, ISV, KJV, NAB, NET, NJB, NRSV, REB], 'to invoke the benediction' [ICC], 'to say the blessing' [HNTC], 'to offer a blessing over' [NIGTC], 'to consecrate' [BAGD], 'to praise, to speak well of' [LN (33.356)].
  d. οὐχί (LN 69.12): 'not' [all versions except TEV]. This question is also rendered as a positive statement: 'The cup we use...and for which we give thanks...we are sharing...' [TEV]. Οὐχί is a marker of questions expecting a somewhat more emphatic positive response than οὐ [LN]. See this word also at 1:20.
  e. κοινωνία (LN 34.5, 57.98) (BAGD 3. 4. p. 439): 'sharing' [LN (57.98); ISV, NAB, NET, NJB, NLT, NRSV], 'fellowship, close association' [LN (34.5)], 'communion' [Lns; KJV], 'means of sharing' [REB], 'participation' [BAGD, Herm, NTC; NIV], 'common participation' [HNTC], 'communal participation' [NIGTC], 'partnership' [AB], 'a means of communion' [ICC]. 'a means for attaining a close relationship' [BAGD]. The phrase κοινωνία ἐστίν 'it is a sharing' is translated 'that is sharing' [CEV], 'we are sharing' [NLT, TEV, TNT]. The primary meaning of κοινωνία is 'to fellowship or share with someone in something' [EGT, NIC2].

QUESTION—What is Paul's intention in talking about the Last Supper here?
He mentions it to draw attention to the sacred pagan meals referred to in 10:19–21 [NIC2]. He wants to convince the Corinthians that if a pagan feast is held in a temple, it was an act of idolatry to attend the feast. By analogy he shows that attendance at the Lord's Supper is to commune with Christ, the object of Christian worship, and to join in fellowship with all who attend it. The conclusion is that to join in the sacrificial feasts of the heathen is to join in their worship of idols [Ho].

QUESTION—To what does τὸ ποτήριον τῆς εὐλογίας 'the cup of blessing' refer?
'The cup of blessing' was a technical term for the cup of wine drunk at the conclusion of the Jewish meal [Alf, Gdt, HNTC, MNTC, NIC2, TNTC]. It 0

was also term for the third cup of the Passover [AB, Lns, TNTC]. A prayer of thanksgiving or benediction was said over it [Alf, Gdt, HNTC]. Jesus may have used this particular cup at the Last Supper to institute the communion ceremony. The early believers adopted this term to refer to the Communion cup [MNTC, NIC2]. It is called 'the cup of blessing' because Christ blessed the cup at the Last Supper. Reference to the Jewish meal would not be obvious to the Corinthians [EGT]. It contrasts with the 'cup of demons' (10:21) [NIC2].

QUESTION—To what does ποτήριον 'cup' refer?

It refers to its contents, the wine [AB, BAGD, Lns]. It represents the blood of Christ [AB, NIC2].

QUESTION—How are the nouns related in the genitive construction τὸ ποτήριον τῆς εὐλογίας 'the cup of blessing'?

It refers to the cup over which a blessing or benediction is said by the Christian minister [ICC]. It refers to the cup over which the Lord offered a prayer of blessing or thanksgiving [Gdt].

QUESTION—Does εὐλογέω mean 'to give thanks' or 'to consecrate, set apart as holy, make sacred'?

1. It means to give thanks [AB, HNTC, MNTC, NIC, NIC2, TG, TH, TNTC, Vn; NIV, TEV, TNT]: the cup of thanksgiving for which we give thanks. The effect of the prayer of thanksgiving may be to consecrate the cup [TNTC].
2. It means to set apart as holy [Alf, Gdt, Ho, ICC, Lns, My]: the cup of consecration which we set apart as holy. God is asked to bless the cup [Ho, ICC] and make it accomplish its appointed end [Ho]. It was consecrated with a prayer of thanksgiving [Alf].

QUESTION—What reply is expected to these rhetorical questions?

The presence of the particle οὐχί 'not' in a question expects a positive reply to the question [LN (69.12), NIC, NTC, TG, TH; CEV, ISV, TEV]: The cup of blessing which we bless is a sharing in the blood of Christ, is it not?

QUESTION—To whom does 'we' refer?

It refers to Christians in general [TH]. It refers to the congregation that blessed the cup through the agency of the minister [Alf, ICC, Lns].

QUESTION—What does the phrase 'sharing of the blood of Christ' mean?

1. It means that a person shares in the benefits of Christ's death [AB, EGT, HNTC, Ho, Lns, NIC, NIC2, NTC, TG]. At the fellowship meal, by faith they considered Christ's sacrifice and realized its benefits in their own lives [NIC2]. 'Blood' is a metonymy for Christ's sacrificial death. Reminded of the Lord's sacrifice, we commune with him and with his people [MNTC]. Since the comparison is between two liquids, wine and blood, we should keep the literal translation 'blood' [TH]. This is done by actual eating and drinking, not by faith [Lns].
2. It means that a person actually shares in some way in the blood and body of Christ [Alf, ICC]. This supports the following argument that since we all share the same bread we are all a single body [Alf].

The bread which we-break, is-it not a-sharing of-the body of Christ?
QUESTION—Is the word 'body' literal or figurative?
1. It is literal and refers to Christ's physical body, sacrificed for others [EGT, Gdt, Ho, ICC, Lns, NIC, NTC]. Sharing of the body of Christ is to share in the benefits of His body as broken for us [Ho, NIC].
2. It is figurative and refers to the church as the body of Christ [HNTC, NIC2]. Paul's term that refers to the physical body of Christ is σάρξ 'flesh' (whereas σῶμα 'body' is used here). To eat the bread then means to share with other believers who compose the body of Christ [HNTC]. Paul interprets the word body in a figurative sense in 10:17, showing that this is what he meant here [NIC2].

QUESTION—To whom does 'we' refer in 'we break'?
It can either refer to each person of the congregation individually breaking the bread as it is passed to her/him, or simply to the pastor breaking the bread in behalf of the congregation [Gdt].

10:17 Because[a] (there is) one bread, (we) the many are one body, for (we) all partake[b] from[c] one bread.
LEXICON—a. ὅτι (LN 89.33) (BAGD 3. p. 589): 'because' [HNTC, ICC, LN, Lns, NIGTC, NTC; ISV, NAB, NET, NIV, NRSV, REB, TEV, TNT], 'since' [AB, LN], 'for' [Herm, LN; KJV], 'in view of the fact that' [LN], not explicit [CEV, NJB, NLT].
  b. pres. act. indic. of μετέχω (LN 57.6, 23.2) (BAGD p. 514): 'to partake' [Herm, HNTC, Lns, NTC; ISV, NAB, NIV, NRSV, REB], 'to be a partaker' [KJV], 'to share' [AB, BAGD, NIGTC; CEV, NET, NJB, TEV], 'to share in' [LN (57.6)], 'to have a share of' [BAGD, LN (57.6)], 'to have (one's) share' [TNT], 'to eat (food)' [BAGD, LN (23.2); NLT].
  c. ἐκ with genitive object (LN 90.16) (BAGD 4.a.ε. p. 236): 'from' [AB, LN; NLT, TNT], 'of' [Herm, HNTC, Lns, NTC; ISV, KJV, NAB, NIV, NRSV, REB], 'in' [CEV, NJB], not explicit [NIGTC; NET, TEV].

QUESTION—What relationship is indicated by ὅτι 'because'?
1. It indicates the reason for the preceding clause [AB, Alf, Ho, ICC, NIC, NIC2, Vn]: the breaking of the bread is a sharing in the body of Christ *because* it is one bread and we who are many, are one body. This clause explains how we share in Christ's body—all who eat of one bread become one body and that bread is Christ [AB]. The order 'cup-bread' in 10:16 is a reversal of the usual reference to the Eucharist. Paul must have done this to bring the 'bread' of verse 16 together with the 'one bread' in 10:17. Paul states that the 'body' of 10:17 is to be understood as the congregation of believers [NIC2]. What is argued is that breaking of bread is a sharing of the body of Christ because we all partake of one bread [Ho].
2. It indicates the reason for the following clause [EGT, Gdt, HNTC, Lns, NIC, NTC, TNTC]: we who are many are one body *because* there is one bread.

QUESTION—What relationship is indicated by γάρ 'for'.

It indicates the grounds for the previous statement [EGT, NIC, NIC2]: we who are many are one body *since* we all share in one bread. It indicates that its clause is a restatement of the previous statement [Lns]: we who are many are one body, that is, we all share in one bread.

QUESTION—What is Paul trying to show by this verse?

He is showing that the unity of believers in one body in Christ is incompatible with all other unions [NIC2]. He is showing that all participants form one body because of their joint participation with Christ. Similarly those who share in the pagan meals form one religious body because of their joint participation with the demons, the object of their worship [Ho].

DISCOURSE UNIT: 10:18–22 [NTC]. The topic is an example of symmetry.

10:18 Look-at[a] Israel[b] according-to[c] flesh;[d]

LEXICON—a. pres. act. impera. of βλέπω (LN 30.1) (BAGD 4.b. p. 143): 'to consider' [AB, BAGD, HNTC, ICC, LN, NIGTC, NTC; NIV, NRSV, REB, TEV, TNT], 'to think about' [LN; NLT], 'to look at' [Herm; ISV, NAB, NET], 'to behold' [Lns; KJV], 'to compare' [NJB], 'to note' [BAGD], 'to direct (one's) attention to' [BAGD], not explicit [CEV].

b. Ἰσραήλ (LN 93.182) (BAGD 3. p. 381): 'Israel' [BAGD, Herm, HNTC, LN, Lns, NIGTC, NTC; KJV, NAB], 'Israelites' [ICC; ISV], 'the people of Israel' [AB; NJB]. This noun is also translated as an adjective: 'Jewish' [REB, TNT]. The phrase τὸν Ἰσραὴλ κατὰ σάρκα 'Israel according to flesh' is translated 'the people of Israel' [CEV, NET, NIV, NRSV, TEV], 'the nation of Israel' [NLT], 'Jewish practice' [REB], 'Jewish faith and practice' [TNT].

c. κατά with accusative object (LN 89.4): 'according to' [NTC; NAB], 'from' [AB; ISV], 'after' [Lns; KJV], 'in relation to, with regard to' [LN], not explicit [Herm, HNTC, ICC, NIGTC; all versions except ISV, KJV, NAB].

d. σάρξ (LN 8.63, 58.10) (BAGD 4. p. 743): 'flesh' [LN (8.63), Lns, NTC; KJV, NAB], 'human nature, physical nature of people' [LN (58.10)], not explicit [CEV, NET, NIV, NLT, NRSV, REB, TEV, TNT]. The phrase κατὰ σάρκα 'according to flesh' is translated 'from a human standpoint' [AB], 'from a human point of view' [ISV], 'natural' [NJB], 'historic' [HNTC], 'of earthly descent' [NIGTC], 'as we have them in history with their national ritual' [ICC], 'earthly' [BAGD, Herm].

QUESTION—What is Paul's purpose in this verse?

He gives another example to show that participation in the pagan meals is idolatry [Ed, My]. Participation in the pagan meals is communion with the unseen [ICC]. He shows the connection between the sacrifice and those who partake of it [NIC].

QUESTION—To what does Ἰσραήλ κατὰ σάρκα 'Israel according to flesh' refer?
1. It refers to the Israel of history [NIV, REB, EGT, Gdt, Herm, HNTC, Ho, ICC, My, Rb, TNTC, Vn]. It is a reference to Israel as a nation in contrast to being a reference to Christians as spiritual Israel [Alf, BAGD, EGT, Gdt, Ho, My, Rb, TNTC]. It refers all those who were born as Israelites [My, Vn].
2. It is a reference to an unspiritual or sinful Israel [NTC]. Paul is referring back to 10:6–10 in which Israel is seen as worshiping idols from the accounts in Exodus 24:3, 7 and 32:6.

are not the-ones eating the sacrifices[a] partakers[b] of-the altar?[c]
LEXICON—a. θυσία (LN 53.20) (BAGD 2.a. p. 366): 'sacrifice' [AB, BAGD, Herm, HNTC, LN, Lns, NIGTC, NTC; all versions except REB, TEV], 'sacrificial meal' [REB], 'what is offered in sacrifice' [TEV], 'prescribed sacrifice' [ICC].
b. κοινωνός (LN 34.6) (BAGD 1.b.α. p. 439): 'partaker' [Herm, NTC; KJV], 'partner' [AB, HNTC, LN; NET, NRSV, REB], 'communicant' [Lns], 'communal participant' [NIGTC], 'associate, one who joins in with' [LN], 'one who takes part in something' [BAGD]. This noun is also translated as a phrase: 'in fellowship with' [TNT]. The phrase κοινωνοί…εἰσίν 'are…partakers' is translated '(they) share' [NAB, NJB], '(they) participate' [NIV], 'enter into fellowship with' [ICC]. The phrase οὐχ κοινωνοί…εἰσίν 'are they not partakers' is translated 'aren't they sharing in the worship' [CEV], 'they share…, don't they?' [ISV], 'they share' [TEV]. The phrase κοινωνοὶ τοῦ θυσιαστηρίου εἰσίν 'are partakers of the altar' is translated 'are united by that act' [NLT].
c. θυσιαστήριον (LN 6.114) (BAGD 1.a. p. 366): 'altar' [AB, BAGD, Herm, HNTC, LN, NTC; all versions except NLT, TEV, TNT], 'altar's service to God' [TEV], 'sacrificial altar' [Lns], 'altar of sacrifice' [NIGTC], 'the God to whom the sacrifices are made' [TNT], not explicit [NLT].
QUESTION—What answer is expected to this question?
Questions with the negative particle οὐ, οὐχ 'not' expect a positive answer [LN (69.11), NTC; ISV, NJB, NLT, TEV]: Those who eat the sacrifices are partakers of the altar, aren't they?
QUESTION—Did they eat the sacrifices or only parts of them?
Part of the sacrifice was burned on the altar (Leviticus 3:3), part was set aside to be eaten (Leviticus 7:15–18) [Alf]. Both the priests and those who were making the sacrifice could eat [NIC, NTC].
QUESTION—Did the eater of a sacrifice become a partaker of the altar or a partner with others in regard to the altar?
1. The eater entered into fellowship with the altar (i.e., with God) [AB, Alf, BAGD, Ed, Gdt, Herm, Ho, ICC, My, NIC, NTC, Rb, TG, TNTC, Vn; NJB, NLT, TNT]. By eating the sacrifice they are in fellowship with God

1 CORINTHIANS 10:18   37

to whom the altar belongs [Herm, ICC, NTC, Vn]. To eat of a sacrifice, either Jewish or pagan, in a sacred place, was an act of worship—either sacred or profane [Ho]. Altar is a metonymy for God [AB, ICC]: they are partners with God.
2. The eaters became partners with each other in regard to the altar [EGT, HNTC; CEV, ISV]. Both the priests and non-priests ate of parts of the sacrifice and so shared both its physical and spiritual benefits [HNTC]. They share in what is on the altar [ISV]. The share in worship [CEV].

10:19 What then am-I-saying[a]? That food-sacrificed-to-idols[b] is anything
TEXT—Some manuscripts reverse the order of this clause and the following one. GNT does not mention this alternative. However, CEV, KJV, NET, NLT, REB, and TEV reverse the order.
LEXICON—a. φημί (See this word at 10:15): 'to say' [AB, NTC; CEV, KJV, NET, TNT], 'to try to say' [NLT], 'to claim' [Lns], 'to mean' [Herm, HNTC; NIV, NJB], 'to mean to affirm' [NIGTC], 'to imply' [ICC; NRSV, REB, TEV], 'to suggest' [ISV].
b. εἰδωλόθυτος (LN 5.15) (BAGD p. 221): 'food sacrificed to idols' [HNTC; CEV, NET, NRSV, TEV], 'food offered to an idol' [NTC; TNT], 'meat consecrated to an idol' [REB], 'offering made to idols' [ISV], 'idol-offering' [AB], 'meat offered to an idol' [BAGD; NAB], 'that which is offered in sacrifice to idols' [KJV], 'the offering of what is sacrificed' [NIGTC], 'the dedication of food to false gods' [NJB], 'sacrifices to (the) idols' [ICC; NLT], 'meat sacrificed to an idol' [Herm], 'idol sacrifice' [Lns], 'sacrifice offered to an idol' [NIV], 'sacrificial meat, meat of animals sacrificed to an idol' [LN].
QUESTION—What is Paul implying in this verse?
Paul's argument that those who eat the Jewish sacrifices were partners with the altar and its God may have lead some to believe that the same was true about the eating of pagan sacrifices, that those who ate sacrifices offered to idols became partners with the pagan altar and with its god, and therefore that idols were really what they were purported to be [Ho, NIC, TG, TH].
QUESTION—What is meant by τί οὖν φημι 'what I say then'?
Φημί 'I say' is not Paul's usual verb for 'saying'. Here and in 7:29 and 10:15 it has more the meaning of 'I mean' [BAGD, Herm, HNTC, ICC, NIC2; NIV, NJB, NRSV, REB, TEV]: what do I mean then?

or that (an) idol is anything?
QUESTION—What reply is expected to these questions?
They both expect a negative reply [NIC2, NTC, TNTC]: both idols and food offered to them are nothing.
QUESTION—What does τί 'anything' mean in this context (assuming that the reference is chiefly to 'idols' and only then to 'food offered to idols')?
It means to have anything beyond their material value [ICC, NTC; REB, TNT], to be anything exceptional [TNTC; ISV], to have any real existence [Gdt, Vn; NAB], to have any real claim of being a god [Herm, NIC2; NLT],

to have any spiritual power [MNTC], to amount to anything [NET, NJB, TEV].

DISCOURSE UNIT: 10:20b-22 [AB]. The topic is restriction against partaking of both.

10:20 But[a] that what they-sacrifice,[b] [they-sacrifice] to-demons[c] and not to-God;

TEXT—Some manuscripts include τὰ ἔθνη 'the Gentiles' following the first θύουσιν 'they sacrifice'. These words are omitted by GNT with a C rating, indicating difficulty in deciding whether or not to include them in the text. They are also omitted by Herm, HNTC, NIGTC, NTC; CEV, ISV, NET, NLT, REB, TEV and TNT. They are included by AB, ICC, Lns; KJV, NAB, NIV, NJB, NRSV. (AB includes them within square brackets.)

LEXICON—a. ἀλλά (LN 89.125): 'but' [HNTC, LN], 'rather' [AB], 'but I say' [KJV], 'but I do imply' [ICC], 'no, but' [NIV], 'no; however' [NTC], 'no, not at all' [NLT], 'no, I imply' [NRSV], 'no, I mean' [NAB, NET, REB], 'No! What I am saying is' [TEV, TNT], 'Not that! But' [NIGTC], 'instead, on the contrary', [LN], 'on the contrary, I am claiming' [Lns], 'no it does not: simply' [NJB], 'No, I am not!' [CEV], 'Hardly!' [ISV], 'no, rather that' [Herm]. Ἀλλά here means 'No, but rather' [HNTC], 'I do not contend that idols exist, but I do contend…' [NIC]. See this word also at 10:5

b. pres. act. indic. of θύω (LN 53.19) (BAGD 1. p. 367): 'to sacrifice' [AB, BAGD, Herm, HNTC, LN, Lns, NIGTC, NTC; KJV, NET, NRSV], 'to offer' [ICC; ISV], 'to make a sacrifice' [LN], not explicit [NAB]. This active verb is translated as a passive: 'to be sacrificed' [NJB, TEV]. The phrase ἃ θύουσιν 'the things which they sacrifice' is translated 'the/these sacrifices are offered' [NIV, NLT], 'pagan sacrifices are offered' [REB, TNT], 'food is really sacrificed' [CEV].

c. δαιμόνιον (LN 12.37, 12:26): 'demon' [AB, BAGD, Herm, HNTC, ICC, LN (12.37), NIGTC, NTC; all versions except KJV], 'devil' [Lns; KJV], 'evil spirit' [BAGD, LN (12.37)], 'god, lesser god' [LN (12.26)].

QUESTION—To whom does 'they' refer?

It refers to the pagans or the Gentiles [AB, HNTC, ICC, Lns, NIC; KJV, NAB, NIV, NJB, NRSV, REB, TEV, TNT]. It refers to Israel when they worshiped false gods [NTC].

QUESTION—To whom does δαιμόνιον 'demon' refer?

It refers to evil spirits [BAGD, Ho, NIC, TNTC], fallen angels [Ho, Lns], disembodied spirits [Vn], or evil spiritual powers [HNTC, TH].

QUESTION—To whom does θεῷ 'to God/god' refer?

1. It refers to God [Herm, HNTC, NTC; all versions]: they sacrifice to demons and not to God.
2. It refers to a god [AB, ICC, Lns, NIC, NIC2, Rb]. Paul usually includes the article when specifying God when no other markers are present. Here

then he intends 'god' [AB, Lns, NIC, NIC2]: they sacrifice to demons and not to a god. It means: 'a no-god' (see Deut. 32:17) [ICC, NIC2, Rb].

and not I-desire you to-become partakers[a] of-the demons.
LEXICON—a. κοινωνός (BAGD 1.a.β. p. 439): 'partaker' [NTC], 'partner' [AB, BAGD, Herm, HNTC; ISV, NET, NLT, NRSV, REB, TEV], 'sharer' [NAB], 'participant' [NIV], 'communicant' [Lns], 'communal participants' [NIGTC]. The phrase κοινωνοὺς γίνεσθαι 'to become sharers' is translated 'to be in fellowship with' [TNT], 'to have fellowship with' [KJV], 'to enter into fellowship with' [ICC], 'to have anything to do with' [CEV], 'to share with' [NJB]. See this word also at 10:18.
QUESTION—What is implied in this clause?
The gods Jupiter and Minerva do not have a real existence, but those who worship them, worship demons and when a person sacrifices to demons he comes into fellowship with demons [Ho].

10:21 **Not are-you-able to-drink (the) cup of-(the)-Lord and (the) cup of-demons, not are-you-able to-partake-of[a] (the) table[b] of-(the)-Lord and (the) table of-demons.**
LEXICON—a. pres. act. infin. of μετέχω (LN **34.32**, 57.6) (BAGD p. 514): 'to partake of' [Herm, HNTC, Lns, NTC; NAB, NRSV, REB], 'to be a partaker of' [KJV], 'to eat at' [LN (34.32); CEV, ISV, NLT, TEV], 'to eat in common with others' [ICC], 'to take part in' [NET], 'to have a part in' [NIV], 'to have a share of' [BAGD, LN (57.6); NJB], 'to share in' [AB, BAGD, LN (57.6); TNT], 'to participate in' [BAGD, NIGTC]. The idiom τραπέζης μετέχειν 'to share in a table' means that by the ceremonial eating the participant shows that he belongs to that religious group and here the clause means 'you cannot belong to the Lord and belong to demons' [LN (34.32)]. This phrase is an idiom which means to belong to a particular religious group as evidenced by ceremonial eating [LN (34.32)]. Μετέχω refers here to the actual act of eating as it was used in 10:17 [NIC2]. See this word also at 10:17.
b. τράπεζα (LN 6.113, 23.26) (BAGD 2. p. 824): 'table' [AB, BAGD, Herm, HNTC, ICC, LN (6.113), Lns, NIGTC, NTC; all versions], 'meal' [LN (23.26)].
QUESTION—What is the point of this verse?
The point is that eating and drinking at the table of the Lord and the table of demons is mutually exclusive, a person cannot do both. This parallels what Jesus had said, "You cannot serve two masters" (Matt. 6:24) [MNTC, NTC].
QUESTION—What is the meaning of οὐ δύνασθε 'you are not able'?
It means that this is not an option for you [AB]. It means that it is morally impossible [Alf, Gdt, ICC, Lns, Rb, TNTC], that is, one cannot in good conscience, consent to doing this [ICC, TNTC], or one cannot do it without punishment [Gdt].

QUESTION—What does ποτήριον 'cup' stand for?
   It is a metonymy in which 'cup' stands for what is in it [BAGD], it stands for the wine in the cup [TG, TH].
QUESTION—How are the nouns related in the genitive construction ποτήριον κυρίου 'cup of the Lord' (and by extension 'cup of demons')?
   It is a possessive relationship [Lns]: the cup which belongs to the Lord. It is a relationship of unity [Ho, ICC, My]: the cup which brings one into fellowship with the Lord. It indicates 'the cup which the Lord instituted' [Ed, EGT]. It indicates 'the cup used in the Lord's Supper' [TH].
QUESTION—What is meant by ποτήριον κυρίου πίνω 'to drink the cup of the Lord'?
   It means entering into a covenantal relationship with the Lord by the benefits of his blood [NIC2]. It signifies allegiance to the Lord [EGT].
QUESTION—What does ποτήριον δαιμονίων πίνω 'to drink the cup of demons' signify?
   It signifies drinking to honor the gods. The first cup of the pagan banquets were drunk to Jupiter, the second to Jupiter and the Nymphs, and the third to Jupiter Soter [Gdt].
QUESTION—What does τράπεζα 'table' stand for?
   It is a metonymy in which 'table' is used to refer to the food on it [AB, BAGD, ICC, Rb, Vn].
QUESTION—How are the nouns related in the genitive construction τραπέζης κυρίου 'table of the Lord' (and by extension 'table of demons')?
   It indicates 'the table at which the Lord presides' [Ho, TNTC]. It refers to the Lord's Supper [ICC, Lns, Rb].
QUESTION—What is meant by τραπέζης κυρίου μετέχω 'to eat at the table of the Lord' (and by extension, at the table of demons)?
   It means to share a meal with the Lord [AB]. This signifies being in fellowship with the Lord [MNTC, TNTC, Vn]. It signifies being united with the Lord and with his people in one body [HNTC]. Both eating and drinking at the table signify being one with the Lord [NTC]. It signifies being bound to each other [NIC2].

10:22 Or do-we-provoke-to-jealousy[a] the Lord?

LEXICON—a. pres. act. indic. of παραζηλόω (LN 88.164) (BAGD p. 616): 'to provoke to jealousy' [AB, BAGD, ICC, Lns, NTC; ISV, KJV, NET, NRSV], 'to provoke to jealous anger' [NAB], 'to make jealous' [LN; CEV, TEV, TNT], 'to arouse (someone's) jealousy' [NIGTC; NIV, NJB], 'to rouse (someone's) jealousy' [NLT], 'to seek to provoke to jealousy' [Herm], 'to provoke' [HNTC; REB], 'to cause to be envious' [LN]. Παραζηλόω here means 'to intend to provoke' [Ho; NAB], 'to want to provoke' [NJB, TEV, TNT], 'to dare to provoke' [NLT]. The present tense is a conative present meaning 'we try to provoke to jealousy' [AB, NIGTC; ISV, NET, NIV].

QUESTION—What alternative is suggested by the conjunction ἤ 'or'?
It stands as an alternative to the previous verse implying 'or, will we eat and drink from the table of the Lord and the table of demons and thus provoke the Lord to jealousy'? [Ed, EGT, ICC, NIC2, TG, TH, TNTC, Vn]. A person who would eat of the table of demons would be an idolater and would excite God's anger [NIC].

QUESTION—What response is expected to this question?
Paul expects a negative response, assuming that the Corinthians would not want to do such a thing [Ho, Lns, NTC, TG].

QUESTION—To whom does κυρίος 'Lord' refer?
1. It refers to Christ [Alf, Ed, HNTC, Ho, My, NIC2, TH, Vn]. The immediate context demands this where the reference has been to Christ [NIC2].
2. It refers to God since it is a quotation of Deuteronomy 32:16, 21 where it refers to God [NIC, NTC].

QUESTION—What does 'jealousy' denote?
It denotes an emotion aroused in a lover by rejection in favor of someone else. It is the strongest human emotion [Ho]. It has an element of anger [Ho, ICC, MNTC, Vn].

not[a] are-we stronger than-he?
LEXICON—a. μή (LN 69.15) (BAGD C.1. p. 517): 'not' [LN]. This particle marks a negative response to a question [LN].

QUESTION—What reply is expected to this question?
Questions with the negative particle μή 'not' expect a negative reply [AB, ICC, LN, Lns, MNTC, NIGTC, NTC, TG; CEV, ISV, NAB, NET, NLT, TEV]: we are not stronger than he, are we?

QUESTION—What does being stronger than the Lord imply?
It implies that one is able to provoke the Lord and get away with it [HNTC, Ho, Lns, TH, Vn].

DISCOURSE UNIT: 10:23–11:1 [Alf, Ed, EGT, Gdt, GNT, Herm, HNTC, ICC, Lns, MNTC, NCBC, NIC, NIC2, NIGTC, NTC, TG, TNTC; CEV, NET, NIV, NJB]. The topic is conduct in detail [Gdt, Lns], idol sacrifice and conscience (freedom) [Herm], the eating of marketplace food [NIC2], freedom of conscience [NTC], using freedom for God's glory [MNTC], principles and warnings [TG], the practical outcome [TNTC], a practical summary [Ed], liberty and charity [NCBC], liberty and its limits [EGT, HNTC], the believer's freedom [NIV], freedom and love [NIGTC], practical rules about idol-meats [NIC; NJB], do all to God's glory [GNT], always honor God [CEV], living to glorify God [NET].

DISCOURSE UNIT: 10:23–33 [Ho; ISV]. The topic is the eating of meat offered to idols [Ho], doing all to God's glory [ISV].

10:23 All-things are-permissible[a] but not all-things are-helpful;[b]

LEXICON—a. pres. act. indic. of ἔξεστι (LN 71.1) (BAGD 1. p. 275): 'to be permissible' [AB, BAGD, NTC; ISV, NIV, NJB], 'to be permitted' [BAGD, HNTC, TH], 'to be lawful' [Lns; KJV, NAB, NET, NRSV], 'to do as one likes' [ICC], 'to be proper' [BAGD, TH], 'to be possible' [BAGD, LN]. The phrase πάντα ἔξεστιν 'all things are permissible' is translated 'One is free to do anything' [Herm], 'Some of you say, "We can do whatever we want to!"' [CEV], 'You say, "I am allowed to do anything"' [NLT], '"We are free to do anything," you say' [REB], '"We are allowed to do anything," so they say' [TEV], 'You say, "All things are permissible."' [TNT], 'Liberty to do all things' [NIGTC].

b. pres. act. indic. of συμφέρω (LN 65.44) (BAGD 2.a. p. 780): 'to be helpful' [BAGD, NIGTC; ISV, NLT], 'to be beneficial' [NET, NIV, NRSV], 'to benefit' [Lns], 'to be profitable' [NTC], 'to be useful' [BAGD], 'to be advantageous' [AB, LN; NAB], 'to be to (one's) advantage' [LN], 'to be expedient' [HNTC; KJV], 'to be good' [CEV, TEV], 'to be good (for one)' [REB], 'to be for (one's) good' [TNT], 'to be for the best' [Herm], 'to do good' [ICC; NJB], 'to be better off' [LN].

QUESTION—To whom does Paul now address his remarks?

Paul resumes his point from chapter 8 and once again addresses the strong ones among the Corinthians. In the preceding verses he has been addressing the weak [NIC].

QUESTION—What other verse is this similar to?

It parallels 6:12 almost word for word [NIC2].

QUESTION—What does Paul mean by πάντα 'all things'?

He does not mean literally all things but all social practices in themselves [AB]. He means all things that are not essential to the Christian faith, the nonessentials [Gdt, ICC, Lns, NIC2, Vn]. He means all things that are not identified as sinful [MNTC].

QUESTION—Whose words are πάντα ἔξεστιν 'all things are permissible'?

These are the words of a saying used in Corinth and Paul is quoting it [Alf, Gdt, HNTC, NIC, NIC2, NTC, TG, TH; all versions except ISV, KJV]: You say, "All things are permissible." (Other commentaries and versions do not reflect this interpretation.) Paul agreed with the sentiment with self evident limitations [Lns].

QUESTION— What is the specific meaning of συμφέρει 'be helpful'?

It means to be spiritually helpful or beneficial to oneself and to others [Lns]. It means to be helpful to others [Ho, NIC, NIC2]. It means to be profitable for oneself [NTC].

all-things are-permissible but not all-things build-up.[a]

LEXICON—a. pres. act. indic. of οἰκοδομέω (LN 74.15) (BAGD 3. p. 558): 'to build up' [AB, Herm, HNTC, LN, Lns; ISV, NET, NJB, NRSV, REB], 'to build up the life of the church' [ICC], 'to build up the church' [NIGTC], 'to edify' [NTC; KJV], 'to be constructive' [NAB, NIV], 'to be beneficial'

[BAGD; NLT], 'to strengthen, to make more able' [LN], 'to be helpful' [CEV, TEV, TNT].

QUESTION—What is the specific meaning of οἰκοδομεῖ 'build up'?

It means to build up spiritually [Lns, NIC, Vn]. It means to cause someone else to advance spiritually [NIC]. It refers to building up the character and faith of individuals and of their society [ICC]. The verb applies to building up others [Alf, EGT, Gdt, Herm, HNTC, My, NIC, NIC2, NTC, TG, TH], since this refers to how one's actions affects others [TG]. Here it specifically means to build up oneself, agreeing with 10:6, 12 [Ho].

10:24 No-one let-seek[a] his-own-thing but the thing of-the other (person).

LEXICON—a. pres. act. impera. of ζητέω (LN 57.59, 25.9) (BAGD 2.b.α. p. 339): 'to seek' [AB, Herm, HNTC, LN (57.59), Lns, NIGTC, NTC; ISV, KJV, NAB, NET, NIV, NRSV, TNT], 'to look for' [NJB], 'to desire, to want to' [LN (25.9)], 'to think about' [CEV], 'to think of' [NLT], 'to look after' [REB], 'to look out for' [TEV], 'to strive for' [BAGD], 'to try to obtain, to attempt to get' [LN (57.59)].

QUESTION—What is the relationship of this verse to the preceding?

In this verse Paul explains what he means by 'is helpful' and 'build up' of 10:23 [ICC, Rb, Vn]. Paul explains what he means by 'build up' of 10:23 [Gdt, NTC]. This states the principle behind the instructions of 10:23 [NIC].

QUESTION—What is implied in the phrases τὸ ἑαυτοῦ 'his own thing' and τὸ τοῦ ἑτέρου 'the thing of the other person'?

They imply the word 'interest' [AB, Lns, NTC; NAB, REB, TEV]: his own interest…the interest of the other person. They imply the word 'good' [EGT, Rb, TNTC; NET, NIV, NLT, TNT], 'welfare' [Ho; ISV, KJV], 'enjoyment or advantage' [Gdt; NJB, NRSV], 'ends' [HNTC], 'rights' and 'well-being' [ICC, NIGTC].

QUESTION—What is the principle stated in this verse?

The principle stated here does not mean that one should never seek his own good, but that when one's own good conflicts with the good of others, the latter should take precedence over the former [ICC, Lns, Vn]. It is a general principle meant to limit a person's freedom [NIC]. The principle is that even if a thing is helpful, we should not do it if it is not helpful to others [MNTC].

10:25 Eat every thing being-sold[a] in (the) meat-market[b] not asking-questions[c] because-of[d] conscience;[e]

LEXICON—a. pres. pass. participle of πωλέω (LN 57.186) (BAGD p. 731): 'to be sold' [AB, Herm, HNTC, LN, NIGTC, NTC; all versions except CEV, TNT], 'to be on/for sale' [ICC, Lns; TNT], 'to be offered for sale' [BAGD]. The phrase πᾶν τὸ ἐν μακέλλῳ πωλούμενον 'everything being sold in the meat market' is translated 'when you buy meat in the market' [CEV].

b. μάκελλον (LN **57.208**) (BAGD p. 487): 'meat market' [AB, BAGD, ICC, **LN**, NIGTC, NTC; ISV, NIV, NRSV, REB, TEV, TNT], 'market' [Herm,

HNTC; CEV, NAB], 'marketplace' [NET, NLT], 'butchers' shops' [Lns; NJB], 'shambles' [KJV].
c. pres. act. participle of ἀνακρίνω (LN 27.44, 30.109) (BAGD 1.a. p. 56): 'to ask questions' [AB, BAGD, NTC; KJV, NJB, TEV, TNT], 'to raise questions' [Herm; ISV, NAB, NIV, NRSV, REB], 'to ask' [CEV, NLT], 'to ask about to reach a judgment' [NIGTC], 'to make inquiries' [HNTC], 'to ask for information' [ICC], 'to make investigation' [Lns], 'to investigate, to examine carefully, to study thoroughly' [LN (27.44)], 'to judge carefully, to evaluate carefully' [LN (30.109)]. The phrase μηδὲν ἀνακρίνοντες 'questioning nothing' is translated 'without questions' [NET].
d. διά with accusative object (LN 89.26): 'because of' [AB, LN, Lns, NIGTC; TEV], 'on the ground of' [ISV, NRSV], 'based on' [HNTC], 'for the sake of' [NTC; KJV, NJB], 'on account of, by reason of' [LN]. The phrase διὰ τὴν συνείδησιν 'on account of conscience' is translated 'keep your conscience clear' [CEV], 'and then your conscience won't be bothered' [NLT], 'that might perplex your conscience' [ICC], '(question(s)) of conscience' [Herm; NAB, NET, NIV, REB, TNT].
e. συνείδησις (LN 26.13) (BAGD 2. p. 786): 'conscience' [AB, BAGD, ICC, LN, Lns, NTC; all versions except NLT, TEV], 'your conscience' [NLT, TEV], 'conscientious scruples' [HNTC], 'self awareness' [NIGTC].

QUESTION—What is the relationship of this verse to the preceding one?

This verse begins to give specific applications of the principle given in 10:24 [Lns]. To a certain extent it counterbalances the preceding principle. Although the welfare of others should be of primary concern, their standards should not decide everything we do [MNTC]. Freedom in one's personal life is not to be judged by others [NIC2].

QUESTION—Where does the emphasis lie in this verse?

The words πᾶν τό 'everything' are forefronted and are emphatic [NIC2].

QUESTION—What is meant by the phrase διὰ τὴν συνείδησιν 'because of conscience'?

1. They should eat and not ask questions based on conscientious scruples [Ed, EGT, Gdt, Herm, Ho, Lns, My, NIC2, TG, Vn; NAB, NIV, NJB, NRSV, REB, TNT]: eat and do not ask questions in regard to conscience. They need not ask whether or not the meat has been offered to idols because there is no need to have scruples about the matter. This interpretation is supported by the reason given in the next verse [EGT, Ho]. This whole matter lies outside of the concerns of conscience [Lns, NIC2]. They need not ask questions because their strong consciences would not be troubled if the meat had been sacrificed to idols [Ed].
2. They should eat without asking questions because their consciences might be troubled upon finding out that the meat had been sacrificed to idols. [AB, Alf, ICC, NIC]: eat without asking questions, because if you ask, it

might offend your conscience. It is alright to eat as long as one does not know that the meat has been sacrificed to idols [AB].
QUESTION—What is the question to be asked?
The question to be asked is whether the meat had been sacrificed to idols or not [Alf, Ho, ICC, MNTC, NIC2, Rb].

10:26 For the earth and its fullness[a] (are) the Lord's.
LEXICON—a. πλήρωμα (LN **59.36**) (BAGD 1.a. p. 672): 'fullness' [Lns; KJV, NAB, NRSV], 'abundance' [NET], 'that which fills' [LN]. The phrase τὸ πλήρωμα αὐτῆς 'its fullness' is translated 'everything that is in it' [BAGD, **LN**], 'everything in it' [CEV, ISV, NIV, NLT, TEV], 'everything else in the world' [ICC], 'everything it contains' [HNTC], 'all that is in it' [NIGTC; REB, TNT], 'all it contains' [Herm; NJB], 'that which fills it' [AB].
QUESTION—What relationship is indicated by γάρ 'for'?
It indicates the grounds for the principle stated in 10:25 [Herm, HNTC, Ho, ICC, NIC, NIC2, Rb, TH, TNTC]: eat every thing being sold in the meat market, not asking questions because of conscience *since* the earth and its fullness are the Lord's. All that belongs to the Lord includes food that has been sacrificed to idols [TG]. It is implied that if all belongs to God, the fact that it has been offered to idols cannot change that nor contaminate anyone [ICC, MNTC, NIC2]. This shows why no examination is necessary [NIC].
QUESTION—Is this verse a quotation?
Excluding the word 'for', this verse is a quotation [CEV, ISV, NAB, NET, NIV, NJB, NLT, NRSV, REB, TEV]. It quotes Psalm 24:1 [AB, EGT, Gdt, Herm, HNTC, ICC, Lns, MNTC, NIC, NIC2, NTC, TG, TH, Vn].
QUESTION—What words are emphasized in this verse?
The words τοῦ κυρίου 'the Lord's' are emphasized [ICC, TH, Vn]: it is to the Lord that the earth belongs.
QUESTION—Who is 'the Lord'?
In the quotation 'the Lord' is God [AB, Ho, TG, TH].

DISCOURSE UNIT: 10:27–30 [NTC]. The topic is freedom and conscience.

10:27 If anyone of-the unbelievers[a] invites[b] you
LEXICON—a. ἄπιστος (LN 11.19, 31.106) (BAGD 2. p. 85): 'unbeliever' [AB, HNTC, LN (31.106), Lns, NIGTC, NTC; all versions except KJV, NLT], 'one of the heathen' [ICC], '(one) who believes not' [KJV], 'who isn't a Christian' [NLT], 'non-Christian' [LN (11.19)], 'one who is not a believer' [LN (31.106)]. This word is also translated as an adjective: 'unbelieving' [BAGD, Herm]. Ἄπιστος refers to someone who does not believe the good news about Jesus Christ [LN]. See this word also at 6:6.
  b. pres. act. indic. of καλέω (LN 33.315) (BAGD 1.b. p. 399): 'to invite' [AB, BAGD, Herm, LN, Lns, NIGTC, NTC; ISV, NET, TNT], 'to invite to a meal' [ICC; NIV, NJB, NRSV, REB, TEV], 'to invite to dinner' [CEV], 'to invite to (one's) table' [NAB], 'to ask home for dinner' [NLT],

'to bid to a feast' [KJV]. This means to ask a person to accept offered hospitality [LN].

QUESTION—What is implied by τις καλεῖ 'anyone invites'?

It implies that someone invites someone to their home for a meal [LN, NIC2, NTC, TH, TNTC; CEV, NAB, NIV, NJB, NLT, NRSV, REB, TEV]. It implies an invitation to a banquet [Alf, Rb; KJV].

QUESTION—Who is included in ὑμᾶς 'you'?

Although he has been addressing all of the Corinthians, here the meaning must be 'some of you' [ICC].

and you-want^a to-go,

LEXICON—a. pres. act. indic. of θέλω (LN 25.1) (BAGD 1. p. 355): 'to want' [LN, NIGTC; CEV, NAB, NET, NIV, NJB, NLT], 'to wish' [AB, HNTC, LN, NTC; ISV, TNT], 'to desire' [LN, Lns], 'to be disposed' [KJV, NRSV], 'to care (to)' [ICC], 'to decide' [TEV], 'to be willing' [Herm]. This clause is translated 'and you accept' [REB].

QUESTION—What is implied by θέλετε πορεύεσθαι 'you want to go'?

It implies that Paul would not advise their going [ICC]. It does not imply that Paul would not advise their going [HNTC, Lns]. It may imply that there is need for deliberation before deciding [Gdt]. It may imply that they were considering the advisability of going because of possible difficulties [NIC]. It does not imply that Christians did not go to such meals [TH]. It implies that they would not go unless invited [Vn]. All he implies is that for some reason or other they might not wish to go [Lns]. The word θέλω 'want' implies active purpose or will [EGT].

eat every thing being-set-before^a you not asking-questions because-of^b conscience.

LEXICON—a. pres. pass. participle of παρατίθημι (LN 57.116) (BAGD 1.a. p. 623): 'to be set before' [AB, BAGD, HNTC, ICC, NTC; ISV, KJV, NRSV, TEV, TNT], 'to be placed before' [Lns; NAB], 'to be put before' [Herm, NIGTC; NIV, NJB, REB], 'to be served' [BAGD; CEV, NET], 'to be offered' [NLT], 'to be given food, to be provided with food' [LN].

b. διά with accusative object (See this word at 10:25): 'because of' [AB, Lns, NIGTC; TEV], 'on the ground of' [ISV, NRSV], 'based on' [HNTC], 'for the sake of' [NTC; KJV]. The phrase διὰ τὴν συνείδησιν 'on account of conscience' is translated 'to cause a problem for someone's conscience' [CEV], 'your conscience should not be bothered by this' [NLT], '(asking/raising question(s)) of conscience' [Herm; NAB, NET, NIV, NJB, REB, TNT].

QUESTION—What is the question to be asked?

The question to be asked is whether the meat had been sacrificed to idols or not [Vn].

QUESTION—What is meant by διὰ τὴν συνείδησιν 'because of conscience'?
It means because one's conscience tells them it is wrong, or because one's conscience begins to bother them [TH]. This is almost identical language with 10:25 [Lns, NIC].

DISCOURSE UNIT: 10:28–29 [AB]. The topic is when another's conscience is concerned.

10:28 But if someone should-say to-you, "This is (a) temple-sacrifice,"ª (do) not eat

LEXICON—a. ἱερόθυτος (LN **53.21**) (BAGD p. 372): 'temple sacrifice' [TNT], 'temple offering' [AB], 'sacrifice' [NET], 'sacrifice meat' [Lns], 'sacrificial meat' [Herm], 'something which has been sacrificed to a deity' [**LN**], 'sacrificed to a divinity, devoted to a divinity' [BAGD], 'meat offered to an idol' [NTC]. This noun is also translated as a verb phrase: 'to be offered in sacrifice' [ICC, NIGTC; ISV, NIV, NJB, NRSV, REB], 'to be offered in sacrifice unto idols' [KJV], 'to be offered in idol worship' [NAB], 'to be offered to idols' [TEV], 'to be offered to an idol' [NLT], 'to be sacrificed to idols' [CEV]. The word means 'offered to sacred beings' [TH].

QUESTION—What is the point of this verse?
It shows that the liberty of the Christian in 10:27 must be governed by love and consideration for others [Lns].

QUESTION—What relationship is indicated by δέ 'but'?
It is an adversative relationship and contrasts with 10:27 [NIC2]: eat everything set before you, *but* if someone should say…, then don't eat it. It indicates that 10:28 will be something different from the principle stated in 10:27 [Lns]. It is an exception to the general rule [Ho].

QUESTION—Where does this take place?
The action takes place in a private home [HNTC, ICC, NIC2, NTC]. Otherwise if it took place in a temple there would be no need to reveal that the meat had been sacrificed to idols [HNTC, ICC]. A weak Christian would not be present at an idol feast [HNTC].

QUESTION—Who is τις 'someone' likely to be?
1. It refers to a fellow believer [Alf, Ed, Gdt, HNTC, Ho, ICC, Lns, MNTC, My, Rb, TG, TNTC, Vn]. It probably refers to a weak scrupulous Christian [HNTC, ICC, Lns,]. The context has been about weak Christians especially 10:25–27 [Lns]. A weak Christian would warn his brother to keep him from sin [NIC]. The term ἱερόθυτος 'sacrificial meat' would be appropriately used at a pagan's table [Alf, Lns].
2. It refers to a pagan guest. If it were a fellow believer he/she would not use the pagan term ἱερόθυτος 'sacrificial meat' rather than εἰδωλόθυτον 'idol meat', the standard Jewish-Christian word [AB, Herm, NIC2]. Paul cannot mean the host since he repeats the indefinite τις 'anyone' whereas the host is a definite reference. A fellow guest who is an unbeliever would

be trying to help out a Christian whom he assumes would have scruples about food offered to idols [NIC2].

3. It refers either to the non-Christian host or to a fellow guest who may not be a Christian [EGT, HNTC, NTC]. This person would not be a Christian since he would be unlikely to have asked about the meat and then stayed for dinner [NTC].

QUESTION—What is implied in the words ἱερόθυτον ἐστιν 'it is a temple sacrifice'?

It changes the nature of the meal from being harmless to being a sacrificial meal implying participation in sacrifice to idols [Herm].

QUESTION—What is the significance of the present tense imperative μὴ ἐσθίετε 'Do not eat!'?

It means to stop an activity that is in progress [AB]: Stop eating! It means 'do not make a practice of eating' [ICC, Rb].

for-the-sake-of[a] that (person) the-(one) having-informed[b] (you) and (for the sake of) conscience;

TEXT—Some manuscripts include τοῦ γὰρ κυρίου ἡ γῆ καὶ τὸ πλήρωμα αὐτῆς 'for the earth is the Lord's and the fullness thereof' at the end of this verse. GNT omits this clause with an A rating, indicating that the text is certain. Only KJV includes it.

LEXICON—a. διά with accusative object (LN 89.26, 90.38): 'for the sake of' [Herm, LN (90.38), NTC; KJV, NAB, NIV, TEV, TNT], 'out of consideration for' [ISV, NJB, NLT, NRSV, REB], 'out of regard for' [NIGTC], 'because of' [AB, LN (89.26), Lns; NET], 'for' [LN (90.38); CEV], 'on account of, by reason of' [LN (89.26)], 'on behalf of, for the benefit of' [LN (90.38)]. The words δι' εἰκεῖνον τὸν μηνύσαντα 'for the sake of the one who informed' are translated 'so as to avoid shocking your informant' [ICC].

b. aorist act. participle of μηνύω (LN 33.209) (BAGD p. 519): 'to inform' [AB, BAGD, LN, NIGTC, NTC; NRSV, TNT], 'to call attention to' [NAB], 'to tell' [CEV, ISV, NET, NIV, NJB, NLT, TEV], 'to show' [Lns; KJV], 'to reveal' [LN], 'to point out' [Rb]. The phrase ἐκεῖνον τὸν μηνύσαντα 'the one having informed you' is translated 'him' [REB], 'the man who gave you the information' [Herm], '(your) informant' [ICC].

QUESTION—What does δι' εἰκεῖνον τὸν μηνύσαντα 'for the sake of the one who informed you' mean?

It means that eating in this case would be a bad example to the weak Christian [Gdt].

QUESTION—What does δι'…καὶ τὴν συνείδησιν 'and for the sake conscience' mean?

The word καί 'and' is explanatory [Lns]: for the one who informed you, *that is*, for the sake of the conscience of the one who informed you. Here Paul does not specify whose conscience he means; that is explained in the next verse [NIC2, NTC]. It means that care must be taken not to wound that

1 CORINTHIANS 10:28   49

conscience by eating [Alf, Ho, Lns, NIC]. It means to avoid shocking him [ICC]. It means 'out of consideration for' or 'to spare the feelings of' [TG].

10:29 **But conscience I-say not one's-own but the (conscience) of-the other (person).**
QUESTION—What is the function of this clause?
   1. When this refers to the conscience of a weak Christian who informed him. Since he showed that his conscience was offended by eating of the sacrificial meat, his views must be respected [NIC].
   2. When this refers to a non-Christian. The pagan assumed the Christian would not eat sacrificial meat and felt a moral obligation to inform the Christian. The Christian should not offend him by acting contrary to his expectations [NIC2]. If eating discredits the Christian faith in the eyes of the pagan, the Christian will not eat [NTC].

For why is-judged^a my freedom^b by^c another's conscience?
LEXICON—a. pres. pass. indic. of κρίνω (LN 56.30) (BAGD 6.b. p. 452): 'to be judged' [AB, ICC, Lns, NTC; ISV, KJV, NET, NIV, TNT], 'to be subject to the judgment' [NRSV], 'to be exposed to the judgment of' [HNTC], 'to be called in question' [REB], 'to be governed' [NJB], 'to be limited' [CEV, NLT, TEV], 'to be restricted' [NAB], 'to be subject to the judgment of' [Herm], 'to be subjected to' [NIGTC], 'to be judged unfavorably' [BAGD], 'to be criticized' [BAGD], 'to be condemned' [BAGD, LN], 'to be judged as guilty' [LN]. This word is used here in the sense of 'to be condemned' [Alf, EGT, Gdt, Ho, NTC, TNTC, Vn]. See this word also at 10:15.
   b. ἐλευθερία (LN 37.133) (BAGD p. 250): 'freedom' [AB, BAGD, Herm, HNTC, LN, Lns, NIGTC, NTC; CEV, ISV, NIV, NJB, NLT, REB, TNT], 'freedom to act' [TEV], 'liberty' [BAGD, ICC; KJV, NAB, NRSV], 'right' [NET].
   c. ὑπό with genitive object (LN **90.1**) (BAGD 1.a.β. p. 843): 'by' [AB, BAGD, Herm, ICC, **LN**, Lns, NTC; all versions except KJV, NRSV], 'of' [KJV, NRSV], not explicit [HNTC, NIGTC].
QUESTION—What relationship is indicated by γάρ 'for'?
   1. It indicates the reason why they should not eat. They should not eat if their liberty offends someone else's conscience [Alf, EGT, Gdt, Ho, ICC, MNTC, NTC, TNTC, Vn]. It means, for if I eat he will judge my freedom and condemn it and I don't want that to happen. Therefore I will not eat [EGT, Gdt, Ho, ICC]. He will not eat because there is no good to be gained by eating it and letting his liberty incur condemnation [ICC]. Why should he use his freedom to give offence? [Ho].
   2. It indicates the reason why Paul meant another person's conscience. They are to refrain from eating for the sake of someone else's conscience, not their own, because their own consciences are not to be judged by someone else's conscience [AB, Ed, HNTC, Lns, My, NIC]. I abstain for his conscience not my own, because if I abstain for my own conscience it

means that I surrender my freedom. If, on the other hand, I abstain for his conscience I remain free [HNTC]. He will abstain from eating for the sake of the other person, not himself. He will not allow that person's conscience to dictate to his own conscience [AB].
3. This is the voice of an objector who disagrees with Paul about not eating [Rb, TG; NAB, REB, TEV, TNT]: You say, "Why should my freedom be judged by another person's conscience?" A believer with a weak conscience should not restrict freedom of one with a strong conscience [TG].
4. This is a rhetorical outburst of Paul reverting back to the defense of his freedom against his accusers and is not connected with the context here [NIC2]. Paul's main concern here is with the theme of freedom and the idea of someone else's conscience limiting freedom provokes him to return to his defense from 9:19–23.

QUESTION—Is this question real or rhetorical?

It is rhetorical [EGT, NIC, TH] and could be rendered as a statement [TH]: For my freedom should not be judged by another person's conscience.

QUESTION—What is meant by ἐλευθερία 'freedom'?

It is the Christian's liberty to use all of God's gifts, including sacrificial meat [NIC]. Here freedom refers to the right to eat food sacrificed to idols [TG].

DISCOURSE UNIT: 10:30–11:1 [AB]. The topic is Paul's Christian example.

10:30 If I with-thankfulness/grace[a] partake,[b]

LEXICON—a. χάρις (LN 33.350) (BAGD 5. p. 878): 'thankfulness' [BAGD, Herm, Lns; ISV, NET, NIV, NRSV, REB], 'thanksgiving' [HNTC, NIGTC; TNT], 'gratitude' [NJB], 'grace' [AB; KJV], 'to say grace (for food)' [ICC], 'thanks' [LN]. This noun is also translated as an adverb: 'thankfully' [NAB]; as a verb: 'to thank' [NLT, TEV], 'to thank and to enjoy' [NLT]. This word plus the phrase ὑπὲρ οὗ ἐγὼ εὐχαριστέω 'regarding the thing for which I give thanks' in the following clause is translated 'I give thanks' [CEV].

b. pres. act. indic. of μετέχω (LN **23.2, 23.2 fn 3**): 'to partake' [Herm, Lns; NAB, NET, NRSV, REB], 'to be a partaker' [KJV], 'to eat food' [**LN** (23.2)], 'to partake of food' [HNTC, LN 23.2 fn 3], 'to eat' [LN (23.2); CEV, ISV, NLT], 'to share (a) meal' [TNT], 'to take part in (a) meal' [NIGTC; NIV], 'to share in' [AB], 'to accept' [NJB], not explicit [ICC; TEV]. This entire phrase is translated 'if I thank God for my food' [TEV]. See this word also at 10:17, 21.

QUESTION—What is meant by χάριτι 'with thankfulness/grace'?

1. It refers to eating food with thanksgiving [Alf, BAGD, Ed, EGT, Gdt, Herm, HNTC, Ho, ICC, Lns, My, NIC, NIC2, NTC, Rb, TG, TH; NIV, NJB, NRSV, REB, TEV, TNT]. The words 'I give thanks' show that the idea of 'gratitude' is intended here [EGT, Lns, NIC, TH].

2. It refers to receiving a share of God's grace [AB, Vn; KJV]. This can mean God's gift of grace that makes food suitable to eat or it may refer to one's life with God on the basis of grace [AB].

why am-I-blamed[a] for[b] (the-thing) for-which I give-thanks?[c]
LEXICON—a. pres. pass. indic. of βλασθημέω (LN 33.400) (BAGD 1. p. 142): 'to be blamed' [HNTC; NAB, NET, NJB, REB], 'to be slandered' [AB, Lns; TNT], 'to be evil spoken of' [KJV], 'to be denounced' [Herm; ISV, NIV, NRSV], 'to be condemned' [NLT], 'to be accused of doing wrong' [CEV], 'to be criticized' [TEV], 'to be involved in blame' [ICC], 'to be blasphemed' [LN], 'to suffer defamation of character' [NIGTC], 'to be reviled, to be defamed' [BAGD, LN], 'to have one's reputation injured' [BAGD].
  b. ὑπέρ with genitive object (LN **89.28**, 90.24) (BAGD 1.d. p. 839): 'for' [BAGD, Herm, HNTC, Lns; KJV, NAB, NET, NJB, NLT, REB], 'because of' [AB, BAGD, **LN**; ISV, NIV, NRSV, TNT], 'about' [TEV], 'over' [NIGTC], 'in view of' [LN], 'for the sake of' [BAGD].
  c. pres. act. indic. of εὐχαριστέω (LN **33.349**, 25.100) (BAGD 2. p. 328): 'to give thanks' [AB, BAGD, Herm, HNTC, NIGTC; CEV, KJV, NAB, NET, NJB, NRSV, TEV, TNT], 'to thank God (for)' [**LN** (33.349); NIV, NLT], 'to be thankful for' [ISV], 'to say grace' [REB], 'to render thanks' [BAGD], 'to return thanks' [BAGD], 'to thank' [LN (33.349)], 'to be thankful, to be grateful' [LN (25.100)].
QUESTION—Is this question real or rhetorical?
  It is a rhetorical question [EGT, ICC, Lns, NIC2, TG, TH]: 'Fancy my 'saying grace' for food which causes offence and involves me in blame!' [ICC]. There is no just reason for blaming him [Lns, TG].
QUESTION—What is the function of this question?
  1. It reinforces the reason why they should not eat [Alf, EGT, Gdt, Ho, ICC, MNTC, NTC, TNTC]. The lack of a conjunction on this verse shows that it restates and explains 10:29. If the strong Christian gives thanks and eats, it will result in his being blamed by the other person [Gdt].
  2. It continues the reason why Paul meant the other person's conscience [Ed, Herm, HNTC, My, NIC].
  3. This is a continuation of the voice of an objector who disagrees with Paul about eating [TG; NAB, REB, TEV, TNT].
  4. This continues Paul's rhetorical outburst reverting back to the defense of his freedom against his accusers and is not connected with the context here [NIC2]. This rhetorical outburst about freedom refers back to 10:25 and 26. Verse 10:26 is the Jewish prayer of thanks said over the food and the second verb of this verse refers back to that prayer [NIC2].
QUESTION—Where is the emphasis in this verse?
  There is emphasis on the twice repeated ἐγώ 'I' [Alf, EGT, Lns]. The emphasis serves to contrast the good intentions of Paul in face of the blame he receives [EGT].

DISCOURSE UNIT: 10:31–11:1 [NTC]. The topic is a conclusion.

10:31 **Whether therefore you-eat or you-drink or what you-do, do everything for^a (the) glory^b of-God.**

LEXICON—a. εἰς with accusative object (LN 89.57) (BAGD 4.d. p. 229): 'for' [AB, BAGD, NIGTC; NAB, NET, NIV, NJB, NLT, NRSV, TEV, TNT], 'to' [Herm, HNTC, Lns, NTC; ISV, KJV, REB], 'for the purpose of, in order to' [LN]. The phrase εἰς δόξαν 'for the glory' is translated 'the promotion of (God's) glory' [ICC].

b. δόξα (LN 33.357, 87.4) (BAGD 3. p. 204): 'glory' [AB, Herm, HNTC, ICC, Lns, NIGTC, NTC; all versions except CEV], 'praise' [BAGD, LN (33.357)], 'honor, respect, status' [LN (87.4)]. The phrase εἰς δόξαν 'for the glory' is translated 'to honor' [CEV].

QUESTION—What relationship is indicated by οὖν 'therefore'?

It indicates the conclusion to what has gone before [AB, Alf, Ed, EGT, Herm, ICC, Lns, My, NIC, NIC2; ISV, KJV, NET, NIV, NJB, NRSV]. It logically concludes the argument of chapters 8–10 [NIC2]. This is the beginning of a summary of all that has gone before from chapter 8 on [TH]. It states a general principle which should underlie all activity. In 10:24 Paul had said that Christians should seek the good of others. Now he gives a principle that is more basic even than this. It is that all activity should be to bring glory to God [Lns].

QUESTION—What is meant by δόξα θεοῦ 'glory of God'?

It refers to God's greatness and therefore people should live so that people will think of God as being great [TG]. It refers to God's honor and therefore people should conduct their lives so that other people will honor God [TH]. It refers especially to God's love and holiness. A person should therefore live so as to help others to understand God's love and holiness [Gdt]. It refers to God's character and actions seen in people's lives [Lns, Vn].

10:32 **Be inoffensive^a both to-Jews and to-Greeks^b and to-the church^c of God,**

LEXICON—a. ἀπρόσκοπος (LN **25.184**, 88.318) (BAGD 2. p. 102): 'inoffensive' [AB], 'blameless, without blame' [LN (88.318)], 'devoid of offense' [Lns], 'never a cause of offence' [NJB], 'men who lay no stumbling-block' [HNTC], 'not a cause of stumbling' [TNT], 'not to cause offense' [**LN** (25.184)], 'without causing offense, without causing trouble' [LN (25.184)]. The phrase ἀπρόσκοποι γίνεσθε 'become blameless' is translated 'to give no offense' [BAGD, Herm, NTC; KJV, NAB, NLT, NRSV, REB], 'not to give offense' [NET], 'not to cause problems' [CEV], 'to live in such a way as to cause no trouble' [TEV], 'not to cause anyone to stumble' [NIV], 'to stop being (a) stumbling block' [ISV], 'to put difficulties in the way' [ICC], 'to avoid doing damage' [NIGTC].

b. Ἕλλην (LN 11.40; 11.90) (BAGD 2.a. p. 252): 'Greek' [AB, Herm, HNTC, ICC, LN, Lns, NTC; all versions except KJV, NLT, TEV],

'Gentile' [BAGD, LN, NIGTC; KJV, NLT, TEV], non-Jew [LN (11.40)]. See this word also at 1:22.

c. ἐκκλησία (LN 11.32) (BAGD 4.b. p. 241): 'church' [AB, BAGD, Herm, HNTC, ICC, LN, Lns, NIGTC, NTC; all versions], 'congregation' [BAGD, LN]. See this word also at 1:2 and 11:16.

QUESTION—What is the function of this verse?

It describes how we are to do all things to God's glory [Lns]. It is a consequence of loving God [NIC]. This gives in positive terms what is implied in the questions of 10:27–30 [NTC].

QUESTION—What is meant by ἀπρόσκοπος 'inoffensive'?

It means a lack of offensive behavior, that is, behavior over which men can stumble [Ho], or that can cause them to sin [Ho, NIC, TG]. Causing offense refers to causing someone trouble of a moral or spiritual nature [TG, TH]. Causing offense can mean making it difficult for others to believe or making others lose their faith [HNTC]. It refers to actions that prevent others from hearing the Good News or action that offends other believers [NIC2].

QUESTION—What is the significance of the present tense in the imperative ἀπρόσκοποι γίνεσθε 'be inoffensive'?

It indicates that the action was already going on [ISV]: Stop being offensive. It indicates action that continues to go on [AB, NIC; NJB]: Continue to be inoffensive.

QUESTION—To whom does Ἰουδαῖος 'Jew' refer?

It refers to Jews who are not Christians [Alf, EGT, Ho, ICC].

QUESTION—To whom does Ἕλλην 'Greek' refer?

It refers to the heathen [Alf, Gdt]. It refers to Gentiles or all non-Jews [HNTC, Ho, NIC2, NTC, TH; KJV, NLT, TEV]. It refers to Greeks who are not Christians [EGT, ICC]. It refers to non-Jews who are not Christians [Ho, NIC2].

QUESTION—To whom does τῇ ἐκκλησίᾳ τοῦ θεοῦ 'the church of God' refer?

It refers to Christian believers [EGT, Gdt]. It refers to the local assembly of God's people [HNTC, NIC2, TH, Vn]. It refers to God's people [Ho].

DISCOURSE UNIT: 10:33–11:1 [MNTC]. The topic is the pattern of Christian freedom.

10:33 just-as I-also in-everything please[a] everyone

LEXICON—a. pres. act. indic. of ἀρέσκω (LN 25.90) (BAGD 1. p. 105): 'to please' [LN, Lns, NTC; KJV, TNT], 'to try to please' [AB; CEV, ISV, NAB, NET, NIV, NLT, NRSV, TEV], 'to seek to please' [HNTC], 'to try to accommodate' [NJB], 'to try to be considerate' [REB], 'to try to win the approval of' [ICC], 'to be obliging to' [Herm], 'to strive to please' [BAGD], 'to accommodate' [BAGD], 'to take account of all the interests of' [NIGTC]. This means 'to comply with' or 'to accommodate oneself to' [EGT]. Ἀρέσκω carries the sense of 'trying to do' [AB, Ed, HNTC, ICC, NIGTC; CEV, ISV, NAB, NIV, NJB, NLT, NRSV, REB, TEV]: I try to please.

QUESTION—What is meant by ἀρέσκω 'I please' and how was this action limited?

This word means to please in ways that would win people for God [Gdt, HNTC, Lns]. This does not mean currying people's favor, but rather doing for them what from Paul's viewpoint should please them [ICC, Lns]. This approaches the idea of being a benefactor to someone [ICC, Vn]. Paul's pleasing men is limited to acting in ways that brings glory to God (10:31) [NIC]. The following participial clause, 'not seeking my own advantage', shows that Paul does not mean to merely please men for his own advantage [Herm, ICC].

QUESTION—How inclusive is πᾶσιν 'in everything'?

It means everything allowable within Christian liberty [Gdt, Ho].

not seeking[a] my-own advantage[b] but the-(advantage) of-the many,[c]

LEXICON—a. pres. act. participle of ζητέω (See this word at 10:24): 'to seek' [Herm, LN, NIGTC; KJV, NAB, NET, NIV, NRSV, REB, TNT], 'to look for' [ISV, NJB], 'to think of' [TEV], 'to do' [NLT], 'to strive for' [BAGD], 'to try to obtain, to attempt to get, to desire' [LN], not explicit [CEV].

b. σύμφορον (LN 65.45) (BAGD p. 780): 'advantage' [AB, BAGD, Herm, ICC, LN, Lns, NIGTC; ISV, NAB, NJB, NRSV], 'benefit' [BAGD, LN; NET, TNT], 'profit' [NTC; KJV], 'profitable' [HNTC], 'good' [NIV, REB, TEV], not explicit [CEV]. This noun is also translated as a phrase: 'what I like or what is best for me' [NLT]. This has the meaning of 'spiritual profit' [ICC, Vn].

c. πολύς (LN 59.1) (BAGD I.2.a.β. p. 688): 'many' [AB, BAGD, Herm, ICC, LN, Lns, NIGTC, NTC; ISV, KJV, NAB, NET, NIV, NRSV, REB], 'many of them' [CEV], 'everybody else' [NJB], 'everyone' [NLT], 'all' [TEV, TNT], 'majority' [HNTC, NIC], 'a great number of' [LN].

in-order-that they-may-be-saved.[a]

LEXICON—a. σῴζω (LN 21.27) (BAGD 2.b p. 798): 'to be saved' [AB, Herm, HNTC, LN, Lns, NTC; all versions], 'to be saved from perdition' [ICC], 'to attain salvation' [BAGD], 'their salvation' [NIGTC]. See this word at 1:18.

QUESTION—What is the function of this clause?

This statement of purpose serves to modify what Paul meant by pleasing everyone and seeking their advantage [EGT]. It gives content to what Paul means by the word σύμφορον 'advantage' [Herm, Lns]. It defines what Paul meant by 'I please everyone in everything' [ICC].

QUESTION—Who is the actor of the passive verb σωθῶσιν 'they may be saved'?

God is the actor [Lns]: in order that God may save them.

DISCOURSE UNIT: 11:1–2 [ISV]. The topic is an exhortation to be imitators of the writer.

1 CORINTHIANS 11:1

11:1 Be imitators[a] of-me just-as I-also (am) of-Christ.

LEXICON—a. μιμητής (LN **41.45**) (BAGD 1. p. 522): 'imitator' [AB, BAGD, HNTC, **LN**, Lns, NTC; ISV, NET, NRSV], 'follower' [KJV], 'one who does what others do' [LN]. This noun is also translated as a verb: 'to follow in one's footsteps' [ICC]. The phrase μιμηταί μου γίνεσθε 'become imitators of me' is translated 'imitate me' [NAB, TEV, TNT], 'follow my example' [Herm; NIV, NLT, REB], 'you must follow my example' [CEV], 'take me as your pattern' [NJB, NIGTC].

QUESTION—To which chapter does this verse belong?

It belongs with chapter 10 [AB, HNTC, Ho, ICC, NIC, NIC2, NTC, Rb, Vn; CEV, KJV, NAB, NET, NIV, NJB, NLT, NRSV, REB, TEV, TNT]. This verse serves to conclude Paul's argument for this section [Ho, NIC2, NTC]. He has just given his own principle of action (10:33) and he urges them to follow his example. There is no connection with what follows [ICC].

QUESTION—What aspect of γίνεσθε 'be' is in view?

It should be translated 'become' rather than 'be' [Gdt, ICC, My, NIC2]: Become imitators of me. Γίνεσθε has the force of moral effort or striving to do this [ICC]. So far there was no evidence that they were trying to imitate him [My].

QUESTION—What specific point of similarity does Paul have in mind?

He is thinking of Christ's sacrifice on the cross [EGT, Herm, NIC2]. He is thinking primarily of the sacrifice of one's own rights in order to benefit others [Alf, Gdt, ICC, Lns, MNTC, NIC, Rb, Vn]. Paul asks them to imitate him since his life is more visible to them than Christ's is [HNTC]. There is no arrogance in asking them to imitate him; he is asking them to do what he himself does in imitating Christ [ICC].

DISCOURSE UNIT: 11:2–14:40 [EGT, Herm, ICC, NTC, TG, TNTC]. The topic is disorders in worship and church life [EGT, ICC], questions of divine worship [Herm], worship [NTC], decorum in public worship [NJB], church life and worship [TG, TNTC].

DISCOURSE UNIT: 11:2–34 [AB, Alf, Ed, HNTC, NIGTC]. The topic is the Christian assembly [HNTC], scandals in church services [AB, Ed], men and women and rich and poor at worship [NIGTC].

DISCOURSE UNIT: 11:2–16 [AB, Alf, Ed, Gdt, Herm, Ho, ICC, Lns, MNTC, NIC, NIGTC, TNTC]. The topic is women in public worship [Herm], the veiling of women in public worship [ICC, Lns, NIC, TNTC], head coverings of women and its significance [AB], the impropriety of women appearing unveiled in public [Ho], the subordination and equality of women [MNTC], gender identity at public worship [NIGTC].

11:2 Now[a] I-praise[b] you that in-everything/always you-have-remembered[c] me

TEXT—Some manuscripts include ἀδελφοί 'brothers' after ὑμᾶς 'you'. GNT does not deal with this variant. It is included by KJV and NLT.

56   1 CORINTHIANS 11:2

LEXICON—a. δέ (LN 89.124, 89.87): 'now' [HNTC, Lns; ISV, KJV], 'now, as to another question' [ICC], 'but, on the other hand' [LN (89.124)], 'and, and then' [LN (89.87)], not explicit [AB, Herm, NIGTC, NTC; all other versions].
 b. pres. act. indic. of ἐπαινέω (LN 33.354) (BAGD p. 281): 'to praise' [AB, BAGD, HNTC, LN, Lns, NTC; ISV, KJV, NAB, NET, NIV, TEV], 'to be proud of' [CEV], 'to congratulate' [NJB], 'to commend' [Herm, ICC; NRSV, REB, TNT], 'to give full credit' [NIGTC]. The phrase ἐπαινῶ ὑμᾶς 'I praise you' is translated 'I am so glad' [NLT].
 c. perf. mid. (deponent = act.) indic. of μιμνῄσκομαι (LN 29.7, **29.16**) (BAGD 1.a.β. p. 522): 'to remember' [AB, BAGD, HNTC, ICC, **LN** (29.16), Lns, NTC; all versions except NLT, REB], 'to keep (someone) in mind' [NIGTC; REB], 'to keep (someone) in (one's) thoughts' [NLT], 'to be mindful of' [Herm], 'to recall' [LN (29.16)], 'to think about again' [LN (29.7)], 'to recall to mind, to think of, to keep in mind' [BAGD]. The perfect tense of this verb indicates action that occurred in the past and is still going on [AB, EGT, Lns, MNTC, NIC, NTC]: you continue to remember.
QUESTION—What relationship is indicated by δέ 'now'?
 1. It indicates a transition to a new subject [AB, Gdt, ICC, Lns, My, TH]. This verse introduces the new topic of public worship [ICC].
 2. It indicates a contrast with the preceding mood of blame and instruction [Alf, Ed, EGT]. Along with the contrast, it introduces a new topic [EGT].
QUESTION—Why does Paul praise the Corinthians?
 He may praise them because of their words in a previous letter to him in which they said they remembered him in all things [EGT, HNTC, ICC, TNTC]. He praises them in order to prepare them psychologically for the correction that follows [AB, Herm, NIC2, Vn]. The praise seems to intentionally anticipate 11:17 where he has to tell them that he does not praise them [Ed, ICC, NIC, NIC2].
QUESTION—What is meant by πάντα 'everything/always'?
 1. It functions as an adverb indicating the extent of their remembrance [EGT, Gdt, Lns, NIC, NIC2, NTC; ISV, KJV, NET, NIV, NRSV]: you remember in everything. They remembered Paul in respect to all things [NIC]. Some of the Corinthians have fond memories of Paul and followed his instructions; however it is evident from what follows that many other Corinthians did not obey him [NTC]. It is not the object of remember because it is in the accusative case and this verb typically takes the genitive case for objects [EGT, Lns].
 2. It functions as a temporal adverb meaning 'always' [HNTC, TG; CEV, NAB, NLT, REB, TEV, TNT]: you always remember.
QUESTION—What did the Corinthians remember about Paul?
 They remembered Paul's conduct and his teaching [TG, TH]. They remember the rules he had taught them [Ho]. They remember the directions for public worship he had taught them [TNTC]. To remember him means to

keep and observe his teachings [NIC]. In regard to every question that came up, they thought of Paul and asked what he had taught them on the subject [Lns].

and, just-as I-passed-on[a] to-you, you-hold-fast[b] the traditions.[c]
LEXICON—a. aorist act. indic. of παραδίδωμι (LN 33.237, 57.77) (BAGD 3. p. 615): 'to pass on' [BAGD, Herm; ISV, NET, NIV, NJB, NLT], 'to hand on' [HNTC; NAB, NRSV, REB, TEV, TNT], 'to give' [CEV], 'to deliver' [AB, Lns, NTC; KJV], 'to hand on' [NIGTC], 'to hand down' [BAGD], 'to hand over, to give over' [LN (57.77)], 'to instruct' [LN (33.237)], 'to teach' [BAGD, LN (33.237)], 'to transmit' [BAGD, ICC], 'to relate' [BAGD]. Παραδίδωμι means to pass on traditional instruction [LN (33.237)]. This term brings out that Paul was not the originator of these teachings, he had just passed them on [TNTC]. Note the relationship between this word παραδίδωμι 'I handed on' and παράδοσις 'traditions' in this same verse [Lns].

b. pres. act. indic. of κατέχω (LN **31.48**) (BAGD 1.b.β. p. 423): 'to hold fast (to)' [AB, BAGD, HNTC, Lns, NIGTC; NAB, TNT], 'to maintain' [Herm; NET, NJB, NRSV, REB], 'to continue to believe and practice' [**LN**], 'to hold to' [NIV], 'to keep' [KJV], 'to obey' [CEV], 'to follow' [NLT, TEV], 'to follow carefully' [ISV], 'to loyally hold to' [ICC], 'to guard' [BAGD, NTC], 'to continue to follow' [LN], 'to retain (faithfully)' [BAGD]. The present tense indicates that they were continuing to hold fast [Alf, Lns]: you continue to hold fast.

c. παράδοσις (LN 33.239) (BAGD 2. p. 616): 'tradition' [AB, BAGD, Herm, HNTC, ICC, LN, Lns, NIGTC, NTC; ISV, NAB, NET, NJB, NRSV, REB, TNT], 'teaching' [LN; CEV, NIV, TEV], 'Christian teaching' [NLT], 'ordinance' [KJV].

QUESTION—To what does παράδοσις 'tradition' refer?

It refers to instructions that Paul had received from others and had passed on to the Corinthians [MNTC, NTC, TG, TH, TNTC, Vn]. See 11:23 for an example of this [NTC, TG]. It was a technical term used by Jews to refer to religious instructions passed on orally. Here it refers not to teachings but to traditions that have to do with worship [NIC2]. The early church had only the Old Testament as authoritative. It was necessary therefore to carefully preserve the traditions of the apostles. Tradition indicates something that they received and passed on from Christ [NIC]. It refers to customs regarding church order and not doctrinal teaching [Gdt]. It refers to any instruction of faith and practice, either oral or written [Alf, Ho]. It refers to history, teaching, and rules for practical living [EGT]. It refers to the basic truths of Christianity [HNTC]. The definite article with this word indicates that this was *the* teaching that had apostolic authority for all the churches [Vn]. The article indicates that they were well-known Christian traditions [TNTC].

DISCOURSE UNIT: 11:3–16 [ISV]. The topic is advice about uncovering the head in worship.

11:3 But/now^a I-want you to-know^b that the head^c of-every man is Christ,

LEXICON—a. δέ (See this word at 11:2): 'but' [AB, HNTC, ICC, NTC; KJV, NET, NJB, NLT, NRSV, REB, TEV, TNT], 'however' [Herm, NIGTC], 'now' [Lns; CEV, ISV, NIV], not explicit [NAB].
  b. perf. (pres. in meaning) act. infin. of οἶδα (LN 28.1, 32.4): 'to know' [AB, Herm, HNTC, LN (28.1), Lns; CEV, KJV, NAB, NET, NLT, TNT], 'to realize' [ISV, NIV], 'to understand' [LN (32.4), NIGTC, NTC; NJB, NRSV, REB, TEV], 'to grasp' [ICC], 'to comprehend' [LN (32.4)], 'to know about, to have knowledge of, to be acquainted with' [LN (28.1)].
  c. κεφαλή (LN **87.51**) (BAGD 2.a. p. 430): 'head' [AB, BAGD, Herm, HNTC, ICC, LN, Lns, NTC; all versions except NLT, TEV], 'one who is supreme over, one who is the head of, one who is superior to' [LN]. This noun is also translated as an adjective: 'supreme over' [**LN**; TEV], 'responsible to' [NLT], 'preeminent' [NIGTC]. Κεφαλή 'head' is used figuratively here, meaning supreme or preeminent status with respect to authority to command [LN].

QUESTION—What relationship is indicated by δέ 'but/now'?
  1. It indicates a contrast [Gdt, HNTC, Ho, NIC2, Rb, TG, TH]: you hold fast the traditions *but* I want you to know this. The contrast is between ways in which the Corinthians were holding fast to the traditions and now the ways in which they were not [Gdt, Ho, Rb, TG]. The contrast is between the teaching Paul had given before and the new teaching he was about to give [TH].
  2. It indicates transition [Lns, Vn; CEV, ISV, NIV]: now. Paul wants to point to the principle behind the custom of women covering their heads and so confirm the Corinthians in this practice [Lns].

QUESTION—What does κεφαλή 'head' imply?
  1. It implies a hierarchical meaning of authority of one over another [AB, Alf, BAGD, Ed, EGT, Gdt, Herm, Ho, ICC, Lns, MNTC, My, NIC, NTC, TG, TNTC, Vn]: Christ has authority over every man. The principle given in this verse is that order and subordination are givens in the universe and its essential makeup [Ho]. 'Head' implies supremacy [ICC, TG]. It implies that which governs or rules [NIC, TG]. It implies superiority. In all three cases the idea of subjection to a head is indicated [Lns]. It implies superior authority [TNTC]. If we interpret 'head' as source, while this may hold for the woman and man, it does not hold for Christ and God. 'Head' as authority applies equally in all three cases [NTC].
  2. It implies that one is the source of the other [HNTC, NIC2, TNTC]: Christ is the creator of every man. Christ is the source of every man in that he was God's agent in creation [HNTC]. The meaning of head as chief or ruler is rare in Greek literature. The Corinthians would have understood head as source, that being the meaning of the Greek word. This

interpretation is also supported by 11:8–9. Christ is the source of the believer in that He is the head of the body [NIC2]. This term was never used for leader of a group but for the source as the head of a river [TNTC].

QUESTION—Does παντὸς ἀνδρός 'of every man' include only believers, or every man in the absolute sense?

1. It is limited to only believers [Gdt, Ho, My, NIC2, Vn]: Christ is the head of every man who is a believer. Since Christ is the head of the body, He is the source of its life [NIC2]. Verses 11:4–5 refer to every man who prays and every woman who prays, and this indicates that believers are in focus here [Gdt].
2. It means every man in the absolute sense [Alf, EGT, HNTC, ICC, Lns, MNTC, NIC]: Christ is the head of absolutely every man. Unbelievers may not recognize this, but it is true nevertheless [NIC].

and (the) head of-(a)-woman/wife[a] (is) the man/husband,[b]

LEXICON—a. γυνή (LN 9.34, 10.54) (BAGD 1. p. 168): 'woman' [AB, BAGD, Herm, HNTC, ICC, LN (9.34), Lns, NIGTC, NTC; all versions except NRSV, TEV], 'his wife' [NRSV, TEV], 'wife' [LN (10.54)].

b. ἀνήρ (LN 9.24, 10.53) (BAGD 1. p. 66): 'man' [AB, BAGD, Herm, HNTC, LN (9.24), Lns, NIGTC, NTC; CEV, ISV, KJV, NET, NIV, NJB, REB, TNT], 'husband' [ICC, LN (10.53); NAB, NLT, NRSV, TEV].

QUESTION—What is meant by γυνή 'woman/wife' and ἀνήρ 'man/husband'?

1. The relationship between woman and man in general is in focus here [AB, Herm, Lns, MNTC, NIC, NIC2, TG, TNTC, Vn]: the head of woman is man. Marriage is not in focus, but the makeup of a community and the nature of man and woman as such [Herm]. The relation of man and woman in the Christian assembly is being referred to here, not marriage [Vn]. Unmarried women should cover their heads also [TNTC].
2. The relationship between wife and husband is in focus [Gdt, ICC, NTC, TH; NAB, NLT, NRSV, TEV]: the head of a wife is her husband.

QUESTION—What does it mean that the man is the head of the woman?

1. When 'head' is understood as authority.
   In marriage a community of life is formed as well as an inequality, namely that man is the strong directing one, and woman is the receptive and dependent one [Gdt]. The idea of subjection to a head is indicated [Lns]. In the Corinthian church there was a desire to put man and woman on the same level. Here Paul puts the man above the woman [NIC]. The meaning of head as supreme does not mean that the two cannot at the same time be equal. This is true of Christ and God as well as man and woman [NTC]. Man has authority over the woman in the Christian congregation (see 1 Tim. 2:11–12) [Vn].
2. When 'head' is understood as source.
   This refers back to creation where woman was taken out of man [HNTC, NIC2, TNTC]. Woman was created to be a helper to man and was created

from man's rib (see Gen. 2:18–23) [HNTC]. This interpretation is supported by 11:8–9 [HNTC, NIC2]. The meaning is that woman derives her being from man (see Gen. 1:21, 22) [TNTC].

and the head of Christ (is) God.
QUESTION—What does it mean that God is the head of Christ?
1. When 'head' is understood as authority.
The idea of being subject to a head is indicated [Lns]. Christ is subordinate to God in the same way that a son is subordinate to his father or a word is to the speaker [Gdt]. Christ is subordinate to God in the sense of his becoming a man and rescuing man from sin [Ho]. God is the head of Christ in respect to having sent him [ICC, Lns, NIC]. Christ is subordinate to God, not in essence, but in His role as Savior of man, a role he willingly accepted [MNTC, Vn]. The meaning of head as supreme does not mean that the two cannot at the same time be equal. This is true of Christ and God as well as man and woman [NTC].
2. When 'head' is understood as source.
God is the source of Christ's life in the sense of Christ's becoming a man [NIC2]. Christ owes his being to the Father [HNTC].
QUESTION—What is the significance of the definite article with the word 'head' when referring to Christ and the man versus its absence when referring to the other two relationships.
It indicates that the same relationship does not hold for all three, each is unique but all three indicate the subjection to a head [Lns]. The lack of article in the case of woman indicates that the relationship for man and woman is not the same as for the man and Christ [NTC].

11:4 **Every man praying or prophesying[a] having down-to[b] his-head dishonors[c] his head.[d]**
LEXICON—a. pres. act. participle of προφητεύω (LN 33.459) (BAGD 1. p. 723): 'to prophesy' [AB, Herm, HNTC, ICC, LN, Lns, NTC; all versions except TEV, TNT], 'to speak God's message' [TNT], 'to proclaim God's message in public worship' [TEV], 'to expound the will of God' [ICC], 'to make inspired utterances' [LN], 'to utter prophetic speech' [NIGTC], 'to proclaim a divine revelation' [BAGD]. The word means to speak under the influence of divine inspiration with or without reference to future events [LN].
   b. κατά (LN 84.21, 89.4) (BAGD I.1.a. p. 405): 'down to, down, downward' [LN (84.21)], 'in relation to, with regard to' [LN (89.4)], 'on' [BAGD]. Κατὰ κεφαλῆς ἔχω 'having down on the head' is an idiom which means to wear a covering over one's head [LN (49.16)]. The phrase is translated 'having his head covered' [LN; KJV], 'with his head covered' [NIGTC], 'who has any covering on his head' [ICC], 'with a veil hanging down from his head' [HNTC], 'with his head covered' [**LN**, Lns; NAB, NET, NIV, NJB, TEV, TNT], 'with something on his head' [AB, Herm, NTC;

1 CORINTHIANS 11:4

CEV, ISV, NRSV], 'who keeps his head covered' [REB], 'if he covers his head' [NLT].
c. pres. act. indic. of καταισχύνω (LN 25.194) (BAGD 1. p. 410): 'to dishonor' [Herm, Lns; ISV, KJV, NIV, NLT, TNT], 'to shame' [NIGTC], 'to bring shame upon' [NAB], 'to bring shame on' [REB], 'to bring shame to' [CEV], 'to disgrace' [AB, BAGD, HNTC, LN; NET, NRSV, TEV], 'to dishonor' [BAGD, ICC, NTC], 'to show disrespect for' [NJB], 'to put to shame, to humiliate' [LN].
d. κεφαλή (LN **8.10**) (BAGD 1.a. p. 430): 'head' [AB, BAGD, Herm, HNTC, ICC, **LN**, Lns, NIGTC, NTC; all versions except NLT, TEV, TNT], 'Christ, his head' [TNT], 'Christ' [NLT, TEV]. The whole head is not covered, only the top is [LN].

QUESTION—What are these next two verses teaching?

Paul applies the principles concerning headship to customs existing in Corinth [Lns]. In the same way that man prays to God with uncovered head because of his spiritual subjection to Christ, so the woman should pray with her head covered because of her spiritual subjection to man [AB, EGT].

QUESTION—What is meant by προφητεύω 'to prophesy'?

It means to proclaim God's message to people [TG]. God gives both the message and the power to declare it. It does not necessarily mean to predict the future [TH]. It was inspired speech for the edification and encouragement of the congregation [NIC2]. It means speaking in the spirit [Alf]. It means to speak under the divine inspiration God's messages of teaching, exhortation, consolation, or prediction [Ho]. It means public teaching, correction, comforting, or delivering God's message to the people [ICC]. It means the ability to present and apply the Word of God by teaching others [Lns]. While prayer is talking to God about people, prophesying is talking to people about God [MNTC]. It means to preach, teach, and explain God's Word [NTC]. It is a sudden revelation given to one by the Holy Spirit [Gdt]. It refers to the charismatic activity of intercession for others in an assembly of people [NIC].

QUESTION—Was 'praying' and 'prophesying' in private or in public.

The praying and prophesying here refers to that which was done in public [Alf, HNTC, MNTC, NIC2, NTC, TG]. It implies that the congregation was at worship [NIC2, NTC]. There is no mention of where or when this takes place, it is wherever and whenever it is proper to pray or prophesy [Lns].

QUESTION—What kind of head covering is intended?

This is a cloth which covered the head [NIC2]. It is probably a garment hanging down from the head and covering the hair and upper part of the body but not the face [HNTC, TH]. It refers to a veil [EGT, MNTC, Rb]. It is a kerchief or veil worn over the head and falling over the shoulders [Gdt]. This is a hypothetical argument and it is improbable that the Corinthian men actually veiled their heads [Alf, Gdt, ICC, NIC2].

QUESTION—What is meant by καταισχύνει τὴν κεφαλὴν θυτοῦ 'he dishonors his head'?
1. It means that he dishonors his physical head, that is, he dishonors himself [AB, Ho, ICC, Lns, MNTC, My, NIC]. Since the first occurrence of 'head' is literal, it would mean that this occurrence should also be literal [AB, Ho]. In 11:5 both uses of 'head' are literal so they should be here as well. Further, it is more obvious that a person would dishonor himself by behaving incorrectly than that he would dishonor his superior [Ho]. The reference is literal because the definite article here refers back to the first part of the verse [Lns].
2. It means that he dishonors Christ who is his head [Alf, EGT, Gdt, NIC2, TG, TH, Vn; TEV, TNT]. If he appears in the assembly covered, he is thereby showing he is subject to the assembly and therefore dishonors Christ to whom alone he is subject [Alf]
3. It means that he dishonors both Christ and his own head [Ed, HNTC, NTC, TNTC]. The thought is that since man is the glory of Christ (2 Corinthians 3:18), if he were to cover his head, he would veil the glory of Christ and thus dishonor Him and at the same time dishonor his own head that should reflect Christ's glory [HNTC].

QUESTION—What did 'covering the head' signify?
1. It signified that the person who covered his head was subject or inferior to someone else [Alf, Gdt, Ho, ICC, TG]. There may be a hint that in covering his head the man would be recognizing some other head than Christ [ICC, TG]. The woman covered her head to show her subjection to man. If the man covers his head, he thereby shows he has a human head over him other than Christ. By throwing away his true honor he dishonors himself [Lns]. Christ is man's true superior, not another man which would be signified by the covered head. By covering his head then, a man would dishonor Christ [TG]. In Corinthian society praying or prophesying without one's head covered was a sign of authority over women. If his head were covered it would be a disgrace to him [MNTC].
2. It signified mourning among the Jews and that may be its significance here [NIC2]. For a man to cover his head as though in mourning while praying or prophesying would dishonor Christ.
3. It signified the practice of idol worshipping. The Romans would cover their heads when offering sacrifices, praying, or prophesying. Paul's advice then to the Corinthians is to turn away from the practice of idol worshippers since covering their heads would suggest this kind of practice [NTC].

QUESTION—Why is the case of the man presented?
Man's case is presented probably as an introduction to the more pressing problem of women [Alf, Gdt, ICC, Lns]. In preparation for his argument with the woman, Paul sets up a hypothetical situation for the man. He does this in order to show that for man, praying with his head covered was as

shameful to his Head. Similarly praying with her head uncovered was shameful to her head [NIC2].

11:5 But/and[a] every woman praying or prophesying with-the head uncovered[b] dishonors her head;[c]

LEXICON—a. δέ (See this word at 11:2): 'but' [AB, HNTC, NTC; CEV, KJV, NET, NLT, NRSV, REB], 'whereas' [ICC], 'however' [Herm], 'and' [Lns; NIV, NJB, TEV], 'similarly' [NAB], not explicit [NIGTC; ISV, TNT].

b. ἀκατακάλυπτος (LN **79.116**) (BAGD p. 29): 'uncovered' [BAGD, ICC, **LN**, Lns, NIGTC, NTC; ISV, KJV, NAB, NET, NIV, NJB], 'unveiled' [AB, Herm, HNTC; NRSV, TNT], 'bareheaded' [REB], 'with nothing on' [TEV], 'without something on' [CEV], 'without a covering on' [NLT]. Two kinds of covering were worn. One covered the head and the whole body. The other just covered the face leaving the eyes uncovered [Ho].

c. κεφαλή (LN **8.10**) (BAGD 1.a. p. 430): 'head' [AB, BAGD, Herm, HNTC, ICC, **LN**, Lns, NTC; all versions except NLT, TEV, TNT], 'husband' [NLT, TEV], 'husband, who is her head' [TNT].

QUESTION—What relationship is indicated by δέ 'but/and'?

1. It indicates a contrastive relationship [AB, HNTC, ICC, My, NIC2, NTC; CEV, KJV, NET, NLT, NRSV, REB]: every man…dishonors his head, *but* every woman.
2. It indicates a conjoining relationship [Lns; NIV, NJB, TEV]: every man…dishonors his head, *and* every woman. It indicates a comparative relationship [NAB]: every man…dishonors his head, *similarly* every woman.

QUESTION—Was 'praying' and 'prophesying' in private or in public.

The praying and prophesying here refers to that which was done in public [AB, Gdt, HNTC, Ho, ICC, Lns, NIC, NIC2, NTC, TNTC, Vn; TEV]. A meeting of the assembly or congregation of believers is indicated here [AB, Gdt, HNTC, Ho, ICC, NIC2, NTC]. Verse 11:13 makes no sense if it did not take place in an assembly of believers [NIC2]. A meeting of the congregation or assembly of believers cannot be where this took place [Lns, NIC, Vn], because the teaching of this verse clashes with the command that they be silent in 14:34 [Vn].

QUESTION—To what does κεφαλή 'head' refer?

1. It refers to the woman's own head, that is, to herself [EGT, HNTC, Ho, ICC, Lns, My, NIC, TNTC]. The reading ἑαυτῆς 'one's own' is correct [EGT, Ho]: her own head.
2. It refers to the man or to her husband who is her head [AB, Alf, MNTC, NIC2, NTC, TG, TH; NLT, TEV, TNT]. This probably refers to disgracing the man in terms of male-female relationships [NIC2].
3. It refers to both her own head and her husband [Ed].

1 CORINTHIANS 11:5

QUESTION—How did the 'uncovering of the head' dishonor the woman's head?

It made the woman look more like a man and resulted in a blurring of the sexes, thus dishonoring the man [NIC2]. Being uncovered meant an attempt to look like a man [Lns, NIC], and to be honored as such. To take an honor that was not rightfully hers meant disgrace for her [Lns]. Among Greek women, only the immoral went unveiled [Vn]. The veil was a sign of subjection to one's husband. If the woman wore no veil it would bring disgrace on him [MNTC, NTC, TG]. The veil was not worn until a woman was married. Once married she could not go out without being properly covered. To do so disgraced her husband and he could use it as a grounds for divorce [AB]. The veil was a recognition of the authority of the man over her. If she refused to wear it, it was an affront to him [Alf]. An absence of the veil was considered indecent and a claim of equality with man. She dishonors her head since that is where the indecency is seen [ICC]. It was customary for all respectable women to appear in public with a veil as a cover [Ho]. Being uncovered was considered indecent and a sign that a woman was claiming equality with man [ICC].

for^a it-is one and the same as being-shaved.^b

LEXICON—a. γάρ (See this word at 10:1): 'for' [AB, Herm, HNTC, ICC, Lns, NIGTC, NTC; KJV, NET, NLT], 'in fact' [CEV], not explicit [all other versions].

b. perf. pass. participle of ξυράω (LN **19.24**) (BAGD p. 549): 'to be shaved' [BAGD, LN, NIGTC; KJV, NIV, REB, TEV], 'to be shaven' [Herm], 'to have (one's) head shaved' [BAGD, **LN**; ISV, NAB, NET, NRSV], 'to have (one's) hair shaved off' [NJB]. This passive participle is translated actively: 'to shave (one's) head' [CEV, NLT]. This was done with a razor [Ho, TG].

QUESTION—What relationship is indicated by γάρ 'for'?

It indicates the grounds for the first part of the verse [Ho, Lns, NIC, TH]: Every woman praying or prophesying with her head uncovered dishonors her head *since* it is the same as having her head shaved.

QUESTION—In what way does having one's head shaved indicate disgrace?

A shaved head indicated that that woman was being disgracefully punished. This meant that she bore the mark of a disreputable woman [Ho]. Short hair may have been a mark of a prostitute. If a woman wore short hair it was a sign of immorality and therefore disgrace [NIC]. It was a sign of a loose woman [TG]. For a woman to have her head shaved was a sign of humiliation and disgrace [NTC, TH]. In those days slaves had their heads shaved [EGT, Gdt, Rb, TG, Vn]. Adulteresses were also shaved as a punishment [Alf, EGT, Rb]. Only a prostitute or extreme feminist would have her head shaved [MNTC]. (But note: The shaving of the head did not signify that a woman was a prostitute [Herm]. There is no contemporary evidence to support the view that short hair or shaving was a sign of a prostitute [NIC2].)

11:6 For[a] if (a) woman (does) not cover-her-head,[b] let-her-cut-her-hair[c] also;

LEXICON—a. γάρ (See this word at 10:1): 'for' [Herm, HNTC, Lns, NIGTC, NTC; KJV, NRSV], 'indeed' [NAB], 'in fact' [NJB], not explicit [ICC; all other versions].
  b. pres. mid. indic. of κατακαλύπτω (LN **49.16**) (BAGD 2. p. 411): 'to cover (one's) head' [LN, NTC; ISV, NET, NIV, REB, TEV], 'to have (one's) head covered' [**LN**], 'to wear something on (one's) head' [CEV], 'to wear a head covering' [NLT], 'to cover (oneself)' [BAGD], 'to be covered' [Lns; KJV], 'to wear a veil' [NAB], 'to go with a veil' [NJB], 'to veil (oneself)' [NRSV], 'to be veiled' [AB, Herm, HNTC; TNT], 'to retain one's head covering' [NIGTC]. The words οὐ κατακαλύπτεται 'does not cover her head' are translated 'to be unveiled like a man' [ICC]. The present tense of this verb here indicates what was habitual or customary [Alf, Vn].
  c. pres. mid. impera. of κείρω (LN **19.23**) (BAGD p. 427): 'to cut (one's) hair' [BAGD, **LN**; TEV], 'to have (one's) hair cut' [BAGD; TNT], 'to cut off (one's) hair' [CEV, ISV, NAB, NET, NRSV], 'to cut off all (one's) hair' [NLT], 'to have (one's) hair cut off' [NTC; NIV, NJB, REB], 'to cut one's hair short' [HNTC], 'to cut one's hair short like a man' [ICC], 'to have oneself shorn' [Herm, Lns], 'to shear' [LN]. This is also translated in passive voice 'to be shorn' [AB; KJV], 'to have it cropped close to the head' [NIGTC]. This is done with scissors [TG]. This means 'to cut one's hair short' [NIC, NIC2, Rb].

QUESTION—What relationship is indicated by γάρ 'for'?
  It explains why he said that it is the same as being shaved [Ed, HNTC, Lns, My, NIC, NIC2, NTC, TH]. A woman who does not cover herself is as much a shame to her husband as a close-cut and shaven head would be to herself [NTC]. It teaches that a woman needs to act consistently. If she wants to act as a respectable woman, let her cover her head like respectable women. Otherwise she should go ahead and act completely like a disrespectable one [Ho]. If a woman thinks it is a disgrace to have her hair cut short or her head shaved, it is equally a disgrace to pray or prophesy with her head uncovered [TNTC]. What a woman must do in public life she also must do when she prays or prophesies [NIC].

QUESTION—What is implied by 'having one's hair cut'?
  It had the appearance of being masculine [ICC, NIC2]: to cut one's hair short like a man. The logic is that if she goes uncovered to appear like a man, she may as well cut her hair short and go all the way to appearing like a man [ICC]. It meant people would think of her as a lewd woman [Rb]. The cutting of hair or shaving of heads was not the sign of a prostitute [Lns].

QUESTION—Is Paul serious or is he using irony?
Paul is using irony here and this is brought out in the way TEV renders the verse [TG]: she might as well cut her hair.

but[a] if (it is) shameful[b] for-(a)-woman to-cut-her-hair or to-have-her-head-shaved, let-her-cover-her-head.[c]

LEXICON—a. δέ (See this word at 11:2): 'but' [Herm, HNTC, ICC, Lns, NTC; CEV, KJV, NET, NJB, NRSV, REB, TNT], 'and' [AB; NIV, NLT, TEV], 'however' [NIGTC], not explicit [ISV, NAB].
  b. αἰσχρός (LN **88.150**) (BAGD p. 25): 'shameful' [BAGD, **LN**; NAB, NJB, NLT, TEV, TNT], 'disgraceful' [AB, BAGD, HNTC, LN, NTC; NET, NRSV], 'base, ugly' [BAGD]. This adjective is also translated as a noun: 'disgrace' [Herm; CEV, ISV, NIV, REB], 'shame' [Lns; KJV]. This word includes the senses of 'ugliness' and 'moral indecency' [Gdt].
  c. pres. mid. impera. of κατακαλύπτω (See this word in the first part of this verse): 'to cover (one's) head' [NTC; NET, NIV, REB, TEV], 'to be covered' [KJV], 'to wear a covering' [NLT], 'to cover (one's own) head' [ISV], 'to have oneself covered' [Lns], 'to wear something on (one's) head' [CEV], 'to wear a veil' [ICC; NAB, NJB, NRSV], 'to retain one's head covering' [NIGTC]. This is also translated as a passive: 'to be veiled' [AB, Herm, HNTC; TNT].

QUESTION—What relationship is indicated by δέ 'but/and'?
  1. It indicates a contrastive relationship [Herm, HNTC, ICC, Lns, NIC2, NTC; CEV, KJV, NET, NJB, NRSV, REB, TNT]: but.
  2. It indicates a conjoining relationship [AB; NIV, NLT, TEV]: and.

QUESTION—Is this sentence hypothetical or affirmative?
It is affirmative [ICC, Lns, NIC, NIC2, Rb; CEV, NLT, TEV]: since it is a shameful thing for a woman to shave her head or cut her hair, she should cover her head. The 'if' implies that it would certainly be a shame [ICC, Lns].

DISCOURSE UNIT: 11:7–16 [EGT]. The topic is man and woman in the Lord.

11:7 For[a] (a) man on-the-one-hand ought[b] not to-cover his head

LEXICON—a. γάρ (See this word at 10:1): 'for' [AB, Herm, HNTC, Lns, NIGTC, NTC; KJV, NET, NRSV], 'but' [NJB], not explicit [ICC; CEV, ISV, NAB, NIV, NLT, REB, TEV, TNT].
  b. pres. act. indic. of ὀφείλω (LN 71.25, 71.35) (BAGD 2.a.β. p. 599): '(one) ought' [AB, BAGD, HNTC, LN (71.25), Lns, NIGTC, NTC; KJV, NAB, NIV, NRSV, TNT], '(one) should' [CEV, ISV, NET, NLT], '(one) must' [BAGD, Herm, LN (71.35); REB], 'to be right for someone' [NJB], 'to need' [TEV], 'to have (a) right' [ICC], 'to be under obligation' [LN (71.25)], 'to be necessary, to have to' [LN (71.35)].

QUESTION—What relationship is indicated by γάρ 'for'?
It indicates further grounds for his position that men should not be covered while women should be (11:4–6). The contrasting particles μέν...δέ '(man)

1 CORINTHIANS 11:7 67

on the one hand…(woman) on the other' support this [NIC2]. It indicates that 11:7–12 is the explanation of 11:5–6 [NTC]. It indicates further support for the claim made in 11:5a [TH]: every woman who prays or prophesies with her head uncovered dishonors her head *because* man has no need to cover his head…but the woman…. It indicates that this verse is a second grounds for the imperative 'let her cover her head' [Alf, My]. It is the woman who should cover her head since the man ought not cover his [Ho].

QUESTION—What is meant by οὐκ ὀφείλω 'ought not to'?

It means moral obligation [EGT, HNTC, ICC, NIC2; REB]. It indicates need or simple obligation [NIC, TH; TEV]. It indicates that it is right or appropriate [NJB]. This applies to prayer and prophesying and not to covering one's head because of weather [NTC].

being^a (the) image^b and glory^c of-God;

LEXICON—a. pres. act. participle of ὑπάρχω (LN 13.5) (BAGD 2. p. 838): 'to be' [AB, BAGD, Herm, HNTC, LN, Lns, NTC; all versions except ISV, TEV, TNT], 'to exist' [ISV], 'to be by constitution' [ICC]. The phrase εἰκών…ὑπάρχων 'being…the image' is translated 'because he reflects the image' [TEV], 'since he reflects the likeness' [TNT].

b. εἰκών (LN 58.35) (BAGD 1.b. p. 222): 'image' [AB, BAGD, Herm, HNTC, ICC, Lns, NTC; all versions except CEV, TNT], 'likeness' [BAGD, LN, Lns; TNT], 'same form' [LN]. This noun is also translated as a preposition: 'like' [CEV]. Εἰκών indicates a visible representation of something [TG, Vn].

c. δόξα (LN 79.18) (BAGD 1.c. p. 204): 'glory' [AB, HNTC, LN, Lns, NTC; ISV, KJV, NET, NIV, NLT, TEV, TNT], 'honor' [CEV], 'reflection' [BAGD, Herm; NRSV], 'splendor' [BAGD, LN], 'brightness, radiance' [BAGD]. This word is also translated as a phrase: 'mirror of (one's) glory' [REB], 'reflection of (one's) glory' [NAB], 'to reflect (one's) glory' [ICC; NJB], 'manifests his glory' [NIGTC]. See this word also at 10:31.

QUESTION—What relationship is indicated by the participial construction εἰκὼν καὶ δόξα θεοῦ ὑπαρξων 'being the image and glory of God'?

It indicates grounds [AB, HNTC, Lns, NIC, NIGTC, NTC, TG, TNTC; all versions]: a man ought not to cover his head, *since* he is the image and glory of God. For a man to veil his head would be to veil the image and glory of God [EGT, HNTC].

QUESTION—What is implied by the action κατακαλύπτεσθαι τὴν καφαλὴν 'to cover his head'?

It implies that to cover his head would be to cover or diminish the image and glory of God [EGT, Gdt, HNTC].

QUESTION—In what way(s) is man the εἰκών 'image' of God?

He is the image of God in a moral, not physical, sense [Rb]. He is the image of God in a moral, mental, and spiritual way [MNTC]. He is the image of God in the characteristics of goodness, wisdom, and power [Vn]. Man, as distinct from woman, is the image of God in the domains of dominion, sovereignty, or authority [Gdt, Ho, MNTC, My, NTC, Rb]. As God is the invisible sovereign over all things, so man reflects visibly this sovereignty over creation [Gdt].

QUESTION—In what way(s) is man the δόξα 'glory' of God?

Glory has to do with God's character so man reflects the features of God's character [Lns]. The glory of God has to do with his nature. Man is a visible representation of God's nature [TG, TH]. In man, God's splendor, dignity, and majesty are seen [Alf, EGT, Ho, NIC, TG, Vn]. Glory has to do with honor or praise. So man brings honor to God [Gdt, NIC, NIC2]. In view of the fact that he was given dominion and authority over the world, he is the glory of God in that he reveals God's authority and dominion [MNTC]. Man is the pinnacle of God's creation and as such honors God by showing His creativity at its best [Lns, NIC, Rb].

the woman on-the-other-hand is (the) glory[a] of-man.

LEXICON—a. δόξα (See this word in the previous clause): 'glory' [AB, HNTC, Lns, NIGTC, NTC; ISV, KJV, NET, NIV, NLT, REB], 'splendor' [LN], 'honor' [CEV], 'reflection' [Herm; NRSV]. It is also translated as a phrase: 'reflection of (one's) glory' [NAB, NJB]. The phrase δόξα... ἐστιν 'is the glory' is translated 'reflects the glory' [ICC; TEV, TNT].

QUESTION—What information is left implicit in this clause?

It is implied that the woman needs to veil herself because she is the glory of man [AB, EGT, ICC, TNTC]. It is implied that the woman ought to have authority on her head (11:10) [NIC2].

QUESTION—If it is implied that the woman must be covered when she worships, what is the logic behind it?

Man does not need to be covered when he worships because he reflects God's glory. But because woman reflects man's glory, she should be covered when she worships since God alone should be glorified [TNTC].

QUESTION—What is meant by woman's being δόξα ἀνδρός 'glory of man'?

Woman reveals how beautiful a creature God could create out of man [NIC]. She shows how magnificent is the creature God has made from a man [MNTC]. She is man's glory in that she was made to reflect his authority and will [MNTC, TNTC]. She is man's glory in that she reveals his majesty. She reveals to others the wealth and honor of her husband [Ho]. She seeks to honor her husband by recognizing his headship [NTC]. Woman is the image of God, not the image of man, but she is the glory of man, not the glory of God. [ICC, MNTC, NIC, NIC2, TNTC]. She exists to bring honor to man [NIC2].

11:8 For man is[a] not from[b] woman but woman from man;

LEXICON—a. pres. act. indic. of εἰμί (LN 13.69) (BAGD III.3. p. 225): 'to be' [AB, LN, Lns; KJV], 'to come' [BAGD, HNTC, NIGTC, NTC; ISV, NET, NIV, NJB, NLT, TNT], 'to be made' [CEV, NAB, NRSV], 'to

originate' [Herm], 'to be created' [ICC; TEV], 'to spring originally' [REB], 'to exist' [LN]. Εἰμί here indicates 'to takes one's being' [Alf].
b. ἐκ with genitive object (LN 89.3, 84.4, 90.16) (BAGD III.3. p. 225): 'from' [AB, BAGD, Herm, HNTC, LN (89.3, 84.4, 90.16), NIGTC, NTC; all versions except KJV, REB], 'out of' [LN (84.4), Lns; REB], 'of' [KJV], 'out from' [LN (84.4)], 'by' [LN (90.16)]. The phrase ἐστιν ἐκ 'to be from' is translated 'to owe one's origin to' [ICC].

QUESTION—What relationship is indicated by γάρ 'for'?
It indicates the grounds for saying that the woman is the glory of man [EGT, ICC, Lns, MNTC, NIC2; KJV, NIV, NRSV, REB, TEV]: the woman is the glory of man *since* man is not from woman but woman from man. It indicates the grounds for saying that the man is the glory of God and the woman is the glory of the man [Alf, Ed, Gdt, NIC]. It proves that the woman is subordinate to the man [Ho].

QUESTION—In what sense is woman ἐκ 'from' man?
She is from man in the sense that Eve was created from Adam's rib (see Genesis 2:18–23) [HNTC, Ho, MNTC, NIC2, NTC, TNTC]. Adam was created directly, then Eve was derived from Adam [Lns].

11:9 For also man not was-created^a for-the-sake-of^b the woman, but woman for-the-sake-of the man.

LEXICON—a. κτίζω (LN 42.35) (BAGD p. 455): 'to be created' [AB, BAGD, Herm, HNTC, ICC, LN, Lns, NIGTC, NTC; all versions except NLT], 'to be made' [ICC; NLT], 'to be formed' [Rb].
b. διά with accusative object (See this word at 10:28): 'for the sake of' [AB, Herm, HNTC, ICC, NTC; NET, NJB, NRSV, REB, TEV, TNT], 'for the benefit of' [NLT], 'for' [CEV, ISV, KJV, NAB, NIV], 'on account of' [Lns], 'on one's account' [NIGTC], 'because of' [EGT, Rb].

QUESTION—What relationship is indicated by γάρ 'for'?
It stands, with 11:8, as an additional grounds for 11:7 [Alf, Ed, EGT, Gdt, HNTC, Ho, ICC, Lns, NIC, NIC2, NTC, TNTC]: the woman is the glory of man *since*...woman was created for man's sake. Woman cannot claim priority either in her origin or in the purpose for which God created her [TNTC].

11:10 Because-of^a this the woman ought^b to-have^c authority^d on^e her head because-of^f the angels.

LEXICON—a. διά with accusative object (See this word at 10:28): 'because of' [AB, NIGTC; CEV]. The phrase διὰ τοῦτο 'because of this' is translated 'this is why' [ISV, NJB], 'for this reason' [Herm, HNTC, NTC; NAB, NET, NIV, NRSV], 'for this cause' [KJV], 'therefore' [REB, TNT], 'so' [NLT], 'then' [TEV].
b. pres. act. indic. of ὀφείλω (See this word at 11:7): '(one) ought' [AB, HNTC, NIGTC, NTC; CEV, KJV, NAB, NIV, NRSV, TNT], '(one) should' [ISV, NET, NLT, TEV], '(one) must' [Herm; REB], 'to be right

for someone' [NJB]. Moral obligation is indicated here [ICC, Rb]. Simple obligation is indicated here [Lns].
   c. pres. act. infin. of ἔχω (LN 57.1, 49.13): 'to have' [AB, Herm, HNTC, LN (57.1), NTC; all versions except CEV, NJB, NLT], 'to wear' [LN (49.13); CEV, NJB, NLT].
   d. ἐξουσία (LN **37.37**, 76.12) (BAGD 5. p. 278): 'authority' [AB, BAGD, HNTC, NTC; ISV], 'a sign of authority' [NIV, TNT], 'symbol of authority' [LN (37.37); NET, NRSV], 'power' [Herm, LN (76.12); KJV], 'a covering as a sign of authority' [NLT], 'something as a sign of her authority' [CEV], 'the sign of her authority' [REB], 'a sign of the authority over her' [NJB], 'a covering to show that she is under her husband's authority' [TEV], 'a sign of submission' [NAB], 'a means of exercising power… (the) veil' [BAGD], 'a symbol of authority (over her)' [**LN** (37.37)], 'symbol of subjection to authority' [LN (37.37)]. The clause is translated 'a woman ought to keep control of her head' [NIGTC].
   e. ἐπί with genitive object (LN 37.9, 83.46) (BAGD I.1.a.α. p. 286): 'on' [BAGD, Herm, HNTC, LN (83.46), NTC; all versions except ISV, TEV], 'upon' [BAGD, LN (83.46)], 'over' [AB, LN (37.9); ISV, TEV], 'with responsibility for' [LN (37.9)].
   f. διά with accusative object (LN 90.44): 'because of' [Herm, LN, NTC; all versions except NLT, REB, TEV], 'on account of' [HNTC, LN, NIGTC; TEV], 'because…are watching' [NLT], 'out of regard for' [REB], 'for the sake of' [AB], 'for this reason' [LN].
QUESTION—What relationship is indicated by διὰ τοῦτο 'because of this'?
   1. It indicates the logical conclusion of 11:7 [AB, ICC, TG, TH]: the woman is the glory of man, *therefore* the woman should have authority on her head. The two verses 10:8–9 are parenthetical in the argument [ICC, TH].
   2. It indicates the logical conclusion of 11:8–9 [Gdt, Herm, Lns, NIC]: the woman was created from man and for his sake, *therefore* the woman should have authority on her head. Verses 11:8–9 are parenthetical [AB].
   3. It indicates the logical conclusion of 11:7–9 [Alf, EGT, HNTC, My, NTC, TG]. This verse completes the thought of 11:7a, that a man ought not to cover his head. Here the thought is that a woman should cover her head since, as 11:7–9 argues, her being is derived from man and auxiliary to him [EGT].
   4. It indicates that the angels are the reason she should have authority on her head [ISV, TEV, TNT]: the woman should have authority on her head *because of* the angels.
   5. It indicates the logical conclusion of 11:7 and from the following phrase 'because of the angels' [NIC2, TG; CEV, NIV]. The words 'because of this' look both ways, back to the woman being the glory of man and forward to the angels [NIC2].

QUESTION—What is meant by ἐξουσίαν ἔχειν ἐπὶ τῆς κεφαλῆς 'to have authority on her head'?
1. It means that she should wear a veil as a symbol of her subjection to another's authority [Alf, EGT, Gdt, Ho, Lns, My, Rb, TG; NAB, TEV]. Ἐξουσία 'authority/power' should be σημεῖον ἐξουσίας 'a sign of authority' [Alf, EGT, Gdt, Ho, Rb]. This is a sign of power, but not power used, rather power submitted to [Gdt].
2. It means that she also has authority from God to pray and to declare His word in prophesy that she did not have before [HNTC, MNTC, NIC, NTC, TH, TNTC]. The head covering symbolized this authority and served to cover her head in worship so as to veil man's glory in God's presence [HNTC, TH, TNTC]. The covered head was the woman's authority to worship since it showed her submissiveness [MNTC]. Her authority for praying or prophesying is the covering of man's glory [TNTC]. It may mean that the woman has authority to pray or prophesy as she shows respect by covering her head in the presence of the angels [NTC].
3. It means that she should exercise her freedom in a responsible manner [AB, NIC2]. The primary meaning of this phrase is to have freedom or the right to choose. It means then that a woman should have the freedom to do as she chooses. But because of the preceding argument and because of the angels, she should choose responsibly to remain covered [NIC2].

QUESTION—What is indicated by the phrase διὰ τοὺς ἀγγέλους 'because of the angels'?

It indicates that angels are present in the assembly of believers at worship [AB, Alf, EGT, Ho, ICC, Lns, Rb, TNTC]. Violation of proper order would offend the angels [Alf, EGT, HNTC, Lns, MNTC, My, Rb, TNTC]. Proper order would indicate that the woman's head be covered while praying or prophesying [Lns]. Angels are the guardians of the created order and would be offended by violations of the principles set down in 11:3 [HNTC, NIC, TH]. Angels were concerned with appropriate respect of God in worship [AB]. The angels are watching to see that the women are behaving properly [TH]. If an unveiled woman shocks the sensibilities of men, she will also be shocking the sensibilities of angels who are present at worship [ICC]. The angels were the most submissive of all creatures and would be offended by non-submissiveness [MNTC, Rb]. It indicates that the woman's veiled condition displays the authority of Christ before the heavenly powers referred to in Ephesians 3:10 [Vn]. This phrase indicates an additional reason why the woman should cover her head [TG]: she should cover to show that she is under her husband's authority and because of the angels.

QUESTION—What does the word ἄγγελος 'angel' indicate?

Here ἄγγελος does not indicate an 'evil spirit' but God's good angels [Alf, EGT, Gdt, HNTC, ICC, Lns, NIC2, Rb, TNTC]. This term only refers to holy angels in the New Testament [Alf].

11:11 However^a neither (is) woman without^b man nor man without woman in^c (the) Lord;

LEXICON—a. πλήν (LN 89.130) (BAGD 1.c. p. 669): 'however' [BAGD, NTC; ISV, NIV, NJB, TEV, TNT], 'nevertheless' [ICC, LN, NIGTC; KJV, NRSV], 'yet' [NAB, REB], 'but' [BAGD, LN; NLT], 'in any case' [AB, BAGD; NET], 'only' [BAGD, HNTC, Lns], 'except' [LN], 'of course' [Herm], not explicit [CEV].
  b. χωρίς (LN **89.120**) (BAGD 2.a.α. p. 890): 'without' [AB, Herm, LN, Lns; KJV], 'apart from' [BAGD]. The phrase οὔτε...χωρίς 'neither (is)...without' is translated 'nor is without some relationship to' [**LN**], 'is not independent of' [**LN**; ISV, NAB, NET, NIV, NLT, NRSV, TEV], 'is nothing without' [NJB], 'is nothing apart from' [NIGTC; TNT], 'is essential to' [REB]. This word is also translated as a verb: 'to need' [CEV].
  c. ἐν with dative object (LN 13.8, 83.13, 89.119): 'in' [AB, Herm, HNTC, ICC, LN, Lns, NIGTC, NTC; ISV, KJV, NAB, NET, NIV, NJB, NRSV, TNT], 'inside, within' [LN (83.13)], 'joined closely to, in union with' [LN (89.119)], 'in our life in' [TEV]. The phrase ἐν κυρίῳ 'in the Lord' is translated 'in the Lord's fellowship' [REB], 'in relationships among the Lord's people' [NLT].

QUESTION—What relationship is indicated by πλήν 'however'?

It indicates a contrastive relationship and limits 11:10 [EGT, ICC, NIC, NIC2, NTC, Rb, Vn]: *however*. The thought is that while it is true that woman is dependent on man, yet he cannot despise her [EGT, Ho, ICC, My]. It indicates an interruption in the flow of the argument to summarize [AB; NET]: *in any case*. It carries the idea that the following should not be overlooked [Lns]. Paul typically uses this word to break off a discussion and give emphasis to what is important [NIC2]: *nonetheless*. Paul is writing something new and wants the readers to remember it lest they draw the wrong conclusions from 11:10 [NIC]. It indicates that Paul is returning to the main point of his argument [NTC, TH].

QUESTION—What is the significance of the changed order of man-woman in this verse from the preceding context?

It serves to support the interpretation in 11:10 of the woman's authority rather than her subordination to man. Had the latter been the case, one would have expected the reversed order here. Nevertheless the man is not independent of the woman [NIC2].

QUESTION—What is meant by ἐν κυρίῳ 'in the Lord'?

  1. It means that they are both in the Christian circle or family as believers in Christ [Alf, EGT, Gdt, ICC, Lns, MNTC, My, NIC, NIC2, TG, TNTC, Vn; NLT, REB, TEV]. To be 'in the Lord' means to be subject to the Lord [EGT, NIC], and to enjoy the benefits he acquired [NIC]. It refers to living in union with the Lord [TG], to be in fellowship with him [TNTC].

2. It means as the Lord intended or willed they are interdependent [HNTC, Ho]. It means 'by divine appointment' [Ho] as He originally intended that they be and as they are now restored to be [HNTC].

QUESTION—To whom do γυνή 'woman' and ἀνήρ 'man' refer?

They refer to man and woman in general and not to husband and wife [NIC, TH]. They refer to Christian spouses [Gdt, My].

11:12 For just-as[a] the woman (is) from[b] the man,

LEXICON—a. ὥσπερ (LN 64.13) (BAGD 2. p. 899): 'just as' [AB, Herm, LN, NIGTC; NET, NRSV], 'as' [HNTC, ICC, LN, NTC; ISV, KJV, NIV, TEV, TNT], 'even as' [Lns], 'in the same way that' [NAB], 'though' [NJB], 'although' [NLT], not explicit [CEV, REB]. See this word also at 8:5.
  b. ἐκ with genitive object (BAGD 3.c., 3.h. p. 235): 'from' [AB, BAGD, NIGTC, NTC; NET], 'out of' [BAGD], 'of' [Lns; KJV]. This is also translated with an implied verb: 'to come from' [CEV, ISV, NIV, NJB, NLT, NRSV], 'to come out of' [TNT], 'to be made out of' [REB], 'to be made from' [NAB, TEV], 'to originate from' [Herm], 'to be taken out of' [HNTC], 'to come into being from' [ICC]. Ἐκ indicates origin [Lns, TH, TNTC]. See this word also at 11:8.

QUESTION—What relationship is indicated by γάρ 'for'?

It indicates the grounds for the preceding verse [Alf, Ho, ICC, NIC, Vn]: woman is not independent of man, nor is man independent of woman, *since* as woman came from man, so also man is born of woman. This verse proves the mutual dependence of man and woman [Ho].

QUESTION—What historical event is referred to here?

This is a reference to the creation story of Genesis 2:21–23 [Alf, Herm, TG]. Woman was originally formed out of man [Ho]. It might be good to translate 'the first man' and 'the first woman' [TG].

so[a] also the man (is) through[b] the woman;

LEXICON—a. οὕτως (LN 61.9) (BAGD p. 597): 'so' [AB, Herm, HNTC, ICC, LN, Lns; ISV, NAB, NET, NIV, NJB, NRSV, TNT], 'even so' [NIGTC, NTC; KJV], 'in the same way' [TEV], 'thus, in this way' [LN], not explicit [CEV, NLT, REB].
  b. διά with genitive object (LN 90.4): 'through' [AB, HNTC, LN, NTC; NET, REB, TNT], 'by' [LN, Lns; KJV]. This is also translated with an implied verb: 'to be born of' [NAB, NIV, TEV], 'to be born from' [NLT], 'to be given birth by' [CEV], 'to come from' [NJB], 'to exist through' [Herm], 'to come through' [ISV, NRSV], 'to come into being by means of' [ICC], 'to derive existence through' [NIGTC]. Διά indicates the 'means by which' [TH].

QUESTION—What is the significance of ὥσπερ...οὕτως 'just as...so'?

The similarity of the two events lies in the source of their existence. The man is the initial source of the woman while she is the instrumental source of the man [EGT, ICC, Vn].

QUESTION—In what way is ὁ ἀνὴρ διὰ τῆς γυναικός 'the man through the woman'?

This refers to natural childbirth [Ho, My, NIC, TG; CEV, NAB, NIV, NLT, TEV]. This refers to ordinary conditions where every man has a mother; the exception of Adam is not in view [NIC].

and/but all-things (are) from^a God.

LEXICON—a. ἐκ with genitive object (See this word above in this verse): 'from' [AB, HNTC, ICC, NTC; NAB, NET, TNT], 'of' [Lns; KJV]. This word is also translated with an implied verb 'to come from' [Herm; ISV, NIV, NJB, NLT, NRSV]. This entire clause is translated 'yet God is the one who created everything' [CEV], 'and God is the source of all' [REB], 'and it is God who brings everything into existence' [TEV], 'and the source of everything is God' [NIGTC].

QUESTION—What relationship is indicated by δέ 'and/but'?
  1. It indicates a continuative relationship [HNTC, ICC, Lns, NIC2; NAB, NJB, NLT, REB, TEV]: *and*.
  2. It indicates a contrastive relationship [AB; CEV, ISV, KJV, NET, NIV, TNT]: *but*.

QUESTION—What is the significance of the definite article in τὰ πάντα 'the all things'?

It does not refer to all things in general as it would without the article, but specifically to both the man and woman [Lns].

QUESTION—How does this clause modify the preceding two?

It qualifies their existence by stating that the ultimate source of both man and woman is God. It seems to be designed to show that the preceding argument should not be viewed from a point of view that makes the woman subordinate [NIC2]. That God is ultimately the source of man and woman is further reason why man must not be contemptuous of the woman [ICC].

DISCOURSE UNIT: 11:13–16 [NIC2, NTC]. The topic is an argument from propriety [NIC2], man and woman again [NTC].

11:13 Judge^a among^b yourselves;

LEXICON—a. aorist act. impera. of κρίνω (LN 30.75): 'to judge' [AB, NTC; KJV, NAB, NET, NIV, NRSV, REB, TEV, TNT], 'to decide' [HNTC, LN, Lns; ISV, NJB], 'to use one's power of discernment' [ICC], 'to come to a decision' [NIGTC], 'to make up one's mind, to come to a conclusion' [LN]. This entire clause is translated 'ask yourselves' [CEV], 'what do you think about this?' [NLT]. See this word also at 10:15.

  b. ἐν with dative object (LN 83.9): 'among' [HNTC, LN], 'for' [AB, NIGTC, NTC; all versions except CEV, KJV, NLT], 'in' [KJV], 'in regard to' [Lns], not explicit [ICC; CEV, NLT].

1 CORINTHIANS 11:13　　　　75

QUESTION—What is meant by ἐν ὑμῖν αὐτοῖς κρίνατε 'judge among yourselves'?
1. They should judge in their own minds for themselves [Alf, HNTC, ICC, My; probably all versions except KJV]. These words are translated 'judge for yourselves' [NAB, NET, NIV, NRSV, REB, TEV, TNT], 'ask yourselves' [CEV], 'decide for yourselves' [ISV, NJB], 'what do you think about this' [NLT].
2. They should decide together among themselves [EGT, Lns, TH]. Paul is addressing a community, so 'among yourselves' is the meaning [TH].

QUESTION—What words are emphasized in this clause?
The words ἐν ὑμῖν αὐτοῖς 'among yourselves' is emphasized both by its position at the beginning [Lns], and the addition of the word αὐτοῖς 'selves' [Lns, TNTC].

is-it being-fitting[a] for-a-woman to-pray[b] to-God uncovered?[c]

LEXICON—a. pres. act. participle of πρέπω (LN 66.1) (BAGD p. 699): 'to be fitting' [BAGD, HNTC, LN; NJB, REB, TNT], 'to be proper' [AB, Herm, Lns, NTC; CEV, ISV, NAB, NET, NIV, NRSV, TEV], 'to be right' [BAGD, LN; NLT], 'to be appropriate' [NIGTC], 'to be decent' [ICC], 'to be comely' [Ho; KJV], 'to be seemly, to be suitable' [BAGD]. This refers to what is culturally acceptable [NTC].
b. pres. mid. (deponent = act.) infin. of προσεύχομαι (LN 33.178) (BAGD p. 713): 'to pray' [AB, BAGD, Herm, HNTC, LN, Lns, NTC; all versions except TEV, TNT], 'to pray in public worship' [TEV], 'to offer prayer' [TNT], 'to publicly offer prayers' [ICC], 'to conduct prayer' [NIGTC], 'to speak to God, to ask God for' [LN]. 'Praying' here does not refer to private, but to public prayer [TG].
c. ἀκατακάλυπτος (See this word at 11:5): 'uncovered' [LN, Lns, NTC; KJV], 'bareheaded' [REB], 'unveiled' [AB, Herm, HNTC; NAB, TNT], 'without a veil' [NJB], 'with (one's) head unveiled' [NRSV], 'with nothing on (one's) head' [TEV], 'without something on (one's) head' [CEV], 'with (one's) head uncovered' [ISV, NET, NIV], 'without covering (one's) head' [NLT], 'without wearing a hood' [NIGTC], 'to have one's head uncovered' [ICC].

QUESTION—What reply is expected to this question?
The question is rhetorical [NIC2, NTC] and expects the answer 'No!' [HNTC, NIC2, NTC, TG, TH]. Because they are to judge for themselves, the question is not strictly rhetorical, although Paul clearly expected them to answer "No" [TH].

QUESTION—What is the significance of the words τῷ θεῷ 'to God'?
They are added to show that this is public worship [Gdt]. They show that the woman is not only in church, but is an active participant in the worship [NIC2]. The words add solemnity to prayer [EGT]. The words are added to stress that when praying she should neither be asserting her equality with men nor drawing their attention to herself [ICC].

11:14 (Does) not-even[a] nature[b] itself teach you

LEXICON—a. οὐδέ (LN 69.7, 69.8) (BAGD 3. p. 591): 'not even' [BAGD, LN (69.8), Lns, NIGTC; KJV], 'not' [AB, Herm, HNTC, NTC; CEV, NET, NJB, NLT, NRSV, REB, TNT], 'not…the very' [NIV], 'neither…nor' [ISV], 'and not, nor, neither' [LN (69.7)], 'even' [ICC], not explicit [TEV].

b. φύσις (LN 58.8) (BAGD 3. p. 869): 'nature' [AB, BAGD, Herm, HNTC, ICC, LN, Lns, NTC; all versions except CEV, NIV, NLT], 'very nature of things' [NIV], 'the very ordering of how things are' [NIGTC], 'the regular natural order' [BAGD]. This entire phrase is translated 'isn't it unnatural?' [CEV], 'isn't it obvious?' [NLT].

QUESTION—What is the function of 11:14–15?

It supports the argument of the previous verse [ICC, Lns, NIC, NIC2]. A woman's glory is her long hair and nature gives a hint that at appropriate occasions a woman needs to have her head covered and her hair is given to her as a covering [TNTC]. A woman's long hair is given to her as a covering, a natural veil, and so the veil itself must be becoming to a woman [Ho]. Since women by nature have been given long hair as a covering, this points to the need to be covered when praying or prophesying [NIC2]. Her hair is a natural covering and a veil is a cultural symbolic covering, both showing her subordinate role [NTC]. Since long hair is an honor for a woman because it is given to her in place of a covering, then any proper custom which emphasizes this honor should be prized [Lns]. She should follow the hint her long hair implies [HNTC].

QUESTION—What is meant by φύσις 'nature'?

It is a sense of what is appropriate [Ho]. It refers to the common feelings of mankind [ICC]. It refers to what a person instinctively feels as being normal or correct [EGT, MNTC]. It has to do with mankind's inherent moral makeup [EGT]. It means the general opinion all people share by virtue of their being human beings [NIC]. It refers to the way things are or as people perceive them to be in view of their shared culture [NIC2]. It means the natural world as God made it without any artificial change [HNTC, Lns, NTC]. It means the law of creation, not propriety [Alf]. It means both a person's culture and Christian convictions. Here it has to do with the order God has ordained in the world and particularly in human society [TH].

QUESTION—What answer is expected to this question which ends in the middle of 11:15?

1. The question expects a positive reply [AB, ICC, Lns, NIC2, NTC, Rb, TH; TEV]: Nature itself teaches you that if a man wears long hair, it is a dishonor to him, but if a woman wears long hair, it is her glory.
2. The question expects a negative reply [ISV]: Nature itself teaches you neither that it's disgraceful for a man to have long hair nor that hair is a woman's glory.

that (a) man on-the-one-hand if he-wears-long-hair[a] it-is (a) dishonor[b] to-him,

LEXICON—a. pres. act. subj. of κομάω (LN 49.25) (BAGD p. 442): 'to wear long hair' [AB, BAGD, LN, Lns; NRSV], 'to wear (one's) hair long' [ICC; NAB], 'to have long hair' [Herm, HNTC, LN; CEV, ISV, KJV, NET, NIV, NJB, NLT, TNT], 'to appear with long hair' [LN], 'to let one's hair grow long' [BAGD, NTC]. This clause and the following clause are translated 'while long hair disgraces a man' [REB], 'that long hair on a man is a disgrace' [TEV], 'long hair degrades a man' [NIGTC]. Having long hair carries the sense of 'like a woman' [Gdt, Lns]. We cannot assume that Paul had in mind the short hair that modern men wear [Lns].

b. ἀτιμία (LN 87.71) (BAGD p. 120): 'dishonor' [AB, BAGD, HNTC, LN, Lns; TNT], 'disgrace' [BAGD, Herm, NTC; NET, NIV, NJB, TEV], 'shame' [BAGD; KJV], 'disrespect' [LN]. This noun is also translated as an adjective: 'degrading' [ICC; NRSV], 'disgraceful' [CEV, ISV, NLT], 'dishonorable' [NAB]. It is also translated as a verb: 'to disgrace' [REB], 'to degrade' [NIGTC].

QUESTION—Do men physiologically have shorter hair than women?
1. Men have shorter hair due to a physiological difference from women [Alf, Gdt, Herm, Ho, ICC, Lns, MNTC, NTC, TNTC]. The testosterone of men's physical makeup causes their hair to fall out at an earlier stage than women giving them naturally shorter hair [MNTC].
2. Men and women's hair is physiologically capable of being equally long, so Paul must have been referring to the custom of his day [AB, NIC, NIC2]. This only refers to the contemporary custom of Paul's day since how short a person's hair is depends on how short they cut it [NIC2].

QUESTION—What was the custom of Paul's day regarding to short hair in men?

Long hair was not the custom for either Hebrew or Greek men [Ho]. It was considered a mark of effeminacy to have long hair [Ho, Lns]. At that time, Jews, Greeks, and Romans wore their hair short [ICC]. In Paul's time, long hair was a disgrace for men [NTC].

11:15 But if (a) woman has-long-hair[a] it is (a) glory[b] to-her?

LEXICON—a. pres. act. subj. of κομάω (LN **49.25**): 'to have long hair' [Herm, HNTC, LN; KJV, NET, NIV, NJB, NRSV, TNT], 'to wear long hair' [AB, **LN**, Lns], 'to let one's hair grow long' [NTC]. It is also translated as a noun: 'long hair' [NIGTC; CEV, NAB, NLT], 'hair' [ISV], not explicit [ICC; REB, TEV]. See this word also in 11:14.

b. δόξα (LN 25.205): 'glory' [AB, Herm, HNTC, ICC, Lns, NIGTC, NTC; ISV, KJV, NAB, NET, NIV, NJB, NRSV], 'honor' [LN (87.4); TNT], 'pride and joy' [NLT], 'a beautiful way (to cover)' [CEV], 'a thing of beauty' [TEV], 'pride' [LN]. This word contrasts with 'dishonor' of 11:15 and here means 'honor' or 'distinction' [NIC2]. It refers to a woman's natural beauty [EGT, NTC]. It means that her hair is like an ornament

[Ho]. It is that which distinguishes her and gives her dignity as a woman [NIC, Vn]. See this word also at 10:31.

QUESTION—What relationship is indicated by δέ 'on the other hand'?

It indicates a contrast with the previous verse about the man [AB, HNTC, ICC, Lns, NIC2, NTC; CEV, KJV, NET, NIV, NJB, NRSV, TEV, TNT]: the man...*but*...the woman.

Because[a] the hair[b] has-been-given [to-her] for/instead-of[c] (a) covering.[d]

TEXT—Some manuscripts omit αὐτῇ 'to her'. GNT includes this word in brackets in the text with a C rating, indicating difficulty in deciding whether or not to include it in the text. It is included by ICC, Lns, NTC; all versions except CEV, ISV, REB. It is omitted or not translated by AB, HNTC, NIGTC; CEV, ISV, and REB.

LEXICON—a. ὅτι (See this word at 10:17): 'because' [AB, ICC, Lns, NIGTC, NTC], 'for' [Herm, HNTC; ISV, KJV, NET, NIV, NLT, NRSV, REB], 'after all' [NJB], not explicit [all other versions].

b. κόμη (LN **8.14**) (BAGD p. 442): 'hair' [AB, Herm, **LN**; ISV, KJV, NAB, NET, NJB, NRSV, REB], 'long hair' [BAGD, HNTC, ICC, Lns, NIGTC, NTC; NIV, TEV, TNT], 'it' [NLT], not explicit [CEV].

c. ἀντί with genitive object (LN 57.145, 89.24) (BAGD 2. p. 73): 'for' [AB, BAGD, LN (57.145); KJV, NAB, NET, NRSV, TNT], 'as' [BAGD, HNTC, NIGTC, NTC; NIV, NLT, REB, TEV], 'as a substitute for' [ISV], 'for the purpose of' [LN (89.24)], 'in place of' [BAGD, LN (57.145)], 'instead of' [Lns], not explicit [CEV]. This preposition is also translated as a verb phrase: 'to be (a covering)' [NJB], 'to serve as' [ICC]. Ἀντί is used here in the sense of 'to serve as' [HNTC].

d. περιβόλαιον (LN **6.163**) (BAGD p. 646): 'covering' [AB, BAGD, Herm, HNTC, ICC, Lns, NIGTC, NTC; all versions except CEV, ISV], 'clothing' [**LN**], 'apparel' [LN], 'wrap, cloak, robe' [BAGD]. This singular noun is translated as a plural noun: 'coverings' [ISV]. It is also translated as a verb: 'to cover' [CEV]. This word literally refers to some kind of wrapper or a garment which enveloped. It may have referred to the *peplum* or shawl worn by Greek women [Alf]. It denotes a *peplum* of sorts that would cover the whole body [Gdt]. It refers to a 'hood' [EGT].

QUESTION—What relationship is indicated by ὅτι 'because'?

It indicates reason [HNTC, NIC, NIC2, NTC]: if a woman has long hair, it is her glory *because* long hair is given to her as a covering.

QUESTION—Who is the actor of the passive verb δέδοται 'it is given'?

The actor is God [NTC, TG, TH]: God gave her the hair for a covering

QUESTION—What is meant by ἀντί 'for/instead of'?

1. The word ἀντί denotes 'as' or 'for' [AB, Gdt, HNTC, Ho, MNTC, My, NIC2, NTC, TNTC; KJV, NAB, NET, NIV, NLT, NRSV, REB, TEV, TNT]: her hair has been given to her for a covering. He is arguing that since a woman has long hair naturally which acts as a covering for her, this is further support from nature itself that a woman should be covered

when praying or prophesying. It should not be taken here to mean 'instead of' as though a woman's hair itself served her as a veil and she need not cover her head [NTC]. The word κόμη can mean both 'long hair' and 'a neat hairdo' [MNTC].
2. It means 'instead of' [Lns, NIC; ISV]: her hair has been given to her instead of a covering. He is arguing that since a woman's long hair has been given to her in place of a covering and all she needs to do is to have an orderly hairdo. The word κόμη means 'hairdo' [NIC]. Long hair is an honor for a woman since it is given her in place of a covering. Therefore they should follow a custom that accentuates this honor [Lns]. Hair is given as a substitute for coverings [ISV].

11:16 But/and if anyone wants/seems[a] to-be contentious,[b]

LEXICON—a. pres. act. indic. of δοκέω (LN **25.7**, **30.96**, 31.30) (BAGD 1.b. p. 201): 'to want' [**LN** (25.7); ISV, NAB, NIV, NJB, NLT, TEV, TNT], 'to be disposed' [BAGD, **LN** (25.7); NRSV], 'to be inclined' [NTC], 'to be minded' [NIGTC], 'to intend' [NET], 'to insist on' [REB], 'to think (one) must be' [Herm], 'to mean' [HNTC], 'to be' [ICC], 'to choose' [**LN** (30.96)], 'to appear' [LN (31.30)], 'to think' [BAGD, LN (31.30)], 'to believe, to consider, to suppose' [BAGD], 'to assume' [LN (31.30)], 'to seem' [AB, LN (31.30), Lns; KJV], not explicit [CEV].

b. φιλόνεικος (LN **33.450**) (BAGD 1. p. 860): 'contentious' [AB, BAGD, Herm, HNTC, Lns, NIGTC, NTC; KJV, NIV, NJB, NRSV], 'quarrelsome' [BAGD, **LN**], 'argumentative' [BAGD; TNT], 'given to arguing' [LN]. The phrase φιλόνεικος εἶναι 'to be contentious' is translated 'to quarrel' [NET], 'to argue' [CEV, ISV, NAB, NLT, TEV], '(insists on) arguing' [REB], 'so contentious as to dispute this conclusion' [ICC]. Φιλόνεικος refers to a person who loves strife [Lns, Rb, TNTC].

QUESTION—What relationship is indicated by δέ 'and/but'?
1. It indicates a contrast [HNTC, ICC, Lns, NTC; ISV, KJV, NLT, NRSV, REB, TEV]: the long hair is given to her as a covering *but* if anyone wants to be contentious.
2. It indicates a conjoining relationship [REB]: the long hair is given to her as a covering *and* if anyone wants to be contentious. It helps to indicate that Paul is concluding the discussion he began in 11:4 and 5 [TH].

QUESTION—What is the significance of the kind of condition or formula used here?

When εἰ 'if' is used with the present indicative it signifies a condition assumed to be true by the speaker. Here Paul assumes that there is such a person (or persons) in Corinth [Lns]. A similar formula is used in four places in this epistle each making reference to something some of the Corinthians were doing (see 3:18, 8.2, 14:37) [NIC2].

80   1 CORINTHIANS 11:16

QUESTION—What is meant by δοκέω 'to want/to seem'?
1. It refers to desire or intent [EGT, Gdt, Ho, ICC, MNTC, My, NIC2, NTC, TG, TNTC, Vn; all versions except ISV, KJV]: if anyone wants to be contentious.
2. It refers to appearance [AB, Alf, NIC; KJV]: if anyone seems to be contentious.

we (do) not have[a] such[b] (a) custom,[c] nor (do) the churches[d] of God.
LEXICON—a. pres. act. indic. of ἔχω (See this word at 11:10): 'to have' [AB, Herm, HNTC, Lns, NIGTC, NTC; all versions except CEV, NAB, REB], 'to recognize' [NAB], 'there is' [REB], not explicit [ICC; CEV].
b. τοιοῦτος (LN 64.2) (BAGD 2.a.β. p. 821): 'such' [AB, Herm, HNTC, LN, Lns, NIGTC, NTC; KJV, NJB, NRSV, REB], 'like this' [ISV], 'any other' [NAB, TEV], 'other' [NET, NIV, NLT, TNT], 'like such, like that' [LN], 'of such a kind, such as this' [BAGD], not explicit [ICC; CEV].
c. συνήθεια (LN 41.25) (BAGD 2.b. p. 789): 'custom' [AB, BAGD, Herm, HNTC, LN, Lns, NIGTC, NTC; ISV, KJV, NJB, NLT, NRSV, REB, TNT], 'custom in worship' [TEV], 'usage' [BAGD; NAB], 'Christian usage' [ICC], 'practice' [NET, NIV], 'habit' [BAGD, LN]. This is also translated as a clause: 'this is how things are done' [CEV].
d. ἐκκλησία (LN 11.78) (BAGD 4.e.α. p. 241): 'church' [AB, BAGD, Herm, HNTC, ICC, NIGTC, NTC; all versions except REB], 'congregation' [BAGD; REB], 'Christian authority' [ICC], 'assembly, gathering' [LN]. Ἐκκλησία here refers to a local Christian community [TH]. 'Churches of God' would be 'churches that worship God' [TG]. 'Churches of God' is Paul's way of referring to all of God's people combined [HNTC]. See this word also at 10:32.
QUESTION—To whom does ἡμεῖς 'we' refer?
1. It refers to Paul and the other apostles and teachers [EGT, Ho, ICC, MNTC, NTC, TG, Vn]. These instructions have apostolic authority [ICC].
2. It refers to Paul and the Christians closely associated with him [Alf, Gdt, Lns, NIC2].
3. It refers to Paul alone [HNTC, NIC, TH]. If this refers to Paul and the Christian community, then the next phrase must be translated 'the other churches of God'. But here Paul is using the editorial 'we' meaning 'I' [TH].
QUESTION—What words are implied at the beginning of this clause?
Words like the following are implied: 'let him know that' [Gdt], 'remember that' [NAB], 'I say that' [NJB], 'I tell you' [TNT], 'all I can say is that' [NLT], 'all that I have to say is that' [TEV]
QUESTION—What word is emphasized in this clause?
The word ἡμεῖς 'we' is emphatic [Lns, NTC]: we ourselves. This word contrasts with 'anyone' [NTC].

QUESTION—To what does συνήθεια 'custom' refer?
1. It refers to the custom of women being unveiled in public meetings [Alf, EGT, Gdt, Herm, HNTC, Ho, ICC, NIC2, TG, TNTC, Vn]. Four times Paul uses this kind of sentence (3:18, 8:2, 11:16, and 14:27) and each time it refers to something that was actually going on. Here it probably refers to some women who were not wearing the veil when praying. When Paul therefore refers to 'such custom' he is must be referring to their practice of uncovering. The matter of the covering of women is also what has been under discussion through this section [NIC2].
2. It refers to the custom of arguing or being contentious [Ed, Lns, My, NIC]: If anyone wants to be contentious about this, we have no such practice (of being contentious).

DISCOURSE UNIT: 11:17–34 [AB, Alf, Ed, Gdt, Herm, HNTC, Ho, ICC, Lns, MNTC, NCBC, NIC, NIC2, NIGTC, NTC, TG, TH, TNTC, Vn; NET, NIV, NJB, NLT, TEV]. The topic is the abuse of the Lord's Supper [AB, Alf, Ed, Gdt, NIC], the Lord's Supper [Herm, HNTC, Ho, ICC, Lns, MNTC, NCBC, NTC, TNTC; NET, NIV, NJB, TEV], order at the Lord's Supper [NLT].

11:17 Now/but[a] (concerning) this giving-of-instruction[b] I-praise[c] (you) not
LEXICON—a. δέ (See this word at 11:2): 'now' [ICC, NIGTC; KJV, NET, NJB, NRSV], 'what I now have to say' [NAB], 'but' [Herm, NTC], 'however' [TEV], 'yet' [Lns], 'but now' [NLT], not explicit [AB, HNTC; CEV, ISV, NIV, REB, TNT].
b. pres. act. participle of παραγγέλλω (LN 33.327) (BAGD p. 613): 'to give instruction' [AB, BAGD, Herm, NTC; ISV, NET, REB], 'to declare' [KJV], 'to have to say' [NAB], 'to give a charge' [HNTC, ICC], 'to give a directive' [NIGTC], 'to transmit' [Lns], 'to order' [LN], 'to command' [BAGD, LN], 'to instruct, to give orders, to direct' [BAGD], not explicit [CEV]. The phrase τοῦτο παραγγέλλων 'this giving of instruction' is translated 'in the following directives' [NIV], 'in the following instructions' [NRSV, TEV], 'while giving you these instructions' [TNT], 'now that I am on the subject of instructions' [NJB], 'when I mention this next issue' [NLT].
c. pres. act. indic. of ἐπαινέω (See this word at 11:2): 'to praise' [AB, Lns, NTC; CEV, ISV, KJV, NET, NLT, TEV], 'to say in praise' [NAB], 'to have praise for' [HNTC; NIV], 'to approve of the fact that' [Herm], 'to commend' [ICC; NRSV, REB], 'to continue a commendation' [NIGTC], 'to congratulate' [NJB]. The phrase οὐκ ἐπαινῶ 'I do not praise' is translated 'I have a criticism to make' [TNT].
QUESTION—What relationship is indicated by δέ 'but/now'?
1. It indicates a contrastive relationship [Lns, NIC2, NTC; NLT, TEV]: I praise you that you have remembered me (11:2)...*but* concerning giving this teaching I do not praise you.
2. It indicates a transitional relationship [AB, ICC; KJV, NAB, NET, NJB, NRSV]: *now* concerning giving this teaching I do not praise you.

3. It indicates a conjoining relationship [EGT]: *moreover*, concerning giving this teaching.

QUESTION—Does τοῦτο παραγγέλλων 'this giving of instruction' refer to what follows or to what precedes?

1. It refers to what follows [AB, EGT, MNTC, NIC2, NTC, TH, Vn; CEV, ISV, NAB, NET, NIV, NLT, NRSV, TEV]. This verse constitutes a complete break with the preceding section. There Paul praised them (11:2). Here he does not praise them. Also the second half of the verse gives the content of why he does not praise them. The direction is forward not back [NTC].
2. It refers to what precedes [Alf, Ed, Gdt, HNTC, ICC, Lns, My, NIC, Rb, TNTC; NJB, REB, TNT]. Τοῦτο 'this' refers to the warning in 11:16 and would mean 'Giving you this warning I do not praise you (about the following)' [Gdt]. If τοῦτο refers to what follows, some definite command should follow it [Alf]. It refers not to 11:16 as there is no command there, but to 11:2–16 [NIC].

QUESTION—What figure of speech is 'I do not praise'?

It is a litotes, an understatement, in which something is expressed by negating its opposite [Gdt, ICC, Lns, My; TNT]: I blame you. It is a gentle way of expressing blame [Lns]. This contrasts with the praise he expressed in 11:2 [Gdt, ICC, Lns, My, NIC, TG, TNTC].

because/that you-come-together[a] not for[b] the better[c] but for the worse.[d]

LEXICON—a. pres. mid. (deponent = act.) indic. of συνέρχομαι (LN 15.123) (BAGD 1.a. p. 788): 'to come together' [BAGD, LN, Lns, NTC; KJV, NET, NRSV], 'to assemble' [AB, BAGD, HNTC, LN], 'to gather' [BAGD; ISV], 'to meet together' [NLT], 'to meet' [LN], 'to hold (one's) meetings' [BAGD]. This verb is also translated as a noun phrase: 'worship services' [CEV], 'your assemblies' [TNT], 'your meetings' [Herm; NAB, NIV, REB], 'your meetings for worship' [TEV], 'the meetings you hold' [NJB], 'the meetings you hold as a church' [NIGTC], 'your religious gatherings' [ICC]. This is a reference to the Corinthians coming together for a meeting [Herm, NIC], for worship [Gdt, NIC2], for public worship [Lns]. The present tense indicates that this was a regular activity rather than an occasional one [Lns].

b. εἰς with accusative object (LN 89.48): 'for' [AB, Herm, Lns, NTC; ISV, KJV, NET, NRSV], 'with the result that, so that as a result, to cause' [LN]. This preposition is also translated as a verb: 'to make (things)' [HNTC]. The phrase οὐκ εἰς τὸ κρεῖσσον ἀλλὰ εἰς τὸ ἧσσον 'not for the better but for the worse' is translated '(your meetings are) not profitable but harmful' [NAB], '(they) do more harm than good' [NJB], '(your meetings) tend to do more harm than good' [REB], '(your meetings)...actually do more harm than good' [TEV], '(your meetings) do more harm than good' [NIGTC; NIV], '(your assemblies) do more harm

than good' [TNT], 'more harm than good is done' [NLT], '(your religious gatherings) do (you) more harm than good' [ICC; CEV].
  c. κρείσσων (LN 65.21) (BAGD 2. p. 449): 'better' [AB, BAGD, Herm, HNTC, LN, Lns, NTC; ISV, KJV, NET, NRSV], 'good' [ICC, NIGTC; CEV, NIV, NJB, NLT, REB, TEV, TNT], 'profitable' [NAB], 'superior' [LN], 'more useful' [BAGD], 'more advantageous' [BAGD]. This entails building up [Alf, Gdt, HNTC], stimulation of spiritual life [ICC], spiritual enrichment [Lns, MNTC], benefit [NIC], advantage [Vn].
  d. ἥσσων (LN **65.29**) (BAGD p. 349): 'worse' [AB, BAGD, Herm, HNTC, **LN**, Lns, NTC; ISV, KJV, NET, NRSV], 'harm' [ICC, NIGTC; CEV, NIV, NJB, NLT, REB, TEV, TNT], 'harmful' [NAB], 'lesser, inferior, weaker' [BAGD]. This implies damage of the community [HNTC], misconduct [ICC], spiritual detriment [Lns], spiritual deterioration [Vn], lack of appropriateness and hindrance to faith [Alf].
QUESTION—What relationship is indicated by ὅτι 'because/that'?
  1. It indicates grounds for not praising them [AB, Ed, HNTC, NTC; NAB, NET, NIV, NLT, NRSV, TEV]: I do not praise you *since* your meetings do more harm than good.
  2. It indicates the contents of 'praise' [ICC, Lns; KJV, TNT]: I do not praise you (for this,) *that* your meetings do more harm than good.
  3. It functions to give both the grounds and the content [EGT].

DISCOURSE UNIT: 11:18–22 [MNTC]. The topic is the perversion of the Lord's Supper.

11:18 For in-the-first-place[a] on-the-one-hand you coming-together[b] in[c] church[d]

LEXICON—a. πρῶτος (LN 60.46) (BAGD 2. b. p. 726): 'in the first place' [Herm, HNTC, NTC; ISV, NET, NIV, NJB, TEV], 'first' [BAGD, LN; TNT], 'first of all' [AB, ICC, NIGTC; KJV, NAB, NLT], 'to begin with' [NRSV, REB], not explicit [Lns; CEV].
  b. pres. mid. (deponent = act.) participle of συνέρχομαι (See this word at 11:17): 'to come together' [HNTC, Lns, NTC; KJV, NET, NIV, NJB, NRSV], 'to assemble' [AB; TEV, TNT], 'to hold (church) meetings' [Herm], 'to meet' [ICC; NLT, REB], 'to meet together' [NIGTC], 'to gather' [ISV, NAB], 'to worship' [CEV].
  c. ἐν with dative object (LN 83.13): 'in' [AB, HNTC, LN, Lns, NTC; KJV, NJB, TEV], 'as (a)' [ICC, NIGTC; ISV, NET, NIV, NLT, NRSV, REB, TNT], 'for' [NAB], not explicit [Herm; CEV].
  d. ἐκκλησία (BAGD 4.a. p. 240): 'church' [AB, BAGD, Herm, HNTC, NTC; ISV, KJV, NET, NIV, NLT, NRSV], 'congregation' [BAGD; REB, TNT], 'assembly' [Lns; NJB], 'meeting' [NAB, TEV], 'Christian congregation' [BAGD, ICC], not explicit [CEV]. Ἐκκλησία does not refer to a building [Gdt, Ho, ICC, NTC, TH, Vn]. It refers to an assembly or gathering [Alf, BAGD, EGT, Gdt, ICC, Lns, NIC, NIC2, Rb, TH, TNTC, Vn]. Church indicates the people of God assembled [HNTC]. It refers to God's people

gathered for worship. Here it means the physical meetings of Corinthian Christians [TH]. It refers here to the Body of Christ at worship services [NTC]. See this word also at 10:32 and 11:16.

QUESTION—What relationship is indicated by γάρ 'for'?
1. It indicates the grounds for why Paul could not praise them [Gdt, ICC]: I do not praise you, *since* when you assemble there are divisions among you.
2. It indicates the grounds for saying that their meetings are for the worse rather than the better [EGT, Ho, NIC, NIC2]: you come together for the worse, *since* when you assemble there are divisions among you.
3. It indicates an explanation of how they came together for the worse [HNTC, My, TH]: you come together for the worse *in that* there are divisions among you. This gives an example of what 'worse' means [HNTC, TH].

QUESTION—What is indicated by πρῶτον μέν 'in the first place, on the one hand'?
1. It indicates the first of a series or list of items [Alf, EGT, Gdt, HNTC, Ho, ICC, Lns, NIC2, NTC, Rb, TH, TNTC; all versions except CEV]: first. Πρῶτον μὲν calls for a second item but Paul does not give one that we can positively identify [HNTC, ICC, NIC2]. The second item of correction begins with Chapter 12 and the topic of spiritual gifts [Alf, EGT, Ho, Lns]. The second item begins at 11:20 where Paul begins to talk about the Lord's Supper [Gdt].
2. It indicates a degree of importance [AB, NIC, Vn]: mainly. Since there is no second in the context, it means that this was the main thing that Paul wanted to bring up with them [NIC].

I-hear (that there) are divisions[a] among you

LEXICON—a. σχίσμα (LN 39.13) (BAGD 2. p. 797): 'division' [AB, BAGD, Herm, HNTC, LN; ISV, KJV, NAB, NET, NIV, NLT, NRSV, TNT], 'faction' [NTC], 'separate faction' [NJB], 'opposing group' [TEV], 'clique' [Lns], 'split' [NIGTC], 'discord' [LN], 'dissension, schism' [BAGD]. The phrase σχίσματα ἐν ὑμῖν ὑπάρχειν 'divisions among you' is translated 'you fall into sharply divided groups' [REB], 'you can't get along with each other' [CEV], 'you are split into sets' [ICC].

QUESTION—What is the significance of the present tense in ἀκούω 'I hear'?
Some think it means that Paul kept on hearing this kind of report from various people [Ed, EGT, ICC, Rb]. Another view is that it does not indicate repeated hearings, but simply that he hears and therefore knows [Lns].

QUESTION—Who told Paul about this?
It could have been Chloe's people (1:11) or Stephanas, Fortunatus, and Achaicus (16:17) [HNTC].

QUESTION—To what does σχίσματα 'divisions' refer?
It refers to the problems that existed when they came together as is shown in the following verses [Alf, HNTC, Ho, ICC, MNTC, NIC, NIC2, NTC, Rb,

TH, TNTC]. The divisions referred to are those between the rich and the poor [HNTC, Ho, ICC, NIC, NIC2, NTC, TNTC]. It refers to the fact that they did not wait for each other [Alf]. It refers to their forming separate groups and to lack of unity among them [NIC]. It refers to the divisions already addressed in chapters 1–4 [Gdt].

and partly[a] I-believe.
LEXICON—a. μέρος τι (LN **78.49**) (BAGD 1.d. p. 506): 'partly' [BAGD, Herm, LN (78.49); ISV, KJV, TEV, TNT], 'to some degree' [**LN** (78.49)], 'in part' [AB, Lns, NTC; NET], 'to some extent' [ICC, NIGTC; NIV, NJB, NLT, NRSV]. This entire clause is translated 'and I am inclined to believe it' [NAB], 'and I am sure that some of what I have heard is true' [CEV], 'I believe there is some truth in it' [REB].
QUESTION—Why does Paul only partly believe?
He only partly believes because he is hesitant to believe so shameful a report, yet he trusts his sources [HNTC]. Paul wants to believe the best about the Corinthians [ICC, Lns]. He hopes his sources were exaggerating [Vn]. He expects the reports may be exaggerated and wants to give them the benefit of the doubt [MNTC]. He recognizes that his informants may not be disinterested observers [NIC2]. He is cautious lest he be considered rash [NTC]. He does not want to appear gullible [TNTC].

11:19 For indeed/even[a] divisions/differences[b] must[c] be among you,
LEXICON—a. καί (LN 89.93, 91.12): 'indeed' [AB, Herm, ICC, LN (91.12); NRSV], 'even' [LN (89.93), Lns; NAB], 'in addition' [LN (89.93)], 'also' [LN (89.93); KJV], 'in fact' [NET], 'of course' [ISV, NLT], 'no doubt' [NIV, TEV], 'either' [NJB], 'then' [LN (91.12)], not explicit [NIGTC, NTC; CEV, REB, TNT]. The καί functions to indicate that there is a further reason for Paul to believe the reports [NIC2]. The καί functions to indicate a further step which strengthens the idea of the existence of divisions in 11:18. Here it is 'even' necessary that they be [Gdt].
b. αἵρεσις (LN **63.27**, 33.241) (BAGD 1.c. p. 24): 'division' [**LN** (63.27), Lns; NET, NLT, REB, TEV], 'faction' [AB, BAGD, Herm, HNTC; ISV, NAB, NRSV], 'party-divisions' [ICC], 'dissension' [BAGD, NIGTC, NTC], 'heresy' [LN (33.241); KJV], 'difference of opinion' [TNT], 'differing group' [NJB], 'difference' [NIV], 'untrue doctrine, false teaching' [LN (33.241)], 'separate group' [LN (63.27)], 'sect, party, school' [BAGD].
c. pres. act. indic. of impersonal verb δεῖ (LN 71.34) (BAGD 5. p. 172): 'must' [BAGD, Herm, HNTC, LN, Lns, NTC; ISV, KJV, NET, NLT, TEV, TNT], 'to be necessary' [AB, BAGD, LN], 'to have to be' [BAGD; NAB, NIV, NRSV], 'to be bound' [REB], 'it is no bad thing that there should be' [NJB]. This entire clause is translated 'you are bound to argue with each other' [CEV], 'party-divisions among you can hardly be avoided' [ICC] 'for "dissensions are unavoidable," it is claimed among you' [NIGTC]. Δεῖ is often used to indicate God's purposes [Alf, Ed, My,

TH]. Divisions are inevitable because of sinful human nature and its divisive character [Vn].

QUESTION—What relationship is indicated by γάρ 'for'?

It indicates the reason why Paul partly believes the reports of 11:18 [Ho, Lns, NIC2, TH]: and I partly believe it *because* there must be divisions among you. It functions as a theological digression to support Paul's belief in the reports he had heard. Divisions were repulsive to Paul but he probably says they are inevitable in anticipation of what will come in the future and in anticipation of 11:28–32 [NIC2]. It should be taken as parenthetical and not a part of the flow of the argument [TEV]. The verse may be ironical (conveying the opposite meaning) so TEV translates 'No doubt there must be' [TG].

QUESTION—To what does αἱρέσεις 'divisions/differences' refer?

1. It refers to the same thing as σχίσμα 'division' in 11:18 [Herm, HNTC, Ho, ICC, My, NIC2, TG, TH, TNTC]. If the meaning were distinct from σχίσμα the chain of thought would break down [HNTC, NIC2]. Both words have the general meaning of division [Ho, NIC2]. Αἵρεσις is based on the verb 'to choose' and therefore indicates those who have chosen the same thing and belong to a party such as the Sadducees [TNTC].

2. It refers to something other than 11:18, but is still undesirable [AB, Alf, Ed, EGT, Gdt, Lns, Vn]. The αἵρεσις is the outward expression of the σχίσμα of 11:18 [AB]. This word indicates a further step away from mere divisions toward the idea of choice and willful maintenance of party distinction [Alf]. This word is more specific than σχίσμα and indicates mental attitude or school of thought [EGT, Vn]. This word indicates not simple division based on personal preference, but deep-seated doctrinal opposition to the truth [Gdt]. This is a more serious word than σχίσμα, 'clique' which already existed. Αἵρεσις 'division' only threatened to occur [Lns].

3. It refers to something other than 11:18 and is desirable [NIC, NTC]. The word here denotes choice or selection and indicates that there should be discussions in the congregation, but not those which end in divisions [NIC]. The word denotes dissension, the kind of dissension in which true believers voluntarily separate from those who do not follow Christ's true teaching [NTC].

so-that [also] the genuine[a] (ones) may-become evident[b] among you.

LEXICON—a. δόκιμος (LN 73.4) (BAGD 1. p. 203): 'genuine' [HNTC, LN; ISV, NRSV, REB], 'approved' [AB, Lns; KJV, NET], 'tried and true' [BAGD, NIGTC; NAB], 'trusted' [NJB], 'right' [NLT], 'in the right' [TEV], 'sound' [Herm], 'sincere' [LN]. This adjective is also translated as a noun phrase: 'men of proved worth' [ICC], 'men of real worth' [TNT], 'proven (believers)' [NTC]. It is also translated as a clause: 'which of you have God's approval' [CEV, NIV]. Δόκιμος denotes the quality of having stood the test [Vn]. The one who approves here is God [HNTC, ICC, Lns,

TNTC, Vn; CEV, NIV]. Here the word 'genuine' implies the noun 'believers' [NTC, TG].
   b. φανερός (LN 28.58) (BAGD 1. p. 852): 'evident' [BAGD, LN, NTC; NET], 'manifest' [Lns; KJV], 'plain' [BAGD, LN], 'clear' [BAGD, LN; NRSV], 'known' [AB, BAGD], 'clearly seen' [TEV], 'clearly recognized' [NJB], 'recognized' [NLT], 'easily known, clearly known' [LN], 'visible, open, plainly to be seen' [BAGD], 'visibly revealed' [NIGTC]. The phrase φανεροὶ γένωνται 'may become manifest' is translated 'to come to light' [Herm], 'to stand out' [HNTC], 'to stand out clearly' [NAB], 'to see' [TNT], 'to be easy to see' [CEV], 'to show' [ISV, NIV, REB], 'to not be lost in the crowd' [ICC]. The ones to whom these will be evident are other men [EGT].
QUESTION—What relationship is indicated by ἵνα 'so that'?
   1. It indicates the purpose of there being divisions [AB, EGT, Herm, HNTC, ICC, Lns, NTC; ISV, NAB, NET, NJB, NLT, REB, TEV, TNT]: there must be divisions *in order that* the genuine ones among you may become evident. This is God's purpose in permitting such divisions [Alf, EGT, Gdt, Ho, ICC, My, Rb]. God uses divisions to bring good [ICC]. God permits these divisions so as to reveal who the true Christians are [Gdt].
   2. It indicates the result of having divisions [NRSV]: there must be divisions *which will result* in the genuine ones among you becoming evident.
QUESTION—How do divisions reveal the 'genuine ones'?
   When the evil factions separate from the rest, only the true members remain [Lns]. The 'genuine' will be revealed by the nobler attitude that they display [Alf]. They would be revealed either by their support of unity or their remaining detached from divisions [ICC, Vn].

11:20 You therefore gathering[a] together[b]
LEXICON—a. pres. mid. (deponent = act.) participle of συνέρχομαι (See this word at 11:17): 'to gather' [ISV], 'to come together' [KJV, NET, NIV, NLT, NRSV], 'to meet' [CEV, NJB, REB], 'to assemble' [Herm; NAB, TNT], 'to meet together' [NIGTC; TEV].
   b. ἐπὶ τὸ αὐτό (LN 58.31) (BAGD 4.b. p. 123): 'together' [AB, BAGD, HNTC; CEV, NJB, TNT], 'as a group' [TEV], 'as a congregation' [REB], 'for a meeting' [Herm], 'at/in the same place' [BAGD, NIGTC, NTC; ISV, NET], 'in/into/to one place' [ICC, Lns; KJV], not explicit [NAB, NIV, NLT, NRSV]. This phrase corresponds to ἐν ἐκκλησίᾳ 'in church' of 11:18 and has roughly the same meaning in both places [Gdt, HNTC, NIC2]. This phrase means 'at the same place' [Alf, Ed, EGT, Gdt, ICC, Lns, NTC]. It indicates 'together' more than 'in the same place' [AB, HNTC, NIC].
QUESTION—What relationship is indicated by οὖν 'therefore'?
   It indicates a resumption of the argument in 11:18 [Alf, EGT, Ho, Lns, My, NIC2] since 11:19 is an interruption [Ho]. The repetition of the verb 'come together' supports this as well, as do the words ἐπὶ τὸ αὐτό 'at the same

it-is not to-eat (the) Lord's^a Supper;^b

LEXICON—a. κυριακός (LN **12.10**) (BAGD p. 458): 'Lord's' [BAGD, Herm, LN, NIGTC; all versions], 'belonging to the Lord' [BAGD, LN]. This word is emphasized in the clause [Alf, ICC, Vn]. It contrasts with ἴδιον 'his own' of 11:21 [Alf].

b. δεῖπνον (LN 23.22, 23.25) (BAGD 1. p. 173): 'Supper' [BAGD, Herm, NIGTC; all versions except KJV, NRSV], 'supper' [LN (23.25); KJV, NRSV], 'main meal' [LN (23.25)], 'dinner' [BAGD], 'meal, banquet, feast' [LN (23.22)].

QUESTION—How are the nouns related in the genitive construction κυριακός δεῖπνον 'the Lord's supper'?

It means the supper which the Lord instituted [Alf, Gdt, Ho], the supper which the Lord gives, invites to, and presides over [Gdt], the supper in memory of, under the authority of, or in the presence of the Lord [HNTC], the supper which received its character from the Lord [NIC], the supper which belongs to the Lord [My, NTC, TH]. It may mean the supper which is consecrated to or in honor of the Lord [HNTC, Ho, NIC2]. It is the supper celebrated in commemoration of the Lord's death [Ho].

QUESTION—What is the meaning of this clause?

1. It means that they did not come together for the purpose of eating the Lord's Supper [Alf, HNTC; NAB, TNT]. Their selfish greed and over indulgence shows that their intention was not to celebrate the Lord's Supper [Alf].
2. It means that it was not really the Lord's Supper that they ate [AB, Gdt, Herm, ICC, MNTC, NIC2, TG, TH, TNTC, Vn; NJB]. The presence of social distinctions at the supper changed the original character of the Lord's Supper [NIC2]. The word κυριακός 'Lord's' is emphatic due to its position—it was not the *Lord's* supper they ate [ICC, Vn].
3. It means that it was impossible for them to eat the Lord's Supper correctly [Ed, EGT, Ho, Lns, My, NIC, NTC, Rb]. They intended to eat the Lord's Supper, but their behavior made it impossible for them to be doing so [EGT, Lns]. The phrase οὐκ ἔστιν φαγεῖν 'it is not to eat' means 'it is impossible to eat' [Ho, Lns].

QUESTION—What was the 'Lord's Supper' supposed to be in the observance of the Corinthian church?

It was the combination of a love feast in which the believers came together and shared their food and ate together. This was accompanied by an observance of the Lord's Supper or Communion [Alf, EGT, Gdt, HNTC, ICC, Lns, MNTC, NIC, NIC2, Rb, TG]. The original Lord's Supper consisted of a δεῖπνον 'supper' followed by the institution of Holy Communion by the Lord. It was this that the Corinthians were trying to emulate [Gdt]. It was Holy Communion itself [Ed, Ho].

1 CORINTHIANS 11:21 89

11:21 For each-one takes-before[a] his-own[b] supper in[c] the eating,

LEXICON—a. pres. act. indic. of προλαμβάνω (LN 90.49) (BAGD 2.a. p. 708): 'to take before' [NTC; KJV], 'to go ahead with' [NRSV, TEV], 'to take' [BAGD, Herm; NET, REB], 'to consume in advance' [Lns], 'to have first' [NJB], 'to get ahead with' [HNTC], 'to get on with' [TNT], 'to be in haste' [NAB], 'to rush to eat' [ISV], 'to take ahead of time' [AB], 'to be before hand in getting' [ICC], 'to do in advance, to undertake ahead of time, to make before' [LN], not explicit [NIGTC]. The phrase τὸ ἴδιον δεῖπνον προλαμβάνει 'takes before his own supper' is translated 'goes ahead without waiting for anybody else' [NIV], 'hurry to eat…without sharing with others' [NLT]. This entire clause is translated 'You even start eating before everyone gets to the meeting' [CEV]. The prefix πρό 'before' has lost the meaning of 'beforehand' here [BAGD].

b. ἴδιος (LN **57.4**): 'his own' [AB, Herm, HNTC, ICC, **LN**, Lns; ISV, KJV, NAB, NET, NJB, REB], 'his' [NTC], 'your own' [NLT, NRSV, TEV, TNT], 'his or her own' [NIGTC], 'one's property' [LN], not explicit [AB; CEV, NIV].

c. ἐν with dative object (LN 67.33, 83.13): 'in' [HNTC, LN (83.13), Lns; KJV], 'as' [NTC; ISV, NIV, TEV], 'when it comes' [REB], 'when the time comes' [NRSV], 'when it is time' [NET], 'when (the eating) begins' [NJB], 'at (the meal)' [Herm], 'at the time of' [LN (67.33), NIGTC], 'when' [LN (67.33)], not explicit [AB, ICC; CEV, NAB, NLT, TNT].

QUESTION—What relationship is indicated by γάρ 'for'?

It indicates the grounds for saying that the Lord's Supper was not what they were celebrating (11:20) [Ho, Lns, NIC2]: it is not to eat the Lord's Supper, *since* each one takes his own supper before. There was no communion or eating together [Ho]. At the same time, it explains the divisions mentioned in 11:18 [NIC, NIC2].

QUESTION—Who is included in ἕκαστος 'each'?

It does not refer to each and every one, but to the rich who were at fault [Alf, NIC2, NTC]. The poor had no meal of their own to take [Alf]. The word ἕκαστος is emphasized [NIC2, TH] accenting the individualistic behavior of the rich who ate their own meals instead of partaking together as a unit [NIC2].

QUESTION—What is meant by προλαμβάνω 'to take before'?

1. It means to take food before others do [AB, Alf, Ed, EGT, Gdt, HNTC, Ho, ICC, My, Rb, TG, TH, TNTC; KJV, NIV]. Here the emphasis is on the prefix πρό 'before'. The Corinthians were taking the provisions they had brought before any distribution had been made and without sharing them [Gdt]. The rich hurried in order to avoid sharing a common dish with slaves and lower class people [EGT]. They took before the others in contrast to 'waiting for each other' as 11:33 commands [HNTC].

2. It means simply to take food [BAGD, Herm, Lns, NIC2]. It means here to consume food [Herm]. It is difficult to know which meaning to take, but it could be that Paul is focusing not on when they took as much as on their

eating of their own private meals and not sharing with others [NIC2]. Rather than sharing their food, cliques formed and sat together at private tables—the rich here, the poor there. The problem focused on the selfish behavior rather than on their eating before the others [Lns].

QUESTION—What was expected of the Corinthians at the Lord's Supper?

They were expected to share their meals, the rich bringing more than they needed so as to provide for others less able [HNTC]. There is an implication that the Lord's Supper was eaten in conjunction with a common meal [NIC2, TG]. The common meal, the love feast, was followed by the Communion [MNTC].

and on-the-one-hand one goes-hungry,[a] on-the-other-hand another gets-drunk.[b]

LEXICON—a. pres. act. indic. of πεινάω (LN 23.29) (BAGD 1. p. 640): 'to go hungry' [Herm, HNTC, NIGTC; CEV, ISV, NAB, NJB, NLT, NRSV, REB, TNT], 'to be hungry' [AB, BAGD, LN; KJV, NET, TEV], 'to remain hungry' [Lns, NTC; NIV], 'to not be able to get enough to eat' [ICC], 'to hunger' [BAGD], 'to have hunger' [LN]. The present tense of this verb and the next indicate repetition showing that this was a regular practice in Corinth [Lns]. It was the poor who went hungry [Alf, Gdt, ICC, Lns] as they had little if anything to bring and no one shared with them [Lns]. The poor would have to finish their work before they could come and the slaves also were typically late [TNTC].

b. pres. act. indic. of μεθύω (LN 88.283) (BAGD 1. p. 499): 'to get drunk' [HNTC; CEV, ISV, NAB, NIV, NJB, NLT, TEV, TNT], 'to be drunk' [AB, BAGD, Herm, LN, NIGTC, NTC], 'to be drunken' [Lns; KJV], 'to become drunk' [NET, NRSV], 'to have too much to drink' [REB], 'to take too much even to drink' [ICC].

QUESTION—How did this state qualify as the 'worse' of 11:17?

The poor going hungry while the rich were intoxicated would have disgraced a heathen guild-feast and this was happening at the Lord's Supper! [EGT]. There is no fellowship if one is hungry and another is drunk [Herm].

QUESTION—What is meant by their being drunk?

The real meaning of this word is 'to be drunk' [Gdt, HNTC, Ho, ICC], but whether Paul intended to convey this or just that they overindulged we cannot say [Ho]. It was the rich who were intoxicated [AB, Alf, Ed, Herm, ICC, Lns, My, NIC]. Paul is expressing the extremes: one group gets nothing and the other group is gorged on food and wine, thus being drunk [NIC2].

11:22 For not[a] have-you not houses for[b] eating and drinking?

LEXICON—a. μή (See this word at 10:22): 'not' [CEV, ISV, KJV, NAB, NLT, NRSV, REB, TEV, TNT]. Μή expects a negative response to the question, implying 'you do have' [AB, BAGD, HNTC, ICC, LN, Lns, NIGTC, NTC, TH; all versions]. The double negative could be translated, 'It isn't that you don't have homes, is it?' [AB].

b. εἰς with accusative object (See this word at 10:31): 'for' [AB, HNTC, Lns, NIGTC; NJB, NLT], 'so that (one) can' [NET], 'for the purpose of' [NTC], 'to (eat and drink) in' [Herm; KJV, NIV, NRSV, REB], 'in which' [ICC; ISV, TEV], 'where' [CEV, NAB]. The whole clause is rendered 'Can you not eat and drink at home?' [TNT].

QUESTION—What is Paul's overall point in this verse?

He is showing the difference between the Lord's Supper and other feasts [Gdt]. Paul is concerned about their unity at the Lord's Supper without considerations of the kind or amount of food eaten [NIC2]. Paul is concerned with separating the Lord's Supper from the matter of satisfying one's hunger [Herm]. Refusal to join with the whole assembly in a meal intended to express social unity and Christian love is an expression of contempt for the whole congregation [AB].

QUESTION—What relationship is indicated by γάρ 'for'?

It indicates the grounds for the accusation of 11:21 [Alf, Gdt, Ho]: this should not be, *since* you have homes. It is used here as an exclamation [BAGD (p. 152), HNTC, Lns; KJV, NLT, NRSV]: 'What!' It is used to express surprise and irony along with the double negative μή οὐ [Ed]. It is used to indicate a justified conclusion arising from the previous verse [Lns].

QUESTION—What is the function of this rhetorical question and those that follow?

The first question functions to express indignation [Gdt, HNTC, NIC2]. It expresses irony and means something like 'It seems you do this because you are homeless and need to fill your stomachs at church!' [Ed, EGT, ICC, NIC2]. It functions as a reprimand [Gdt, TG]. The questions function to express Paul's revulsion at the disrespect of the Corinthians for the church of God [Rb]. They function to shame the rich as they have brought shame on the poor [NIC2]. They function to attack the evil of the situation [TNTC]. The first question was to teach them why they were coming together as a congregation [Vn]. Paul does not mean that they should abandon the practice of eating together, but that if they want to eat on their own and have their own special food, they should do it at home [HNTC]. Paul addresses the rich home owners and implies that they should not attend if they do not love and respect the poor [NTC].

Or do-you-despise[a] **the church of God,**

LEXICON—a. pres. act. indic. of καταφρονέω (LN 88.192) (BAGD 1. p. 420): 'to despise' [AB, BAGD, Herm, HNTC, LN, Lns, NTC; ISV, KJV, NIV, TEV, TNT], 'to show contempt for' [NIGTC; NAB, NET, NRSV], 'to be contemptuous of' [REB], 'to have disregard for' [NJB], 'to disgrace' [NLT], 'to hate' [CEV], 'to have no reverence for' [ICC], 'to scorn' [BAGD, LN], 'to treat with contempt' [BAGD], 'to look down on' [BAGD, LN]. The present tense should be taken as having a conative aspect [NET, NLT, TEV]: do you want to show contempt? The basic meaning of despise is to treat someone or something as though he or it were unimportant [TH].

QUESTION—What is implied by ἤ 'or'?

It is elliptical and means 'If it is true that you have homes, then the alternative is' that you despise...and humiliate... [EGT, ICC].

QUESTION—How did their action show disrespect for the church of God?

By not eating with the rest they showed that they considered them in some way not fit to eat with [Ho, My]. Their behavior showed that the church amounted to nothing in their opinion [NIC2]. Their behavior showed that membership with others in the church of God meant nothing to them [TH]. By not eating with the rest, they broke the unity of the church [NIC, NIC2].

QUESTION—What is the function of τοῦ θεοῦ 'of God'?

It functions to add grave dignity to the word 'church' [EGT]. It not only adds an aspect of solemnity [ICC], but by contrast also stresses the seriousness of their bad behavior [ICC, Lns, Vn]. It brings out the holy character of the church [Vn].

and do-you-humiliate[a] the-ones not having?[b]

LEXICON—a. pres. act. indic. of καταισχύνω (BAGD 2. p. 410): 'to humiliate' [AB, BAGD, Herm; ISV, NIV, NRSV], 'to embarrass' [CEV, NAB], 'to shame' [KJV, NET, NLT, REB], 'to treat with contempt' [ICC], 'to put to shame' [BAGD, Lns, NIGTC, NTC; NJB, TEV, TNT], 'to want to put to shame' [HNTC]. This word means to embarrass and humble people by making them conscious of their inferiority [Ho]. The present tense should be taken as having a conative aspect [HNTC]: do you want to put to shame those who have nothing? See this word also at 11:4.

b. pres. act. participle of ἔχω (BAGD I.2.a. p. 332): 'to have' [AB, BAGD, Herm, Lns, NIGTC, NTC; CEV, ISV, KJV, NAB, NET, NIV, NJB, NRSV], 'to be poor' [ICC]. The phrase τοὺς μὴ ἔχοντες 'the ones not having' is translated 'the poor' [HNTC; NLT, TNT], 'its poorer members' [REB], 'the people who are in need' [TEV]. The implied object 'anything' or 'nothing' is supplied [AB, BAGD, Lns, NIGTC, NTC; CEV, ISV, NAB, NET, NIV, NJB, NRSV]. See this word also at 11:10.

QUESTION—What is the function of the second and third rhetorical questions, 'Do you despise the church of God' and 'Do you humiliate the ones not having'?

They also function as a reprimands [Gdt]: You should not despise the church of God or humiliate those who have not!

QUESTION—What is it that τοὺς μὴ ἔχοντας 'those not having' lack?

1. This means those who do not have houses [Alf]. This reference to 'not having' refers to the first part of the verse, to those 'having' houses, and carries the same reference here.
2. This refers to those who do not have material goods, the poor [Ed, EGT, Gdt, HNTC, Ho, ICC, My, Rb, TG, TH, Vn; NLT, REB, TNT]. This not only refers to poverty in general but the context indicates that these are

those who have no food [Gdt]. Οἱ ἔχοντες 'the ones having' in Classical Greek referred to 'the men of property'. Here τοὺς μὴ ἔχοντας refers to the poor [EGT]. This is an exaggeration and means those who have only a few material possessions [TH].

QUESTION—To whom are these questions especially directed?

They are directed to the more well-to-do of the Corinthian church who were guilty of spoiling the Lord's Supper by their behavior [NIC, NIC2, NTC].

What should-I-say to-you?

QUESTION—What is the function of this question?

It shows Paul's bewilderment [Rb]. He is considering what he should say to them [TH]. It shows Paul's embarrassment as he tries to describe their behavior without using too harsh language [Gdt]. It shows that Paul is baffled and shocked [Lns]. Paul is at a loss for words as he considers the obvious denial of Christian principle [HNTC].

Should-I-praise[a] you? In this I-praise (you) not.

LEXICON—a. aorist act. subj. of ἐπαινέω (See this word at 11:2): 'to praise' [AB, BAGD, HNTC, LN, Lns, NTC; ISV, KJV, NAB, NET, NIV, NLT, TEV], 'to commend' [Herm, ICC; NRSV, REB, TNT], 'to congratulate' [NIGTC; NJB], not explicit [CEV].

QUESTION—Should the words ἐν τούτῳ 'in this' go with the question or the statement?.

1. They go with the question [Alf; KJV, NIV]: Should I praise you in this matter? I do not praise you.
2. They go with the statement [AB, Ed, EGT, Gdt, GNT, HNTC, ICC, Lns, My, NTC, TH, Vn; ISV, NAB, NET, NJB, NRSV, REB, TEV, TNT]: Should I praise you? In this matter I do not praise you.

QUESTION—What figure of speech is οὐκ ἐπαινῶ 'I praise you not'?

It is a form of understatement called litotes [EGT, Gdt, Lns]: I blame you.

DISCOURSE UNIT: 11:23–34 [EGT; CEV]. The topic is the Lord's Supper [CEV], unworthy participants of the Lord's Supper [EGT].

11:23 For I received[a] from the Lord, that-which also I-passed-on[b] to-you,

LEXICON–a. aorist act. indic. of παραλαμβάνω (LN **33.238**, 27.13, 34.53) (BAGD 2.b.γ. p. 619): 'to receive' [BAGD, Herm, **LN** (33.238, 34.53); ISV, KJV, NAB, NET, NIV, NJB, NRSV, TEV], 'to receive a tradition' [NIGTC], 'to receive instruction from, to be taught by' [LN (33.238)]. The phrase ἐγὼ γὰρ παρέλαβον 'for I received' is translated 'and it came' [CEV], 'the tradition came' [TNT], 'for the tradition came to me' [REB], 'to learn from someone, to learn about a tradition' [LN (27.13)]. This entire clause is translated 'For this is what the Lord himself said…just as I received it' [NLT].

  b. aorist act. indic. of παραδίδωμι (See this word at 11:2): 'to pass on' [Herm; ISV, NET, NIV, NLT, TEV], 'to hand on' [HNTC, NIGTC; NAB,

NJB, NRSV, REB], 'to deliver' [AB, Lns, NTC; KJV], 'to give' [TNT], 'to tell' [CEV], 'to transmit' [ICC].

QUESTION—What relationship is indicated by γάρ 'for'?

It indicates the grounds for his not praising them [Ed, HNTC, Ho, ICC, Lns, NIC, NIC2]: I cannot praise you, *since* I received from the Lord.... This was one tradition they had not been keeping even though they may have claimed to be doing so (11:2) [NIC2]. It indicates that Paul cannot praise them because the way they celebrated the Lord's Supper was not consistent with how it was originally given [HNTC, Ho]. It indicates that this account of the Lord's Supper is the reason for the reprimands of 11:22 [Gdt].

QUESTION—What word is emphasized in this clause?

The word ἐγώ 'I' is emphatic [Ed, Lns, NTC, TH, TNTC, Vn]. Both ἐγώ 'I', and ὑμῖν 'to you' are emphatic [NTC]. The emphasis on 'I' functions to contrast Paul's instruction with the bad behavior of the Corinthians [TH]. Paul contrasts himself with the Corinthians pointing out the difference between what they were doing and what he had passed on to them [Lns].

QUESTION—How did Paul receive this information?

1. He received it directly from the Lord [Alf, Ed, Gdt, Ho, Lns, MNTC, Rb, TNTC, Vn]. If Paul were referring to a tradition that he had received from others rather than from the Lord, he would have used the plural 'we received' [Alf, Gdt]. If Paul received this indirectly, then anyone else along the chain of transmission could similarly claim that he also had received some tradition from the Lord [Gdt]. Galatians 1:11, 12 indicates that Paul received the Gospel from the Lord directly. This certainly includes the Lord's Supper [Lns]. It can only mean that he received it directly from Christ for Paul's purpose in saying this was to give authority to his account of the Sacrament [Ho]. Paul uses the emphatic pronoun ἐγώ 'I'. Why would Paul emphasize himself if he received it from other men? [TNTC]. 'I', being emphatic, shows that Paul had received it personally from the Lord serving to verify his account of the Lord's Supper [Ed, Vn]. The similarity with Luke can be explained that Luke read Paul's letter before he wrote the Gospel [Rb].

2. He received it indirectly from the Lord by being taught by other people what the Lord had taught them [Herm, NIC, NIC2, NTC, TG, TH]. The close similarity between Paul's account and Luke's account suggest that Paul is relying on tradition and not direct revelation [TH]. Paul means that what he received did come from the Lord in the sense that He was the ultimate source of it but not necessarily his immediate source. The words Paul uses for 'received' and 'passed on' probably indicate that he was rather talking about an apostolic tradition of which he was a recipient [NIC2].

QUESTION—What is the significance of παραλαμβάνω 'to receive' and παραδίδωμι 'to pass on'?
They are technical terms for the oral transmission of religious instruction. Παραδίδωμι 'to pass on' is the verb from which παραδόσις 'tradition' (11:2) is derived.

that the Lord Jesus on the night on-which he-was-being-betrayed[a] took bread

LEXICON—a. imperf. pass. indic. of παραδίδωμι (LN 37.111) (BAGD 1.b. p. 614): 'to be betrayed' [Herm, LN; all versions except REB, TNT], 'to be delivered up' [BAGD; TNT], 'to be handed over' [BAGD, LN, NIGTC], 'to be turned over' [BAGD, LN], 'to be given up' [BAGD]. The clause ᾗ παρεδίδετο 'on which he was being betrayed' is translated 'of his arrest' [REB]. The imperfect tense indicates that while Jesus was being betrayed he took bread [Alf, Ed, EGT, Ho, ICC, Lns, My, NIC, NTC, Vn].

QUESTION—What is the significance of the word Ἰησοῦς 'Jesus' to 'Lord'?
It functions to bring out the historical earthly aspect of the Lord's life [Gdt, NIC2, NTC].

QUESTION—Who is the actor of this passive παρεδίδετο 'he was being betrayed'?
Judas is the actor [Ed, NIC2, TG, Vn]: when Judas was betraying him. The actors would have included Judas, God, in his act of delivering Jesus up, and even Jesus himself in his own self-sacrifice [ICC].

QUESTION—What time of νύξ 'night' is indicated?
It probably refers to sometime soon after sunset and not the middle of the night [TH].

11:24 **and having-given-thanks[a] he-broke (it) and said,**

LEXICON—a. εὐχαριστέω (See this word at 10:30): 'to give thanks' [AB, Herm, HNTC, ICC, Lns, NIGTC, NTC; all versions].

QUESTION—For what and to whom did Jesus 'give thanks'?
Jesus apparently gave thanks for the bread and for the gift of God that it represented [Lns]. Jesus thanked God for the bread [TH; REB, TEV].

QUESTION—What is the significance of ἔκλασεν 'he broke'?
1. It is symbolic of the breaking of Christ's body [Ed, My, NIC].
2. It has no symbolic significance and is only incidental to the Sacrament [Herm, Lns, Rb, Vn]. Jesus broke the bread only for the purpose of distributing it. The Lord's body was not broken on the cross [Lns]. Scripture says that none of His bones will be broken and it does not suggest that His wounds represented the breaking of His body [NIC2, Vn].

"This is my body the-(one) for[a] you;
TEXT—Some manuscripts include λάβετε φάγετε 'take, eat' before τοῦτο 'this'. It is omitted by GNT with an "A" rating, indicating that the text is certain. These words are included only by KJV.
TEXT—Some manuscripts include κλώμενον 'broken' after ὑμῶν 'you'. It is omitted by GNT with an "A" rating, indicating that the text is certain. This word is included by Ed and KJV.
LEXICON—a. ὑπέρ with genitive object (LN 90.36) (BAGD 1.a.ε. p. 838): 'for' [AB, BAGD, Herm, HNTC, ICC, LN, Lns, NIGTC, NTC; all versions], 'on behalf of' [BAGD, LN], 'for the sake of' [BAGD, LN]. Ὑπέρ signifies 'for one's advantage' [EGT].
QUESTION—To what does τοῦτο 'this' refer?
It refers to the bread Jesus held in his hand [EGT, Ho, Lns, NIC, NTC]. It cannot refer to the ἄρτος 'bread' since it is masculine and τοῦτο 'this' is neuter [Lns, TNTC] and it may refer to the complete action [TNTC].
QUESTION—What is meant by ἐστιν 'is'?
1. It indicates the idea of a symbol or something that stands for, signifies, or represents something else [EGT, Gdt, Ho, NIC2, NTC, TNTC, Vn]: this represents my body.
2. It means 'is', not 'represents'. It was Christ's own body that was given for men. This gift is no longer mere bread, but bread which is sacramentally one with Christ's body [Lns]. It cannot indicate complete identity between bread and Christ's body, but it does indicate a very close connection [NIC].
QUESTION—What does σῶμα τὸ ὑπέρ ὑμῶν 'body which is for you' signify?
It signifies that Christ's work on the cross was the giving of himself 'on their behalf' [Herm, Ho, Lns, TNTC, Vn]. It signifies that the sacrifice of Christ and the deliverance he achieved were 'for them' [HNTC]. It signifies the removal of the guilt of sin for the benefit of the recipient (15:3) [Herm, NIC2]. The purpose of Christ's suffering was for the good of people [TNTC].

do this in[a] my remembrance."[b]
LEXICON—a. εἰς with accusative object (LN 90.23, 89.57) (BAGD 4.d. p. 229): 'in' [Herm, ICC, LN (90.23), Lns, NIGTC, NTC; all versions except CEV], 'for' [AB, BAGD], 'concerning, with respect to, with reference to, about' [LN (90.23)], 'for the purpose of, in order to' [LN (89.57)], 'as' [BAGD, HNTC], not explicit [CEV].
b. ἀνάμνησις (LN 29.11) (BAGD p. 58): 'remembrance' [AB, BAGD, Herm, ICC, Lns, NIGTC, NTC; KJV, NAB, NET, NIV, NJB, NLT, NRSV, TNT], 'memory' [ISV, REB, TEV], 'memorial' [HNTC], 'reminder' [BAGD, LN], 'means of remembering' [LN]. The phrase εἰς τὴν ἐμὴν ἀνάμνησιν 'for my remembrance' is translated 'and remember me' [CEV].

QUESTION—What is the significance of the present tense imperative ποιεῖτε 'Do!'?

It signifies continuous or repeated action [Lns, TNTC]: Keep on doing! The present tense is not to be taken as an imperative but as an indicative [AB]: you are doing this.

QUESTION—To what does τοῦτο 'this' refer?

It refers to taking the bread, giving thanks, breaking it, distributing it, and eating it, the whole ceremony [Herm, Ho, NTC, TH]. It refers to the giving of thanks, the breaking, the distributing, and the eating of the bread [NIC2]. It refers to the giving of thanks, the breaking, and distributing of the bread [HNTC]. It refers to taking, thanking, and breaking of the bread [ICC]. It refers to the thanking and breaking of the bread [Vn]. It refers to giving of thanks and distributing [Lns]. It refers to the eating of the bread [TG].

QUESTION—How are the nouns related in the genitive construction τὴν ἀνάμνησιν 'my remembrance'?

'Me' is the object of 'remember' [Ed, Gdt, HNTC, Ho, ICC, Lns, NIC, NIC2, NTC, TG, TH, TNTC, Vn; all versions]: (you) remember me.

QUESTION—What is to be remembered?

Jesus himself is to be remembered [TG, TH]. Both Jesus and his sacrifice are to be remembered [Gdt, Ho]. Both Jesus and the deliverance he accomplished are to be remembered [HNTC, NIC, NIC2]. Jesus' suffering for us is to be remembered [TNTC]. Jesus' deliverance of people is to be remembered [Ed]. All that Jesus has done for us and all that he is to us are to be remembered [ICC]. His spiritual presence and his sacrifice are to be remembered [Vn].

QUESTION—What words are emphasized in this verse?

The word ἐμήν 'my' in 'in my remembrance' is emphasized [Ed, NTC]. They are to remember the person of Jesus and His work [NTC]. The word μού 'my' in 'my body' is emphatic [Ed]. The word σῶμα 'body' is probably emphatic [NTC].

11:25 In-the-same-way[a] also the cup[b] after eating-supper[c] saying,

LEXICON—a. ὡσαύτως (LN **64.16**) (BAGD p. 899): 'in the same way' [AB, BAGD, HNTC, LN, NIGTC, NTC; all versions except CEV, ISV, KJV], 'after the same manner' [Lns; KJV], 'he did the same with' [ISV], 'likewise' [Herm], 'similarly' [BAGD, **LN**], 'in like manner' [ICC, LN], 'just as' [LN], not explicit [CEV].

b. ποτήριον (See this word at 10:16): 'cup' [AB, BAGD, Herm, HNTC, ICC, Lns, NIGTC, NTC; all versions except CEV, NLT], 'cup of wine' [CEV, NLT].

c. aorist act. infin. of δειπνέω (LN 23.20) (BAGD p. 173): 'to eat supper' [AB], 'to have supper' [HNTC], 'to sup' [KJV], 'to eat' [BAGD, Lns], 'to eat a meal, to have a meal' [LN], 'to dine' [BAGD]. This infinitive is also translated as a noun: 'meal' [CEV], 'supper' [Herm, ICC, NIGTC, NTC; all versions except CEV, KJV].

QUESTION—What is included by the word ὡσαύτως 'in the same way'?
It would include taking and thanking [Ho, NIC, NIC2, TH]. It would include taking, thanking, and giving out [HNTC, ICC]. It would include taking, thanking, giving out, and speaking words parallel to those that were spoken about the bread [Lns]. It may imply that thanking was also included for the wine [TG]. It simply means as he had done with the bread [Vn].

QUESTION—What is implied in the phrase ὡσαύτως καὶ τὸ ποτήριον 'in the same way also the cup'?
The verb 'to take' is implied [AB, EGT, HNTC, NIC, NIC2, NTC, TNTC; all versions except NJB]: in the same way also *taking* the cup.

QUESTION—What does the word 'cup' here refer to?
It refers to the wine in the cup [ICC, NIC, TG, Vn; CEV, NLT]. It refers to the cup and its contents [Lns]. The Lord used the word 'cup' here as it was not possible to pass around the wine without it [NIC]. The wine in turn represents the blood which seals the covenant [ICC].

QUESTION—What is the significance of the definite article in τὸ ποτήριον '*the* cup'?
It refers to a cup which was well-known to his readers [ICC, TH]. It was probably the cup of wine drunk at the Lord's Supper celebration [Lns, TH]. It refers to the cup which was there before Him [Gdt].

QUESTION—Does this mean after the whole meal or only part of the meal?
1. It means that the Lord's Supper was begun by the breaking of the bread, continued by the regular meal, and ended with the drinking of the cup [Ed, EGT, Gdt, ICC, My, NIC2, NTC, TG, TH, TNTC]. At a Jewish meal, the host would start the meal by breaking and blessing the bread and would conclude the meal by a blessing over the cup. It seems likely that such a practice was also observed in Corinth [NIC2]. In translating 'after supper' it is important to indicate that a real meal was in progress [TH].
2. It means either after the eating of the bread or after the Lord's Supper [Herm, Lns, NIC, Vn]. The Lord's Supper which takes place here occurred in both parts after the Passover Feast [Vn]. It means that during the meal He took bread and distributed it, then after the eating of the bread he took the cup and passed it around [NIC]. The 'love feast' was originally enclosed in two sacred observances, but in Corinth both followed the meal [Herm].

"This cup is the new covenant[a] in[b] my blood;
LEXICON—a. διαθήκη (LN 34.44) (BAGD 2. p. 183): 'covenant' [AB, BAGD, Herm, HNTC, LN, NIGTC, NTC; all versions except CEV, KJV], 'agreement' [CEV], 'testament' [Lns; KJV], 'pact' [LN].
b. ἐν with dative object (LN 89.76, 90.10): 'in' [Herm, HNTC, Lns, NIGTC, NTC; ISV, KJV, NAB, NET, NIV, NJB, NRSV], 'by' [AB, LN (89.76, 90.10)], 'in virtue of' [ICC], 'sealed by' [REB], 'sealed by the shedding of' [NLT], 'sealed with' [TEV], 'made by' [TNT], 'with' [LN (90.10); CEV], 'by means of, through' [LN (89.76)].

QUESTION—What is meant by ποτήριον 'cup' here?
It indicates what it contains [Lns]: what the cup contains is the new covenant in my blood.

QUESTION—What is meant by διαθήκη 'covenant'?
It means a unilateral arrangement established by God in man's favor [ICC, Lns, NTC, TH, Vn]. In this arrangement, it is God who takes the initiative [EGT]. It means a will in which God confers on us all the benefits that Christ brought [Lns]. In Greek διαθήκη indicates 'last will and testament'. However, in the Septuagint, διαθήκη is used 277 times to translate the Hebrew word 'covenant', so that is its sense here [TNTC].

QUESTION—In what sense is the covenant καινή 'new'?
It is new in that it replaces the Mosaic covenant between God and the people of Israel described in Exodus 24 [Ho]. The covenant is new in the benefits it offers—forgiveness [EGT, ICC], and undeserved favor [ICC]. It is new in that it grants spiritual renovation [EGT]. It is new in that it freely confers eternal life on the believer [Vn]. It is new in the sense of Jeremiah 31:31ff. [NIC2, TNTC], in which there is free forgiveness, God's law written on the hearts of the people, and the Holy Spirit working in the hearts of people [TNTC].

QUESTION—What is meant by ἐν 'in'?
It means 'ratified or validated by' [AB, Alf, Ed, Ho, MNTC, NIC2, NTC, TG, TH, Vn], 'sealed by/with' [ICC, My, TG, Vn; NLT, REB, TEV], 'established by' [AB, HNTC, Lns, TH, TNTC], 'by means of' [AB, HNTC, TH], 'resting/grounded on' [Ed, EGT, NIC], 'in connection with' [Lns], 'guaranteed by' [TH], 'made by' [TH; TNT], 'in virtue of' [ICC, Vn], 'at the cost of' [HNTC, TH], 'the benefits of which are secured by' [Ho]. The new covenant was established by the shedding of Christ's blood [HNTC].

QUESTION—What does αἷμα 'blood' imply?
It implies the death of Christ [AB, NIC, NIC2, TNTC]. It implies sacrificial death [Lns].

QUESTION—What is implied by ἐστίν 'is'?
It implies 'the sign of' [NIC]: this cup is *the sign of* the new covenant. It implies 'represents' [Ed, Vn]: this cup *represents* the new covenant. It also implies 'the means of communion' [Ed]: this cup *is the means of communion* with the new covenant (that is, with the blood of Christ).

QUESTION—What word is emphasized in ἐν τῷ ἐμῷ αἵματι 'in my blood'?
The words τῷ ἐμῷ, 'my', a strong possessive adjective, is emphatic [Lns, NTC]: in my own blood.

do this, as-often-as[a] you-drink (it), in my remembrance."

LEXICON—a. ὁσάκις ἐάν (LN **67.36**) (BAGD p. 585): 'as often as' [AB, BAGD, Herm, HNTC, ICC, LN; ISV, NLT, NRSV, TNT], 'as oft as' [KJV], 'whenever' [**LN**, NIGTC; NAB, NIV, NJB, REB, TEV], 'every time' [NET], not explicit [CEV].

QUESTION—What things are included in τοῦτο 'this'?
It is not the cup, but the act of drinking from the cup [NIC]. The giving of thanks for the cup and its distribution among the rest are included [Ho]. It includes saying the words as well as performing the ceremony [EGT].

QUESTION—What is meant by ὁσάκις ἐάν 'as often as'?
It does not mean every time that believers drank wine together, but every time the Communion is observed [Alf, Ed, EGT, Gdt, Ho, ICC, Lns, TH]. It implies that it should be done regularly [NTC], frequently [NIC, NIC2], repeatedly [NIC2, Rb]. It indicates that it should be done on the first day of the week [Vn]. It indicates that the timing is put at the discretion of the church [Gdt].

QUESTION—What word is emphasized in εἰς τὴν ἐμὴν ἀνάμνησιν 'in my remembrance'?
The words τὴν ἐμὴν 'my' is emphatic [NTC]: in remembrance of *me*. The phrase 'in my remembrance' is emphasized [Alf].

11:26 For[a] as-often-as you-eat this bread and drink the cup,

LEXICON—a. γάρ (See this word at 10:1): 'for' [AB, Herm, HNTC, Lns, NIGTC, NTC; ISV, KJV, NET, NIV, NLT, NRSV, REB, TNT], 'Yes, He gave this command; for' [ICC], 'this means that' [TEV], 'then' [NAB, NJB], 'the Lord meant that' [CEV].

QUESTION—What relationship is indicated by γάρ 'for'?
1. It indicates the grounds for stating that the Lord's Supper is a remembrance of the Lord [Alf, Ed, EGT, Gdt, Herm, HNTC, Ho, ICC; KJV, NIV, NRSV, REB, TNT]. The connection is most naturally to the words of 11:25 'in remembrance of me': *since* each time you celebrate the Lord's Supper it is a memorial of Christ's person [Gdt]. It either explains why they observe the Lord's Supper, or it explains 11:23–25 [ICC]. The Lord's Supper is in remembrance of him because the act of eating the bread and drinking the cup proclaim his death [Alf]. It emphasizes the solemn nature of the Lord's Supper, that it was a commemoration of his death and was therefore not a place to satisfy one's hunger or to socialize [Ho].
2. It indicates the grounds for referring to the tradition of the Lord's Supper in his argument [NIC2]. It was to emphasize that the bread and cup signified Christ's death and it was intended to proclaim that death, a point that the Corinthians were neglecting [NIC2].
3. It indicates a conclusion drawn from the account of the Lord's Supper [Lns, My, NTC, TH; NAB, NJB, TEV]. 'For' draws a conclusion from the whole citation of the institution of the Lord's Supper, and indicates, 'These facts being so, *therefore*...' [My]. Paul now gives his own summary and insight into the Lord's Supper [NTC]. This shows the gravity of the Corinthian disorders [Lns].

you-proclaim[a] **the death of-the Lord until**[b] **he-comes.**

LEXICON—a. pres. act. indic. of καταγγέλλω (LN 33.204) (BAGD 1. p. 409): 'to proclaim' [BAGD, Herm, HNTC, ICC, Lns, NIGTC, NTC; all versions except CEV, KJV, NLT], 'to announce' [AB, LN; NLT], 'to tell about' [CEV], 'to show' [KJV], 'to speak out about, to proclaim throughout' [LN]. The force of the present tense is that it be done continually [ICC], or repeatedly [Lns].

  b. ἄχρις οὗ (LN **67.119**) (BAGD 2.a. p. 129, I.11.f. p. 585): 'until' [AB, BAGD, Herm, HNTC, ICC, **LN**, Lns, NIGTC, NTC; all versions except KJV], 'till' [KJV].

QUESTION—Does this mean that the Lord's Supper in itself is an announcement or is the use of words also intended?

  1. It means that the Lord's Supper in itself is a proclamation of the Lord's death [BAGD, Ed, EGT, Lns, Rb, TG, Vn]. The acts of breaking the bread and drinking the cup are a silent declaration of the fact of Christ's death [Vn]. The Lord's supper is the great proclaimer of Christ's death [Rb].

  2. It means that the Lord's Supper is accompanied by words which tell of his death [Herm, HNTC, ICC, My, NIC2, NTC, TNTC]. 'Announce' could be taken in the sense of 'represent symbolically' in which the act speaks for itself. But it is almost certain that it indicates 'proclaim' and actual words are implied and the believers verbally recalled the background events of the institution during the celebration [HNTC]. The event itself is an observance in word and symbol [TNTC].

QUESTION—What word is emphasized in this clause?

The word θάνατος 'death' is put first in the clause thereby emphasizing it [Lns, NIC2]. This emphasis along with the term 'the Lord' (as in 11:23) lends gravity to these words [Lns].

QUESTION—What is the significance of the words ἄχρις οὗ ἔλθῃ 'until he comes'?

The repetition of that proclamation is to continue until he comes back from heaven [HNTC]. It implies that the observance of the Lord's Supper will end at that time [Gdt, ICC, Vn]. It marks the last boundary of the observance of the Lord's Supper and the age of the church extending from the Resurrection until the Second Coming of the Lord [Herm]. It serves to promise the Lord's Second Coming just as the Passover observance promised His First Coming [Ho]. The aorist subjunctive, ἔλθῃ 'he comes', indicates the certainty of a future event [Lns, TH].

DISCOURSE UNIT: 11:27–34 [GNT, MNTC, NTC, TG, TH, TNTC; KJV]. The topic is partaking of the supper unworthily [GNT; KJV], preparation for the Lord's Supper [MNTC, NTC], instructions and warnings [TG], practical conclusions [TH], the practical outcome [TNTC].

11:27 Therefore[a] **whoever eats the bread or drinks the cup of-the Lord unworthily,**[b]

LEXICON—a. ὥστε (See this word at 10:12): 'therefore' [NTC; ISV; NIV, NJB, NRSV], 'wherefore' [Lns; KJV], 'thus' [Herm], 'so' [AB; NLT, TNT], 'consequently' [NIGTC], 'this means that' [NAB], 'it follows that' [HNTC; REB, TEV], 'it follows therefore' [ICC], 'for this reason' [NET], 'but' [CEV]. This word is strongly inferential [NIC2].

b. ἀναξίως (LN **65.19, 66.7**) (BAGD p. 58): 'unworthily' [HNTC, LN (65.19), Lns, NTC; KJV, NAB, NJB, NLT, REB, TNT], 'in an unworthy manner' [AB, BAGD, Herm; ISV, NET, NIV, NRSV], 'in a way that isn't worthy' [CEV], 'in a way that dishonors (him)' [ICC; TEV], 'without being worthy' [**LN** (65.19)], 'in an improper manner' [**LN** (66.7)], 'in a way that is not fitting' [NIGTC], 'improperly' [LN (66.7)], 'not meriting' [LN (65.19)], 'in a careless manner' [BAGD].

QUESTION—What relationship is indicated by ὥστε 'therefore'?

It indicates the conclusion to be drawn from the preceding verse [Alf, Gdt, Herm, HNTC, Ho, ICC, Lns, NIC, NIC2, TH, TNTC, Vn]: the Lord's Supper is a proclamation of the Lord's death, *therefore* whoever eats.... It indicates the logical result of 11:20–26 [EGT]. It indicates that Paul is now resuming the main discussion from 11:22 [AB].

QUESTION—Do the words τοῦ κυρίου 'of the Lord' modify 'cup' or both 'bread' and 'cup'?

1. They should be taken as modifying both words [Ed, HNTC, Lns, NIC, NIC2, TH; TEV]: the bread of the Lord and the cup of the Lord.
2. They should be taken only with 'cup' as there is no precedent for the phrase 'body of the Lord' [AB].

QUESTION—What is indicated by ἤ 'or'?

It indicates that in either case, unworthy partaking would involve the person in guilt [Ed, EGT, Gdt, Ho, ICC, NTC]. Since the drinking of the cup was separated by a significant interval from the eating of the bread one could be taken in one manner and another in another manner [EGT, Gdt, ICC, My]. 'Or' is used here in a conjunctive sense [Lns]: *and*.

QUESTION—What is meant by ἀναξίος 'unworthily'?

1. It refers to the way the Corinthians were abusing the Lord's Supper as seen in 11:18 and following [AB, EGT, Herm, HNTC, Ho, NIC, NIC2, TG]. Unworthily basically means to not acknowledge the worth or value of a thing. Therefore to partake without acknowledging the value of the elements was to do so unworthily. In particular, celebrating the Lord's Supper after a love feast ruined by quarreling would be doing so unworthily [NIC]. It specifically refers to the way that some were mistreating the others by going ahead with their own private meals and not waiting for the others [NIC2]. It refers to breaking the unity of the body as seen in 10:16, 17 and insulting the poor [AB]. It refers to eating the Lord's Supper as though it were one's own supper [Herm, Ho]. It refers to partaking carelessly and greedily [HNTC]. It includes partaking

in an irreverent manner without a desire to remember the death of Christ, eating merely to satisfy hunger and refusing to fellowship with their poorer brothers [Ho].
2. It has a broader definition [Alf, ICC, Lns, MNTC, NTC, Vn]. It includes all sorts of unworthiness and should not be restricted to the ways in which the Corinthians were being unworthy [Lns]. It includes irreverence in the form of selfish and greedy behavior but also an interior attitude of the soul [ICC]. Things like low thinking about the Father, Son, and Holy Spirit, lack of love for fellow believers, bitterness or hatred toward others, or refusing to repent of some sin, all constitute unworthiness [MNTC]. It also could include lack of self examination, contempt for the poor, turning the Lord's Supper into a lighthearted feast, and feeling oneself unworthy of such holy food and drink [NTC]. Also included could be considering the bread and cup of no significance [Alf, Vn], that is, not thinking of them as symbolizing Christ's death and partaking while in an unspiritual state [Vn].
3. Other views [Ed, Gdt, Rb, TH]. This does not mean that a person must be worthy in order to partake of the Lord's Supper. What he means by this term is defined in 11:29 [Ed, Rb]. The phrase 'not discerning the Lord's body' means not understanding correctly the purifying effect of fellowship with Christ [Ed]. Partaking unworthily means partaking without being thankful for the sufferings of Christ [Gdt]. It means partaking in a way that dishonors Christ [TH].

will-be guilty[a] of-the body and of-the blood of-the Lord.
LEXICON—a. ἔνοχος (LN **88.312**) (BAGD 2.b.γ. p. 268): 'guilty' [AB, BAGD, HNTC, **LN**, Lns; KJV, NET, REB], 'guilty of sinning against' [NIV, NLT, TEV, TNT], 'guilty of offending against' [REB], 'guilty of an offense against' [Herm], 'guilty of profaning' [NTC], 'held responsible (for)' [ICC; ISV], 'held accountable' [NIGTC], 'answerable (for)' [BAGD; NJB, NRSV], 'liable' [BAGD, LN]. The phrase ἔνοχος ἔσται 'will be guilty' is translated 'to sin against' [BAGD; CEV, NAB], 'can rightly be accused of sinning against' [**LN**]. The word denotes liability [Ed, EGT, NIC, NIC2, Vn]. It indicates a state of being bound by a fault one has committed [Gdt, Lns].
QUESTION—What is meant by ἔνοχος ἔσται τοῦ σώματος καὶ τοῦ αἵματος τοῦ κυρίου 'will be guilty of the body and blood of the Lord'?
1. It means that such a person is as responsible for the death of the Lord as those who originally crucified Him [Herm, HNTC, NIC, NIC2, NTC, TNTC, Vn]. To act irreverently toward the Lord's Supper as the Corinthians were doing means to deny the purpose of Christ's self-sacrifice and therefore to join those who crucified Him [HNTC].
2. It means that such a person profanes or dishonors Christ or Christ's death on the cross [Ho, ICC, MNTC, TG, TH]. To dishonor the bread and the

cup is the same as dishonoring the one whose body and blood are represented [MNTC].

QUESTION—What are the implications of being 'guilty of the body and the blood of the Lord'?

It means being guilty of sin against the Lord himself, for to despise a symbol means to despise the person who is symbolized [EGT, Gdt, ICC, MNTC, NTC].

11:28 But/and (a) man[a] let-him-examine[b] himself

LEXICON—a. ἄνθρωπος (LN 9.1, 9.24) (BAGD 3.a.γ. p. 69): 'man' [Herm, HNTC, ICC, LN (9.24), Lns, NTC; KJV, NAB, NIV, TNT], 'person' [AB, LN (9.1), NIGTC; ISV, NET], 'everyone' [NJB, REB], 'you' [CEV, NLT, NRSV], 'you each' [TEV], 'one' [BAGD], 'human being, individual' [LN (9.1)]. Ἄνθρωπος is used here in the sense of 'each' [Ed, NIC, NTC, Vn].

b. pres. act. impera. of δοκιμάζω (LN **27.45**) (BAGD 1. p. 202): 'to examine' [AB, BAGD, Herm, **LN**, NTC; all versions except REB], 'to test' [HNTC, LN, Lns; REB], 'to scrutinize one's own spiritual condition and motives' [ICC], 'to examine one's own genuineness' [NIGTC], 'to try to determine the genuineness of' [LN], 'to put to the test' [BAGD]. This verb is cognate with δόκιμος 'genuine, approved' of 11:19 [HNTC, NIC2, TH]. It implies that one should check to see if all is right [TH]. It implies the checking against a standard of correctness [AB]. It means to prove with the purpose of approving [ICC, NIC, Vn].

QUESTION—What relationship is indicated by δέ 'but/and'?

1. It indicates a contrast with 'eating unworthily' [Alf, Ed, EGT, ICC, Lns, NIC2, NTC; KJV]: such a man eats or drinks unworthily *but instead* let him examine himself.
2. It indicates a result relationship, 'that's why' [CEV, ISV, NLT], 'so then' [TEV]: such a man eats or drinks unworthily *and that is why* he must examine himself. The word implies 'if one is partaking unworthily, this is what must be done' [Gdt].

QUESTION—What word is emphasized in this verse?

Δοκιμάζω 'to examine' is emphasized [ICC, Vn].

and so[a] let-him-eat of the bread and let-him-drink from the cup;

LEXICON—a. οὕτως (See this word at 11:12): 'so' [Herm, Lns; KJV], 'then' [ISV, TEV], 'then, and not until then' [ICC], 'only then' [NAB, NJB, NRSV], 'and only in this way' [NIGTC], 'in this spirit' [NET], 'thus' [AB, NTC], 'that is how he should' [HNTC], not explicit [CEV]. The phrase καὶ οὕτως ἐσθιέτω...καὶ πινέτω 'and thus let him eat... and let him drink' is translated 'before he eats...and drinks' [NIV], 'before eating...and drinking' [NLT, REB, TNT].

QUESTION—What is implied by οὕτως 'so'?

It implies that the eating and drinking be done only after the examining has been done [Alf, Ed, Gdt, Ho, ICC, My, NIC, TH] and the person is not guilty of doing so in an unworthy manner [Ho, My, NIC]. Paul implies that they should examine their behavior and then, if necessary, change from unworthy to worthy behavior before partaking [EGT, HNTC, Ho, ICC, Lns, MNTC, NIC, NTC, TG, TNTC, Vn]. Οὕτως is emphatic meaning that only after examining himself should he partake [TH].

QUESTION—What is the significance of the present tense in the verbs of this verse?

The present tense indicates that this should be repeated or habitual action [Lns, NTC]. The present tense imperative of δοκιμάζω 'to examine' indicates habitual action [EGT].

11:29 **For the-one eating and drinking eats and drinks judgment[a] to-himself**

TEXT—Some manuscripts include ἀναξίως 'unworthily' after πίνων 'drinking'. It is omitted by GNT with an A rating, indicating that the text is certain. It is included by KJV and NLT.

LEXICON—a. κρίμα (LN 56.30, 30.110) (BAGD 4.b. p. 450): 'judgment' [AB, Herm, HNTC, LN (30.110), NIGTC, NTC; ISV, NAB, NET, NIV, NLT, NRSV, REB, TEV], 'a judgment' [LN (30.110), Lns], 'condemnation' [BAGD, LN (56.30); NJB], 'damnation' [KJV], 'sentence' [ICC], 'judicial verdict, sentence of condemnation, punishment' [BAGD], 'decision, evaluation' [LN (30.110)]. This entire clause is translated 'you will condemn yourself by the way you eat and drink' [CEV], 'he is condemning himself in the very act of eating and drinking' [TNT]. Κρίμα indicates 'judgment' in a negative sense like punishment [Ho, ICC, MNTC, NIC2, TH]. It indicates rather a temporal punishment than eternal condemnation [Alf, Ed, EGT, Gdt, HNTC, ICC, Lns, MNTC, NTC, TG, Vn]. The judgments themselves are seen in 11:30, namely, illness and death [Ho, NIC2]. The actor of judgment is God [Ho, NCBC, NIC, NIC2, NTC, TH].

QUESTION—What relationship is indicated by γάρ 'for'?

It indicates the grounds for the command to examine oneself (11:28) [Ed, Gdt, HNTC, Ho, Lns, NCBC, NIC2, NTC, TH]: a man ought to examine himself before he eats of the bread and drinks of the cup *since* the one eating and drinking eats and drinks judgment to himself not discerning the body. It also functions as a restatement of the reason given in 11:27 [HNTC]. It should be understood as 'for otherwise' [Lns].

not discerning[a] the body.

TEXT—Some manuscripts include τοῦ κυρίου 'of the Lord' after σῶμα 'body'. It is omitted by GNT with an A rating, indicating that the text is certain. It is included by KJV, NIV, and TEV.

LEXICON—a. pres. act. participle of διακρίνω (LN 30.109) (BAGD 1.c.β. p. 185): 'to discern' [Lns, NTC; KJV, NRSV, REB], 'to recognize' [BAGD; ISV, NAB, NIV, NJB, TEV, TNT], 'to recognize the sanctity of' [ICC], 'to understand' [CEV], 'to honor' [NLT], 'to distinguish' [Herm,

HNTC], 'to discriminate' [AB], 'to judge, to judge correctly' [BAGD], 'to judge carefully, to evaluate carefully' [LN], 'to recognize what characterizes (the body) as different' [NIGTC]. The phrase μὴ διακρίνων 'not discerning' is translated 'without careful regard for' [NET].

QUESTION—What relationship is indicated by the use of the participle διακρίνων 'discerning'?

1. It indicates the circumstance of eating and drinking [ISV, NAB, NIV, NJB, NRSV]: the person who eats and drinks *without* discerning the body, eats and drinks a judgment on himself.
2. It indicates a condition for being judged [AB, HNTC, ICC, My, Rb, TG, TH; CEV, NLT, REB, TEV, TNT]: *if* a person does not discern the body when he eats and drinks, he will eat and drink a judgment on himself.
3. It indicates the grounds for being judged [Lns]: he who eats and drinks (unworthily), eats and drinks a judgment on himself, *since* he does not discern the body.

QUESTION—What is meant by διακρίνω 'to discern'?

1. It means to recognize the Lord's body in the bread which he eats [Alf, EGT, Gdt, HNTC, Ho, ICC, Lns, MNTC, NTC, Rb, TG, TH, TNTC, Vn]. The Corinthians were not recognizing in the symbol (the bread and wine) what was being symbolized (Jesus crucified) and so their meals became just a matter of ordinary food and drink [EGT]. It means to recognize the sacredness of Christ's body as one eats [TH]. It means to recognize that the bread and the cup represent the Lord's sacrificial death for us [Alf, Ho, TG]. It means to perceive the body of Christ in the elements as being truly present and received [Lns]. It means to recognize the distinctiveness of the Lord's Supper from other meals [TNTC].
2. It means to recognize that the 'body' is the Lord's body being made up of all the believers joined together, each having equal value and each worthy of respect [AB, NCBC, NIC2]. In 10:17 Paul brings up the word ἕν σῶμα 'one body' which refers to all being 'one body' because all eat one bread. Here again he brings up τό σῶμα 'the body' without any modifier as there. Because 10:17 was a digression from the argument there, it is arguable that it was to anticipate the argument here and in 12:12–26. As such it serves to explain that the Corinthian failure to discern 'the body' was seen in their making a distinction between themselves and the poor during the Lord's Supper [NIC2]. The Corinthians were guilty of dividing the body apart and mistreating the poor. To discern means to recognize that people together form the actual presence of Christ and should be treated accordingly [AB].
3. It means to recognize the purifying influence of fellowship with Christ. Τὸ σῶμα 'the body' here refers to Christ's heavenly glorified manhood [Ed].

11:30 Because-of-this[a] many among you (are) weak[b] and sick[c] and a-considerable-number[d] are-sleeping.[e]

LEXICON—a. διὰ τοῦτο (See this phrase at 11:10): 'that is why' [HNTC; all versions except KJV, NRSV, TNT], 'this is why' [Herm; TNT], 'for this cause' [Lns; KJV], 'for this reason' [NRSV], 'it is for this reason' [NIGTC], 'the proof of this is within your own experience; for it is because' [ICC], 'because of this' [NTC], 'on account of this' [AB].

b. ἀσθενής (LN 23.145, 79.69) (BAGD 1.a. p. 115): 'weak' [AB, Herm, LN (23.145, 79.69), Lns, NTC; all versions except NAB, REB], 'weakness' [NIGTC], 'feeble' [REB], 'ill' [BAGD, LN (23.145)], 'sick' [BAGD, ICC, LN (23.145); NAB], 'sickly' [HNTC], 'disabled' [LN (23.145)], 'powerless' [BAGD]. Ἀσθενής refers to illness of any kind [EGT].

c. ἄρρωστος (LN 23.147) (BAGD p. 109): 'sick' [BAGD, Herm, LN; CEV, ISV, NET, NIV, NLT, REB, TEV, TNT], 'sickly' [AB, Lns; KJV], 'ill' [BAGD, HNTC, ICC, LN, NTC; NJB, NRSV], 'ill-health' [NIGTC], 'infirm' [NAB], 'powerless' [BAGD].

d. ἱκανός (LN 59.2) (BAGD 1.c. p. 374): 'a considerable number' [AB, Lns; ISV], 'considerable, quite a number of' [LN], 'a number' [HNTC; NIV, REB, TNT], 'a good number' [NIGTC; NJB], 'in large numbers' [BAGD], 'quite a few' [NET], 'not a few' [ICC], 'several' [TEV], 'so many' [NTC; NAB], 'many' [BAGD, LN; KJV], 'a lot of others' [CEV], 'some' [Herm; NLT, NRSV]. This would indicate less than the πολλοί 'many' who were sick [EGT, TH], but sufficient numbers to merit serious attention [EGT]. It means 'enough to be considerable' [ICC, NIC, Rb].

e. pres. mid. (deponent = act.) indic. of κοιμάω (LN 23.104, 23.66) (BAGD 2.a. p. 437): 'to sleep' [Herm, HNTC, LN, Lns; KJV], 'to fall asleep' [BAGD; NIV], 'to be asleep' [LN (23.66)], 'to have died' [ICC, LN (23.104), NIGTC, NTC; CEV, NAB, NJB, NLT, NRSV, REB, TEV, TNT], 'to be dying' [AB; ISV], 'to be dead' [LN (23.104); NET], 'to die' [BAGD], 'to pass away' [BAGD]. This is a euphemistic way of referring to the state of being dead [HNTC, LN (23.104), NIC, NTC, TG, TH]. This term was used to refer only to believers who had died [EGT, Lns, MNTC, NIC2, TH, Vn]. This refers to the body as sleeping, not the soul [Lns].

QUESTION—What relationship is indicated by διὰ τοῦτο 'because of this'?

It indicates the result of being judged for not discerning the body in 11:29 [AB, Alf, Ed, EGT, Ho, ICC, NIC, NIC2, NTC, TG, TH]: anyone who eats and drinks without discerning the body of the Lord eats and drinks judgment on himself, *and as a result* many of you are weak and sick and sleeping. The word 'this' refers roughly to 11:27–29, but specifically to 11:29 and not discerning the body [AB].

QUESTION—Are the words ἀσθενής 'weak' and ἄρρωστος 'sick' to be taken in a physical or spiritual sense?

They should be taken in a physical sense [Alf, EGT, Gdt, HNTC, Ho, ICC, Lns, NIC2, TH, TNTC, Vn]. The word κοιμάομαι 'to die' shows that Paul was speaking of physical sickness [EGT].

QUESTION—Are the words ἀσθενής 'weak' and ἄρρωστος 'sick' synonymous or distinct in meaning?

Ἄρρωστος and ἀσθενής are virtual synonyms [Lns, My, NIC], both words denote weakness as the result of sickness [My]. The distinction is that ἀσθενής is weakness that occurs by itself while ἄρρωστος is weakness resulting from sickness [Ho]. Ἀσθενής refers to illnesses of any kind while ἄρρωστος refers to weakness and on-going poor health [EGT].

QUESTION—What was the cause of this predicament?

It was the punishment from God [ICC, Lns, MNTC, NIC, NTC, TNTC]. The cause should be linked to 10:20ff in that the offenders were opening themselves to demons who in turn were causing the physical sickness [HNTC].

11:31 But/now if we-were-examining[a] ourselves, not would-we-be-being-judged;[b]

LEXICON—a. imperf. act. indic. of διακρίνω (LN 30.109) (BAGD 1.c.β. p. 185): 'to examine' [HNTC; NAB, NET, NLT, REB, TEV], 'to judge carefully' [LN; CEV], 'to judge correctly' [BAGD, NTC; ISV], 'to judge rightly' [TNT], 'to judge' [KJV, NIV, NRSV], 'to be critical of' [NJB], 'to enter into judgment with' [Herm], 'to discriminate' [AB], 'to discern' [Lns], 'to evaluate carefully' [LN], 'to recognize (one's own) condition and motives' [ICC], 'to recognize what characterizes us as Christian believers' [NIGTC]. The imperfect tense signifies to make a practice of examining [ICC, TNTC]. The force of the prefix διά on the verb is to add the sense of 'truly' to 'judge' [NCBC].

b. imperf. pass. indic. of κρίνω (LN 56.20) (BAGD 4.b.α. p. 452): 'to be judged' [AB, BAGD, Herm, HNTC, LN (56.20), Lns, NTC; ISV, KJV, NET, NRSV, TNT], 'to fall under judgment' [NIGTC; NAB, REB], 'to come under judgment' [NIV, TEV], 'to be examined and judged' [NLT], 'to be condemned' [LN (56.30); NJB], 'to be punished' [CEV], 'to stand trial' [LN (56.20)]. This word is also translated as a noun phrase: '(escape) this sentence' [ICC]. The imperfect tense in both parts of the condition imply action that is going on [NIC2], and refers definitely to the sickness and death of 11:30 [HNTC, Ho, ICC, NIC2, TNTC, Vn]. The actor of this passive verb is Christ [Ed, TH]. The actor is God [Ho, NCBC]. This refers to temporal and not eternal punishment [Ed, Herm, NCBC] as shown by 11:32–34 [Herm]. See this word also at 10:29.

QUESTION—What relationship is indicated by δέ 'but'?

1. It indicates that this verse contrasts with the sickness and death mentioned in 11:30 [Alf, HNTC, ICC, Lns, NTC; ISV, NET, NIV, NLT, NRSV, REB]: but.
2. It indicates a transition [AB, Gdt]: now.

1 CORINTHIANS 11:31

QUESTION—What kind of condition is this sentence?

It is a contrary to fact condition implying that the Corinthians are not examining themselves and that they are being judged [AB, Alf, Ed, Lns, NIC, NIC2, NTC, Rb].

QUESTION—Why does Paul use the pronoun 'we' here?

It functions to soften the reprimand [ICC, Lns]. It shows Paul's care and makes a general rule here that can apply to other cases [NIC]. It functions to identify Paul with the Corinthians even though he himself did not share their behavior [NIC2, NTC].

QUESTION—What is meant by διακρίνω 'to examine'?

It means to determine one's own moral condition in reference to how it either is pleasing or displeasing to God [Gdt]. It means to make an honest estimate of oneself accompanied by remedial action [Ed]. It means to look at our lives and distinguish between what we are and what we ought to be [MNTC, TNTC, Vn], then confess our sins [MNTC]. It means we should truly judge our lives and change accordingly [NCBC]. It means to perceive that in the Lord's Supper we partake of the Lord's own body and blood [Lns]. It means to reach a correct verdict about ourselves [Herm]. It refers back to the δοκιμάζω 'to examine' of 11:28 [ICC, NIC2, TG]. It refers back to διακρίνω of 11:29 [Herm, HNTC, NIC2], and shows that the 'examining' (of 11:28) should take the form of 'discerning the body' (of 11:29) [NIC2].

11:32 **But being-judged by the Lord we-are-being-disciplined,**[a]

LEXICON—a. pres. pass. indic. of παιδεύω (LN 36.10, 33.226) (BAGD 2.b.α. p. 604): 'to be disciplined' [AB, BAGD, HNTC, LN (36.10), NIGTC, NTC; ISV, NET, NIV, NLT, NRSV, REB, TNT], 'to be chastened' [ICC, Lns; KJV, NAB], 'to be punished' [CEV, TEV], 'to be corrected' [NJB], 'to be trained' [LN (36.10, 33.226)], 'to be instructed, to be taught' [LN (33.226)]. It is also translated as a noun: 'discipline' [Herm]. The sense of punishment is also indicated [BAGD, HNTC] but the purpose of punishment is correction and instruction [HNTC]. This is correction by act rather than by word [Ed]. The sense of education is indicated here whether by discipline or simple teaching [Herm]. Παιδεύω implies moral instruction rather than ordinary instruction [ICC]. Discipline is the trademark of being a son for it is sons whom the Father disciplines (Hebrews 12) [Vn]. These two verbs are present tense indicating on-going activity [Lns].

QUESTION—What relationship is indicated by δέ 'but'?

It indicates a contrast [AB, Gdt, HNTC, ICC, Lns, TH; all versions except NIV]: but. It indicates a contrast with the preceding clause [TH]: we would not be judged *but* being judged by the Lord we are disciplined. Δέ implies 'but these judgments are not completely bad because' [HNTC]. It indicates a transition [ISV]: now.

QUESTION—What is the nature of the judgment here?
It refers to the being weak and sickly and dying of the previous verse [Lns]. It is disciplinary and not eternal condemnation [AB, Lns, NIC, NTC]. This judgment is a token of God's favor [NIC]. Judgments are a token of God's love to save people from being eternally condemned with the world [TNTC].

QUESTION—Is ὑπὸ τοῦ κυρίου 'by the Lord' connected with κρινόμενοι 'being judged' or with παιδευόμεθα 'we are being disciplined'?

1. It is connected with κρινόμενοι 'being judged' [Ed, Gdt, Herm, HNTC, Lns; ISV, NAB, NET, NIV, NJB, NRSV, REB, TNT]: we are being judged by the Lord. It goes with 'being judged' and so maintains the contrast with 'ourselves' in 11:31 [Ed, Gdt].
2. It is connected with παιδευόμεθα 'we are being disciplined' [AB, Alf, EGT, ICC, MNTC, My, NTC, Vn; KJV]: we are being disciplined by the Lord.
3. It goes with both [CEV, NLT, TEV]: we are being disciplined and judged by the Lord.

QUESTION—To whom does κυρίος 'Lord' refer?
It refers to God [My, NIC]. It refers to Christ [Ed, TH].

so-that with the world not we-would-be-condemned.[a]

LEXICON—a. aorist pass. subj. of κατακρίνω (LN **56.31**) (BAGD p. 412): 'to be condemned' [AB, BAGD, Herm, HNTC, **LN**, NIGTC, NTC; all versions], 'to be finally judged adversely' [Lns], 'to render a verdict of guilt' [LN]. This word is also translated as a noun phrase: 'the final condemnation' [ICC]. The aorist indicates a final, once for all activity [Lns]. Eternal condemnation is indicated by this verb here [Alf, NIC2, NTC].

QUESTION—What relationship is indicated by ἵνα 'so that'?
It indicates the purpose of the Lord's disciplining [TH]: we are disciplined *in order that* we may not be condemned.

QUESTION—To what does κόσμος 'world' refer?
It refers to unbelieving mankind [Alf, Gdt, HNTC, Ho, Lns, NIC, NTC, TG, Vn]. It refers to God's enemy [ICC]. It refers to the godless world [MNTC]. It refers to the evil world [Rb]. It refers to the world organized in rebellion against God [TH]. It refers to mankind in contrast to those chosen by God out of the world [Ho].

QUESTION—Who is the actor of this passive verb?
God is probably the actor especially if the Last Judgment is indicated [TH]. It refers to Christ and will take place at His Second Coming (11:26) [Ed].

DISCOURSE UNIT: 11:33–34 [AB, Alf, NIC2, TH]. The topic is summary instruction [AB], general conclusion [Alf, TH], the answer: wait for one another [NIC2].

11:33 Therefore,[a] my brothers,[b] coming-together[c] to eat[d] wait-for/receive[e] each-other.

LEXICON—a. ὥστε (See this word at 10:12): 'therefore' [Herm, NTC; ISV, NAB, REB], 'wherefore' [Lns; KJV], 'so then' [ICC, NIGTC; NET, NIV, NJB, NRSV, TEV], 'so' [AB, HNTC; NLT, TNT], not explicit [CEV].

b. ἀδελφός (See this word at 10:1): 'brother' [AB, Herm, HNTC, ICC, Lns, NTC; ISV, KJV, NAB, NIV, NJB, TNT], 'brother and sister' [NET, NLT, NRSV], 'friend' [CEV, REB, TEV], 'dear fellow Christian' [NIGTC]. This term also includes sisters [NTC; NET, NLT, NRSV]. Ἀδελφός 'brother' does not refer to physical kinship relations but to fellow Christians [TH]. The use of 'brothers' here adds a touch of affection to a rather severe scolding [EGT]. It serves to mitigate the severity of Paul's admonition [ICC]. It serves to open the hearts of his readers to the counsel he is about to give [Gdt].

c. pres. mid. (deponent = act.) participle of συνέρχομαι (See this word at 11:17): 'to come together' [Herm, Lns, NTC; KJV, NET, NIV, NRSV], 'to assemble together' [TNT], 'to assemble' [AB, HNTC; NAB], 'to gather' [ISV, NLT], 'to gather together' [NIGTC; TEV], 'to meet' [NJB, REB], 'to get there' [CEV]. This verb is also translated as a phrase: 'at your religious gatherings' [ICC]. The reference is to coming together for a religious gathering [ICC]. The reference is not to the Lord's Supper only, but to all gatherings together to eat [NIC]. It means to come together for the love feast and the Lord's Supper [Gdt]. The use of this verb takes the argument back to its beginning at 11:17 where it was first used [Lns].

d. aorist act. infin. of ἐσθίω (LN 23.1): 'to eat' [AB, Herm, LN, Lns, NTC; CEV, ISV, KJV, NET, NIV, NRSV, TNT], 'to eat the Lord's Supper' [TEV], 'to drink, to consume food' [LN]. The infinitive τὸ φαγεῖν 'to eat' is also translated as a noun: 'the/a meal' [HNTC, NIGTC; NAB], 'the Meal' [NJB], 'this meal' [REB], 'the Lord's Supper' [NLT], 'a common meal' [ICC]. Their coming together to eat a common meal is what is meant [ICC]. The object of 'eat' here is the love feast which preceded the Lord's Supper [Lns]. It is assumed that the Lord's Supper would be included in their gathering [TH].

e. pres. mid. (deponent = act.) impera. of ἐκδέχομαι (LN 85.60) (BAGD p. 238): 'to wait for' [AB, BAGD, Herm, HNTC, LN, Lns, NIGTC, NTC; all versions except CEV, KJV, NET], 'to wait on' [NET], 'to wait' [CEV], 'to wait until all are ready' [ICC], 'to await' [LN], 'to tarry for' [KJV]. The idea is that they are to all begin their meal at the same time [NIC].

QUESTION—What relationship is indicated by ὥστε 'therefore'?

It indicates a conclusion drawn from the preceding discussion [NIC, NIC2, TH, TNTC]. The use of ὥστε 'so then' and the vocative 'my brothers' indicates that Paul is giving the conclusion to his argument [NIC2]. Verses 11:33–34 form a conclusion to the whole argument beginning at 11:17 [TH]. It indicates that Paul now summarizes [NTC].

QUESTION—What is meant by ἐκδέχομαι 'to wait for/receive'?
1. It means 'wait for' [AB, Ed, EGT, Gdt, ICC, NCBC, NIC, NTC, TH, TNTC; all versions]. This verb is used six times in the New Testament and all with the sense of 'wait for' [NTC]. It corresponds to 11:21 where it was seen that the Corinthians were not waiting for each other in their meals together [Ed, EGT, Gdt, HNTC, ICC, Lns, NCBC, NTC, TG, TNTC]. They are not to start the supper until all are gathered so that all may begin eating together and share alike [EGT].
2. It means 'receive' or 'welcome' [NIC2]. In 11:21 it was seen that the meaning of προλαμβάνω 'to take (supper)' had lost the sense of 'before', that is 'to take (supper) before (others)'. This put the focus rather on the Corinthians stuffing themselves on their own food in front of the poor. One sense of ἐκδέχομαι is 'to receive' or 'to welcome'. It has this sense here where Paul is admonishing the wealthy to show normal Christian hospitality to their brothers [NIC2].

11:34 If anyone is-hungry, he-should-eat at home, in-order-that not for[a] judgment[b] you-come-together.

LEXICON—a. εἰς with accusative object (LN 89.48) (BAGD 4.e. p. 229): 'for' [Herm; NRSV], 'to come under' [TEV], 'to fall under' [NIGTC; REB], 'unto' [Lns; KJV], 'to' [AB, BAGD], 'into' [BAGD], 'with the result that, so that as a result, to cause' [LN (89.48)]. The phrase εἰς κρίμα 'for judgment' is translated 'to result in judgment' [NIV]. The phrase ἵνα μὴ εἰς κρίμα 'in order that not for judgment' is translated 'then you won't condemn yourselves' [CEV], 'so you won't bring judgment upon yourselves' [NLT], 'so that it will not bring judgment on you' [ISV], 'so that it does not lead to judgment' [NET]. This entire clause is translated 'so that your assembly may not deserve condemnation' [NAB], 'that your meeting may not result in condemnation' [TNT], 'then your meeting will not bring your condemnation' [NJB], 'that the end of your assembly may not be judgment' [HNTC], 'so that your gatherings may not have these fatal results' [ICC], 'that you may not encounter judgment' [NTC], 'you may not be assembling to be judged' [AB]. See this word also at 10:31.
b. κρίμα (See this word at 11:29): 'judgment' [Herm, HNTC, Lns, NIGTC, NTC; ISV, NET, NIV, NLT, REB], 'condemnation' [KJV, NAB, NJB, NRSV, TNT], 'God's judgment' [TEV], 'fatal results' [ICC]. This noun is also translated as a verb: 'to condemn' [CEV], 'to be judged' [AB]. Judgment is not altogether a good thing even though God can use it as such in a Christian's life [HNTC].

QUESTION—Does this imply that the Lord's Supper was not a real meal for satisfying one's hunger?

It does not imply that the Lord's Supper was not a real meal [EGT, HNTC, NIC, NIC2, TH]. It merely means that if anyone was so hungry that they could not wait until the others arrived to eat, he should eat at home first [HNTC, TH]. 'If anyone hunger' in this context probably means 'If anyone wants to stuff himself...'. In other words, don't eat rich foods before your poorer brothers and so humiliate them [NIC2]. The meaning is that the Lord's Supper is not a place to come to only satisfy one's hunger. If that is the case, then it is better to eat at home as this attitude spoils the love feast [NIC].

QUESTION—Who is the actor of κρίμα 'judgment'?

God is probably the one who judges [HNTC, NTC, TH].

And the other-matters[a] I-will-give-instructions[b] when[c] I-come.

LEXICON—a. λοιπός (LN 63.21) (BAGD 2.b.β. p. 480): 'other matter' [Herm, HNTC; all versions except KJV, NIV, NRSV], 'other matters in which you need instruction' [ICC], 'other things' [BAGD; NRSV], 'rest' [BAGD, LN, Lns; KJV], 'rest of the matter' [AB], 'rest of the things' [NTC], 'remaining matters' [NIGTC], 'remaining, what remains, other' [LN]. The phrase τὰ λοιπά 'the rest' is translated 'further' [NIV].

b. fut. mid. indic. of διατάσσω (LN 62.8, 33.325) (BAGD p. 189): 'to give instructions' [ISV, NAB, NLT, NRSV, TNT], 'to instruct (about)' [LN (33.325); CEV], 'to give directions' [NET, NIV], 'to set in order' [Herm, Lns, NIGTC; KJV], 'to put in order' [AB], 'to put right' [HNTC], 'to arrange' [NTC; NJB], 'to settle' [REB, TEV], 'to regulate' [ICC], 'to arrange for, to plan' [LN (62.8)], 'to order, to command' [BAGD, LN (33.325)], 'to direct' [BAGD], 'to tell' [LN (33.325)]. The most common meaning for this verb in the New Testament is 'to give orders or instructions' [TH].

c. ὡς (LN **67.45**) (BAGD IV.1.c.β. p. 898): 'when' [Herm, LN]. The phrase ὡς ἄν is translated 'when' [AB, BAGD, HNTC, **LN**, Lns, NIGTC; all versions except CEV, NLT], 'whenever' [ICC], 'after' [CEV, NLT], 'as soon as' [BAGD]. Ὡς ἄν plus the aorist subjunctive ἔλθω 'I come' means 'whenever I come' [NTC].

QUESTION—What were the other matters?

'Other matters' probably refer to things having to do with the Love-feasts and Communion [EGT, HNTC, ICC, Lns, NIC, TG, TNTC, Vn]. It must mean other things about the Lord's Supper as he goes on to discuss other matters in the rest of the epistle [Vn].

DISCOURSE UNIT: 12:1–14:40 [AB, Alf, Ed, Gdt, Herm, HNTC, ICC, Lns, NCBC, NIC2, NIGTC, TH, TNTC, Vn; NAB, REB]. The topic is spiritual gifts [AB, Ed, Gdt, HNTC, ICC, Lns, NCBC, TH, TNTC; NAB, REB], the gifts of the Spirit for service in love [NIGTC], spiritual gifts and spiritual people [NIC2], abuse of spiritual gifts [Alf], community, divine service, and the Spirit [Herm].

DISCOURSE UNIT: 12:1–31 [Alf, Ed, Gdt, Ho, Lns, NTC; KJV]. The topic is spiritual gifts.

DISCOURSE UNIT: 12:1–31a [GNT]. The topic is spiritual gifts.

DISCOURSE UNIT: 12:1–11 [EGT, GNT, ICC, NTC, TH, TNTC; CEV, ISV, NAB, NET, NIV, NLT, TEV]. The topic is spiritual gifts [EGT, GNT; CEV, ISV, NAB, NET, NIV, NLT, TEV], variety of spiritual gifts [ICC, TNTC; NAB], the Holy Spirit [NTC].

DISCOURSE UNIT: 12:1–3 [AB, Alf, Gdt, Herm, HNTC, MNTC, NCBC, NIC, NIC2, NIGTC, NTC, Vn; NJB]. The topic is the Spirit of God and spiritual gifts [AB], spiritual gifts [Alf, NIC; NJB], limits of the Christian spiritual domain [Gdt], the criterion [Herm, Vn], the criterion: Jesus is Lord [HNTC, NIC2], the Christological criterion [NIGTC], discerning spiritual utterances [NCBC], background and testing of counterfeit spiritual gifts [MNTC], the Christian's confession [NTC].

12:1 Now/but about[a] the spiritual[b] (things), brothers, not I-wish you to-be-ignorant.[c]

LEXICON—a. περί with genitive object (LN 89.6, 90.24) (BAGD 1.h. p. 645): 'about' [LN (90.24), NIGTC; CEV, NAB, NIV, NJB, NLT, REB], 'of' [LN (90.24)], 'concerning' [BAGD, Herm, ICC, LN (89.6, 90.24); ISV, KJV, NRSV, TEV, TNT], 'with reference to' [BAGD], 'with regard to' [LN (89.6); NET], 'in relation to' [LN (89.6)].

b. πνευματικός (LN **12.21**, 12.20) (BAGD 2.b.α., 2.b.β. p. 679): 'spiritual, pertaining to the spirit' [BAGD, LN (12.21, 26.10)], 'from the Spirit' [LN (12.21)]. The phrase τῶν πνευματικῶν 'the spiritual (things)' is translated 'spiritual gifts' [BAGD (2.b.α.), Herm, **LN** (12.21); CEV, ISV, KJV, NAB, NET, NIV, NRSV, TNT], 'things that "come from the Spirit"' [NIGTC], 'gifts which come from the Spirit' [**LN** (12.21)], 'gifts of the Spirit' [NJB, REB], 'gifts from the Holy Spirit' [TEV], 'special abilities the Holy Spirit gives to each of us' [NLT], 'spiritual manifestations' [ICC], 'ones possessing the Spirit, spirit-filled persons' [BAGD (2.b.β.)], 'ones who are spiritual' [LN (12.20)]. See this word also at 10:3.

c. pres. act. infin. of ἀγνοέω (See this word at 10:1): 'to be ignorant' [Herm; ISV, KJV, NET, NIV], 'to leave (one) in ignorance' [NAB], 'to be uninformed' [NRSV], 'to remain without knowledge' [NIGTC], 'to be under delusions' [ICC]. The phrase οὐ θέλω ὑμᾶς ἀγνοεῖν 'I do not wish you to be ignorant' is translated 'I want you to be quite certain' [NJB], 'I want you to know the truth about them' [TEV], 'I want you to understand the facts' [TNT], 'I want there to be no misunderstanding' [REB], 'for I must correct your misunderstandings about them' [NLT], not explicit [CEV].

QUESTION—What relationship is indicated by δέ 'now/but'?
  1. It indicates a transition to a new topic [Alf, Ed, EGT, Gdt, Ho, ICC, Lns, My, NIGTC, TH; ISV, KJV, NAB, NIV, NLT, NRSV, TEV]: now. It is the counterpart to the πρῶτον μέν 'first, on the one hand' of 12:11:18 [Ho, Lns, MNTC]: first, I hear there are divisions among you…*now* concerning spiritual gifts.

2. It indicates a contrast with the words 'other matters' of 12:11:34 [Gdt]: concerning the other matters I will give instructions when I come, *but* concerning spiritual gifts I tell you now.

QUESTION—What is indicated by the phrase περὶ δέ 'now concerning'?

It indicates that Paul is now addressing a topic that the Corinthians have written to him about. The same formula is used in 7:1 and 8:1 [ICC, Lns, NIC, NIC2, NIGTC, NTC, Rb, TG, TNTC; TEV]. It may indicate Paul's response to matters that others have told him about the Corinthians as given in 1:11 and 11:18 [Alf, TH].

QUESTION—To what does τῶν πνευματικῶν 'the spiritual (things)' refer?

1. It refers to spiritual gifts [AB, Alf, Ed, EGT, Gdt, Herm, HNTC, Ho, ICC, Lns, MNTC, My, NIC, NIC2, NTC, Rb, TG, TH, Vn; all versions]. Verse 12:4 shows that 'gifts' are in focus [Vn]. These are spiritual 'gifts' [all versions]. It probably refers to 'spiritual gifts' but the emphasis is more on 'the Spirit' than on 'the gifts', so that 'things of the Spirit' would be a better rendering. When 'gifts' are in focus, Paul uses χαρίσματα 'gifts' [NIC2].
2. It refers to spiritual people. The reference is probably to people who have been given spiritual gifts (see 2:15 and 3:1) [NCBC].
3. It refers to both people and gifts. The question asked by the Corinthians was probably how they were to judge whether specific people and specific gifts were truly from the Spirit. Some people claim that they are from the Spirit, but how is one to know? [NIGTC]

QUESTION—What is the function of the vocative ἀδελφοί 'brothers'?

Together with the words 'now concerning' it functions to introduce a new topic [NIC, NIC2, TH]. It introduces a section which might contain a reprimand [TNTC]. It functions to get their attention but also to soften the humiliation of the reference to their being ignorant [Gdt]. The term 'brothers' also includes 'sisters' [NTC]. This term does not indicate physical kinship relations but refers to fellow believers [TH].

QUESTION—What is the figure of speech is οὐ θέλω ὑμᾶς ἀγνοεῖν 'I do not want you to be ignorant'?

It is a litotes, an understatement, in which something is expressed by negating its opposite [NIC; NJB, TEV, TNT]: I want you to know. It functions to strengthen his argument [NIC]. See this same phrase at 10:1.

12:2 You-know that when you-were pagans[a] how[b] to mute[c] idols[d] being-led-away[e] (you were) being-led.[f]

TEXT—Some manuscripts omit ὅτε 'when' after ὅτι 'that'. GNT includes it but does not deal with this variant. It is omitted by KJV.

LEXICON—a. ἔθνη (LN 11.37) (BAGD 2. p. 218): 'pagan' [AB, Herm, LN, NIGTC; NAB, NET, NIV, NJB, NLT, NRSV, REB], 'heathen' [ICC, LN; TEV, TNT], 'Gentile' [HNTC, Lns, NTC; ISV, KJV]. The phrase ὅτε ἔθνη ἦτε 'when you were pagans' is translated 'before you became followers of the Lord' [CEV]. Ἔθνος is used here to non-Jews [HNTC],

to non-Christians [Ed, MNTC, NTC, TG, TH, TNTC; CEV]. The majority of Christians in the Corinthian church had been Gentiles [Lns].
b. ὡς (LN 89.86) (BAGD p. 899): 'in what manner, how' [LN]. The phrase ὡς ἄν is translated 'however' [NET], 'somehow or other' [NIV], 'how' [Herm, HNTC], 'even as' [Lns; KJV], 'in all the wrong ways' [CEV], 'as impulse (drove you)' [NAB], 'irresistibly' [NJB], 'by some impulse or other' [REB], 'just as the impulse (might take you)' [ICC], 'in many ways' [TEV], 'in one way or another' [TNT], 'as if, as it were, so to speak' [BAGD], 'in whatever way' [NTC], 'whenever' [AB], not explicit [NIGTC; ISV, NLT, NRSV]. The presence of the ἄν gives the verb an iterative or repetitive aspect [Alf, Ed, HNTC, Lns, NIC2, NTC, TNTC]: being led again and again, or continually being led, or being led from time to time. The ἄν indicates capriciousness that at one time they would go to this god, another time to another [Gdt].
c. ἄφωνος (LN 33.106) (BAGD 1. p. 128): 'mute' [LN, NTC; NAB, NIV], 'dumb' [AB, BAGD, Herm, HNTC, ICC, LN, Lns; KJV, REB, TNT], 'speechless' [NET, NLT], 'inarticulate' [NJB], 'that cannot even talk' [CEV], 'that could not speak' [NRSV], 'that were incapable of speech' [NIGTC], 'that couldn't even speak' [ISV], 'silent' [BAGD], 'unable to speak, incapable of talking' [LN], 'lifeless' [TEV]. The word ἄφωνος is literally 'voiceless' [MNTC, TH], but it is implied that they are lifeless and therefore cannot speak. In the light of the next verse where men speak under the influence of an evil spirit, it would be better to render this as 'lifeless' [TG, TH]. This is an understatement which means that they are lifeless [Lns].
d. εἴδωλον (LN **6.97**) (BAGD 1. p. 221): 'idol' [AB, BAGD, Herm, HNTC, ICC, **LN**, Lns, NIGTC, NTC; all versions except NJB, REB], 'heathen god' [NJB, REB], 'image' [BAGD].
e. pres. pass. participle of ἀπάγω (LN 15.177, **88.152**) (BAGD 4. p. 79): 'to be led away' [ICC, LN (15.177), Lns], 'to be led astray' [BAGD, **LN** (88.152), NTC], 'to be carried away' [BAGD, Herm, HNTC, NIGTC], 'to be led off' [AB, LN (15.177)], 'to be taken away' [LN (15.177)], 'to be misled' [BAGD, LN (88.152)], 'to be deceived' [LN (88.152)]. See the next word for various version renderings of these two verbs together. This verb has the idea of being led away by force rather than by any kind of persuasion [EGT, Ho, ICC]. The verb was often used to describe prisoners being taken away to prison or execution [MNTC]. The basic meaning is 'led away' not 'led astray' [Alf, ICC]. Although the meaning is 'to be led away', the resulting meaning of 'to be led into error' is indicated here [Lns, TH]. They were led away from the truth [Ed]. This verb, comprising Paul's main point in the verse and strengthened by ἄγω 'to be led', suggests times of ecstatic experience in their pagan religion when a person would be possessed by a supernatural being [HNTC].
f. imperf. pass. indic. of ἄγω (LN 15.165) (BAGD 3. p. 14): 'to be led' [AB, BAGD, ICC, LN, Lns, NTC], 'to be led astray' [HNTC], 'to be drawn'

[Herm], 'to be brought' [LN], 'to be attracted, to allow oneself to be led' [BAGD]. The phrase ὡς ἂν ἤγεσθε…ἀπαγόμενοι 'how you were being led, being led astray' is translated 'you were enticed and led away' [ISV], 'somehow or other you were influenced and led astray' [NIV], 'you were enticed and led astray' [NRSV], 'you were led astray as impulse drove you' [NAB], 'you were often led astray…, however you were led' [NET], 'you were led astray in many ways' [TEV], 'you were irresistibly drawn' [NJB], 'you were led astray and swept along' [NLT], 'you were led away, in one way or another' [TNT], 'you were led in all the wrong ways' [CEV], 'you used to be carried away by some impulse or other' [REB], 'you used to be carried away' [NIGTC], 'carried away even as ye were led' [KJV]. The imperfect plus the particle ἄν gives the verb a repetitive aspect [Ed, NTC]: led from time to time.

QUESTION—Why is this verse ungrammatical?

It is ungrammatical because it has a participle where it seems to need a finite verb. It literally reads: "You know that when you were pagans however you were led to mute idols *being led away*." It is better to supply the finite verb 'you were' with the final participle and to make it the main verb of the verse as follows: "You know that when you were pagans *you were being led away* however you were being led to mute idols" [AB, EGT, Gdt, Lns, NIC, NIC2, NIGTC, NTC, Rb]. It is better to just let the participle hang [Ed].

QUESTION—Who is the agent of ἀπαγόμενοι 'being led away'?

The agent by whom they were led astray was Satan [ICC, Lns], evil spirits [Ed, Herm, HNTC, Lns, NCBC, Rb], the mute idols [TH], pagan priests [Lns, Vn], an irrational influence [Ho], or impure gusts of power [Gdt].

QUESTION—Who is the agent of ἤγεσθε 'you were led'?

The agent by whom they were led was Satan or his representatives [NTC], local custom or the priests or rulers [ICC], strong impulses [AB], some influence which they could neither understand nor resist [Ho, TG], teachers [NIC], or irrational directing powers [EGT]. Note that we have separated the two passives simply because the commentaries tended to comment on them separately or to not specify about which verb they were commenting. However, for all practical purposes the agent of one should be the agent of the other.

QUESTION—What is implied by the phrase 'being led away to mute idols'?

It implies that they were led away to worship mute idols [Ho, ICC, My].

QUESTION—What is the significance of the phrase τὰ εἴδωλα τὰ ἄφωνα 'the idols the mute'?

This formation with the adjective following the noun with an article gives as much importance to the adjective as to the noun [Lns]. The grammatical import of the phrase emphasizes the quality of the adjective [Gdt].

QUESTION—What is the function of the clause ὡς ἂν ἤγεσθε 'however you were led' appended to ἀπαγόμενοι 'being led away'?

It functions to emphasize the notion that the act of following was rather senseless and almost unconscious [ICC]. It carries the idea that they are being controlled by something that they could neither understand nor resist [Ho]. The idea of being helplessly led by others at any time is expressed [Lns].

12:3 Therefore[a] I-make-known[b] to-you that no-one speaking by[c] (the) Spirit of-God says, "Accursed[d] (be/is) Jesus,"

TEXT—Instead of the nominative case Ἰησοῦς 'Jesus', some manuscripts have the accusative case Ἰησοῦν, giving the sense '(calls) Jesus accursed'. GNT does not mention this alternative. Only KJV reads Ἰησοῦν.

LEXICON—a. διό (LN 89.47) (BAGD p. 198): 'therefore' [BAGD, Herm, LN, NIGTC, NTC; NIV, NRSV, TNT], 'wherefore' [Lns; KJV], 'so' [HNTC; ISV, NET, NLT], 'that is why' [NAB], 'because of that' [NJB], 'for this reason' [BAGD, LN; REB], 'on this account' [AB], 'those experiences do not help you now; and therefore' [ICC], 'now' [CEV], 'for this very reason, so then' [LN], not explicit [TEV]. This is a relatively emphatic marker of result [LN, NIC2].

b. pres. act. indic. of γνωρίζω (LN 28.26) (BAGD 1. p. 163): 'to make known' [BAGD, LN, NTC; TNT], 'to want (someone) to know' [CEV, ISV, NLT, TEV], 'to want (someone) to understand' [NET, NRSV], 'to give (someone) to understand' [Lns; KJV], 'to impart "knowledge"' [NIGTC], 'to want to make quite clear' [NJB], 'to make plain to' [HNTC], 'to impress upon' [ICC; REB], 'to tell' [NAB, NIV], 'to inform' [AB, Herm], 'to reveal' [BAGD].

c. ἐν with dative object (LN 90.6) (BAGD I.5.d. p. 260): 'by' [AB, LN, NTC; CEV, ISV, KJV, NET, NIV, NLT, NRSV, TEV], 'under the influence of' [BAGD, ICC; REB, TNT], 'through the agency of' [NIGTC], 'under divine/demonic inspiration' [BAGD], 'in' [Herm, HNTC; NAB, NJB], 'in union with' [Lns], 'from' [LN].

d. ἀνάθεμα (LN 33.474) (BAGD 2.a. p. 54): 'accursed' [Herm, LN, Lns; KJV], 'cursed' [BAGD, LN, NIGTC, NTC; ISV, NAB, NET, NIV, TNT], 'a curse on' [NJB, REB, TEV], 'damned' [AB], 'anathema' [HNTC, ICC]. The phrase λέγει, Ἀνάθεμα 'no one says, "Accursed be/is"', is translated 'you will (never) curse' [CEV], 'no one...can curse' [NLT], 'no one...says, "Let...be cursed!"' [NRSV]. This word denoted anything that was dedicated to God. But in the LXX it was used to designate anything dedicated to be destroyed or cursed and this is its usage here [Gdt, Ho].

QUESTION—What is the point of this verse?

What marks something as spiritual is not that it is an inspired utterance, but that its content is intelligible and able to stand the test of the Lordship of Jesus [NIC2]. Ecstasy does not indicate the working of the Spirit. It is the declaration that Jesus is Lord that indicates it [Herm, NCBC]. The confession that Jesus is Lord is the critical test of spiritual gifts [Ed].

QUESTION—What relationship is indicated by διό 'therefore'?

It indicates the conclusion drawn from his previous statement [Alf, HNTC, Ho, ICC, Lns, My, NIC, NIC2, NTC, Vn]: when you were pagans you were led away to mute idols, *therefore* know that no one says by the Spirit of God that Jesus is cursed. Paul is basing his conclusion on his statement 'you know' of 12:2 which told of their being led astray [HNTC, Lns]. Paul is basing his conclusion on his not wanting them to be ignorant as in 12:1 [Ho, Vn]. Paul is basing his conclusion on their knowing nothing about spiritual gifts or how to discern their authenticity [ICC]. Paul is basing his conclusion both on his not wanting them to be ignorant and on their knowledge as pagans of inspired utterances [NIC2]. Paul is basing his conclusion on the fact that as pagans they could not know about spiritually gifted men [My].

QUESTION—What relationship is indicated by the preposition ἐν 'by'?

It indicates 'under the influence of' [AB, EGT, HNTC, Ho, ICC], or 'entirely possessed by' [Ed], or '(the element) in which' [Alf, EGT, My]. It indicates that the Holy Spirit is that in which the speaking occurs [My]. It indicates that the Holy Spirit is guiding the person [NIC, NIGTC, TH]. It indicates that the Holy Spirit is the instrument by which the speaking is accomplished [Vn].

QUESTION—In what way is the name Ἰησοῦς 'Jesus' used here?

It is used to signify the historical person of Jesus rather than his office [Gdt, Ho, Lns].

QUESTION—What verb is to be supplied in this quotation?

1. The optative 'may...be' should be supplied [AB, BAGD; NAB, NIV, NJB, NLT, NRSV, REB, TEV, TNT]: May Jesus be cursed!
2. The indicative 'is' should be implied [Alf, EGT, HNTC, ICC, Lns, NIGTC, NTC; ISV, NET]: Jesus is cursed. The indicative 'is' should be supplied in that it parallels the following declaration 'Jesus is Lord' [NTC]. This is a confession [NIGTC].

QUESTION—Who might say that Jesus is cursed?

It is conceivable that in the mixed group that came to a Christian gathering, someone would suddenly shout this out and the Corinthians, who were used to the frenzied shouts of worshippers at the cult of Dionysus, might think the shout was inspired. Paul corrects this [ICC, TNTC]. Paul himself tried to make Christians blaspheme (Acts 25:11) [AB]. The Jews knew from Deuteronomy 21:23 that anyone who hung on a tree was under God's curse. Jesus' crucifixion would put him in that class of men if one believed he were an imposter [MNTC]. They said that Jesus was a malefactor justly condemned to die [Ho]. This is an extreme example to make the point that no false witness to Jesus can be from God's Spirit [NCBC]. *Anathema* summarizes everything that could be said against Jesus [NIC]. Paul could have been using this example as being purely hypothetical and no one actually said it [NIC2]. It is said that a requirement to join the sect of Ophite was to declare that Jesus was cursed [NCBC].

and no-one is-able to-say, "Jesus (is) Lord," except by (the) Holy[a] Spirit.
LEXICON—a. ἅγιος (LN 88.24) (BAGD 1.b.δ. p. 9, 5.c. p. 676): 'Holy' [AB, Herm, HNTC, ICC, Lns, NTC; all versions], 'holy' [BAGD (p. 9), LN],

'sacred' [BAGD (p. 9)], 'pure, divine' [LN]. Ἅγιος indicates possessing superior moral and divine qualities [LN]. God's Spirit is called 'holy' because of his heavenly origin and nature [BAGD (p. 676)].

QUESTION—What is the significance of the quote 'Jesus (is) Lord?
It was the earliest confession of New Testament Christians [AB, NIC2, NTC].

QUESTION—What does it mean to say "Jesus is Lord"?
It was the same as claiming that the man Jesus was truly God [Ho, MNTC, NIC2], since the Greek word κύριος was used to translate the Hebrew word for Yahweh in the Septuagint [Ho]. It was a declaration of allegiance to Jesus as one's God [NIC2, NTC]. It meant more that just saying the words [NIC, TNTC, Vn]. By saying this, a person both acknowledges who Jesus is and acknowledges his authority over himself [Vn]. The one who says this accepts Jesus' authority over his life and declares that he is Jesus' servant [HNTC].

QUESTION—What is the significance of saying this ἐν πνεύματι ἁγίῳ 'by the Holy Spirit'?
Paul means that a person can realize that Jesus is Lord only when the Holy Spirit is in that person's heart [TNTC]. It signifies that every true Christian is inspired and that those who have received special gifts should not think of those who have not received them as being without the Holy Spirit [Alf, EGT, ICC, Lns, NCBC]. In this context, it refers to speaking in tongues [NIC].

QUESTION—What other New Testament passage is similar to this?
1 John 4:1–3 is a similar test that focuses on those who would deny the true manhood of Jesus [NCBC].

DISCOURSE UNIT: 12:4–31 [Herm, HNTC, NIC2]. The topic is the diversity of gifts in one body [HNTC], the need for diversity [NIC2], the multiplicity and unity of spiritual gifts [Herm].

DISCOURSE UNIT: 12:4–12 [Gdt]. The topic is the unity of spiritual forces in their diversity.

DISCOURSE UNIT: 12:4–11 [AB, NCBC, NIC, NIC2, Vn; NJB]. The topic is diversity in the Godhead and the gifts [NIC2], varieties of gifts, different persons, one Spirit [AB], varieties of spiritual gifts [NCBC, NIC], the Divine Source and the variety and purpose of the gifts [Vn], the variety and the unity of gifts [NJB].

DISCOURSE UNIT: 12:4–7 [MNTC, NIGTC]. The topic is the source and purpose of spiritual gifts [MNTC], varied gifts from one source [NIGTC].

DISCOURSE UNIT: 12:4–6 [Alf, NTC]. The topic is different but divinely derived gifts [NTC].

12:4 Now/but[a] there-are varieties/distributions[b] of-gifts,[c] but the same Spirit;[d]

LEXICON—a. δέ (See this word at 11:2): 'now' [ICC, Lns; ISV, KJV, NET, NLT, NRSV], not explicit [AB, Herm, HNTC, NIGTC, NTC; CEV, NAB, NIV, NJB, REB, TEV, TNT].

b. διαίρεσις (LN **57.91** or **58.39**) (BAGD 1. p. 183): 'variety' [LN (58.39), NTC; NRSV, REB], 'different kind' [CEV, NIV, NLT, TEV], 'diversity' [KJV], 'apportionment' [AB, BAGD], 'assignment' [Herm], 'distribution' [HNTC, **LN** (57.91), Lns], 'difference' [**LN** (58.39)], 'division' [BAGD, LN (57.91)], 'different apportionings' [NIGTC], 'allotment' [BAGD]. This noun is also translated as an adjective: 'different' [NAB, NET], 'many different' [NJB]; and as a verb: 'to vary' [ISV]. The plural is translated 'various distributions' [ICC], 'many kinds' [TNT].

c. χάρισμα (LN 57.103) (BAGD 2. p. 879): 'gift' [BAGD, HNTC, ICC, LN, NIGTC, NTC; ISV, KJV, NAB, NET, NIV, NJB, NRSV, REB], 'spiritual gift' [BAGD; CEV, NLT, TEV, TNT], 'divine gift' [AB], '(the gift of) grace' [Herm], 'charismata' [Lns], 'gracious gift' [LN], 'gift (freely and graciously given), a favor bestowed' [BAGD]. (Also see this word at 1:7.)

d. πνεῦμα (LN 12.18) (BAGD 6.d. p. 677): 'Spirit' [AB, Herm, HNTC, LN, Lns, NIGTC, NTC; all versions except NLT], 'Spirit who bestows them' [ICC], 'Holy Spirit' [LN; NLT], 'Spirit of God' [BAGD, LN].

QUESTION—What relationship is indicated by δέ 'now/but'?
1. It indicates transition [AB, Lns; ISV, KJV, NET, NLT, NRSV]: now. Paul is now extending the range of the Holy Spirit's activities to show that the Spirit is the one who distributes the divine gifts [AB].
2. It indicates a contrast [Alf, EGT, ICC, My]: but. There is this unity of spiritual influence, *but* there is also variety [Alf]. Everyone who testifies that Jesus is Lord is inspired, yet the Spirit distributes special gifts [EGT, ICC, My].

QUESTION—What is Paul saying in 12:4–6?
Paul's point here is that while spiritual gifts vary, unity lies in the three persons: the Spirit who gives, the Lord who is served, and God who is at work [HNTC].

QUESTION—What is meant by διαίρεσις 'varieties/distributions' here and in the following verses?
1. It means varieties of gifts [Gdt, MNTC, NIC2, NTC, TH; all versions]: there are various kinds of gifts. The context indicates that 'variety' is the correct choice [NIC2].
2. It means distributions of gifts [AB, BAGD, EGT, HNTC, ICC, Lns, My, NCBC, NIC, NIGTC]: the gifts are distributed to people by the Holy Spirit. In 12:11, the Spirit is seen as διαιροῦν 'distributing' to each as He wills, and this determines the sense intended here [Herm, ICC]. It is the giving out of the gifts rather than their variety that is in focus [ICC]. The

meaning is that no one gets all the gifts, but that they are distributed [NIC].
3. Paul intends to convey both senses [Ed]: a variety of gifts are distributed to people by the Holy Spirit.

QUESTION—What is meant by χάρισμα 'gift'?

This word does not mean natural abilities which men inherit from their parents, but gifts that the Holy Spirit gives to benefit the church [AB]. The word comes from χάρις 'grace' which focuses on the freeness of it. Here it refers to the special workings of the Holy Spirit in men [TNTC]. This would include such gifts as tongues, miracles, healing, and prophesying as well as such gifts as teaching, exhortation, and knowledge for the building up of the church [Alf]. It means an extraordinary ability made available by the loving favor of God and given through the Holy Spirit for the benefit of the Christian assembly. They could be either newly granted powers or those already possessed but filled with greater strength [My]. It means supernatural gifts given to believers to enable them to minister supernaturally to others [MNTC]. Verse 12:1 has the term πνευματικός 'spiritual gifts' which emphasizes the spiritual nature of the gift. Here χάρισμα emphasizes the giving nature of the gifts [TH].

QUESTION—What relationship is indicated by δέ 'but' in the phrase 'but the same Spirit'?

It indicates a contrast between the variety of the gifts and the single source [AB, HNTC, ICC, Lns, NIC, NTC; all versions]: there are a variety of gifts, *but* the same Spirit.

QUESTION—What is the relationship of the 'Spirit' and the 'gifts'?

The Spirit is the author or source of the gifts [Alf, Gdt, Ho, ICC, Lns, My, NIC, NIC2, NIGTC, NTC, TG, TH, TNTC, Vn; CEV, NLT, TEV, TNT].

QUESTION—What is the significance of the repetition of the words ὁ αὐτός 'the same' in the same Spirit, the same Lord, and the same God (12:4–6)?

The repetition emphasizes that the same Spirit/Lord/God reveals himself in a variety of gifts and services [NIC2]. It emphasizes that these three persons work together [TG].

12:5 And there-are varieties/distributions[a] of-services,[b] but/and the same Lord;

LEXICON—a. διαίρεσις (See this word at 12:4): 'variety' [NIGTC, NTC; NRSV, REB], 'different kind' [NIV, NLT], 'difference' [KJV], 'different way' [CEV, TEV], 'apportionment' [AB], 'assignment' [Herm], 'distribution' [HNTC, Lns]. This noun is also translated as an adjective: 'different' [NAB, NET], 'many different' [NJB]. The plural form is translated 'many kinds' [TNT], 'various distributions' [ICC]. The phrase διαιρέσεις διακονιῶν 'varieties of services' is translated 'ministries vary' [ISV].

b. διακονία (LN 35.19, 35.21) (BAGD 3. p. 184): 'service' [BAGD, HNTC, LN (35.19); NIV, NLT, NRSV, REB, TNT], 'ministry' [LN (35.21), NTC; ISV, NAB, NET], 'serving ministries' [AB], 'acts of service'

[Herm], 'ministration' [ICC, Lns], 'serving' [TEV], 'ways of serving' [NIGTC], 'administration' [KJV], 'activity' [NJB], 'task' [LN (35.21)], 'help' [LN (35.19)], 'office' [BAGD]. This noun is also translated as a verb: 'to serve' [CEV]. Διακονία indicates 'service' [AB, Alf, Ed, Herm, HNTC, Ho, ICC, Lns, MNTC, NCBC, NIC2, NTC, TG, TH, TNTC, Vn], or 'ministry' [AB, Alf, EGT, ICC, NTC].

QUESTION—What kinds of services are indicated?

It indicates all Christian services rendered either by an Apostle or the humblest believer. It would also include the giving of alms and ministering to the needs of the body [ICC]. The work of a missionary and teaching may be indicated [AB]. All the 'spiritual gifts' must be intended [Ed, My]. Paul is showing that everyday services are now equal to the supernatural phenomena of the Spirit [Herm, TNTC]. The services of apostles, evangelists, bishops, and deacons may be indicated [Gdt]. Preaching, teaching, singing in the choir, worshiping, counseling, outreach, encouraging, administration, and governing are all means of service [NTC].

QUESTION—Are the following nouns χάρισμα, διακονία, ἐνέργημα 'gift, service, activity' distinct categories from services or are they all aspects of the same thing?

They are all different aspects of the same thing [EGT, Ho, Lns, My, NCBC, NIC2, TH]. They are probably three different ways of viewing the expressions of the Spirit of 12:7 [NIC2]. They are all spiritual gifts; when seen as a gift it is viewed from the perspective of its quality, when seen as a service it is viewed from the perspective of its usefulness, and when seen as an activity it is viewed from the perspective of what makes it operate [EGT].

QUESTION—What relationship is indicated by δέ 'but/and' in the phrase 'but/and the same Lord'?

1. It indicates a contrast between the variety of the services and the single source or recipient [AB, HNTC, ICC, Lns, NIC, NTC; all versions]: there are a variety of services, *but* the same Lord. This is parallel with 12:4 and 12:6 [all versions].
2. It indicates conjoining [AB, HNTC, ICC, Lns]: there are a variety of services, *and* the same Lord. Instead of a contrast between the many and the one, here the facts are stated in parallel. There are distributions of service and there is the Lord who is glorified by these ministries [ICC].

QUESTION—To whom does ὁ κύριος 'the Lord' refer?

It refers to Jesus Christ [AB, Alf, NTC, TNTC, Vn]. In 12:3 the declaration 'Jesus is Lord' supports this interpretation [AB].

QUESTION—To whom is the διακονία 'service' rendered?

It is rendered to the Lord [EGT, Gdt, Ho, ICC, NTC, TG, TH, Vn; CEV, NLT, TEV]. It is rendered to other members of the Christian community [Lns, TNTC]. Christ indwelling the believer enables him to serve others [TNTC]. It is rendered to the Christian community and through it to the Lord [HNTC].

QUESTION—What is the relationship of 'the Lord' to the 'service'?
1. The Lord is the recipient of the service [CEV, NLT, TEV]: there are a variety of services, but the same Lord is served.
2. The Lord is the one who calls people to the services [NIC, NIGTC]. It is by the authority of the Lord that the service is rendered [Gdt, Ho]. The services are directed and enabled by the Lord [EGT, TNTC].

12:6 **and there-are varieties/distributions of working,[a] but the same God the-(one) working[b] all[c] (things) in all.[d]**

LEXICON— a. ἐνέργημα (LN **42.11**) (BAGD 1. p. 265): 'working' [NIV], 'activity' [AB, BAGD, NTC; NJB, NRSV, REB], 'operation' [Herm, HNTC; KJV], 'work' [NAB], 'result' [ISV, NET], 'distribution of effect' [ICC], 'energy' [Lns], 'deed' [**LN**], 'act' [LN]. This noun is also translated as a phrase: 'ability to perform service' [TEV], 'divine power at work' [TNT], 'what activates effects' [NIGTC]. This noun is also translated as a verb: 'to do' [CEV], 'to work' [NLT].

b. pres. act. participle of ἐνεργέω (LN 42.3, **42.4**) (BAGD 2. p. 265): 'to work' [BAGD, Herm, LN (42.3), NTC; CEV, KJV, NIV], 'to be at work' [NJB, TNT], 'to do work' [NLT], 'to produce' [AB, BAGD], 'to produce results' [ISV, NET], 'to operate' [HNTC], 'to give ability to (someone) for his/her service' [**LN**; TEV], 'to activate' [NRSV], 'to energize' [Lns], 'to be active' [REB], 'to accomplish works' [NAB], 'to cause' [ICC], 'to bring about' [NIGTC], 'to cause to function' [**LN**], 'to grant the ability to do' [LN (42.4)], 'to effect' [BAGD].

c. πᾶς (LN 58.28, 59.23, 63.2): 'all' [Herm, LN (59.23); KJV], 'every' [LN (59.23)], 'every kind of' [LN (58.28)], 'whole' [LN (59.23, 63.2)], 'entire' [LN (63.2)]. The phrase τὰ πάντα 'the all things' is translated 'all things' [AB, HNTC, Lns, NTC], 'all of them' [NAB, NET, NIV, NJB, NRSV, REB], 'all the results' [ISV], 'everything' [NIGTC; CEV], 'every one of them' [ICC], 'the work' [NLT]. 'their particular service' [TEV], not explicit [TNT].

d. πᾶς (See this word just above): 'all' [Herm; KJV, TEV], 'all of us' [CEV, NLT], 'all men' [Herm, HNTC; NIV], 'all people' [AB, NTC], 'everyone' [NIGTC; ISV, NAB, NET, NRSV, REB], 'everybody' [NJB], 'every case' [TNT], 'all ways' [Lns], 'every Christian that manifests them' [ICC].

QUESTION—What is meant by ἐνέργημα 'working'?
It means effective activity [Ed, EGT, NIC2]. It means the effect or result of action [ICC, Rb, Vn] or the effect of energy [Alf, ICC]. It means the ability to perform service [TG, TH]. It is similar to διακονία 'service' of 12:5 but here the focus is on the power to perform this service [TG]. It means something that is worked out [MNTC]. It means a visible expression of power [ICC] or power in action [Gdt, NTC, TNTC]. It is the result of the working of the gifts [Alf].

QUESTION—What relationship is indicated by δέ 'but'

It indicates contrast [AB, Gdt, HNTC, ICC, Lns, NTC; all versions]: varieties of activities, *but* the same God. It contrasts the singleness of the operator and the diversity of operations [ICC].

QUESTION—The first πᾶς 'all' is neuter, meaning 'all things', but to what does it refer?

It refers to the spiritual gifts [Alf, Ed, TNTC]: all gifts. It is close in meaning to gifts [Herm, ICC, NTC], but focuses on the power rather than the endowment. It refers to gifts and ministries [NIC2]. It refers to the whole sphere in which the gifts function [EGT].

QUESTION—The second πᾶς 'all' can either be masculine or neuter. How should it be taken here?

1. It should be taken as a masculine pronoun [AB, Alf, Ed, EGT, Gdt, HNTC, Ho, ICC, MNTC, NCBC, NIC, NIC2, NTC, TNTC, Vn; NIV, NJB, REB, TEV]: all men. It means all who have been given gifts [Alf, ICC]. It means both those who serve and those who are served [Gdt]. It means in all Christians [Ed].
2. It should be taken as a neuter pronoun [Herm, Lns; probably TNT]: all things. It means that God is active in every way [Lns] or in every case [TNT].

DISCOURSE UNIT: 12:7–11 [Alf, NTC]. The topic is gifts for the common good [NTC].

12:7 **But/now the manifestation**[a] **of-the Spirit is-given to-each for**[b] **profit.**[c]

LEXICON—a. φανέρωσις (LN **28.36**) (BAGD p. 853): 'manifestation' [AB, Herm, ICC, Lns, NTC; KJV, NAB, NET, NIV, NJB, NRSV], 'his own manifestation' [HNTC], 'public manifestation' [NIGTC], 'ability to display' [ISV], 'presence…clearly made known' [LN; TEV], 'revelation' [LN], 'announcement, disclosure' [BAGD]. The phrase ἡ ανέρωσις τοῦ πνεύματος 'the manifestation of the Spirit' is translated 'a spiritual gift' [NLT], 'spiritual enlightenment' [TNT], 'the Spirit is seen to be at work' [REB]. This entire clause is translated 'the Spirit has given each of us a special way of serving others' [CEV]. Φανέρωσις denotes making something fully known by revealing it clearly and in detail [LN].

b. πρός with accusative object (LN 89.60): 'for' [AB, NIGTC, NTC; ISV, NAB, NET, NIV, NJB, NRSV, REB, TEV, TNT], 'as a means of' [NLT], 'for the purpose of' [LN, Lns], 'with a view to' [Alf, Ed, EGT, Herm, HNTC, ICC], 'in order to' [Herm, LN], 'for the sake of' [LN], not explicit [CEV]. The phase πρὸς τὸ συμφέρον 'for the thing being advantageous' is translated 'to profit withal' [KJV].

c. pres. act. participle of συμφέρω (BAGD 2.b.γ. p. 780): 'to profit' [KJV], 'to be to someone's advantage' [BAGD], 'to help (the entire church)' [BAGD; NLT], 'to serve others' [CEV], 'to make use of it' [Herm], 'to confer a benefit, to be profitable or useful' [BAGD]. This participle is also translated as a noun phrase: 'the common good' [NTC; ISV, NAB, NIV,

NRSV, TNT], 'the common advantage' [AB, NIGTC], 'the general good' [NJB], 'the good of all' [TEV], 'the benefit' [Lns], 'the benefit of all' [NET], 'some useful purpose' [REB], 'mutual profit' [HNTC], 'some beneficent end' [ICC]. See this word also at 10:23.

QUESTION—What relationship is indicated by δέ 'but/now'?
1. It indicates a contrast [Alf, EGT, Herm, Ho, ICC, NTC; KJV]: but. Although the gifts have the same source, *yet* they have different expressions [Ho]. It indicates a contrast with 'the same' of the last verse. Now it is 'to each' [Alf].
2. It indicates a transition or continuation [HNTC, Lns, TH; NIV]: now. With this new paragraph he sums up the argument so far [HNTC]. From the topic of gifts, he advances to the persons who were given these gifts [Lns].

QUESTION—What words are emphasized in this verse?
The word ἑκάστῳ 'to each' is emphasized [Alf, EGT, NIC2], in this way stressing the diversity of the gifts [NIC2]. The emphasis is on πρὸς τὸ συμφέρον 'for profit' [Herm, My]. Both ἑκάστῳ 'to each' and πρὸς τὸ συμφέρον 'for profit' are emphasized [Ed, ICC, Lns], the one stressing diversity, the other the unity of the gifts [Ed].

QUESTION—How inclusive is ἕκαστος 'to each'?
1. It means to each believer [Ed, Herm, HNTC, Ho, Lns, NCBC, NTC, TH, TNTC]. The long description of the body from 12:12 shows that this includes everyone, those who have gifts as well as those who do not [Lns].
2. It means to each person who receives a gift [My, NIC]. Verses 12:28 and following show that it means only those who receive a gift are meant here [NIC].

QUESTION—Who is the actor of the passive verb δίδοται 'is given', and what is the significance of the present tense?
The implied actor is God [NIC2, NIGTC, NTC]: God gives. The actor is the Holy Spirit [NIC]: the Holy Spirit gives. The actors are the Persons of the Trinity [MNTC]. The present tense indicates indefinite frequency [Ed], or continual impartation [EGT].

QUESTION—What is implied by φανέρωσις 'manifestation'?
It implies spiritual gifts [Herm, HNTC, Lns, NCBC, NIC2, TNTC]. It implies spiritual gifts, services, and activities [Alf]. Paul's focus, however, is not on the gifts but on the revealing of the Spirit's work among them [NIC2].

QUESTION—How are the nouns related in the genitive construction ἡ φανέρωσις του πνεύματος 'the manifestation of the Spirit'?
1. It means that God manifests or reveals the Spirit [NIC2, NTC, TG, TH]. In view of the fact that δίδοται 'is given' has God as its implied agent, and the focus is on revealing the activity of the Spirit through the gifts, it is better to take this as meaning that God is one who reveals [NIC2].

1 CORINTHIANS 12:7

2. It means that the person using the gifts manifests or reveals the Spirit [EGT, ICC, My, NCBC]. Each receives some gift by which he reveals the Spirit [EGT]. It is the gift which reveals the Spirit [ICC, MNTC].
3. It means that the Spirit manifests or reveals himself [Alf, Ed, Gdt, Ho, Lns, Vn]. The Spirit reveals himself by giving the gifts [Gdt]. The Spirit reveals himself in one way in one person, in another way in another [Ho]. The Spirit reveals himself in us by his gift [Lns].

QUESTION—What is meant by πρὸς τὸ συμφέρον 'for profit'?

It means that the benefit of the gift is not primarily for the individual, but for the whole Christian community [AB, Alf, Ed, EGT, Gdt, Herm, HNTC, Ho, ICC, Lns, MNTC, NIC, NIC2, NTC, TG, TH, TNTC]. The purpose of the gifts are for the edification of the church as seen in Ephesians 4:12 [NTC]. The words 'for profit' point to what Paul brings out in 10:23 about the importance of activity being beneficial and edifying [NIC].

DISCOURSE UNIT: 12:8–11 [MNTC, NIGTC]. The topic is the gifts of the Spirit [NIGTC], varieties of spiritual gifts [MNTC].

12:8 For on-one-hand (a) message^a of-wisdom^b is-given to-one (person) through^c the Spirit

LEXICON—a. λόγος (LN 33.98) (BAGD 1.a.β. p. 477): 'message' [AB, LN; ISV, NET, NIV, TEV], 'word' [HNTC, LN, NTC; KJV], 'statement, saying' [LN], 'utterance' [ICC; NJB, NRSV], 'discourse' [NAB], 'power to speak' [TNT], 'speech' [REB], 'articulate utterance' [NIGTC], 'ability to give advice' [NLT], 'expression' [Lns], 'speaking' [BAGD]. This word is also translated as a verb: 'to speak' [Herm; CEV]. The phrase λόγος σοφία 'word of wisdom' is translated 'proclamation of wisdom, speaking wisely' [BAGD]. The word λόγος here means the ability to communicate to others [ICC]. It means the ability to speak [MNTC].

b. σοφία (LN 32.32, 32.37) (BAGD 2. p. 759): 'wisdom' [AB, BAGD, Herm, HNTC, ICC, LN (32.32), Lns, NIGTC, NTC; all versions except REB], 'insight, understanding' [LN (32.37)]. This noun is also translated as an adjective: 'wise' [NLT, REB]. See this word also at 1:17.

c. διά with genitive object (See this word at 11:12): 'through' [AB, Herm, HNTC, ICC, Lns, NTC; NET, NIV, NRSV, REB, TNT], 'by' [ISV, KJV], 'from' [NJB]. The phrase διὰ τοῦ πνεύματος δίδοται 'through the Spirit is given' is translated 'the Spirit gives' [NAB, NLT, TEV], 'God gives through the Spirit' [NIGTC]. This preposition is also translated by a verb: 'to come from' [CEV]. Διά denotes instrumentality here [ICC, Lns]. It denotes that the Spirit is the cause [Herm]. It denotes that the words are produced by the Spirit [Gdt, Rb]. It denotes agency [AB, NTC]. The three prepositions διά 'through', κάτα 'according to', and ἐν 'by' (12:8–9) mean the same thing and are only used for sake of variety [HNTC, NTC].

QUESTION—What relationship is indicated by γάρ 'for'?

It indicates the grounds for using the words 'is given' and 'for profit' of 12:7 [Alf]. It explains what is meant by each person having his own gift [Lns]. It indicates that what follows supports the facts that each has his gift, that the gifts are given by the Spirit and that God gives the gifts for building up the church [Ed]. It illustrates and confirms what precedes [EGT, Ho].

QUESTION—How are the nouns related in the genitive construction λόγος σογίας 'word of wisdom'?

It means a wise word [NLT, REB], a word full of wisdom [NIC, NIC2, Rb, TG, TH; TEV], or a word characterized by wisdom [NIC2], articulate utterance relating to "wisdom" [NIGTC]. It refers to the ability to speak with divine wisdom [NTC], the ability to teach [Herm, HNTC], or reveal [Herm]. It is the ability to communicate wisdom [Ho, ICC], specifically the ability to communicate the Good News as something to be believed [Ho, ICC, Lns]. It is the ability to explain spiritual truths [Ed]. It is speaking about the truth and how to apply it [Gdt, MNTC].

QUESTION—What does Paul mean by σογία 'wisdom'?

Paul means that the true wisdom of God is seen in the crucifixion of Christ (see 2:6–16) [NIC2]. Wisdom is the Good News, the revealed truth in its entirety [Ho]. It is the understanding of God's will and the ability to apply truth to everyday situations [MNTC]. Wisdom is personified in Jesus Christ and seen in the Good News [Lns]. The word implies knowing the truth and being able to apply it [Gdt]. The word mean God's truth internalized in man [EGT].

on-the-other-hand to-another, (a) message of-knowledge[a] (is given) according-to[b] the same Spirit,

LEXICON—a. γνῶσις (LN 28.17) (BAGD 2. p. 164): 'knowledge' [AB, Herm, HNTC, ICC, LN (28.17), Lns, NIGTC, NTC; all versions except NLT, REB], 'what is known' [LN], 'special knowledge' [NLT], 'deepest knowledge' [REB]. Here Christian (supernatural mystical) knowledge is meant [BAGD]. See this word also at 1:5.

b. κατά with accusative object (LN 89.8) (BAGD II.5.a.δ. p. 407): 'according to' [Herm, Lns, NTC; ISV, NET, NRSV], 'according to the leading of' [ICC], 'in accordance with' [AB, HNTC, LN, NIGTC; NJB, TNT], 'by' [KJV], 'by means of' [NIV], 'by the power of' [REB], 'from' [CEV], 'because of, on the basis of, as a result of' [BAGD], 'in relation to' [LN], not explicit [NAB, NLT]. The phrase κατὰ τὸ αὐτὸ πνεῦμα 'according to the same Spirit' is translated 'the same Spirit gives' [TEV]. The change in preposition from διά 'through' to κατά 'according to' is probably intentional. Here knowledge is effective when it agrees with the Spirit [AB]. Κατά has the sense of 'agreeing with' [NIC]. By this we see that the Spirit is a standard that serves to measure or validate a thing [EGT, Gdt, Herm, NIC]. Κατά indicates 'according to the measure of' since the Spirit is the giver [Ed]. Κατά indicates 'according to' the will of the Spirit [Ho].

QUESTION—What does Paul mean by γνῶσις 'knowledge'?

The words σοφία 'wisdom' and γνῶσις 'knowledge' are either synonymous or are difficult to distinguish between [Alf, Herm, HNTC, ICC, Lns, NIC, TNTC], yet the corresponding pronouns 'to one' and 'to another' suggest that a distinction be made between them [Herm]. Paul probably means some kind of revelation [NIC2]. It means insight [Rb]. It means the ability to understand the meaning of God's revelation [MNTC]. It means the ability to understand the Good News [Lns]. The word implies investigation and discovery [Gdt]. The word means the truth of God understood [EGT]. Paul means an intimate personal knowledge of God based on love and God's knowledge of man [NTC].

QUESTION—How are the nouns related in the genitive construction λόγος γνώσεως 'word of knowledge'?

It means a word full of knowledge [NIC, TG, TH; TEV] or a spiritual word of revelation of some kind [NIC2]. It is the ability to effectively declare the truths of the Christianity [AB]. It is the ability to teach [Herm, HNTC] or reveal [Herm]. It is the ability to communicate knowledge, specifically the truths revealed by the apostles and prophets [Ho]. It is the ability to use knowledge to build others up [ICC]. It is the ability to share our understanding of the Good News with others [Lns]. It means speaking about the investigation and discovery of truth [Alf, Ed]. The Spirit enables the person to discover truth from the facts of Scripture and explain those truths to others [MNTC].

12:9 to-another, faith[a] by[b] the same Spirit,

LEXICON—a. πίστις (LN 31.85) (BAGD 2.d.ζ. p. 664): 'faith' [AB, BAGD, Herm, HNTC, LN, Lns, NIGTC, NTC; all versions except CEV, NLT], 'special faith' [NLT], 'great faith' [CEV], 'potent faith' [ICC], 'trust' [LN]. Here 'faith' refers to a special gift of faith as a firm belief in God's power to help people by means of miracles [BAGD]. See this word also at 2:5.

b. ἐν with dative object (See this word at 12:3): 'by' [AB, NIGTC, NTC; ISV, KJV, NET, NIV, NRSV, REB, TNT], 'through' [NAB], 'by means of' [ICC], 'from' [NJB], 'in' [Herm, HNTC, Lns]. The phrase ἐν τῷ αὐτῷ πνεύματι 'by the same Spirit' is translated 'the Spirit has given' [CEV], 'the Spirit gives' [NLT]. This phrase is combined with the phrase ἐν τῷ ἑνὶ πνεύματι 'by the one Spirit' in the following phrase to read 'one and the same Spirit gives' [TEV]. Here ἐν means 'in the power of' [HNTC]. It means 'by' and 'through' as the cause and means [Alf]. It has an instrumental sense in addition to denoting the sphere in which the Spirit works [NIC]. It denotes the element in which something is done [EGT, Vn]. It denotes 'grounded on' the Spirit [EGT]. It has the same meaning as the διά and κατά of 12:8 [HNTC, NTC].

QUESTION—What is meant by πίστις 'faith'?
It means a supernatural assurance that God will act in a powerful way on a given occasion [NIC2]. It means the ability to trust God in spite of obstacles and impossibilities [Gdt, MNTC]. It means a trust that makes it possible for God's power to function through the person who possesses it [AB]. It means faith to perform miracles such as are indicated in Matthew 17:20 or 1 Corinthians 13:2 [Gdt, Herm, Ho, ICC, Lns, NIC, NIC2, NTC, Rb, TG, TNTC, Vn]. It does not mean the faith by which a person becomes a Christian [AB, Gdt, HNTC, Ho, ICC, Lns, NCBC, NIC, NIC2, NTC, Rb, TG, TNTC, Vn]. It means a greater amount of faith than usual [Ho, TH], more like what would enable a man to become a martyr [Ho]. It means a firm trust that God will perform miracles [NTC]. It means a trust in Christ [TH].

and to-another, gifts^a of-healings^b by the one^c Spirit,

TEXT—Instead of ἑνί 'one' some manuscripts read αὐτῷ 'same'. GNT reads ἑνί 'one' with an A rating, indicating that the text is certain. Αὐτῷ 'same' is read by KJV and NAB.

LEXICON—a. χάρισμα (See this word at 12:4): 'gift' [AB, Herm, HNTC, NIGTC, NTC; ISV, KJV, NET, NIV, NJB, NRSV, REB], 'spiritual gift' [TNT]. This plural noun is translated 'manifold gifts' [ICC], 'charismata' [Lns]. 'gift' [NAB], 'power' [CEV, NLT, TEV].
b. ἴαμα (LN **23.138**) (BAGD p. 368): 'healing' [BAGD, Herm, HNTC, ICC, Lns, NIGTC, NTC; all versions except CEV, NLT, TEV], 'the power to heal' [**LN**], 'the capacity to heal' [**LN**]. This noun is also translated as a verb phrase: 'to heal' [TEV], 'to heal the sick' [CEV, NLT]. It is also translated as an adjective: 'healing (gifts)' [AB]. The plural of this noun indicates different kinds of diseases were to be healed [Alf, Ed, Gdt, MNTC].
c. εἷς (LN 60.10) (BAGD 2.a. p. 231): 'one' [Herm, LN, NIGTC; NET, NRSV, REB, TEV, TNT], 'one and the same' [BAGD]. It is emphatic [BAGD]. The phrase τῷ ἑνὶ 'the one' is translated 'the one' [HNTC, ICC, Lns, NTC], 'that one' [ISV, NIV], 'this one' [AB; NJB]. This word focuses on the unity of the diversity of gifts [Ed].

QUESTION—What is meant by ἴαμα 'healing'?
It means miraculous healing [Alf, Ho], of diseases [Ho]. It refers to the ability to heal various kinds of diseases [TH]. It does not mean healing by means of a doctor's skill [Ed, NCBC]. It refers to acts of healing as seen in Acts 4:30 [Rb]. It was a gift possessed by the apostles who instantaneously healed people with a word or with a touch [MNTC].

QUESTION—How are the nouns related in the genitive construction χαρίσματα ἰαμάτων 'gifts of healing'?
It indicates gifts which produce healings [ICC].

QUESTION—What is the significance of the plural 'gifts'?

It signifies that one person does not have a permanent gift but that each gift is complete in itself; and that the gift is given to the person performing the activity, rather than to the person being healed [NIC2]. It signifies that different gifts are necessary to heal different kinds of sickness [Ed, Lns, NIC, TNTC]. It signifies that each gifted person has a disease or group of diseases which he or she could cure, not that one person could cure all diseases [ICC]. The word 'healings' is plural to emphasize the many kinds of afflictions that needed healing [MNTC, NIC].

QUESTION—What is the significance of the variation in the phrases 'by the same Spirit' and 'by the one Spirit'?

There is no difference, the change is only for stylistic reasons [Herm, TH].

QUESTION—What is the significance of the variation in the words ἄλλῳ 'to another' (in 12:8, 9 and 10) and ἑτέρῳ 'to another' (in 12: 9)?

There is no difference, they are used synonymously for variation [HNTC, NIC].

12:10 and to-another, workings^a of-miracles,^b

LEXICON—a. ἐνέργημα (See this word at 12:6): 'working' [Herm, HNTC; KJV, NJB, NRSV], 'performance' [NET], 'power to work' [CEV, TEV], 'power to do' [TNT], 'power to perform' [NLT], 'power' [NAB, NIV, REB], 'energy' [Lns], 'result' [ISV], 'effect' [ICC], 'activity' [AB], 'activity that elicits' [NTC], 'actively effective (deeds of power)' [NIGTC].

b. δύναμις (LN 76.7) (BAGD 4. p. 208): 'miracle' [BAGD, Herm, HNTC, LN, Lns, NTC; KJV, NET, NJB, NLT, NRSV, TEV], 'mighty miracle' [CEV], 'mighty work' [TNT], 'mighty deed' [LN], 'deed of power' [BAGD, NIGTC], 'wonder' [BAGD]. This word is also translated as an adjective modifying ἐνέργημα 'workings': 'miraculous' [ICC; ISV, NAB, NIV, REB], 'miracle-working' [AB].

QUESTION—What is meant by δύναμις 'miracle'?

It means supernatural activities [Ed, Gdt, Ho, ICC, Lns, MNTC, NCBC, NIC2, NTC, Rb, TG, TH, TNTC, Vn] such as: stilling a storm, feeding a multitude [TNTC], driving out demons [Gdt, MNTC, TNTC], making Elymas go blind (Acts 13:11) [Ho, ICC, Rb, TNTC], the deaths of Ananias and Sapphira (Acts 5:1–11) [Ho, TNTC], exorcising of evil spirits [ICC, NIC2], extraordinary exertions (2 Corinthians 11:23) [NIC], turning water into wine (John 2) [NCBC], the raising of Dorcas (Acts 9:36–42) [Gdt, Ho], the deliverance at Malta (Acts 28:1) [Gdt], or healing (Luke 5:17, Acts 19:11) [Ed]. This gift was a distinctive mark of an apostle (2 Corinthians 12:12) [NTC].

and to-another, prophecy,^a

LEXICON—a. προφητεία (LN 33.460, 33.461) (BAGD 2. p. 722): 'prophecy' [Herm, HNTC, LN (33.460), Lns, NIGTC, NTC; ISV, KJV, NAB, NET, NIV, NJB, NRSV], 'gift of prophecy' [AB, BAGD; REB], 'ability to prophesy' [LN (33.461); NLT], 'gift of speaking God's message' [TEV], 'power to preach' [TNT], '(some of us are) prophets' [CEV], 'inspired utterance' [ICC, LN (33.460)], 'to be able to speak inspired messages' [LN (33.461)]. Προφητεία comes from the verb προφητεύω that means 'to speak forth or proclaim' [MNTC].

QUESTION—What is meant by προφητεία 'prophecy'?

Prophesy is a message inspired by the Holy Spirit [Alf, Ed, Gdt, Ho, Lns, MNTC, My, NIC2, NIGTC, Rb, TH, TNTC, Vn]. It may also contain predictions about the future but not necessarily [AB, Ho, ICC, MNTC, NIC2, NTC, Rb, TNTC]. It is intended to edify believers [EGT, Gdt, NIC2]. It is intended to instruct believers [Alf, Ed, Ho, Lns, MNTC, My, NTC]. It is intended to encourage believers [Alf, Gdt, My, NTC]. It is intended to convince people of sin [AB, Ho]. It is spontaneous, intelligible, and is spoken in the assembly of believers [NIC2]. It may reveal secret things of God [Alf, EGT, My]. It is a revelation from God [Ho, NIC]. It may be preaching under the inspiration of God [ICC, Lns, MNTC, TH]. Examples of it may be seen in Agabus (Acts 11:28) and Philips's daughters (Acts 21:9) [TNTC]. It is the ability to proclaim the Word of God. At first it included new revelation, but since the completion of the Scriptures it is proclaiming what has been revealed in Scripture [MNTC].

and to-another, discernings[a] of-spirits,

LEXICON—a. διάκρισις (LN **30.112**) (BAGD 1. p. 185): 'discerning' [Lns; KJV], 'discernment' [NET, NRSV], 'ability to distinguish between' [BAGD; ISV, TNT], 'distinguishing' [Herm], 'power to distinguish' [HNTC; NAB, NJB], 'ability to judge the genuineness of' **[LN]**, 'ability to discriminate among/between' [AB, ICC], 'ability to make judgments, ability to decide' [LN]. This noun is also translated as a verb: 'to distinguish between' [NIV], 'to distinguish' [NTC]. The phrase διακρίσεις πνευμάτων 'discernings of spirits' is translated 'the ability to distinguish true spirits from false' [REB], 'the ability to tell the difference between gifts that come from the Spirit and those that do not' [TEV], 'the ability to know whether it is really the Spirit of God or another spirit that is speaking' [NLT], 'to recognize when God's Spirit is present' [CEV], 'discernment of what is "of the Spirit"' [NIGTC]. Διάκρισις indicates the distinguishing between the genuine and the spurious [MNTC].

QUESTION—Who are the πνεῦμα 'spirit(s)'?

They refer to the sudden inspirations of the Holy Spirit as they come on a prophet [Gdt]. They refer to the Holy Spirit and other possible sources of inspiration [HNTC]. They refer to prophetic utterances [NIC2]. They refer to the Holy Spirit and demons [Alf, HNTC, MNTC, NTC, TNTC]. They are spirits of people and evil spirits [AB].

QUESTION—What is meant by διακρίσεις πνευμάτων 'discernings of spirits'?

An example of this gift is seen in Paul's recognition of the spirit that was inspiring Elymas in Acts 13:8–10 [EGT]. It is the gift of being able to recognize what spirit is inspiring a person to speak, that is, whether it is the Spirit of God or an evil spirit [Gdt, HNTC, Ho, NIC2, TNTC, Vn], or whether it is the person himself who is speaking [Gdt, Ho]. It is the gift of being able to judge between good and evil spirits [NIC, TNTC]. This was an intuitive discernment, it did not come from any kind of testing [ICC]. It is not limited to the testing of prophecy only, but includes the recognition of the identity of what spirit is inspiring various kinds of activity [Ed, ICC, Lns, NTC]. It means the ability to tell if the particular gift was inspired by the Holy Spirit or by evil spirits or was from the person himself/herself [Rb]. It is the gift of being able to judge between the activity of the Holy Spirit, the activity of evil spirits [AB, Alf, MNTC, TH], and the activity of the person himself [AB, Alf]. 1 John 4:1 reads, "try the spirits, whether they are of God; for many false prophets are gone out into the world". The gift of discernment made it possible to identify and expose these [Ho, NIC]. It concerns distinguishing false information, counterfeit miracles, and false teachers from the true [NTC]. It is the ability to distinguish between the activity of the Holy Spirit and mere human attempts and the ability to discern the various ways the Holy Spirit is working [NIGTC].

to-another, kinds[a] of-tongues,[b]

LEXICON—a. γένος (LN 58.23) (BAGD 4. p. 156): 'kind' [AB, BAGD, Herm, LN], 'variety' [Lns], 'class' [BAGD], 'type' [LN], 'gift' [NAB], 'species' [NIGTC]. This plural noun is also translated 'different kinds' [ICC, NTC; CEV, NET, NIV, TNT], 'various kinds' [HNTC; ISV, NRSV, REB], 'diverse kinds' [KJV]. This noun is also translated as an adjective: 'different' [NJB], 'strange' [TEV], 'unknown' [NLT].

b. γλῶσσα (LN 33.3, 33.2) (BAGD 3. p. 162): 'tongue' [AB, Herm, HNTC, LN (33.3), Lns, NIGTC, NTC; all versions except CEV, NLT], 'Tongue' [ICC], 'language' [LN (33.2); CEV, NLT], 'ecstatic language, ecstatic speech' [LN (33.3)], 'dialect, speech' [LN (33.2)]. Γλῶσσα refers to speech which has the form of language but requires an inspired interpreter to know its meaning [LN (33.3)]. It refers here to speech in religious ecstasy [BAGD]. Tongues were highly valued in Corinth because they were unintelligible and gave to the speaker the command of a language of heaven (see 13:1) [Herm].

QUESTION—Is γλῶσσα 'tongue' a foreign language or a spiritual language?

1. It is a spiritual language [AB, EGT, Gdt, NIC, NIC2, NTC, TNTC]. It is a form of speech that is inspired by the Holy Spirit and unintelligible without translation, and it is addressed to God [AB, NIC2, NTC, TNTC]. This was mystical utterance different from all forms of known language [EGT]. Paul compares it to the language of angels 13:1 [Gdt, NIC2]. It

was not an ecstatic language or out of control of the speaker [NIC2]. It was different from the 'tongues' in Acts 2 where it means speaking in foreign languages [EGT, TNTC]. 'Tongues' is plural to indicate that this miraculous language was spoken at different times, and 'kinds' is plural to show that with the same person the tongue did not always have the same character [NIC].
2. It was an ecstatic language [Alf, ICC, NIGTC, Rb, TG, TH]. It is a form of speech that is not an intelligible language but consists of strange sounds springing from an emotional and spiritual experience [TG]. It was an ecstatic language in which the Holy Spirit enabled the speaker to express his/her otherwise inexpressible emotions [ICC, Rb]. It is the language of the unconscious self and unintelligible to others and to the speaker unless interpreted [NIGTC].
3. It is an actual foreign language [Ho, Lns, MNTC]. The meaning of this word is seen in Acts 2 where the apostles were enabled by the Holy Spirit to speak the foreign languages of those various peoples who had come to Jerusalem without having learned them [Ho, Lns]. The plural form 'tongues' refers to real languages used to bring a supernatural message to people whom God wanted to reach and was a sign to verify the gospel and apostolic authority. The singular form in chapter 14 refers to spurious ecstatic utterances common in pagan religions [MNTC].
4. It can be either a foreign language or a spiritual language. It is Spirit-inspired prayer and praise in either a language unknown to the speaker or in a spiritual language [Alf, Ed, NCBC]. It was unintelligible to both speaker and hearer, but could have included those languages which were understood by some hearers [NCBC].

and to-another, interpretation[a] of-tongues;
LEXICON—a. ἑρμηνεία (LN 33.147) (BAGD p. 310): 'interpretation' [AB, BAGD, HNTC, ICC, **LN**, Lns, NTC; ISV, KJV, NET, NIV, NJB, NRSV], 'interpreting' [Herm, LN; NAB], 'ability to interpret' [NLT, REB, TNT], 'ability to explain' [TEV], 'intelligible articulation of what is spoken' [NIGTC], 'translation' [BAGD, LN]. This entire phrase is translated 'and still others can tell what these languages mean' [CEV].
QUESTION—What was the gift of interpretation of tongues?
1. When the tongues are not foreign languages.
It could not be a learned skill [TG]. The gift was needed for a spiritual language that had no human characteristics and was unintelligible to ordinary people [NIC]. Rather than 'interpret', it means to put into words what the tongue speaker said [NIC2]. It was the power to give a meaning to what was ecstatically said [EGT].
2. When the tongues are known foreign languages.
If the person using a foreign language understood it, he needed a distinct gift to make himself an instrument of the Holy Spirit in its interpretation. If he did not understand that language, he would need an interpreter who

did and had such a gift [Ho]. The gift of interpretation utilized a natural ability in one who knew the language and sanctified it and used it for spiritual ends [Lns].

12:11 But^a the one and the same Spirit produces^b all these-things

LEXICON—a. δέ (See this word at 11:2): 'but' [Herm, ICC; CEV, KJV, NAB, NJB, REB, TEV], 'now' [Lns], not explicit [AB, HNTC, NIGTC, NTC; ISV, NET, NIV, NLT, NRSV, TNT]. Δέ shows the contrast between the many gifts and the single source for them all [Ho, ICC].

b. pres. act. indic. of ἐνεργέω (See this word at 12:6): 'to produce' [AB, Lns; ISV, NAB, NET], 'to work' [NTC; KJV], 'to be at work in' [NJB], 'to do' [CEV, TEV], 'to put into operation' [HNTC], 'to activate' [NIGTC], not explicit [NLT]. This active voice is also translated as a passive: 'to be activated by' [NRSV], 'to be caused by' [ICC]. It is also translated as a phrase: 'to be the work of' [Herm; NIV, TNT], 'to be the activity of' [REB]. This is the same verb used about God in 12:6 [Ho, ICC, NIC2, Rb, Vn].

QUESTION—What is the function of this verse?

It functions to sum up all that has been said so far in 12:4–10 [Ed, EGT, NIC2]. It functions as an emphatic conclusion to 12:4–10 [TH]. It functions to restate and stress 12:4–7 and stands as a corrective over against thinking that one gift is better than another [Lns]. It functions to sum up and restate that all the gifts were gifts of one Spirit [NIC]. It functions to emphatically stress the variety of the gifts along with their unity and individual value [EGT]. It functions to stress the action of the Holy Spirit in the distribution of the gifts [Ed].

QUESTION—What is the significance of the words τὸ ἕν καὶ τὸ αὐτὸ πνεῦμα 'the one and the same Spirit'?

It is a more emphatic way of saying 'the same Spirit' as used in 12:4 and 8 [TH]: God's Spirit alone. The same phrase was used in 12:9 but here emphasizes the identity of the subject [TG]. Paul stresses that all nine gifts have one single source implying that the Spirit forbids all boasting about what he or she has received [NTC]. Since there is one giver of all the gifts, they should not be used to produce rivalry among the recipients [TNTC].

QUESTION—What word is stressed in this clause?

The word πάντα 'all' is emphatic [ICC, NIC2, TNTC, Vn]. There is a contrast between the many gifts and a single source [ICC]. This serves to emphasize the variety of the gifts [TNTC]. The antecedent of πάντα ταῦτα 'all these' is the preceding list of gifts [HNTC, Lns, NIC, NIC2, TH].

distributing^a individually^b to-each-one just-as he wills.^c

LEXICON—a. pres. act. participle of διαιρέω (LN 57.91) (BAGD p. 183): 'to distribute' [HNTC, ICC, LN; NAB, NET, NJB, NLT, REB, TNT], 'to divide' [LN; KJV], 'to allot' [NRSV], 'to give' [CEV, ISV, NIV, TEV], 'to assign' [Herm], 'to apportion' [AB, BAGD, Lns, NIGTC, NTC].

b. ἴδιος (LN **92.21**) (BAGD 4. p. 370): 'individually' [AB, HNTC, **LN**, NIGTC, NTC; NRSV, TNT], 'severally' [Lns; KJV], 'to each in particular' [Herm], 'separately' [LN], 'singly' [ICC], 'privately, by oneself' [BAGD], not explicit [CEV, ISV, NAB, NET, NIV, NLT, TEV]. This adverb is also translated as a noun: '(to each) individual' [NJB, REB]. See this word also at 11:21.

c. pres. pass. (deponent = act.) indic. of βούλομαι (LN 25.3, 30.56) (BAGD 2.b. p. 146): 'to will' [HNTC, ICC, LN (25.3), Lns, NIGTC; KJV, NAB, TNT], 'to want' [LN (25.3); ISV], 'to wish' [AB, BAGD; TEV], 'to decide' [CEV, NET], 'to choose' [NRSV], 'to determine' [NIV], 'to desire' [LN (25.3), NTC], 'to plan, to intend, to purpose' [LN (30.56)]. The phrase καθὼς βούλεται 'just as he wills' is translated 'what he wants' [ISV], 'at will' [NJB, REB], 'whatever he pleases' [Herm].

QUESTION—What is the significance of ἰδίᾳ ἑκάστῳ 'individually to each one'?

Ἰδίᾳ 'individually' implies that the gift each receives is his own [HNTC, NTC]. Ἰδίᾳ ἑκάστῳ 'individually to each one' indicates in a way suitable to that person [EGT, Lns]. It recalls the word ἑκάστῳ 'to each one' of 12:7 but is more emphatic here: 'to each individual' [TH]. It implies that no person is left out of the distribution of gifts [HNTC, NTC] and no one receives all the gifts [NTC]. The addition of the word ἰδίᾳ 'individually' stresses the individual nature of the Holy Spirit's attention to each person [EGT, NIC2]. The words 'to each' are strongly stressed [Herm].

QUESTION—What is implied by βούλεται 'he wills'?

It implies that the Holy Spirit is a person with a will [Ed, EGT, Gdt, Ho, ICC, NTC, TNTC, Vn].

QUESTION—What are the implications of the clause, 'distributing individually to each one just as he wills'?

It should exclude all pride [AB, Ed, Gdt, ICC, Rb], and envy on the part of the recipients [Ed, Gdt]. It should exclude placing more value on one gift above another [NIC]. It should exclude party faction [Rb].

DISCOURSE UNIT: 12:12–31 [ICC, NIGTC, NTC, TG, TNTC, Vn; CEV, ISV, NET, TEV]. The topic is one body with many parts [ICC, NTC, TG; CEV, TEV], different members in one body [NET], diversity in unity [TNTC; ISV], the image of the body of Christ [NIGTC].

DISCOURSE UNIT: 12:12–31a [GNT, NIC, TH; NAB, NIV, NLT]. The topic is an illustration of Christian unity [NIC], the analogy of the body [NAB], one body with many members [GNT; NIV, NLT].

DISCOURSE UNIT: 12:12–30 [Alf, Vn; NJB]. The topic is the analogy of the body.

DISCOURSE UNIT: 12:12–26 [AB, NCBC]. The topic is analogue: the body and its parts.

DISCOURSE UNIT: 12:12–20 [EGT]. The topic is the one body of many members.

DISCOURSE UNIT: 12:12–19 [MNTC]. The topic is unified and diversified.

DISCOURSE UNIT: 12:12–14 [NIC2]. The topic is the body: diversity in unity.

DISCOURSE UNIT: 12:12–13 [AB, NTC]. The topic is the nature of the body of Christ [AB], the body and the Spirit [NTC].

12:12 **For just-as the body is one^a and has many parts,^b**

LEXICON—a. εἷς (See this word at 12:9): 'one' [AB, Herm, HNTC, Lns, NIGTC, NTC; ISV, KJV, NAB, NET, NLT, NRSV, REB, TEV], 'a unit' [NIV], 'a unity' [NJB, TNT], 'one whole' [ICC], not explicit [CEV].

b. μέλος (LN 8.9, 63.17) (BAGD 1. p. 501): 'part' [AB, BAGD; CEV, ISV, NIV, NJB, NLT, TEV, TNT], 'member' [BAGD, Herm, HNTC, LN (8.9, 63.17), Lns, NTC; KJV, NAB, NET, NRSV], 'organ' [ICC], 'limbs and organs' [NIGTC; REB], 'body part' [LN (8.9)].

QUESTION—What relationship is indicated by γάρ 'for'?

It indicates the grounds for the point of 12:4–11, that there are various gifts but one Spirit [Lns, NIC2]. It indicates the grounds for using the phrase 'one and the same Spirit' of 12:11 [Alf]. It illustrates the idea of unity in diversity seen in the preceding verses [Ho].

QUESTION—What is the significance of the repetition of σῶμα 'body' twice in the verse and to what does it refer?

It functions to emphasize the unity of the parts in one body [Alf, ICC]. The body refers to a physical body [TH].

and all the parts of-the body being many are one body, so also (is) Christ;

QUESTION—What is the significance of the emphatic πάντα 'all (the parts)' and the repetition of the words ἕν 'one' and πολλά 'many' in the phrase 'the body is *one* and has *many* parts, and *all* the parts of the body being *many* are *one* body'?

They function to emphasize the extent of the Holy Spirit's working in contrast to the tendency of the Corinthians to form parties and focus on gifts [EGT].

QUESTION—What is the meaning of ὁ Χριστός 'Christ'?

It means the Church as the body of Christ [AB, Alf, Ed, EGT, Herm, HNTC, Ho, ICC, NCBC, NIC, NIC2, NTC, Rb, TG, TNTC, Vn]. This is evident from 12:27 'Now you are the body of Christ...' [NIC, NIC2, Vn]. This is also seen in 6:15 'your bodies are members of Christ himself' [Alf]. This is also seen in Acts 9:4 'Saul, Saul, why do you persecute me?' [NTC]. Here Christ and the church are joined together as a unit [Lns]. This is a figure known as metonymy where a part is named while intending the whole. Here Christ is named for the body of Christ [EGT, NIC2, NTC]. It means that Christ the head has a body consisting of parts (members who have gifts) like the different part of a human body [Rb]. 'Christ' means the personal glorified Christ [Gdt].

QUESTION—Who are the parts of 'Christ'?

All Christians are the parts of Christ's body [AB, Alf, EGT, NTC, Rb, TNTC].

QUESTION—If the image is the body and its parts, and the topic is Christ and the church, what is the point of similarity.

The point of similarity is that there is unity in diversity [NIC].

12:13 **For also we all were-baptized^a in/by^b one Spirit into^c one body,**

LEXICON—a. aorist pass. indic. of βαπτίζω (See this word at 10:2): 'to be baptized' [AB, Herm, HNTC, ICC, Lns, NIGTC, NTC; all versions except CEV, REB, TNT]. The phrase ἐβαπτίσθημεν εἰς 'we were baptized into' is translated 'by our baptism we all became' [TNT], 'we were brought into one body by baptism' [REB]. This passive is also translated actively: '(God's Spirit) baptized (each of us)' [CEV].

b. ἐν with dative object (LN 89.119): 'in' [Herm, HNTC, LN (89.119); NAB, NET, NJB, NRSV, REB, TNT], 'by' [AB, NIGTC, NTC; ISV, KJV, NIV, NLT, TEV], 'by means of' [ICC], 'in union with' [LN, Lns], 'joined closely to, one with' [LN]. This preposition is also translated as an agent and left implicit: 'God's Spirit baptized each of us' [CEV]. Ἐν here denotes 'with' [MNTC, TNTC]. See this word also at 12:3.

c. εἰς with accusative object (LN 84.22): 'into' [AB, Herm, LN, NIGTC, NTC; all versions except CEV, TNT], 'unto' [Lns]. This preposition is also translated by a phrase: 'so as to become (one body)' [HNTC, NIC2], 'to become (one body)' [TNT], 'to make someone part of something' [CEV], 'in order to form (one body)' [ICC]. Εἰς here indicates 'so as to form' [Ed, Ho, ICC, TG]. It indicates result, that is, it resulted in making us one body [Gdt, Lns]. It indicates motion from outside to inside the body of Christ. For Paul becoming a part of the Body of Christ is the same as becoming a Christian [NTC].

QUESTION— What relationship is indicated by γάρ 'for'?

It explains the words 'the body is one' of 12:12. It is because the Corinthians' common experience of the Spirit unites them as one [NIC2]: the body is one, *you see,* we all are baptized into one body. It explains the words 'so also is Christ' of 12:12 [Lns, NIC]: so also is Christ, you see, we all are baptized into one body. It explains how it can be said that Christ is a body [HNTC]. It indicates another reason why the many are one [ICC]. It indicates the reason why the comparison between the human body and Christ is valid [Gdt]. It indicates that the following proves how the church is one [Ho].

1 CORINTHIANS 12:13

QUESTION—Should ἐβαπτίσθημεν 'we were baptized' be taken literally or figuratively?

1. It is literal and refers to baptism in water [AB, Alf, Ed, EGT, Gdt, HNTC, ICC, Lns, NIC, TH, Vn]. Paul refers to Christian baptism which symbolizes the regenerating work of the Holy Spirit [EGT].
2. It is figurative and refers to baptism in, with, or by the Spirit [Ho, MNTC, NCBC, NIC2, NTC, Rb, TNTC]: Christ baptized us with the Spirit. Paul is referring to conversion in terms of receiving of the Spirit [NIC2, NTC]. Paul's focus here is not baptism but 'the Spirit' which he repeats in both clauses. If he were referring to water baptism he would have either used 'baptism' alone or have added 'in water'. Here he adds 'in the one Spirit' [NIC2]. It refers to baptism by Christ with the Holy Spirit and is in effect the equivalent of salvation [MNTC]. It refers to the baptism in the Holy Spirit referred to in John 1:33 where John says, "the one who sent me to baptize with water told me, 'the man on whom you see the Spirit come down and remain is he who will baptize with the Holy Spirit'." The baptism with the Holy Spirit is spiritual regeneration. It is not by baptism with water, but by the Holy Spirit that we become part of the body of Christ [Ho]. Paul is referring to the spiritual reality which was symbolized by water baptism [TNTC].

QUESTION—What relationship is indicated by ἐν 'in/by/with/in union with' in the phrase ἐν ἑνὶ πνεύματι ἡμεῖς...ἐβαπτισθημεν 'in one Spirit we...were baptized'?

1. It indicates location or the element in which something takes place [EGT, HNTC, ICC, NCBC, NIC2, TNTC; NAB, NET, NJB, NRSV, REB, TNT]: We were baptized in the Spirit. Nowhere else in the NT does the word 'baptize' with the dative case denote agency. It rather denotes the element in which a person is baptized. We were baptized/immersed in one Spirit so as to become one body. This happened at conversion when we received the Spirit [NIC2]. It indicates the person in whom we were all baptized [NCBC]. We were baptized by means of one Spirit in order to form one body [ICC]. Christ baptizes with the one Spirit, giving us new life and placing us into the one body. Baptism with the one Spirit makes the church one Body [MNTC]. We were literally baptized and this seal of personal salvation placed us in union with the one Spirit, introducing us into the one body [EGT].
2. It indicates agency [AB, NIGTC; CEV, ISV, KJV, NIV, NLT, TEV]: We were baptized by the Spirit. 'God's Spirit baptized each of us and made us part of the body of Christ' [CEV].
3. It indicates instrument or means [Gdt, Ho, MNTC, NIC]: By means of the one Spirit, into which they had all been baptized, they now find themselves fused into one spiritual body [Gdt]. We were baptized by Christ with the Spirit. Any communication of the Spirit is called baptism, so by the communication of the Spirit we are made members by Christ [Ho]. The baptizer is the Son and the agent of the baptism is the Holy

Spirit. By one Spirit we are baptized so as to become incorporated into one body. When spiritual regeneration takes place, they enter the body of Christ, that is, the Church [NTC]. When we were baptized, by the one Spirit we became one body [NIC].

4. It indicates close association. We were baptized in vital connection with the Spirit who creates a new spiritual life. John 3:5 shows this where it reads, "…born of water and the Spirit…" [Lns].

whether Jews or Greeks whether slaves[a] or free[b] (persons),

LEXICON—a. δοῦλος (LN 87.76) (BAGD 1.b. p. 205): 'slave' [AB, BAGD, Herm, HNTC, ICC, LN, Lns, NIGTC, NTC; all versions except KJV], 'bond' [KJV], 'bondservant' [LN].

b. ἐλεύθερος (LN 87.84) (BAGD 1. p. 250): 'free' [AB, BAGD, Herm, HNTC, Lns, NTC; all versions except NJB, TNT], 'free person' [LN, NIGTC], 'free man' [ICC, LN; NJB, TNT].

QUESTION—What is the function of this clause?

It functions to emphasize the many becoming one and to show that the distinctions of race and social status have no significance in view of their common life in the Spirit [NIC2]. It functions to show how varied the members are and how close the oneness of the body (Galatians 3.28; Col. 3.11) [ICC].

and all we-were-made-to-drink[a] one Spirit.

TEXT—Some manuscripts include εἰς 'into' before ἕν 'one'. GNT does not mention this variant. Εἰς 'into' is included by KJV.

LEXICON—a. aorist pass. indic. of ποτίζω (LN 23.35) (BAGD 1. p. 695): 'to be made to drink' [BAGD, Lns, NTC; KJV, NET, NRSV], 'to be given (something) to drink' [AB, HNTC, LN; NAB, NIV, NJB, REB, TEV, TNT], 'to be given to drink one's fill' [NIGTC], 'to be made to drink deeply of' [ICC], 'to be privileged to drink' [ISV], 'to be imbued with' [BAGD, Herm]. This passive voice is translated actively: 'to drink' [CEV], 'to receive' [NLT].

QUESTION—To what does ποτίζω 'to be made to drink' refer?

1. It refers to the same thing as 'being baptized in one Spirit into one body' [EGT, HNTC, ICC, Lns, MNTC, NIC, NIC2, Rb, TNTC]. The figure of drinking symbolizes a very close association as is seen in John 6:53 where Jesus talks of drinking his blood. This refers here to being united closely with the Spirit [NIC]. This is an instance of Semitic parallelism where both statements refer to the same concept and signify the conversion experience through the receiving of the Spirit [NIC2]. This couples with baptism to refer to the same experience, since in baptism, the Spirit surrounds them from the outside; in drinking, the Spirit is absorbed into their beings [EGT, HNTC, Rb]. Baptism in union with the Spirit means being made to drink the Spirit (John 7:37–39, 4:14) [Lns]. Being born again we become a part of Christ's body but we also have the Holy Spirit placed in us [MNTC]. 'To drink' means very close communion [NIC].

2. It refers to the same thing as 'being baptized in one Spirit' but the verb does not refer to drinking but to watering [Ed, ICC, NTC]. Ἐποτίσθημεν can either mean 'were given one Spirit to drink' or 'were watered with one Spirit'. The first meaning would refer to the Lord's Supper. Here, however, it refers to being watered and carries the idea of abundance, that in baptism the Spirit is given so profusely that we receive all the gifts and powers as well [Ed]. When a person becomes a part of the body of Christ he is saturated with the Holy Spirit who then flows out of him producing the fruit of the Spirit (John 4:10; 7:38–39) [NTC].
3. It indicates a separate event [Gdt, Ho, TG, TH, Vn]. Mark 1:8 states, "I baptize you with water, but he will baptize you with the Holy Spirit." This coupled with John 7:37–39 may refer to the gift of the Holy Spirit [TH]. It may have reference to the Lord's Supper but the translation should bring out that it is figurative of having the Holy Spirit in our hearts [TG]. It refers to the giving of the gifts of the Spirit with the laying on of hands after baptism (Acts 8:17, 19:6). The following focus on the diversity of the gifts fits well with this interpretation [Gdt]. Baptism signifies the beginning of the Christian life, this partaking of 'the spiritual rock' (10:4) refers to the Spirit's role in maintaining of the Christian life [Vn]. Drinking the Spirit signifies receiving the Spirit. By doing this we become parts of the one body of Christ [Ho]. Drinking brings to mind John 7:37–39 where in reference to drinking, the Spirit is promised to those who believed on Jesus [NCBC].

QUESTION—Who is the actor of the passive ἐποτίσθημεν 'we were made to drink'?

The actor is God [Lns, TG, TH]: God made us drink. Christ is the actor [MNTC]: Christ made us drink. He not only put us into his body but he put the Holy Spirit into us [MNTC].

DISCOURSE UNIT: 12:14–21 [AB]. The topic is the interrelationship of parts of the body.

DISCOURSE UNIT: 12:14–20 [NTC]. The topic is the physical body.

12:14 **For indeed/also**[a] **the body**[b] **is not one part but many.**
LEXICON—a. καί (See this word at 11:19): 'indeed' [Herm, NTC; NJB, NRSV], 'also' [Lns], 'in fact' [AB; NET], 'I repeat' [ICC], not explicit [HNTC, NIGTC; all versions except NET, NJB, NRSV]. This is the intensive use of καί 'indeed' as in 13:2 [NIC2].
b. σῶμα (LN 8.1) (BAGD 1.b. p. 799): 'body' [AB, Herm, HNTC, ICC, LN, Lns, NIGTC, NTC; all versions except TNT], 'human body' [ICC; TNT], 'living body' [BAGD]. Σῶμα refers here to the physical body in general, not to any one body in particular [HNTC, TH].

QUESTION—What is the function of this verse?

It functions to state the theme of what follows [Lns]. The negative-positive restatement 'not one, but many' functions to indicate the thrust of his whole argument at this point [NIC2].

QUESTION—What relationship is indicated by γάρ 'for'?

It adds a further reason to 12:13 for the statement 'so also is Christ' of 12:12 [NIC]: so also is Christ...because the body is not one part but many. It indicates another reason for the unity and diversity of the body [ICC]. It indicates the reason why the Corinthians should not expect to have identical gifts [HNTC]. It indicates the reason for diversity in unity [Alf]. It indicates an expansion on the idea in 12:12 that the body is not one part but many [NIC2]. It indicates that this verse resumes the idea presented in 12:12 that there are many parts and one body [NTC]. It proves that the diversity of gifts is necessary to the unity of the church [Ho]. It indicates another example of the unity of the body [My]. It functions to show that Paul will explain further [Lns]. It indicates that this verse will explain the reference to 'we all' in 12:13 and that the plural refers to the local church [Vn].

QUESTION—What is the function of the negative statement οὐκ ἔστιν ἓν μέλος ἀλλὰ πολλά, 'is not one part but many'?

It functions to bring out the major focus of his argument [NIC2].

DISCOURSE UNIT: 12:15–26 [Gdt, NIC2]. The topic is a twofold application of the metaphor.

12:15 **If the foot should-say, "Because I-am not (a) hand, I-am not of^a the body,"**

LEXICON—a. ἐκ with genitive object (LN 63.20) (BAGD 4.a.δ. p. 236): 'of' [NTC; KJV], '(a) part of' [LN, Lns; CEV, ISV, NET, NLT], 'one of, one among' [LN]. The phrase εἰμὶ ἐκ 'I am of' is translated 'I belong to' [AB, BAGD, Herm, HNTC, NIGTC; NAB, NIV, NJB, NRSV, REB, TEV, TNT], 'I count as part of' [ICC]. See this word at 11:8 and 11:12.

not because-of^a this is-it not of the body?

LEXICON—a. παρά with accusative object (LN **89.25**) (BAGD III.5. p. 611): 'because of' [**LN**, NIGTC; NET], 'for' [NJB]. The phrase παρὰ τοῦτο 'by this' is translated 'for that/this reason' [AB, BAGD, Lns, NTC; NIV, TNT], 'therefore' [KJV, NAB]. This entire clause is translated 'that would not keep it from being a part of the body' [TEV], 'that does/would not make it any less a part of the body' [NLT, NRSV], 'it belongs to the body none the less' [REB], 'wouldn't the foot still belong to the body?' [CEV], 'that doesn't make it any less a part of the body, does it?' [ISV], 'yet it does belong to the body all the same' [Herm], 'saying this will not mean that it does not belong to the body' [HNTC], 'not for all it can say does it cease to belong to the body' [ICC].

QUESTION—What is the focus of the analogy between the foot and hand and the ear and eye? [Note: because of the similarity of 12:15 and 16 these following questions apply to both].
   1. The focus is on the relative value of each, the foot and ear being inferior to the hand and eye respectively [AB, Ed, EGT, Gdt, Ho, ICC, MNTC, NIC, NTC, TNTC, Vn]. Paul's point is that one member should not be envious of another's gift [NTC]. He focuses on the dissatisfaction of the members with their roles or gifts [Ed, Ho, ICC, My, Vn]. The person with an inferior gift has no right to envy one who has a superior gift because they are both part of Christ's body [Ed].
   2. The focus is on the claim of the foot and ear that they are not part of the body [Herm, HNTC, Lns, NIC2]. Paul's intent is against those in the Corinthian church who would separate themselves from the assembly [Herm]. There is no reference here to inferiority. The point is the need for all parts of the body to be present for it to be complete [NIC2]. No matter how much a part complains it remains a member of the body [Lns].

QUESTION—If the foot, hand, ear, and eye in relation to the body form the image, and the various spiritual gifts in relation to the Church form the topic, what is the point of similarity?

The point of similarity is the notion of essentiality; just as the parts are essential to the body, so the gifts are essential to the Church [NCBC].

QUESTION—Should this clause be taken as a question or a statement?
   1. It should be taken as a statement [AB, EGT, Herm, HNTC, ICC, Lns, MNTC, My, NIC2, NTC, Rb, TG, TNTC; NET, NIV, NJB, NLT, NRSV, REB, TEV, TNT]: If the foot should say, "Because I am not the hand, I am not of the body," it is not part of the body for this reason. This being a present general condition argues against its being an interrogative without further internal evidence [NIC2].
   2. It should be taken as a question [Alf, Ed, Gdt, NIGTC; CEV, ISV, KJV, NAB]: If the foot should say, "Because I am not the hand, I am not of the body," is it for this reason not part of the body? Although a question, it should be a kind of half question that expects a negative reply, contrary to the indications of grammar [Ed]: it is not, is it? Although these take the clause as a question, the end result is the same as those who take it as a statement [NIGTC].

QUESTION—What is the function of this clause either as a rhetorical question or a statement?

It functions to show the absurdity of the claim of the hand and ear [AB, Ho]. It shows how foolish it would be to make such a claim [Lns]. Paul intends to show that these attitudes are ridiculous [AB].

12:16 **And if the ear should-say, "Because I-am not (an) eye, I-am not of the body," is-it not by this not of the body?**
QUESTION—What is the function of this verse?
It functions as a repetition of 12:15 with different parts and as such emphasizes Paul's point; the member remains a part of the body no matter what it may say. This duplication serves to emphasize the point [Lns].

12:17 **If all the body (were) (an) eye[a], where (would-be) the hearing?[b]**
LEXICON—a. ὀφθαλμός (LN 8.23, **24.16**) (BAGD 1. p. 599): 'eye' [AB, BAGD, Herm, HNTC, LN (8.23), Lns, NIGTC, NTC; all versions], 'one monstrous eye' [ICC], 'a matter of sight' [**LN** (24.16)], 'seeing' [LN (24.16)]. The word can mean 'capacity to see' as a figurative extension of meaning of 'eye' [LN]. [Note: The choice to translate 'a matter of sight' instead of 'an eye' may be dictated by the use of 'hearing' in place of 'ear', and 'sense of smell' in place of 'nose' in what follows.]
b. ἀκοή (LN **24.53**) (BAGD 1.a. or c. p. 30): 'hearing' [AB, Herm, HNTC, ICC, **LN**, Lns, NIGTC, NTC; KJV, NAB, NET, NJB, NRSV], 'sense of hearing' [ISV, NIV], 'ability to hear' [LN], 'ear' [BAGD, LN; TNT], 'faculty of hearing' [BAGD]. The phrase ποῦ ἡ ἀκοή 'where (would be) the hearing?' is translated 'how could it hear?' [REB, TEV], 'then how would you hear?' [NLT], 'we couldn't hear a thing' [CEV].

If all (were) hearing, where (would-be) the sense-of-smell?[a]
LEXICON—a. ὄσφρησις (LN **24.71**) (BAGD p. 587): 'sense of smell' [AB, BAGD, Herm, **LN**, NTC; ISV, NIV, NRSV, TNT], 'smelling' [HNTC, ICC, Lns, NTC; KJV, NAB, NET, NJB], 'nose' [BAGD, NIGTC]. The phrase ποῦ ἡ ὄσφρησις 'where (is) the sense of smell?' is translated 'how could you smell anything?' [NLT], 'how could (it) smell?' [**LN**, REB, TEV], 'we couldn't smell a thing' [CEV]. The word can mean either 'the sense of smell' or simply the 'nose'. Since Paul is distinguishing between the organs of the body, 'nose' is slightly to be preferred [NIGTC].
QUESTION—Are these questions real or rhetorical?
They are rhetorical [NIC2, TG]. The questions make the statements that if the whole body were an eye, there would be no hearing; and if the whole body were hearing, there would be no smelling [TG; CEV].
QUESTION—What is the point of what Paul is saying?
Paul's point is that the body needs all of its members to function properly [AB, NIC2, TNTC]. An effectively functioning body takes diversity for granted [Ed, MNTC]. The body requires the union of parts having diverse functions [Ho]. Each part has its own essential function and that it should neither despise that function nor envy the function of another part [ICC, Vn]. Both the dissatisfaction of the inferior parts and the disdain of the superior parts are individualistic and indifferent to the good of the whole body [EGT]. Paul's point is unity and mutual dependence. He points out how absurd it is to cultivate jealousy over diverse gifts [NTC].

12:18 But-now^a God placed^b the parts,

LEXICON—a. νυνὶ δέ (LN 91.4) (BAGD 2.b. p. 546): 'but now' [Lns, NTC; KJV], 'but as a matter of fact' [AB, BAGD, ICC; NET], 'but in fact' [HNTC; NIV, REB], 'but as it is' [NIGTC; NRSV], 'as it is however' [Herm; TEV], 'but' [CEV, NLT], 'as it is' [NAB, NJB, TNT], 'at this very time' [ISV], 'but as the case really stands' [Alf], 'now, however, as things are' [Ed, EGT], 'the way things are/but the fact is that' [TG].

b. aorist act. indic. of τίθημι (LN 85.32, 37.96) (BAGD II.1.a. p. 816): 'to place' [LN (85.32), NIGTC, NTC; NET, TNT], 'to arrange' [AB, BAGD; ISV, NIV, NRSV], 'to put' [HNTC, LN (85.32); NJB, NLT, TEV], 'to set' [Lns; KJV, NAB], 'to put together' [CEV], 'to appoint' [LN (37.96); REB], 'to give something its proper place in the body' [ICC], 'to designate, to assign, to give a task to' [LN (37.96)].

QUESTION—What relationship is indicated by νυνὶ δέ 'but now'?

Νυνὶ δέ functions to introduce a summary statement and translates 'and so, accordingly, meanwhile' [LN (91.4)]. Here νυνί is logical indicating, 'now as the situation is' [EGT, Ho, NIC2, NIGTC], 'as a matter of fact' [NTC]. Νυνί is an emphatic form of νῦν without any change in meaning [BAGD]. Δέ is adversative and indicates that this will be a response to the rhetorical questions of 12:17 [NIC2]. Δέ is contrastive [Alf, EGT, Gdt, NIC2, NIGTC, Rb] and contrasts with the absurd questions of 12:17 [Rb].

each one of-them in the body just-as he-wanted.^a

LEXICON—a. aorist act. indic. of θέλω (LN **25.1**, 30.58) (BAGD 2. p. 355): 'to want' [**LN** (25.1); ISV, NAB, NIV, NLT, TEV], 'to will' [AB, BAGD, ICC, Lns; TNT], 'to choose' [NJB, NRSV, REB], 'to decide' [NET], 'to please (oneself)' [KJV], 'to desire' [LN (25.1), NTC], 'to decide what is best' [CEV], 'to see fit' [HNTC], 'to wish' [LN (25.1)], 'to purpose' [LN (30.58)]. This is also translated as a phrase: '(as) it has pleased him' [Herm], '(just as) it seems good to him' [NIGTC]. This corresponds to the word βούλεται 'he wills' of 12:11 where the Spirit is the actor [Alf, EGT]. See this word also at 10:27.

QUESTION—What is the function of ἓν ἕκαστον 'each one' in this clause?

They are in apposition to the word 'parts' and modify them [Lns]: the parts, each one. These words are emphasized by the fact that they are a separate phrase in the clause [TH]. They show that God's attention goes beyond the more important or showy members to include every member [TNTC].

QUESTION—What is the significance of the two aorist tenses ἔθετο 'he placed' and ἠθέλησεν '(just as) he wanted'?

They refer to the act of creation [ICC, Lns, NIC, NTC, TNTC, Vn].

QUESTION—What is the implication of this verse?

It implies that to be dissatisfied with one's gift is to rebel against the will of God [ICC, Vn]. It implies that dissatisfaction with one's gift indicates that a person does not trust God's wisdom [EGT]. It implies that the gifts of each believer in the Church are decided by the Lord [Ho].

12:19 And[a] if all were one part, where (would be) the body?
LEXICON—a.(See this word at 11:2): 'and' [Lns, NTC; KJV], 'now' [ICC], 'but' [NIGTC], not explicit [AB, Herm, HNTC; all versions].
QUESTION—What relationship is indicated by δέ 'and'?
The logic of 12:12–20 is summarized in 12:19–20 [NIGTC]. Since each person has his/her role in the function of the body, it is wrong for any one member to assume the role of the whole body [AB]. If one part made up the body, then the body could not be identified as having an existence of its own, apart from that part [NIC].
QUESTION—Is this question real or rhetorical?
It is a rhetorical question [EGT, Herm, ICC, NIC2, NIGTC, NTC, TG, TH, TNTC]: if all were one part, there would be no body.
QUESTION—What is the function of this rhetorical question?
It shows that a body with a single part would be absurd [Alf, ICC, Lns, TNTC]. It shows the Corinthians that their overstressed admiration for one or other of the gifts is absurd [TNTC]. It shows that such a body would be a monstrosity [NCBC, NIC2]. It shows that a diversity of members is needed for the existence of the body [Ed, EGT, Herm, Ho, ICC, NIC2, TG, TNTC]. It shows that only one part would not equal a body [MNTC]. It stresses the need for the existence of the body, which is one that has many parts [Vn].

DISCOURSE UNIT: 12:20–31 [MNTC]. The topic is interdependence not independence.

12:20 But-now[a] on-the-one-hand (there are) many parts,
LEXICON—a. νυνὶ δέ (See this phrase at 12:18): 'but now' [AB, Lns, NTC; KJV, NET], 'but, as it is' [ICC], 'but in fact' [HNTC], 'in fact however' [REB], 'but as the case stands' [EGT], 'so now' [NET], 'as it is' [NIGTC, TG; NIV, NJB, NRSV, TEV, TNT], 'as it is however' [Herm], 'so' [ISV], 'Yes' [NLT], not explicit [CEV, NAB].
QUESTION—What relationships are indicated by νῦν δέ 'but now'.
Νῦν has a logical sense here [NIC2]. Δέ is adversative [Alf, Gdt, Lns, My, NTC] and indicates a contrast with 12:19 [Alf]: if all were one part there would be no body, *but* there are many parts.

but[a] (there is) one body.
LEXICON—a. δέ (See this word at 11:2): 'but' [Herm, Lns, NTC; all versions except NRSV], 'yet' [NRSV], 'and' [AB, HNTC], not explicit [ICC, NIGTC; CEV]. This δέ 'on the other hand' functions to balance the μέν 'on the one hand' of the first part of the verse [Lns].
QUESTION—What is Paul saying in this verse?
Paul is focusing on the unity of the body as over against the diversity of its parts [Herm, NIC2, TNTC]. Paul is saying that diversity of parts is completely consistent with the unity of the body [Ho]. The fact that God has designed there to be diversity in the body is true of the human as well as the Christian body [HNTC]. This is a repetition of 12:12 except that there one

body was seen to have many parts while here the many parts are seen to exist in one body [NIC, NTC].

DISCOURSE UNIT: 12:21–31a [EGT]. The topic is the mutual dependence of the body's members.

DISCOURSE UNIT: 12:21–26 [Alf, NTC]. The topic is the honorable and unpresentable parts [NTC], spiritual gifts necessary to each other [Alf].

12:21 And/but[a] **the eye not is-able to-say to-the hand, "I-have no need[b] of-you,"**

LEXICON—a. δέ (See this word at 11:2): 'and' [ICC, Lns; KJV], 'so then' [TEV], not explicit [AB, Herm, HNTC, NIGTC, NTC; all versions except KJV].
  b. χρεία (LN 57.40) (BAGD 1. p. 885): 'need' [AB, BAGD, HNTC, LN, Lns, NTC; KJV, NJB, NRSV]. This noun is also translated as a verb: 'to be of use to' [ICC], 'to need' [Herm, NIGTC; CEV, ISV, NAB, NET, NIV, NLT, REB, TEV, TNT].

QUESTION—What relationship is indicated by δέ 'and'?
  1. It indicates a conclusion [Ho, NIC, NIGTC; TEV]: therefore. This verse is a conclusion drawn from the fact of 12:10 that the body is one [NIC]. Paul is teaching the need for mutual dependence among the members of the church [Ho].
  2. It indicates contrast [Ed, Gdt, ICC]: but. It has an adversative sense here: 'on the other hand' [Ed]. In 12:15–16 he spoke of the foot and ear which said, 'The body does not need us'. Here he speaks of the eye and head that say, "We don't need the body" [ICC, MNTC]. Paul is teaching that there is no such thing as independence either in the human body or in society [ICC].

or again the head to-the feet, "I-have no need of-you."

QUESTION—What is indicated by πάλιν 'again'?
  It indicates a further example [Ed, EGT]. It indicates something more that belongs in the same category [My].

QUESTION—In what sense can the eye and the head not say these things?
  They cannot say them and be truthful to things as they are [AB, TG]. They cannot say them without rendering themselves useless [ICC].

QUESTION—What is implied by the choice of the 'eye' and the 'head' as representative parts?
  It is implied that they represent superior parts of the body having a condescending attitude toward the 'hand' and 'feet' respectively [AB, Alf, Ed, EGT, Gdt, Ho, ICC, Lns, MNTC, NIC2, Rb, TNTC, Vn].

QUESTION—How does this interpretation apply to the Church?
  It signifies that the members of the church having greater gifts should not despise those having lesser gifts [Alf, Ho, Lns, MNTC, NTC]. It probably does not signify relative gifts here as much as indicating that the 'haves' should not despise the 'have-nots'. This is more in keeping with the context

of what was happening at Corinth as referred to in 11:17–34. Further, it also does not focus as much on pride as on the self-sufficiency of the superiors and their thinking that they did not even need the 'have-nots' [NIC2].

12:22 On-the-contrary[a] much-more[b] the parts of-the body appearing to-be weaker[c] are indispensable,[d]

LEXICON—a. ἀλλά (See this word at 10:5): 'on the contrary' [ICC, Lns, NIGTC, Rb; ISV, NET, NIV, NRSV, TEV, TNT], 'quite the contrary' [REB], 'however' [AB], 'by contrast' [NTC], 'no' [Ed; KJV, TNT], 'even' [NAB], 'in fact' [CEV, NLT], 'but' [Herm], not explicit [HNTC; NJB]. Ἀλλά is a strong adversative [NIC2].

b. πολύς μᾶλλον (BAGD I.2.c.α. p. 688): 'much more' [AB, BAGD, Lns; KJV], 'even more' [NTC], 'much rather' [HNTC], 'all the more' [Herm], 'what is more, it is precisely' [NJB], 'it is much truer to say' [ICC], 'even more to the point' [NIGTC], 'in fact' [ISV, NAB], 'to a much greater degree' [BAGD], 'most' [NLT], not explicit [CEV, NET, NIV, NRSV, REB, TEV].

c. ἀσθενής (BAGD 2.a. p. 115): 'weak' [AB, BAGD, HNTC, NTC; all versions except KJV, NAB, REB], 'feeble' [ICC, Lns; KJV], 'frail' [REB], 'specially weak' [Herm], 'less important' [BAGD; NAB], 'less endowed with power or status' [NIGTC]. See this word also at 11:30.

d. ἀναγκαῖος (LN 71.39) (BAGD 1. p. 52): 'indispensable' [LN, NTC; ISV, NAB, NIV, NJB, NRSV, REB], 'as indispensable as any' [ICC], 'necessary' [AB, BAGD, Herm, HNTC, LN, Lns; KJV, TNT], 'essential' [NIGTC; NET], 'the most necessary' [NLT]. The phrase ἀναγκαῖά ἐστιν 'are necessary' is translated 'we cannot do without' [TEV], 'we cannot get along without' [CEV].

QUESTION—What is the function of πολλῷ μᾶλλον 'much more'?

1. It modifies ἀναγκαῖος 'indispensable' [AB, Alf, Herm, Lns, NTC, Rb; NLT]: much more indispensable. It indicates that the necessity to the body of the weaker parts is brought out much more than the other parts [Alf].

2. It strengthens the ἀλλά 'on the contrary' [Ed, EGT, Gdt, NIGTC; TNT]. Paul is contrasting this verse with the idea that the superior parts can do without the inferior ones [Ed]. On the contrary, it is 'much more' the case that the weaker parts are necessary. These words indicate that the idea of 12:21 is more than negated. Far from being useless, those parts are indispensable [EGT]. It points out the *a fortiori* argument: 'it is much more the case that' [NIGTC].

QUESTION—What parts of the body may be considered weak?

They may be the internal organs [AB, HNTC, MNTC, NIC2, NTC, Rb]. The eyes may be weak in that they cannot protect themselves [AB, HNTC, TG]. They may be the arms and legs which make it possible for the hands and feet to work, or possibly the intestines [NIC]. They may be the heart, lungs, liver, and kidneys [Rb]. They may be the lungs and stomach on which the health of the body depends [Gdt].

QUESTION—Are these parts really weak?

The point is that these parts only *appear* (δοκέω) to be weak and even this supposed weakness has nothing to do with their real value [NIC2]. They seem to be weak, but in reality they are not [Lns, MNTC, NIC]. 'Weak' means apparently unimportant, but they are indispensable [TNTC]. Another view is that this is a correct opinion, they really are weaker, and it means 'the parts which, because they are weaker, are considered less valuable, but they are necessary' [Herm].

12:23 and (the-parts) of-the body that we-think[a] to-be less-honorable[b]

LEXICON—a. pres. act. indic. of δοκέω (LN 31.29) (BAGD 1.c. p. 202): 'to think' [LN, Lns; ISV, KJV, NIV, NRSV, TEV, TNT], 'to consider' [BAGD, HNTC; NAB, NET, NJB], 'to regard as' [Herm, ICC; NLT, REB], 'to believe, to suppose, to presume, to assume, to imagine' [LN], 'to deem' [AB, NIGTC, NTC], not explicit [CEV].

b. ἀτιμός (LN 87.72) (BAGD 2. p. 120): 'less honorable' [AB, BAGD, ICC, Lns, NIGTC, NTC; all versions except CEV, NJB, TEV], 'relatively less honorable' [HNTC], 'least dignified' [NJB], 'specially dishonorable' [Herm], 'dishonored, lacking in honor' [LN], 'insignificant' [BAGD], not explicit [CEV]. The phrase ἀτιμότερα εἶναι 'to be less-honorable' is translated 'aren't worth very much' [TEV].

QUESTION—What parts would be considered ἀτιμός 'less honorable'?

They may be the hands, feet, and limbs [AB]. They may be the arms, throat, legs, or belly [Gdt]. They may be the torso, thighs, or paunch [MNTC]. They would be a part that we normally cover, but if uncovered it would not be considered indecent [Alf].

these we-clothe-with[a] greater[b] honor,[c]

LEXICON—a. pres. act. indic. of περιτίθημι (LN **13.10**, 85.39) (BAGD 2. p. 652): 'to clothe with' [HNTC, ICC; NAB, NET, NLT, NRSV], 'to bestow on' [AB, BAGD, Lns; KJV], 'to assign to' [**LN** (13.10)], 'to surround (with)' [LN (85.39); NJB], 'to treat with' [Herm; NIV, TEV, TNT], 'to place on' [NTC], 'to put around' [BAGD, LN (85.39)], 'to invest with' [BAGD, NIGTC], 'to cause to have' [LN (13.10)]. This active voice is translated as a passive: 'to be treated with' [ISV, REB]. This entire phrase is translated 'we take special care to dress up' [CEV].

b. περισσότερος (LN 78.31) (BAGD 1. p. 651): 'greater' [AB, BAGD, NIGTC, NTC; NAB, NET, NRSV, TEV, TNT], 'more abundant' [Lns; KJV], 'special' [Herm, HNTC, ICC; ISV, NIV, REB], 'greatest' [NJB, NLT], 'excessive, very great, surpassing, much greater, all the more' [LN], 'more' [BAGD], not explicit [CEV].

c. τιμή (LN **65.1**, 87.4) (BAGD 2.b. p. 817): 'honor' [AB, BAGD, Herm, HNTC, LN (87.4), Lns, NIGTC, NTC; ISV, KJV, NET, NIV, NRSV, REB], 'respect' [BAGD, LN (87.4); TNT], 'dignity' [NJB], 'care' [ICC; NAB, NLT, TEV], 'value, importance' [**LN** (65.1)], 'status' [LN (87.4)], not explicit [CEV].

QUESTION—What is indicated by the phrase τιμὴν περισσοτέραν περιτίθεμεν 'we clothe with greater honor'?
It means to put clothes on those parts [Alf, Ed, HNTC, ICC, Lns, MNTC, NIC, NTC, TG, TNTC, Vn]. It means to adorn those parts [AB, ICC]. Τιμή 'honor' is a covering as a sign of honor [Ed]. The comparative 'greater' implies a comparison with the parts that we do not cover [NIC].

QUESTION—How should 'honoring' be applied in the Church?
Those in the Church who have greater gifts should make it a point to show appreciation to those with lesser gifts and they should protect and encourage them [MNTC].

QUESTION—What is indicated by the two occurrences of καί 'and' in this clause and the next?
The first καί means 'and moreover', the second means 'and even' [Gdt]: *And moreover* the parts of the body…*and even* our unpresentable parts….

and our unpresentable^a (parts) have greater attractiveness,^b

LEXICON—a. ἀσχήμων (LN **79.16**) (BAGD p. 119): 'unpresentable' [AB, BAGD, LN, NIGTC, NTC; NET, NIV], 'less presentable' [NAB, NJB], 'not presentable' [**LN**], 'unattractive' [**LN**], 'less respectable' [NRSV], 'less attractive' [ISV], 'unseemly' [Herm, HNTC; TNT], 'personal' [CEV], 'uncomely' [ICC, Lns; KJV], 'ugly' [LN], 'private (parts)' [BAGD]. This adjective is also translated as a clause: '(the parts) which don't look very nice' [TEV], '(the parts) we are modest about' [REB], '(those parts) that should not be seen' [NLT].

b. εὐσχημοσύνη (LN **79.13**) (BAGD p. 327): 'presentability' [AB, BAGD], 'modesty' [BAGD], 'comeliness' [ICC, Lns; KJV], 'seemliness' [Herm, HNTC], 'beauty, loveliness' [LN], 'propriety' [BAGD; NAB]. The phrase εὐσχημοσύνην περισσοτέραν ἔχει 'have greater attractiveness' is translated 'are made more seemly' [TNT], 'we make more attractive' [ISV], 'we are modest about' [CEV], 'we carefully protect from the eyes of others' [NLT], 'are clothed with dignity' [NET], 'are treated with special modesty' [NIV, TEV], 'are treated with special respect' [REB], 'are treated with greater respect' [NRSV], 'are treated with greater modesty' [NTC], 'are given greater presentability' [NJB], 'have greater adornment to make them presentable' [NIGTC], 'acquire more than ordinary attractiveness' [**LN**]. Εὐσχημοσύνη refers to external elegance or decorum [ICC].

QUESTION—Which parts would be considered ἀσχήμων 'unpresentable'?
This word is concerned with decency and refers to parts that should not be seen in public [TH]. These may be the feet, torso, or breasts [AB]. They may be the genitals [AB, Ed, Lns, My, NIC, NIC2, TG, TH]. They may be the buttocks [Lns]. They may be the sex organs and organs of secretion that we are right in thinking to be less honorable and cover with special care [NIC, TNTC], being the parts which are considered indecent or cause shame if exposed [NTC].

QUESTION—What is the meaning of εὐσχημοσύνην περισσοτέραν ἔχει 'they have greater attractiveness'?
1. It means that we make them more attractive [Alf, HNTC, Ho, ICC, MNTC, NIC, NIC2, NTC, TNTC; all versions except KJV]. 'Have' means to receive clothing from us [Alf, HNTC]. We should supply the words 'and in this way' from the first clause [ICC]: we surround with greater honor, *and in this way* our unpresentable parts have greater respect. The words 'greater attractiveness' refer to the greater care we take to cloth these parts at all times [ICC].
2. It means that they naturally have respect or attractiveness [AB, Ed, EGT, Lns, Rb; KJV]. These parts have greater loveliness in their function; marriage is honorable (Hebrews 13:4) [Ed]. The mother's womb and breast are the most sacred of all parts [EGT, Rb]. The respect consists in the greater degree of shame or modesty which they evoke [Lns].

12:24 but^a our attractive^b (parts) have no need.^c

LEXICON—a. δέ (See this word at 11:2): 'but' [CEV, NET], 'however' [ISV], 'whereas' [Herm, ICC, Lns; NRSV, REB, TNT], 'and' [NTC], 'for' [KJV], 'while' [HNTC; NIV, NLT], not explicit [AB, NIGTC; all other versions].
b. εὐσχήμων (LN **79.15**) (BAGD 1. p. 327): 'attractive' [LN; ISV], 'presentable' [AB, BAGD, LN, NIGTC; NET, NIV, NJB], 'respectable' [NTC; REB], 'comely' [ICC, Lns; KJV], 'seemly' [Herm, HNTC; TNT], 'other' [NLT], 'proper' [BAGD]. This adjective is also translated as a comparative: 'more presentable' [**LN**; NAB], 'more respectable' [NRSV], 'more beautiful' [TEV]. This entire phrase is translated 'but we don't have to be modest about other parts' [CEV].
c. χρεία (See this word at 12:21): 'need' [AB, Lns; KJV, REB], 'need of this' [Herm, HNTC, NTC]. The phrase χρείαν ἔχει 'have need' is translated 'to need' [NIGTC; ISV, NET, NJB, NRSV, TEV, TNT], 'to need without special attention' [ICC], 'to require special care' [NLT], 'to need special treatment' [NIV], 'to have already' [NAB]. The phrase οὐ χρείαν ἔχει 'do not have need' is translated '(we) don't have to be modest about' [CEV].

QUESTION—To which verse does this first clause belong?
It belongs to the last clause of 12:23 [AB, EGT, Gdt, Herm, HNTC, ICC, My, NIC, NIC2, NTC, TNTC, Vn; CEV, NAB, NET, NIV, NJB, NLT, NRSV, REB, TEV, TNT]: our unpresentable parts have greater attractiveness, but our attractive parts have no need.

QUESTION—What does χρεία 'need' imply?
It implies the need to be honored by being covered [Gdt, Ho, Lns]. It implies that they need no help [TNTC].

QUESTION—To what particular parts do our 'attractive' parts refer?
They may refer to our faces [EGT, Ho, NIC, NIC2]. They may refer to our heads. Note 11:7 where man does not cover his head because he is the image

of God [EGT]. They refer to the parts which we think are good-looking [TNTC]. They are the parts that we feel we do not need to cover [Vn].

But[a] God put-together[b] the body having-given greater honor to-the lacking[c] (part),

LEXICON—a. ἀλλά (See this word at 10:5): 'but' [AB, Herm, Lns, NIGTC; ISV, KJV, NIV, NRSV, REB, TNT], 'instead' [NET], 'however' [NTC], 'so' [NLT], 'Why, yes' [ICC], not explicit [HNTC; CEV, NAB, NJB, TEV]. Ἀλλά is emphatic [Lns, NIC2]: but, as it is.

b. aorist act. indic. of συγκεράννυμι (LN **62.2**) (BAGD 2. p. 773): 'to put together' [HNTC, **LN**; CEV, ISV, NLT, TEV, TNT], 'to blend (together)' [AB, BAGD; NET], 'to fit together' [Herm], 'to combine' [NTC; NIV, REB], 'to compose' [BAGD, LN, NIGTC; NJB], 'to temper together' [KJV], 'to construct' [NAB], 'to arrange' [NRSV], 'to frame on principles of compensation' [Alf, ICC], 'to mix together' [BAGD, Lns], 'to structure' [**LN**]. Συγκεράννυμι means to compose by unifying so as to form one organism [BAGD, NIC2]. It means to make parts to fit together in an overall arrangement [LN].

c. pres. act. participle of ὑστερέω (LN **87.65**) (BAGD 2. p. 849): 'to lack' [BAGD, HNTC, NTC; ISV, KJV, NIV, TNT], 'to need' [TEV], 'to show deficiency' [ICC], 'to be without' [NJB], 'to fall short' [Lns], 'to have less dignity' [NLT], 'to be inferior, to lack in honor' [**LN**], 'to feel inferior' [NIGTC], 'to come short of' [BAGD]. This participle is also translated as an adjective: 'lowly' [NAB], 'humbler' [REB], 'lesser' [NET], 'inferior' [AB; NRSV], 'least important' [CEV]. This is also translated with a phrase: 'the member that is in need' [Herm]. The feature that is lacking is honor [TH].

QUESTION—What relationship is indicated by ἀλλά 'but'?

It indicates a strong contrast with all erroneous concepts about the true makeup of the body [Lns, NIGTC]. It indicates a contrast with the thought that vital bodily functions are only dishonorable and unpresentable [EGT]. It indicates a contrast as a transition from Paul's main discussion to his conclusion [NTC]. It indicates a break from Paul's discussion of the mutual relationship of the members to a view of God's role [My]. This part of 12:24 marks a major transition from the theme of diversity (12–21) and of divisions in the church at Corinth (1:10 and 11:18), back to the theme of unity (4–11), [TH].

QUESTION—What words have the emphasis in this clause?

The emphasis is on the word 'God' [Ed, ICC, NIC2, Vn]: It was God who put the body together.

QUESTION—To what event does ὁ θεὸς συνεκέρασεν τὸ σῶμα 'God put together the body' refer?

It refers to the act of the creation of man [Alf, NTC].

QUESTION—What does τῷ ὑστερουμένῳ περισσοτέραν δοὺς τιμήν 'giving greater honor to the lacking part' mean?

It means that man's natural instinct to honor the less honorable organs of the body has been given by God [Ed, EGT, Vn]. He probably means that God has given that weak or less worthy part a more important function or caused it to receive greater attention [NIC2]. God decided which parts of the body are put on display and which parts are essential for survival [NIGTC]. It means that God has mixed together the weak and strong parts of the human body in such a way that the strong give special care and attention to the weak so that whole body gives the appearance of being one beautiful whole [Gdt]. Greater honor here refers to the need which men recognize for these lacking parts to be dressed in an honorable and lovely way [My]. It means that God has so structured the body of Christ that the strong parts compensate for the weak so that the weak receive more recognition [NTC].

12:25 **so-that there-might-be no division[a] in the body**
LEXICON—a. σχίσμα (See this word at 1:10, 11:18): 'division' [AB, Herm, HNTC, NTC; NET, NIV, REB, TEV, TNT], 'disagreement' [NJB], 'disharmony' [ISV], 'dissension' [NAB, NRSV], 'disunion' [ICC], 'schism' [Lns; KJV], 'split' [NIGTC]. This entire phrase is translated 'he did this to make all parts of the body work together smoothly' [CEV], 'this makes for harmony among the members' [NLT]. Σχίσμα in reference to a group of people means a feeling of alienation [Ho]. He is referring to the envy and scorn as seen in 12:16 and 21 [EGT]. This is the word used in 1:10 [NIGTC].

QUESTION—What relationship is indicated by ἵνα 'so that'?

It indicates the purpose for which God put the body parts together as he did [AB, Ed, Lns, NIC2, NIGTC, TH]: God put together the body *in order* that there may be no division in the body but that the members should have the same concern for each other.

but (that) the parts should-have-care[a] the same[b] for[c] each-other.
LEXICON—a. pres. act. subj. of μεριμνάω (LN 25.225) (BAGD 2. p. 505): 'to have care' [AB, HNTC, NTC; KJV, NRSV, TNT], 'to care' [BAGD; CEV, NLT], 'to secure anxious care in' [ICC], 'to be concerned' [NAB, NJB], 'to have concern' [BAGD; ISV, NET, NIV, TEV], 'to share a concern' [NIGTC], 'to feel concern' [REB], 'to (harmoniously) provide (for)' [Herm], 'to be anxious about' [LN, Lns], 'to be worried about' [LN]. Μεριμνάω is a term indicating anxiety and strong emotion [TNTC]. It indicates anxious concern about possible danger or misfortune [LN]. It indicates deep concern [Ed, Lns].

b. αὐτός (LN 58.31): 'same' [AB, HNTC, LN, NIGTC, NTC; ISV, KJV, NRSV, REB, TEV, TNT], 'mutual' [NET], 'equal' [NIV], not explicit [CEV, NAB]. The phrase τὸ αὐτό 'the same' is also translated 'equally' [NJB, NLT], 'harmoniously' [Herm], '(in all organs) alike the same (anxious care)' [ICC]. This adjective is also translated with a phrase: 'in the same way' [Lns].

c. ὑπέρ with genitive object (See this word at 11:24): 'for' [AB, Herm, HNTC, Lns, NTC; all versions except CEV], 'for (one another's) welfare' [ICC], 'about' [CEV].

QUESTION—What is the function of ἀλλά 'but'?

It is a strong adversative [TNTC]: on the contrary. It is the positive side of God's purpose [Lns].

QUESTION—What is the significance of the present subjunctives of the verbs ᾖ 'there may be' and μεριμνῶσιν 'they may have care'?

The second subjunctive is the subjunctive of habitual feeling [EGT]: (so that) they may habitually have concern. If Paul used aorist subjunctives it would indicate that God's purpose had been realized as it was in the case of the human body. He uses present subjunctives to indicate that in the case of the members of the church his purpose was yet to be realized [Lns].

QUESTION—What is meant by τὸ αὐτό 'the same' in the phrase 'the same care'?

It means that the concern shown to another member be the same as for oneself [EGT, HNTC, Ho, NTC, TG]. In regard to the Lord's Supper, some were not caring for the needs of others as they did for themselves [NIC2]. The concern shown to one member should be the same as for any other member so that there may be no partiality [MNTC, TNTC]. There should be the same care for the nursery worker as there is for the pastor [MNTC]. It means that all should have the same care for the well-being of the whole [Alf, Gdt, Lns]. Specifically, in regard to eating food sacrifices to idols, the stronger member should think not only about his own freedom but also about the conscience of his weaker brother [HNTC].

QUESTION—What words are emphasized in this clause?

The words 'the same' are emphasized [ICC, Lns, NIGTC].

12:26 And[a] if one part[b] suffers,[c] all the parts suffer-with[d] (it);

LEXICON—a. καί (See this word at 11:19): 'and' [Herm, LN, NTC; KJV], 'and so' [AB, ICC, NIGTC], 'and also, in addition' [LN], 'and accordingly' [ICC], 'and accordingly, in matter of fact' [Alf], 'and really' [Gdt], 'moreover' [Lns], not explicit [HNTC; all versions except KJV].

b. μέλος (See this word at 12:12): 'part' [AB, LN; CEV, ISV, NIV, NJB, NLT, REB, TEV, TNT], 'member' [Herm, HNTC, Lns, NTC; KJV, NAB, NET, NRSV], 'limb or organ' [NIGTC], 'aspect, feature' [LN], 'one of them' [ICC].

c. pres. act. indic. of πάσχω (LN 24.78) (BAGD 3.a.α. p. 634): 'to suffer' [AB, BAGD, Herm, HNTC, LN, Lns, NIGTC, NTC; all versions except CEV, NJB], 'to hurt' [CEV], 'to be in pain' [ICC, LN]. This active voice is translated as a passive: 'to be hurt' [NJB].

d. pres. act. indic. of συμπάσχω (LN 24.84) (BAGD p. 779): 'to suffer with' [BAGD, Herm, HNTC, Lns, NIGTC, NTC; ISV, KJV, NAB, NET, NIV,

NLT, TEV, TNT], 'to suffer together' [AB, **LN**; REB], 'to suffer together with' [NRSV], 'to share (one's) pain' [NJB], 'to be in pain with' [ICC], 'to join in suffering, to assume one's share of suffering' [LN], 'to suffer the same thing as' [BAGD]. The clause συμπάσχει πάντα τὰ μέλη 'all the members suffer together' is translated 'we hurt all over' [CEV].

QUESTION—What relationship is indicated by καί 'and'?

It indicates a conjoining relationship [Alf, Gdt, ICC, Lns, Vn]: the parts should have the same care for each other *and* if one part suffers.... Paul means to add this as a result of God's blending the body together [ICC, Lns]. Paul means that the mutual caring of 12:25 must be a part of the body because, in fact, if one member suffers all suffer with it [Gdt].

QUESTION—In what way do all parts of a body suffer if one part suffers?

If a person hurts one of his parts he says he has a pain in that part, he does not say that his part has a pain. His whole body suffers when one part suffers [ICC, TNTC]. An ulcer in the stomach makes the rest of the body feel ill at ease [NTC].

if (one) part is-honored,ᵃ all the parts rejoice-withᵇ (it).

LEXICON—a. pres. pass. indic. of δοξάζω (LN 33.357, 87.8) (BAGD 1. p. 204): 'to be honored' [AB, BAGD, Herm, LN (87.8), NTC; CEV, KJV, NAB, NET, NIV, NJB, NLT, NRSV], 'to be praised' [BAGD, LN (33.357), NIGTC; ISV, TEV, TNT], 'to be glorified' [HNTC, LN (33.357), Lns], 'to be respected' [LN (87.8)], 'to have honor done to' [ICC]. This passive voice is also translated as actively: 'to flourish' [REB].

b. pres. act. indic. of συγχαίρω (LN **25.126**) (BAGD 1. p. 775): 'to rejoice with' [BAGD, Herm, HNTC, **LN**, Lns, NTC; ISV, KJV, NET, NIV, TNT], 'to rejoice together' [AB; REB], 'to share (one's) joy' [NAB, NJB], 'to rejoice together with' [NRSV], 'to be glad' [NLT], 'to share (one's) happiness' [TEV], 'to share in the congratulations' [NIGTC], 'to enjoy with' [LN], 'to feel joy with' [BAGD]. The whole phrase 'all the members rejoice together' is rendered 'the rest of the body will be honored too' [CEV], '(honor done to one) is a joy to all' [ICC].

QUESTION—How can one part of the body be honored?

A body part may be honored by beautifying it with lovely clothing or jewelry, by nourishing it or by paying attention to its development [ICC, My]. In the case of the stomach, it would be by feeding it a delicious meal [NTC].

QUESTION—In what way do all parts of a body rejoice if one part is honored?

If a person's head is crowned, his whole body feels the honor and is happy with the head [Ed, EGT, Gdt, TNTC]. If one part feels pleasure it can cause pleasure to the whole body. Good news to the mind is felt in the body thanks to the nervous system [Rb]. When one's stomach is honored by the care of a good meal, the whole body is strengthened [NTC].

QUESTION—What causes suffering and pleasure on the part of one part to be felt by all the others?

The close connection of the parts of the body causes it to suffer or feel pleasure of the other parts [NIC]. In a body there is a principle of sympathy in which benefit to one part benefits the whole and harm to one part means harm to the whole [Ho, ICC, Vn]. The nervous system of the body causes pain and pleasure in one part to be sensed by all parts [AB, EGT].

QUESTION—How does this principle apply to the body of Christ?

What is true of the human body is not always true of the Body of Christ, but Paul is pointing out what should be. The members of the Church should suffer with the member who is suffering, and rejoice with the member who is honored [Lns]. If spiritual gifts thought to be inferior are looked down on and discouraged, the whole Church will feel the loss [Gdt]. God's gift to one member is a gift to the whole body and so all members should be glad when one is honored [HNTC].

DISCOURSE UNIT: 12:27–31 [NCBC, NIC2, NTC]. The topic is the exercise of spiritual gifts [NCBC], the fact of diversity once more [NIC2], members and gifts [NTC].

DISCOURSE UNIT: 12:27–31a [AB; NAB]. The topic is the functions of members in the church [AB], the one body of Christ [NAB].

DISCOURSE UNIT: 12:27–30 [Gdt, Vn]. The topic is a spiritual application [Vn].

12:27 Now[a] you are (the) body of-Christ and members[b] in-part.[c]

LEXICON—a. δέ (See this word at 11:2): 'now' [AB, HNTC, ICC, Lns, NIGTC; all versions except CEV, NAB, TEV], 'then' [NAB], 'but' [Herm], not explicit [NTC; CEV, TEV].

b. μέλος (See this word at 12:12): 'member' [Herm, HNTC, ICC, Lns, NTC; KJV, NAB, NET, NRSV], 'part' [AB; ISV, TNT], 'a separate and necessary part' [NLT], 'a part to play (in the whole)' [NJB], 'limb or organ' [REB], not explicit [CEV, NIV, TEV].

c. ἐκ μέρος (LN **63.15**) (BAGD 1.c. p. 506): 'in part' [BAGD, LN (63.14); NIV, TEV], 'individually' [AB, BAGD, Herm, HNTC, ICC, NTC; NRSV, TNT], 'in particular' [KJV], 'individual (parts)' [ISV], 'each in his part' [Lns], 'being part of, as a part of, partially' [LN (63.15)], not explicit [NAB, NET, NLT, REB]. The phrase μέλη ἐκ μέρους 'members in part' is translated 'each (of you) with a part to play in the whole' [NJB], 'each one is a part of' [**LN** (63.15); CEV], 'and each (of you), for his or her part, limbs or organs of it' [NIGTC], 'each member is a part of' [**LN** (63.15)].

QUESTION—What relationship is indicated by δέ 'now'?

It indicates that Paul is now returning to the thought of 12:12, that the body is one and has many parts [ICC]. It functions to apply to the Corinthians the figure that he has just been drawing [AB, Alf, Ed, EGT, Gdt, Ho, Lns, NIC,

TG]. It forms a bridge between Paul's figure and his functional summary [AB]. It functions as a summary, returning from the figure to the thing symbolized [Herm]. It functions to complete Paul's argument [HNTC].

QUESTION—What word is emphasized in this verse?

The word ὑμεῖς 'you' is emphatic [Ed, NCBC, NIC, NIC2, NTC, TNTC, Vn], by being placed first in the clause [NIC2, NTC, TNTC]: you yourselves. It means 'you, in spite of your imperfections' [Ed].

QUESTION—How are the nouns related in the genitive construction σῶμα Χριστοῦ 'body of Christ'?

It means the body that belongs to Christ [HNTC, Lns, NIC2, NTC, TH]. The body belongs to Christ because he lives in it [Lns]. It also means the body over which Christ rules [HNTC]. It means that Christians collectively provide a body for Christ as a human body provides a body for the spirit of a man [EGT]. It indicates that the body has been founded and maintained by Christ [NIC]. It indicates that the body of Christ is made up of Corinthian believers [TH]. Body of Christ does not mean his physical body, but is figurative of the church [NTC].

QUESTION—What is the significance of the lack of an article in σῶμα Χριστοῦ 'body of Christ'?

It has no significance since this genitive construction must either be composed of article–noun—article-noun or noun—noun, and either way it means the same [NCBC]. It neither indicates that the Corinthians were *a* body of Christ, as though there were many such bodies, nor that they were *the* body of Christ, as though they made up the whole body of Christ by themselves [ICC, Lns, NIC2], rather the lack of the article focuses on the quality of the noun, that is, whatever the term 'body of Christ' signified qualitatively, the Corinthians were [ICC, Lns]. It means that the Corinthians are what Christ's body is in respect to its nature and quality (see 12:12) [Lns]. It means that it is the body of Christ and not any other kind of entity [ICC]. It means that the Corinthians' relationship to Christ consisted in collectively being His body [NIC2]. It means that they were the unique body of Christ, that is, that there was no other body that could be called that [NTC]. It indicates that it is a distinguishing feature of the Corinthian believers that they are members of Christ's body [TNTC]. It indicates that there are many such churches and that each has the same characteristics, each being a small replica of the Body of Christ universal [Alf, NIC, NTC]. It means that they were *a* body of Christ, not *the* universal body of Christ. Other churches shared the same distinction. They were a group in which Christ dwelled and over which He ruled [Gdt].

QUESTION—What is meant by ἐκ μέρους 'in part'?

It means 'individually' [AB, BAGD, Ed, HNTC, Ho, ICC, Lns, NCBC, NIC2, NTC, TNTC; NRSV, TNT]. It probably means that each has his own assigned part or distinct role to play for the benefit of the body [ICC, NCBC, Rb]. As a group they were the body of Christ, but they were members individually [Ho]. Individually they composed the many parts of the body

158   1 CORINTHIANS 12:27

[NIC2]. It means that every individual member was a part of Christ's body [NTC, TNTC].

12:28 And^a on-one-hand those-whom^b God placed^c in the church^d

LEXICON—a. καί (See this word at 12:26): 'and' [AB, Herm, ICC, Lns, NIGTC, NTC; KJV, NET, NIV, NJB, NRSV, TNT], 'further' [HNTC], 'furthermore' [NAB], not explicit [CEV, ISV, NAB, REB, TEV].

b. ὅς (LN 92.27) (BAGD II.2. p. 585): 'those whom' [NJB], 'some' [AB, BAGD, Herm, Lns, NIC; KJV], 'some people' [CEV], 'here is a list of some of the members that' [NLT], 'all' [TEV], 'each' [ICC], 'who, which, what, the one who, that which' [LN], not explicit [NIGTC, NTC; ISV, NAB, NET, NIV, NRSV, REB, TNT]. The phrase οὓς μέν 'those whom on one hand' is translated 'there are some whom' [HNTC]. The phrase οὓς μέν 'those whom on one hand' should be grammatically followed by οὓς δέ 'those whom on the other hand', but having said the first, Paul changes to a numerical listing [Alf, EGT, Gdt, HNTC, ICC, NIC2, Rb].

c. aorist act. indic. of τίθημι (BAGD II.2.b. p. 816): 'to place' [NIGTC; NET, NLT, TNT], 'to put in place' [TEV], 'to set' [HNTC, Lns; KJV], 'to set up' [NAB], 'to give (someone) his proper place' [ICC], 'to appoint' [AB, Herm, NTC; ISV, NIV, NJB, NRSV, REB], 'to choose' [CEV], 'to make (someone something)' [BAGD]. See this word also at 12:18.

d. ἐκκλησία (See this word at 10:32): 'church' [AB, Herm, HNTC, ICC, Lns, NIGTC, NTC; all versions except NLT, REB], 'body of Christ' [NLT], 'our community' [REB].

QUESTION—What relationship is indicated by καί 'and'?

It indicates an explanation of the previous verse [Ed]. It indicates a conjoining relationship [HNTC, Lns, NIC2] as Paul adds a second fact to their being the body of Christ [Lns]: and. Paul proceeds to enlarge on the many parts that compose the body [EGT, My, NIC2]. Paul now enlarges on the thought of the church as an organic entity [HNTC]. Paul enlarges on the thought of 12:27 [Ho].

QUESTION—What is the significance of the middle voice in ἔθετο ὁ θεός 'God placed'?

It signifies that God did it for himself or for his own purposes [Ed, ICC, Rb, Vn].

QUESTION—What sense of ἐκκλησία 'church' is indicated here?

1. The sense of the whole or universal church is indicated, not just the local assembly [Alf, Ed, EGT, Gdt, ICC, Lns, NIC, NTC, TNTC]. The definite article functions to indicate the universal church [NIC]. The local church is also indicated because it is included in the universal church [Ed]. The sense probably shifts in the verse; the universal church is indicated in the case of apostles but the local church for prophets [HNTC].

2. The local church is mainly indicated [NIC2, Vn]. This verse is parallel with 12:27 where the emphatic words *'you are* (the body of Christ)' indicated the church at Corinth [NIC2].

first[a] apostles,[b]
LEXICON—a. πρῶτος (See this word at 11:18): 'first' [AB, HNTC, ICC, Lns, NIGTC, NTC; CEV, KJV, NAB, NET, NJB, NLT, NRSV, TNT], 'first of all' [Herm; ISV, NIV], 'in the first place' [REB, TEV].

b. ἀπόστολος (LN 53.74, 33.194) (BAGD 3. p. 99): 'apostle' [AB, BAGD, Herm, HNTC, ICC, LN (53.74), Lns, NIGTC, NTC; all versions], 'special messenger' [LN (53.74)], 'messenger' [LN (33.194)]. See this word also at 1:1.

QUESTION—What is meant by πρῶτος 'first'?

The sense of primary rank or importance is in focus [AB, Ed, EGT, Herm, ICC, NCBC, TG, TNTC]. The ranking does not refer to relative importance but rather to a kind of precedence of one over others growing out of the role of establishing and building up of the church [NIC2]. Although the idea of importance is in focus, there may be a sense of timing as well [Gdt, TH]. The gift of being an apostle is first as those so gifted were the witnesses of the facts which are foundational to the whole system [Ed]. It may be that Paul is giving a ranking of apostles here to establish his authority over those in the Corinthian church who were opposing him [Gdt].

QUESTION—If the enumeration of gifts is on the basis of rank, are all eight ranked?

Only the first three are intended to be ranked [NCBC, NIC2, TNTC]. Although apostles and prophets are highest ranked, in view of the fact that the other lists of gifts in the New Testament do not mesh with this, no precise ranking of importance of all the gifts is intended [AB].

QUESTION—Who are included in the term ἀπόστολος 'apostle'?

1. It includes only the original twelve, minus Judas, plus Matthias and Paul for a total of thirteen [Ed, Lns, Rb]. To extend the meaning to include more than these makes the term too indefinite. These thirteen were directly called by Christ and form the foundation of the church (Ephesians 2:20) [Lns].

2. It includes more that the thirteen listed above [Alf, Gdt, HNTC, ICC, MNTC, My, NTC, TG, TH, TNTC, Vn]. See 15:7 where other apostles than the twelve existed [HNTC]. Beyond the thirteen we can also include Barnabas [NTC]. We can also include Barnabas, James, and Paul [TNTC]. The primary group was thirteen, but others, like Barnabas, Silas, Timothy, and other leading men, were also called apostles [MNTC]. In addition to the twelve there were Paul, Barnabas, and James the Lord's brother, Andronicus, and Junias (see Romans 16:7) [Alf, ICC, Vn]. The term includes James, Barnabas, Silas, Timothy, Titus, Andronicus, and Junias [Gdt]. If the number were restricted to the original twelve, there could not have been false apostles (2 Corinthians 11:13) [ICC].

QUESTION—What were the qualifications of an apostle?

They were those men who had witnessed the resurrection or seen Jesus after he rose from the dead (9:1, 2; Luke 24:48; Acts 1:8, 21–23) [Ed, ICC, MNTC, NTC, TNTC, Vn]. They were men who had been with the Lord from his baptism until his ascension (Acts 1:21–22). They functioned to announce, teach, and record the Good News [NTC]. They were also directly chosen by Christ [Ho, Lns, MNTC, NIC] and performed signs and miracles (2 Corinthians 12:12) [MNTC]. They were men whom Christ chose to be with him, whom he sent out to preach and drive out evil spirits (Mark 3:14–19). They preserved the truth of the Good News [TNTC].

second[a] prophets,[b]
LEXICON—a. δεύτερος (LN 60.49) (BAGD 4. p. 177): 'second' [AB, HNTC, LN, NIGTC; ISV, NAB, NET, NIV, NLT, NRSV], 'secondly' [BAGD, Herm, LN, Lns; NJB, TNT], 'in the second place' [LN; REB, TEV], 'secondarily' [KJV], 'next' [ICC, NTC], not explicit [CEV].
b. προφήτης (LN 53.79) (BAGD 5. p. 724): 'prophet' [AB, BAGD, Herm, HNTC, LN, Lns, NIGTC, NTC; all versions], 'inspired preacher' [ICC, LN]. A prophet is a person who proclaims inspired utterances on behalf of God [LN]. See προφητεία 'prophecy' also at 12:10 for discussion of this activity.
QUESTION—What was the function of the prophet?
A prophet is one who proclaims God's message to people [AB, Ho, LN, NCBC, NIC2, Rb, TG, TH, TNTC]. The prophet was inspired by the Holy Spirit [Alf, Gdt, HNTC, Ho, ICC, NCBC, NIC2, NTC, Rb, TNTC]. His/her functions are to edify believers [Gdt, ICC, NIC2, Vn], to encourage believers [Gdt, Vn], to console believers [Alf, ICC], to enlighten believers [Alf, Gdt], to exhort believers [Alf], to convict of sin [ICC], to predict the future [ICC, NIC2, NTC], to win unbelievers [Alf, HNTC], to teach about Christian conduct [NTC], to proclaim the deep things of God [ICC, Rb]. The prophets along with the apostles were the foundation of the church Ephesians 2:20 [Gdt, MNTC, NTC]. An apostle could also be a prophet [Gdt, NTC]. By the enabling of the Holy Spirit, the prophets interpreted the truth that the apostles declared [Ed].
QUESTION—Is a prophet a permanent role or a gift given on a particular occasion?
1. The gift of being a prophet is a person's role or office rather than a gift which comes to a person from time to time [Gdt, Herm, MNTC, NIC, NIC2, TNTC]. It can be either a role or a gift, but the role is more in focus here [NIC2, TNTC].
2. It is a gift which is given to a person on a specific occasion [Alf, Ho, Lns, My, NCBC, NTC, Rb, Vn].
QUESTION—Did prophets function in the local assemblies or the universal church?
1. Prophets belonged to the local assemblies rather than to the universal church [HNTC, MNTC, NTC, TNTC]. This is supported by Chrysostom who wrote that each church had many who prophesied [TNTC].
2. Prophets belonged to the universal church rather than the local assemblies [Gdt].

third[a] teachers,[b]

LEXICON—a. τρίτος (LN 60.50) (BAGD 3. p. 826): 'third' [AB, BAGD, HNTC, ICC, LN, NIGTC, NTC; ISV, NAB, NET, NIV, NLT, NRSV], 'thirdly' [Herm, Lns; KJV, NJB, REB, TNT], 'in the third place' [BAGD; TEV], not explicit [CEV].

b. διδάσκαλος (LN 33.243) (BAGD p. 191): 'teacher' [AB, BAGD, Herm, HNTC, ICC, LN, Lns, NIGTC, NTC; all versions], 'instructor' [LN].

QUESTION—To what does διδάσκαλος 'teacher' refer?

This refers to those who had the gift of explaining the meaning of Scripture and applying it to daily life [Alf, Gdt, HNTC]. They explained the meaning of the Old Testament [HNTC]. They were people who taught the Christian faith [TG, TH]. They were men whose natural abilities and acquired knowledge were improved and strengthened by a special gift [ICC]. People who had this gift used it more in their local assemblies rather than traveling from church to church [Gdt]. The emphasis of this gift was not on its being an office or role, but on the gift itself. A person would receive a teaching and deliver it to the gathered believers [NIC2].

QUESTION—Is the ranking of these first three meant to be precise?

The ranking is probably not meant to be precise since here the order is: apostles, prophets, teachers; in Ephesians 4:11 the order is apostles, prophets, evangelists, pastors, and teachers; while in Romans 12:8–10 the order is prophecy, ministry, teaching [AB].

then[a] miracles,[b]

LEXICON—a. ἔπειτα (LN 67.44) (BAGD 2.b. p. 284): 'then' [AB, Herm, HNTC, LN, Lns, NIGTC, NTC; all versions except KJV, NJB], 'after that' [KJV], 'after them' [NJB], 'afterwards, later' [LN], 'besides these' [ICC]. Ἔπειτα 'then' here denotes succession as the fourth and fifth member of a list [BAGD]. It indicates a point in time following another point [LN].

b. δύναμις (BAGD 1. p. 207): 'miracle' [Herm, HNTC, Lns, NTC; KJV, NET], 'miraculous power' [ICC; NJB], 'deed of power' [NRSV], 'effective deed of power' [NIGTC], 'worker of miracles' [NIV], 'miracle worker' [AB; NAB, REB], 'might, strength, force, power (that works wonders)' [BAGD]. The plural is translated 'some to work miracles' [CEV], 'those who do miracles' [NLT], 'those who perform miracles' [ISV, TEV], 'those who do mighty works' [TNT]. The abstract word 'miracle' is here used in place of the concrete 'people given the power of working miracles' [Ho]. See this word also at 12:10.

QUESTION—What is indicated by ἔπειτα 'then'?

It indicates a break from the ranking function of the first three to begin a generic sequence [Ho, ICC, NIC2]: then. It indicates that a different class follows—gifts instead of offices [AB, NIC, TNTC]. It indicates that the following gifts are of lesser importance than the first three [ICC]. The fact that the order of miracles and healings is reversed here from the list 12:8–10 suggests that rank is no longer in focus [NIC2].

QUESTION—What is indicated by the change from people to abstract gifts?

The change indicates that these gifts were not as much associated with particular persons as were those of apostle, prophet, and teacher [Ed, EGT]. It focuses attention on the gift and not on the person possessing it [EGT, HNTC, TH]. It perhaps only indicates variety of presentation [EGT, ICC]. Most translations make the nouns refer to people rather than the gifts: 'those who perform miracles, those who heal', etc. [TH].

then gifts[a] of-healings,[b]

LEXICON—a. χάρισμα (See this word at 12:4): 'gift' [AB, Herm, HNTC, ICC, NIGTC, NTC; ISV, KJV, NET, NJB, NRSV], 'charismata' [Lns]. The plural of this noun is translated 'those who have the gift' [NLT], 'those having gifts' [NIV], 'those who have gifts' [ISV, REB], 'those who have spiritual gifts' [TNT], 'those who are given the power (to heal)' [TEV], not explicit [CEV].

b. ἴαμα (See this word at 12:9): 'healing' [AB, Herm, HNTC, ICC, Lns, NIGTC, NTC; all versions except CEV, NAB, TEV]. This noun is also translated as a verb: 'to heal' [TEV]. The phrase χαρίσματα ἰαμάτων 'gifts of healings' is translated 'healers' [NAB], '(some to) heal the sick' [CEV]. This indicates those who have the gift to heal diseases [Ho].

helps,[a]

LEXICON—a. ἀντίλημψις (LN **35.9**) (BAGD p. 75): 'help' [BAGD, Lns; KJV, NET], 'act of helping' [Herm], 'helpful act' [NJB], 'form of assistance' [NRSV], 'assistant' [NAB], 'ministry of aid' [AB], 'gift of support' [HNTC], 'power of succoring' [ICC], 'the ability to help others' [**LN**], 'helpful deed' [BAGD, NTC]. The plural is translated '(some to) help others' [CEV], 'those who do helpful deeds' [TNT], 'those who help others' [ISV], 'those who can help others' [NLT], 'those who have ability to help others' [REB], 'those able to help others' [NIV], 'those who are given the power to help others' [TEV], 'various kinds of administrative support' [NIGTC].

QUESTION—Does this refer to helping people in need or assisting church officers in their work?

1. It refers to helping people in need [Ed, Gdt, HNTC, ICC, Lns, My, NCBC, NIC2, NTC, TG, TH, TNTC, Vn]. In keeping with Acts 20:35, this refers to helping the poor and sick among believers [Ed]. It refers to helping all kinds of suffering and need [Gdt].
2. It refers to helping church officers in their work [AB, Ho, NIC, NIGTC]. It refers helping other officers in the church to care for the poor and sick [Ho]. It refers to a variety of services among which may have been the finances and the order of divine services [NIC].

1 CORINTHIANS 12:28 163

administrations,ᵃ kindsᵇ of-tongues.ᶜ
LEXICON—a. κυβέρνησις (LN **36.3**) (BAGD p. 456): 'administration' [BAGD, NTC], 'administrative ability' [AB], 'administrative gift' [NIV, TNT], 'administrator' [ISV, NAB], 'act of administration' [Herm], 'government' [KJV], 'power of governing' [ICC], 'power to direct' [TEV], 'gift of direction' [HNTC], 'power to guide' [REB], 'ability to formulate strategies' [NIGTC], 'guidance' [LN; NJB], 'leadership' [**LN**], 'form of leadership' [NRSV], 'leader' [CEV], 'management' [Lns; NET]. The plural is translated '(those who) can get others to work together' [NLT].
  b. γένος (See this word at 12:10): 'kind' [AB, NTC], 'diversity' [KJV], 'variety' [Lns], not explicit [NAB]. This noun is also translated as an adjective: 'unknown' [NLT], 'strange' [TEV], 'ecstatic' [ICC]. The plural is translated 'different kinds' [CEV, NET, NIV, TNT], 'various kinds' [Herm, HNTC, NIGTC; ISV, NJB, NRSV, REB].
  c. γλῶσσα (See this word at 12:10): 'tongue' [AB, Herm, HNTC, Lns, NIGTC, NTC; all versions except CEV, NLT], 'language' [CEV, NLT], 'utterance' [ICC].
QUESTION—What is meant by κυβέρνησις 'administration'?
  This word only occurs here in the New Testament. In its three occurrences in the Septuagint it has the sense of giving 'guidance'. Here it means 'acts of guidance' both to the individual and to the community of believers [NIC2]. It is related to the noun meaning 'pilot' or 'sea captain' in Acts 27:11 and Revelation 18:17. Here it seems to indicate the ability to direct the affairs of the church [NTC]. It has the sense of being able to give direction [TNTC]. It probably indicates the ability to oversee the organization of the church [ICC]. It perhaps refers to spiritual leadership in the church [NIC]. It indicates the ability to manage and direct others [Lns].

12:29 **Surely not all (are) apostles? Surely not all (are) prophets? Surely not all (are) teachers? Surely not all (are) miracles?**
QUESTION—What reply is expected to these rhetorical question using the negative particle μή 'not'?
  They all expect a negative reply [AB, Gdt, HNTC, ICC, Lns, MNTC, NCBC, NIC, NIC2, NIGTC, NTC, Rb, TG, TH, TNTC, Vn; CEV, ISV, NET, NLT, TEV]: Surely all are not apostles, are they?
QUESTION—What is the function of these rhetorical questions?
  They function to show that it is preposterous for all to have the same gift [NCBC]. They show that it is wrong to think that all should have all the gifts [HNTC] or desire to have the same gift [Ho]. They explain 12:27, that the Corinthians were individually members of the one body and they also refer back to 12:14 which says the body is one and has many members. For one member to be the complete body would have meant the death of the other parts [ICC]. They make clear 12:28, that only some, not everyone, received gifts [NIC]. They function to stress the concept of the diversity of gifts

[NIC2, TNTC]. They function to counter the spirit of independence and self-sufficiency [Vn].

QUESTION—Where is the emphasis in these questions?

The repeated πάντες 'all' is emphasized [EGT].

QUESTION—What is meant by μὴ πάντες δυνάμεις 'Surely all are not miracles, are they'?

We should supply the verb 'to have' [Ed, EGT, ICC, Lns, My; NLT, TEV]: Surely not all have miracles, do they? / Surely all do not have (the power to work) miracles, do they? We should make the abstract noun into an agentive noun [AB, Gdt, HNTC, NTC; all versions except NLT, TEV]: All are not miracle-workers, are they?

12:30 **Surely not all have gifts of-healings? Surely not all speak in-tongues? Surely not all interpret?**[a]

LEXICON—a. pres. act. indic. of διερμηνεύω (LN 33.145) (BAGD 1. p. 194, 2. p. 194): 'to interpret' [AB, BAGD (2), Herm, HNTC, LN, Lns, NTC; ISV, KJV, NET, NIV, NJB, NRSV, REB, TNT], 'to translate' [BAGD (1), LN]. This verb is also translated as a phrase: 'to interpret unknown languages' [NLT], 'to have the gift of interpretation of tongues' [NAB], 'to explain what is said' [TEV], 'to tell what a language means' [CEV], 'to put the deepest secret things into articulate speech' [NIGTC]. Διερμηνεύω refers to interpreting ecstatic speech [BAGD].

QUESTION—To what does διερμηνεύω 'to interpret' refer?

See ἑρμηνεία 'interpretation' at 12:10 for a discussion of whether this refers to unknown or known languages.

QUESTION—Why does Paul mention only these seven gifts here?

The gifts he mentions are only intended to be representative of them all [Lns].

QUESTION—Is there any meaning to the order in which he lists the gifts?

That he lists 'tongues' and 'the interpretation of tongues' last in all three lists in this chapter may indicate that there was a problem regarding this gift among the Corinthians [AB]. This is the third time he places 'tongues' last [ICC].

DISCOURSE UNIT: 12:31a–13:13 [NJB]. The topic is the order of importance in spiritual gifts. Hymn to love.

12:31a **But/now**[a] **set-your-hearts-on**[b] **the greater**[c] **gifts.**

TEXT—Instead of μείζονα 'greater', some manuscripts have κρεί(ττ)ονα 'better'. GNT does not mention this alternative. Gdt, CEV, ISV and KJV seem to support κρεί(ττ)ονα 'better'.

LEXICON—a. δέ (See this word at 11:2): 'but' [AB, Ed, EGT, Gdt, Herm, HNTC, Ho, ICC, Lns, NTC; KJV, NET, NIV, NRSV, TNT], 'and in any event' [NLT], 'then' [TEV], 'now' [My], 'so' [ISV], not explicit [NIGTC; CEV, NAB, NJB, REB].

b. pres. act. impera. of ζηλόω (LN **25.76**) (BAGD 1.a. p. 338): 'to set one's heart on' [**LN**; NAB, TEV], 'to set one's mind on' [NJB], 'to desire eagerly' [NTC; NIV], 'to desire' [CEV, ISV, NLT], 'to strive for' [BAGD, Herm, HNTC; NRSV, TNT], 'to strive zealously for' [Lns], 'to be zealously concerned about' [NIGTC], 'to covet earnestly' [KJV], 'to be eager for' [NET], 'to prize' [REB], 'to be zealous for' [AB], 'to persistently long for' [ICC], 'to be earnest, to be completely intent upon' [LN]. Ζηλόω means to be deeply committed to something with accompanying desire [LN].

c. μείζων (LN **87.28**) (BAGD 2.b.β. p. 498): 'greater' [HNTC, LN, Lns, NTC; NAB, NET, NIV, NRSV], 'yet greater' [ICC], 'more important' [AB, BAGD; TEV], 'better' [LN; ISV], 'higher' [Herm; NJB, REB], 'superior to' [LN]. This comparative adjective is also translated as a superlative: 'best' [CEV, KJV], 'greatest' [NIGTC; TNT], 'most helpful' [NLT].

QUESTION—What relationship is indicated by δέ 'but/now'?

1. The δέ is adversative [AB, Ed, EGT, Gdt, HNTC, Ho, ICC, Lns, NTC; KJV, NET, NIV, NRSV, TNT]: but. All cannot have every gift, but they should covet the better ones [Ho]. All cannot have the best gifts, but they should strive to obtain them [ICC]. The contrast is between lower and higher gifts and between the sovereignty of God in their distribution as over against each believer's desire for the greater ones [Ed]. The contrast is between God's sovereignty in giving and people's striving [EGT, ICC].
2. The δέ is transitional [My]: now. Paul is making a transition to a new point.

QUESTION—Should the verb ζηλόω 'to set one's heart on' be taken as imperative or indicative mood?

1. It should be taken as imperative mood [AB, Alf, EGT, Gdt, HNTC, Ho, ICC, Lns, NCBC, NIC, NIC2, NIGTC, NTC, TG, TH; all versions]: set your heart on the greater gifts. This decision is supported by the fact that in 14:1 the same verb form is used and there it is almost certainly imperative [AB]. The word does not mean to strive to obtain the greatest gift since God is the one who distributes the gifts and it is not a question of striving for a particular gift. Rather, they are not to stop being zealously concerned about them [NIGTC].
2. It should be taken as indicative mood [MNTC]: you are setting your hearts on greater gifts. In view of the fact that ζηλόω more commonly has a negative sense of jealously desiring something and because the imperative and indicative forms are identical, it seems more in keeping with the context that Paul is stating what they were eagerly doing, that is, desiring the (apparently) greater gifts. They were to stop doing this.

QUESTION—What is the implication of the present imperative of ζηλόω 'to set one's heart on' and what is meant by desiring the greater gifts?

It implies that the action should be continually done [ICC, NIC2]: keep on setting your hearts on the greater gifts. God determines what gifts to give, but they can have an earnest desire for them and prepare themselves to receive them [HNTC, ICC, TNTC]. The believers are to attain the goal of receiving and developing their spiritual gifts for the benefit of the church [NTC]. They can do this by putting themselves at God's disposal, being content with what he gives [Vn]. The greater gifts were related to the inspired exercise of their conscious faculties [EGT]. They are to pray that the greater gifts be given to the church at Corinth, leaving it to the Lord to choose which gifts are to be given. This does not mean that each individual will strive to receive the greater gifts [NIC]. The command is general and does not imply that each person should strive for any or all of the greater gifts [Lns].

QUESTION—What does Paul mean by μείζων 'greater' gifts?

He means the gifts that are intelligible to others and therefore of benefit to the whole community, as over against tongues without interpretation. This is seen in the passage 14:1–25 [NIC2]. It may mean gifts that are *more constructive* than tongues and interpretation of tongues [AB]. The greater gifts are those which are more beneficial or useful [EGT, Ho, ICC, Lns, NIGTC; NLT]. Prophecy and teaching would be of maximum benefit to the whole body of believers [Alf, HNTC]. The gifts which come at the beginning of the lists in 8–10, 28 and 29 are perhaps the greater ones, especially prophecy [NCBC]. He probably has in mind prophecy as suggested by 14:1 [TH]. He means those higher in rank than tongues which he has put at the bottom of two lists [NIC]. The reading κρείττονα 'better' is preferable and has the sense of 'more useful' or 'resulting in the building up of the whole' [Gdt].

DISCOURSE UNIT: 12:31b–14:1a [AB]. The topic is excursus: love highest of the higher gifts.

DISCOURSE UNIT: 12:31b–13:13 [GNT, NIC; NAB, NIV, NJB, NLT]. The topic is the significance of love [NIC], love [GNT; NIV], the excellence of the gift of love [NAB], the order of importance in spiritual gifts and hymn to love [NJB], love is the greatest [NLT].

DISCOURSE UNIT: 12:31b–13:3 [AB, EGT, TH]. The topic is the way to Christian eminence [EGT], worthlessness of all gifts without love [AB].

12:31b And yet/still[a] (a) more-excellent[b] way[c] I-show[d] you.

LEXICON—a. ἔτι (LN 67.128, 59.75, 89.135): 'yet' [HNTC, LN (67.128); KJV], 'still' [Herm, LN (67.128)]; NRSV, TNT], 'now' [ISV, NET, NIV, NJB], 'even' [NTC; REB], 'further' [AB], 'besides' [LN (59.75), Lns], 'in addition' [LN (59.75)], 'nevertheless' [LN (89.135)]. The phrase καὶ ἔτι 'and yet' is translated 'so' [CEV], 'however' [TEV], 'first, however' [NLT], 'now' [NAB], 'yes' [NIGTC].

b. καθ' ὑπερβολή (LN **78.33**) (BAGD II.5.b.β. p. 407, p. 840): 'more excellent' [Herm, ICC, NTC; KJV, NRSV], 'exceedingly excellent' [Lns], 'the most excellent' [NIV], 'better' [HNTC; TNT], 'much better' [CEV],

'far better' [BAGD (p. 840), **LN**], 'even better' [REB], 'even great' [NIGTC], '(that is) better than any of them' [NLT], 'best of all' [TEV], 'the best of all' [ISV, NJB], 'beyond comparison' [BAGD (p. 407); NET], 'beyond measure' [BAGD (p. 407)], 'more extraordinary' [AB], '(which) surpasses all the others' [NAB], 'supremely excellent' [Gdt, Rb]. The word ὑπερβολή alone is translated 'extreme, far more, supreme, extraordinary, much greater, to a far greater degree' [LN], 'excess, extraordinary quality or character' [BAGD (p. 840)]. This should be superlative, not comparative, 'a super-excellent way' [EGT].
  c. ὁδός (LN 41.16) (BAGD 2.c. p. 555): 'way' [BAGD, Herm, NIGTC; all versions except NLT], 'something else' [NLT], 'way of life, way to live', a figurative extension of the word 'road' [LN].
  d. pres. act. indic. of δείκνυμι (LN **28.47, 33.150**, 33 fn 27) (BAGD 1.b. p. 172): 'to show' [AB, BAGD, Herm, HNTC, ICC, LN (28.47, **33.150**), NIGTC, NTC; all versions except NJB, NLT, TEV], 'to make known' [BAGD, **LN** (28.47)], 'to tell about' [NLT], 'to point out' [BAGD, Lns], 'to put before (one)' [NJB], 'to make clear, to explain' [LN (33.150)], 'to demonstrate' [LN (28.47)], 'to cause to know' [LN (33 fn 27)]. The phrase ὑμῖν δείκνυμι 'I show you' is translated 'is the following' [TEV].
QUESTION—With what word is ἔτι 'yet/still' to be construed?
  1. It should be construed with the preceding καί 'and' [AB, Alf, EGT, Gdt, Ho, Lns; CEV, ISV, KJV, NAB, NET, NIV, NJB, NLT, TEV]: and now / and yet / moreover / besides.
  2. It should be construed with the following καθ' ὑπερβολὴν ὁδόν 'more excellent' [Herm, HNTC, ICC, NIC, NTC, Rb, TH; NRSV, REB, TNT]: a still more excellent way.
QUESTION—What is meant by καθ' ὑπερβολὴν ὁδόν 'a more excellent way'?
  1. It means that love is the only proper way to use spiritual gifts [Alf, HNTC, ICC, NIC2, NTC]. Paul is not contrasting love and the gifts but is saying that love is the only framework in which the gifts properly operate [NIC2]. Love is the way to test and evaluate other gifts and is the way to maintain unity in the body [HNTC].
  2. It means that love is a way of life that is more excellent than obtaining spiritual gifts [Gdt, Herm, NIC, TG, TNTC]. Paul's 'way' is better than the earnest desire for greater gifts he has just spoken about [NIC]. Paul is saying that love should be sought for its own sake [TNTC].
  3. It indicates that love is a way to obtain spiritual gifts [Ed, EGT, Ho, My, Rb]. Love is a means to obtain spiritual gifts for the benefit of the body of believers and to protect the possessor from any evil influence that might accrue from their possession [Ed]. This is the way to set one's heart on the greater gifts [EGT].
  4. It indicates that love should be the dominant motive for seeking and using gifts [Lns].

DISCOURSE UNIT: 13:1–13 [Alf, Ed, Gdt, Herm, HNTC, Ho, ICC, Lns, NIGTC, NTC, TG, TNTC, Vn; CEV, ISV, KJV, NET, TEV]. The topic is the panegyric of love [Alf], the praise of love [Ed, ICC, TNTC], Christian love [Ho], the fundamental test: love [HNTC], the better way: love [Lns], the more excellent way [Gdt, Herm, NIC2], letter of love [NTC], love [TG; CEV, TEV], the way of love [NET], the supremacy of love [NCBC; ISV], love is the essential and lasting criterion [NIGTC].

DISCOURSE UNIT: 13:1–3 [Alf, Ed, Gdt, Herm, MNTC, NIC2, NIGTC, NTC, TH, Vn]. The topic is the prominence of love [MNTC], the necessity of love [NIC2, Vn], the fruitlessness of all gifts without love [NIGTC], prerequisite of love [NTC].

13:1 If I-speak with-the tongues^a of men^b and of angels,

LEXICON—a. γλῶσσα (See this word at 12:10, 28): 'tongue' [AB, Herm, HNTC, ICC, Lns, NIGTC, NTC; ISV, KJV, NAB, NET, NIV, NRSV, REB, TNT], 'language' [CEV, NJB, NLT, TEV]. Γλῶσσα is not a reference to eloquent speaking but to the gift of tongues as referred to in 12:28 [AB, Ed, EGT, Gdt, HNTC, Ho, ICC, Lns, My, NIC, NIC2, TH, TNTC, Vn].

b. ἄνθρωπος (BAGD 1.a.β. p. 68): 'man' [BAGD, Herm, HNTC, ICC, Lns, NTC; KJV, NET, NIV, REB, TNT], 'human being' [AB, BAGD; TEV], 'human' [CEV, ISV], 'mortal' [NRSV]. This noun is also translated as an adjective: 'human (tongues)' [NIGTC; NAB], 'human (language)' [NJB]. The phrase τῶν ἀνθρώπων καὶ τῶν ἀγγέλων 'of men and of the angels' is translated 'in heaven or on earth' [NLT]. Ἄνθρωπος includes both men and women [AB, BAGD, TH; CEV, ISV, NRSV, TEV]. See this word also at 11:28.

QUESTION—What kind of language is referred to in γλώσσαις τῶν ἀνθρώπων 'tongues of men'?

1. This refers to foreign languages spoken by human beings [Alf, HNTC, Ho, Lns, MNTC, TG, TH, Vn]. It refers to common human speech [HNTC]. It refers to languages and dialects that the speaker has not learned such as happened at Pentecost [Ho, Lns]. It refers to being able to speak all sorts of languages with the eloquence of the greatest men [MNTC].
2. This refers to the gift of tongues [AB, Ed, EGT, ICC, My, NIC, NIC2, NIGTC, NTC, TNTC]. He means people speaking under the inspiration of the Holy Spirit but not understanding what they are saying [NIC2]. It refers to tongues, but coupled with angelic speech, is general enough to include all kinds of speech [TNTC]. Both the preceding and following context argues for the sense of glossolalia [AB].

QUESTION—Why does Paul mention γλῶσσα 'tongues' first?

He mentions 'tongues' first since that was the prominent topic in the discussion [Ho]. He mentions them first because the Corinthians were placing too high a value on them [ICC, Lns, Rb]. The gift of tongues was most valued at Corinth [Ed, EGT]. This was the topic that was causing the problem with the Corinthians [AB, NIC2].

QUESTION—What is meant by γλώσσαις τῶν ἀγγέλων 'the tongues of angels'?

It indicates that angels spoke among themselves in different languages than people [TG]. He refers to, but does not endorse, a view held by some in Corinth that the gift of tongues was an angelic language [NIGTC]. This phrase coupled with 'tongues of men' indicates all languages, human and divine [Ho]. This phrase coupled with 'tongues of men', indicates mystical utterance at its highest realization [EGT]. He refers to speaking with even angelic eloquence [MNTC]. The plural 'tongues' does not imply that angels spoke a number of languages. This is simply an addition meant to surpass what the Corinthians practiced in regard to tongues [Lns].

but do-not have love,[a]

LEXICON—a. ἀγάπη (LN 25.43) (BAGD I.1.a. p. 5): 'love' [AB, BAGD, Herm, HNTC, ICC, LN, Lns, NIGTC, NTC; all versions except CEV, KJV, NLT], 'charity' [KJV], 'loving concern' [LN]. This noun is also translated as a verb: '(if I did not) love others' [CEV], '(but didn't) love others' [NLT].

QUESTION—Who is meant as the recipient of such love?

This means love for others [NIGTC, TG; CEV, NLT], our neighbors [Gdt], all people [Lns]. No distinction between love for God and love for people is intended, but the following verses show that it is especially in its application to people that is praised [ICC]. Love is an attitude that manifests itself in acts that indicate regard, respect, and concern for the welfare of others [NIGTC].

I-have-become (a) sounding[a] **gong**[b] **or (a) clanging**[c] **cymbal.**[d]

LEXICON—a. pres. act. participle of ἠχέω (LN **14.80**) (BAGD p. 349): 'to sound' [BAGD, Lns; KJV, REB], 'to resound' [AB, LN; NIV, TNT], 'to reverberate' [ISV], 'to resonate' [NIGTC], 'to boom' [NJB], 'to produce a sound, to make noise' [LN], 'to ring out' [BAGD], 'to clang' [HNTC, LN], 'to echo' [NTC]. This participle is also translated as an adjective: 'noisy' [Herm, **LN**; CEV, NAB, NRSV, TEV]. It is also translated as a phrase: 'meaningless noise like a loud (gong)' [NLT]. The basic meaning of ἠχέω is 'to make a noise'. In translating it is often given the sound or noise that a gong makes [LN].

b. χαλκός (LN 2.54, **6.95**) (BAGD 2. p. 875): 'gong' [AB, Herm; all versions except KJV], 'brass' [LN (2.54), Lns; KJV], 'brass gong' [BAGD, **LN** (6.95)], 'jar' [NIGTC], 'bronze' [HNTC, LN (2.54), NTC], 'copper' [LN (2.54)]. Χαλκός is the word for the metals brass, bronze, or copper, and thus indicates anything made from them [BAGD, LN]. It probably refers to bronze, an alloy of copper and tin [TNTC]. It probably referred to a gong [AB, ICC, TNTC; all versions except KJV]. It was not a musical instrument but a piece of clanging brass which made a meaningless noise [Ho].

c. pres. act. participle of ἀλαλάζω (LN **14.82, 6.95**) (BAGD p. 34): 'to clang' [Herm, **LN** (6.95, 14.82), Lns, NTC; CEV, NAB, NET, NIV, NLT, NRSV, REB, TEV], 'to clash' [BAGD; ISV, NJB, TNT], 'to tinkle' [KJV], 'to reverberate' [AB, **LN**, NIGTC]. This verb is also translated as an adjective: 'shrill' [HNTC]. Ἀλαλάζω indicates a loud reverberating sound [ICC, LN (14.82)].

d. κύμβαλον (LN **6.94, 6.95**) (BAGD p. 457): 'cymbal' [AB, BAGD, Herm, HNTC, **LN** (6.94, 6.95), Lns, NIGTC, NTC; all versions except TEV], 'bell' [TEV]. The phrase χαλκὸς ἠχῶν ἢ κύμβαλον ἀλαλάζον 'resounding gong or clanging cymbal' is also translated 'the senseless din in heathen worships' [ICC]. Cymbals were a pair of metal basins used like our modern cymbals [TH]. Cymbals were used in the worship of the goddess Cybele and the god Dionysus and the god Corybantes [ICC].

QUESTION—With the image being a resounding gong or a clanging cymbal, and the topic being a person speaking in tongues with no love, and what is the point of similarity.

The point of similarity is the lack of intelligent communication [AB, HNTC, ICC, TNTC]. The point of similarity is the empty hollow sound of heathen worship [ICC, NIC2, Vn]. The point of similarity is the lack of heart in both resounding gongs and people speaking in tongues without love [NIC]. Paul is saying that such action without love is without meaning [HNTC, NTC, TG, TNTC] and, in fact, pagan [HNTC].

13:2 And if I-have[a] prophecy[b] and I-know[c] all the mysteries[d] and all the knowledge[e]

LEXICON—a. pres. act. indic. of ἔχω (LN 74.12) (BAGD I.2.e. β. p. 332): 'to have' [AB, BAGD, Herm, HNTC, ICC, LN, Lns, NIGTC, NTC; all versions except CEV], 'to be able to' [LN; CEV], 'to have the capacity to' [LN]. See this word also at 11:10.

b. προφητεία (LN **33.461**, 33 fn76): 'prophecy' [Lns; NET], 'the gift of prophecy' [AB, Herm, HNTC, NIGTC, NTC; ISV, KJV, NAB, NIV, NLT, REB, TNT], 'the power of prophecy' [NJB], 'prophetic powers' [NRSV], 'the gift of inspired preaching' [ICC; TEV], 'capacity to prophesy' [**LN**], 'ability to prophesy, to be able to speak inspired messages' [LN]. This noun is also translated as a verb: 'to prophesy' [CEV]. 'To have prophecy' indicates more than 'to prophesy', it means that the person has become a prophet [NTC]. See this word also at 12:10.

c. perf. (with pres. meaning) act. subj. of οἶδα (BAGD 1.b. p. 555): 'to know' [BAGD, Herm, HNTC, Lns; NET, NLT], 'to understand' [AB, NTC; CEV, ISV, KJV, NRSV, TNT], 'to comprehend' [LN (32.4); NAB], 'to fathom' [NIV], 'to penetrate' [NIGTC; NJB], 'to see one's way through' [ICC]. The phrase εἰδῶ τὰ μυστήρια πάντα καὶ πᾶσαν τὴν γνῶσιν 'I know all the mysteries and all the knowledge' is translated 'I have...the knowledge of every hidden truth' [REB], 'I may have all knowledge and understand all secrets' [TEV]. See this word also at 11:3.

d. μυστήριον (LN 28.77) (BAGD 2. p. 530): 'mystery' [AB, BAGD, Herm, HNTC, LN, Lns, NTC; KJV, NAB, NET, NIV, NJB, NRSV], 'secret' [LN; CEV, ISV, TEV], 'mystery of the future' [NLT], 'mystery of the kingdom of God' [ICC], 'hidden secret' [TNT], 'hidden truth' [REB], 'depths too profound for mere human discovery' [NIGTC]. See this word also at 2:1.

e. γνῶσις (See this word at 12:8): 'knowledge' [AB, Herm, HNTC, ICC, Lns, NTC; all versions except NAB, NLT, REB], 'knowledge'" [NIGTC], 'with full knowledge' [NAB], not explicit [REB]. The phrase πᾶσαν τὴν γνῶσιν 'all knowledge' is translated 'knew everything about everything' [NLT].

QUESTION—What relationship is indicated by the initial καί 'and'?

It indicates a conjoining relationship with the first verse [Lns]: if...*and* if. The two καὶ ἐάν 'and if' phrases of this verse plus two in the next verse have a cumulative overwhelming effect [Lns].

QUESTION—What is meant by μυστήριον 'mystery'?

It means 'that which was not known before' but now is revealed to some [LN]. It means truth that people could only know if God revealed it to them [Ho, TNTC]. It may refer to God's secret plans for mankind (see 2:6, 7) [TG]. It refers to the secrets of God's thinking (see Rom. 11:25, 16:25) [Alf]. It refers to truths of God's plans revealed by the Holy Spirit only to believers [Vn]. It refers God's secret plans to save people from their sins [Gdt, Ho, NIC2]. He speaks of understanding all unrevealed mysteries of God and all the mysteries that have been revealed [MNTC].

QUESTION—What is meant by γνῶσις 'knowledge'?

Γνῶσις means supernatural mystical knowledge [BAGD]. It means the intellectual grasping of truth as revealed [Ho]. It means a human understanding of all facts, being virtually omniscient [MNTC]. It is similar in meaning to the 'word of wisdom' referred to in 12:8. It is not mere intellectual knowledge, but has a mystical sense [NIC].

and if I-have all faith[a] so-as[b] to-remove[c] mountains,[d]

LEXICON—a. πίστις (LN 31.85, 31.102): 'faith' [AB, Herm, HNTC, ICC, LN (31.85), Lns, NTC; all versions except NLT], 'the gift of faith' [NIGTC; NLT], 'Christian faith' [LN (31.102)]. It refers to a special gift of faith in God's power to help people by means of miracles [BAGD]. See this word at 12:9.

b. ὥστε (See this word at 10:12): 'so as' [Herm, HNTC, ICC, Lns, NTC; NRSV, TNT], 'so that' [AB; KJV, NET, NLT], 'that' [CEV, NIV], 'enough' [REB], 'great enough' [NAB], '(all) needed' [TEV], 'necessary' [NJB], 'sufficient to' [NIGTC], not explicit [ISV].

c. pres. act. infin. of μεθίστημι (LN 15.9) (BAGD 1. p. 499): 'to remove' [AB, BAGD, Herm, HNTC, **LN**, NIGTC, NTC; KJV, NET, NRSV, TNT], 'to move' [ICC; CEV, ISV, NAB, NIV, NJB, REB, TEV], 'to transfer' [Lns], 'to cause to move' [LN], 'to remove from one place to another' [BAGD]. The phrase ὄρη μεθιστάναι 'to remove mountains' is translated 'I could speak to a mountain and make it move' [NLT].

d. ὄρος (LN 1.46) (BAGD p. 582): 'mountain' [AB, BAGD, Herm, HNTC, ICC, LN, Lns, NIGTC, NTC; all versions], 'hill' [BAGD].

QUESTION—What is the significance of the present tense infinitive μεθιστάναι 'to remove'?

The present infinitive indicates a continuous aspect [Ed, EGT]: to keep on removing mountains. It means to remove mountain after mountain from its place and transfer the whole mass to another location [Ed].

QUESTION—What is the function of the repetition of the word πᾶς 'all' with 'mysteries', 'knowledge', and 'faith'?

It means to possess each of these in its individual perfection [Gdt].

QUESTION—What is meant by πίστις 'faith'?

It means miracle-working faith [Gdt, Herm, HNTC, Ho, ICC, Rb, TNTC, Vn]. It does not mean the faith which brings salvation [HNTC, ICC, Vn]. It refers to faith as a gift of the Spirit as seen in 12:9 [MNTC, NCBC, NIGTC, TNTC]. All faith does not indicate absolutely all the faith in the world, but rather to enough faith to accomplish a given goal [Alf].

QUESTION—What does ὄρη μεθιστάναι 'to remove mountains' imply?

It is a proverb which implied the doing of what was thought to be impossible [BAGD, HNTC, Lns, NTC]. A mountain represents a possible obstacle [Gdt, NIGTC]. This is hyperbole (overstatement) [EGT, MNTC, NCBC] and means completely trusting God to do mighty things on behalf of his people [MNTC].

but I-have not love, I-am nothing.

QUESTION—What is meant by οὐθέν εἰμι 'I am nothing'?

It means I am worth nothing [EGT, Ho, NIC, TG, TH, Vn]. None of these attainments are of any value without love and so he is worthless [Ho].

13:3 And-if[a] I-give-away[b] all the-(things) belonging-to[c] me

LEXICON—a. κἄν (LN89.73) (BAGD 1. p. 402): 'and if' [AB, BAGD, Herm, HNTC, Lns, NTC], 'even if' [LN, NIGTC; ISV], 'if' [NAB, NET, NIV, NLT, NRSV], 'and what if' [CEV], 'even though' [LN], 'and though' [KJV], 'though' [NJB], not explicit [ICC; REB, TEV, TNT]. Κἄν is a contraction of καί plus ἐάν, 'and if' [LN].

b. aorist act. subj. of ψωμίζω (LN 23.5, **57.113**) (BAGD 2. p. 894): 'to give away' [**LN**, NTC; CEV, ISV, NET, NRSV, TEV], 'to give to others' [**LN**], 'to give to the needy' [REB], 'to give to the poor' [NIV, NLT], 'to give away to the poor' [NJB], 'to give to feed the poor' [KJV, NAB], 'to spend on feeding the poor' [TNT], 'to use for feeding others' [HNTC], 'to distribute' [Herm], 'to divide up' [NIGTC], 'to give away bit by bit, to divide in small pieces' [BAGD], 'to dole out' [AB, BAGD, LN (57.113)], 'to dole out with one's own hands' [ICC], 'to feed' [LN (23.5), Lns], 'to give to eat' [LN (23.5)]. The aorist tense indicates a single action in which the person gives all of his possessions away [Ed, Gdt, ICC, TNTC].

c. pres. act. participle of ὑπάρχω (LN 57.2) (BAGD 1. p. 838): 'to belong to' [LN], 'to have' [LN; ISV, NAB, NLT, TEV, TNT], 'to own' [CEV, NET], 'to possess' [ICC; NIV, NJB, REB]. It is also translated as a noun: '(one's) goods' [KJV], '(one's) property' [AB, BAGD, HNTC], '(one's) possessions' [BAGD, Herm, Lns, NIGTC, NTC; NRSV], '(one's) means' [BAGD].

QUESTION—What relationship is indicated by καί 'and'?

It indicates a conjoining relationship [AB, Lns, NTC; KJV]: and.

QUESTION—What is implied in ψωμίσω πάντα τὰ ὑπάρχοντά μου 'I give away all the things that belong to me'?

The basic idea is selling ones goods and giving away the proceeds [TH]. The verb implies that the gifts be given to many people and be given personally [Ed, Gdt, ICC]. The verb implies giving away in small amounts to a large number of people [TNTC]. It implies giving away bit by bit over a long time [NTC]. The implied indirect object is 'to the poor' [Gdt, HNTC; KJV, NAB, NIV, NJB, NLT, TNT], 'to others' [HNTC, LN], 'to the needy' [NIGTC, TG; REB]. The implied purpose is 'to feed (others/the poor)' [HNTC; KJV, NAB, TNT]. The Greek has no overt indirect object since the focus is on the giver [ICC, TNTC].

and if I-hand-over[a] my body in-order-that I-may-boast[b]/burn,[c]

TEXT—Instead of καυχήσωμαι 'I may boast' some manuscripts have καυθήσωμαι 'I may be burned' or καυθήσομαι 'I will be burned'. GNT selects the reading καυχήσωμαι 'I may boast' with a C rating, indicating difficulty in deciding which variant to place in the text. The reading καυχήσωμαι 'I may boast' is also taken by AB, EGT, NIC2, NIGTC, Rb, TNTC; NET, NLT and NRSV. The reading καυθήσωμαι 'I may burn' or καυθήσομαι 'I will burn' is taken by Alf, Gdt, Herm, HNTC, Ho, ICC, Lns, NTC, Vn; CEV, KJV, NAB, NIV, NJB, REB, TEV, and TNT.

LEXICON—a. aorist act. subj. of παραδίδωμι (BAGD 1.a. p. 614): 'to hand over' [AB, BAGD, HNTC, LN, NIGTC; NAB, NRSV], 'to give over' [NET], 'to give up' [BAGD, Herm, NTC; NJB, TEV], 'to give' [KJV, REB], 'to surrender' [ICC; ISV, NIV], 'to deliver up' [TNT], 'to deliver over' [Lns], 'to sacrifice' [NLT], 'to let oneself (be burned alive)' [CEV]. See this word also at 11:2.

b. aorist mid. (deponent = act.) subj. of καυχάομαι (LN 33.368) (BAGD 1. p. 425): 'to boast' [AB, BAGD, LN; ISV, NET, NLT, NRSV], 'to brag' [ISV], 'to glory' [BAGD, NIGTC].

c. aorist mid. (deponent = act.) subj. of καυσόω (LN 14.63) (BAGD p. 425): 'to burn' [LN], 'to be on fire' [LN], 'to burn up' [BAGD], '(surrender my body) to the flames' [ICC; NIV]. This middle is also translated as a passive: 'to be burned' [Herm, HNTC, Lns, NTC; CEV, KJV, NAB, NJB, REB, TEV, TNT], 'to be consumed by heat' [BAGD].

174 1 CORINTHIANS 13:3

QUESTION—What is the purpose of giving one's body if the reading meaning 'to burn' is understood, and what does it indicate?

The purpose is voluntary martyrdom [Gdt, My, TG], which is the greatest show of dedication to a cause [My, TG]. The context indicates dying for the good of others [Ho]. The words imply 'in self-sacrifice' [Alf]. The words indicate the pinnacle of self-sacrifice [Ho, Lns, NIC]. It probably indicates self-sacrifice for a cause by the most painful of deaths [HNTC, ICC]. Martyrdom is probably not in focus [Ho, Lns, NIC2]. Martyrdom by fire was not used until after Paul's time [AB, HNTC, Lns, NIC2]. The giving of one's body to be burned should not be taken literally, but as figurative of self-sacrifice [NTC]. Paul could have in mind the dramatic sacrifice of either giving his body for burning or selling himself into slavery, both amount to the same without love [TNTC]. It can either indicate martyrdom by fire or the self-immolation of an ascetic [Herm].

QUESTION—What is the purpose of giving one's body if the reading meaning 'to boast' is understood?

We must assume that Paul had a good sense of boasting in mind. Paul does use this word elsewhere in a positive sense (see 1:29–31, 9:15; 2 Cor. 1:14, 11:23–29, 12:10). He means then that if he performed the self-sacrifice of giving his body so that he could boast about it (as he could about his other sufferings), but lacked love, it would benefit him nothing. Clement of Rome referred in his writings of people who would sell themselves into slavery and use the payment received to feed others [NIC2]. The reading 'boast' is likely and giving one's body could imply to be burned [TNTC] or to be a slave [TNTC; NET].

but have not love, I-am-benefited[a] nothing.

LEXICON— a. pres. pass. indic. of ὠφελέω (LN 35.2) (BAGD 1.a. p. 900): 'to be benefited' [BAGD; TNT], 'to be helped' [BAGD, LN]. This passive is also translated as a simple active: 'to gain something' [CEV, NAB, NIV, NRSV, REB], 'to profit' [Lns], 'to get something out of it' [ISV], 'to be of value' [NLT], 'to count for' [NIGTC], 'to be one whit the better' [ICC], 'to receive benefit' [NET]. This passive voice is also translated as an active with 'it/this/what' as subject: 'to avail (someone)' [Herm], 'to profit (someone)' [NTC; KJV], 'to benefit (someone)' [AB], 'to do (someone) good' [BAGD, HNTC; NJB, TEV].

QUESTION—Why does Paul use first person in these three verses?

Paul uses first person to lessen the idea that he is scolding the Corinthians [EGT]. He uses first person to show that he personally endorses what he is saying [AB].

QUESTION—What is meant by 'I am benefited nothing'?

There is a different result for each of these attainments: I produce nothing of value (13:1), I am of no value (13:2), and I gain nothing of value (13:3) [EGT, ICC, MNTC]. This changes from 'I am nothing' (13:2) to 'I am benefited nothing' because the focus changes from the worth of the person to

1 CORINTHIANS 13:3 175

the worth of the acts [Gdt]. Everyone who serves the Lord will receive a reward only if he has love [NIC]. At God's judgment he will receive no credit [HNTC].

DISCOURSE UNIT: 13:4–7 [AB, Alf, Ed, Gdt, ICC, MNTC, NIC2, NIGTC, NTC, TH, Vn]. The topic is the characteristics of love [AB, Alf, ICC, Vn], the character of love [NIC2], the nature and action of love [NIGTC], the portrayal of love [NTC], the qualities of love [MNTC].

13:4 Love is-patient,ᵃ love is-kind,ᵇ (is) not jealous,ᶜ

LEXICON—a. pres. act. indic. of μακροθυμέω (LN 25.168) (BAGD 2. p. 488): 'to be patient' [AB, BAGD, ICC, LN, NTC; all versions except ISV, KJV, NJB], 'to be very patient' [ISV], 'to be always patient' [NJB], 'to wait patiently' [NIGTC], 'to suffer long' [Lns; KJV], 'to be long-suffering' [Herm, HNTC], 'to remain patient, to wait patiently' [LN], 'to be forbearing' [BAGD]. Μακροθυμέω indicates patience with people rather than circumstances [EGT, ICC, Lns, MNTC, NIC2, NTC, TNTC]. It indicates a self-restraint with the hurts inflicted by others without retaliation [ICC, Lns, Vn]. It is the opposite of anger [Vn]. It receives injuries over a long period without complaint [AB].

b. pres. mid. (deponent = act.) indic. of χρηστεύομαι (LN **88.67**) (BAGD p. 886): 'to be kind' [AB, BAGD, Herm, HNTC, ICC, LN, NTC; all versions except ISV], 'to be very kind' [ISV], 'to be benignant' [Lns], 'to act kindly' [**LN**], 'to show kindness' [NIGTC], 'to be loving, to be merciful' [BAGD]. Χρηστεύομαι indicates doing good to someone as an act of kindness [LN]. While μακροθυμέω 'to be patient' is passive, χρηστεύομαι 'to be kind' is active in seeking the good of others [ICC, NIC2]. It indicates action which alleviates the pain, worries and fears of others and contributes positively to their happiness [AB].

c. pres. act. indic. of ζηλόω (LN 88.163) (BAGD 2. p. 338): 'to be jealous' [AB, LN, NTC; CEV, NAB, NJB, NLT, TEV, TNT], 'to be envious' [HNTC, LN; ISV, NET, NRSV], 'to envy' [Lns; KJV, NIV, REB], 'to know hatred or envy' [ICC], 'to burn with envy' [NIGTC], 'to be filled with jealousy, envy' [BAGD]. Ζηλόω indicates experiencing strong resentment and jealousy against someone [LN]. It can be either positive or negative. When negative, as here, it indicates 'jealous longing for one's own improvement to another's detriment' [NIC2]. It indicates displeasure at the success of others [TNTC]. It is to envy gifted persons [ICC]. It indicates any wrong emotion stimulated by seeing the good of others such as envy, hatred and emulation [Ho]. It basically means 'to have a strong desire' and is the same word as the verb in 12:31, 'earnestly desire (the greater gifts)' [MNTC]. See this word also at 12:31.

QUESTION—What is implied in this personification of 'love'?

It is implied that a person who loves behaves in these ways [TG, TH]. It describes a character which is ruled by love [NCBC].

love (does) not brag,[a] (is) not puffed-up,[b]

TEXT—Some manuscripts omit ἡ ἀγάπη 'love'. It is included by GNT in brackets with a C rating, indicating difficulty in deciding whether or not to include it in the text. It is included by Lns, NTC; KJV, NET, NJB, TNT. It is omitted or not translated by AB, Herm, HNTC, ICC; CEV, ISV, NAB, NIV, NLT, NRSV, REB, TEV.

LEXICON—a. pres. mid. (deponent = act.) indic. of περπερεύομαι (LN **33.369**) (BAGD p. 653): 'to brag' [AB, BAGD, HNTC, **LN**, NIGTC, NTC; NET], 'to boast' [BAGD; NIV, TNT], 'to be boastful' [Herm; CEV, NJB, NLT, NRSV, REB], 'to vaunt (oneself)' [Lns; KJV], 'to put on airs' [NAB], 'to be conceited' [TEV], 'to be a braggart' [ICC, LN], 'to behave as a braggart (windbag)' [BAGD, NIC2, NTC]. This verb is also translated as a prepositional phrase: '(to be vaunted up) with pride' [ISV], '(to be puffed up) with pride' [AB]. Περπερεύομαι indicates the desire to have the praise of others [Ho]. Pretension is the main sense of this word [ICC]. It carries the idea of people being self-centered and having an excessive desire to have others notice them [NIC2] and to make them jealous [MNTC]. It means to talk conceitedly [MNTC].

b. pres. mid./pass. indic. of φυσιόω (LN 88.217) (BAGD p. 869): 'to be puffed up' [BAGD, HNTC, Lns; KJV, NET], 'to be puffed' [AB], 'to swell with self-adulation' [ICC], 'to be proud' [CEV, NIV, NLT, TEV], 'to be conceited' [BAGD; NJB, REB], 'to be arrogant' [Herm, NTC; NRSV], 'to be snobbish' [NAB], 'to be vaunted up' [ISV], 'to behave arrogantly' [TNT], 'to be inflated with its own importance' [NIGTC], 'to be made proud, to be made arrogant, to be made haughty, to be inflated' [LN], 'to put on airs' [BAGD]. Φυσιόω indicates 'to be conceited' [Ho]. It has a connotation of arrogance [NIC2]. The Corinthians considered themselves to have arrived at perfection [MNTC].

13:5 (is) not rude,[a]

LEXICON—a. pres. act. indic. of ἀσχημονέω (LN **88.149**) (BAGD 1. p. 119): 'to be rude' [Herm; all versions except KJV, TEV, TNT], 'to be ill-mannered' [TEV], 'to act improperly' [TNT], 'to behave shamefully' [**LN**, NIC2], 'to act shamefully' [LN], 'to behave unseemly' [KJV], 'to behave in an unseemly way' [HNTC], 'to act unseemly' [Lns], 'to behave with ill-mannered impropriety' [NIGTC], 'to behave indecently' [BAGD, NTC], 'to behave unpresentably' [AB], 'to behave disgracefully' [BAGD, NIC2], 'to behave dishonorably' [BAGD], 'to offend good feeling' [ICC]. Ἀσχημονέω means to act in defiance of social and moral standards, with shame as a result [LN, NTC]. It means to fail to show respect, honor, or consideration for others [Lns]. It means to act with poor manners [ICC, MNTC]. An example of this kind of behavior among the Corinthians is seen at 11:21 where some would eat without waiting for the others [MNTC]. Another example is when the women brought shame on themselves by dressing more like men [NIC2]. Positively it means to act becomingly or politely [MNTC]. See this word also at 7:36.

(does) not seek[a] the-things of-itself,
LEXICON—a. pres. act. indic. of ζητέω (See this word at 10:24): 'to seek' [AB, Herm, HNTC, Lns, NTC; KJV, NJB, TNT], 'to insist on' [ICC; NRSV], 'to demand' [NLT], 'to think of' [ISV] 'to be preoccupied with' [NIGTC]. This clause is translated 'love isn't selfish' [CEV], 'love is never selfish' [REB], 'or selfish' [TEV], 'it is not self-seeking' [NAB, NIV], 'it is not self-serving' [NET]. To seek not one's own is to be unselfish and to seek the interests of others [Lns, MNTC]. 'One's own' implies 'one's own interests' [ICC]. Love does not seek one's own pleasure, profit, or honor [Lns].

not is-irritable,[a]
LEXICON—a. pres. pass. indic. of παροξύνω (LN **88.189**) (BAGD p. 629): 'to be irritable' [Herm; NLT, NRSV, TEV], 'to be irritated' [TNT], 'to be easily angered' [NET, NIV], 'to be upset' [**LN**], 'to be provoked' [LN, Lns], 'to be easily provoked' [KJV], 'to be touchy' [HNTC], 'to get annoyed' [ISV], 'to blaze with rage' [ICC], 'to become exasperated into pique' [NIGTC]. This passive voice is also translated as an active: 'to take offence' [NJB], 'to be quick to take offence' [REB], 'to be quick-tempered' [Ho; CEV], 'to be prone to anger' [NAB], 'to become irritated' [AB, BAGD, NTC], 'to become angry' [BAGD]. Παροξύνω means 'to yield to provocation' [ICC]. One who loves avoids being angered by what is said or done against him [MNTC].

(does) not keep-a-record-of[a] evil,[b]
LEXICON—a. pres. mid. (deponent = act.) indic. of λογίζομαι (LN **29.4**) (BAGD 1.a. p. 476): 'to keep a record (of)' [**LN**, NTC; CEV, NIV, NLT, TEV], 'to keep (a) score of' [Herm; REB], 'to take/keep an account of' [Lns; TNT], 'to keep a reckoning up' [NIGTC], 'to put down to someone's account' [HNTC], 'to brood over' [NAB], 'to store up' [NJB], 'to calculate' [AB], 'to think' [KJV], 'to remember, to bear in mind' [LN], 'to take into account' [BAGD]. The phrase λογίζεται τὸ κακόν 'keep a record of evil' is translated 'to be resentful' [ISV, NET, NRSV], 'to store up resentment' [ICC]. Λογίζομαι means to keep a mental record of something for future action [LN].
  b. κακός (LN 88.106, 65.26) (BAGD 1.c. p. 397): 'evil' [BAGD, LN (88.106), NIGTC], 'bad, harmful' [LN (88.106)], 'difficult, harsh' [LN (65.26)], not explicit [ICC; ISV, NET, NRSV]. This adjective is also translated as a noun: 'evil' [AB, HNTC; KJV, TNT], '(the) bad' [Lns], 'wrong that others do' [CEV], 'wrongs' [Herm, NTC; NIV, REB, TEV], 'grievances' [NJB], 'injuries' [NAB]. It is also translated as a clause: 'when it has been wronged' [NLT]. Κακός refers here to moral evil,

178   1 CORINTHIANS 13:5

things that are contrary to law, crime, or sin [BAGD]. The definite article, 'the evil', indicates '*the* evil done to it' [ICC, Lns].

QUESTION—What is the meaning of οὐ λογίζεται τὸ κακόν 'does not keep a record of evil'?

1. It means not to hold unforgiven the person who does it evil [AB, Alf, Gdt, HNTC, Ho, ICC, Lns, MNTC, NCBC, NIC2, NTC, Rb, TG, TH, TNTC, Vn; all versions except KJV]. It means that love takes evil on itself and so does away with it [HNTC]. Love absorbs evil and disposes of it by forgiving it [AB]. One who loves does not keep remembering the evil someone has done to him [TG].
2. It means that love does not suspect others of evil motives [KJV].
3. It means that love does not think about how to harm to others [NIC].

13:6 (does) not rejoice[a] in[b] unrighteousness,[c]

LEXICON—a. pres. act. indic. of χαίρω (LN 25.125) (BAGD 1. p. 873): 'to rejoice' [AB, BAGD, Herm, HNTC, LN, Lns, NTC; CEV, KJV, NAB, NJB, NRSV], 'to be glad' [LN; ISV, NET, NLT], 'to be happy' [TEV], 'to delight' [ICC; NIV], 'to take pleasure' [NIGTC; REB], 'to applaud' [TNT].

b. ἐπί with dative object (LN 90.23): 'in' [LN, NTC; CEV, KJV, NAB, NIV, NRSV, REB], 'with' [ISV, TEV], 'at' [AB, HNTC, NIGTC; NJB], 'about' [LN; NET, NLT], 'over' [Herm, ICC, Lns], 'with reference to, with respect to' [LN], not explicit [TNT].

c. ἀδικία (LN 88.21) (BAGD 2. p. 18): 'unrighteousness' [BAGD, HNTC, LN, Lns], 'injustice' [AB, BAGD; NET, NLT], 'evil' [NTC; CEV, NIV, TEV], 'what is wrong' [NAB], 'wrongdoing' [Herm, NIGTC; NJB, NRSV], 'wrong that men do' [ICC], 'iniquity' [KJV], 'wickedness' [BAGD; TNT], 'sin' [ISV], 'sin of others' [REB], 'unjust deed, doing what is unjust' [LN]. Ἀδικία indicates moral evil of every kind [Ho].

QUESTION—What does it mean not to rejoice in unrighteousness?

It means not to be happy when others do what is wrong [TG]. Loves does not take pleasure in criticizing those who do wrong and does not have a sense of superiority [HNTC, NIGTC]. It grieves over the sins committed against others [NTC].

but rejoices-in[a] the truth;[b]

LEXICON—a. pres. act. indic. of συγχαίρω (See this word at 12:26): 'to rejoice in' [Herm, NTC; CEV, KJV, NET, NRSV], 'to rejoice with' [Lns; NAB, NIV, TNT], 'to rejoice over' [AB], 'to rejoice (whenever truth wins out)' [NLT], 'to delight in' [REB], 'to be happy with' [TEV], 'to find one's joy in' [NJB], 'to be glad to side with' [ISV], 'to join in rejoicing at' [HNTC], 'to respond with delight to' [ICC], 'to joyfully celebrate' [NIGTC].

b. ἀλήθεια (LN 72.2) (BAGD 2.b. p. 36): 'truth' [AB, Herm, HNTC, Lns, NIGTC, NTC; all versions except NLT], 'true dealing' [ICC]. This noun is also translated as a clause: 'whenever the truth wins out' [NLT]. See this word also at 5:8.

QUESTION—What sense of ἀλήθεια 'truth' is contrasted here with ἀδικία 'unrighteousness'?

1. Ἀλήθεια in the sense of 'truth' is contrasted here with ἀδικία 'unrighteousness' [AB, Alf, Ed, EGT, Gdt, HNTC, Lns, MNTC, My, NIC, NIC2, NTC, Rb, TNTC, Vn; all versions]. 'Truth' is personified [Alf, Ed, EGT, Gdt, My, NIC, Rb, Vn] and refers to the Gospel [Alf, Ed, EGT, Lns, My, NIC2, TNTC] and its spread among people [Alf]. Probably what is intended is the gospel in the broad sense (each victory achieved, forgiveness offered, kindness in action) in contrast to all that opposes it (war, moral indiscretion of a brother or sister, or a child's misbehavior) [NIC2]. 'Truth' here should not be limited to the Gospel but should have a more general meaning to contrast with falsehood [Gdt]. The speaking of the truth as intellectual good is opposed to all unrighteous acts [NIC].

2. Ἀλήθεια in the sense of 'righteousness' or 'goodness' is contrasted here with ἀδικία 'unrighteousness' [BAGD, Ho, ICC, TG]. 'Truth' in the sense of 'goodness' is indicated [ICC]. 'Truth' not as an abstract quality, but a concrete quality of 'right behavior' is intended [TG]. Christianity is absolute truth and has a strong practical side indicating righteousness and holiness as opposed to wrong [BAGD].

13:7 Bears/covers[a] all-things,

LEXICON—a. pres. act. indic. of στέγω (LN 25.176) (BAGD 1. or 2. p. 766): 'to bear' [BAGD (2.); KJV, NET, NRSV], 'to bear up under' [ISV], 'to suffer' [Lns], 'to put up with' [LN; TNT], 'to make allowances' [NJB], 'to be tolerant' [ICC], 'to be supportive' [CEV], 'to support' [HNTC], 'to protect' [NIV], 'to keep confidence' [AB], 'to cover' [BAGD (1.), Herm, NTC], 'to pass over in silence, to keep confidential' [BAGD (1.)], 'to endure' [BAGD (2.), LN], 'to stand' [BAGD (2.)]. The phrase πάντα στέγει 'bears all things' is translated 'there is no limit to (love's) forbearance' [NAB], 'there is nothing (love) cannot face' [REB], 'never gives up' [NLT, TEV], 'never tires of support' [NIGTC]. See this word also at 9:12.

QUESTION—What sense of στέγω 'bears/covers' is meant here?

1. It means to bear hardships of any kind [Alf, Herm, Ho, ICC, Lns, My, NIC2, TH, TNTC; ISV, KJV, NAB, NET, NLT, NRSV, REB, TEV, TNT]. In 9:12 Paul used this word to express that he could endure everything in order to avoid putting an obstacle in the way of the gospel of Christ [NIC2]. It means to bear in silence all that would annoy or trouble a person [Ho].

2. It means to cover or conceal the faults of others in silence [AB, Gdt, MNTC, NCBC, NTC; NIV, NJB]. This interpretation avoids redundancy with the last verb in the verse ὑπομένω 'to endure', and it is supported by

1 Peter 4:8 where 'love covers a multitude of sins' (also see Proverbs 10:12; 17:9) [NTC]. Love protects other persons from being exposed, ridiculed, or harmed. When sin is known to have been committed, it tries to correct it with the least possible harm to the sinner [MNTC].
3. It means to bear with the injuries of others against it [Ed]. If others injure the person who loves, he/she bears it without resentment [Ed].
4. It means that it supports all things [HNTC; CEV].

believes[a] all-things,
LEXICON—a. pres. act. indic. of πιστεύω (LN 31.35, 31.85) (BAGD 1.a.α. p. 660): 'to believe' [Herm, HNTC, LN (31.35), Lns, NTC; KJV, NET, NRSV], 'to believe the best in' [ISV], 'to have faith in' [LN (31.85); TNT], 'to trust' [LN (31.85); NIV, NJB], 'to be trustful' [ICC], 'to have confidence in' [LN (31.85)], 'to be loyal' [CEV], 'to maintain faithfulness' [AB], 'to believe in' [BAGD, LN (31.85)], 'to be convinced of something' [BAGD]. The phrase πάντα πιστεύω 'believes all things' is translated '(its) faith never fails' [TEV], 'there is no limit to (its) faith/trust' [NAB, REB], '(love) never loses faith' [NIGTC; NLT].

QUESTION—What is meant by πάντα πιστεύει 'believes all things'?
It does not mean that a person who loves will believe that black is white [ICC, NTC, TNTC], but rather means that in doubtful cases he/she will err on the side of believing others rather than suspecting them [Ho, ICC]. It means that a person believes that God will work out his plans even when everything seems to indicate otherwise [NTC]. It means that love is always ready to give the benefit of the doubt [MNTC, NCBC, TNTC]. The implied object of believing is either God or the success of His purposes in the world [TG]. The object is the potential good in others and in God's ability to bring good out of evil [AB].

hopes[a] all-things,
LEXICON—a. pres. act. indic. of ἐλπίζω (LN 25.59, 30.54) (BAGD 2. p. 252): 'to hope' [Herm, HNTC, LN (25.59, 30.54), Lns, NTC; KJV, NET, NIV, NJB, NRSV], 'to hope for' [BAGD, LN (29.59); TNT], 'to be hopeful' [ICC; CEV, NLT], 'to maintain hope' [AB], 'to expect' [LN (30.54)]. This verb is also translated as a noun: 'its hope (never fails)' [TEV], '(there is no limit to its/her) hope' [ISV, NAB, REB], 'never exhausts hope' [NIGTC]. Ἐλπίζω means to look forward with confidence to something beneficial [LN (29.59)].

QUESTION—What is meant by πάντα ἐλπίζει 'hopes all things'?
It means that this hope is directed toward others and expects the best of them [Ho, Lns]. It means a refusal to take failure as defeat and a trust in the ultimate success of God's plan [NTC, TNTC]. A key feature of hope is confidence, here confidence in God [TH]. It hopes that God will show mercy in a person's behalf [NTC]. Hope is the conviction that there is God's purpose in life, and that his purposes will be realized no matter how grim things look [AB].

1 CORINTHIANS 13:7

endures[a] **all-things.**
LEXICON—a. pres. act. indic. of ὑπομένω (LN 25.175) (BAGD 2. p. 846): 'to endure' [BAGD, Herm, HNTC, LN, Lns, NTC; KJV, NET, NJB, NLT, NRSV, TNT], 'to persevere' [NIV], 'to be strong' [ICC], 'to be trusting' [CEV], 'to maintain steadfastness' [AB], 'to put up with, to bear up, to demonstrate endurance' [LN], 'to hold out, to stand one's ground' [BAGD]. The phrase πάντα ὑπομένει 'endures all things' is translated 'its patience never fails' [TEV], 'there is no limit to its endurance' [REB], 'there is no limit to its power to endure' [NAB], 'never gives up' [NIGTC], 'and never will she fall' [ISV]. Στέγω 'to bear' has reference to present troubles but ὑπομένω 'to endure' applies to the future as well. Στέγω has reference to troubles while ὑπομένω has reference to persecution and suffering [Ho]. The two verbs are synonymous [TG].
QUESTION—What is meant by πάντα ὑπομένει 'endures all things'?
It means to bear up under suffering and persecution [Ho]. It continues to love people and to refuse to stop bearing, believing, and hoping [MNTC, TG].

DISCOURSE UNIT: 13:8–14:1a [AB]. The topic is the permanence of love.

DISCOURSE UNIT: 13:8–13 [Gdt, ICC, MNTC, NIC2, NIGTC, NTC, TH, Vn]. The topic is the permanence of love [MNTC, NIC2], the permanence and perfection of love [NTC], love's eternal durability [Gdt, ICC], the eschatological permanence of love [NIGTC], the permanency and superiority of love [Vn].

DISCOURSE UNIT: 13:8–12 [Alf, Ed]. The topic is the eternal abiding of love.

13:8 **Love never**[a] **fails;**[b]
LEXICON—a. οὐδέποτε (LN 67.10) (BAGD p. 592): 'never' [AB, BAGD, Herm, HNTC, ICC, LN, Lns, NIGTC, NTC; all versions except NLT, TEV], 'not ever, at no time' [LN]. The phrase οὐδέποτε πίπτει 'never fails' is translated 'will last forever' [NLT], 'is eternal' [TEV].
b. pres. act. indic. of πίπτω (LN 13.97, 15.118, **68.49, 75.7**) (BAGD 2.b.δ. p. 660): 'to fail' [BAGD, Herm, LN (68.49, **75.7**); CEV, KJV, NAB, NIV, TNT], 'to end' [NET, NRSV], 'to come to an end' [BAGD, LN (13.97); NJB, REB], 'to break down' [ISV], 'to fall apart' [NIGTC], 'to cease' [LN (13.97, **68.49**)], 'to stop' [LN (68.49)], 'to become invalid' [BAGD], 'to become inadequate' [LN (75.7)], 'to fall' [LN (13.97, 15.118)]. The phrase οὐδέποτε πίπτει 'never fails' is translated 'will last forever' [NLT], 'is eternal' [TEV], 'is always sufficient' or 'is always adequate for anything' [LN (**75.7**)]. Πίπτω has the primary sense of 'to fall' with the extended meanings of 'to fail' or 'to become inadequate' as here [LN (68.49, 75.7)]. It may indicate either an active sense of 'to be defeated' or a more passive sense of 'to come to an end'. It may be that Paul intended both senses [NIC2]. It indicates 'to become obsolescent' or 'become invalid' here [AB]. See this word also at 10:8.

but if[a] (there are) prophecies,[b] they-will-be-done-away-with;[c]

LEXICON—a. εἴτε (LN 89.69): 'if' [LN; ISV, NET, NJB, TNT], 'whether' [LN, NIGTC; KJV], 'where' [NIV], 'as for' [NRSV], not explicit [Herm; NAB, NLT, REB, TEV]. Εἴτε...εἴτε (as here) means 'if...if' or 'whether...or' [LN].

b. προφητεία (LN **33.460**): 'prophecy' [LN, NIGTC; ISV, KJV, NAB, NET, NIV, NJB, NLT, NRSV, REB, TNT], 'inspired message' [TEV], 'inspired utterance' [**LN**], 'gift of prophecy' [Herm]. The phrase εἴτε δὲ προφητεῖαι 'if there are prophecies' is translated 'everyone who prophesies' [CEV]. Προφητεία indicates the spiritual gift of prophecy referred to in 12:10 [MNTC]. See this word also at 12:10.

c. fut. pass. indic. of καταργέω (LN 13.100, **13.162**, 13.163) (BAGD 2. p. 417): 'to be done away with' [ISV, NJB], 'to be brought to an end' [NIGTC; NRSV, TNT], 'to be set aside' [NET], 'to be temporary' [TEV], 'to be destroyed' [Herm], 'to be put an end to' [LN (13.100)], 'to be put a stop to' [LN (13.163)]. It is also translated in active voice: 'to cease' [BAGD, LN (13.162); NAB, NIV, REB], 'to stop' [CEV], 'to fail' [KJV], 'to disappear' [NLT], 'to pass away' [BAGD], 'to no longer take place' [LN (13.162)]. Prophecies will no longer be needed and therefore will not be continued [Ho, NIC]. See this word also at 1:28, 2:6 and 6:13.

QUESTION—What relationship is indicated by δέ 'but'?

It indicates contrast [AB, HNTC, Ho, ICC, Lns, NIC, NTC, TG, TNTC; KJV, NET, NIV, NJB, NLT, NRSV]: love never fails *but* if there are prophecies they will be done away with. Love endures forever, in contrast with the gifts being considered [Ho, ICC, NIC, TG, TNTC].

if (there are) tongues,[a] they-will-cease;[b]

LEXICON—a. γλῶσσα (See this word at 12:10): 'tongue' [Herm, NIGTC; ISV, KJV, NAB, NET, NIV, NJB, NRSV, TNT], 'unknown language' [CEV], 'tongue of ecstasy' [REB], 'speaking in unknown languages' [NLT], 'gift of speaking in strange tongues' [TEV].

b. fut. mid. (deponent = act.) indic. of παύομαι (LN 68.34) (BAGD 2. p. 638): 'to cease' [BAGD, Herm, LN; ISV, KJV, NET, NRSV, TEV, TNT], 'to stop' [NIGTC], 'to be stilled' [NIV], 'to be spoken no longer' [CEV], 'to fall silent' [NJB, REB], 'to be silent' [NAB], 'to disappear' [NLT], 'to stop' [LN], 'to come to an end' [BAGD]. The gift of tongues will no longer be given [Ho]. The speaker will speak no more [Lns]. Their cause will be gone at the coming of Christ [NIGTC].

if (there is) knowledge,[a] it-will-be-done-away-with.[b]

LEXICON—a. γνῶσις (See this word at 12:8): 'knowledge' [Herm, NIGTC; all versions except CEV, NLT], 'special knowledge' [NLT]. The phrase εἴτε γνῶσις 'if there is knowledge' is translated 'all that we know' [CEV]. Γνῶσις indicates the spiritual gift of knowledge referred to in 12:8 [Ho, Lns, MNTC, NIC2]. It refers to knowledge that is acquired by hard work here on earth [TNTC].

b. fut. pass. indic. of καταργέω (LN **13.162**) (See this word above in this verse): 'to be done away with' [ISV, NJB], 'to be brought to an end' [TNT], 'to be set aside' [NET], 'to be destroyed' [Herm], 'to be rendered obsolete' [NIGTC], 'to be forgotten' [CEV]. This is also translated in active voice: 'to cease' [**LN**], 'to come to an end' [NRSV], 'to vanish' [REB], 'to vanish away' [KJV], 'to pass away' [NAB, NIV], 'to pass' [TEV], 'to disappear' [NLT]. Knowledge in general will not cease, but the gift of knowledge will [Ho, NIC2, NTC]. Imperfect human knowledge will be replaced by with the new knowledge of God [TNTC].

QUESTION—What is implied by the repeated use of εἴτε 'if'?

It implies a depreciation of these gifts: if there *be* any prophesy, tongues, knowledge, they will come to an end [ICC].

QUESTION—Why are only these three gifts mentioned?

The three prominent gifts of prophesy, tongues and knowledge, are probably meant to be representative of the transitory character of all the gifts [ICC].

13:9 For[a] we-know[b] in-part[c] and we-prophesy[d] in-part;

LEXICON—a. γάρ (See this word at 10:1): 'for' [AB, Herm, HNTC, ICC, Lns, NIGTC, NTC; ISV, KJV, NET, NIV, NRSV, REB, TEV], 'now' [NLT], not explicit [CEV, NAB, NLT, TNT].

b. pres. act. indic. of γινώσκω (LN 28.1) (BAGD 1.a. p. 160): 'to know' [AB, BAGD, HNTC, LN, Lns, NIGTC, NTC; CEV, ISV, KJV, NET, NIV, NJB, NLT, NRSV]. This verb is also translated as a noun or noun phrase: 'knowledge' [Herm, ICC; NAB, REB, TNT], 'gift of knowledge' [TEV].

c. ἐκ μέρος (See this phrase at 12:27): 'in part' [HNTC, Lns, NTC; KJV, NET, NIV], 'partially' [AB], 'only in part' [NRSV], 'imperfectly' [NJB], 'only a little' [NLT], 'in fragmentary ways' [NIGTC]. This adverbial phrase is also translated as an adjective: '(is) partial' [REB, TEV], '(is) incomplete' [ISV], '(is) imperfect' [NAB], '(is) fragmentary' [Herm]. It is also translated as a phrase: 'of fragments' [ICC]. The clause ἐκ μέρους γάρ γινώσκομεν 'for we know in part' is translated 'we don't know everything' [CEV], 'our knowledge is not enough' [TNT].

d. pres. act. indic. of προφητεύω (See this word at 11:4): 'to prophesy' [AB, HNTC, Lns, NIGTC, NTC; ISV, KJV, NET, NIV, NJB, NRSV]. This verb is also translated as a noun: 'prophecy' [CEV, REB], 'prophesying' [Herm, ICC; NAB, TNT], 'gift of prophecy' [NLT], 'gift of inspired messages' [TEV].

QUESTION—What relationship is indicated by γάρ 'for'?

It indicates the reason for the demise of knowledge and prophesying of 13:8 [Ed, EGT, Gdt, Herm, Ho, ICC, Lns, My, NIC, NIC2]: knowledge and prophecy will be done away with *because* they are incomplete. Paul means that all the gifts are 'in part' but he lists only knowledge and prophecy [MNTC, NIC2]. He omits tongues because it has little meaning to say that we speak in tongues in part [Ed, NIC2]. He omits tongues perhaps because it needs no grounds [My].

QUESTION—How do we know and prophesy only in part now?

We know only fragments of the truth, not the whole truth [ICC]. The prophet only gives a glimpse of the whole truth [Ho, TNTC]. We know God's truth but partially and we prophesy it in segments. Both are incomplete [NTC].

13:10 But[a] when the perfect[b] comes,

LEXICON—a. δέ (See this word at 11:2): 'but' [AB, Herm, HNTC, ICC, Lns, NIGTC, NTC; all versions except NAB, REB], 'and' [REB], not explicit [NAB].

b. τέλειος (LN 68.23, 88.100) (BAGD 1.a.β. p. 809): 'perfect' [Herm; NAB], 'complete' [LN (68.23); NRSV], 'the completed whole' [NIGTC], 'end' [NLT], 'mature, grownup' [LN (88.100)]. The phrase τὸ τέλειον 'the perfect' is translated 'that which is complete' [AB], 'absolute completeness' [ICC], 'perfect completeness' [TNT], 'the complete' [Lns], 'what is perfect' [BAGD; CEV, KJV, NET, TEV], 'perfection' [NTC; NIV, NJB], 'totality' [HNTC], 'what is fully developed' [ISV], 'wholeness' [REB].

QUESTION—What is meant by τὸ τέλειον 'the perfect'?

Τέλειος 'perfect' refers to the time when God's final purpose of salvation through Christ will be realized. Then the gifts of the Spirit that are part of this era and are only in part, will be done away with because 'the complete' will have arrived. So it has the sense of 'having attained the end or purpose' or of being 'complete' [NIC2]. The 'perfect' comes at the Second Coming of Christ [Ed, EGT, Gdt, Herm, Lns, My, NCBC, NIC, NIC2, NTC, Vn]. The perfect is not a form of perfection in this present age, it is the final purpose of God's saving work in Christ that will have been reached at Christ's coming [NIC]. It is the eternal state entered into at death or at the rapture [MNTC]. The gifts will cease to be needed and will be replaced by a perfect state of knowledge [NTC]. It means the totality of the truth about God [HNTC].

the in-part[a] will-be-done-away.[b]

LEXICON—a. ἐκ μέρος (LN **78.49**): 'in part' [LN (63.15)], 'partial' [NET, NRSV, REB], 'imperfect' [NAB, NIV], 'fragmentary' [Herm]. The phrase τὸ ἐκ μέρους 'the in-part' is translated 'that which exists only in part' [**LN**], 'that which is in part' [Lns, NTC; KJV], 'what is partial' [AB, HNTC; TEV], 'what is piece by piece' [NIGTC], 'all imperfect things' [NJB], 'what is incomplete' [ISV], 'what isn't perfect' [CEV], 'all deficiencies' [TNT], 'these special gifts' [NLT], 'that which is of fragments' [ICC]. The gifts of the Spirit are part of this present age and are partial in the sense that what is 'complete' has not yet come [NIC2]. See this phrase also at 12:27.

b. aorist pass. indic. of καταργέω (See this word at 13:8): 'to be done away' [Lns, NIGTC; KJV], 'to be done away with' [HNTC; ISV, NJB], 'to be destroyed' [Herm], 'to be set aside' [NTC; NET], 'to be nullified' [AB], 'to have no use' [ICC]. This passive is also translated in active voice: 'to disappear' [CEV, NIV, NLT, TEV, TNT], 'to vanish' [REB], 'to pass away' [NAB], 'to come to an end' [NRSV]. They will no longer be needed [Ho, MNTC]

13:11 **When I-was (a) child,**[a]
LEXICON—a. νήπιος (LN 9.43) (BAGD 1.a. p. 537): 'child' [AB, Herm, HNTC, ICC, Lns, NIGTC, NTC; all versions except CEV, TNT], 'small child' [LN], 'infant' [TNT]. Νήπιος refers to a child above the age of a helpless infant but probably not more than three or four years old [LN]. It indicates a very young child [BAGD, Ho, NIC2].
QUESTION—What is the function of this verse?
It illustrates the preceding verses [NIC]. It illustrates what Paul means by 'the perfect' replacing that which was only in part. He means that maturity replaces immaturity [NCBC, TG]. It illustrates that activity that is appropriate at one stage of life is done away with at another stage [NIC2]. Paul is saying that he wants the Corinthians to recognize that the things they value now are transient and that they should begin to value the things that are eternal [NCBC].

I-used-to-speak[a] **like**[b] **(a) child, I-used-to-think**[c] **like (a) child, I-used-to-reason**[d] **like (a) child;**
LEXICON—a. imperf. act. indic. of λαλέω (LN 33.70) (BAGD 2.a.ε. p. 463): 'to speak' [AB, BAGD, Herm, HNTC, LN, Lns; ISV, KJV, NLT, NRSV, REB, TNT], 'to talk' [ICC, LN, NIGTC, NTC; NAB, NET, NIV, NJB], not explicit [CEV]. This verb is also translated as a noun: 'speech' [TEV]. No reference to 'speaking in tongues' is intended [Ho, Lns, NIC2]. The imperfect tenses of 'speaking', 'thinking', and 'reasoning' refer to habitual actions of the past [Lns, Rb].
b. ὡς (LN 64.12) (BAGD I.2.a. p. 897): 'like' [LN, NIGTC; ISV, NAB, NET, NIV, NJB, NRSV, REB, TNT], 'as' [AB, BAGD, Herm, HNTC, ICC, LN, Lns, NTC; CEV, KJV, NLT], not explicit [TEV]. This is an ellipsis meaning 'as a child is accustomed to speak' [BAGD].
c. imperf. act. indic. of φρονέω (LN 26.16) (BAGD 1. p. 866): 'to think' [AB, BAGD, Herm, HNTC, ICC, NTC; all versions except KJV, NJB, TEV], 'to understand' [Rb; KJV], 'to see' [NJB], 'to have the interests of' [Lns], 'to think in a particular manner, to have an attitude' [LN], 'to form opinions' [NIGTC], 'to form or hold an opinion, to judge' [BAGD]. This verb is also translated as a noun: 'feelings' [TEV]. Φρονέω refers more to opinion, judgment and attitude than to emotion [TH]. It refers to thinking in general, not to feeling [TNTC].
d. imperf. mid. (deponent = act.) indic. of λογίζομαι (LN 30.9) (BAGD 2. p. 476): 'to reason' [AB, BAGD, Herm, ICC, **LN**, Lns, NTC; all versions except KJV, NJB, TEV], 'to reckon' [HNTC], 'to think' [KJV, NJB], 'to think about' [BAGD, LN], 'to reason about, to ponder' [LN], 'to count

values' [NIGTC], 'to make plans' [BAGD]. This verb is also translated as a participle: 'thinking' [TEV]. Λογίζομαι refers to logical processes [TH]. It refers to the reflective activity of the mind [My]. See this word also at 13:5.

when I-became (a) man,ᵃ I-put-an-end-toᵇ the-things of-the child.
LEXICON—a. ἀνήρ (LN **9.24**) (BAGD 2. p. 66): 'man' [AB, BAGD, Herm, HNTC, ICC, **LN**, Lns, NTC; ISV, KJV, NAB, NIV, TNT], 'adult' [NET, NJB, NRSV, TEV]. The phrase γέγονα ἀνήρ 'I became a man' is translated 'to grow up' [CEV, NLT, REB], 'to reach adulthood' [NIGTC]. See this word also at 11:3.
  b. perf. act. indic. of καταργέω (LN **13.163**): 'to put an end to' [NRSV], 'to put a stop to' [**LN**], 'to put/set aside' [NTC; NAB, NET], 'to put away' [KJV, NLT], 'to do away with' [Herm, ICC], 'to be done with' [HNTC], 'to put behind (one)' [NIV], 'to discard' [AB], 'to give up' [ISV], 'to finish with' [NJB, REB], 'to turn one's back on' [NIGTC], 'to have no more use for' [TEV], 'to bring to an end' [TNT], 'to quit' [CEV]. Καταργέω indicates a decision to leave his childish ways [TNTC]. The perfect aspect indicates decision and finality [Lns, TNTC]. See this word also at 13:8.
QUESTION—What is meant by ὅτε γέγονα 'when I have become'?
  It means 'when I became' [NTC; CEV, ISV, KJV, NAB, NET, NIV, NLT, NRSV, REB]. It means 'since/now that I have become' [AB, Alf, Ed, EGT, HNTC, ICC, Lns; NJB, TEV, TNT].

13:12 **For now we-see by-means-of/through/inᵃ (a) mirrorᵇ indistinctly,ᶜ**
LEXICON—a. διά with genitive object (LN 89.76): 'by means of' [LN, Lns, NIGTC], 'through' [HNTC, LN; KJV], 'in' [AB, Herm, NTC; CEV, ISV, NAB, NET, NJB, NRSV, REB, TEV, TNT], 'from' [ICC], 'as in' [NIV, NLT].
  b. ἔσοπτρον (LN 6.221) (BAGD p. 313): 'mirror' [AB, BAGD, Herm, ICC, LN, Lns, NIGTC, NTC; all versions except KJV, NLT], 'poor mirror' [NLT], 'glass' [HNTC; KJV]. Ἔσοπτρον indicates a flat highly polished piece of metal used to reflect an image [LN]. Some of the highest quality bronze mirrors of that time were made in Corinth [NIC2]. Even the best polished metal mirrors could only give an imperfect and imprecise reflection [ICC]. The phrase 'to see through a mirror in a riddle' means to see dimly or indirectly in a mirror (because it is the mirror-image and not the thing itself which is seen) [BAGD].
  c. ἐν αἰνίγμα (LN **24.37, 32.21**) (BAGD p. 23): 'indistinctly' [AB; NAB], 'imperfectly' [NLT], 'dimly' [BAGD, **LN** (24.37); NRSV], 'obscurely' [HNTC], 'by reflection' [BAGD], 'like a dim image' [TEV], 'like a cloudy picture' [CEV], 'indirectly' [NIGTC; NET], 'darkly' [KJV], 'in a dark saying' [Lns], 'enigmatically' [Herm]. It is also translated as the direct object of 'see': 'a dim reflected image' [**LN** (24.37)], 'but a poor reflection' [NIV], 'only puzzling reflections' [**LN** (32.21); REB, TNT],

1 CORINTHIANS 13:12

'only reflections' [NJB], 'only a blurred reflection' [ISV], 'an indistinct reflection' [NTC]. It is also translated as an adjectival clause: '(a mirror) which clouds and confuses things' [ICC]. Αἴνιγμα seems to indicate difficulty in understanding and comprehension rather than physical sight [LN (32.21)]. The idiom probably refers to seeing things indirectly rather than to seeing them obscurely [NIC2; NET, NJB]. Since making of good mirrors was a matter of pride in Corinth, for Paul to say that they were obscure or indistinct would have been offensive to them [NIC2]. We see enigmatically or indistinctly because we do not see the objects themselves but only the objects as described in words and symbols [Ho]. Αἴνιγμα itself means 'riddle' [LN (32.21)], 'dim image, reflected image' [LN (24.37)], 'puzzle, that which is puzzling, that which is difficult to understand' [LN (32.21)], 'indirect image, indistinct image' [BAGD].

QUESTION—What relationship is indicated by γάρ 'for'?

1. It indicates the grounds for 13:10 [Ed, HNTC, Ho, NIC, NIC2]: when the perfect comes then the imperfect will pass away *since* now we see in a mirror dimly.... Paul is saying that what we know now is imperfect because we now see as through a glass [Ho].
2. It indicates the grounds for 13:11 [Alf, Gdt, ICC, Lns, My]: When I was a child I spoke like a child...when I became a man I gave up childish things *since* we see now in a mirror dimly.... This verse verifies the previous verse with an increase in the level of argumentation: if one puts off childish ways when becoming an adult, how much more will seeing in a mirror be replaced when a person sees face to face [ICC].

QUESTION—Who is included in the pronoun 'we'?

The 'we' is inclusive and implies all Christians [Lns, TG]. In 13:11 Paul uses 'I' in speaking about what is true for all. Here his change to 'we' shows that every 'I' in the paragraph refers to all [Lns].

QUESTION—What is the meaning of διά 'by means of/through/in'?

1. It has the instrumental sense of 'by means of' [EGT, ICC, Lns, Rb, Vn]: we see *by means of* a mirror. To see a friend's face in a mirror is different from seeing him/her face to face [ICC, Vn].
2. It has the local sense 'through' [Alf, Ed, HNTC, Ho, My; KJV]: we see *through* a mirror. The impression of looking in a mirror puts the object behind the mirror. So we look through the mirror to see the person [Ho].
3. It has the local sense 'in' [AB, NTC; all versions except KJV]: we see *in* a mirror.

QUESTION—What or whom do we see 'in a mirror' and 'face to face'?

The illustration breaks down somewhat, since instead of seeing one's own face, one sees God or understands the 'mysteries' indirectly [NIC2]. We will see God [Ed, EGT, MNTC, My, NIC, TH]. The mirror refers to all that reveals God to us now like creation, Jesus' earthly life, and the Gospel [Ed]. We will see Christ [Lns, MNTC, TNTC]. We will see Jesus (1 John 3:2) and we will see God (Matthew 5:8) [Lns]. We will see God, but we will also see or understand everything [NIC]. No object is necessary since the 'seeing' itself is emphasized [Lns]. Seeing face to face refers to God's gift of perfect knowledge to understand his truth [NTC]. We cannot grasp God's truth fully today, but then God will give us perfect knowledge to understand his revelation [NTC]. It means that our knowledge will no longer be mediate, partial, and confused, but will be immediate, complete, and clear [Ho, ICC].

but then[a] face[b] to face;
LEXICON—a. τότε (LN 67.47) (BAGD 1.b. p. 823): 'then' [AB, BAGD, Herm, HNTC, LN, Lns, NIGTC, NTC; all versions except CEV, REB], 'later' [CEV], 'one day' [REB], 'in the next world' [ICC]. Τότε 'then' implies 'when the perfect comes' [ICC, NIC]. It implies when Christ comes again [TG].
  b. πρόσωπον (LN 8.18, **83.37**) (BAGD 1.b. p. 721): 'face' [AB, BAGD, Herm, HNTC, ICC, LN (8.18), Lns, NIGTC, NTC; all versions except NLT]. The phrase πρόσωπον πρὸς πρόσωπον 'face to face' is translated 'with perfect clarity' [NLT]. The idiomatic phrase indicates direct personal interaction, as though one was seeing something directly [**LN** (83.37), NIC2], which in turn implies clear understanding [**L N** (83.37)]. This phrase is used in the Old Testament at Numbers 12:8 and other places to refer to clear and direct communication [NTC]. There will be nothing between us [NIC].

now I-know[a] in-part,[b]
LEXICON—a. pres. act. indic. of γινώσκω (LN 32.16): 'to know' [AB, Herm, HNTC, Lns, NTC; CEV, KJV, NET, NIV, NJB, NRSV], 'to come to know' [NIGTC], 'to come to understand, to perceive, to comprehend' [LN], 'to have knowledge' [ICC]. This verb is also translated 'what I know' [ISV, TEV], 'all that I know' [NLT], 'my knowledge' [NAB, REB, TNT]. See this word also at 13:9.
  b. ἐκ μέρος (See this word at 13:9): 'in part' [Herm, HNTC, Lns, NTC; KJV, NET, NIV, NRSV], '(is) partial' [REB], '(is) only partial' [TEV], 'partially' [AB], 'only imperfectly' [NJB], 'of fragments' [ICC], 'part by part' [NIGTC]. This phrase is also translated as an adjective: '(is) incomplete' [ISV, TNT], '(is) partial and incomplete' [NLT], '(is) imperfect' [NAB]. The clause γινώσκω ἐκ μέρους 'I know in part' is translated 'we don't know everything' [CEV].
QUESTION—Why does Paul change from first person plural 'we' to first person singular 'I' here?
  It may be because this 'knowing in part' was a problem in Corinth and Paul refers to himself to make the reference to them more indirect and thus more acceptable [NIC2]. Paul returns to his own personal experience [ICC].

but then I-will-know-fully[a] just-as[b] also I-was-fully-known.[c]
LEXICON—a. fut. mid. (deponent = act.) indic. of ἐπιγινώσκω (LN 28.2, 32.16) (BAGD 1.a. p. 291): 'to know fully' [AB, Herm, Lns, NIGTC, NTC; ISV, NET, NIV, NJB, NRSV, TNT], 'to know' [CEV, KJV, NAB],

'to know completely' [HNTC], 'to know everything completely' [NLT], 'to know exactly, to know completely, to know through and through' [BAGD], 'to know about, to know definitely about' [LN (28.2)], 'to come to understand, to perceive, to comprehend' [LN (32.16)]. This verb is also translated '(my) knowledge...will be whole' [REB], 'what I know...will be complete' [TEV]. Ἐπιγινώσκω means not just knowing but *fully* knowing [Ed, EGT, Gdt, HNTC, Lns, NCBC, NIC, NIC2, Rb, TH, TNTC, Vn]. We cannot be sure that ἐπιγινώσκω implies any more than simply 'knowing' [ICC].

b. καθώς (See this word at 10:6): 'just as' [AB, NIGTC; CEV, NET, NLT, TNT], 'even as' [Herm, HNTC, Lns, NTC; ISV, KJV, NAB, NIV, NRSV], 'as complete(ly) as' [ICC; TEV], 'as fully as' [NJB], 'like' [REB]. See this word also at 1:6.

c. aorist pass. indic. of ἐπιγινώσκω (See this word just above): 'to be fully known' [AB, Herm, Lns, NIGTC, NTC; ISV, NET, NIV, NJB, NRSV], 'to be known completely' [HNTC], 'to be known' [HNTC; KJV, NAB]. The clause καθὼς καὶ ἐπεγνώσθην 'even as also I was fully known' is translated 'just as God knows me now' [NLT], 'just as God fully knows me' [TNT], 'like God's knowledge of me' [REB], 'as complete as God's knowledge of me' [TEV], 'just as God completely understands us' [CEV]. The aorist, 'I was fully known', may refer to Christ's knowledge of a person at conversion [ICC, My]. The aorist is a constative aorist meaning that all of God's knowledge of Paul is summed up and included in a single act [Lns]. God's knowledge of a man during the entire course of his life is meant [Alf, Gdt]. God's knowledge is perfect or complete, not something that is growing [TNTC].

QUESTION—Who is the object of ἐπιγνώσομαι 'I will fully know'?
The object is God [HNTC, NTC, TH]: I will fully know God.

QUESTION—Who is the actor of the passive ἐπεγνώσθην 'I was fully known'?
The actor is God [AB, Alf, Ed, EGT, Gdt, HNTC, ICC, Lns, NIC, NIC2, NTC, TH, TNTC, Vn; REB, TEV, TNT]: as God fully knew me.

13:13 And-now[a] remains[b] faith, hope, love, these three;

LEXICON—a. νυνὶ δέ (LN 91.4) (BAGD 2.b p. 546): 'and now' [Lns; KJV, NET, NIV, NRSV], 'now' [**LN**, NTC], 'but now' [AB, BAGD, Herm, HNTC], 'for now' [CEV], 'right now' [ISV], 'meanwhile' [LN; TEV], 'in the end' [NAB], 'as it is' [NJB], 'so then' [ICC; TNT], 'so now' [NIGTC], 'but now, as the situation is' [BAGD], not explicit [NLT, REB]. See this phrase also at 12:18.

b. pres. act. indic. of μένω (LN 13.89) (BAGD 2.c.β. p. 504): 'to remain' [BAGD, Herm, LN, Lns, NIGTC, NTC; ISV, NET, NIV, NJB, TEV], 'to last' [BAGD; NAB], 'to last on' [ICC], 'to be lasting' [TNT], 'to last for ever' [REB], 'to endure' [AB; NLT], 'to abide' [HNTC; KJV, NRSV], 'to be' [CEV], 'to continue, to continue to exist, to still be in existence' [LN], 'to persist, to continue to live' [BAGD].

QUESTION—What relationship is indicated by νυνὶ δέ 'now and/but'?

The phrase is logical and means 'and so we see'. The δέ has no contrastive meaning [Ed]. Νυνὶ is logical, meaning 'now' and the δέ contrasts with the temporal gifts just mentioned [ICC]. The phrase is inferential, meaning 'now, since things are so' [Ho]. Νυνὶ 'now' is not temporal but logical [Ed, ICC, Lns, NIC, NTC, TNTC, Vn]. The phrase indicates that 13:13 is a conclusion [NIC, TH, Vn]. Νυνὶ has some temporal sense here referring to the present condition as over against what will be [NIC2]. This phrase means 'in truth', 'as a fact', or 'as things are'. It has the same meaning as at 12:18 [TG].

QUESTION—What is the significance of the phrase τὰ τρία ταῦτα 'these three'?

It indicates that the three were referred to often in early Christian preaching and therefore might indicate "these well-known three" [NIC2, NTC].

QUESTION—What is meant by μένω 'to remain'?

1. It means to remain in a temporary sense [MNTC, NCBC, NIC2]. In view of 2 Corinthians 5:7 and Romans 8:24 that seem to suggest the temporary nature of faith and hope, it is better to take 'remain' as meaning 'remain for the present'. Further, this also serves to stress the present nature of love as well, in addition to its eternal nature [NIC2]. Faith and hope seem to change in the age to come but love remains unchanged [NCBC]. Faith and hope will have no purpose in heaven where everything that is true will be known and everything good will be possessed [MNTC].
2. It means to remain in an eternal sense [Alf, Ed, EGT, Gdt, HNTC, Ho, ICC, Lns, NIC, NIGTC, NTC, Rb, TNTC, Vn]. Although one aspect of faith and hope come to an end, in another sense our trust in the Lord and our hope in Christ continue (see 15:19) [NTC].

But/and[a] greatest[b] of-these (is) love.

LEXICON—a. δέ (See this word at 11:2): 'but' [AB, Herm, HNTC, ICC, NIGTC; CEV, ISV, KJV, NET, NIV, TNT], 'yet' [Lns], 'and' [NTC; NAB, NJB, NLT, NRSV, REB, TEV].

b. μείζων (See this word at 12:31): 'greatest' [AB, Herm, HNTC, Lns, NIGTC, NTC; all versions], 'chiefest and best' [ICC]. This comparative form is functioning as a superlative [BAGD, NTC, Rb].

QUESTION—Why is 'love' greater than 'faith' or 'hope'?

Love is greater because it alone makes us like God [Lns, MNTC, NTC]. Love is greater because faith and hope are born out of love [Alf, ICC, MNTC, Vn]. Love is greater because it is eternal while faith and hope are temporary [NIC2]. Love is greater because it is the end while faith and hope are the means to it [Gdt]. Love is greater because it is more useful; faith is self-directed but love is directed toward others [Ho]. Love is greater because it is unchanging while faith and hope change when the age to come arrives

[NCBC]. Love is greater because it is basic to the relationship between God, His Son and His people. It is the foundation on which the relationship between God and man is laid [NTC].

DISCOURSE UNIT: 14:1–40 [Ed, Gdt, Herm, HNTC, ICC, Lns, NIGTC; KJV]. The topic is the superiority of prophecy over tongues [Ed], practical rules of the exercise of the gifts [Gdt], tests applied to tongues and prophecy [HNTC], the conclusion of the subject of spiritual gifts [ICC], prophecy and tongues [Herm, Lns], speaking in tongues [KJV], evaluating prophecy and tongues [NIGTC].

DISCOURSE UNIT: 14:1–25 [Alf, Gdt, GNT, Ho, ICC, NIC2, NIGTC, NTC, TH, TNTC, Vn; CEV, ISV, NET, NIV, NJB, NLT, TEV]. The topic is the need for intelligibility in the assembly [NIC2, NIGTC], the gifts of tongues and prophecy [Alf, Gdt, GNT, Ho, NTC; CEV, ISV, NET, NIV, NLT], superiority of prophecy over tongues [ICC, TNTC, Vn], more about gifts from the Spirit [TEV], the respective importance of spiritual gifts in the community [NJB].

DISCOURSE UNIT: 14:1–19 [MNTC, NIC]. The topic is the position of the gift of tongues [MNTC], love and spiritual gifts [NIC].

DISCOURSE UNIT: 14:1–12 [NCBC]. The topic is prophecy being preferable to tongues.

DISCOURSE UNIT: 14:1–6 [EGT]. The topic is the gifts of tongues and of prophecy.

DISCOURSE UNIT: 14:1–5 [NIC2, NIGTC, NTC; NAB]. The topic is the greater gift is prophecy [NIC2], eager pursuit [NTC], the gift of prophecy [NAB], self or others in the use of gifts [NIGTC].

14:1 Pursue^a love,

LEXICON—a. pres. act. impera. of διώκω (LN 15.158, 68.66) (BAGD 4.b. p. 201): 'to pursue' [BAGD, LN (15.158), Lns, NIGTC, NTC; ISV, NET, NRSV], 'to aim at' [Herm], 'to pursue as one's aim' [HNTC], 'to strive for' [AB, BAGD, LN (68.66); TEV], 'to seek eagerly after' [NAB], 'to follow after' [KJV], 'to follow the way of' [NIV], 'to make (something one's) aim' [NJB, REB], 'to make (something one's) chief aim' [TNT], 'to seek after, to aspire to' [BAGD]. This clause is translated 'love should be your guide' [CEV], 'let love be your highest goal' [NLT]. The present imperative indicates a continuative action [NIC2]: keep on pursuing love. Paul means by this command that love is to be the proper context in which the gifts are to function [NIC2]. By this command he means that love is to be the motivation for the spiritual gifts [MNTC].

QUESTION—What is the function of this verse?

It resumes Paul's argument from 12:31 [NIC2, NTC]: Set your hearts on the greater gifts. And yet I show you a more excellent way, it is to pursue love.... It summarizes the two previous chapters and refers back to 12:31

[ICC]. In 12:31 Paul spoke of setting one's heart on the greater gifts. Here Paul specifies which gifts he had in mind [NIC2].

DISCOURSE UNIT: 14:1b–33a [AB]. The topic is the superiority of prophecy over speaking in tongues.

DISCOURSE UNIT: 14:1b–5 [AB]. The topic is prophecy, tongues, and building up.

but/and[a] set-your-hearts-on[b] spiritual-gifts.[c]

LEXICON—a. δέ (See this word at 11:2): 'but' [HNTC, NIGTC], 'but also' [NLT], 'but…too' [NJB], 'yet' [Lns; TNT], 'and' [ISV, KJV, NET, NIV, NRSV], 'then' [REB], not explicit [AB, Herm, ICC, NTC; CEV, NAB, TEV].

  b. pres. act. impera. of ζηλόω (LN 25.46): 'to set (one's) heart on' [NAB, TEV], 'to strive for' [Herm, HNTC; NRSV, TNT], 'to strive eagerly for' [NTC], 'to strive zealously for' [Lns], 'to strive to make one's own' [ICC], 'to desire' [ISV, KJV, NLT], 'to be zealous for' [AB], 'to be eager for' [NIGTC; NET, NJB, REB], 'to be eager to have' [CEV], 'to desire eagerly' [NIV], 'to have a deep concern for, to be devoted to' [LN (25.46)]. The present imperative indicates a continuative aspect [NTC]: keep on setting your heart on. See this word also at 12:31.

  c. πνευματικός (See this word at 12:1 and 10:3): 'spiritual gift' [AB, Herm, HNTC, Lns, NTC; all versions except CEV, NLT, REB], 'gift of the Spirit' [ICC, NIGTC; REB], 'a gift that comes from the Holy Spirit' [CEV], 'a special ability the Spirit gives' [NLT]. Πνευματικός probably refers to here to 'utterances inspired by the Spirit'. In 12:31 Paul used the term χαρίσματα 'spiritual gifts'. Here in chapter 14 there will be emphasis on the Spirit's activity in worship so he uses the word πνευματικός indicating 'the things of the Spirit' [NIC2]. With this term there may be more emphasis on 'spiritual' than on 'gifts' [NTC].

QUESTION—What relationship is indicated by δέ 'but/and'?

  1. It indicates a contrastive relationship [Alf, Ed, HNTC, Ho, Lns, My, NIGTC, TH; NET, NJB, NLT]: pursue love, *but* set your heart on spiritual gifts. Paul had said, "Pursue love." He means pursue love, *but* it does not replace the gifts. Rather, they should be desired as well [Ed]. They should pursue love, but at the same time they should desire spiritual gifts [Ho].
  2. It indicates a conjoining relationship [ISV, KJV, NET, NIV, NRSV]: pursue love, *and* set your heart on spiritual gifts.

but rather[a] that[b] you-may-prophesy.[c]

LEXICON—a. μᾶλλον (LN 78.28) (BAGD 3.d. p. 489): 'rather' [BAGD, Lns; KJV], 'especially' [AB, Herm, HNTC, ICC, NTC; all versions except NAB, REB], 'above all' [NAB, REB], 'more' [Alf, BAGD, LN], 'chiefly' [Alf], 'most particularly' [NIGTC], 'even more, to a greater degree' [LN]. Μᾶλλον here it carries the meaning of 'instead' [BAGD]. It indicates that

1 CORINTHIANS 14:1

Paul will specify what he especially chooses for them to desire among the spiritual gifts [NIC2]. See this word also at 12:22.

b. ἵνα (LN 89.59, 90.22) (BAGD II.1.a. α. p. 377): 'that' [AB, BAGD, Herm, HNTC, LN (90.22), Lns, NIGTC, NTC; KJV, NET, NRSV], 'to' [ICC], 'in order that, so that, for the purpose that' [LN (89.59)], not explicit [all other versions].

c. pres. act. subj. of προφητεύω (See this word at 11:4): 'to prophesy' [AB, HNTC, Lns, NIGTC, NTC; KJV, NET, NRSV], 'to be inspired to preach' [ICC]. This verb is also translated as a participle or noun phrase: 'prophesying' [Herm; NJB], 'prophecy' [REB], 'the gift of prophecy' [CEV, NAB, NIV, NLT], 'the ability to prophesy' [ISV], 'the gift of proclaiming God's message' [TEV], 'the gift of speaking God's message' [TNT]. The present imperative indicates a continuative aspect [NTC, Rb]: that you may continue to prophesy. Προφητεύω does not mean preaching a carefully prepared sermon but expressing a message directly inspired by God [NTC, TNTC]. Prophecy includes preaching and teaching [NIGTC].

QUESTION—What relationship is indicated by ἵνα 'that/in order that'?

1. It indicates what they are to desire [Ed, ICC, Lns, NIC, NIC2, NIGTC, NTC]: earnestly desire spiritual gifts, but rather *desire that* you may prophesy. The ἵνα 'that' depends on ζηλοῦτε 'earnestly desire' [Ed, NIC]. The ἵνα explains more specifically what Paul meant by desiring spiritual gifts [NIC2]: earnestly desire spiritual gifts, *that is, that* you may prophesy.
2. It indicates purpose [Alf, EGT, Gdt, My]: earnestly desire spiritual gifts *in order that* you may prophesy.

QUESTION—What is the significance of the plural form of the verb προφητεύητε 'you (plural) may prophesy'?

It indicates that the desire of the whole church should be that the gift of prophecy be used in their meetings, not that each individual should desire to personally have the gift of prophecy [Lns, MNTC]. They may all eagerly desire the gift of prophesy, but, being a gift, only those to whom it is given will be able to prophesy [ICC, NTC]. 'Pursue love' is directed to the entire congregation while 'set your hearts' is directed to those who have spiritual gifts [NIC]. Each one should want to pursue love, to have spiritual gifts, and especially to prophesy [HNTC].

14:2 For the-(one) speaking in-(a)-tongue[a] speaks not to-men[b] but to-God;

LEXICON—a. γλῶσσα (LN 33.3): 'tongue' [AB, Herm, HNTC, ICC, **LN**, Lns, NIGTC, NTC; all versions except CEV, KJV, TEV], 'languages that others don't know' [CEV], 'unknown tongue' [KJV], 'strange tongue' [TEV]. See this word at 12:10.

b. ἄνθρωπος (See this word at 13:1): 'man' [Herm, HNTC, ICC, Lns; KJV, NAB, NIV, TNT], 'human being' [NIGTC], 'people' [AB; ISV, NET, NLT], 'other people' [NJB, NRSV], 'others' [TEV], 'someone else' [CEV], 'men and women' [NTC; REB].

QUESTION—What relationship is indicated by γάρ 'for'?
It indicates the grounds for the advice to desire prophesy [EGT, My, NIC]: desire that you may prophesy *since* no one understands what is said when you speak in a tongue.

QUESTION—What does ὁ λαλῶν γλώσσῃ οὐκ ἀνθρώποις λαλεῖ ἀλλὰ θεῷ 'he who speaks in a tongue speaks not to men but to God' mean?

1. When this refers to a human foreign language.
   It means that he speaks in a foreign language that is unknown to the people present but is known to God [Ho, Lns].
2. When this refers to a non-human heavenly language.
   It means that he speaks to God in this heavenly language that only God can understand [HNTC]. This language is given by the Holy Spirit and is not addressed to men [NIC]. Paul understands this term to mean a language of prayer and praise to God [NIC2]. It is private worship of God [NTC]. This language was used to commune with God and was partly addressed to God, partly to oneself [ICC]. What is spoken is between the speaker and God and is not understood by others [Gdt].
3. When this refers to a pseudo speaking in tongues.
   A better translation for θεῷ 'to God' is 'to a god' since there is no article. The carnal Christians in Corinth were not exercising the true gift of tongues, but a kind of tongues (ecstatic utterances) that was a left-over from their pagan past. Their concern was for excitement and self-gratification rather than building up others. The singular use of γλῶσσα refers to the counterfeited gift of tongues both here and in 14:4. The true gift of speaking in human languages is referred to by the plural form (14:5, 6, 18, 22, 23, 39) and one instance in the singular (14:27) where a single man speaks in a genuine language [MNTC].

for no-one understands[a] (him), but he-speaks mysteries[b] in-(the)-Spirit/ spirit;[c]

LEXICON—a. ἀκούω (LN 32.1) (BAGD 7. p. 32): 'to understand' [BAGD, Herm, **LN**, Lns, NIGTC, NTC; all versions except CEV], 'to be able to understand' [HNTC, ICC], 'to know what (one) means' [CEV], 'to comprehend' [LN], 'to hear' [AB, BAGD]. Ἀκούω here means 'to hear and understand' [NIC2].

b. μυστήριον (See this word at 13:2): 'mystery' [AB, Herm, HNTC, Lns, NIGTC, NTC; CEV, KJV, NAB, NET, NIV, NRSV], 'divine mystery' [REB], 'secret' [ISV, TNT], 'mystic secrets' [ICC], 'secret truth' [TEV]. This noun is also translated as a clause: 'and the meaning is hidden' [NJB], 'it will all be mysterious' [NLT].

c. πνεῦμα (LN 12.18, 26.9) (BAGD 6.e. p. 677): 'Spirit' [BAGD, Herm, HNTC, LN (12.18), NIGTC, NTC; CEV, ISV, NAB, NET, NJB, NRSV, REB], 'the power of the Spirit' [NLT, TEV], 'Spirit of God, Holy Spirit' [LN (12.18)], 'spirit' [AB, LN (26.9), Lns; KJV, NIV], 'inner being' [LN

(26.9)]. The word πνεύματι 'in spirit' is translated 'by inspiration' [TNT], 'one who is in a state of rapture' [ICC].

QUESTION—What does οὐδεὶς ἀκούει 'no one understands him' mean?
1. When γλῶσσα refers to a human foreign language.
   He does not mean that no one could understand the language, but only that no one present could understand it [Ho, Lns]. 'No one' here means 'no one who does not have the gift of interpretation', that is, no one who is not conversant with that particular foreign language [Lns].
2. When γλῶσσα refers to a non-human heavenly language.
   It means that such a language is not understandable either to speaker or hearer [NIC2].
3. When γλῶσσα refers to a pseudo speaking in tongues.
   The utterance is unintelligible gibberish [MNTC].

QUESTION—What relationship is indicated by δέ 'but'?
1. It indicates a contrastive relationship [Ed, EGT, Gdt, Lns, NTC; CEV, KJV, NLT]: no one understands him, *but* in the Spirit he speaks mysteries. The contrast indicates that even though no one understands him yet he does speak things that are of value [EGT].
2. It indicates a reason relationship [ICC; ISV, NAB, NRSV, REB]: no one understands him, *because* in the Spirit he speaks mysteries.

QUESTION—What is meant by πνεύματι λαλεῖ μυστήρια 'he speaks mysteries in the Spirit/spirit'?
1. It refers to the Holy Spirit who speaks mysteries [BAGD, HNTC, Ho, NCBC, NIC2, NIGTC, NTC, TG, TH; NAB, NRSV, TEV].
   1.1 When this refers to human foreign languages.
       The Holy Spirit guides the person to speak mysteries or divine truth. Though spoken through a foreign language which is not understood, still the language has meaning [Ho].
   1.2 When this refers to non-human heavenly languages.
       This indicates communing with God in a heavenly language by the enabling of the Holy Spirit. Since the speaker is addressing only God, Paul thinks of these mysteries as prayer and praise [NIC2]. God enables people to speak unintelligible mysteries by the Holy Spirit (see 2:6–16 and 1 Peter 1:10–12) [NTC]. The speech may be called mysteries simply because it is unintelligible [TG].
2. It refers to the person's own spirit which speaks mysteries [Alf, Ed, EGT, Gdt, Lns, MNTC, My, NIC, TNTC, Vn; KJV, NIV, NJB].
   2.1 When this refers to human foreign languages.
       The Holy Spirit inspires a person's spirit and gives him/her words to speak which he/she may or may not understand. This happens without conscious thought on the part of the speaker [Lns].
   2.2 When this refers to non-human heavenly languages.
       The Holy Spirit works directly with a person's spirit enabling him/her to speak without understanding. What he/she speaks is not understood and

so is mysterious [NIC]. It refers to a state of rapture in which the person speaks mysteries [ICC]. The speaker's spirit is lifted up in ecstasy [Gdt].
2.3 When this refers to a pseudo speaking in tongues.

The Corinthians were speaking mysteries, as people did in pagan religions in which the mysteries were secret truths that only the initiated were allowed to know. This was done in (locative sense) the person's own spirit [MNTC].

14:3 But[a] the-(one) prophesying[b] speaks upbuilding[c] and encouragement[d] and comfort[e] to men.

LEXICON—a. δέ (See this word at 11:2): 'but' [AB, HNTC, Lns, NTC; CEV, ISV, NET, NIV, NLT, TEV, TNT], 'on the other hand' [KJV, NAB, NJB, NRSV, REB], 'however' [Herm, NIGTC], 'it is otherwise with' [ICC].
  b. pres. act. participle of προφητεύω (See this word at 11:4): 'to prophesy' [AB, HNTC, Lns, NIGTC, NTC; all versions except NAB, TEV, TNT], 'to speak God's message' [TNT], 'to proclaim God's message' [TEV], 'to be inspired to preach' [ICC]. This participle is translated as a noun: 'prophet' [NAB]. It is implied that he prophesies to people in their own language so they could easily understand [Lns].
  c. οἰκοδομή (LN 74.15) (BAGD 1.b.α. p. 559): 'upbuilding' [BAGD; ISV, NAB, NRSV], 'edification' [BAGD, Herm, HNTC, Lns; KJV], 'strengthening' [NET, NIV], 'words which build up' [TNT], 'words that edify' [BAGD], 'words of hope to quicken' [ICC], 'constructive message' [AB]. This noun is also translated as a verb: 'to build' [REB], 'to build up' [LN, NIGTC; NJB], 'to strengthen, to make more able' [LN], 'to give help' [TEV], 'to help (someone) grow in the Lord' [NLT], 'to be helped' [CEV]. Οἰκοδομή indicates the process of increasing the potential of someone [LN]. It is used here to refer to the building up of a person's spiritual life [ICC, NIC]. It refers to making a person's faith and spiritual life strong [Lns]. It refers to growth both in a person's individual life as well as in the body of the church [NIC2]. See the verbal form of this word at 10:23 and 14:4.
  d. παράκλησις (LN 25.150) (BAGD 1. p. 618): 'encouragement' [BAGD, LN; ISV, NAB, NET, NIV, NRSV], 'exhortation' [BAGD, Herm, HNTC; KJV], 'admonition' [Lns], 'words which encourage' [TNT], 'words of exhortation' [BAGD], 'words of love to hearten' [ICC], 'encouraging message' [AB]. This noun is also translated as a verb: 'to encourage' [NIGTC; NLT], 'to give encouragement' [NJB, TEV], 'to be encouraged' [CEV], 'to stimulate' [REB].
  e. παραμυθία (LN **25.154**) (BAGD p. 620): 'comfort' [BAGD, HNTC; ISV, KJV, NIV], 'consolation' [BAGD, LN, Lns; NAB, NET, NRSV], 'encouragement' [BAGD, Herm, LN], 'words which comfort' [TNT], 'words of love to console' [ICC], 'consoling message' [AB]. This noun is also translated as a verb: 'to console' [**LN**], 'to comfort' [NLT], 'to give

comfort' [TEV], 'to bring comfort' [NIGTC], 'to encourage' [REB], 'to give reassurance' [NJB], 'to be made to feel better' [CEV].

QUESTION—Are these three separate terms here?
1. The three terms are separate terms [EGT, Gdt, ICC, Lns, MNTC, NIGTC]: upbuilding, encouragement, and comfort.
2. The first term is a general term and the next two are specifics of it [Alf, Herm, Ho, My]: upbuilding, that is, encouragement and comfort. The person prophesying builds people up either by encouraging or comforting them [Ho].

QUESTION—What is the difference between παράκλησις 'encouragement' and παραμυθία 'comfort'?

The two words are nearly synonymous in meaning [Herm, NIC]. Παράκλησις has the meaning of 'encouragement' or 'exhortation' while παραμυθία has the sense of 'comfort' or 'consolation' [ICC]. Παράκλησις means to help and support the church while παραμυθία means to promote a good spirit in the Christian assembly [TH]. Since παραμυθία has the meaning of 'comfort' here, it is best to give the meaning of 'exhortation' to παράκλησις [Ho, NIC]. Παράκλησις refers to 'admonition' of any kind while παραμυθία refers to enabling a Christian to face persecution and hardship and to hold out cheerfully to the end [Lns]. Παράκλησις refers to persuasion and urging a course of action while παραμυθία refers to sympathy [Ed].

14:4 **The-one speaking in-(a)-tongue builds-up[a] himself;**

LEXICON—a. pres. act. indic. of οἰκοδομέω (See this word also at 10:23): 'to build up' [AB, HNTC, ICC, NIGTC; ISV, NAB, NET, NJB, NRSV, REB, TNT], 'to edify' [Herm, Lns, NTC; KJV, NIV], 'to help' [CEV, TEV], 'to be strengthened personally in the Lord' [NLT].

QUESTION—Was Paul sincere in what he says here?
1. Paul was sincere in saying that speaking in tongues builds a person up [AB, Alf, Ed, EGT, Gdt, HNTC, Ho, ICC, Lns, My, NIC, NIC2, NIGTC, NTC, TG, TNTC].
2. Paul was using this word sarcastically here referring to the supposed value that the Corinthians placed on their particular mode of speaking in tongues that was not the true gift of tongues. [MNTC].

QUESTION—What does ἑαυτὸν οἰκοδομεῖ 'builds himself up' mean?
1. When speaking in tongues refers to a human foreign language.
The speaker builds himself up because he understands what he is saying [Ho]. Speaking in tongues consists of prayer, singing, blessing, and giving thanks [Lns].
2. When speaking in tongues refers to a non-human heavenly language.
Communing with God by the Holy Spirit in this way by-passes the brain but builds up the person himself/herself [NIC2]. In speaking in tongues, God receives praise and gives the speaker comfort and encouragement [NTC]. Since he does not understand what he says, it must be that the act

of speaking in tongues itself builds the speaker up because the speaker is assured by the act that he/she possesses the Holy Spirit [NIC]. The fact that the speaker is communing with God is what builds him up [Gdt, ICC]. The speaker may not understand what he says, but he is built up by the strong feeling of the prayer or praise that the Holy Spirit inspires in him [Alf].

3. When speaking in tongues refers to pseudo speaking in tongues.
It was emotional self-satisfaction rather than spiritual edification [MNTC].

but the-one prophesying builds-up (a) church.[a]

LEXICON—a. ἐκκλησία (See this word at 10:32): 'church' [AB, Herm, HNTC, ICC, Lns, NTC; all versions except NJB, REB], 'Christian community' [REB], 'community' [NJB], 'church community' [NIGTC], 'assembled company' [HNTC], 'congregation' [LN (11.32)]. Ἐκκλησία here indicates the local congregation not the universal church [HNTC, Lns, NTC, Rb, TH, Vn]. There is no article with ἐκκλησία so 'a church' is a correct translation. But the meaning is 'the church of which one is a member' [HNTC]. It refers to the universal church [NIC].

14:5 Now[a] I-wish[b] you all to-speak in-tongues,

LEXICON—a. δέ (See this word at 11:2): 'now' [AB, Gdt, ICC, NTC; NRSV], 'for' [Lns], not explicit [Herm, HNTC, NIGTC; all versions except NRSV].

b. pres. act. indic. of θέλω (See this word at 10:27): 'to wish' [Herm, HNTC, ICC, NTC; ISV, NET, NLT], 'to want' [AB], 'to be glad for' [CEV], 'to be happy for' [REB], 'to take pleasure in' [NIGTC]. This verb is also translated 'I would like' [NIV, NRSV, TEV, TNT], 'I should like (it)' [NAB, NJB], 'I would that' [KJV], 'I would have' [Lns].

QUESTION—Does Paul think that they should all speak in tongues?
This is said for the sake of emphasis [MNTC, TNTC]. Paul wishes what is impossible. He knew that not all do not have the same gifts but here he is making it clear that he did not despise the true gift of tongues [Ho, MNTC, NTC]. He would like if they did [NIC2, TH] and it would be a good thing [NIC].

but[a] rather[b] that you-should-prophesy;

LEXICON—a. δέ (See this word at 11:2): 'but' [AB, Herm, HNTC, ICC, NIGTC; all versions except CEV, NJB], 'although' [CEV], 'yet' [Lns], not explicit [NTC; NJB].

b. μᾶλλον (See this word at 14:1): 'rather' [Lns, NIGTC; CEV, KJV, NIV, TEV], 'even more' [HNTC; NET, NLT, NRSV], 'especially' [AB, NTC; ISV], 'still more' [Herm], 'much rather' [NJB], 'much more' [TNT], 'happier still' [REB]. This adverb is also translated as a clause: 'I much prefer' [NAB], 'I would greatly prefer' [ICC].

QUESTION—Does Paul think that they should all prophesy?

This was an impossibility since Paul knew that all do not receive the gift of prophecy (12:29) [MNTC, NIC]. Paul meant that although the Corinthians greatly desired the gift of tongues, it would be much better if they changed their desires to the gift of prophecy [MNTC].

and[a] greater[b] (is) the-one prophesying than the-one speaking in-tongues

TEXT—Instead of δέ 'and' some manuscripts have γάρ 'for'. GNT does not mention this alternative. Herm, HNTC; KJV, NJB, NLT, and TEV either read γάρ 'for' or render δέ as 'for'.

LEXICON—a. δέ (See this word at 11:2): 'and' [Lns, NTC], 'in fact' [CEV], not explicit [AB, ICC, NIGTC; ISV, NAB, NET, NIV, NRSV, REB, TNT]. (Herm, HNTC, KJV, NJB, NLT and TEV have some form of 'for'.) Δέ is used here with the sense of 'besides that' indicating a further reason for the benefit of prophecy [EGT, ICC]. Δέ is contrastive 'but' [Gdt]. Δέ is transitional 'now' [Alf].

b. μείζων (BAGD 2.b.α. p. 498): 'greater' [Herm, HNTC, Lns, NTC; KJV, NAB, NET, NIV, NRSV, TNT], 'greater and more useful' [NLT], 'more important' [ISV], 'of greater importance' [NIGTC; NJB], 'of greater value' [TEV], 'worth more' [REB]. This adjective is also translated as a clause: '(prophesying) does much more good' [CEV], '(this being) far more important' [ICC]. Μείζων here means 'more prominent' or 'outstanding' because of certain advantages [BAGD].

QUESTION—What is meant by μείζων 'greater'?

Μείζων now defines what Paul meant by this word in 12:31 where he spoke of 'greater gifts' [NIC2]. It implies that he is more useful than one who speaks in tongues [Ho]. 'Greater' is used in the sense of being of more value to the Christian community [NIC2, NIGTC, TH]. He is of more worth because he builds up others [My]. It is greater in the fact that it is intelligible and can therefore build up [NIC2]. Paul is not comparing people here as prophet and tongue-speaker, but he is comparing their gifts [NTC]. See this word also at 12:31.

unless[a] he-interpret,[b]

LEXICON—a. ἐκτός εἰ μή (LN **89.138**) (BAGD 1. p. 246): 'unless' [AB, BAGD, Herm, HNTC, ICC, Lns, NIGTC, NTC; all versions except KJV, REB], 'unless indeed' [REB], 'except' [BAGD, **LN**; KJV]. Ἐκτός εἰ μή is a combination of ἐκτός εἰ 'except if' and εἰ μή 'unless' meaning 'with this exception—unless' [EGT].

b. pres. act. subj. of διερμηνεύω (See this word at 12:30): 'to interpret' [AB, Herm, HNTC, Lns, NTC; ISV, KJV, NAB, NET, NIV, NJB, NLT, NRSV], 'to be interpreted' [ICC], 'to explain its meaning' [CEV, REB], 'to explain what is said' [TEV], 'to articulate an utterance intelligibly' [NIGTC]. This verb is translated as a clause: 'there is an interpreter' [TNT]. This can be translated as 'unless someone interprets' since 'he' is a generic singular and Paul is probably thinking of a congregation which has some who have the gift of interpretation [TH].

QUESTION—What is intended by making this exception?

Paul is saying that speaking in tongues when interpreted has value in that it builds up other members of the church. The Corinthians may have previously spoken in tongues in their pagan rites and Paul wanted them to make sure that the gift they now exercised was genuinely from the Holy Spirit [NTC]. Interpreted tongues had the same benefit as prophecy [Ho, NIC, TNTC]. Prophecy and interpreted tongues can both edify the church. The interpretation of the tongue may not be directed toward the congregation in the same way that prophecy is, but the congregation could benefit from what the person said to God [Lns, NIC2, NTC].

QUESTION—To whom does διερμηνεύῃ 'he interpret' refer?

1. It refers to the same person who speaks in a tongue [AB, Alf, EGT, Gdt, Herm, HNTC, Ho, ICC, Lns, My, NIC, NIC2, NTC, Vn; ISV, KJV, NAB, NET, NIV, NJB, REB]. This implies that the same person had two gifts, speaking in tongues and interpretation of tongues [Lns, NIC]. The reference is to the speaker himself. However, there is the possibility that another could do it (see 14:27) [Gdt].
2. It can refer to a different person than the one who speaks in a tongue [My, TG, TH; CEV, NLT, NRSV, TEV, TNT]. Verses 12:10, 30 indicate that it may be another person who interprets [TH].

so-that the church may-receive edification.

QUESTION—What is the significance of this purpose clause?

This purpose clause is the point of the exception [Lns]. The Corinthian problem was very likely not speaking in tongues as such, but doing so without interpretation. This may highlight Paul's major concern: intelligible speaking with a view to edification [NIC2].

DISCOURSE UNIT: 14:6–19 [AB; NAB]. The topic is tongues, interpretation, and building up [AB], the interpretation of tongues [NAB].

DISCOURSE UNIT: 14:6–12 [NIC2, NIGTC, NTC]. The topic is analogies that argue for intelligibility [NIC, NTC], examples of the useless of unintelligible noise [NIGTC].

14:6 But-now,[a] brothers,[b] if I-come to you speaking in-tongues,

LEXICON—a. νυνὶ δέ (See this phrase at 12:18): 'but now' [Herm, NTC], 'but now…think' [HNTC], 'now' [AB; ISV, KJV, NET, NIV, NRSV], 'well now' [NIGTC], 'and now' [Lns], 'so' [TEV], 'so then' [TNT], 'suppose' [REB], 'now suppose' [NJB], 'just suppose' [NAB], 'but…suppose' [ICC], 'but as it is' [NIC2], 'but because things are so' [NTC], not explicit [CEV, NLT].

b. ἀδελφός (See this word at 10:1): 'brother' [AB, Herm, HNTC, Lns, NTC; ISV, KJV, NAB, NIV, NJB, TNT], 'brother and sister' [NET, NLT, NRSV], 'dear fellow believers' [NIGTC], '(one's) friends' [CEV, REB,

1 CORINTHIANS 14:6   201

TEV]. Ἀδελφός also includes 'sisters' [NIC2, NTC]. The use of ἀδελφός puts Paul on their level and permits him to correct them with tenderness [NTC].

QUESTION—What is the function of νῦν 'now'?
It is logical [Alf, Ed, Gdt, Herm, Ho, ICC, Lns, My, NIC, NIC2, NTC, TH, Vn; NAB, NJB, REB, TEV, TNT]: now then. The combination of vocative plus the νῦν δέ, indicates a change in Paul's argument [NIC2, TH]. Νῦν δέ 'but now' indicates that Paul will now conclude and sum up what he has been saying [NIC]. Νῦν δέ 'but as it is' means, in view of the fact that in order to edify there must be intelligible communication [Alf, Ho, ICC, My]. Νῦν δέ ἀδελφοί 'and now, brothers' indicates that Paul will illustrate in terms that they can understand even better [Lns]. The opening sentence serves to introduce a pattern of analogies that reason for the intelligibility in the use of the gifts [NIC2]. Νῦν 'now' indicates that Paul will at this time turn his attention to the present situation at Corinth [EGT]. Paul now looks at the facts and takes a concrete example [NIGTC].

what will-I-benefit[a] you unless I-speak to-you either in[b] revelation[c] or in[b] knowledge[d] or in[b] prophecy[e] or [in][b] (a) teaching?[f]

LEXICON—a. fut. act. indic. of ὠφελέω (See this word at 13:3): 'to benefit' [AB; NRSV, TNT], 'to do good' [Herm, HNTC; CEV, NAB, NJB, REB], 'to be of good to' [ISV, NIV], 'to be of use to' [TEV], 'to help' [NET, NLT], 'to profit someone' [Lns, NIGTC, NTC; KJV].

b. ἐν with dative object (LN 89.5, 90.23): 'in' [HNTC, LN (89.5, 90.23); ISV, NRSV], 'by' [AB, NTC; KJV], 'by way of' [Lns; REB], 'with' [Herm; NET], 'in terms of' [NIGTC], 'with regard to, about' [LN (89.5, 90.23)], 'with respect/reference to' [LN (90.23)], not explicit [NIV, NJB, NLT, TEV]. The phrase λαλήσω ἢ ἐν 'I speak either in' is translated 'I use words of' [TNT]. The phrase ἐὰν μὴ ὑμῖν λαλήσω ἢ ἐν ἀποκαλύψει 'unless I speak to you either in revelation' is translated 'if my speech does not have some revelation' [NAB], 'unless I told you what God had shown me' [CEV]. See this word also at 12:3.

c. ἀποκάλυψις (LN 28.38) (BAGD 2. p. 92): 'revelation' [AB, BAGD, Herm, HNTC, LN, Lns, NTC; all versions except CEV], 'disclosure' [BAGD, NIGTC], 'what God had shown me' [CEV]. It is translated as an infinitive clause 'to explain some glimpse of the unseen' [ICC]. Ἀποκάλυψις is divine truth which a person receives directly from God [Lns]. It implies the disclosure of the mysteries of God concerning either the Gospel or things hidden from natural man [NIC2]. It means pieces of information that would go into the makeup of the New Testament; disclosure of the truth of God's Word which a person would then share with the church; and instructions from God regarding where to go and why (see Galatians 2:2 and 2 Corinthians 12:1, 7) [NTC].

d. γνῶσις (See this word at 12:8): 'knowledge' [AB, Herm, HNTC, Lns, NIGTC, NTC; all versions except NLT, REB], 'special knowledge'

[NLT], 'enlightenment' [REB], 'knowledge of truth' [ICC]. Γνῶσις indicates the understanding of divine truth [Lns].

e. προφητεία (BAGD 3.b. p. 722): 'prophecy' [AB, Herm, HNTC, Lns, NTC; all versions except KJV, TEV], 'prophesying' [KJV], 'prophetic speech' [NIGTC], 'inspired message' [TEV], 'glimpse of the unseen to inspire you' [ICC], 'the form of a prophetic saying' [BAGD]. Προφητεία combines receiving a revelation from God and sharing it with others [Lns]. See this word also at 12:10.

f. διδαχή (LN 33.224, 33.236) (BAGD 1. p. 192): 'teaching' [AB, BAGD, Herm, HNTC, LN (33.224, 33.236), Lns, NIGTC, NTC; CEV, ISV, NET, NLT, NRSV, TEV, TNT], 'instruction' [BAGD; NAB, NJB, REB], 'word of instruction' [NIV], 'knowledge of truth to instruct you' [ICC], 'doctrine' [LN (33.236); KJV]. Διδαχή indicates instructing others in divine truth [Lns].

QUESTION—What reply does Paul expect from his question?

He expects a negative reply to his question [NTC]: you will benefit us nothing if you come without giving us a revelation, knowledge, prophecy, or teaching.

QUESTION—Are revelation, knowledge, prophecy, and teaching separate from speaking in tongues or the content of what was spoken in tongues?

1. They are separate from speaking in tongues [AB, Alf, EGT, Gdt, Ho, ICC, Lns, NIC, NIC2, NIGTC, NTC, TNTC]. The first and second conditions are complementary to each other—one positive, the other negative—showing that they are mutually exclusive. That is, (a) "If I speak in tongues" and (b) "If it does not bring some revelation,…how will it benefit you?" This shows that revelation, knowledge, prophecy, and teaching were in place of speaking in tongues [Alf, ICC]. It means that revelation, knowledge, and so on needed to be in addition to speaking in tongues apart from interpretation [Gdt]. By this verse Paul is indicating his unwillingness to come to them speaking in tongues [NIC2, NTC].

2. They are the content of what was spoken in tongues [Ed, MNTC, My, TG]. Paul means that his speaking in tongues would only be of value if there were an interpretation which would result in some revelation from God and so on [TG].

QUESTION—What is the relationship between revelation, knowledge, prophecy, and teaching?

They form two pairs: prophecy-revelation and teaching-knowledge. What a prophet does is to give a revelation, and what a teacher does is to transmit knowledge [Ho, My, NIC, NTC]. Revelation and knowledge are internal while prophecy and teaching are external [MNTC]. The four gifts overlap and merge into each other [Lns]. Paul intended no particular grouping as some have suggested. What he does intend is to give a list of Spirit-inspired utterances that are all intelligible [NIC2].

DISCOURSE UNIT: 14:7–13 [EGT]. The topic is the uselessness of utterance if there is no clear sense.

14:7 Similarly[a] lifeless[b] things giving sound, whether flute[c] or harp,[d]

LEXICON—a. ὅμως (LN 64.11, **89.74**) (BAGD p. 569): 'similarly' [LN (64.11), NIGTC], 'similarly, in the case of' [**LN** (89.74)], 'in the same way' [AB, HNTC, NTC; ISV], 'likewise' [BAGD, LN (64.11)], 'even in the case of' [NAB, NIV], 'even (musical instruments) like' [NLT], 'even with' [REB], 'and even' [KJV], 'for' [Herm], 'also' [BAGD], 'though' [LN (89.74), Lns], 'although' [LN (89.74)], 'yet' [Ho], not explicit [CEV, NJB]. This adverb is also translated as a clause: 'it is the same way with' [NRSV, TNT], 'it is similar for' [NET], 'take such' [TEV], 'Why, there are instruments which, although (lifeless)' [ICC].
  b. ἄψυχος (LN **23.98**) (BAGD p. 129): 'lifeless' [BAGD, ICC, **LN**, NTC; ISV, NAB, NET, NIV, NLT, NRSV, TEV], 'without life' [KJV], 'soulless' [Lns], 'inanimate' [AB, BAGD, Herm, HNTC, LN, NIGTC; NJB, REB, TNT], not explicit [CEV].
  c. αὐλός (LN **6.86**) (BAGD p. 121): 'flute' [AB, BAGD, Herm, HNTC, **LN**, NIGTC, NTC; all versions except CEV, KJV], 'pipe' [ICC, Lns; KJV]. Αὐλός 'flute' and κιθάρα 'harp' are translated together as 'musical instruments' [CEV]. This is said as representative of all wind instruments [Gdt, ICC, TNTC].
  d. κιθάρα (LN **6.83**) (BAGD p. 432): 'harp' [AB, BAGD, ICC, LN, Lns, NTC; all versions except CEV, NJB, REB], 'lyre' [BAGD, Herm, HNTC, LN, NIGTC; NJB, REB], not explicit [CEV]. This is a small stringed instrument, held in the hands and plucked [LN]. This is said as representative of all stringed instruments [Gdt, ICC, TNTC].

QUESTION—What sense of ὅμως is in focus here?
  1. It has the sense of 'similarly, likewise, in the same way' [AB, BAGD, HNTC, LN (89.74), NIC2, NIGTC, NTC; ISV, NET, NRSV, TNT]. Ὅμως has two senses, 'similarly' and 'though'. Since the concessive sense is doubtful here, it may be preferable to use the sense of 'similarly' [LN]. The position of ὅμως requires the introduction of a comparison so the sense of 'likewise' or 'just as' is indicated [NTC]. If sounds come from a lifeless musical instrument or from a living person and make no sense, then the sounds of the instruments or of the person do not benefit the listener [NIC2].
  2 It has the sense of 'nevertheless, yet', or 'though' [Ed, EGT, Gdt, Ho, ICC, Lns]. Ὅμως should be placed between the clauses: 'Lifeless things give a sound, *yet*, unless they give a distinct sound…' [Ho]. Its use is concessive: '*Although* lifeless things give a sound…unless they give a distinct sound…' [Lns].
  3. It has the sense of 'even' [NCBC; KJV, NAB, NIV, REB].

if it-gives not (a) distinction[a] in-the notes,[b]

LEXICON—a. διαστολή (LN **58.42**) (BAGD p. 188): 'distinction' [AB, BAGD, HNTC, ICC, LN, Lns; KJV, NAB, NET, NIV, NJB], 'clear distinction' [BAGD, **LN**], 'distinct difference' [NIGTC], 'difference' [BAGD, LN; ISV]. This noun is also translated as an adjective: 'distinct' [NTC; NRSV, REB], 'distinguishable' [TNT]. It is also translated as an adverb: 'distinctly' [TEV], 'clearly' [NLT]. It is also translated as a verb phrase: '(its notes) cannot be distinguished' [Herm]. The phrase διαστολή…μὴ δῷ 'distinction… gives not' is translated 'to sound alike' [CEV]. Διαστολή refers to the interval between notes [Alf, EGT, NIC2], or to the pitch [EGT, NIC2]. A distinction of notes may refer to the playing or hearing of a melody [Lns, NIC2]. It contrasts with playing all the notes at once [HNTC].

b. φθόγγος (LN **14.74**) (BAGD p. 857): 'note' [ICC, **LN**, Lns, NTC; all versions except CEV, KJV], 'sound' [BAGD, HNTC, LN; KJV], 'tone' [AB, BAGD], 'pitch' [NIGTC], not explicit [CEV].

how will-be-known what is-being-played-on-the-flute[a] or what is-being-played-on-the-harp?[b]

LEXICON—a. pres. pass. participle of αὐλέω (LN 6.87, **6.84**) (BAGD p. 121): 'to be played on (the) flute' [AB, BAGD, HNTC, **LN**, NTC; NET, NJB], 'to be piped' [Lns; KJV]. This passive is also translated as an active: 'the tune which the pipe is playing' [ICC]. The phrase τὸ αὐλούμενον ἢ τὸ κιθαριζόμενον 'the thing being played on the flute or the thing being played on the lyre' is translated 'what is being played' [NAB, NRSV], 'what is produced by wind or by string' [NIGTC], 'the tune that is blown or played' [Herm], 'what tune is being played' [ISV, NIV, REB], 'the tune that is being played' [TEV], 'their tune' [TNT], 'the melody' [NLT], 'the difference between a flute and a harp' [CEV].

b. pres. pass. participle of κιθαρίζω (LN **6.84**) (BAGD p. 432): 'to be played on the harp' [AB, BAGD, LN, NTC; NET], 'to be played on (the) lyre' [BAGD, HNTC, **LN**; NJB], 'to be played' [Herm], 'to be harped' [Lns; KJV], not explicit [all other versions]. This passive verb is also translated as an active: 'the tune which the harp is playing' [ICC].

QUESTION—What does the figure mean?

It means that as in the case of musical instruments, we must be able to recognize the tune being played in order to benefit by the playing, so in the case of speaking, we must understand the language in order to benefit from what is being said [Ho].

QUESTION—What reply is expected to this question?

The expected reply is that under that condition no one will be able to recognize what is being played [Ho, TG, TH].

QUESTION—If a flute or harp playing unclear tunes is the image, and speaking in tongues without an interpretation is the topic, what is the point of similarity?

The point of similarity is that sound alone is meaningless, it must be accompanied by meaning or something recognizable to the hearer [Alf]. The point of similarity is the lack of benefit to the listener [Ho].

14:8 For-also[a] if (a) trumpet[b] gives (an) unclear[c] sound,

LEXICON—a. καὶ γάρ (BAGD 1. b. p. 151): 'for also' [BAGD], 'for even' [BAGD], 'for' [NTC; KJV], 'for moreover' [Lns], 'for example' [ISV, NET], 'and indeed' [AB], 'still stronger (instance)' [ICC], 'again' [NIV], 'or again' [REB], 'furthermore' [NIGTC], 'and' [Herm, HNTC; NLT, NRSV, TEV, TNT], not explicit [CEV, NAB, NJB].

b. σάλπιγξ (LN **6.89**) (BAGD 1. p. 741): 'trumpet' [AB, BAGD, HNTC, **LN**, Lns, NIGTC, NTC; KJV, NET, NIV, NJB, REB, TNT], 'trumpet blast' [ICC], 'bugle' [Herm; CEV, ISV, NAB, NRSV]. This instrument is also translated by the person who uses it: 'bugler' [NLT], 'the one who plays the bugle' [TEV]. The bugler would sound different tunes on his bugle that served as commands to the soldiers. The tunes had to be played in a way that the soldiers could recognize them or they would not know what to do when the command was given [TG].

c. ἄδηλος (LN 24.95) (BAGD 2. p. 16): 'unclear' [AB, Herm; NET], 'not clear' [CEV, ISV, NIV, NLT, REB, TEV], 'indistinct' [BAGD, NTC; NRSV, TNT], 'uncertain' [ICC, Lns; KJV, NAB], 'unrecognizable' [NJB], 'undistinguishable' [HNTC], 'ambivalent as a signal' [NIGTC], 'not evident' [LN], 'not perceived' [LN].

QUESTION—What relationship is indicated by καὶ γάρ 'for also'?

Καὶ γάρ indicates another and even stronger illustration [ICC, My, Vn]. The καὶ 'also' indicates another example, the γάρ 'for' indicates that it is an explanation of the previous verse [Lns]. The γάρ indicates that this is the reason of the final clause of 14:7 [Ho, My]: how will anyone know what is being played *because* if the bugle gives an indistinct note, no one will get ready for battle. Γάρ indicates a further reason to 14:7 for not speaking in tongues without an interpretation [NIC].

who will-prepare[a] for battle?[b]

LEXICON—a. fut. mid. indic. of παρασκευάζω (LN **77.8**) (BAGD 2. p. 622): 'to prepare' [AB, Herm, **LN**, NIGTC; REB, TEV, TNT], 'to get ready' [ICC; ISV, NAB, NET, NIV, NJB, NRSV], 'to prepare oneself' [BAGD, Lns, NTC; KJV], 'to arm oneself' [HNTC], 'to make ready' [**LN**], 'to become ready' [LN], 'to know to get ready' [CEV]. The phrase τίς παρασκευάσεται 'who will get ready?' is translated 'how will the soldiers know they are being called' [NLT]. Παρασκευάζω indicates 'to make ready' or 'to make preparations' rather than 'to prepare oneself' since the older middle voice sense is more commonly used than the reflexive [ICC]. This refers to a soldier getting his equipment ready [TH].

b. πόλεμος (LN 55.5) (BAGD 1.b. p. 685): 'battle' [AB, BAGD, Herm, HNTC, Lns, NIGTC, NTC; all versions except NJB], 'the attack' [NJB], 'war, fighting' [LN]. 'Battle' fits better in this context for πόλεμος than 'war' [Ed, Gdt, ICC, NIC].

QUESTION—What reply is expected to this question?

The expected reply is that given the condition, that no one will get ready for battle [MNTC, NTC, TG]. To ask the question is to answer it. Paul is teaching that speaking in tongues without communicating a spiritual message is as useless as a soldier playing an unclear tune to call men to battle [NTC].

QUESTION—If playing a bugle call indistinctly is the image, and speaking in tongues without an interpretation is the topic, what is the point of similarity?

The point of similarity is utter futility [NTC]. The point of similarity is the lack of benefit to the audience [NIC2].

14:9 So[a] you also with[b] the tongue unless/if-not[c] you-give (an) intelligible[d] message,[e]

LEXICON—a. οὕτως (See this word at 11:28): 'so' [AB, NTC; NRSV], 'so likewise' [KJV], 'even so' [NIGTC], 'similarly' [NAB], 'in the same way' [ISV, REB, TEV, TNT], 'thus' [Lns]. This adverb is also translated by a clause: 'it is the same' [NET, NJB, NLT], 'it is just the same' [ICC], 'so it is' [Herm, HNTC; NIV], 'that's how it is' [CEV].

b. διά with genitive object (BAGD A.III.1.a. p. 180): 'with' [BAGD, Herm, HNTC, ICC, NTC; ISV, NET, NIV, TNT], 'in' [NIGTC; NAB, NLT, NRSV, REB, TEV], 'by' [AB, LN, Lns; KJV], not explicit [CEV, NJB]. See this word also at 13:12.

c. ἐὰν μή: 'unless' [HNTC, Lns, NTC; ISV, NIV, TNT], 'except' [KJV], 'if (you do) not' [Herm, ICC; NAB, NET, NJB]. The phrase ἐὰν μὴ εὔσημον λόγον δῶτε 'if not intelligible message you give' is translated 'if you talk to people in a language they don't understand' [NLT], 'if no one can understand what you are talking about' [CEV], 'if you utter speech that is not intelligible' [NRSV], 'if you produce unintelligible speech' [AB], 'if what you say yields no precise meaning' [REB].

d. εὔσημος (LN **32.19**) (BAGD p. 326): 'intelligible' [AB, BAGD, HNTC, ICC, **LN**; ISV, NAB, NIV, NRSV], 'readily intelligible' [NIGTC], 'easily understandable' [LN, Lns], 'easy to be understood' [KJV], 'that can be readily understood' [NJB], 'clear' [BAGD; TEV, TNT], 'precise meaning' [REB], 'plain' [Herm], 'distinct' [BAGD, NTC], 'easily recognizable' [BAGD]. This adjective is also translated with an adverb: '(speak) clearly' [NET]. The phrase μὴ εὔσημον 'not intelligible' is translated 'no one can understand' [CEV], 'they don't understand' [NLT]. Εὔσημος indicates 'well-marked, definite, significant' [ICC].

e. λόγος (See this word at 12:8): 'message' [NIGTC, NTC; ISV, TEV], 'word' [Herm; KJV, NIV], 'speech' [AB, ICC, Lns; NAB, NJB, NRSV, TNT], 'discourse' [HNTC]. The phrase λόγον δῶτε 'message you give'

is translated 'what you say' [REB], 'you talk to people' [NLT], 'what you are talking about' [CEV], 'you...speak' [NET].
QUESTION—What words are emphasized in this verse?
The word ὑμεῖς 'you' is emphasized, pointing out the Corinthians [Ed, TH, TNTC]: you yourselves. The words διὰ τῆς γλώσσης 'with the tongue' is forefronted and stressed [EGT, TNTC]. This stress is in contrast with the inanimate musical instruments of verses 7 and 8 [EGT].
QUESTION—Does this refer to the act of speaking or to speaking in tongues?
1. It refers to the act of speaking in general [Alf, EGT, Ho, ICC, Lns, My, NIC, NIC2, NIGTC, NTC, Vn; ISV, KJV, NET, NIV, NJB, TNT]. 'Tongue' should be understood as the organ of speech, not the gift of tongues [Ho, ICC, Lns, NIC, NIC2, NTC]. The speech organ must be referred to since it is modified by 'your'. It is parallel with the musical instruments of 14:7–8, and the preposition διά 'with' denotes instrumentality [NTC]. Paul is adding another example along with musical instruments, but this time from human speech [NIC].
2. It refers to speaking in tongues [AB, Ed, Gdt, Herm, HNTC, TG, TH; CEV, NAB, NLT, NRSV, REB, TEV]. The reference to 'tongue' is to speaking in tongues as is has been throughout this chapter. It is made intelligible by means of an interpretation [Gdt]. To speak in tongues intelligibly is a contradiction. It is implied that the speaking in tongues must be accompanied with an interpretation in order to make it intelligible [Herm, TH].

how will-be-known the-thing being-said? For you-will-be speaking into air.[a]
LEXICON—a. ἀήρ (LN **1.6**) (BAGD p. 20): 'air' [AB, Herm, HNTC, **LN**, Lns, NTC; all versions except CEV, NLT, REB], 'empty air' [NIGTC; REB], 'wind' [BAGD, ICC; CEV], 'an empty room' [NLT].
QUESTION—What reply is expected to the question, "How will anyone know what is being said?
A negative reply is expected—given the condition, it is impossible to know what was spoken [NIC].
QUESTION—What relationship is indicated by γάρ 'for'?
It indicates the reason why it is impossible to know what was spoken [NIC]: no one will know what is being said *because* you will just be speaking into the air
QUESTION—What is the meaning of the phrase ἔσεσθε εἰς ἀέρα λαλοῦντες 'you will be speaking into the air'?
It means that the speaking would be completely in vain [HNTC, Ho, Lns, NIC]. It indicates ineffectual speaking [EGT]. It indicates that the hearers do not receive it [Alf]. They will be speaking into the air instead of into the minds of the hearers [HNTC, Lns].

14:10 There-are probably[a] many[b] kinds of-languages[c] in (the) world
LEXICON—a. εἰ τύχοι (LN **71.13**) (BAGD I.3. p. 219; 2.b. p. 829): 'probably' [BAGD (829), **LN**; NET], 'doubtless' [NRSV], 'undoubtedly' [NTC;

NIV], 'it may be' [BAGD (219), Lns, NIGTC; KJV], 'it would seem' [AB], 'I suppose' [ISV, TNT], 'I don't know' [HNTC], 'perhaps, if it should turn out that way' [BAGD (829), NTC], 'for example' [BAGD (219)], not explicit [Herm; CEV, NAB, NJB, NLT, REB, TEV]. Εἰ τύχοι may indicate 'who knows (how many)' [Herm, NIC2]. Εἰ τύχοι is used to soften a statement that may be too strong [BAGD].
   b. τοσοῦτος (LN 59.6) (BAGD 1.b. p. 823): 'many' [CEV, ISV, NAB, NET, NRSV, TEV], 'so many' [AB, BAGD, Herm, LN, Lns; KJV, NLT], 'ever so many' [NTC], 'how many' [HNTC], 'however many' [NJB], 'any number' [REB], 'innumerable' [TNT], 'all (sorts)' [NIV]. 'varieties' [NIGTC].
   c. φωνή (LN 14.74, **33.1**, 33.103) (BAGD 3. p. 871): 'language' [BAGD, Herm, HNTC, **LN** (33.1), NIGTC, NTC; CEV, ISV, NAB, NET, NIV, NJB, NLT, REB, TEV], 'sound' [LN (14.74); NRSV, TNT], 'voice' [AB, LN (33.103), Lns; KJV].
QUESTION—Does φωνή mean 'language' or 'sound' here?
   1. It means language [Alf, BAGD, Gdt, Herm, HNTC, Ho, LN, MNTC, My, NIC2, NIGTC, NTC, TG, TH, TNTC, Vn; all versions except KJV, NRSV, TNT]. The classical meaning of φωνή is 'language'. Paul probably chose it in place of γλώσση to avoid confusion with the meaning of speaking in tongues [NIC2]. The context indicates that human speech is referred to [Ho].
   2. It means sound or voice [AB, Ed, Lns, NIC; KJV, NRSV, TNT]. The word ἄφωνος 'voiceless' that follows forces us to give the meaning of 'voice' to φωνή here. There are many voices and not one is without sound so that it cannot be heard [Lns]. Paul refers to oral communication [AB].

and none (is) without-meaning/sound;[a]
LEXICON—a. ἄφωνος (LN **33.135**) (BAGD 2. p. 128): 'without meaning' [**LN**, NTC; ISV, NET, NIV, TEV], 'meaningless' [LN; TNT], 'without signification' [KJV], 'incapable of conveying meaning' [BAGD], 'without sound' [NRSV], 'voiceless' [AB, Lns], 'without language' [REB], 'without its own language' [HNTC]. The whole clause is translated 'there is nothing that has no language' [Herm], 'and none fails to use sound' [NIGTC]. This word is also translated positively: '(all of them) make sense' [CEV], '(all) are marked by sound' [NAB], '(all of them) use sound' [NJB], '(all) are excellent for those who understand them' [NLT].
QUESTION—To what does οὐδέν 'none' refer?
   1. It refers to 'kind' [Alf, Ed, EGT, Gdt, Ho, ICC, Lns, My; KJV, NET, NIV, NRSV, TNT]: and no kind of language/voice is without meaning/sound.
   2. It refers to things in general [NIC]: and nothing is without sound. Paul is referring to the sound of musical instruments and the human voice and

drawing the conclusion that all of these have a unique sound by which it can be distinguished [NIC; NRSV].
3. It refers to an implied 'nation' or place [Herm, HNTC; REB]: and no nation is without a language. We must supply the word ἔθνος 'nation' here [Herm]. 'There are any number of different languages in the world; nowhere is without language' [REB].

QUESTION—What is meant by οὐδέν ἄφωνος 'none (is) meaningless/ soundless'?
1. It means that no language is without meaning [Alf, Ed, EGT, Gdt, Ho, ICC, MNTC, My, NIC2, NTC, TG, TH; CEV, ISV, NET, NIV, NLT, TEV].
2. It means that no sound or voice is without sound/meaning [Lns, NIC, NIGTC; KJV, NRSV, TNT]. All objects have their own unique sound when struck [NIC]. 'There are...innumerable kinds of sounds...and not one of them is meaningless' [TNT]. Every language uses sound but this is no reason to use unintelligible noises in meetings [NIGTC].
3. It means that no nation or place is without language [Herm, HNTC; REB]. The correct meaning of ἄφωνος is 'without language' [Herm].

QUESTION—In comparison with speaking in tongues, what is Paul's point in citing this analogy?

He is implying that the difficulty lies with those who *hear* these languages without understanding them [NIC2].

14:11 If then/but[a] I-know not the meaning[b] of-the language,[c]

LEXICON—a. οὖν (LN 89.50, 89.127) (BAGD p. 593): 'then' [AB, Herm, HNTC, LN (89.50), Lns, NTC; NET, NIV, NRSV], 'well then' [ICC; REB], 'therefore' [LN (89.50); KJV], 'it follows' [NIGTC], 'so' [LN (89.50); TNT], 'consequently, accordingly' [LN (89.50)], 'but' [LN (89.127); CEV, NAB, NJB, NLT, TEV], not explicit [ISV, REB]. See this word also at 4:16.

b. δύναμις (LN **33.134**) (BAGD 3. p. 208): 'meaning' [AB, BAGD, Herm, HNTC, ICC, **LN**, Lns, NTC; ISV, KJV, NAB, NET, NIV, NJB, NRSV, TNT], 'what is intended' [LN], not explicit [CEV]. This noun is also translated as a verb: 'to mean (something)' [NLT]. The phrase εἰδῶ τὴν δύναμιν τῆς φωνῆς 'I know the meaning of the language' is translated 'I...know the language being spoken' [TEV], 'I...know the speaker's language' [REB], 'I...understand what has been said' [**LN**] 'I...know the force of the sound' [NIGTC]. Δύναμις literally means 'power' or 'force' [NTC, TNTC]. This implies that a language must convey meaning or it is without power or ineffective [NTC].

c. φωνή (See this word at 14:10): 'language' [Herm, HNTC, ICC; CEV, ISV, NET, REB, TEV], 'sound' [NIGTC; NJB, NRSV, TNT], 'voice' [AB, Lns; KJV], 'what someone is saying' [NIV], not explicit [NAB, NLT]. Φωνή refers to the human voice [Ed].

QUESTION—What relationship is indicated by οὖν 'then/but'?
1. It indicates the result of 14:10 [Alf, Herm, HNTC, Ho, ICC, Lns, My, NIC2; KJV, NET, NIV, NRSV, REB, TNT]: there are no languages without meaning, *therefore* if I don't know the meaning of a language, the speaker will be a foreigner to me and I to him. The idea is that since the sounds spoken are *meaningful*, therefore if I don't know the *meaning* of what another is saying, we are as foreigners to each other [Ho].
2. It indicates a contrastive relationship [CEV, NAB, NJB, NLT, TEV]: there are no languages without meaning, *but* if I don't know the meaning of a language, the speaker will be a foreigner to me and I to him.

I-will-be (a) foreigner[a] to-the-one speaking and the-one speaking (a) foreigner to me.

LEXICON—a. βάρβαρος (LN **11.94**, 41.31) (BAGD 1. p. 133): 'foreigner' [Herm, HNTC, LN (**11.94**), NTC; CEV, ISV, NAB, NET, NIV, NRSV, TEV, TNT], 'alien' [NIGTC], 'barbarian' [AB, LN (41.31), Lns; KJV, NJB]. This noun is also translated as an adjective: 'foreign, strange, unintelligible, barbarous, non-Greek (language)' [BAGD], 'uncivilized' [LN (11.94, 41.31)]. This clause is translated 'I will not understand people who speak those languages and they will not understand me' [NLT], 'his words will be gibberish to me, and mine to him' [REB], 'the person who speaks to me will conclude that I talk gibberish, just as from my point of view he is talking gibberish to me' [ICC]. Βάρβαρος here implies being a foreigner from outside of the civilized world [LN (11.94)]. Βάρβαρος is onomatopoeic with a meaning like 'speaking gibberish', that is, it sounded like 'bar-bar' to the listener, speech that had no sense [MNTC, NIC2, TNTC]. Originally the word meant someone who could not speak Greek. Then it developed to mean 'strange' or 'unintelligible' [NIC].

QUESTION—How will Paul appear to be a foreigner to the speaker?
Paul assumes that the speaker understands that his listener does not understand what he is saying [ICC].

QUESTION—What is indicated by ἐν 'to' in the phrase ἐν ἐμοί 'to me'?
It indicates 'in my opinion or judgment' [Alf, Ed, Herm, HNTC, ICC, My, TH]: the one speaking will be a foreigner in my opinion. It indicates 'in my case' similar to a dative [Rb].

14:12 So[a] you also, since[b] you-are zealous-persons[c] of-spirits,[d]
TEXT—Instead of the noun πνευμάτων 'spirits', some manuscripts have πνευματικῶν 'spiritual (things)'. GNT does not mention this alternative.
LEXICON—a. οὕτως (See this word at 11:28): 'so' [AB, HNTC, NTC; KJV, NJB, NRSV, TNT], 'in the same way' [ISV], 'thus' [Lns]. This word is also translated as a clause: 'so it is with' [Herm; NIV], 'it is just the same with' [ICC; NET], '(you yourselves) are in this situation' [NIGTC], not explicit [CEV, NAB, NLT, REB, TEV].
b. ἐπεί (LN 89.32) (BAGD 2. p. 284): 'since' [AB, BAGD, Herm, HNTC, LN, Lns, NIGTC, NTC; ISV, NAB, NET, NIV, NLT, NRSV, TEV,

TNT], 'forasmuch as' [KJV], 'as' [NJB], 'inasmuch as' [LN], 'seeing that' [ICC], 'for, because' [BAGD, LN], not explicit [CEV]. This word is also translated as a clause: 'I know' [REB].

c. ζηλωτής (LN 25.77) (BAGD 1.a.β. p. 338): 'zealous person, enthusiast' [LN], 'zealots' [Lns], 'men who strive for' [HNTC]. The phrase ζηλωταὶ ἐστε 'you are zealous persons' is translated 'you are zealous for' [AB], 'you are zealous of' [KJV], 'you are eager to have' [NIV, NJB, NLT, TEV], 'you are eager for' [Herm, NTC; NET, NRSV, REB, TNT], 'you are so enthusiastic for' [ICC], 'you are so desirous of' [ISV], 'you are eager to possess' [BAGD], 'you have a burning concern about' [NIGTC], 'you have set your hearts on' [NAB], 'you really want' [CEV].

d. πνεῦμα (LN 12.33) (BAGD 6.d. p. 677): 'spirit' [AB, Herm, LN, Lns], 'spiritual gift' [BAGD, HNTC, NTC; CEV, ISV, KJV, NAB, NIV, NLT, NRSV, TNT], 'spiritual power' [NJB], 'gift of the Spirit' [REB, TEV], 'manifestation of the Spirit' [NET], 'the powers of the Spirit' [NIGTC], 'inspirations' [ICC]. The reference is to the various workings of the Holy Spirit [BAGD]. See this word also at 14:2.

QUESTION—What is implied by the expression οὕτως καὶ ὑμεῖς 'so also you'?

1. It indicates that this is a separate proposition meaning 'You also are barbarians to each other when you speak in tongues without an interpretation'. A new proposition then is begun with the word 'since' [NIC].
2. It indicates that this is an introduction to 14:12 and an inference is to be drawn from 14:11 [Alf, Ed, Gdt, Ho]. Such an inference would be 'So, since communication has to be meaningful to be understood, thinking of the church's welfare, you should be careful to make yourselves increasingly more intelligible' [Gdt].

QUESTION—What is meant by πνεῦμα 'spirit/spiritual things'?

1. It means the spiritual gifts or manifestations of the Holy Spirit [AB, Alf, Ed, EGT, Gdt, Herm, HNTC, Ho, Lns, MNTC, NIC2, NIGTC, NTC, TG, TH, TNTC; all versions]. The reference is clarified by noting 12:7 where each person received a manifestation of the Holy Spirit. Such manifestations are called 'spirits'. See also 14:32, 12:11, 1 John 4:1 and Revelation 4:5 in which each reference to 'spirits' indicates manifestations of the Holy Spirit [Ho]. The plural 'spirits' refers to the Holy Spirit allocating many spiritual gifts to his people [NTC]. The Holy Spirit is only one and yet he reveals himself through each believer. These manifestations are termed 'spirits' [Lns]. The plural 'spirits' refers to the Holy Spirit revealing himself through the individual spirits of the Corinthians and in this context probably refers specifically to speaking in tongues rather than to spiritual gifts in general. Their zeal was for the Holy Spirit to speak in tongues through their spirits [NIC2]. It refers to all supernatural abilities regardless of their nature [Ed, EGT]. It refers to the Spirit of God

revealing himself in different kinds of inspirations in the churches [Gdt, NIGTC].
2. It means spirits [AB, My, NIC]. It indicates that the Corinthians were striving for spirits that could obtain special gifts. This does not seem to be a significant error as Paul does not correct them for it [NIC]. It refers to the individual spirits that were part of the makeup of each individual believer, that is, each person is part mind, part spirit. What is in focus is the ability of the Holy Spirit to accommodate himself to each person's unique spirit [AB].

seek[a] that you-may-excel[b] for the upbuilding[c] of-the church.
LEXICON—a. pres. act. impera. of ζητέω (BAGD 2.b.γ. p. 339): 'to seek' [Herm, HNTC, ICC, LN (57.59), Lns, NTC; KJV, NET, TNT], 'to try' [NAB, NIV, TEV], 'to aim' [BAGD; NJB], 'to desire' [BAGD, LN (25.9); ISV], 'to want to' [LN (25.9)], 'to aspire' [REB], 'to strive' [AB; NRSV], 'to ask God' [NLT], 'to choose' [CEV], 'to try to obtain, to try to get, to attempt to get' [LN (57.59)], 'to strive for, to wish' [BAGD], 'to direct one's eagerness toward' [NIGTC]. The present tense imperative indicates a continual seeking [MNTC]: keep on seeking. See this word also at 10:24.
  b. pres. act. subj. of περισσεύω (LN 59.54, 57.24) (BAGD 1.b.α. p. 651): 'to excel' [AB, BAGD, NIGTC, NTC; KJV, NIV, NRSV, REB, TNT], 'to make greater use (of those)' [TEV], 'to abound' [HNTC, ICC, Lns; NET], 'to be rich in' [Herm; NAB, NJB], 'to have (much) more than enough, to have an overabundance' [LN (57.24)], 'to provide in abundance, to provide a great deal of, to cause to be abundant' [LN (59.54)], not explicit [CEV, NLT]. The two verbs, ζητέω 'to seek' and περισσεύω 'to excel' together are rendered 'you must keep on desiring them' [ISV].
  c. οἰκοδομή (LN 65.20 fn. 6): 'upbuilding' [AB; ISV], 'building up' [HNTC, NIGTC; NRSV], 'edification' [Herm, Lns], 'edifying' [KJV], 'spiritual advantage' [ICC]. This noun is also translated as a verb: 'to build up' [NAB, NIV, NJB, REB, TNT], 'to edify' [NTC], 'to help to build up' [TEV], 'to be of real help' [NLT], 'to strengthen' [NET], 'to be most helpful' [CEV]. See this word also at 14:3.

QUESTION—What words are emphasized in this verse?
The words πρὸς τὴν οἰκοδομὴν τῆς ἐκκλησίας 'for the upbuilding of the church' are placed forward for emphasis [Lns].

QUESTION—The Greek simply states πρὸς τὴν οἰκοδομὴν τῆς ἐκκλησίας ζητεῖτε ἵνα περισσεύτε 'for the upbuilding of the church, seek that you may excel'. In what are they to excel?
  1. They are to seek to excel in building up the church by the spiritual gifts [Ed, Gdt, Herm, HNTC, Ho, ICC, Lns, NCBC, NIC, NIC2, NIGTC, NTC, Rb, TG, TH, TNTC, Vn; KJV, TNT].
  2. They are to seek spiritual gifts to build up the church so that they may excel in spiritual gifts [AB, Alf, My].

DISCOURSE UNIT: 14:13–19 [NCBC, NIC2, NIGTC]. The topic is 'tongues' must be interpreted, [MNTC], application to the believing community [NIC2], intelligibility versus use of the mind [NIGTC].

DISCOURSE UNIT: 14:13–17 [NTC]. The topic is praying and praising.

14:13 Therefore[a] the-(one) speaking in-(a)-tongue let-him-pray that he-may-interpret.[b]

LEXICON—a. διό (See this word at 12:3): 'therefore' [AB, ICC, NTC; ISV, NRSV, TNT], 'wherefore' [Lns; KJV], 'then' [TEV], 'so then' [LN; NET], 'so' [Herm, HNTC; NLT], 'hence' [NIGTC], 'this means that' [NAB], 'for this reason' [LN; NIV], 'that is why' [NJB], not explicit [CEV, REB].

b. pres. act. subj. of διερμηνεύω (See this word at 12:30): 'to interpret' [AB, HNTC, ICC, Lns, NTC; KJV, NET, NIV], 'to be given the interpretation' [NJB], 'to be able to interpret' [Herm], 'to put what is uttered into words' [NIGTC]. The phrase ἵνα διερμηνεύῃ 'so that he may interpret' is translated 'for the power to interpret (it)' [NRSV, TNT], 'for the ability to interpret' [REB], 'for the ability to interpret it' [ISV], 'for the gift of interpretation' [NAB, NLT], 'for the gift to explain what is said' [TEV], 'for the power to explain what we mean' [CEV].

QUESTION—What relationship is indicated by διό 'therefore'?

It indicates a conclusion based on 14:12 [EGT, Ho, NIC, NIC2, NTC]: since you should seek to excel for the upbuilding of the church, the one speaking in a tongue should *therefore* pray that he may interpret. Having an interpretation is the only way that one speaking in a tongue can upbuild the church [EGT]. This is a logical admonition from what he wrote about speaking in a language that can be understood [NIC]. Not only the preceding verse but the whole preceding argument stands as the grounds. It is useless to speak in an unintelligible language [Ho, NIC2, NIGTC, NTC].

QUESTION—What relationship is indicated by ἵνα 'that'?

1. It indicates the content of what he should pray [AB, EGT, Herm, HNTC, Ho, ICC, Lns, MNTC, NCBC, NIC, NIC2, NIGTC, NTC, TNTC; NAB, NJB, NRSV, TEV, TNT]: let him pray *that* he may interpret.

    1.1 When this refers to human foreign languages.
    This indicates that the speaker should pray for the gift of interpretation so that he/she might declare intelligibly the 'wonderful works of God' (Acts 2:5–11) [Ho].

    1.2 When this refers to non-human heavenly languages.
    He should interpret what he has said in order to make it intelligible and in this way build up the church [NIC2]. He might pray this either before or after speaking in tongues but presumably he would not do this in his ecstatic language [ICC].

    1.3 When this refers to a pseudo speaking in tongues.
    In this section Paul is speaking sarcastically about counterfeited tongues and is not really telling them to pray for the true gift of interpretation. In

this way he reproaches them, saying that with their unintelligible jabbering, they could at least ask God to give them a means of making it beneficial to the congregation. As it is, their 'tongues' are pagan and pointless [MNTC].
2. It indicates the purpose they should have when praying in tongues [Alf, Ed, Gdt, My]: let him pray (in tongues) *with the purpose of* interpreting that prayer. It means that he should pray in tongues having purposed beforehand to interpret the contents of his prayer afterwards [Ed, Gdt].

DISCOURSE UNIT: 14:14–20 [EGT]. The topic is the need for the mind to be the ally of the spirit.

14:14 [For]ª if I-pray in-a-tongue, my spiritᵇ prays,

TEXT—Some manuscripts omit γάρ 'for'. GNT places this word in brackets, indicating difficulty in deciding to include it in the text, but does not deal with it in the apparatus.

LEXICON—a. γάρ (See this word at 10:1): 'for' [AB, Herm, HNTC, ICC, Lns, NIGTC, NTC; all versions except CEV, NAB, REB], 'for example' [CEV], not explicit [NAB, REB].
  b. πνεῦμα (See this word at 14:2 and 14:12): 'spirit' [AB, Herm, HNTC, ICC, Lns, NTC; all versions], 'innermost spiritual being' [NIGTC].

QUESTION—What relationship is indicated by γάρ 'for'?
  It indicates that this verse is the reason why a person should pray that he may interpret [EGT, Ho, Lns, NIC]: let him pray that he may interpret *because* if I pray in a tongue my mind is unfruitful. It indicates that this verse explains 14:13 [NTC]: let him pray that he may interpret *you see* if I pray in a tongue my mind is unfruitful.

QUESTION—What is meant by τὸ πνεῦμα μου προσεύχεται 'my spirit prays'?
  1. It means that the man's own spirit prays [Alf, Ed, EGT, Gdt, ICC, Lns, My, NCBC, NIC, NIC2, NTC, TG, Vn; KJV, NAB, NIV, NJB, NRSV, TEV, TNT].
    1.1 When this refers to human languages.
      The 'spirit' is the immaterial part of a person's self that is able to receive impressions from the Holy Spirit. It can sense that the Holy Spirit is causing it to speak spiritual words as a prayer in an unknown language [Lns].
    1.2 When this refers to non-human, heavenly languages.
      It means that the person's spirit is praying as the Holy Spirit enables him/her [NIC2].
  2. It means that the person prays using his spiritual gift given by the Holy Spirit [HNTC, Ho]. 'My spirit' refers to the Holy Spirit manifesting himself in the person. The Holy Spirit is active in the person so that his spiritual gift is exercised [Ho]. Three things are indicated: (a) that God's Spirit is acting, (b) that he gives a spiritual gift, and (c) that the gift is so personal that the person can speak of it as 'his spirit' [HNTC].

3. It means that only the person's breath 'prays' [MNTC]. Paul is still speaking sarcastically to the Corinthians. Here he means if he were to speak gibberish (like the Corinthians do), he would only be producing air from his mouth as meaningless as the ecstatic languages spoken in pagan temples [MNTC].

but my mind[a] is unfruitful.[b]
LEXICON—a. νοῦς (LN 26.14) (BAGD 1. p. 544): 'mind' [AB, BAGD, HNTC, ICC, LN, Lns, NIGTC, NTC; all versions except KJV, NLT], 'understanding' [Herm, ICC, Lns; KJV]. This noun is also translated as though it were metonymy, the part for the whole: 'I' [NLT].
b. ἄκαρπος (LN 65.34) (BAGD 2. p. 29): 'unfruitful' [NTC; KJV, NIV], 'unproductive' [AB, BAGD, LN; ISV, NET, NRSV, TNT], 'useless' [LN; CEV], 'barren' [Herm, Lns; REB], 'inactive' [HNTC]. This adjective is also translated as a verb phrase: 'contributes nothing' [NAB], 'has no part in it' [LN (26.14); TEV], 'derives no fruit from it' [NJB], 'produces no fruit from it' [NIGTC], 'is doing no good' [ICC]. This entire clause is translated 'but I don't understand what I am saying' [NLT].
QUESTION—What is meant by ὁ νοῦς μου ἄκαρπός ἐστιν 'my mind is unfruitful'?
1. It means that the person's mind is unfruitful to others [Alf, Gdt, Ho, ICC, My, NIGTC, NTC, Vn]. It does not build up others [NTC].
1.1 When this refers to human foreign languages.
Although it may mean that he does not understand what he said, this interpretation would contradict the passages that teach that a person speaking in tongues did understand what he was saying. It must therefore mean that Paul's understanding did not benefit others [Ho].
1.2 When this refers to non-human heavenly languages.
It means that what Paul says is not rational and so does not benefit the congregation [ICC, NTC]. It is essential that the spirit and the mind work together for the activity to be productive [NTC].
2. It means the person's mind is unfruitful to himself [Ed, EGT, HNTC, Lns, NCBC, NIC2, Rb, TG, TH, TNTC; NJB].
2.1 When this refers to human foreign languages.
It means that a person's mind generates no intelligible thoughts [Lns]. It means that the person does not understand what he/she has prayed [NCBC].
2.2 When this refers to non-human heavenly languages
It means that the person's mind remains inactive and that is not good for the person himself/herself or for others [HNTC]. It means that the person's intelligence is not involved [TG]. It means that he receives no intellectual benefit, but also he will later point out, that neither does anyone else [NIC2].

14:15 What[a] then is-it?

LEXICON—a. τίς (LN 92.14) (BAGD 1.b.ε. p. 819): 'what' [LN; KJV]. This whole clause is translated 'what then?' [NJB, REB], 'what does this mean?' [ISV], 'what is to be done then?' [HNTC], 'what should I do?' [NET], 'what should I do then?' [CEV, NRSV, TEV], 'so what shall I do?' [NIV], 'well then, what shall I do?' [NLT], 'what follows then?' [Lns; TNT], 'so what follows' [NIGTC], 'what is my point here?' [NAB], 'what is the conclusion from this?' [Herm], 'what does that imply?' [ICC], 'what then is the result?' [NTC]. This clause in Greek functions to call attention to what has just been said [EGT].

I-will-pray with-the spirit, and I-will-pray with-the mind also;

QUESTION—What does this statement mean?

1. It means that Paul will pray in ordinary language in which both his mind and spirit participate [AB, EGT, HNTC, Ho, MNTC, NIGTC, NTC, TNTC, Vn]. It means that praying in a tongue leaves the intellect inactive and this is not good for the speaker or the listeners [HNTC]. It was possible to speak under the direction of the Spirit so as to be intelligible to others [Ho]. What Paul is saying is that it is useless to pray without bringing in one's mind [NTC].
2. It means that he will at times pray in tongues with his spirit only, and at other times he will pray in ordinary language with his mind as well [Alf, Ed, Gdt, ICC, Lns, My, NIC, NIC2, TG; CEV]. One can pray in the spirit by praying in tongues and one can pray with the mind by interpreting the prayer [Alf, Gdt, My]. Paul means that for his own sake he will pray with the spirit, but for the sake of others he will pray with the mind [ICC]. He means he prays in church with the mind while in private he can pray with either spirit or mind [NIC]. He means that he will not pray in tongues without interpreting [Lns].

QUESTION—What is the significance of the future tenses in this verse?

They function to indicate what Paul's will, determination or desire was in these matters [Lns, NTC; CEV, NAB, TNT].

I-will-sing[a] with-the spirit, and I-will-sing with-the mind also.

LEXICON—a. fut. act. indic. of ψάλλω (LN 33.111) (BAGD p. 891): 'to sing' [AB, Herm, ICC, LN, Lns, NTC; CEV, KJV, NAB, NIV, NLT, TEV], 'to sing praise(s)' [BAGD, HNTC, LN; NET, NJB, NRSV, TNT], 'to sing hymns' [REB], 'to sing (a) psalm(s)' [LN; ISV], 'to sing a song of praise' [LN].

QUESTION—How is singing related to prayer?

Singing is a second form of speaking with tongues [AB, Lns, NIC2]. Not only is he to pray with the mind, but he is to sing praises to God with the mind also [NTC]. The setting for prayer and singing is a worship service held by a congregation [Ho, NTC, TG].

14:16 For[a] if you-praise[b] [with][c] spirit,

TEXT—Some manuscripts omit the preposition ἐν 'in'. GNT places this word in brackets, indicating doubt about including it in the text.

LEXICON—a. ἐπεί (BAGD 2. p. 284): 'for' [HNTC; NLT, TNT], 'otherwise' [AB, NIGTC, NTC; ISV, NET, NJB, NRSV], 'else' [ICC, Lns; KJV], not explicit [Herm; CEV, NAB, NIV, REB, TEV]. Ἐπεί 'for, since, because' is used elliptically here and means 'for otherwise' [BAGD]. See this word also at 14:12.

b. pres. act. subj. of εὐλογέω (BAGD 1. p. 322): 'to praise' [LN (33.356)], 'to praise God' [CEV, NET, NIV, NLT, REB], 'to give thanks' [TNT], 'to give thanks to God' [TEV], 'to bless' [AB, LN (33.470), Lns, NTC; KJV], 'to utter praises' [Herm], 'to bless God' [ICC, NIGTC], 'to say a blessing' [HNTC; ISV, NRSV], 'to say (one's) blessing' [NJB], 'to give thanks and praise' [BAGD]. This verb is translated as a noun phrase: '(one's) praise of God' [NAB]. Εὐλογέω is almost synonymous with the verb εὐχαριστέω 'to thank' which underlies εὐχαριστία 'thanksgiving' in the next clause [EGT, Herm, Ho, NIC2, NIGTC]. One sense of εὐλογέω means 'to bless' in the sense of asking God to confer his favor on something [LN (33.470)]. See this word also at 10:16.

c. ἐν with dative object (LN 83.13, 90.10): 'with' [AB, LN (90.10), NIGTC; all versions except NLT, TEV], '(only) with' [NTC], 'in' [Herm, HNTC, ICC, LN (83.13), Lns; NLT, TEV], 'by' [LN (90.10)].

QUESTION—What relationship is indicated by ἐπεί 'for'?

It indicates that he will now give an example to show that tongues without interpretation does not build up the church [Ed]. It means 'in case I do not speak intelligibly' [Ho]. It implies that we need to pray and supply an interpretation because if... [Gdt].

QUESTION—What is the significance of Paul's use of the singular in 'you praise'?

It probably means that he is addressing an imagined correspondent who is on the opposite side of the question [NIC2]. This may signify that this is what the Corinthians were doing [NIC]. Paul uses the singular to give more emphasis to his words [Lns].

QUESTION—What is the meaning of ἐν πνεύματι 'in spirit'?

The lack of an article here probably indicates that the person, by the enabling of the Holy Spirit, is praising God in tongues in a meeting [NIC2]. It means the same as the similar phrase in 14:15, that is, 'using one's spiritual gift' or 'enabled by the Spirit' [Ho]. The dative case indicates that the person's spirit is being used since he is speaking in tongues [Lns]. It implies 'in spirit only', that is, without the mind [EGT, HNTC, NTC]. It means 'in ecstasy' [ICC].

the-one occupying[a] the place of-the uninstructed[b] how will-he-say the "Amen"[c] to your thanksgiving?[d]

LEXICON—a. pres. act. participle of ἀναπληρόω (LN **85.24**) (BAGD 4. p. 59): 'to occupy' [AB, HNTC, **LN**, Lns; KJV], 'to fill up' [NTC], 'to fill, to take' [BAGD]. The phrase ὁ ἀναπληρῶν τὸν τόπον τοῦ ἰδιώτου 'the one occupying the place of the uninstructed' is translated 'one who takes part in the service as an ordinary person' or 'who occupies the place of an ordinary person' [**LN**], 'anyone in the position of an outsider' [NRSV], 'an ordinary person who is present' [REB], 'ordinary people taking part in the meeting' [TEV], 'the person in a layman's position' [Herm], 'the ordinary man in the congregation' [TNT], 'some strangers in your worship service' [CEV], 'an otherwise uneducated person' [ISV], 'the one who does not comprehend' [NAB], 'one who finds himself among those who do not understand' [NIV], 'those who don't understand you' [NLT], 'the uninitiated person' [NIGTC; NJB], 'someone without the gift' [NET], 'he who has no experience of such things' [ICC].

b. ἰδιώτης (LN 27.26) (BAGD 2. p. 370): 'uninstructed' [AB, BAGD], 'uneducated person' [ISV], 'unlearned' [Lns; KJV], 'uninformed' [NTC], 'ordinary person' [REB, TNT], 'uninitiated person' [NIGTC; NJB], 'ordinary, uninitiated person' [**LN**; NJB], 'outsider' [NRSV], 'stranger' [CEV], 'simple listener' [HNTC], 'layman' [Herm, LN], 'inquirer' [BAGD], 'one who does not comprehend' [NAB], 'someone without the gift' [NET]. This singular noun is translated as a plural: 'ordinary people' [TEV], 'those who do not understand' [NIV, NLT]. Ἰδιώτης means a person who was neither an unbeliever nor a fully-instructed Christian, a kind of inquirer or learner [LN].

c. ἀμήν (LN 72.6) (BAGD 1. p. 45, 3. p. 46): 'amen' [AB, BAGD, Herm, HNTC, ICC, Lns, NIGTC, NTC; all versions except NLT], 'truly' [BAGD, LN], 'indeed, it is true that' [LN], 'so let it be' [BAGD]. The phrase πῶς ἐρεῖ τὸ Ἀμήν ἐπὶ τῇ σῇ εὐχαριστίᾳ 'how will he say the "Amen" to your thanksgiving' is translated 'how can they join you in giving thanks' [NLT]. Ἀμήν indicated whole-hearted agreement with something another person has said [Alf, Ed, Gdt, Ho, MNTC, NIC2, NTC]. It was the custom in the Jewish synagogue to say this at the end of prayers that had been said to signify agreement with the prayer [Ho]. "To say *the* Amen" meant to say the familiar formula of assent to what had been said [Alf, Ed, Gdt, Ho, NIGTC].

d. εὐχαριστία (LN 33.349) (BAGD 2. p. 328): 'thanksgiving' [AB, HNTC, LN, Lns, NIGTC, NTC; ISV, NAB, NET, NIV, NJB, NRSV, REB, TNT], 'giving of thanks' [ICC; KJV], 'prayer of thanksgiving' [BAGD; TEV], 'thankfulness' [LN], 'prayer' [Herm], not explicit [CEV]. This noun is also translated as a verb: 'to give thanks' [NLT].

QUESTION—Should the word 'place' be taken literally or figuratively?

    1. It should be taken figuratively [Alf, BAGD, Ed, EGT, Gdt, HNTC, Ho, ICC, Lns, NIC, NIC2, NTC, Rb]. It should be taken to mean role, position, part, function or status [Gdt, HNTC, NIC, NIGTC, NTC, TH]: the one having the status of the uninstructed.

    2. It should be taken literally. It means that there was a separate section in the church for such people to occupy [BAGD (2. p. 370)].

1 CORINTHIANS 14:16 219

QUESTION—To whom was Paul referring when he used the term ἰδιώτης 'uninstructed'?

He was referring simply to a person who does not understand what is being said [Alf, Ho, ICC, MNTC, My, NIC2, NTC; NAB, NIV, NLT]. This refers to a full member of the church who either does not have the gift of speaking in tongues or the gift of interpretation [NTC]. It probably refers to those who did not have the gift of interpretation [ICC, TH]. It refers to those who did not have the gift of tongues [Alf, Ho, ICC, My]. It refers to one who is unlearned, that is, he/she does not know about the gift of tongues [NIC]. It refers to a person who does not know the language being used by the speaker [Ho]. It refers to all the members of the church who, like a stranger, do not understand what a person who is speaking in tongues is saying [Gdt, NIC2]. It refers to all people, Christian and non-Christian, who did not have the gift of tongues [Herm, NIGTC]. It refers to those who were not Christians, but were interested in becoming Christians [BAGD, TNTC].

since what you-are-saying he-understands[a] not;

LEXICON—a. perf. (with pres. meaning) act. indic. of οἶδα (LN **32.4**) (BAGD 4. p. 556): 'to understand' [AB, BAGD, HNTC, **LN** (32.4), NTC; CEV, KJV, NJB, NLT], 'to comprehend' [LN], 'to know' [Herm, ICC, Lns, NIGTC; ISV, NAB, NET, NIV, NRSV, REB, TEV, TNT]. See this word also at 11:3.

14:17 **For you indeed[a] give-thanks[b] well[c]**

LEXICON—a. μέν (LN 91.6, 89.136) (BAGD p. 1.a.β.): 'indeed' [AB, Herm, HNTC, LN (91.6), Lns; NAB], 'to be sure' [BAGD], 'although' [ICC], 'on the one hand' [LN (89.136)], 'on your side' [NIGTC], 'no doubt' [NLT], not explicit [all versions except NAB, NLT]. Μέν is a marker of weak emphasis [LN]. It is used here in combination with the following ἀλλά to mean 'to be sure…but' [BAGD, NIC2]. Μέν…ἀλλά indicates a sharp contrast between the two people [Ed, ICC, NIC2, NTC]. The ἀλλά indicates 'but what of that?' [Ed]. The ἀλλά indicates 'but none the less' [ICC].

b. pres. act. indic. of εὐχαριστέω (See this word at 10:30): 'to give thanks' [AB, HNTC, ICC, Lns, NIGTC, NTC; ISV, KJV, NET, NIV, NLT, NRSV], 'to make (one's) thanksgiving' [NJB], 'to utter praise' [NAB], 'to worship God' [CEV], 'to say a prayer' [Herm]. This verb is also translated as a noun phrase: 'prayer of thanksgiving' [REB], 'thanksgiving prayer' [TNT], 'prayer of thanks' [TEV]. Εὐχαριστέω is used synonymously with εὐλογέω 'to praise' of 14:16 [ICC].

c. καλῶς (LN 78.21, 72.12) (BAGD 1. p. 401): 'well' [Lns; NET, NJB], 'very well' [LN (78.21)], 'very well indeed' [NAB], 'well enough' [BAGD, HNTC, NIGTC, NTC; NIV, NRSV], 'verily…well' [KJV], 'nicely' [AB], 'very nicely, no doubt' [NLT], 'in a wonderful way' [CEV], 'beautifully' [ICC], 'certainly, correctly' [LN (72.12)]. This adverb is also translated as an adjective: '(your prayer may be) splendid'

[REB], 'quite good' [TEV], 'fine' [Herm], 'excellent' [TNT]. It is also translated as a clause: 'it's good (for you)' [ISV]. Καλῶς here is used to indicate that Paul concedes that thanksgiving in a tongue is good as a gift of the Spirit, but it does not benefit others [Alf].

QUESTION—What relationship is indicated by γάρ 'for'?

It indicates that this verse is the reason for the rule in 14:16 that there should be no speaking in tongues in church without interpretation [NIC]. It indicates that this is the explanation of who the speaker and hearer of 14:16 are [Lns].

QUESTION—What word is emphasized?

The pronoun 'you' is emphasized [ICC]: you yourself.

QUESTION—Is Paul sincere or speaking ironically?

1. He is being sincere [Alf, Ed, NIC2, NTC]. To say that it is ironical does not take 14:15 into account that shows that Paul believes that this kind of prayer is genuine and good [NIC2]. It is not the expression of thanksgiving that is faulty, but the manner in which it is expressed [NTC].
2. Καλῶς may be being used ironically (intending its opposite) [Gdt, ICC, MNTC]. He may mean that the person's prayer was in reality of no good to the poor listener or that Paul considers God's gifts to be good when used correctly, but tongues are of no good to an uninstructed hearer [ICC]. This is how the tongues speaker feels, but no one else knows what is said [MNTC].

but the other (person) not is-built-up.[a]

LEXICON—a. pres. pass. indic. of οἰκοδομέω (See this word at 10:23): 'to be built up' [AB, HNTC; NJB, NRSV], 'to be edified' [Herm, Lns, NTC; KJV, NIV], 'to be strengthened' [NET], 'to be helped' [CEV, NAB, TEV, TNT], 'to get spiritual advantage' [ICC]. This entire clause is translated 'but it doesn't build up the other person' [ISV], 'but it doesn't help the other people present' [NLT], 'but it is no help to the other person' [REB].

QUESTION—To whom does ἕτερος 'the other person' refer?

It refers to the 'uninstructed' person of 14:16 [Alf, EGT]. It refers to anyone else [Lns, MNTC, NIC, TG]. It refers to all the members of the congregation individually [Gdt].

DISCOURSE UNIT: 14:18–19 [NTC]. The topic is thanksgiving.

14:18 **I-thank God, I-speak in-tongues more**[a] **than-you all;**

TEXT—Some manuscripts include μου 'of me' following θεῷ 'God'. GNT does not mention this reading. Only KJV includes μου 'of me'.

TEXT—Some manuscripts include ὅτι 'that' following θεῷ 'God'. GNT does not mention this reading.

LEXICON—a. μᾶλλον (BAGD 1. p. 489): 'more' [BAGD, Herm, LN; all versions except TEV], 'much more than' [TEV], 'more (gifted in tongues)' [NIGTC]. Μᾶλλον 'more' is used here with the genitive of comparison, πάντων ὑμῶν 'than you all' [NIC2]. See this word also at 14:1.

QUESTION—What does Paul mean by πάντων ὑμῶν μᾶλλον γλώσσαις λαλῶ 'I speak in tongues more than you all'?
1. When this refers to human foreign languages.
It means that he speaks in foreign languages more than the Corinthians did [Ho]. The number of foreign languages spoken is not in focus. It rather means that Paul had received from the Spirit a greater ability to speak in tongues than the Corinthians had [Lns]. The word γλώσσαις 'in tongues' is plural indicating that this was the true gift of tongues not a pseudo gift. Paul may have used this gift to bring a message to people God wanted to reach and to function as a miraculous sign verifying the message and his authority as an apostle [MNTC].
2. When this refers to non-human heavenly languages
'More' includes both quantity and quality, but perhaps more in the sense of quantity [HNTC, NIC2, NTC], indicating that he speaks more often in tongues [NIC, NIC2]. This verse gives evidence that the gift of tongues does not mean foreign languages [ICC, NIC]. 'More' indicates the intensity of Paul's gift [ICC]. 'More' indicates a special measure of this gift [NIC, NIGTC]. The focus is not so much on how often he spoke in tongues, but on the quality of his gift [NTC].

QUESTION—What is the significance of the words εὐχαριστῶ τῷ θεῷ 'I thank God'?
They should probably be taken as being equivalent to a weak oath in which Paul is invoking God to be a witness to the truth of what he is about to say [NIC2]. It signifies that Paul is serious about what he is saying [HNTC]. It signifies that he thinks seriously about the gift of speaking in tongues [EGT]. It signifies that he does not at all scorn this gift [Gdt]. The verse makes a very strong statement that Paul believes that the gift of tongues is valid [NCBC].

QUESTION—What is the significance of the lack of the conjunction 'that' before 'I speak'?
The lack of a conjunction tends to signify that the following clause is highlighted [Herm, ICC, NIC2].

14:19 But[a] in church I-want[b] to-speak five words with-my mind,

LEXICON—a. ἀλλά (See this word at 10:5): 'but' [AB, Herm, HNTC; CEV, ISV, NAB, NET, NIV, NLT, REB, TEV, TNT], 'yet' [ICC, Lns; KJV], 'nevertheless' [NRSV], 'however' [NTC], 'all the same' [NJB], 'but all the same' [NIGTC]. Ἀλλά 'but' indicates that this verse contrasts with what Paul would do in private [EGT, ICC].
b. pres. act. indic. of θέλω (See this word at 10:27): 'to want' [NET], 'to prefer' [TNT], 'to desire' [HNTC], 'to be resolved' [Lns]. This verb is also translated 'I would rather' [AB, Herm, ICC, NIGTC, NTC; ISV, NAB, NIV, NJB, NRSV, REB, TEV], 'I would much rather' [NLT], 'I had rather' [CEV, KJV]. Θέλω here has a sense close to 'prefer' [NIC2].

so-that I-may-instruct[a] others also,
LEXICON—a. aorist act. subj. of κατηχέω (LN 33.225) (BAGD 2.a. p. 423): 'to instruct' [AB, BAGD, Herm, HNTC, LN, Lns; ISV, NAB, NET, NIV, NJB, NRSV, TNT], 'to teach' [BAGD, LN, NTC; KJV, TEV], 'to give solid instruction' [ICC], 'to communicate instruction' [NIGTC]. This entire clause is translated 'that will help others' [NLT], 'for the benefit of others as well as myself' [REB], 'but words that make sense can help the church' [CEV]. Κατηχέω indicates teaching in a systematic or detailed manner [LN]. This word refers to instructing others in religious matters [NIC2]. It implies a question-and-answer method of teaching and is the word from which the English word *catechism* is derived [NTC].

than ten-thousand[a] words in (a) tongue.
LEXICON—a. μυρίος (LN 60.7, 60.45) (BAGD p. 529): 'ten thousand' [Herm, LN (60.45), Lns, NTC; CEV, KJV, NAB, NET, NIV, NJB, NLT, NRSV], '10,000' [ISV], 'tens of thousands' [HNTC], 'thousands and thousands' [ICC], 'thousands upon thousands' [NIGTC], 'thousands' [AB; REB, TEV, TNT], 'countless' [BAGD, LN (60.7)], 'innumerable' [BAGD, LN (60.7)], 'very very many' [LN]. It would be possible to translate 'ten thousand' but the context calls for an emphasis on an indefinitely large number [LN (60.7)]. It is a term meaning the highest number conceivable [NIGTC].
QUESTION—What is the significance of the singular use of ἐν γλώσσῃ 'in a tongue'?
There is no real significance between singular and plural uses. Here it could indicate 'in any given instance of tongues' [NIC2]. The singular use of 'tongue' indicates that Paul is now referring to the gibberish of pagan tongue speaking [MNTC].

DISCOURSE UNIT: 14:20–28 [MNTC]. The topic is the purpose and procedure for the gift of tongues.

DISCOURSE UNIT: 14:20–25 [AB, NCBC, NIC, NIGTC, NTC; NAB]. The topic is tongues and unbelievers [AB], a sign for unbelievers [NCBC], decorum in the exercise of gifts [NIC], tongues and Scripture [NTC], the function of the gifts [NAB], maturity as love for others [NIGTC].

14:20 **Brothers,[a] (do) not be children[b] in (your) thinking[c]**
LEXICON—a. ἀδελφός (See this word at 10:1): 'brother' [AB, Herm, HNTC, ICC, Lns, NTC; ISV, KJV, NAB, NIV, NJB, TNT], 'brother and sister' [NET, NLT, NRSV], 'my friend' [CEV, REB, TEV], 'fellow Christian' [NIGTC]. Ἀδελφός refers to fellow Christians, not to physical kin [TH].
b. παιδίον (LN 9.42) (BAGD 3.a. p. 604): 'child' [AB, BAGD, Herm, HNTC, ICC, LN, Lns, NIGTC, NTC; all versions except NAB, NLT]. This noun is also translated as an adjective: 'childish' [NAB, NLT].
c. φρήν (LN **26.15**) (BAGD p. 866): 'thinking' [AB, BAGD, NTC; ISV, NET, NJB, NRSV, REB, TEV, TNT], 'understanding' [BAGD; KJV,

NLT], 'discernment' [Herm], 'outlook' [LN; NAB], 'mind' [ICC, Lns], 'intelligence' [HNTC], 'how one thinks' [NIGTC], 'the way you think' [**LN**]. This noun is also translated as a verb: 'to think' [CEV, NIV]. Φρήν primarily denotes 'diaphragm', a physical organ of the body. To the Greeks it connoted 'thought' [Lns, TNTC]. It could be translated 'outlook' or 'attitude' [TG].

QUESTION—What is the function of the vocative ἀδελφοί 'brothers'?

It marks a turn in Paul's argument [ICC, NIC2, Vn]. It signifies that Paul is broaching a sensitive topic. By using this term he puts himself on a level with the Corinthians [NTC]. It softens the reprimand [Ed, EGT, HNTC, TNTC]. It serves to appeal to their weakened sense of Christian dignity [Gdt]. With this affectionate term Paul makes a new start [ICC]. The vocative serves to show Paul's affection and draws attention to what follows [TNTC].

QUESTION—What is the significance of the present imperative μὴ παιδία γίνεσθε 'do not be children'?

It signifies that the action was going on and should be stopped [Gdt, NIC2, NIGTC, NTC, Rb, TNTC, Vn; ISV, NIV, NJB]: stop being children.

QUESTION—If the image is children, and the topic is the Corinthians, what is the point of similarity?

The point of similarity is immaturity or childishness [Ed, Herm, MNTC, NCBC, NIC2, NTC; NAB, NLT], the tendency to be pleased with trifles [Ho], a love of display and thoughtless self-centeredness [NIGTC]. The point of similarity is the disposition to value external appearances [HNTC, NIC], the disposition to be preoccupied with a gift and not realize the implications of using the gift inconsiderately [Lns], the disposition to be enthralled by exciting novelty [AB]. The child chooses what is entertaining over what is useful [Gdt, ICC].

but be-infants[a] in evil,[b]

LEXICON—a. pres. act. impera. of νηπιάζω (LN **9.44**) (BAGD p. 537): 'to be infants' [ISV, NET, NIV, NRSV, REB], 'to be like infants' [TNT], 'to be mere infants' [HNTC], 'to be children' [KJV, NAB, TEV], 'to be children, nay be very babes' [ICC], 'to be like children' [AB, LN], 'to remain infants' [NJB], 'to be babes' [Herm, Lns, NTC], 'to be as a child' [BAGD, LN], 'to be a child' [BAGD, NIGTC], 'to be childlike' [LN]. This word is also translated with the point of comparison made explicit: 'to be innocent as tiny babies' [CEV], 'to be innocent as babies' [NLT].

b. κακία (LN 88.105) (BAGD 1.a. p. 397): 'evil' [AB, Herm, LN, NTC; ISV, NAB, NET, NIV, NLT, NRSV, REB, TEV], 'wickedness' [BAGD, HNTC, LN; NJB, TNT], 'matters of wickedness' [NIGTC], 'malice' [KJV], 'baseness' [Lns], 'jealousy and ill-will' [ICC], 'badness' [LN], not explicit [CEV]. Κακία refers in general to everything that is wrong or sinful [TH]. See this word also at 5:8.

QUESTION—What is the significance of the dative case in τῇ κακίᾳ 'in evil'?
It is a dative of reference [AB, Alf, NTC; NIV, NLT, TEV, TNT]: *in reference to* evil. All three datives in this verse are datives of reference [NIC2].

QUESTION—If the image is children and the topic is the Corinthians, what is the point of similarity?
The point of similarity is innocence [AB, Ed, NIC2, NIGTC, TH; CEV, NLT]: be as innocent as children. The point of similarity is naiveté [NTC]. The point of similarity is lack of experience or knowledge [Lns, TG]. Children are unaware of the trickery of evil [AB]. Paul's desire was for the Corinthians to be inexperienced in knowing how to practice evil [Lns]

and in (your) thinking[a] become mature.[b]

LEXICON—a. φρήν (See above in this verse): 'thinking' [AB, NTC; ISV, NET, NIV, NJB, NRSV, REB, TEV, TNT], 'understanding' [KJV], 'discernment' [Herm], 'mind' [ICC, Lns; NAB], 'intelligence' [HNTC]. The phrase ταῖς φρεσίν 'in the thinking' is translated 'in understanding matters of this kind' [NLT], 'in matters of the mind' [NIGTC]. This noun is also translated as a verb: 'to think' [CEV].

b. τέλειος (LN 9.10, 88.100) (BAGD 2.a.α. p. 809): 'mature' [AB, BAGD, Herm, HNTC, LN (88.100), Lns, NTC; NAB, NET, TNT], 'mature and wise' [NLT], 'grown-up' [LN (88.100); REB, TEV], 'adult' [BAGD, LN (9.10)], 'mature adult' [NIGTC], 'full grown' [BAGD]. This adjective is also translated as a noun: 'mature people' [CEV], 'full-grown men' [ICC], 'men' [KJV], 'adults' [ISV, NIV, NRSV], 'grown-ups' [NJB], 'grown person' [LN (9.10)]. Paul's desire is to have people who are able to make full use of their thinking and judgment [Lns].

DISCOURSE UNIT: 14:21–25 [EGT]. The topic is the strange tongues being an occasion of unbelief.

14:21 It is-written in the Law[a]

LEXICON—a. νόμος (LN 33.55, 33.56) (BAGD 4.b. p. 543): 'Law' [LN (33.55), Lns, NIGTC, NTC; ISV, NET, NIV, NJB, TNT], 'law' [BAGD, Herm; KJV, NAB, NRSV, REB], 'Scriptures' [LN (33.56); CEV, NLT, TEV], 'holy writings, sacred writings' [LN (33.56)], 'the great Prophet of the old Covenant' [ICC]. By metonymy (part for whole) this word refers to the Holy Scripture in general [BAGD]. Specifically it refers to the Torah, the first five books of the OT [LN (33.55)]. The reference is to Isaiah 28:11, 12 [ICC, NIGTC]. Paul cites the prophet Isaiah as part of the Law. This was according to Jewish custom [NIC2]. See this word also at 9:8.

"In strange-tongues[a] and by (the) lips[b] of-others[c] I-will-speak to this people[d]

LEXICON—a. ἑτερόγλωσσος (LN **33.4**) (BAGD p. 314): 'strange tongue' [AB, Lns, NTC; NAB, NJB, REB], 'foreign tongue' [NIGTC], 'unknown language' [NLT], 'speaking in a strange language, in a strange language'

[LN]. This word is also translated with its actor supplied: 'men of other tongues' [KJV], 'men of foreign tongues' [TNT], 'people/men of strange tongues' [BAGD, Herm, HNTC; ISV, NET, NIV, NRSV], 'those who speak strange languages' [**LN**; TEV], 'strangers who speak unknown languages' [CEV]. In the Isaiah passage these men are Assyrians [ICC, NIC, NTC].
- b. χεῖλος (LN 33.74) (BAGD 1. p. 879): 'lip' [AB, BAGD, Herm, HNTC, LN, Lns, NIGTC, NTC; KJV, NET, NIV, NLT, NRSV, REB, TEV, TNT], 'mouth' [ISV], 'speech' [NAB]. The phrase χείλεσιν ἑτέρων 'lips of others' is translated 'a foreign language' [NJB], not explicit [CEV]. Χεῖλος is a reference to 'speaking' [Alf].
- c. ἕτερος (LN 58.36, 58.37) (BAGD 2. p. 315): 'other' [LN (58.37); KJV], 'different' [LN (58.36)], 'alien' [NIGTC; NAB]. This adjective is also translated as a noun: 'foreigner' [NTC; ISV, NIV, NLT, NRSV, REB, TEV, TNT], 'stranger' [AB, BAGD, Herm, HNTC, Lns; CEV, NET], 'Assyrian' [ICC], 'foreign language' [NJB].
- d. λαός (LN 11.55): 'people' [AB, Herm, HNTC, LN, Lns, NIGTC, NTC; all versions except NJB, NLT], 'nation' [LN; NJB], 'my own people' [NLT], 'Israel' [ICC]. Λαός refers to the Israelites, which here refers in general to unbelievers [Alf].

and not-even so[a] will-they-listen-to[b] me," says the-Lord.
LEXICON—a. οὕτως (See this word at 11:28): 'so' [AB, HNTC, NTC; NAB, NJB, REB, TNT], 'then' [NIGTC; ISV, NIV, NLT, NRSV, TEV], 'in this way' [NET], 'still' [CEV], 'thus' [Lns]. The phrase οὐδ' οὕτως 'not even so' is translated 'yet for all that...not' [KJV], 'yet...not' [Herm].
- b. fut. mid. indic. of εἰσακούω (LN 24.60, **36.15**) (BAGD 1. p. 232): 'to listen to' [AB, Herm, HNTC, LN (24.60), Lns; CEV, ISV, NET, NIV, NLT, NRSV, TEV, TNT], 'to hear' [NIGTC; KJV], 'to heed' [LN (24.60); NAB, REB], 'to obey' [BAGD, **LN** (36.15), NTC], 'to pay attention to what is said' [LN (24.60)]. This verb is joined with the negative and translated 'to refuse to listen' [NJB]. This verb is also translated as a noun: 'obedience' [ICC].

QUESTION—To whom does κύριος 'Lord' refer?
It probably refers to God rather than Christ [TH].

QUESTION—What is the background of the Scripture that Paul quotes?
God spoke to the people of Israel in their own language through his prophets and they did not believe Him. So he promises to speak to them through the language of foreigners (the Assyrians). This predicted their exile to Assyria and was a curse and still resulted in their unbelief [NTC].

QUESTION—What is Paul's point in quoting these verses here?
Paul wants to show that God's speaking in tongues through foreigners did not cause the people of Israel to believe. His point is that a similar rejection will be realized when unbelievers hear the Corinthians speaking in tongues [NIC2]. The point is that unintelligible tongues do not have any effect on

unbelievers [Lns]. Paul means that as people did not listen to God when he spoke by means of strange tongues, so strange tongues are not an effective means of communicating with others [HNTC]. The Jews did not listen to prophets who spoke in their own language and so God judged them by bringing to them a people whose language they could not understand. From this the Corinthians could deduce that being taught by men speaking in strange tongues was not a sign of God's good will, but of his disfavor. The gift of tongues was given to help spread the Gospel among people who spoke foreign languages. But to use strange tongues for show with those who could not understand, was to make it a curse [Ho]. Perhaps Paul means that as that the people of Israel who refused to hear the prophet were disciplined by having to listen to unintelligible speech, so with the Corinthians, those who would not believe would hear tongues but would not be able to understand their wonderful content [TNTC].

14:22 Therefore[a] tongues are for[b] (a) sign[c] not to-the-ones believing[d] but for unbelievers,[e]

LEXICON—a. ὥστε (See this word at 10:12): 'therefore' [AB, NTC], 'wherefore' [Lns; KJV], 'so then' [NIGTC; NET, NJB, TEV], 'then' [ISV, NIV, NRSV], 'so' [TNT], 'so you see' [NLT], 'thus' [NRSV], 'clearly then' [REB], 'accordingly' [Herm], 'it follows' [HNTC], 'this shows us' [ICC], not explicit [CEV, NAB].

b. εἰς with accusative object (LN 89.57) (BAGD 4.d. p. 229): 'for' [Lns; KJV], 'meant to be' [ISV], 'meant as' [TNT], 'intended for/as' [AB; REB], 'for the purpose of' [LN], not explicit [Herm, ICC, NTC; CEV, NAB, NET, NIV, NJB, NLT, NRSV, TEV]. The phrase εἰς...εἰσιν 'are...for' is translated 'serve as' [BAGD, HNTC, NIGTC].

c. σημεῖον (LN 33.477) (BAGD 1. p. 748): 'sign' [AB, Herm, HNTC, ICC, LN, Lns, NTC; all versions except CEV, NJB, TEV], 'proof' [TEV], 'warning sign' [BAGD], 'a sign for judgment' [NIGTC]. This noun is also translated as an adjective: '(are) significant' [NJB]. The phrase εἰς σημεῖον 'for a sign' is translated 'may mean something' [CEV]. Σημεῖον indicates an event that is considered to have a special meaning [LN].

d. pres. act. participle of πιστεύω (LN 31.102) (BAGD 2.b. p. 661): 'to believe' [AB, BAGD, HNTC, ICC, Lns, NTC; all versions except CEV], 'to believe in, to have confidence in, to have faith in, to trust' [LN (31.85)], 'to be a believer, to be a Christian' [LN (31.102)]. This verb is also translated as a noun phrase: 'the Lord's follower' [CEV], 'believer' [Herm, NIGTC], 'Christian' [BAGD]. Πιστεύω means to believe in the good news about Jesus Christ and become his follower [LN (31.102)]. Τοῖς πιστεύσουσιν 'to the ones believing' is a common designation for 'Christians' in his letters [NIC2]. See this word also at 13:7.

e. ἄπιστος (See this word at 10:27): 'unbeliever' [AB, Herm, Lns, NIGTC, NTC; all versions except KJV, NAB], 'unbelieving' [HNTC], 'one who does not believe' [KJV, NAB], 'those who fail to believe' [ICC].

1 CORINTHIANS 14:22

QUESTION—What relationship is indicated by ὥστε 'therefore'?

It indicates a conclusion based on 14:21 [Alf, Ho, ICC, NIC, NIC2, TH]: I will speak with strange tongues but they will not listen to me, *therefore* tongues are a sign for unbelievers not believers. It is a conclusion based on the final clause of 14:21 [HNTC, Lns]. He will show that there is still another facet of tongues than the one given in 14:2 and following [NIC]. He is saying that the sending of foreigners among the Israelis was a sign of God's disapproval and therefore speaking in tongues in the assembly would also be a curse [Ho].

QUESTION—What is meant by 'tongues are a sign for unbelievers'?

1. When tongues refers to human foreign languages.

   Tongues are a sign of God's judgment [Lns]. Tongues are a sign of God's presence. Paul is not referring to the gift of tongues here, but to 'tongues' as referred to in 14:21, that is, to foreign languages. When the people were obedient, God sent them prophets who spoke Hebrew. When they were disobedient, he sent them those who spoke foreign languages. It follows that 'tongues' are for the unbelieving and disobedient, while prophecy is for believers [Ho].

2. When tongues refers to non-human heavenly languages.

   They were a sign of God's judgment [AB, HNTC, ICC, MNTC, NIC2, NIGTC, NTC, TNTC, Vn]. As unbelieving Jews were punished by being made to listen to the unintelligible communication of foreigners, so now those not believing the Good News are punished by having to hear magnificent sounds without comprehension [ICC]. The gift of speaking in tongues is meant by God to show people the extent to which they are failing to believe [Gdt]. This verse should be interpreted in the light of the following verses (14:23–25). He first counters the Corinthian belief (that tongues were a sign to believers of God's presence in their meetings) by saying that they were a sign to unbelievers that worked to their disadvantage. That is, unintelligible tongues had the effect of driving away unbelievers, for they thought the speakers were crazy. Paul wants them therefore to stop the use of this gift in their public assemblies [NIC2]. He may mean that tongues are a sign of God's power, to impress unbelievers and that the power was shown in the ability of believers to understand them [TH].

3. When it refers to either human languages or non-human heavenly languages: Tongues are a sign of God's judgment [Ed, NCBC]. Paul means that speaking in tongues to unbelievers will only serve to cause them to remain unbelievers [NCBC].

but prophecy (is) not for unbelievers but for-the-ones believing.

QUESTION—Is this clause elliptical?

1. The words 'is a sign' is implied from the previous clause [EGT, Gdt, HNTC, Ho, Lns, My, NIC, NIC2, NTC; TEV]: prophecy *is a sign* not for unbelievers but for believers. The clause is probably elliptical since both

'sign' and the verb 'to be', from the first clause, are omitted here [NIC2]. The two clauses are exact parallels so both 'is' and 'sign' must be supplied [Lns]. The sign is one of God's favor [Lns, NIC, NIC2]. The sign speaks of God's approval and presence among them [NIC2, TG]. Prophecy was a sign of judgment on the Corinthians as they tended to reject it [HNTC]. Prophecy is a sign of faith or a readiness to believe. Such a readiness results in faith in the unbeliever in 14:24 who comes to faith through prophecy [Gdt]. While it is a warning sign for judgment in respect to unbelievers, it signals the presence of God in respect to believers [NIGTC].

2. 'Sign' is not implied [AB, ICC, MNTC; all versions except TEV]: prophecy is *for the benefit of* believers. Prophecy is given to those who believe for edification and it is not given as a sign pointing to something else [MNTC].

14:23 If then[a] the whole church assembles at the same-place and all speak in-tongues,

LEXICON—a. οὖν (See this word at 14:11): 'then' [AB, Herm, HNTC; TEV], 'so' [NTC; NET, NIV, NJB, REB], 'therefore' [NIGTC; KJV, NRSV], 'consequently' [ICC], 'accordingly' [Lns], 'even so' [NLT], 'now' [ISV], 'suppose that' [NJB], not explicit [CEV, NAB, TNT].

QUESTION—What relationship is indicated by οὖν 'then'?

It indicates the logical conclusion of 14:22 [Alf, My]. The conclusion drawn in 14:23 is from the first half of 14:22 while 14:24 is a conclusion drawn from the second half of 14:22 [My]: tongues are a sign not for believers but for unbelievers, *therefore* if the whole church assembles.... Prophecy is for believers, not unbelievers, *therefore* if an unbeliever comes in.... It indicates that Paul is returning to his main argument after a digression of two or three verses [TH]. It indicates that Paul is returning to his subject of speaking in tongues in church. At the same time he draws on the facts he has just presented [NIC]. It indicates that the following will support the implied conclusion to 14:22 that speaking in tongues without interpretation is useless [Ho].

QUESTION—To whom does πάντες 'all' refer?

'All' is probably overstated [NIC2, NTC], but it implies that the potential for it was there. This hypothesis may give a glimpse of what was going on in the assembly in Corinth. The guidelines in 14:27–33 imply that many were speaking in tongues in the meetings at the same time [NIC2]. 'All' simply means that all who spoke used foreign languages [Ho]. 'All' here refers only to all who could speak in tongues, not that everyone could [TH, Vn]. It may mean that everyone there spoke in tongues at the same time [Ed, HNTC, My] and in disorder [Ed, My]. Paul does not mean that all spoke at once but rather that they spoke in tongues one after another [Alf, Gdt, ICC, Lns, My]. Paul may be using an extreme example for the sake of the argument [ICC].

and uninstructed-persons[a] or unbelievers enter,

LEXICON—a. ἰδιώτης (BAGD 2. p. 370): 'uninstructed person' [AB; REB], 'ordinary person' [TEV], 'uneducated person' [ISV], '(one) who is unlearned' [Lns; KJV], 'outsider' [CEV, NRSV], 'uninitiated' [NAB], 'uninitiated person' [NIGTC; NJB], 'uninformed person' [NET], '(one) who does not understand' [NIV, NLT], 'lay person' [Herm], 'those who have no experience of such things' [ICC], 'novice' [NTC], 'inquirer' [BAGD]. The phrase ἰδιῶται ἢ ἄπιστοι 'uninstructed persons or unbelievers' is translated 'ordinary unbelievers' [TNT], 'unbelieving outsider' [HNTC]. See this word also at 14:16.

QUESTION—Who were the ἰδιώτης 'uninstructed'?

1. They were the same as unbelievers [Herm, HNTC, Ho, Lns, NIC2, NTC; TNT]: uninstructed unbelievers. Verse 14:21 and the comment, "You are mad," show that this person was neither a member of the church nor a learner under instruction. This person was an 'unbelieving outsider' [HNTC]. The 'unlearned' were so called because they did not know the language being used; the 'unbelievers' were non-Christians. In this verse and the next it is obvious that the 'unlearned' were similarly non-Christian since the same effect is created on them as is on 'unbelievers'. One person could be described by both of these designations [Ho]. 'Unlearned' indicates someone who has not been tutored in the Christian faith. The fact that this term is used together with 'unbelievers' and that they both respond in the same way to tongues and prophecy indicates that the 'unlearned' was not a believer. It is possible that Paul is describing a single class of unbeliever [NIC2].
2. They were not believers but they were still different from unbelievers [BAGD, EGT, Gdt, TNTC]: uninstructed persons and unbelievers. They were a class of persons under instruction to become Christians but were not yet full Christians. They were 'inquirers' [BAGD, Gdt]. The ἰδιώτης was a person unfamiliar with the Christian faith [EGT].
3. They were a class of believers [Alf, Ed, ICC, My, TG, TH, Vn]: uninstructed believers and unbelievers. They were uninstructed Christians [TH]. This person was a 'plain believer' in the sense that he/she was not familiar with the gift of tongues and its use [Alf].

not will-they-say that you-are-out-of-your-minds?[a]

LEXICON—a. pres. mid. (deponent = act.) of μαίνομαι (LN 30.24) (BAGD p. 486): 'to be out of one's mind' [BAGD, LN, NIGTC, NTC; ISV, NAB, NIV, NRSV], 'to be mad' [AB, BAGD, Herm, HNTC, ICC, LN, Lns; KJV, REB, TNT], 'to be crazy' [CEV, NET, NLT, TEV], 'to rave' [NJB], 'to be insane, to be not in one's right mind' [LN]. Μαίνομαι refers here not to mental derangement but to demon possession [Ed, HNTC, TH]. It means 'to be in a frenzied rage, to be beside oneself in anger' [MNTC]. This response on the part of the unbeliever compares the Christian gathering to the disorder that was typical of some of the mystery cults [NIC2].

QUESTION—What reply is expected to this rhetorical question?

The presence of the negative particle οὐ requires a positive reply [AB, Alf, BAGD, EGT, Gdt, ICC, Lns, NIC2, Rb, TG, Vn; ISV, NJB, NLT]: They will say you are out of your mind, won't they?

14:24 **But if all prophesy, and some unbeliever or uninstructed-person enters,**

QUESTION—What relationship is indicated by δέ 'but'?

It indicates a contrastive relationship [EGT; all versions]: they will say you are out of your minds. *But* if all prophesy.... This verse is the second part of the conclusion that was begun at 14:23 [Ho].

QUESTION—What is indicated by the present subjunctive προφητεύωσιν 'they prophesy'?

It functions to picture the action in progress [Lns]: if they are all engaged in prophesying.

QUESTION—What is the significance of the change from the plural 'unbelievers' and 'uninstructed persons' of 14:23 to the singular here?

It would be more probable that the good result would happen to a single person than to a group [Ed, Gdt, ICC].

he-is-convicted[a] by all, he-is-judged[b] by all,

LEXICON—a. pres. pass. indic. of ἐλέγχω (LN 33.417) (BAGD 2. 249): 'to be convicted' [BAGD; ISV, NET], 'to be convicted of sin' [NLT], 'to be convinced' [BAGD, Herm; KJV, NIV], 'to be convinced of (one's) sin' [TEV], 'to undergo conviction' [NIGTC], 'to hear something that searches (one's) conscience' [REB], 'to be put to the test' [NJB], 'to be taken to task' [NAB], 'to be reproved' [NRSV], 'to be rebuked, to be reproached' [LN]. This clause is translated 'they will realize that they are sinners' [CEV], 'everything he hears will challenge him' [TNT].

b. pres. pass. indic. of ἀνακρίνω (BAGD 2. p. 56): 'to be judged' [BAGD; KJV, NIV, NJB, TEV], 'to be called to account' [BAGD; NAB, NET, NRSV], 'to be examined' [BAGD, Herm; ISV], 'to be condemned' [NLT], 'to undergo judgment' [NIGTC], 'to hear something that brings conviction' [REB]. This clause is translated 'and they will want to change their ways because of what you are saying' [CEV], 'and cause him to think seriously' [TNT]. See this word also at 2:14 and 10:25.

QUESTION—To what does ὑπὸ πάντων 'by all' refer?

1. It refers to all those prophesying [Alf, ICC, My; REB]: convicted and judged by you all. It means convicted by each in his turn [Alf]. The person is convicted by all but it is their words that awaken the person's conscience [ICC, My].

2. It refers to all that was said [Ho, Lns, NTC, TG, TH; CEV, NLT, TEV, TNT]: convicted and judged by all you say. It would be what he heard from everyone that would convict him [Ho]. It is the Word of God that

brings conviction and judges or examines the person's heart (Hebrews 4:12) [Ho]. In the case of the verb 'convicted', it is the Word of God spoken by the Corinthians that exposes the person's sin but in the case of the word 'judged' it is the Corinthians who judge the genuineness of the person's conversion [NTC].

QUESTION—What does it mean that the unbeliever is 'convicted'?

It means that the person will become aware of his sins [Ed, Gdt, NIC2, TG]. It means that the prophesying would have the effect of making the person conscious of sin and guilt [Lns]. It means that the person will be convinced of the truth of what he/she has heard [Ho, MNTC]. John 16:8 indicates that the Holy Spirit would convince the person of sin, righteousness and judgment [Ho, NTC]. God's Spirit, using the Word of God causes people to turn from their sin to the salvation of the Lord [NTC]. It means that the person becomes convinced of that he/she is a sinner [ICC].

QUESTION—What does it mean that the unbeliever is 'judged'?

It means that the unbeliever will realize that he is a sinner and is under God's judgment [TG]. It means that the person would become aware that he/she will be judged on their response to the truth [MNTC]. It means that the Holy Spirit will judge or examine the person's heart [Gdt, Ho, NIC2], and lead him/her to turn from their sin to God [NIC2]. It means that all the believers will judge whether or not the person's conversion is genuine [NTC]. It means that the prophesying examines the person, as is done in a law court, and makes him/her conscious of sin and guilt [Lns]. It means that there is an investigation of the person and the facts of his condition are shown to him/her [ICC].

14:25 the secrets[a] of-his heart[b] become laid-bare,[c]

TEXT—Some manuscripts include καὶ οὕτως 'and so' at the beginning of this verse. GNT does not mention with this variant. Only KJV includes these words.

LEXICON—a. κρυπτός (LN **28.75**, 28.69) (BAGD 2.a. p. 454): 'secret' [Herm, HNTC, **LN** (28.75), Lns; all versions except CEV, NLT, TEV], 'what is hidden' [CEV], 'secret thoughts' [BAGD; NLT, TEV], 'hidden secret' [AB], 'secret depth' [NIGTC], 'secret evil' [ICC], 'hidden thing' [NTC], 'secret information, secret knowledge' [LN (28.75)]. Κρυπτός is primarily an adjective meaning 'secret, hidden, not able to be made known' [LN (28.69)]. The 'secrets of one's heart' refers to a person's true character and moral state [Ho].

b. καρδία (LN **26.3**) (BAGD 1.b.α. p. 403): 'heart' [AB, BAGD, Herm, HNTC, ICC, **LN**, Lns, NTC; all versions except NLT, TEV], 'mind' [LN], 'inner self' [LN], 'depths of one's very being' [NIGTC], not explicit [NLT, TEV]. Καρδία is used figuratively to refer to the source of a person's psychological life, especially his/her thoughts [LN]. It refers to the center and source of a person's whole inner life, his thoughts, feelings and volition [BAGD]. See this word also at 2:9.

c. φανερός (See this word at 11:19): 'laid bare' [Herm, HNTC; NAB, NIV, NLT, REB], 'evident' [Lns], 'disclosed' [NET, NRSV], 'revealed' [NJB], 'exposed' [AB, NIGTC], 'brought into the open' [TEV], 'brought to light' [TNT], 'known' [ISV], 'manifest' [Lns; KJV], 'clear' [BAGD, LN]. The phrase φανερὰ γίνεται 'become laid bare' is translated 'to be revealed' [ICC], 'they will tell (what is hidden)' [CEV]. See the verbal form of this word at 4:5.

QUESTION—What is meant by τὰ κρυπτὰ τῆς καρδίας αὐτοῦ φανερὰ γίνεται 'the secrets of his heart become laid bare'?

It shows clearly that a function of prophecy is to reveal facts that man has hidden [NIC, NIC2]. 'Laid bare' seems to imply public confession of sin [TG]. It is a moral illumination in which a man's past and present are shown in their true perspective [Gdt]. The person's sinful intentions and acts are reveled to him [MNTC].

QUESTION—To whom are the secrets of the heart laid bare?

They are laid bare to the person himself [ICC, Lns, MNTC, NIC, TG, TH], so that he sees them and turns from them to God [Lns]. They are laid bare before all those who are present [My, TH].

QUESTION—Who is the actor in the passive construction φανερὰ γίνεται 'become laid bare'?

The Holy Spirit working through the prophets lays bare the secrets of the heart of the unbeliever [NIC2, TH]. The Lord shines his light on a person's life through his Word and Spirit [NTC].

and so having-fallen-down[a] on (his) face he-will-worship[b] God

LEXICON—a. aorist act. participle of πίπτω (LN 17.22) (BAGD 1.b.α.β. p. 659): 'to fall down' [BAGD; NIV, REB], 'to prostrate oneself before, to fall down before' [LN], 'to throw oneself to the ground' [BAGD]. The phrase πεσὼν ἐπὶ πρόσωπον 'having fallen on his face' is translated 'to fall (down) on one's face' [Herm, HNTC, Lns, NTC; KJV, NET, NJB, TNT], 'to fall down' [NIV, REB], 'to fall prostrate' [AB; NAB], 'to kneel down' [CEV], 'to fall down on one's knees' [NLT], 'to fall to one's knees in obeisance' [NIGTC], 'to bow down to the ground' [ISV], 'to bow down' [TEV], 'to bow down before God' [NRSV], 'to humble oneself before God and man' [ICC]. This is a sign of devotion [BAGD]. See this word also at 10:8.

b. fut. act. indic. of προσκυνέω (LN 53.56) (BAGD 2.a. p. 717): 'to worship' [AB, BAGD, Herm, HNTC, LN, Lns, NIGTC, NTC; all versions except CEV], 'to bow down and worship' [LN], 'to prostrate oneself in worship' [LN], not explicit [ICC]. The clause προσκυνήσει τῷ θεῷ ἀπαγγέλλων ὅτι 'he will worship God, declaring that' is translated 'and say to God' [CEV].

QUESTION—What is implied by πεσὼν ἐπὶ πρόσωπον προσκυνεήσει τῷ θεῷ 'having fallen on (his) face he will worship God'?

It implies that he is converted and becomes a Christian [Ho, NIC, NIC2, NTC]. It implies that the unbeliever now believes and confesses that he does as is indicated by his falling prostrate. His worship shows that he submits to God and declares that He is the true God [Lns].

declaring[a] that "Really[b] God is among you."
LEXICON—a. pres. act. participle of ἀπαγγέλλω (LN 33.198) (BAGD 2. p. 79): 'to declare' [HNTC, Lns, NTC; ISV, NET, NJB, NLT, NRSV, REB, TNT], 'to proclaim' [AB, BAGD, ICC], 'to exclaim' [NIV], 'to cry out' [NAB], 'to confess' [Herm, NIGTC; TEV], 'to say' [CEV], 'to report' [KJV], 'to tell, to inform' [LN]. It is implied that the declaration was said aloud [Alf, My].

b. ὄντως (LN 70.2) (BAGD 1. p. 574): 'really' [BAGD, LN; NET, NIV, NLT, NRSV, TNT], 'truly' [AB, Herm, HNTC, LN, Lns, NTC; ISV, NAB, TEV], 'of a truth' [KJV], 'in truth' [BAGD], 'indeed' [NJB], 'indeed really' [NIGTC], 'certainly' [BAGD, LN; REB], not explicit [ICC]. This adverb is also translated as an adjective: '(to be) certain' [CEV].

DISCOURSE UNIT: 14:26–40 [Gdt, GNT, Ho, NIC2, NIGTC, NTC; CEV, ISV, NAB, NET, NIV, NJB, NLT, TEV]. The topic is rules for the exercise of gifts [Gdt], the ordering of gifts [NIC2], orderly conduct [NTC; NAB], all things being done in order [GNT], orderly worship [CEV, NIV, NLT], church order [Ho; ISV, NET, TEV], regulating spiritual gifts [NJB], controlled speech and building up [NIGTC].

DISCOURSE UNIT: 14:26–35 [Alf]. The topic is regulations respecting the exercise of spiritual gifts in the assemblies.

DISCOURSE UNIT: 14:26–33 [EGT, ICC, NIC2, TNTC, Vn]. The topic is self control in religious exercises [EGT], the ordering of tongues and prophecy [NIC2], the practical outcome [TNTC], rules regarding the gifts [ICC, Vn].

DISCOURSE UNIT: 14:26–33a [AB, NCBC, NIC]. The topic is tongues, prophecy, and order [AB], edification and orderliness are paramount [NCBC], order in the assembly [NIC].

DISCOURSE UNIT: 14:26–28 [NTC]. The topic is edification.

14:26 What is-it then,[a] brothers?[b]
LEXICON—a. οὖν (See this word at 14:11): 'then' [AB, Herm, HNTC, ICC, Lns, NIGTC, NTC; KJV, NET, NIV, NJB, NRSV, TNT], 'so' [ISV], not explicit [CEV, NAB, NLT, REB, TEV].

b. ἀδελφός (See this word at 10:1): 'brother' [Herm; ISV, KJV, NAB, NIV, NJB, TNT], 'brother and sister' [NET, NLT], 'friend' [CEV, NRSV,

REB, TEV], 'dear friend' [NIGTC]. Ἀδελφός indicates 'fellow Christians' [TH].

QUESTION—What is the significance of this question and vocative?

The combination of this question with the vocative indicates that Paul is moving to another part of his argument [NIC2]. The combination signals a change of subject, and here it gives a conclusion [NIC]. The question is rhetorical and indicates that Paul will now explain himself [TEV]. It indicates that Paul is concluding or summing up his argument [TG; NLT, REB]. The question is used to provoke interest as at 14:15 [Herm]. The question is an invitation to the Corinthians to draw the logical conclusion from the principles he has given [Gdt]. Paul is asking the Corinthians what now should be done in light of the facts that uninterpreted tongues cause people to think you are crazy and that prophecy causes the conversion of unbelievers [Ed]. The answer to the question is that if disorder blocks understanding and faith then the Corinthians were failing to edify [NTC]. The οὖν 'then' functions to resume the discussion taking into consideration the complete state of the Corinthian church as it has been viewed [EGT]. Paul uses the term 'brothers' when he talks about something personal. Here he corrects their disorderly conduct in church [NTC].

When you-assemble, each has (a) psalm,[a] has (a) teaching,[b] has (a) revelation,[c] has (a) tongue,[d] has (an) interpretation;[e]

TEXT—Some manuscripts include ὑμῶν 'of you' following ἕκαστος 'each'. GNT does not mention this variant. The reading 'of you' seems to be taken by KJV, NJB, and REB.

TEXT—Some manuscripts place γλῶσσαν ἔχει 'has a tongue' before ἀποκάλυψιν ἔχει 'has a revelation'. GNT does not mention this variant. Only KJV makes this transposition.

LEXICON—a. ψαλμός (LN 33.112) (BAGD 2. p. 891): 'psalm' [AB, BAGD, LN, Lns, NTC; ISV, KJV, NAB, NJB, TNT], 'hymn' [Herm, HNTC, NIGTC; NIV, NRSV, REB, TEV], 'song of praise' [BAGD, LN], 'song' [NET]. This noun is also translated as a verb: 'to sing' [CEV, NLT], 'to sing a song of praise' [ICC].

b. διδαχή (See this word at 14:6): 'teaching' [AB, Lns, NTC; ISV, TEV, TNT], 'piece of teaching' [HNTC], 'item of teaching' [NIGTC], 'piece of instruction' [Herm], 'lesson' [NET, NRSV], 'doctrine' [KJV], 'word of instruction' [NIV], 'some instruction' [NJB, REB], 'some instruction to give' [NAB]. This noun is also translated as a verb: 'to teach' [CEV, NLT], 'to give instruction' [ICC].

c. ἀποκάλυψις (See this word at 14:6): 'revelation' [AB, Herm, HNTC, Lns, NTC; ISV, KJV, NET, NIV, NJB, NRSV, REB, TNT], 'revelation from God' [TEV], 'revelation to share' [NAB], 'something disclosed' [NIGTC]. This noun is also translated as a verb: 'to tell what God has said' [CEV], 'to tell some special revelation God has given' [NLT], 'to

1 CORINTHIANS 14:26 235

reveal a truth' [ICC]. This gift may have been contributed by a prophet [Gdt, Ho, NCBC, NIC, NIC2, TNTC].

d. γλῶσσα (See this word at 12:10): 'tongue' [AB, HNTC, Lns, NTC; ISV, KJV, NAB, NET, NIV, NJB, NRSV, TNT], 'ecstatic utterance' [REB], 'message in strange tongues' [TEV], 'speech in tongues' [Herm]. This noun is also translated as a verb: 'to utter a tongue' [ICC], 'to speak in a tongue' [NIGTC], 'to speak in an unknown language' [CEV, NLT].

e. ἑρμηνεία (See this word at 12:10): 'interpretation' [AB, Herm, HNTC, Lns, NTC; ISV, KJV, NET, NIV, NJB, NRSV, REB, TNT], 'the explanation of what is said' [TEV]. This noun is also translated as a verb: 'to interpret' [NAB], 'to explain what the language means' [CEV], 'to interpret what is said' [NLT], 'to interpret a tongue' [ICC], 'to put the tongues language into words' [NIGTC]. Ἑρμηνεία here implies the interpretation of a tongue [HNTC, Ho, ICC, TNTC].

QUESTION—What is implied in συνέρχησθε 'you assemble'?

It implies that they assemble in order to worship [TH, TNTC].

QUESTION—What does ἕκαστος ἔχει 'each has' indicate?

It does not indicate that each person had the ability to perform all five gifts [Gdt, TG], but that one had one gift and another had another [AB, Herm, NIGTC, TG]. It indicates that each should or may have something [Gdt]. It does not mean that everyone there has a gift but that each one who has a gift will use it in that particular meeting [Lns]. It indicates that everyone had a gift unique to himself/herself [Ed, EGT, NIC]. Paul stresses in 14:23, 34, 26, 31 that each either had or could and should have spiritual gifts [TH]. It does not mean that all present must take part but that any of them might be expected to do so [TNTC]. It implies that all wanted to participate at the same time [MNTC]. Paul is mentioning some of the parts of the service at random [NTC].

QUESTION—What is meant by ἔχει 'to have' a gift?

'To have' means that the person has been enabled by the Holy Spirit to do that activity [NIC]. It means to possess as one's special gift so as to use it in the assembly [Gdt]. It means 'to be ready with' a gift [TNT]. It means 'to bring' a gift [NJB]. It means 'to contribute' a gift [REB]. It means 'to do the action of' a gift, such as each sings a psalm [ICC; CEV, NLT].

QUESTION—What is the meaning of ψαλμός 'psalm'?

It could mean a psalm from the Old Testament [EGT, MNTC, TG], or a Christian song [NIC, TG, TH]. It may have been improvised or composed [EGT, Gdt, HNTC, ICC, NIC, TNTC]. It could have been accompanied or unaccompanied [NTC]. It was given in a language which all could understand [Gdt, Lns]. It was like the psalms, hymns, and spiritual songs mentioned in Colossians 3:16 and Ephesians 5:19 [Gdt, TH]. It was a song prepared for the meeting [Ho]. These were songs like those of Moses and Miriam in Exodus 15, or like Balaam in Numbers 23, 24, or like Deborah in Judges 5, and like the songs in Luke 1, 2 [ICC]. It was not a psalm from the

Old Testament [Gdt, HNTC, Ho]. It was not an already existing Christian hymn [Gdt].

QUESTION—Does the order in which these gifts are presented have any significance?

The order is random and does not mean to suggest anything else [Herm, ICC, NIC2, NTC]. The order presented suggests the normal order for a worship service [EGT, Gdt].

QUESTION—Is 'prophecy' missing from this list?

Prophecy is left out of this list, but is included in the following verses [NIC2]. The gifts of teaching and revelation correspond to the gifts of knowledge and prophecy of 14:6 [NTC]. There are actually only two gifts in focus in this verse, prophecy and tongues. Prophecy includes a psalm, a teaching and a revelation, tongues implies speaking in tongues and its interpretation [Lns].

let-happen everything for upbuilding.[a]

LEXICON—a. οἰκοδομή (See this word at 14:3): 'upbuilding' [ISV], 'building up' [AB; NRSV], 'edification' [Herm, NTC], 'edifying' [Lns; KJV], 'the building up of the congregation' [TNT], 'building up of the community' [HNTC, NIGTC], 'strengthening of the church' [NET, NIV], 'the good of everyone there' [CEV]. The phrase πρὸς οἰκοδομήν 'for edification' is translated 'with a constructive purpose' [NAB], 'in a way that will build up the community' [NJB], 'of help to the church' [TEV], 'aim to build up the church' [REB], 'must be useful to all and build them up in the Lord' [NLT], 'to build up the spiritual life of others' [ICC].

QUESTION—What relationship is indicated by πρός 'for'?

It indicates purpose [Ed, Lns, NTC]: let everything happen *for the purpose of* upbuilding. The first rule for the use of the gifts is that they be used to edify [Ed]. The principle of love must be realized in edification [NTC].

14:27 If anyone speaks in-a-tongue, by-two[a] or the most[b] three and in-turn,[c]

LEXICON—a. κατὰ δύο (BAGD II.3.a. p. 406): 'two' [BAGD; CEV, NIV, NLT, TEV], 'only two' [ISV, REB], 'let two' [TNT], 'let only two' [ICC, NIGTC], 'let it be two' [Lns; NAB], 'let it be two at a time' [AB], 'let there be only two' [NJB, NRSV], 'let it be by two' [HNTC, NTC; KJV], 'it should be two' [Herm; NET].

b. πλεῖστος (LN **59.8**) (BAGD III.2.b.β. p. 689): 'most' [BAGD]. The phrase τὸ πλεῖστον 'the most' is translated 'at the most' [BAGD, **LN**, Lns, NIGTC, NTC; ISV, KJV, NET, NIV, NJB, TEV], 'at most' [AB, Herm, HNTC, ICC; NAB, NRSV, REB, TNT], 'not/no more than' [LN; CEV, NLT].

c. ἀνὰ μέρος (LN **61.4**, 63.14) (BAGD 1.c. p. 506): 'in turn' [LN (61.4), Lns, NIGTC; TNT], 'each (one) in turn' [AB, NTC; NAB, NRSV], 'one at a time' [HNTC, ICC; ISV, NIV, NJB, NLT, REB], 'one after another/the other' [BAGD, Herm, **LN** (61.4); NET, TEV], 'in succession'

[BAGD, LN (61.4)], 'by course' [KJV]. This phrase is also translated by a clause: 'you must take turns' [CEV]. This phrase indicates that each speaker should speak in his turn and not at the same time as someone else [EGT, NIC, TG].

QUESTION—Does the limitation on number of speakers refer to a single meeting or at any given time in the meeting?

1. It refers to a single meeting [AB, EGT, Gdt, Lns, MNTC, NIC2, NTC, TH]. Two factors argue for this position. The first is the phrase 'at the most'; the second is the general concern of this chapter that tongues not dominate the church [NIC2].
2. It refers to a given time in the meeting [Ed]. Paul is only limiting the number of speakers who may speak in tongues with interpretation. He does not mean that only that number may speak in the meeting [Ed].

QUESTION—What is implied in the phrase κατὰ δύο ἢ τὸ πλεῖστον τρεῖς 'by two or at most three'?

The verb 'to speak' is implied [EGT, ICC, NIC; CEV, ISV, NIV, NLT, REB, TEV, TNT]: if anyone speaks in a tongue, let two or at most three speak. The verb 'to be' is implied [Alf, Lns; KJV, NAB, NET, NJB, NRSV]: (If anyone speaks in a tongue), let it be two or at most three. The preference is for just one to speak, but there is a concession for two, or, reluctantly, three at the most [NIGTC].

QUESTION—What is implied by the phrase ἀνὰ μέρος 'in turn'?

It may indicate that the Corinthians were not doing this but were speaking in tongues simultaneously [AB, Gdt, ICC, Lns, MNTC, NIC2, NIGTC, TNTC].

and one[a] let-interpret;

LEXICON—a. εἷς (LN 60.10): 'one' [AB, LN, NTC; KJV, NRSV], 'one member' [HNTC], 'one man' [TNT], 'one interpreter' [ICC], 'one person' [Lns], 'one of these' [NJB], 'the one who speaks' [NIGTC], 'someone' [Herm; CEV, NET, NIV, NLT, REB], 'someone else' [TEV], 'somebody' [ISV], 'another' [NAB].

QUESTION—How many interpreters were there to be?

1. There is a single interpreter for all the messages in tongues [Ed, EGT, Gdt, ICC, MNTC, NTC, Vn]. In the Greek the word εἷς 'one' is in an emphatic position indicating that a single interpreter is indicated. The interpreters in Corinth each tried to outdo the other. Paul therefore lays down the rule that there is to be only one interpreter [MNTC]. Having a single interpreter would prevent two from speaking at the same time [Vn].
2. There can be as many interpreters as necessary to interpret the messages in tongues [Herm, Lns]. Paul simply means that each message in tongues should be followed by an interpretation.

QUESTION—How often should an interpretation be given?

The interpretation should probably follow the two or three messages in tongues [NIC2, Vn]. Each message should be followed by an interpretation [Lns, NCBC].

QUESTION—Who could give an interpretation?
It might be the person who spoke in tongues or someone else [AB, EGT, Gdt, Lns, NIC, NIC2]. It is more likely that the interpreter was someone other than the speaker himself [AB]. Someone other than the one who spoke in tongues is implied [TH; TEV].

14:28 But^a if there-be not (an) interpreter,^b

LEXICON—a. δέ (See this word at 11:2): 'but' [AB, Herm, HNTC, ICC, NTC; KJV, NAB, NET, NLT, NRSV, TEV], 'yet' [Lns], 'however' [NIGTC], not explicit [CEV, ISV, NIV, NJB, REB, TNT].
  b. διερμηνευτής (LN **33.146**) (BAGD p. 194): 'interpreter' [AB, BAGD, Herm, ICC, **LN**, Lns, NTC; ISV, KJV, NET, NIV, NJB, REB, TNT], 'one to interpret' [HNTC; NAB, NRSV], 'one able to interpret' [NLT], 'one able to explain' [CEV, TEV], 'one who puts it into words' [NIGTC], 'translator' [BAGD, LN]. It refers to interpreting ecstatic speech [BAGD].

QUESTION—What is implied by this condition?
It implies that the person could anticipate that he/she would speak in tongues [AB, TNTC]. It implies that the person could discover if an interpreter were present or not [AB, Lns, Vn]. It implies that the gift of interpretation was a permanent gift since the speaker could know if there were someone there with that gift or not (see 12:10) [Gdt]. It implies that the members of the assembly knew who those were who had the gift of interpretation [MNTC]. This shows that tongues involved actual foreign languages. In this way a person could easily look over the congregation to see if there were any present who knew the language of his particular gift [Lns].

let-him-be-silent^a in church,

LEXICON—a. pres. act. impera. of σιγάω (LN 33.121) (BAGD 1.a. p. 749): 'to be silent' [AB, ICC, Lns, NTC; NET, NLT, NRSV], 'to keep silent' [BAGD; CEV, REB, TNT], 'to keep silence' [HNTC; KJV], 'to remain silent' [Herm, NIGTC; ISV], 'to be quiet' [NJB, TEV], 'to keep quiet' [NIV], 'to keep quiet about, to say nothing about' [LN], 'to say nothing' [BAGD]. This verb is also translated 'there should be silence' [NAB].

QUESTION—Who is to keep silent?
The person who has the gift to speak in tongues is to keep silent [Alf, EGT, Ho, ICC, NIGTC, NTC, TH, TNTC].

QUESTION—What is implied by the command to keep silent?
It implies that the person who spoke in tongues had control over the gift [MNTC, NIC, NTC, TNTC]. It shows that a tongue is not an irresistible urge of the Spirit which makes a man speak ecstatically [TNTC].

and let-him-speak to-himself and to God.

QUESTION—What is meant by the dative ἑαυτῷ 'to himself'?
It is a dative of advantage meaning 'for his own benefit', not that he should speak 'to himself' [HNTC, NIC, NIC2, NTC, TH]. Speaking in tongues

indicates that God's Spirit is present and the speaker is benefited when he/she uses this gift [NIC].

QUESTION—What is implied by speaking to oneself and to God?

1. It implies that the person is to speak to God outside of the congregation in private [Herm, ICC, Lns, NIC, NIC2, NIGTC, NTC]. It implies that the person is to speak to God at home [Herm, NIC]. Ἑαυτῷ is emphatic [ICC, Lns, Vn], and contrasts with being in the congregation and implies that the person should wait until he is alone [ICC, NIC2]. The verb λαλεῖν 'to speak' implies audible utterance [ICC, Lns].
2. It simply implies that the person is to speak to God quietly [EGT, Gdt, Ho, MNTC, NIC2, Rb, TG, Vn]. The person should talk quietly, whisper or commune with God silently [TG]. The speaker may continue to exercise his gift in thanksgiving and mental prayer [Gdt].

DISCOURSE UNIT: 14:29–40 [MNTC]. The topic is the procedure for prophecy.

DISCOURSE UNIT: 14:29–33a [NTC]. The topic is prophets and revelation.

14:29 And/but prophets[a] two or three let-them-speak

LEXICON—a. προφήτης (See this word at 12:28): 'prophet' [AB, Herm, HNTC, Lns, NIGTC, NTC; ISV, KJV, NAB, NET, NIV, NJB, NRSV, REB], 'who are given God's message' [TEV], 'as for those who have messages from God' [TNT], 'those who are inspired to preach' [ICC]. This noun is also translated as a verb: 'to prophesy' [CEV, NLT].

QUESTION—What relationship is indicated by δέ 'and/but'?

1. It indicates transition to something else [Alf]: *next*.
2. It indicates a contrast with 'tongues' of 14:27 [Gdt, NIGTC, TH]: *on the other hand*, prophets, let two or three speak. Verse 14:27 began with an εἴτε 'whether' anticipating another εἴτε 'or'. Paul however changes this pattern and writes a simple δέ meaning 'but' or 'as to' [Gdt].

QUESTION—To what time period does this rule apply?

1. It applies to any single meeting [Alf, EGT, HNTC, Ho, ICC, MNTC]: let two or three prophets speak at a meeting.
2. It applies to the number that could prophesy before any judged the prophecies [NIC2]. This does not limit the number of prophets speaking in any one meeting, only the number that may speak in sequence before there is a discerning. Paul's concern is to make sure that tongues, not prophecies, do not dominate the meeting. Further, he suggests in 14:24 and 31 that all might prophesy.

QUESTION—What is the significance of the omission of the words τὸ πλεῖστον 'the most' from the phrase 'two or three' as in 14:27?

There is no particular significance intended and the rule governing both tongues and prophecy is the same [Lns, NIC]. It indicates that Paul does not want to limit such a gift of edification [Alf]. It indicates that while the rule for tongues was an absolute maximum, the rule for prophecy was just a convenient limit [ICC]. The omission indicates that Paul will treat prophecy more positively than he has tongues [TH].

and the others let-them-judge;[a]

LEXICON—a. pres. act. impera. of διακρίνω (LN **30.109**) (BAGD 1.c.α. p. 185): 'to judge' [LN; KJV], 'to judge what (one) says' [TEV], 'to judge the worth of what (one) says' [NAB], 'to exercise (one's) judgment upon what is said' [REB], 'to judge carefully' [LN], 'to pass judgment (on)' [BAGD, NTC], 'to test' [Herm, HNTC], 'to discriminate' [AB], 'to evaluate what is said' [NET, NLT], 'to evaluate carefully' [**LN**], 'to sift' [NIGTC], 'to weigh carefully what is said' [ISV, NIV], 'to weigh what is said' [NRSV], 'to weigh (one's) words' [NJB, TNT], 'to listen carefully' [CEV], 'to discern' [Lns], 'to exercise the gift of discernment' [ICC]. See this word also at 11:29 and its nominal form at 12:10.

QUESTION—To whom does ἄλλοι 'others' refer?

    1. It refers to all others present in the meeting [HNTC, NIC2, NTC]. There are several reasons why it must refer to the whole congregation: (a) In 14:1 Paul encourages them all to desire the spiritual gifts and especially that they may prophesy; (b) In 14:12 he encourages them to excel in building up the church, that is, by prophecy; (c) In 14:24 he hints that all may prophesy; (d) In 14:31 he urges them all to prophesy. Paul is therefore not so much concerned with a class of prophets as such as with the use of the gift of prophecy in the assembly. Further, the pronoun οἱ ἄλλοι refers primarily to 'others different than the subject'. If Paul had wished to refer to the prophets, he could have used οἱ λοίποι referring to 'the rest of the same class' [NIC2]. 1 Thessalonians 5:21 and 1 John 4:1 seem to indicate that any Christian could discern spirits. Further, the test given in 12:3 is one that any believer may apply [HNTC]. 'Others' is used in a general way, but probably it was the leaders of the congregation [NIGTC].

    2. It refers to the other prophets in the meeting [EGT, Lns, MNTC, NIC]. It refers to the other prophets to the extent that they also had the gift of discernment [NIC]. The presence of the definite article indicates that it refers to the other prophets [Lns].

    3. It refers to the others present in the meeting who had the gift of discernment [Gdt, TNTC]. It is most likely that it refers to those who have the gift of discernment (12:10), but it could also refer to other prophets or to the whole congregation [TNTC]. While it must refer to those who have the gift of discernment, 1 Thessalonians 5:20, 21 seems to support the idea that all the members of the church could be indicated [Gdt].

    4. It refers either to other prophets present or to someone else [Alf, TG, TH]. It refers either to other prophets or to those present who had the gift of discernment [Alf, TG]. It refers either to other prophets or to other members of the Christian community [TH].

QUESTION—What is the implied object of διακρινέτωσαν 'let them judge'?
The implied object is the prophecies of the prophets [HNTC, ICC, NIGTC; ISV, NAB, NET, NIV, NJB, NLT, NRSV, TEV, TNT].

QUESTION—What was to be the criterion by which they were 'to judge'?
They were to judge whether the prophecy was from the Spirit of God or not [Alf, ICC, NIC2, NIGTC, Rb, Vn]. They were to judge between true and false prophets [AB, TG]. They were to distinguish between God-given speech, which would agree with the gospel and the pastoral situation, and self-generated speech, which would come from the speaker's self interests and self deceptions or errors [NIGTC]. They were to judge the prophecy to see if it honored Christ (see 12:3) [Gdt]. They were to judge the spirits according to 12:3 and 1 John 4:1 as to whether they were from God or not and to discern if the prophecy was of value to the church or not [NIC]. They were to evaluate the prophecy as to whether it corresponded to the Word of God like the Bereans of Acts 17:11 did [NTC]. The judging prophets may have had the special gift of discernment or perhaps they merely judged what was said by their own knowledge of God and Scripture. New revelations could be tested as to truth and consistency [MNTC]. They were to apply the prophecies to the Corinthian situation [TH]. This was the same judging as is referred to in the gift of discernment mentioned in 12:10 [Alf, Ho, NIC2].

14:30 But/and[a] if (something)-is-revealed[b] to-another sitting,[c]

LEXICON—a. δέ (See this word at 11:2): 'but' [AB, Herm, ICC, NTC, TH; NLT, TEV], 'and' [Lns; NET, NIV, NJB], not explicit [HNTC, NIGTC; CEV, ISV, KJV, NAB, NRSV, REB, TNT].

b. aorist pass. subj. of ἀποκαλύπτω (LN 28.38) (BAGD 2. p. 92): 'to be revealed' [BAGD, LN; KJV], 'to be disclosed' [LN, NIGTC], 'to be made fully known' [LN]. This verb is also translated as a noun: 'a revelation (is made)' [ICC, Lns; ISV, NRSV], 'a revelation (comes)' [NTC; NIV, NJB, TNT], 'a revelation (is given)' [HNTC], '(receive a) revelation' [Herm; NAB, NET, REB], '(receive) a message from God' [CEV, TEV], '(receive) a revelation from the Lord' [NLT], '(God gives) a revelation' [AB]. This shows that prophecy and revelation are closely connected [NIC]. Revelation is essentially what was given in a prophecy [NIC2]. See the nominal form of this word at 14:6 and 26.

c. pres. mid. (deponent = act.) participle of κάθημαι (LN 17.12) (BAGD 1.a.γ. p. 389): 'to sit' [BAGD, LN], 'to sit by' [Herm, HNTC, Lns; KJV, NAB, NJB], 'to be sitting nearby' [NRSV], 'to be sitting in the meeting' [TEV], 'to sit there' [BAGD; CEV], 'to be sitting down' [LN, NIGTC; NIV], 'to sit listening' [ICC], 'to be seated' [AB, LN; ISV, NET, TNT], not explicit [NLT]. This verb is also translated as an adjective: 'present' [REB]. The speaking person stood to give his message [AB, Ed, EGT, Gdt, Herm, ICC, Lns, NIC2, TH, TNTC].

QUESTION—Who is the actor of the passive ἀποκαλυφθῇ 'it is revealed'?
God is the actor [AB, NIC, Vn; CEV, NLT, TEV]: if God gives a revelation.
The actor is the Spirit [Ed, HNTC, Ho, Lns]: if the Spirit gives a revelation.

let-be-silent the first (person).
QUESTION—Why should the person speaking yield to the one who received a revelation?
The person speaking may have already given his message and is only prolonging it [EGT, ICC, Vn]. It is assumed that the freshest revelation will be the purest form of prophecy. The first speaker may be in danger of mixing his own message with the message God has given him [Gdt]. The newer message was more urgent [AB]. If a revelation is received it must be that the Spirit of God himself wants to reveal a fresh truth [HNTC, MNTC, NIC, NIGTC]. When God spoke directly, everyone was to hear what he said [MNTC]. The Spirit determines how long each prophet should prophesy and when he/she should yield to another [NTC].
QUESTION—What is meant by σιγάτω 'let him be silent'?
It means that they should draw their message to a close [ICC, Vn]. It does not say that they should be silent at once [ICC]. It means that the person speaking should yield to the one receiving the new revelation [AB, Lns, MNTC, TH, TNTC]. It probably means that the person receiving the revelation should wait for the speaker to become silent before he begins. This is in keeping with the fact that it was disorderly to interrupt and therefore against Paul's concern for order. It also agrees with the idea that 14:31 gives the reason why the person who receives a new revelation should wait [Ho]. Neither the person who speaks in tongues nor the prophet is out of control [NIC2].

14:31 For[a] you-are-able all one-by-one[b] to-prophesy,
LEXICON—a. γάρ (See this word at 10:1): 'for' [AB, HNTC, ICC, Lns, NIGTC, NTC; ISV, KJV, NIV, NRSV], 'indeed' [NET], 'surely' [Herm], 'in this way' [NLT], not explicit [CEV, NAB, NJB, REB, TEV, TNT].
  b. καθ' ἕνα (See this construction at 14:27): 'one by one' [AB, HNTC, ICC, Lns, NIGTC, NTC; KJV, NAB, NRSV, TEV, TNT], 'one after the other' [BAGD, Herm; NLT], 'in turn' [ISV, NIV], 'one at a time' [NJB, REB], 'one after another' [NET], 'one person...at a time' [CEV], 'singly' [BAGD]. The classical meaning of this phrase is 'one by one' but here it rather has the meaning of 'all without one exception'. It would be absurd to think that they could prophesy simultaneously [Gdt].
QUESTION—What relationship is indicated by γάρ 'for'?
It indicates the justification for the rule of 14:30 [NIC2]: if a revelation is made to another sitting nearby, let the first person be silent *since* you can all prophesy in turn. This verse gives the reason why it was wrong for two prophets to speak simultaneously [Ho]: two prophets should not speak simultaneously *since* you can all prophesy one by one. This verse gives the reason why it is necessary at times for a prophet to be silent [NIC]. If each

prophet stops when another receives a message, all will be able to prophesy [ICC]. Paul means that only by observing the rule of 14:30 could they all be able to prophesy [Gdt].

QUESTION—Who is included in the word δύνασθε...πάντες προφητεύειν 'you are all able to prophesy one by one'?

1. It includes the whole congregation [HNTC, NCBC, NIC2, NTC]. It does not mean that absolutely everyone has this gift, but that they can potentially have it [NIC2]. It means that all the members of the church may at some time prophesy depending on the will of the Spirit. Prophecy is a function a person performs, not an office [HNTC].
2. It includes all the prophets [ICC, MNTC, TNTC]. It could possibly mean the whole congregation, but more likely it means all the prophets [TNTC].

QUESTION—Can all prophesy at one meeting or over the course of several?

1. It means over the course of several meetings [Ho, ICC, NTC, Vn]. It must mean over the course of several meetings since that would violate Paul's overall concern for orderliness [NTC]. It meant over the course of several meetings since Paul had laid down the rule for two or three prophets in any one meeting [Ho, ICC, Vn].
2. It means at a single meeting [NIC2]. It must refer to a single meeting otherwise the rule would make no sense. Paul's concern has been what takes place in a single gathering (see 14:26).

QUESTION—Where is the emphasis in this verse?

1. The emphasis is on the word δύνασθε 'you can' [Alf, Ed, Lns]. The primary emphasis is on the fact that they were able, the secondary emphasis is on 'one by one' [Alf, Lns]. That is, they all *had the power* to prophesy *in turn* if they wished [Alf]. The emphasis is on the fact that they all were able to prophesy so they should not be afraid that they could not. If not at one service then at another, but all would have their turn [Lns]. Paul knows that there is potential for all Christians to be come prophets [Gdt].
2. The emphasis is on the word πάντες 'all' [NIC2, TH]. The word 'all' is repeated three times showing emphasis which the translator should try to preserve [TH]. Paul emphasizes that all may contribute so that all may be edified as he had urged in chapter 12 and in 14:26 [NIC2].
3. The emphasis is on the phrase καθ' ἕνα 'one by one' [Herm]. The emphasis is on speaking in turn so that each may be understood.

so-that all may-learn[a] and all may-be-encouraged.[b]

LEXICON—a. pres. act. subj. of μανθάνω (LN **27.12**) (BAGD 1. p. 490): 'to learn' [AB, BAGD, Herm, HNTC, ICC, **LN**, Lns, NIGTC, NTC; CEV, KJV, NET, NLT, NRSV, TEV, TNT], 'to learn something' [NJB], 'to receive instruction' [REB]. This active voice is also translated as a passive: 'to be instructed' [LN; ISV, NAB, NIV], 'to be taught' [LN].

b. pres. pass. subj. of παρακαλέω (LN 25.150) (BAGD 2. p. 617): 'to be encouraged' [AB, BAGD, Herm, LN, NTC; all versions except KJV,

NJB, REB], 'to be encouraged or exhorted' [NIGTC], 'to be comforted' [KJV], 'to receive encouragement' [NJB, REB], 'to be quickened' [ICC], 'to be admonished' [Lns], 'to receive exhortation' [HNTC], 'to be exhorted' [BAGD]. Παρακαλέω is nearly synonymous with οἰκοδομή 'edification' of 14:26 [TH]. See this word also at 4:13 and its nominal form at 14:3.

QUESTION—What relationship is indicated by ἵνα 'so that'?

It indicates the purpose for such prophesying [Lns, MNTC]: all can prophesy one by one *in order that* all may learn and all may be encouraged.

14:32 And[a] spirits[b] of-prophets are-subject[c] to-prophets,

LEXICON—a. καί (See this word at 11:19): 'and' [Lns, NIGTC, NTC; KJV, NRSV], 'indeed' [AB; NET], 'Yes, he can stop' [ICC], not explicit [Herm, HNTC; all versions except KJV, NET, NRSV].

b. πνεῦμα (BAGD 6.d. p. 677): 'spirit' [AB, Herm, ICC, Lns, NTC; ISV, KJV, NAB, NET, NIV, NJB, NLT, NRSV], 'inspiration' [TNT], 'prophetic inspiration' [REB], 'spiritual utterances' [NIGTC], 'the gift of proclaiming God's message' [TEV], not explicit [CEV]. The phrase πνεύματα προφητῶν 'spirits of prophets' is translated 'the spirits by which prophets speak' [HNTC]. It refers to the prophetic spirit [BAGD; NJB]. See this word at 14:2 and 14:12.

c. pres. pass. indic. of ὑποτάσσω (LN 37.31) (BAGD 1.b.β. p. 848): 'to be subject to' [AB, BAGD, LN, Lns, NIGTC, NTC; ISV, KJV, NET, NRSV], 'to be subject to the control of' [NIV], 'to be under the control of' [Herm, HNTC, ICC; NAB, NJB], 'to be brought under control' [LN]. This entire clause is translated 'remember that people who prophesy are in control of their spirit and can wait their turn' [NLT], 'an inspired man's spirit is under the inspired man's control' [ICC], 'it is for prophets to control prophetic inspiration' [REB], 'the gift of proclaiming God's message should be under the speaker's control' [TEV], 'those who would deliver God's message must keep their inspiration under control' [TNT], 'a prophet should be willing to stop and let someone else speak' [CEV].

QUESTION—What relationship is indicated by καί 'and/indeed'?

It indicates a conjoining relationship [Alf, Ed, EGT, Ho, ICC, Lns, NIC, NTC; KJV, NRSV]: all can prophesy one by one.... *And* the spirits of the prophets.... The καί 'and' adds the subjective reason why prophets should observe rules. Verse 14:31 gave the objective reason [EGT]. This verse gives a second reason why one prophet should be yield to another [Ed, Ho, ICC]. This verse adds a new rule for prophets in addition to 14:29: prophets are to judge other prophets and they are to control their own spirits [MNTC]. It indicates an emphatic relationship [AB; NET]: indeed. It indicates an emphatic conjoining relationship [Gdt]: and indeed.

QUESTION—What is the significance of the lack of articles before the nouns of this verse?
It indicates that this is a general maxim, proverb, or principle having a broad application [Alf, ICC, NIC, TNTC, Vn]: spirits of prophets are subject to prophets.

QUESTION—To what does πνεῦμα 'spirit' refer?
1. It refers to the spiritual gift that the prophet receives [Ed, EGT, Gdt, Herm, Ho, ICC, NCBC, NIGTC, TG, TH; NJB, REB, TEV, TNT]. It refers to the spiritual gift of prophecy [TH]. It probably refers to spiritual gifts rather than the person's own spirit, but the interpretation of the verse is almost the same either way [ICC]. It refers to the Spirit's power that enabled the prophet to speak [Ho]. It refers to the inspiration that the prophet receives [Gdt]. It refers to the prophetic utterance in various forms [Ed].
2. It refers to the prophet's own spirit [Alf, HNTC, Lns, MNTC, NIC, NIC2, Vn; CEV, NLT]. It refers to the person's own spirit under the inspiration of the Holy Spirit [Alf, NIC, NIC2]. It refers to the part of the prophet which receives input from God's Spirit, his soul [Lns].

QUESTION—What does the verse mean?
It means that the prophecy given by the Holy Spirit does not dominate the prophet's will or intelligence [AB]. The gift of prophecy does not control the prophet against his will [Gdt, Ho]. The gift of prophecy is under the control and responsibility of the prophet's will [EGT]. The prophet was fully aware of what the message was and recognized that God had given it to him [MNTC]. Each prophet is in control of himself when prophesying [Ed]. The spirits of Sybil and pythonesses of the pagans controlled those they dominated until the inspiration stopped but this was not true of the Spirit of God [ICC]. Paul's point is that the timing of the prophecy is under the control of the prophet. The verse undergirds Paul's rules for tongues and prophecy. By it he removes inspired speech from being uncontrollable ecstasy and distinguishes it from the mania of the pagan cults [NIC2].

14:33a For God is not (a God) of-disorder[a] but of-peace.[b]

LEXICON—a. ἀκαταστασία (LN 39.36) (BAGD 2. p. 30): 'disorder' [BAGD, Herm, HNTC, NIGTC, NTC; all versions except CEV, KJV, NAB], 'turbulence' [ICC], 'confusion' [AB, Lns; KJV, NAB], 'unruliness' [BAGD], 'riot' [LN]. The phrase οὐ ἐστιν...ακαταστασίας ὁ θεός 'God is not of disorder' is translated positively: 'God wants everything to be done...in order' [CEV]. Ἀκαταστασία refers to a whole whose parts are in conflict [Gdt]. It refers to civil disorder or mutiny [EGT]. It refers to moral disorder [Ed]. It refers to the disorder that would occur if the Holy Spirit were at odds with Himself [Herm].

b. εἰρήνη (LN 22.42) (BAGD 1.c. p. 227): 'peace' [AB, Herm, HNTC, ICC, LN, Lns, NIGTC, NTC; all versions except CEV, TEV], 'harmony and peace' [TEV], 'order' [BAGD], 'tranquility' [LN]. The phrase ἐστιν...ὁ

246   1 CORINTHIANS 14:33

θεός…εἰρήνης 'God is of peace' is translated 'God wants everything to be done…peacefully' [CEV]. Εἰρήνη refers to a whole whose parts are in harmony with each other [Gdt]. It indicates 'well-being' or 'quiet satisfaction' [Lns]. It indicates a deep calm of soul [Ed]. See this word also at 1:3.

QUESTION—What relationship is indicated by γάρ 'for'?

It indicates the grounds for giving all the preceding rules [Alf, Ed, Gdt, NIC2]. It indicates why the spirits of the prophets are subject to the prophets [Ho, Lns]. It gives proof for saying that the gift of prophecy is under control and so a prophet can stop and yield to another prophet [ICC].

QUESTION—How is this clause the grounds for Paul's rules of order?

The worship service should reflect the character of God and this means peace rather than disorder [MNTC, NIC2]. God is not a God of disorder and so cannot be the cause of any disorder in Corinth [HNTC]. The spiritual powers enabling the prophets are from God and since God is a God of peace, the enabling that comes from Him must be capable of control [Ho].

QUESTION—How are the nouns related in the genitive constructions οὐ ὁ θεὸς ἀκαταστασίας 'not the God of disorder', ὁ θεὸς εἰρήνης 'the God of peace'?

They are relationships that describe God [Alf, MNTC, NIC, NIC2; NET]: a God who is not characterized by disorder, but characterized by peace. God is the source of peace not of disorder [NIGTC, TH]. God wants things done orderly and peacefully [CEV, TEV].

DISCOURSE UNIT: 14:33b-36 [AB, NCBC, NIC]. The topic is the silence of wives in the church [AB, NIC], the role of women [NCBC].

DISCOURSE UNIT: 14:33b-35 [NTC]. The topic is orderliness.

14:33b As in all the churches^a of-the saints^b

LEXICON—a. ἐκκλησία (See this word at 11:16): 'church' [AB, Herm, HNTC, Lns, NIGTC, NTC; ISV, KJV, NET, NJB, NLT, NRSV, TEV], 'congregation' [NIV, REB, TNT], 'assembly' [ICC; NAB]. This entire clause is translated 'when God's people meet in church' [CEV]. Ἐκκλησία here refers to a local Christian community [TH].

b. ἅγιος (LN 11.27, 53.46, 88.24): 'saint' [AB, Herm, HNTC, Lns, NTC; ISV, KJV, NET, NIV, NRSV]. The plural forms is translated 'God's people' [LN (11.27); CEV, REB, TEV, TNT], 'God's holy people' [NIGTC; NJB], 'His people' [ICC], 'believers' [NAB], not explicit [NLT]. Ἅγιος is basically an adjective meaning 'devout, godly, dedicated' [LN (53.46)], 'holy, pure, divine' [LN (88.24)]. See this word also at 1:2.

QUESTION—Does this part of 14:33 belong to the preceding or following section?

1. It belongs to 14:33a [Alf, Ed, EGT, HNTC, ICC, NIC2, Rb, TH, Vn; ISV, KJV, NLT]: God is not a God of disorder but of peace as is true in all the churches of the saints. The awkward repetition of the phrase ἐν ταῖς

1 CORINTHIANS 14:33 247

ἐκκλησίαις 'in the churches' here and in 14:34, argues against connecting this with 14:34 (As in all the churches of the saints, let the women in the churches be silent) [EGT, HNTC, ICC, NIC2, TH, Vn]. It is more likely that Paul would begin the next paragraph with its subject rather than a generic support like this preceding the subject [Alf, ICC]. There are several reasons that this belongs to 14:33: (a) verses 34 and 35 may very well not be authentic and early Western tradition separates this phrase from verses 34 and 35; (b) the two rhetorical questions in 14:36 make best sense if joined to this phrase rather than to 35; (c) Paul has used this same appeal (what is done in the churches) three other times in 1 Corinthians (4:17, 7:17, and 11:16) and in each instance the phrase concludes its sentence rather than begins a new one; (d) it is more fitting that such a concern conclude Paul's major point of his argument than that it stand as a prelude to such a minor point as in 14:34 [NIC2]. Paul's style is to name the subject of a new sentence first, not to preface it with an introductory general statement, (see 1 Tim 3:8, 11, 12) [Alf].

2. It belongs to 14:34 [AB, Gdt, GNT, Herm, Ho, Lns, MNTC, NCBC, NIC, NTC, TNTC; all versions except ISV, KJV, NLT]: As is true in all the churches of the saints, let the women be silent in the churches. Paul may be appealing to the traditional custom in all the other churches to support his ruling that women should be silent [Lns]. The maxim in 14:33a reject any further modification so the phrase must go with 14:34 where it supports Paul's command for women to be silent in the assemblies; what occurs elsewhere should be true of the Corinthians themselves [NIC]. It is difficult to conceive that the principle of 14:33b should be supported by no more than that it was the custom of the churches [TNTC]. The maxim, "God is not a God of disorder but of peace," is a complete statement and it seems redundant to add to it. Although the repetition of the phrase 'in the churches' seems awkward, its meaning is not the same in both places. The first occurrence refers to churches in general while the second refers to actual worship services [NTC]. It belongs to 14:34 because: (a) 14:33 already has a fitting conclusion, (b) the truth of 34 is undeniable and needs no further support, and (c) the linking of what is customary in the churches to what is correct behavior for women has a parallel in 11:16 [Ho].

QUESTION—What is the function of this clause?

1. When it is related to 14:33.

It states the range of places where it is true that God is a God of peace [Alf, HNTC, NIC2]. It forms a concluding statement to Paul's teachings on order [EGT, NIC2]. It forms the conclusion of the whole paragraph [TH]. It is evidence that God gives peace to His people as seen in all the churches [EGT].

2. When it is related to 14:34.

This functions as a reminder that this command is not for the Corinthians only [NIC]. Paul is appealing to what is done in all the other churches as a

248   1 CORINTHIANS 14:33

basis for what should be done in Corinth [Gdt, Ho, MNTC, NIC, TNTC]. Paul stresses the fact that this command was not merely locally but universally observed [MNTC].

DISCOURSE UNIT: 14:34–40 [EGT]. The topic is final instructions on church order.

DISCOURSE UNIT: 14:34–36 [ICC, TNTC, Vn]. The topic is regulations concerning women [ICC], women in church [TNTC, Vn].

DISCOURSE UNIT: 14:34–35 [NIC2]. The topic is the order of women.

14:34 The women let-them-be-silent in the churches;[a] for not it-is-permitted[b] to-them to-speak,[c]

LEXICON—a. ἐκκλησία (See this word at 11:18): 'church' [AB, HNTC, ICC, LN, NTC; ISV, KJV, NET, NIV, NRSV], 'church meeting' [BAGD; NLT], 'meeting' [Herm; REB, TEV], 'assembly' [HNTC, ICC, Lns; NJB], 'congregation' [NIGTC; TNT], 'gathering' [NAB], not explicit [CEV]. Ἐκκλησία here refers to the public worship services of the church [NIGTC, NTC, TG].

    b. pres. pass. indic. of ἐπιτρέπω (LN 13.138) (BAGD 1. p. 303): 'to be permitted' [AB, BAGD, Herm, LN, Lns, NTC; KJV, NET, NRSV, TNT], 'to be allowed' [ICC, LN; CEV, ISV, NIV, TEV], 'to have permission' [NJB, REB], 'to have leave' [HNTC]. This passive voice is also translated as a stative: 'to be proper' [NLT]. The complete clause is translated 'they may not speak' [NAB], 'the women should allow for silence' [NIGTC].

    c. pres. act. infin. of λαλέω (See this word at 13:11): 'to speak' [Herm, HNTC, Lns, NTC; all versions except ISV, REB], 'to speak out' [ISV], 'to talk' [AB; REB]. This verb is also translated as a noun phrase: 'utterance, whether in a tongue or in preaching' [ICC].

QUESTION—What relationship is indicated by γάρ 'for'?

It indicates the grounds for the command for women to be silent [Ho, Lns]: let the women be silent in church, *since* it is not permitted for them to speak. This is the reason why Paul gives this prohibition: it is contrary to her role of subordination to the man [Ho]. Paul is pointing out that he is not the source of this command [Lns].

QUESTION—Who or what is the agent of the passive ἐπιτρέπεται 'it is permitted'?

The implied agent is probably Christian custom [TH].

QUESTION—What sense of λαλέω 'to speak' is intended here?

It refers to speaking in public [Alf, Gdt, Ho, Lns]. In light of 11:5, praying and prophesying by women in worship are not indicated here [AB, NTC, TNTC]. The command is not absolute, see Acts 2:18 and 21:9 [TNTC]. Verse 11:5 shows that Paul does not forbid women to pray and prophesy or sing psalms and hymns in worship. This prohibition to speak refers back to 14:29 in which it is stated that some prophets judged the prophecies of others. In this context the women are not to take part in the judgment of their husbands' prophecies [NTC]. In light of 14:11:5 this indicates that women may not prophesy when there is an official meeting of the congregation [NIC]. In view of 11:5 it is the public use of prophecy that is prohibited [Ho]. Paul has prophecy especially in mind but also speaking in tongues [MNTC]. The permission to pray and prophesy of 11:5 is now withdrawn [Ed]. Paul has in mind situations in which wives might publicly challenge what their husbands have said or otherwise embarrass them by public verbal give and take [AB, NIGTC]. It is difficult to see that this rule is anything but an absolute prohibition to women to speak in church. At the same time it is difficult to understand how it fits with 11:5 and 13 and with the words "each one" of 11:26 and the word "all" of 11:31 [NIC2]. It must refer to teaching [Alf, EGT, ICC, Vn], or exercising authority over a man (see 1 Timothy 2:12) [EGT]. It refers to any oral leadership or ministry of God's Word [Vn].

but let-them-be-subjected,[a]

LEXICON—a. pres. pass. impera. of ὑποτάσσω (LN 36.18): 'to be submissive' [NTC; NLT], 'to be in submission' [NET, NIV], 'to be in subjection' [HNTC, Lns], 'to place oneself in submission' [ISV], 'to be subordinate' [AB; NRSV], 'to be under obedience' [KJV]. This passive is also translated actively: 'to keep (one's) place' [REB], 'to stay in the background' [TNT], 'to subordinate oneself' [Herm], 'to listen' [CEV], 'to obey, to submit to' [LN]. This verb is also translated as a noun: 'subjection' [ICC]. The complete clause is translated 'they must not be in charge' [TEV], 'submissiveness is indicated for them' [NAB], 'theirs is a subordinate part' [NJB], 'for there exists no permission for them to speak' [NIGTC]. The present tense indicates a continuative aspect [AB, NIC]: continue to be subordinate. See this word also at 14:32.

QUESTION—To whom are the women to be submissive?

The women are to be subject to their husbands [AB, NIC, TG]. See Ephesians 5:21, 22 and Colossians 3:18 where the same verb is used in reference to husbands [TG]. Verses 11:3–15 show that it is to her husband that she is to be subject [NIC]. The reference here is general and does not indicate husbands specifically (see Ephesians 5:21) [TNTC]. It is likely that women are to be subject to the church as a whole in worship [Gdt, NIC2]. It is to man that the woman is subordinate [Ho].

as the law[a] **also says.**

LEXICON—a. νόμος (BAGD 4.a. p. 543): 'law' [AB, BAGD, NIGTC; KJV, NAB, NET, NLT, NRSV, REB], 'Law' [Herm, HNTC, Lns, NTC; ISV, NIV, NJB, TNT], 'Law of Moses' [CEV], 'Jewish Law' [TEV], 'rule (of subjection)' [ICC]. Νόμος here refers to the Pentateuch [BAGD]. See this word also at 14:21.

QUESTION—To what specific law does Paul refer?

It refers to the creation order in Genesis 2:18–24 in which Adam was first created and then Eve as his helper. It is this helper role on which Paul bases the subjection of a woman to her husband [NTC]. The Law does not say this.

When Paul elsewhere refers to the Law he always quotes it (see 9:8 and 14:21). In no other place does he cite the Law like this as a basis for Christian behavior [NIC2]. He may refer to Genesis 3:16 which states, "...your desire shall be for your husband, and he shall rule over you." [AB, Gdt, HNTC, ICC, MNTC, NIC, TH, TNTC]. He may refer to the Old Testament in general [Ho, Lns]. It probably refers to the creation accounts in Genesis 1:26 and 2:21 [NCBC, TNTC]. This principle was in the OT and followed by Jewish synagogues [MNTC].

14:35 And if they-desire to-learn[a] anything, let-them-ask their-own husbands at home;

LEXICON—a. aorist act. infin. of μανθάνω (See this word at 14:31): 'to learn' [AB, HNTC, Lns, NIGTC, NTC; ISV, KJV, NAB], 'to know' [Herm; CEV, NJB, NRSV, REB, TNT], 'to find out about' [NET, TEV], 'to inquire about' [NIV]. This verb is also translated as a phrase: 'questions to ask' [NLT], 'asking questions' [ICC].

QUESTION—What relationship is indicated by δέ 'and/but'?

It indicates a relationship of degree that takes the command of 14:34 and raises it to a finer degree [Gdt, ICC, Lns, NIC]: let them be submissive *and moreover if* they desire.... It indicates a conjoining relationship [NTC; KJV]: *and*. All other versions leave this word untranslated.

QUESTION—What words are emphasized in this clause?

The words ἐν οἴκῳ 'at home' are stressed [ICC, Lns, NTC], in contrast to the words 'in church' [ICC, NTC]. The word μαθεῖν 'to learn' is emphasized [Alf, NTC].

QUESTION—Why did Paul give this prohibition?

It may have been because questioning in public was a problem in Corinth [AB, Alf, Lns, MNTC, NCBC]. The questioning may have been out loud and occasionally inappropriate, rowdy, piercing and excessive and threatened good order in the meetings [AB]. In Corinth there was a movement to put women on a par with men in respect to public speaking and leadership [EGT].

for it-is shameful[a] for-a-woman to-speak in church.

LEXICON—a. αἰσχρός (See this word at 11:6): 'shameful' [ICC, Lns; NJB, NRSV, TNT], 'disgraceful' [AB, NTC; CEV, NIV, TEV], 'shocking' [REB], 'inappropriate' [ISV], 'improper' [NLT], 'unseemly' [Herm]. This adjective is also translated as a noun: 'a shame' [KJV], 'disgrace' [NIGTC; NAB], 'a disgraceful thing' [HNTC], not explicit [NET].

QUESTION—What is implied by αἰσχρός 'shameful'?

It is implied that it is shameful in the sight of God since Paul has appealed to the Law in the previous verse and does not qualify this word further [Lns]. It is implied that it is shameful in the opinion of people in general [HNTC, NIC]. It is implied that she will bring shame on her husband by doing this [AB, NTC]. It is implied that the woman will disgrace herself [TH].

DISCOURSE UNIT: 14:36–40 [Alf, NIC2, NTC]. The topic is concluding confrontation and summary [NIC2], conclusion [Alf, NTC].

14:36 Or (did) the word of God go-out[a] from[b] you,
LEXICON—a. aorist act. indic. of ἐξέρχομαι (LN 15.40) (BAGD 2.b.α. p. 275): 'to go out' [LN, Lns], 'to go forth' [AB, HNTC, NIGTC], 'to originate' [BAGD, NTC; ISV, NAB, NIV, NRSV, REB], 'to start' [CEV, TNT], 'to come out' [KJV], 'to come' [TEV], 'to begin' [NET, NLT], 'to be the source of' [NJB], 'to first go forth' [Herm]. This whole clause was translated 'What? are you the Mother-Church' [ICC].
  b. ἀπό with genitive object (LN 90.15): 'from' [AB, Herm, HNTC, ICC, LN, NIGTC; KJV, TEV, TNT], 'with' [NTC; CEV, ISV, NAB, NET, NIV, NLT, NRSV, REB], not explicit [ICC]. This preposition is also translated as a noun: '(you are) the source' [NJB].
QUESTION—With what does this verse connect or refer?
  It connects logically back to 14:33b [Gdt, NIC, NIC2, NTC, TG, TH, TNTC]: as is true in all the churches of the saints, or did the word of God originate with you? It refers to 14:35 [EGT]: let them ask their husbands at home for it is shameful for a woman to speak in church, or did the word of God originate with you? It refers to everything that Paul has been talking about: women worshiping without veils, people getting drunk at the Supper, people speaking in tongues without interpretation, prophets refusing to yield to each other and women asking questions in public worship [Alf, Ed, ICC]. These questions refer to some confrontation between Paul and the Corinthians over their attitude toward Paul on some issue. This probably had to do with their idea of what it meant to be πνευματικός 'spiritual' and the proper place of tongues in church [NIC2].
QUESTION—What is implied by the word ἤ 'or'?
  The word ἤ 'or' is elliptical and implies, 'Or if this is not what you think, (then was it from you that the Word of God went out?)' The word is elliptical and implies, 'Or if what I have said is not enough, then…' [EGT]. The word is elliptical and implies, 'Or if you will not admit what I say, then…' [Gdt].
QUESTION—To whom does 'you' refer?
  Since μόνους 'only' is masculine, it is likely that Paul is addressing the whole church [AB].
QUESTION—To what does ὁ λόγος τοῦ θεοῦ 'the word of God' refer?
  It refers to the gospel [Ed, Gdt, HNTC, Ho, NIC2, NTC, TH, Vn]. It refers to the message from God [TG].

or did-it-come[a] only to you?
LEXICON—a. aorist act. indic. of καταντάω (LN 15.84) (BAGD 2.b. p. 415): 'to come' [BAGD, Herm, Lns, NTC; KJV, NAB, NET, NJB, REB, TEV, TNT], 'to reach' [HNTC, LN; CEV, ISV, NIV, NRSV], 'to end with' [NLT], 'to draw near' [AB], 'to come to, to arrive' [LN]. This whole

clause was translated 'are you the only church that you make such claims?' [ICC], 'are you the only ones to whom it came?' [NIGTC].

QUESTION—What is implied by the word ἤ 'or'?

This 'or' means, 'Or if not this, then…' [Lns].

QUESTION—What does this verse imply?

It implies that if the Corinthians did not create the Word of God they should obey it, and if the Word of God did not come to only to them then they along with all other Christians should be subject themselves to it [MNTC]. It implies that the condition which this verse addresses actually existed in Corinth [NIC, TNTC]. It implies that Christians should not independently decide how Christians should believe [TH]. It implies that the Corinthians are claiming a huge amount of authority and independence [ICC].

QUESTION—Are these question real or rhetorical?

They are rhetorical and expect a negative response [AB, Lns, NTC, TG, TH, Vn; CEV]: the Word of God did not originate with you and you are not the only ones to whom it came. The truth is that the Gospel originated with Jesus Christ. He sent Paul to be an apostle to Gentiles and the Corinthians were among those Gentiles [NTC]. (No commentary treated these questions as real.)

QUESTION—What is the function of these rhetorical questions?

They function as a reprimand to the Corinthian behavior [NIC, NIC2]. They function to get the Corinthians to see that they must consider the customs and thinking of the other churches [NCBC, NIC, NIC2, TNTC]. They function as an angry protest to the Corinthian behavior [EGT]. They show Paul's indignation [ICC]. They function to sting the haughty Corinthians [Lns]. They challenge the Corinthian behavior [MNTC]. They are sarcastic [Gdt, ICC, MNTC, NIC2]. They are ironical [Lns, TH, TNTC]. Verses 1:17, 11:23 and 15:3 give the correct answers to Paul's questions and show that he was speaking ironically [TH]. They criticize those Corinthians who were disregarding his instructions by reminding them that there were other churches who also had God's message [TG].

DISCOURSE UNIT: 14:37–40 [AB, ICC, NCBC, NIC, TNTC]. The topic is an injunction to proper order [AB], the summing up [NCBC], the conclusion [ICC, NIC, TNTC].

DISCOURSE UNIT: 14:37–39 [Vn]. The topic is use of gifts should be orderly.

14:37 If anyone thinks[a] (himself) to-be (a) prophet or spiritual,[b]

LEXICON—a. pres. act. indic. of δοκέω (See this word at 12:23): 'to think' [Herm, HNTC, Lns, NIGTC, NTC; ISV, KJV, NAB, NIV, TNT], 'to claim' [ICC; NJB, NLT, NRSV, REB], 'to think of oneself' [CEV], 'to consider oneself' [NET], 'to suppose' [TEV], 'to seem' [AB].

b. πνευματικός (See this word at 10:3): 'spiritual' [NTC; KJV], 'very spiritual' [NLT], 'inspired' [REB], 'pneumatic' [Herm], 'spiritually gifted' [Lns; NIV]. This adjective is also translated as a noun phrase: 'a spiritual person' [AB, HNTC; CEV, ISV, NET], 'a man of the Spirit' [NAB], 'a man with spiritual gifts' [TNT], '(to have a) spiritual gift' [TEV], '(to have) spiritual powers' [NJB, NRSV], 'a person "of the Spirit"' [NIGTC]. It is also translated as a verb: 'to be inspired' [ICC].

QUESTION—What is the main point of this verse?

The main point is that any person who claimed to be spiritual should be able to recognize that Paul's authority was from the Lord [EGT]. The main point is that all who have received spiritual gifts should submit to Paul's authority [NIC]. Paul's point is that any person claiming to be a prophet or possessor of any other gift, should show the genuineness of his gift by acknowledging that what Paul taught as an apostle was of God [MNTC].

QUESTION—To what does πνευματικός 'spiritual' refer?

It refers to a person endowed with a spiritual gift by the Holy Spirit [AB, Alf, EGT, Ho, Lns; NIV, NJB, NRSV, TNT]. It refers to a person endowed with the spiritual gift of speaking in tongues [NIC, Rb]. It refers primarily to a person endowed with the gift of tongues but also to one having any spiritual gift [MNTC]. It refers to a spiritual person [HNTC, NIC2; CEV, ISV, KJV, NET, NLT]. Being 'spiritual' was the central issue that Paul was addressing. The Corinthians thought of themselves as spiritual but they were not sure about Paul. They considered the gifts of tongues evidence of their spirituality. It was because they thought of themselves as being spiritual that Paul talked to them in this way [NIC2].

QUESTION—What is the significance of the phrase εἴ τις δοκεῖ 'if anyone thinks'?

Paul has used this expression in three major parts of the epistle (3:18, 8:2 and here) and in each place he is focusing on the Corinthians' own estimate of their spirituality [NIC2].

let-him-know[a] that the-things I-write to-you are a-command[b] of-the Lord;

LEXICON—a. pres. act. impera. of ἐπιγινώσκω (BAGD 2.a. p. 291): 'to know' [NTC; CEV, NAB, TNT], 'to recognize' [AB, BAGD, Herm, HNTC, ICC, NIGTC; NJB, NLT, REB], 'to acknowledge' [ISV, KJV, NET, NIV, NRSV], 'to make acknowledgement' [Lns], 'to realize' [TEV]. The present imperative indicates a continuous aspect [EGT, ICC, Vn]: 'let him continue to acknowledge' [EGT], 'let him continually take knowledge' [ICC], 'let him constantly and completely understand' [Vn]. See this word also at 13:12.

b. ἐντολή (LN 33.330) (BAGD 2.d. p. 269): 'command' [BAGD, Herm, ICC, NIGTC, NTC; ISV, NET, NIV, NLT, NRSV, TEV, TNT], 'order' [BAGD, LN], 'commandment' [AB, BAGD, LN; KJV, NAB, NJB]. It is also translated as a verb: 'to have the Lord's authority' [REB]. This noun is also translated as a clause: 'what the Lord has commanded' [CEV]. The phrase ἐστὶν ἐντολή 'are a command' is translated 'to come from (the Lord)' [HNTC], 'to be of (the Lord)' [Lns].

QUESTION—What is meant by ἐπιγνωσκέτω 'let him know'?
It means 'let him acknowledge' [EGT, Gdt, Lns, NCBC, NIC2, TH; ISV, KJV, NET, NIV, NRSV]. It means 'let him know' or 'understand' [Ed, ICC, NTC; CEV, NAB, TNT]. It means 'let him recognize' [AB, BAGD, HNTC, ICC, NIC2, NIGTC, TNTC; NJB, NLT, REB].

QUESTION—To what does ἃ γράφω 'the things I write' refer?
They refer to the whole letter the Paul has written [EGT, Vn]. It refers to what Paul has written about the order of worship and the things that edify the church [AB]. They refer to the entire contents of this chapter about the use of spiritual gifts [Ho, TH]. They refer to all that Paul has been saying about disorder in public worship [ICC]. They refer to chapters 12–14 [Lns]. They refer to everything Paul has written about this matter but especially about the need to make speech intelligible, to maintain order in worship and to strive to build others up [NIC2].

QUESTION—What word is emphasized in this verse?
The word κυρίου 'of the Lord' is emphasized [Alf, ICC, NIC2, TNTC, Vn]. These words are very emphatic [ICC]. It is Christ who is the source of Paul's instructions [NIC2].

QUESTION—To whom does 'the Lord' refer?
It refers to Jesus Christ [Ed, EGT, Ho, NCBC, NTC, TG, Vn]. It refers to God [MNTC].

QUESTION—What does κυρίου ἐστὶν ἐντολή 'they are a command of the Lord' mean?
It does not mean that Jesus himself gave this as a command but that he used Paul as his spokesman or his authority was behind it [EGT, HNTC, ICC, Lns, NCBC, NIC2, TG, TH, TNTC, Vn]. It means that Paul's authority was received by a direct revelation of Jesus Christ [Ed].

14:38 And if anyone does-not-recognize[a] (this), he-is-not-recognized.[b]

TEXT—Instead of the indicative verb ἀγνοεῖται 'he is not recognized', some manuscripts have the imperative mood ἀγνοείτω 'let him not be recognized'. GNT selects the indicative mood 'he is ignored' with a B rating, indicating that the text is almost certain. The indicative mood 'he is not recognized' is also taken by AB, EGT, Herm, HNTC, Lns, NCBC, NIC, NIC2, NTC, TG, TNTC; NET, NIV, NJB, NLT, and REB. The imperative mood 'let him not be recognized' is taken by Gdt, Ho, ICC, LN (30.38), Vn; CEV, ISV, KJV, NAB, NRSV, TEV, and TNT.

LEXICON—a. pres. act. indic. of ἀγνοέω (LN 30.38) (BAGD 2. p. 11): 'not to recognize' [NIGTC; NET, NJB, NLT, NRSV], 'to not know' [Herm], 'to ignore' [LN; ISV, NAB, NIV, TNT], 'not to pay attention to' [LN; CEV, TEV], 'not to acknowledge' [REB], 'to be ignorant (of)' [KJV], 'to disregard' [BAGD]. See this word also at 10:1 and 12:1.

b. pres. pass. indic. of ἀγνοέω (See this word just above): 'to be not recognized' [NIGTC; NET, NJB, NLT, NRSV], 'to not be known' [Herm], 'to be ignored' [LN; ISV, NAB, NIV, TNT], 'to pay no attention to' [**LN**; CEV, TEV], 'not to be acknowledged' [REB], 'to be ignorant' [KJV], 'to be disregarded' [BAGD].

QUESTION—What is meant by ἀγνοέω 'not to recognize'?

It means to fail to acknowledge something [NIC2; REB]. It means refusal to acknowledge something [Ed, Ho, TG, Vn]. It means to be ignorant of something [ICC; KJV]. It means to ignore something [ISV, NAB, NIV, TNT], not to pay attention to something [LN; CEV, TEV], to disregard something [BAGD].

QUESTION—What is the object of ἀγνοεῖ 'he does not recognize'?

The object is the fact that Christ's or God's authority is behind Paul's instructions [Ed, EGT, HNTC, Ho, ICC, Lns, NCBC, TG, TNTC]: if anyone does not recognize the Lord's authority in my command. The object is both what is best for edifying the church and Paul's instructions concerning this [AB]. The object is the command of the Lord [TH]. The object is Paul's instructions and it means that if a person did not observe Paul's instructions, he would not be recognized [NIC, NTC; CEV]. The object is a knowledge of salvation [Herm].

QUESTION—Who is the agent of the passive indicative ἀγνοεῖται 'he is not recognized'?

1. God is the agent [AB, BAGD, EGT, HNTC, NIC, NIC2, NTC, TG]: God does not recognize him. It means that God will say to the person, "I know you not" (see 8:3, 2 Timothy 2:19 and John 5:42). But Paul also will not acknowledge him [EGT]. This indicates that there is a sentence of judgment on this person [NIC2, NTC].
2. Paul is the agent [HNTC]: Paul does not recognize him. It means that Paul does not recognize him to be truly inspired.
3. Paul and the church are the agents [Herm, Lns]: Paul and the church do not recognize him. They do not acknowledge that person as being a prophet and spiritually gifted [Lns].

QUESTION—What is implied by the reading ἀγνοεῖται 'he is not recognized'?

It implies that he/she is not recognized as a spiritual person [HNTC, Lns, NCBC]. It implies that he will ignore the authority of God in what Paul says to his own peril [TNTC]. It implies that on judgment day God will ignore that person [NTC].

QUESTION—What is implied by the reading ἀγνοείτω 'let him not be recognized'?

It implies 'let him be ignorant' that is, he must be left as he is in his unedifying condition [ICC]. It implies let him be ignorant [Gdt, Ho; KJV] at his own risk [Gdt]. It implies that his appalling spiritual condition must continue [Vn]. It implies that the person's own claim to be a prophet or a spiritual person should not be acknowledged [REB]. It implies not to pay attention to that person [CEV, TEV]. It implies to ignore that person [ISV, NAB, TNT]. It implies that the person is not to be recognized [NRSV].

14:39 So-then,[a] [my] brothers, set-your-hearts[b] to-prophesy,
TEXT—The word μου 'my' does not occur in some manuscripts. It is included by GNT in brackets, indicating difficulty in deciding to include it in the text. Μου is also included by AB, Herm, HNTC, ICC, Lns, NIC2, NIGTC; NTC; all versions except KJV, NET, NLT. It is omitted by KJV, NET, and NLT.
LEXICON—a. ὥστε (See this word at 10:12): 'so then' [ICC, NIGTC; NET, TEV], 'so' [AB, HNTC, NTC; NJB, NLT, NRSV, TNT], 'therefore' [ISV, NIV], 'wherefore' [Lns; KJV], 'in short' [Herm; REB], not explicit [CEV, NAB].
  b. pres. act. impera. of ζηλόω (See this word at 12:31): 'to set one's heart' [NAB, TEV], 'to be eager' [CEV, NET, NIV, NJB, NLT, NRSV, REB, TNT], 'to desire' [ISV], 'to eagerly desire' [NTC], 'to long earnestly' [ICC], 'to be zealous' [AB], 'to strive after' [Herm, HNTC], 'to strive zealously' [Lns], 'to be zealously concerned about' [NIGTC], 'to covet' [KJV]. The present imperative indicates a continuous aspect [ICC, NIGTC, NTC]: continue to set your hearts.
QUESTION—What is the function of ὥστε 'so'?
  It functions as a strong inferential conjunction signaling a conclusion to his argument [NIC2]. It marks the conclusion of Paul's whole argument [TH]. It introduces Paul's summary [NTC]. It marks the transition from discussion to exhortation [EGT, ICC].
QUESTION—What is the function of the vocative ἀδελφοί μου 'my brothers'?
  It functions to mark the transition from the argument to the conclusion [TH]. It functions as an affectionate term following the stern reprimand [ICC, NTC]. It functions as a brotherly appeal to the Corinthians [Lns].

and (do) not forbid[a] to-speak in-tongues;
LEXICON—a. pres. act. impera. of κωλύω (LN 13.146) (BAGD 2. p. 461): 'to forbid' [AB, BAGD, Herm, HNTC, ICC, LN, Lns, NIGTC, NTC; all versions except CEV, ISV, NJB], 'to hinder' [BAGD, LN], 'to suppress' [NJB], 'to prevent' [BAGD, LN; ISV], 'to stop' [CEV]. The present negative imperative indicates that this was going on and should be stopped [NTC]: stop forbidding people to speak in tongues.

14:40 But/and[a] let-be-done everything decently[b] and in order.[c]
LEXICON—a. δέ (See this word at 11:2): 'but' [ICC, Lns, NTC; all versions except KJV, NET, TEV], 'only' [NIGTC], 'and' [HNTC; NET], not explicit [AB; KJV, TEV].
  b. εὐσχημόνως (LN **66.4**, 88.50) (BAGD p. 327): 'decently' [LN (88.50), NTC; KJV, NRSV, REB, TNT], 'properly' [AB, BAGD; CEV, NAB, NLT], 'fittingly' [NIGTC]. This adverb is also translated as a phrase: 'in a proper way' [**LN** (66.4); ISV, TEV], 'in a proper fashion' [NJB], 'in a decent manner' [NET], 'in a fitting way' [NIV], 'in accordance with natural feelings' [ICC], 'in a seemly way' [Herm, Lns], 'with propriety, in a becoming manner' [LN (66.4)]. It is also translated as an adjective: 'decent' [HNTC], 'proper' [LN (66.4)].

c. τάξις (LN **62.7**) (BAGD 2. p. 803): 'order' [CEV, KJV, NAB, NLT, NRSV, REB, TNT], 'orderly way' [ISV, NIV, TEV], 'orderly manner' [NET], 'ordered manner' [NIGTC], 'orderly fashion' [NJB], 'good order' [AB, LN], 'right order' [LN]. The phrase κατὰ τάξιν 'according to order' is translated 'in order' [BAGD, NTC; CEV, KJV, NAB, NLT, NRSV, REB, TNT], 'in good order' [AB], 'in an orderly manner' [BAGD, HNTC, **LN**; NET], 'in an orderly way' [Herm; ISV, NIV, TEV], 'in an orderly fashion' [NJB], 'in an ordered manner' [NIGTC], 'in due order' [Lns], 'in accordance with established rule' [ICC]. Τάξις implies doing things one at a time [HNTC, Lns, MNTC].

QUESTION—What is implied by this verse?

It implies that in Corinth things were not being done decently and in order [NIC2, NTC]. Verse 14:33 also supports this implication [NIC2]. It functions to close the whole section on worship, chapters 11–14 [Gdt]. It functions to summarize the argument of 14:26–33 [NIC2].

QUESTION—What relationship is indicated by δέ 'but/and'?
1. It indicates contrast [ICC, Lns, NTC; all versions except KJV, NET, TEV]: do not forbid to speak in tongues, *but* let everything be done decently and in order.
2. It indicates a conjoining relationship [HNTC; NET]: and. It adds a caution to 14:39 concerning the use of prophecy and tongues [Alf, EGT, ICC]: *only, provided that* everything be done decently and in order.

DISCOURSE UNIT: 15:1–58 [AB, Alf, Ed, EGT, Gdt, Herm, HNTC, Ho, ICC, Lns, NCBC, NIC2, NIGTC, NTC, TG, TH, TNTC, Vn; KJV, NAB, NJB, REB]. The topic is the resurrection [AB, Alf, Ed, EGT, Gdt, Herm, HNTC, Ho, ICC, Lns, NIGTC, NTC, TH, TNTC, Vn; KJV, NAB, NJB, REB], the resurrection of believers [NIC2, TG], the question of resurrection [NCBC].

DISCOURSE UNIT: 15:1–34 [Gdt, Ho; NJB]. The topic is the fact of the resurrection.

DISCOURSE UNIT: 15:1–11 [AB, Alf, Ed, EGT, Gdt, GNT, HNTC, ICC, Lns, MNTC, NCBC, NIC, NIC2, NIGTC, TG, TH, TNTC, Vn; CEV, ISV, NAB, NET, NIV, NLT, TEV]. The topic is the resurrection of Christ [Alf, EGT, GNT, ICC, Lns, NIC2, TG, TH, TNTC, Vn; CEV, ISV, NAB, NET, NIV, NLT, TEV], the received tradition about the resurrection [AB], the gospel [HNTC, NCBC, NIC], the evidence for Christ's resurrection [Ed, MNTC], the reality of Christ's resurrection [NIGTC].

DISCOURSE UNIT: 15:1–8 [NTC]. The topic is the resurrection of Christ [NTC].

DISCOURSE UNIT: 15:1–4 [ICC, Vn]. The topic is the creed delivered to the Corinthians by St. Paul [ICC], the doctrine of faith as delivered by the Apostle [Vn].

15:1 Now[a] I-make-known[b] to-you, brothers, the gospel[c] that I proclaimed[d] to-you,

LEXICON—a. δέ (See this word at 11:2): 'now' [AB, ICC, Lns, NIGTC, NTC; ISV, NET, NIV, NLT, NRSV, TNT], 'and now' [REB, TEV], 'but' [Herm], 'moreover' [KJV], not explicit [HNTC; CEV, NAB, NJB].
- b. pres. act. indic. of γνωρίζω (See this word at 12:3): 'to make known' [Herm, NTC; ISV], 'to want to remind' [NAB, NIV, TEV, TNT], 'to remind' [Lns; NLT, NRSV, REB], 'to have to remind' [ICC], 'to declare' [KJV], 'to want to make clear' [NET], 'to want to make quite clear' [NJB], 'to want someone to remember' [CEV], 'to want to restore one's full knowledge' [NIGTC], 'to inform' [AB], 'to draw attention to' [HNTC].
- c. εὐαγγέλιον (LN 33.217) (BAGD 1.c. p. 318): 'gospel' [BAGD, Herm, LN, Lns, NIGTC, NTC; ISV, KJV, NAB, NET, NIV, NJB, REB], 'Gospel' [HNTC], 'good news' [AB, BAGD, LN; NRSV], 'Good News' [NLT, TEV, TNT], 'message' [CEV], 'Glad-tidings' [ICC].
- d. aorist mid. (deponent = act.) indic. of εὐαγγελίζω (LN 33.215) (BAGD 2.a.α. p. 317): 'to proclaim' [AB, NIGTC; ISV, NRSV], 'to preach' [BAGD, Herm, HNTC, Lns, NTC; CEV, KJV, NAB, NET, NIV, NJB, NLT, REB, TEV, TNT], 'to announce the gospel, to tell the good news' [LN], 'to gladden someone' [ICC].

QUESTION—What relationship is indicated by δέ 'now'?

It indicates a transition [AB, Alf, ICC, Lns, NTC; ISV, NET, NIV, NLT, NRSV, TNT]: now. It indicates a consecutive relationship [NIC2]: next. It indicates a conjoining relationship [Gdt; KJV]: moreover. It indicates that Paul is now taking up a new subject [Ho, NIGTC, TH].

QUESTION—What is the significance of the word ἀδελφός 'brother'?

It indicates the beginning of a new section [NIGTC, TH]. It indicates that Paul is addressing something controversial to the Corinthians [NTC]. Paul wants to assure the Corinthians that he considers them to be fellow Christians [MNTC]. It refers to fellow Christians [MNTC, NIGTC, NTC, TH]. The term includes women as well as men [NIC2, NTC, TH].

QUESTION—What is implied by the words γνωρίζω 'I make known'?

It means here 'to remind' them of something they knew [Alf, HNTC, ICC, Lns, NIC2, NIGTC, NTC; CEV, NAB, NIV, NLT, NRSV, REB, TEV, TNT]. It means 'to inform' them of something [AB, Ho, ICC, NIC, NTC; KJV]. It implies a trace of reprimand [Alf, EGT, ICC, Rb, TNTC]. It implies that Paul is humiliating the Corinthians for the corruption that had crept into their conception of the Gospel [Gdt].

that also you-received,[a] in which also you-stand,[b]

LEXICON—a. aorist act. indic. of παραλαμβάνω (BAGD 3.b. p. 619): 'to receive' [AB, Herm, HNTC, ICC, NIGTC, NTC; KJV, NAB, NET, NIV, NRSV, REB, TNT], 'to accept' [BAGD; ISV, NJB], 'to welcome' [NLT], 'to believe' [CEV, TEV]. It indicates more than simply hearing the

Gospel [TH], it implies that they had become Christians [NIC, NIC2]. See this word also at 11:23.
  b. perf. act. indic. of ἵστημι (LN **13.29**) (BAGD II.2.c.β. p. 382): 'to stand' [Herm, HNTC, Lns, NTC; KJV, NET, NRSV], 'to take one's stand' [AB, NIGTC; ISV, NIV, NJB, REB], 'to stand firm' [ICC; NAB, TEV, TNT], 'to continue firm' [**LN**], 'to remain firmly, to continue steadfastly' [LN], 'to stand in (grace), to be in (grace)' [BAGD]. The phrase ἐν ᾧ καὶ ἐστήκατε 'in which you stand' is translated 'and trusted' [CEV], 'and still do (welcome the Good News) now' [NLT]. See this word also at 10:12.

QUESTION—What is implied by 'standing in the gospel'?

It means to continue to believe the gospel [CEV]. It means that the Corinthians continued to welcome the Good News and that their faith was built on it [NLT]. They remain loyal to the message that Paul had proclaimed [TG]. It implies being established and continuing resolute in faith like a tree stands when well rooted [Lns].

15:2 by^a which also you-are-being-saved,

LEXICON—a. διά with genitive object (See this word at 13:12): 'by' [Herm, NTC; CEV, KJV, NAB, NET, NIV, NJB, REB, TEV], 'through' [HNTC, Lns, NIGTC; NRSV, TNT], 'by means of' [AB, ICC]. This entire clause is translated 'and it is this Good News that saves you' [NLT], 'and which is now bringing you salvation' [REB]. Διά indicates the means by which something is brought about [NIC].

QUESTION—What is the significance of the present indicative σῴζεσθε 'you are being saved'?

The tense is present continuative [TNTC]. The present tense indicates that salvation is both effective and progressive [NTC]. In the past, they received the gospel and on that gospel they took their stand and still do. Salvation is now in the present and it is also in progress until it is completed at the Day of the Lord [NIC2, NIGTC]. The present tense means that they are being saved and could be translated 'you will be saved' since this tense can refer to anticipation of future events [TH].

QUESTION—Who is the agent of the passive σῴζεσθε 'you are being saved'?

The agent is God [NIC, NIC2, NTC]: God is saving you. God, through the gospel, saves someone through Christ [NIC2]. The agent is Christ [TNTC]: Christ is saving you.

with-which word I-proclaimed^a to-you

LEXICON—a. aorist mid. (deponent = act.) indic. of εὐαγγελίζω (See this word at 15:1): 'to proclaim' [AB, NIGTC; ISV, NRSV], 'to preach' [Herm, HNTC, NTC; KJV, NAB, NET, NIV, NJB, TEV], 'to preach the gospel' [Lns; REB], 'to gladden someone' [ICC], not explicit [CEV, NLT]. The clause τίνι λόγῳ εὐηγγελισάμην 'which word I preached' is translated 'my account of it' [TNT].

QUESTION—With what should the clause, 'with which word I preached to you' be connected?

1. It should be connected with the words, 'if you hold fast' [AB, Alf, Gdt, Ho, ICC, MNTC, NIC, NIGTC, NTC, TG, TH; all versions except REB]: if you hold fast *to the word I preached to you*. Τίνι λόγῳ 'with what word' indicates 'in which manner'. The Corinthians are saved by the gospel if they hold it fast *in the way*, that is, with the same contents as Paul had preached it to them [Ho, NIC]. Τίνι λόγῳ 'with what word' means both the content of what Paul said as well as the manner in which he expressed it [ICC].
2. It should be connected with 'I make known' [Ed, Lns, NIC2, Rb, TNTC, Vn; REB]: I make known, (I say), *in what words I preached the gospel to you*. Paul is saying that he reminds the Corinthians by means of what statement he had preached the gospel to them. The emphasis is on τίνι λόγῳ 'by means of what statement' because he has in mind the vital essence of the gospel contained in that statement. The contents of the statement are given in 15:3–4 [Lns]. Paul is saying, 'I make known to you the gospel, that is, with what word I preached to you'. The contents of 'word' are to be given in 15:3–5 [NIC2].
3. It should be connected with the implied words 'I ask/I ask you to note' [EGT, HNTC]: I ask you to note *with what form of words I preached the Gospel to you* [HNTC]. Although grammatically connected with 'I make known', τίνι λόγῳ, being so far from it, forms its own clause and means: 'In what word (I ask) did I preach the gospel to you? (You will recall) if you hold it fast—unless you believed in vain' [EGT].

QUESTION—To what does λόγος 'word' refer?

It refers to the Good News [EGT, Ho, NIC, NTC, TG; NAB, NET, NIV, NJB, NLT, NRSV, TEV]. It refers to the facts named in 15:3–5 [Lns, NIC2]. It refers to the fact of Christ's resurrection [Ed, Vn]. It refers to the actual words Paul used when he proclaimed the Good News [HNTC, TNTC; REB, TNT]. It refers to both the form and the meaning of what Paul preached [ICC].

QUESTION—What words are emphasized in this clause?

The words τίνι λόγῳ 'with what word' are placed forward in its clause for emphasis [Alf, Ho, ICC, Lns].

if you-hold-fast,[a]

LEXICON—a. pres. act. indic. of κατέχω (LN **31.48**) (BAGD 1.b.α. p. 422): 'to hold fast' [AB, BAGD, Herm, HNTC, ICC, Lns, NIGTC, NTC; NAB, REB, TNT], 'to hold firmly' [CEV, ISV, NET, NIV, NRSV, TEV], 'to believe firmly' [NLT], 'to continue to believe and practice' [**LN**], 'to keep' [NJB], 'to keep in memory' [BAGD; KJV]. See this word also at 11:2.

QUESTION—What does κατέχετε 'you hold fast' mean?
It means to continue to believe and practice the Good News [LN]. It means to remain committed to the Good News [TG]. It means to affirm the truth of the resurrection [Vn]. It means believing the Good News in a productive manner [AB].

unless^a in-vain^b you-believed.

LEXICON—a. ἐκτός εἰ μή (See this word at 14:5): 'unless' [AB, Herm, Lns, NIGTC; KJV, NET, NLT, NRSV, TEV], 'unless, of course' [ICC; ISV], 'unless indeed' [HNTC], 'otherwise' [NTC; NAB, NIV, NJB], 'but if you don't' [CEV]. This entire clause is translated 'and if your belief in it was not meaningless' [TNT], '(for I assume) that your conversion was not in vain' [REB].

b. εἰκῇ (LN 89.54, 89.63) (BAGD 4. p. 222): 'in vain' [LN, Lns, NTC; KJV, NAB, NET, NIV, NJB, NRSV, REB], 'for nothing' [TEV], 'all for nothing' [CEV], 'for/to no purpose' [BAGD, Herm, HNTC, LN (89.63)], 'to no avail, with no result' [LN (89.54)], 'without due consideration, in a haphazard manner' [BAGD], 'without thinking' [ICC], 'without coherent consideration' [NIGTC]. This adverb is also translated as a verb: 'to be worthless' [ISV], 'to be meaningless' [TNT], 'not to be true in the first place' [NLT]. It is also translated as an adjective: 'futile (faith)' [AB].

QUESTION—What is the significance of the aorist tense in ἐπιστεύσατε 'you believed'?
It points back to the time when the Corinthians first believed [Ed, Lns; CEV, NJB, NRSV]. It is an ingressive aorist indicating 'began to believe' [Lns]. 'You believed' indicates 'believed in Christ' [Ed, NIC].

QUESTION—What does εἰκῇ 'in vain' mean?
It means that what they believed will not be realized [TH]. Paul addresses the whole membership of the congregation and some may not have a genuine faith [MNTC, TNTC]. This means unless their faith is worthless and they believed without effect [MNTC]. It means believing without due consideration or thoughtlessly [NIGTC]. It means 'at random' so that it led nowhere and resulted in nothing [Lns]. It means worthless [AB, Ho]. It means without consideration, heedlessly, rashly [ICC]. It means of no purpose, which would be true if Christ has not been raised [Vn]. The word refers to 15:14 and the possibility that the faith of the Corinthians might be in vain if Christ has not been raised [Alf, NCBC, NIC2]. Paul is using this ironically to refer to the hypothetical possibility that their faith just might be in vain if it turns out that Christ is not raised [Ho, NIC2].

DISCOURSE UNIT: 15:3–5 [Herm]. The topic is an excursus concerning the Christ formula.

15:3 **For I-passed-on^a to-you among (the) first^b (things),**
LEXICON—a. aorist act. indic. of παραδίδωμι (See this word at 11:2): 'to pass on' [Herm; ISV, NET, NIV, NLT, TEV], 'to hand on' [HNTC, ICC,

NIGTC; NAB, NJB, NRSV, REB, TNT], 'to deliver' [AB, Lns, NTC; KJV], 'to tell' [CEV].

b. πρῶτος (LN 65.52) (BAGD 1.c.α. p. 726): 'first' [BAGD], 'most important' [BAGD, LN]. The phrase ἐν πρώτοις 'among first (things)' is translated 'as of first importance' [NTC; NET, NIV, NRSV, TNT], 'first of all' [HNTC; KJV, NAB], 'in the first place' [Lns; NJB], 'the most important part' [CEV], 'the most important points' [ISV], 'what was most important' [NLT], 'which is of the greatest importance' [TEV], 'first and foremost' [NIGTC; REB], 'with top priority' [AB], 'above all' [Herm], 'in the forefront of everything' [ICC], 'among the most important things' [BAGD]. See this word also at 11:18.

QUESTION—What relationship is indicated by γάρ 'for'?

It indicates an explanatory relationship [Ed, Ho, NIC2]: unless in vain you believed, *you see*.... It is an explanation of what Paul had preached [Ho]. It indicates that he will now restate the λόγος 'word' that he had preached to them [Lns]. It refers back to the words τίνι λόγῳ 'with which word' of 15:2 [ICC].

QUESTION—What is meant by ἐν πρώτοις 'among the first things'?

It has reference to first in importance rather than first in time [AB, Alf, BAGD, EGT, Gdt, Ho, ICC, Lns, NCBC, NIC, NIC2, NIGTC, NTC, Rb, TG, TH, TNTC, Vn; CEV, NET, NIV, NLT, NRSV, REB, TEV, TNT]: as of first importance. It refers to first in order [Herm]: in the first instance. It is ambiguous whether time or importance is intended, perhaps both [HNTC, TH]. If time had been in focus Paul could have used ἐν ἀρχῇ 'at the beginning' [NIC2].

that-which also I-received,[a]

LEXICON—a. aorist act. indic. of παραλαμβάνω (LN **27.13**): 'to receive' [AB, Herm, HNTC, ICC, Lns, NIGTC, NTC; all versions except CEV, NLT], 'to learn from (someone)' [**LN**]. This clause is translated 'and what had also been passed on to me' [NLT], not explicit [CEV]. See this word also at 11:23.

QUESTION—From whom had Paul received this teaching?

He received it from Jesus Christ (see 11:23 and Galatians 1:12) [Alf, Ed, Ho, Lns, NIC, Rb, Vn]. The two verbs 'to pass on' and 'to receive' indicate the way tradition was preserved in those days [NCBC]. Paul's source was both the Lord and others who had passed on to him the tradition [Gdt, NCBC, NTC]. The source of Paul's teaching is not in focus here. What is in focus is that this teaching did not originate with Paul [HNTC, ICC, TNTC]. It was not necessary to state from whom he received it since the later context tells that [Herm].

QUESTION—What is the function of the conjunction καί 'also'?

It functions to stress the identity of what Paul passed on, that is, it was exactly what he received [EGT, Gdt, ICC]: *even* that which I received.

that Christ died[a] for our sins according-to[b] the Scriptures

LEXICON—a. aorist act. ind. of ἀποθνήσκω (LN 23.99) (BAGD 1.a. p. 91): 'to die' [AB, Herm, HNTC, ICC, Lns, NIGTC, NTC; all versions]. The aorist tense points to a single historical action in the past [EGT, Lns, NIGTC, NTC].

  b. κατά with accusative object (See this word at 12:8): 'according to' [AB, Herm, HNTC, Lns, NIGTC, NTC; KJV, NET, NIV, TNT], 'in accordance with' [NAB, NJB, NRSV, REB], 'in keeping with' [ISV], 'as written in' [TEV]. The phrase κατὰ τὰς γραφὰς 'according to the Scriptures' is translated 'as the Scriptures have predicted' [ICC], 'as the Scriptures say' [CEV], 'just as the Scriptures said' [NLT].

QUESTION—How is the word Χριστός 'Christ' used here?

It is used as a personal name [Lns, NIC2]. It had become a name for Jesus, but it still carried Messianic connotations [NIC2]. It is used as a title indicating his official role of Messiah [NIC, NTC].

QUESTION—What is meant by ὑπὲρ τῶν ἁμαρτιῶν ἡμῶν 'for our sins'?

  1. It means that Jesus died in behalf of our sins, that is, that he might atone for them or become the means of their forgiveness [Alf, Ed, Gdt, Herm, Ho, Lns, NIC2, NTC, TG, TNTC, Vn].
  2. It means that Jesus died in reference to our sins [HNTC, ICC, TH]. It cannot mean 'in behalf of our sins' here, but means the same as περί as in Galatians 1:4:'with reference to, in order to deal with, concerning'. The effect of Christ's death on our sins is not discussed here [HNTC]. It means 'on account of our sins' not 'in behalf of them'. Neither ὑπέρ nor περί indicate vicarious substitution. This meaning would be conveyed by ἀντί. Ὑπέρ means 'in behalf of' when used of persons, not things [ICC].

QUESTION—What particular Scripture may be indicated?

It refers to the Old Testament in general [HNTC, Ho, Lns, MNTC, NIC2]. It may refer to Isaiah 53 [Ed, Herm, HNTC, Ho, NIC, NTC, TG, TNTC]. It may refer to Psalms 22 [NTC]. It is a general reference to Scripture [Herm]. See Luke 18:31 and 24:25–27 [Ed].

15:4 and that he-was-buried[a] and that he-was-raised[b] on-the third day according-to the Scriptures

LEXICON—a. aorist pass. indic. of θάπτω (LN 52.4) (BAGD p. 351): 'to be buried' [AB, BAGD, Herm, HNTC, ICC, LN, NIGTC, NTC; all versions], 'to be entombed' [Lns]. The aorist tense points to a single historical action in the past [EGT, Lns, NTC].

  b. perf. pass. indic. of ἐγείρω (LN 23.94) (BAGD 2.c. p. 215): 'to be raised' [AB, Herm, HNTC, ICC, Lns, NIGTC, NTC; ISV, NET, NIV, NRSV, TNT], 'to be raised to life' [LN; CEV, NJB, REB, TEV], 'to be raised from the dead' [NLT], 'to be made to live again' [LN]. This passive verb is also translated actively: 'to rise' [NAB], 'to rise again' [KJV]. See this word also at 6:14.

QUESTION—What is the significance of ἐτάφη 'he was buried'?
It emphasizes the fact that Christ really died [Ed, Herm, Lns, NIC, NIGTC]. It is essential to the fact of the resurrection [Gdt, ICC, TNTC, Vn]. It is basic to the reality of both Christ's death and His resurrection [AB, HNTC, NCBC, NIC, NIC2, NTC]. It shows that Christ's death was like everyone else's [Lns].

QUESTION—What is the significance of the perfect tense of ἐγήγερται 'he was raised'?
The perfect tense indicates an action that was completed in the past but it continues to be true into the present, indicating that Christ was raised and continues to exist as a living person [AB, Alf, Ed, EGT, Gdt, HNTC, ICC, Lns, NCBC, NIC, NIC2, NTC, Rb, TH, TNTC, Vn].

QUESTION—Who is the agent of the passive ἐγήγερται 'he was raised'?
God is the agent [HNTC, NCBC, NIC, NIC2, NTC, TG, TH, TNTC]: God raised Christ. See 15:15 [HNTC, TNTC].

QUESTION—How are days counted to make three days?
The day of death and the day of resurrection are counted [TH].

QUESTION—What does the phrase κατὰ τὰς γραφάς 'according to Scriptures' modify.
It modifies both 'he was raised' and 'on the third day' [AB, Gdt, Herm, HNTC, Ho, ICC, Lns, MNTC, NCBC, NIC, NIC2, NTC]. It modifies only 'he was raised' [TNTC].

QUESTION—What is the Scripture support for the resurrection of Christ on the third day?
In Luke 24:46, Jesus appeals to Scripture as supporting his resurrection after three days [EGT, ICC, Rb]. John 20:9 and Acts 26:23 both point to Scripture as predicting the resurrection [Ho]. Jonah 1:17 coupled with Matthew 12:40 indicate a resurrection after three days [Ed, Gdt, HNTC, Lns, MNTC, NCBC, NIC, NTC]. Psalms 16:10 as referred to in Acts 2:25–31 and 13:35–37 is a possible reference to the resurrection [AB, Ed, Gdt, HNTC, Ho, ICC, NCBC, NIC2, TNTC]. Psalms 110:1 as referred to in Acts 2:25-36 is a possible reference to the resurrection [NIC2]. Isaiah 53 is also a possible reference to the resurrection [Gdt, NCBC, NTC, TNTC]. Hosea 6:2 is a possible Scriptural reference for resurrection after three days [AB, Gdt, Herm, ICC, NTC]. The presentation of firstfruits on the day after the Sabbath is outlined in Leviticus 23:10 and following. This is a supporting reference to the resurrection [NCBC]. In Acts 13:33 Paul cites Psalms 2:7 for support [Ed]. The citing of Scripture should probably be taken as a general reference to Scripture in general and not to any one reference [AB, NIC2, NTC]. Since Scripture predicted the suffering and death of the Messiah and also predicted his everlasting kingdom, the resurrection is also implied [Ho].

QUESTION—What is the significance of the twice repeated κατὰ τὰς γραφάς 'according to the Scriptures'?
It is repeated to emphasize the fact of Scriptural support [ICC, MNTC, NIC].

DISCOURSE UNIT: 15:5-8 [ICC, Vn]. The topic is the official witnesses of the resurrection of Christ.

15:5 **and that he-appeared**[a] **to-Cephas**[b] **then**[c] **to-the twelve;**[d]
LEXICON—a. aorist pass. (or deponent = act.) indic. of ὁράω (LN 24.1) (BAGD 1.a.δ. p. 578): 'to appear' [AB, BAGD, Herm, HNTC, ICC, Lns, NIGTC, NTC; CEV, NET, NIV, NJB, NRSV, REB, TEV, TNT], 'to be seen' [LN; ISV, KJV, NAB, NLT]. 'to become visible' [BAGD].
  b. Κηφᾶς (LN 93.211) (BAGD p. 431): 'Cephas' [AB, BAGD, Herm, HNTC, LN, Lns, NTC; ISV, KJV, NAB, NET, NJB, NRSV, REB, TNT], 'Kephas' [ICC], 'Peter' [NIGTC; CEV, NIV, NLT, TEV]. Κηφᾶς is the Aramaic equivalent of the Greek name Πέτρος 'Peter' [LN].
  c. εἶτα (LN 67.44): 'then' [AB, Herm, HNTC, ICC, LN, Lns, NIGTC, NTC; CEV, KJV, NAB, NET, NRSV, TNT], 'and then' [ISV, NIV, NLT, TEV], 'later' [LN], 'and later' [NJB], 'and afterwards' [REB], 'afterward' [LN]. See this word also at 15:7.
  d. δώδεκα (LN 60.21) (BAGD p. 210): 'twelve' [BAGD, LN; CEV, ISV, KJV, NET, NRSV], 'Twelve' [AB, Herm, HNTC, ICC, Lns, NIGTC, NTC; NAB, NIV, NJB, REB, TNT], 'twelve apostles' [NLT, TEV].

QUESTION—What is indicated by ὤφθη 'he appeared'?
  It functions to indicate that this was not a vision, but actual physical sight with human eyes [Herm, ICC, NIC, NTC, Rb, Vn]. Paul wants to emphasize the bodily resurrection as a physically verifiable fact. This was not a form of spiritual existence but something that was seen by many on several occasions [NIC2]. Ὤφθη with the dative case indicates 'he appeared to' [EGT, Gdt, Herm, NIC2]. The passive indicates that Christ took the initiative [NCBC, NIC2]. The meaning here is 'he was seen' [ICC, Lns], not 'he appeared in a vision' [ICC].

QUESTION—What Scriptural reference substantiates that Christ appeared to Peter?
  In Luke 24:34 the disciples relate to the two men from Emmaus that the Lord had appeared to Peter [Alf, Ed, EGT, Gdt, Herm, HNTC, Ho, ICC, Lns, NCBC, NIC, TNTC].

QUESTION—What Scriptural references substantiate that Christ appeared to the twelve?
  Luke 24:36 and John 20:19 are occasions when Christ appeared to the apostles [Alf, Gdt, HNTC, Ho, Lns, NIC2, TNTC]. Matthew 28:16-17 also supports this event [NIC2].

QUESTION—To whom does οἱ δώδεκα 'the twelve' refer?
  It refers to the original twelve disciples whom Jesus chose to be his apostles [AB, Ed, EGT, Gdt, HNTC, Ho, ICC, Lns, MNTC, NCBC, NIC, NTC, Rb, TH, TNTC, Vn]. There were actually eleven present without Judas, but the reference to the twelve is to the group as a whole [AB, HNTC, Ho, MNTC, NCBC, NIC]. There were actually 10 there without Judas and Thomas but

the reference of twelve is to the group as a whole [EGT, Gdt, ICC, NTC, Rb, TNTC, Vn].

QUESTION—Is the order in which these are named chronological?

The order in which these witnesses are named is chronological [Alf, Ho, Lns, Rb]. Note the words εἶτα 'then' (this verse), ἔπειτα 'afterward' (15:6) and ἔσχατον δὲ πάντων 'last of all' (15:8) [Alf].

15:6 After-that[a] he-appeared to-more-than[b] five hundred brothers at-one-time,[c]

LEXICON—a. ἔπειτα (LN **67.44**) (BAGD 2.a. p. 284): 'after that' [EGT; ISV, KJV, NAB, NIV, NLT, TNT], 'afterwards' [ICC, LN], 'after this' [CEV], 'later' [**LN**], 'then' [BAGD, Herm, HNTC, LN, Lns, NIGTC, NTC; NET, NRSV, REB, TEV], 'next' [AB; NJB]. Ἔπειτα 'thereafter' is a stronger break than the εἶτα 'then' of 15:5 and indicates a new stage in the list [Gdt]. See this word also at 12:28.

b. ἐπάνω (LN **78.30**) (BAGD 1.b. p. 283): 'more than' [AB, BAGD, Herm, HNTC, **LN**, NIGTC, NTC; all versions except KJV, NAB, REB], 'in excess of' [LN], 'over' [REB], 'above' [Lns; KJV], 'upwards of' [ICC], not explicit [NAB].

c. ἐφάπαξ (LN **60.67, 67.34**) (BAGD 1. p. 330): 'at one time' [AB, NTC; ISV, NET, NLT, NRSV, TNT], 'at the same time' [**LN** (67.34); NIV, NJB], 'at once' [BAGD, Herm, HNTC, ICC, Lns; KJV, NAB, REB, TEV], 'once' [**LN** (60.67)], 'one time' [LN (60.67)], 'on a single occasion' [NIGTC], not explicit [CEV].

QUESTION—To what event in the New Testament does this refer?

It may refer to the meeting in Galilee referred to in Matthew 26:32, 28:7, 10, 16; and Mark 14:28, 16:7 [EGT, Gdt, Ho, ICC, Lns, Rb, TNTC, Vn]. Several reasons support Galilee as the place where this occurred: (a) Jesus had told them before he died that when he was raised he would meet them in Galilee (Mark 14:28); (b) The angel at the tomb told the women to remind the disciples that he would go before them into Galilee (Matthew 28:7); (c) Jesus himself meets the women and tells them to tell his brothers to go to Galilee where they would see him (Matthew 28:10); (d) The disciples went to Galilee where they saw Jesus (Matthew 28:16) [Lns]. Otherwise it may refer to Jerusalem before the crowds left after the observance of the Passover [Alf].

QUESTION—What is the significance of the number 500?

To substantiate the truth of an event, Jewish law required only two or three witnesses. When Jesus appeared to over 500 witnesses, he provided overwhelming proof of His resurrection [NTC].

QUESTION—What is the meaning of ἐφάπαξ 'at one time'?

It means 'at one time' or 'at the same time' or 'at once' [AB, Alf, BAGD, Gdt, Herm, HNTC, ICC, LN, Lns, MNTC, NIC2, NIGTC, TG; all versions]. It means 'once' since to some he appeared more than once [Ed, LN]. It means 'once for all'. Nowhere else does this word have the meaning of 'at once'. This was the final revealing of the risen Jesus to his followers [EGT].

QUESTION—To whom does ἀδελφοί 'brothers' refer?

It refers to Christian followers including women [Gdt, NIC2, TG, TH; CEV, NET, NLT, NRSV, TEV]. It refers to fellow believers [LN (24.1)].

of whom the most[a] remain[b] until now,[c]

LEXICON—a. πλείων (See this word at 10:5): 'most' [Lns, NIGTC, NTC; all versions except KJV], 'greater part' [KJV], 'the majority' [AB, Herm, HNTC, ICC].

b. pres. act. indic. of μένω (BAGD 1.c.α. p. 504): 'to remain' [HNTC, Lns, NTC; KJV, TNT], 'to be living' [NET, NIV], 'to be alive' [BAGD, Herm, NIGTC; CEV, ISV, NAB, NLT, NRSV, REB, TEV], 'to remain alive' [AB, BAGD], 'to survive' [Alf, ICC], 'to be with (someone)' [NJB]. See this word also at 13:13.

c. ἄρτι (LN 67.38) (BAGD 3. p. 110): 'now' [LN, NTC; TNT], 'this present' [KJV], 'the present' [AB, ICC], 'this day' [HNTC], 'today' [Lns]. The phrase ἕως ἄρτι 'until now' is translated 'still' [Herm, NIGTC; all versions except KJV, TNT], 'up to the present time' [BAGD].

QUESTION—What is the point of including the note that most remained alive?

Paul may have said this to strengthen his evidence by implying that any of these could be interviewed if desired [AB, Alf, Gdt, NIC2, NTC, TH, TNTC]. The strength in the fact that he appeared to over 500 followers was in the fact that most of them were still alive [Ho, Rb].

QUESTION—To what specific date did ἄρτι 'now' refer?

It referred to approximately 20–25 years after the resurrection of Christ occurred [HNTC, ICC, Rb].

but some have-fallen-asleep;[a]

LEXICON—a. aorist pass. (deponent = act.) indic. of κοιμάω (See this word at 11:30): 'to fall asleep' [Herm, HNTC, Lns, NTC; NAB, NIV, NJB], 'to be fallen asleep' [KJV], 'to die' [AB], 'to have died' [NIGTC; CEV, ISV, NET, NLT, NRSV, REB, TEV, TNT], 'to go to one's rest' [ICC].

QUESTION—How is 'sleep' a metaphor for death?

A person sleeping continues to exist while his body sleeps. So a person dead continues to exist even though his or her location changes. Both sleeping and death are temporary states. A sleeping person will awaken and a dead person will rise [Vn].

15:7 After-that[a] he-appeared to-James,[b]

LEXICON—a. ἔπειτα (See this word at 15:6): 'after that' [NTC; KJV, TNT], 'then' [AB, Herm, HNTC, Lns, NIGTC; NET, NIV, NJB, NLT, NRSV, REB, TEV], 'next' [ICC; ISV, NAB], 'also' [CEV].

b. Ἰάκωβος (LN 93.158) (BAGD 4. p. 368): 'James' [AB, BAGD, Herm, HNTC, ICC, LN, Lns, NIGTC, NTC; all versions].

QUESTION—To whom does Ἰάκωβος 'James' refer?
It refers to James, the brother of Jesus [AB, Alf, BAGD, Ed, EGT, Gdt, Herm, Lns, MNTC, NCBC, NIC, NIC2, NTC, Rb, TG, TH, TNTC, Vn]. The identity of James is uncertain [Ho, ICC, TNTC]. James was Jesus' cousin, son of Clopas and Mary, Jesus' mother's sister [Lns]. Two apostles were named James: James the son of Alpheus, and James the son of Zebedee. But this refers to Jesus' half-brother, early church leader and author of the book of James [MNTC].

then[a] to-all the apostles;
LEXICON—a. εἶτα (BAGD 1. p. 234): 'then' [BAGD, Herm, HNTC, ICC, Lns, NIGTC, NTC; all versions except NLT, REB, TEV], 'next' [AB], 'later' [NLT], 'afterward' [REB, TEV]. See this word also at 15:5.
QUESTION—To whom does ἀπόστολοι 'apostles' refer?
  1. It refers to the twelve apostles, all of them being present [EGT, Gdt, Ho, ICC, MNTC, NTC, Vn]. Paul was aware that Thomas was not present at the first appearance to the twelve so he states that *all* were present this time [EGT, Gdt, ICC]. This appearance was at the Ascension [EGT, Gdt, ICC, NTC, Rb, TNTC]. This was to be Jesus' final appearance to the apostles and it was important that all of them be present. For this reason the word πᾶσιν 'all' is emphatically placed after the noun [Gdt].
  2. It refers to a wider group of people than Jesus' twelve apostles [AB, Alf, HNTC, Lns, NCBC, NIC, NIC2, TG, TH]. The 'apostles' is a group including missionaries [AB, HNTC] and possibly the seven men of Acts 6:1–6 [AB]. It is a group wider than the twelve, but not unlimited in membership [HNTC]. It may include the 70 of Luke 10 and others [Alf]. There were those, other than the twelve who had the title of apostle whose role was more functional than official, more ministerial than jurisdictional. This group had seen Jesus after he rose from the dead and they proclaimed the gospel and founded churches. The phrase 'all the apostles' then would include this group as well as the twelve [NIC2]. The fact that 'all the apostles' occurs following the reference to the twelve shows that it refers to a wider group [Lns, NIC], that included Barnabas, Timothy, and possibly James [Lns].
  3. It cannot be determined exactly to whom it refers [Ed, Herm]. Although it cannot be known for certain, it is natural to think that Paul is referring to those who witnessed the Ascension of Jesus in Acts 1:10 [Ed].
QUESTION—What word is emphasized in this phrase?
The word πᾶσιν 'all' is placed emphatically after the noun [Gdt, HNTC, TH, TNTC]. There is no emphasis on the word 'all' [ICC, Vn]. When the adjective follows the noun, it is the noun (apostles) that receives the emphasis [NTC]: to the apostles, all the apostles.

15:8 And last[a] of-all he-appeared to-me-also as-though[b] to-the untimely-birth.[c]

LEXICON—a. ἔσχατος (LN 61.13) (BAGD 3.b p. 314): 'last' [AB, BAGD, Herm, HNTC, ICC, LN, Lns, NIGTC, NTC; all versions except CEV, ISV], 'final' [LN], 'finally' [LN]. The phrase ἔσχατον πάντων 'last of all' is translated 'finally' [CEV, ISV].

b. ὡσπερεί (LN **64.13**) (BAGD p. 899): 'as though' [BAGD; ISV, NET, NJB, NLT], 'just as if' [ICC], 'as if' [AB, Herm, NIGTC], 'as' [HNTC, **LN**, Lns, NTC; KJV, NAB, NIV, NRSV], 'though' [TNT], 'even though' [CEV, TEV], 'like' [REB], 'just as' [LN], 'as it were' [BAGD].

c. ἔκτρωμα (LN **23.55**, **64.13**) (BAGD p. 246): 'untimely birth' [BAGD, LN], 'an aborted fetus' [NIGTC], 'miscarriage' [BAGD]. The phrase τῷ ἐκτρώματι 'the untimely birth' is translated 'one untimely born' [AB, NTC; NRSV], 'untimely born Apostle' [ICC], 'one who was born at the wrong time' [**LN** (**23.55**, 64.13); CEV, NET], 'one born out of due time' [KJV], 'one hurried into the world before his time' [HNTC], 'I had been born at the wrong time' [NLT], 'one born out of the normal course' [NAB], 'someone whose birth was abnormal' [LN (**64.13**); TEV], 'one abnormally born' [NIV], 'a child born abnormally' [NJB], 'the dead fetus' [Lns]. The phrase ὡσπερεὶ τῷ ἐκτρώματι, 'as though to the untimely birth' was translated 'as though I were born abnormally late' [ISV], 'it was like a sudden, abnormal birth' [REB], 'as if to an abortive creature' [Herm], 'abortion though I was and far from ready for new life' [TNT].

QUESTION—Does ἔσχατον 'last' refer to time or sequence?

It refers to being the last in a series of similar things or last sequentially [Ed, EGT, Gdt, Herm, HNTC, Ho, ICC, MNTC, NCBC, NIC, NIC2, NTC, TNTC]. Paul was the last one to have seen the risen Christ [Ed, Herm]. It refers to being last in time [TH].

QUESTION—To what does the ἔκτρωμα 'untimely birth' refer?

1. It refers to the time Paul was converted and made an apostle [EGT, Gdt, ICC, MNTC, NTC, TH, Vn].

    1.1 It refers to Paul's being born too soon [EGT, Gdt, ICC, Vn]. The others became apostles by maturing normally while Paul was transformed instantly from persecutor to apostle [EGT]. While the other apostles were disciples of Jesus and were trained by him to become apostles, Paul's transformation was sudden and violent. He refers to his conversion on the road to Damascus [Gdt, ICC].

    1.2 It refers to Paul's being born too late [MNTC, NCBC, NTC, Rb; ISV]. Although the word ordinarily referred to a miscarriage or premature birth, it could mean an ill-timed birth, whether too early or too late. Paul came too late to be have been one of the Twelve [MNTC]. Paul was destined to be an apostle but this was frustrated by his opposition to Christians until the time of his conversion on the road to Damascus [NTC]. The figure has reference to Paul's conversion after the Ascension [Rb]. His opponents referred to him as an 'abortion' of an

apostle comparing him to a true apostle as an aborted child would be compared with a healthy one [NCBC].
2. It refers to the abnormality of Paul's becoming an apostle [Alf, Ed, HNTC, Lns, NCBC, NIC, NIC2, TG, TNTC]. If the apostles are a family, the other apostles had normal birth experiences while Paul's birth was abnormal. He was the immature and deformed child who was unworthy to be called an apostle [Alf]. Paul likens himself to a dead fetus. Even though this was true, Jesus honors him and gives him a place among those living apostles [Lns]. The word implies being undeveloped, repulsive, and possibly even lifeless. It may be that his opponents called him this because of his physical appearance or his deficiencies as an apostle in their opinion [HNTC]. The word highlights the monstrosity of a persecutor becoming an apostle [TH]. The article with 'abortion', '*the* abortion' may indicate that the Corinthians viewed Paul as a kind of freak in contrast to the other apostles. But Paul sees his weakness as a true evidence that his apostleship is from the Lord while his opponents in Corinth see it as proof that he is no apostle [NIC2].

QUESTION—Was this a vision or a real appearance?

It was a real appearance like the others in the series [Ed, Gdt, ICC, NCBC, NIC2, NTC, TNTC]. It refers to the appearance on the road to Damascus [Alf, ICC, NIC2, NTC, TG, TNTC].

QUESTION—What words are emphasized?

The words 'to me' are emphasized [TH, TNTC].

DISCOURSE UNIT: 15:9-11 [ICC, NTC, Vn]. The topic is the agreement between St. Paul and the other Apostles [ICC, Vn], the apostolicity of Paul [NTC].

15:9 **For I am the least**[a] **of-the apostles**

LEXICON—a. ἐλάχιστος (LN 87.66) (BAGD 1. p. 248): 'least' [AB, BAGD, HNTC, Lns, NTC; all versions except CEV], 'very least' [ICC, NIGTC], 'least important' [LN; CEV], 'last' [Herm, LN, Lns], 'lowest' [LN]. This refers to being of the lowest status [LN]. 'Last' refers not to time, but to his character as being a persecutor of the church [Lns]. See also Ephesians 3:8 and 1 Timothy 1:15 [Rb]. See this word also at 6:2.

QUESTION—What relationship is indicated by γάρ 'for'?

It indicates that this verse is the explanation of why Paul used the term ἔκτρωμα 'one untimely born' of himself [Alf, EGT, Gdt, ICC, Lns, NCBC, NIC2, NTC]. This verse explains how Paul is 'the abortion' among the Apostles both regarding his small stature and his immature birth into apostleship [EGT]. The main point of Paul's explanation focuses on the words 'I persecuted' [Gdt].

QUESTION—What word is emphasized in this verse?

The word ἐγώ 'I' is emphatic [Alf, Ed, Herm, ICC, TNTC]: I myself.

who am not worthy[a] to-be-called (an) apostle,
LEXICON—a. ἱκανός (LN 75.2) (BAGD 2. p. 374): 'worthy' [HNTC; NLT, TNT], 'fit' [AB, BAGD, Herm, ICC, Lns, NTC; ISV, NJB, REB], 'meet' [KJV], 'adequate' [LN], 'competent' [BAGD, LN, NIGTC] 'appropriate, qualified, able' [BAGD, LN]. The phrase οὐκ εἰμὶ ἱκανός 'I am not worthy' is translated 'unworthy' [NET], 'unfit' [NRSV], 'do not even deserve' [CEV, NIV, TEV]. The phrase οὐκ εἰμὶ ἱκανὸς καλεῖσθαι ἀπόστολος 'I am not worthy to be called an apostle' is translated 'I do not even deserve the name' [NAB]. The word denotes adequacy or competence for a task or office [TH]. Paul did not mean that he was unequal to the other apostles for he claims equality in 2 Corinthians 11:5. What he means is that his role as persecutor of the church made him the least deserving of them all [TNTC].
QUESTION—What is the function of the relative pronoun ὅς 'who'?
It functions to give the grounds for Paul saying the he was the least of the apostles [Alf, EGT, HNTC, ICC]: I am least *since* I am not worthy to be called an apostle. This is the causal use of the relative [EGT]. The relative pronoun makes awkward English. A better rendering is 'indeed' [NTC; NRSV].

because[a] I-persecuted[b] the church of-God;
LEXICON—a. διότι (LN 89.26) (BAGD 1. p. 199): 'because' [AB, BAGD, Herm, ICC, Lns, NIGTC, NTC; all versions except CEV, NLT], 'since' [HNTC], 'after the way' [NLT], 'because of, on account of, by reason of' [LN]. The phrase διότι ἐδίωξα 'because I persecuted' is translated 'I caused so much trouble…that' [CEV].
  b. aorist act. indic. of διώκω (LN 39.45) (BAGD 2. p. 201): 'to persecute' [AB, BAGD, Herm, HNTC, ICC, LN, Lns, NIGTC, NTC; all versions except CEV], 'to cause so much trouble for' [CEV], 'to harass' [LN]. For the times that Paul did this see Acts 8:1, 3; 9:1, 2; 22:4, 5; 26:9 and Galatians 1:13 [HNTC]. See this word also at 4:12 and 14:1.
QUESTION—What relationship is indicated by διότι 'because'?
It indicates the reason why Paul was unworthy to be called an apostle [EGT, Herm]: I am not worthy to be called an apostle *because* I persecuted the church of God.
QUESTION—What is meant by τὴν ἐκκλησίαν τοῦ θεοῦ 'the church of God?'
It refers to the universal group or body of Christians everywhere [HNTC, NIC2, NTC, TH]. It refers to the church in Jerusalem [EGT, Vn] because it was too early for other churches to have formed yet [Vn]. See Galatians 1:13 and 22 [EGT]. These were Christians both in Jerusalem and other places, see Acts 8:3 and 9:1, 2 [TH].

15:10 But by-(the)-grace[a] of-God I-am what I-am,
LEXICON—a. χάρις (LN 25.89, 88.66) (BAGD 4. p. 878): 'grace' [AB, Herm, HNTC, ICC, LN (88.66), Lns, NIGTC, NTC; all versions except CEV, NAB, NLT], 'graciousness' [LN (88.66)], 'favor' [LN (25.89); NAB],

'special favor' [NLT], 'good will' [LN (25.89)], 'kindness' [LN (88.66)]. Χάριτι θεοῦ 'grace of God' is translated 'God was kind' [CEV]. Here χάρις means the power and capability to carry out his work as an apostle [BAGD]. See this word also at 1:3.

QUESTION—What relationship is indicated by δέ 'but'?

It indicates a contrastive relationship [AB, Gdt, HNTC, ICC, Lns, NTC; all versions]: I persecuted the church of God *but* by the grace of God I am what I am. It indicates a strong contrastive relationship between what Paul was without grace and what he was with grace [Gdt].

QUESTION—What is meant by χάρις 'grace'?

It means God's undeserved favor [AB, EGT, Lns, NIC2, NIGTC]. It refers to the influence of God's Spirit in making Paul what he was, which was an undeserved favor [Ho]. It is God's love, favor, and kindness expressed toward people [TG]. It is the power or ability that God gives someone to do a particular task [Alf, HNTC, ICC, NTC].

QUESTION—What relationship is indicated by the dative χάριτι 'by the grace'?

It indicates a causal or instrumental relationship [TG]: I am who I am *because of, by means of* God's grace. Paul indicates the reason why he is an apostle, it was an undeserved gift [NIC2].

QUESTION—What does Paul mean by εἰμι ὅ εἰμι 'I am what I am'?

He is referring to his role as an apostle [Ho, Lns, NIC2, TH]. He is referring both to being a Christian and an apostle [Gdt, HNTC, Lns]. He is referring to being a Christian, apostle, and hard worker [NIC]. He is referring to the fact that he is an apostle who has both seen the Lord and has worked effectively for Him [ICC]. He is referring to himself as an instrument in God's hand [NTC]. He is referring to his character and to what he had accomplished [Rb].

QUESTION—What is emphasized in this verse?

The words χάριτι θεοῦ 'by the grace of God' are forefronted for emphasis [Alf, Lns]. Both its position and the repetition of the word χάρις 'grace' indicate emphatic prominence [Alf].

and his grace to[a] me was not in-vain,[b]

LEXICON—a. εἰς with accusative object (LN 84.16): 'to' [LN (84.16); ISV, NAB, NET, NIV, NJB, REB], 'toward' [Herm, LN, Lns, NTC; NRSV], 'upon' [KJV], not explicit [CEV, NLT]. The phrase ἡ εἰς ἐμέ 'the one to me' is translated 'that he gave me' [TEV], 'he has given me' [TNT], 'that was for me' [AB], 'which he bestowed upon me' [HNTC], 'which he extended to me' [NIGTC], 'which reached even to me' [ICC].

b. κενός (LN **89.53**, 89.64) (BAGD 2.a.β. p. 427): 'in vain' [BAGD, Herm, LN (89.64), NTC; KJV, NET, NRSV], 'without effect' [LN (**89.53**); NIV, TEV], 'vain' [HNTC; REB], 'ineffective' [TNT], 'ineffectual' [ICC], 'without result(s)' [LN 89.53]; NLT], 'void' [AB], 'fruitless' [NIGTC;

NAB], 'empty' [Lns], 'wasted' [CEV, ISV, NJB], 'for no purpose' [LN (89.64)]. Κενός means 'without effect' [Ho, NIC2, NTC, TNTC].

QUESTION—What is indicated by ἡ χάρις αὐτοῦ ἡ εἰς ἐμέ 'his grace to me'?

It means 'the grace that he gave to me' [NIC2, TG, TH]. It means 'the grace he extended to me' [EGT, ICC, NIGTC]. It means 'the grace he revealed to me' [Alf, Gdt, ICC]. It means 'the grace he directed toward me' [Herm]. In this context 'grace' indicates the gift of being an apostle [TH].

QUESTION—What is the positive meaning of ἡ χάρις αὐτοῦ…οὐ κενή ἐγενήθη 'his grace…was not in vain'?

It means 'void of reality' [EGT], 'without contents' [Lns, NIC, TNTC], 'not wasted, worthless' [TH], 'fruitless' [ICC]. 'Not empty' is a litotes indicating 'genuine'. Grace had its exact meaning in Paul's life [Lns]. It means that it bore extraordinary results [NTC]. It means that His grace was effective [TG, TH]. Paul's extraordinary work showed the real effect of God's grace [Ed].

on-the-contrary I-worked[a] more-abundantly[b] than-they all,

LEXICON—a. aorist act. indic. of κοπιάω (LN 42.47) (BAGD 2. p. 443): 'to work' [AB, LN; all versions except KJV, REB, TNT], 'to toil' [ICC, LN; TNT], 'to labor' [Herm, HNTC, LN, Lns, NIGTC, NTC; KJV], 'to work hard' [BAGD, LN]. This verb is also translated as a noun: '(my) labors' [REB]. Κοπιάω here implies work as an apostle [Alf, Lns]. It is implied that Paul worked by means of God's grace [Alf].

b. περισσότερος (BAGD 2. p. 651): 'harder' [HNTC; all versions except CEV, KJV, REB], 'more abundantly' [HNTC, Lns; KJV], 'more effectually' [ICC], 'much harder' [CEV], 'to an even greater degree' [NIGTC], 'more than' [Herm, NTC], 'even more' [BAGD]. This entire clause is translated 'in my labors I have outdone them all' [REB]. See this word also at 12:23.

QUESTION—What does αὐτῶν πάντων ἐκοπίασα 'I worked harder than all of them' mean?

1. It means that Paul worked harder than all of the apostles put together [AB, Alf, EGT, Gdt, Ho, ICC, Lns, NIC, TNTC; all versions except CEV, NRSV, TEV]. The pronoun 'them' refers to the other apostles [NIC; NLT, TEV].
2. It means that Paul worked harder than any one of the apostles [Alf, NIC2, NTC, TH, Vn; CEV, NRSV, TEV]. The pronoun 'them' refers to the other apostles [NIC2, NTC, TH; CEV, TEV]. To say that he worked harder than all of them together seems to exaggerate [Alf].

QUESTION—How did Paul work harder than the others?

Paul worked harder in proclaiming the Good News and founding new churches [HNTC]. It refers to his journeys and labor [NIC]. Paul continually opened new frontiers with the Good News, (see 2 Corinthians 10:13–17) [Alf, NIC2]. Paul had extended Christ's kingdom over a more extensive area than all the Twelve had at the time [EGT].

yet not I but the grace of-God [the-one] with[a] **me.**
TEXT—Some manuscripts omit the definite article ἡ 'the one' before σύν 'with'. Other manuscripts read ἡ εἰς 'the one into'. GNT selects [ἡ] σύν '[the one] with', with the definite article in brackets and with a C rating, indicating difficulty in deciding to include it in the text. The reading ἡ σύν 'the one with' appears also to be taken by Herm, Ho; ISV, KJV, NIV, NJB, NRSV and TNT. The reading σύν (without the article) seems to be taken by Alf, EGT, Gdt, HNTC, Lns, and NET. It is not clear which reading is taken by CEV, NAB, NLT, REB, and TEV.
LEXICON—a. σύν with dative object (LN 89.107) (BAGD 3. p. 782): 'with' [AB, HNTC, LN, Lns, NTC; all versions except CEV, NAB, NLT], 'through' [NLT], not explicit [CEV, NAB]. The phrase ἡ σὺν ἐμοί 'the one with me' is translated 'that was with me' [Herm], 'that came to my aid' [BAGD], 'working with me' [ICC, NIGTC].
QUESTION—What is the meaning of ἡ χάρις τοῦ θεοῦ σὺν ἐμοί 'the grace of God with me'?
The verb 'worked' should be implied after 'grace of God' [Alf, EGT, Gdt, HNTC, ICC, Lns, NIC2, TG; CEV, NLT, REB, TEV]: the grace of God *worked* with me. 'Grace' here refers God's gifts that enabled Paul to do his apostolic work [TG]. Two worked, Paul and grace, but grace made the work effective [ICC]. It implies that Paul was the instrument of grace [EGT; NLT].

15:11 **Therefore whether (it is) I or-whether (it is) those (persons), so we-preach**[a] **and so you-believed.**
LEXICON—a. pres. act. indic. of κηρύσσω (LN 33.207, 33.256) (BAGD 1.b.β. p. 431): 'to preach' [AB, BAGD, Herm, HNTC, ICC, LN (33.256), Lns; all versions except NRSV, REB, TNT], 'to proclaim' [LN (33.207), NIGTC, NTC; NRSV, REB], 'to tell' [LN (33.207)]. The phrase οὕτως κηρύσσομεν 'thus we preach' is translated 'this is our message' [TNT]. The present tense indicates a continuous aspect [Lns, NIC2]: we continue to preach. The present tense indicates a habitual aspect [TNTC]: we habitually preach. See this word also at 1:23.
QUESTION—What relationship is indicated by οὖν 'therefore'?
It indicates that this verse resumes the main argument from 15:8 after the digression of 15:9 and 10 [Ho, ICC, Lns, NTC]. It summarizes the preceding argument and links back to 15:8 [NTC]. It indicates that this verse is the logical conclusion to be drawn from the preceding, to the effect that both Paul and the apostles preach the same Gospel and the Corinthians believed it [Ed]. It does not link back to 15:8, but simply concludes his argument including his defense of his apostleship in verses 9 and 10 [NIC2].
QUESTION—To whom does ἐκεῖνοι 'those (persons)' refer?
It refers to the other apostles [Alf, HNTC, Ho, TG, TH, Vn]. It refers to Peter, the twelve, the 500, James, or anyone else [MNTC]. It refers to Cephas, the twelve, the first disciples, and James [EGT]. It refers to Peter

and the twelve [Gdt, NIGTC]. It refers to Peter, James and the other apostles [NCBC].

QUESTION—What is implied by the words εἴτε ἐγὼ εἴτε ἐκεῖνοι 'whether I or whether those (persons)'?

The words 'preached' are implied [CEV, NLT, TEV, TNT]: whether I *preached* or they. The words 'labored harder' are implied [ICC]: whether I *labored harder* or they after seeing the risen Christ.

QUESTION—To what does οὕτως 'so' refer?

It refers to the essential facts of 15:1–4, especially concerning the resurrection of Jesus [EGT]. It refers to the resurrection of Christ [Ho, ICC, NIC, TNTC, Vn]. It refers to the death and resurrection of Christ [AB]. It refers to the death, burial, and resurrection of Christ [Alf, HNTC, Lns, MNTC, NTC]. It refers back to the words τίνι λόγῳ 'with what word' of 15:2 [Gdt, ICC]. It refers back to 15:1–3a [Herm]. It refers to the message that each preached [TG, TH].

QUESTION—To whom does 'we' in κηρύσσομεν 'we preached' refer?

It includes Paul and the other apostles or evangelists at Corinth but not to the Corinthians themselves [TH].

QUESTION—What is implied by οὕτως κηρύσσομεν 'so we preached'?

It implies that what Paul preached and what the others preached was the same thing [AB, Gdt, NIC, TG].

DISCOURSE UNIT: 15:12–34 [GNT, ICC, Lns, NIC2, NIGTC, NTC, Vn; CEV, ISV, NET, NIV, NLT, TEV]. The topic is that if Christ is risen, the dead in Christ will rise [ICC], the resurrection of the dead [GNT, NTC; ISV, NIV, NLT], the certainty of resurrection [NIC2], God's people will be raised to life [CEV], our resurrection [Lns; TEV], the resurrection of Christ [Vn], consequences of denying the resurrection [NIGTC], no resurrection? [NET].

DISCOURSE UNIT: 15:12–22 [HNTC]. The topic is the implications of the gospel.

DISCOURSE UNIT: 15:12–19 [AB, Alf, Ed, EGT, Gdt, MNTC, NCBC, NIC, NIC2, NTC, TNTC; NAB]. The topic is the consequences if Christ is not risen [AB, Ed, EGT, NIC2, TNTC], the importance of bodily resurrection [MNTC], the pledge of our resurrection [NIC], logical argument [NTC], no resurrection no salvation [NCBC], the resurrection and faith [NAB].

15:12 Now/but if Christ is-preached that he-has-been-raised[a] from (the) dead,[b]

LEXICON—a. perf. pass. indic. of ἐγείρω (See this word at 15:4): 'to be raised' [AB, HNTC, ICC, Lns, NIGTC, NTC; all versions except KJV, NLT]. This passive verb is also translated as an active: 'to rise' [KJV, NLT]. The perfect passive form indicates that Christ was raised and continues to live [NIGTC].

b. νεκρός (LN 23.121) (BAGD 2.a. p. 535): 'dead' [AB, Herm, ICC, LN, Lns, NIGTC, NTC; all versions except CEV, TEV], 'lifeless' [LN], not explicit [HNTC]. This adjective is also translated as a noun: 'death' [CEV, TEV].

QUESTION—What does this verse imply?

It implies that a person cannot believe in the resurrection of Christ from the dead and at the same time deny the resurrection of the dead [Ed, Ho]. It implies that they were admitting the specific to be true (Christ is risen) but denying the generic (the dead are not raised) [Alf].

QUESTION—What relationship is indicated by δέ 'now/but'?

1. It indicates transition [HNTC, ICC, Lns, TH; ISV, KJV, NET, NJB, NRSV, REB, TEV]: *now*. Paul has established the unanimous witness to the resurrection of Christ, now he passes on to the main question [ICC]. The δέ indicates a new thought [TH].
2. It indicates a contrast [Alf, EGT, NIC2, NTC; NIV, NLT]: so we preach and so you believed *but*…how say some of you…. It indicates a contrast to what all Christians proclaim in 15:11 [EGT].

QUESTION—What is assumed by the conditional clause?

This kind of conditional clause assumes something that is already true [Lns, MNTC, Rb, TH]. Paul is arguing against the some who objected, not interacting with the objectors. This does not imply that the objectors agreed that Christ had been raised [Ho].

QUESTION—Who is the agent of the passive verb ἐγήγερται 'has been raised'?

The agent is God [Lns, NTC, TG, TH]: God raised him from the dead. See Romans 6:4 and 8:11 [Lns].

how (do) some among you say that there-is not (a) resurrection[a] of-(the)-dead?

LEXICON—a. ἀνάστασις (LN 23.93) (BAGD 2.b. p. 60): 'resurrection' [AB, BAGD, Herm, HNTC, ICC, LN, Lns, NIGTC, NTC; all versions except CEV, TEV]. The phrase ἀνάστασις νεκρῶν οὐκ ἔστιν 'there is not a resurrection of the dead' is translated 'the dead will not be raised to life' [CEV, TEV].

QUESTION—What is the function of this rhetorical question?

It functions to express surprise [ICC, Lns, TG]: I am amazed! How can you say there is no resurrection! Paul was surprised at their inconsistent thinking [ICC]. It functions to express surprise and censure [TG]: How can you say that? It is not true to say there is no resurrection! (Note: only TG classified this as a rhetorical question. The others simply noted that it expressed surprise.)

QUESTION—Did the Corinthians who denied the resurrection of the dead believe that Christ was raised from the dead?

These Corinthians did believe that Christ was raised from the dead [EGT, Lns, MNTC, NIC, NTC], see 15:1 and 11 [MNTC]. It was not the resurrection of Christ that was denied, but the resurrection of the dead, that is, of corpses [NIC]. They may not have denied Christ's resurrection but only held that His resurrection was one-of-a-kind and did not affect the rest of mankind [ICC]. Paul does not imply that these admitted the resurrection of Christ [Ho].

QUESTION—Who are the τινες 'some'?

They are probably those who opposed Paul, see 4:18 and 9:3 [NIC2]. They were probably influential in the Corinthian church [NIC2, NTC]. They could have been the 'few wise men' referred to in 1:26 [Ed]. They were educated non-Jews who were influenced by Greek philosophy [Alf, ICC, Lns].

QUESTION—What contemporary thinking may have influenced how these Corinthians thought about resurrection?

The Greeks thought that the body was evil and that at death the soul was set free from it. To return to the body was to return to prison [Ho, ICC]. What the Greeks thought about resurrection can be seen in Acts 17:32 where they scoffed [Lns]. The Greeks believed in the immortality of the soul [NCBC, NIC, NTC, TNTC]. The Greeks denied resurrection of the dead as seen in a quote from Aeschylus [NCBC, NIC2]. The Greeks denied bodily resurrection [NCBC, NIC2, TNTC]. The Epicureans taught that death meant the end of bodily existence and in fact ended existence itself either completely or enough to render it worthless [ICC]. Hymenaeus and Philetus taught that the resurrection had already happened (see 2 Timothy 2:18) [HNTC, NCBC]. Some thought that the resurrection was spiritual and that it had already occurred in that they were raised with Christ in baptism [HNTC, NCBC, NTC, TNTC]. Materialists denied any kind of life after death [HNTC].

QUESTION—What kind of resurrection did some at Corinth deny?

It may have been bodily resurrection that they denied [Ho, ICC, NCBC, NIC, NIC2, NTC, TNTC].

15:13 But if there-is not (a) resurrection of-(the)-dead, not-even[a] Christ is-raised;

LEXICON—a. οὐδέ (BAGD 2. p. 591): 'not even' [NTC], 'then not even' [NET, NIV], 'not...either' [BAGD, Herm; NJB, NLT], 'neither' [AB, BAGD, Lns, NIGTC], 'also not' [BAGD], not explicit [TEV]. This word is implied in the translation 'Christ himself' [ICC; CEV, NAB, TNT]. It may also be implied in the translation 'then' [HNTC; ISV, KJV, NRSV, REB]. See this word also at 11:14.

QUESTION—What is Paul saying in this verse?

He is trying to show the Corinthians that their position counters the position established in 15:1–11 [Gdt, NIC2, Vn]. He is showing the Corinthians that to hold their position is to make the resurrection of Christ logically impossible [EGT]. Paul is not merely arguing from general to specific but also from cause to effect: if you deny the effect (the dead are raised) you deny the cause (Christ has been raised) [ICC]. If they were of the opinion that the resurrection was a resurrection of the soul only, then Christ's body is also still in the tomb [NTC].

QUESTION—What relationship is indicated by δέ 'but'?
It indicates a contrast [Alf, EGT, Lns, NIGTC, NTC; KJV, NET]: you say there is no resurrection of the dead, *but* if that is so then neither is Christ raised. It indicates a step in the argument [AB]: *now*.

QUESTION—What is implied by the conditional clause?
Here and in 15:14, 16, 17, 19 it supposes something that is not true [TH].

15:14 And/but if Christ not is-raised, then[a] [also] our preaching[b] (is) in-vain,[c]

TEXT—The word καί 'also' does not occur in some manuscripts. It is included by GNT in brackets indicating difficulty in deciding to include it in the text but without comment. This word seems to be omitted or is not translated by all versions.

LEXICON—a. ἄρα (LN 89.46) (BAGD 3. p. 103): 'then' [BAGD, Herm, HNTC, ICC, LN, Lns, NTC; all versions except CEV, NAB, NIV], 'as a result' [BAGD, LN], 'it follows' [NIGTC], 'so, consequently' [LN], not explicit [AB; CEV, NAB, NIV]. Ἄρα functions to emphasize the if-then inference [BAGD, NIC2]. It indicates the logical consequence of the supposition [TNTC]. It indicates 'then really' or 'the fact is, however some may gloss over it' [Ed]. It means, 'in that case, as an inevitable result' [ICC]. See this word also at 5:10.

b. κήρυγμα (LN **33.258**) (BAGD 2. p. 431): 'preaching' [BAGD, LN, NTC; KJV, NAB, NET, NIV, NJB, NLT], 'proclamation' [AB, Herm, HNTC, Lns, NIGTC; NRSV], 'proclamation of the Gospel' [ICC], 'gospel' [REB], 'message' [CEV, ISV, TNT], 'what is preached' [LN]. This noun is also translated as a verb: 'to preach' [TEV]. The phrase τὸ κήρυγμα ἡμῶν 'our preaching' is translated 'what we have preached' [**LN**]. Κήρυγμα refers back to the corresponding verb of 15:11 [Lns]. The nouns κήρυγμα 'preaching' and πίστις 'faith' of this verse refer back to the corresponding verbs of 15:11 [ICC, NIC2]. See this word also at 1:21 and 15:11.

c. κενός (LN **72.10**, **89.53**, **89.64**) (BAGD 2.a.α. p. 427): 'in vain' [**LN** (89.64); NRSV], 'vain' [BAGD, Herm, NTC; KJV], 'void of content' [NAB], 'worthless' [AB, TG; CEV], 'means nothing' [ISV], 'meaningless' [TNT], 'without substance' [NJB], 'futile' [NET], 'useless' [TNTC; NIV, NLT], 'null and void' [REB], 'empty' [Alf, Ed, Lns, NIC2, Rb, TH], 'hollow and empty' [NIGTC], 'without any result' [**LN** (89.53)], 'without purpose' [**LN** (89.53)], 'untrue' [Gdt, Ho, **LN** (72.10)]. This adjective is also translated as a verb phrase: 'to have nothing (to preach)' [TEV], 'to go for nothing' [HNTC]. It is also translated as a noun: 'empty verbiage' [ICC]. Κενός here means 'lacking contents' [Ed, EGT, ICC, Lns, NIC]. It means 'without reality' [Ho, ICC]. It means 'idle, without result' [Alf]. It means 'void, unsubstantial' [EGT]. It means 'void of power' [Ho]. It indicates 'without basis' [NIC2]. See this word also at 15:10.

1 CORINTHIANS 15:14 279

QUESTION—What relationship is indicated by δέ 'and/but'?
1. It indicates a conjoining of, or a transition to, a new inference [AB, Alf, HNTC, ICC, NTC; all versions]: then Christ is not raised, *and* if he is not raised….
2. It indicates a contrast [Lns, NIGTC]: then Christ is not raised, *but* if he is not raised…. This is a contrast introducing a logical sequence [NIGTC]: *but* if… it follows that…

QUESTION—To whom does ἡμῶν 'our' refer?
It refers to Paul and the apostles [TNTC]. It refers to all the evangelists at Corinth but excludes the readers [TH]. It refers to Paul and his colleagues [EGT].

QUESTION—Does κήρυγμα 'preaching' refer to the activity of preaching or to the contents of what was preached?
It refers to the contents of what was preached [ICC, Lns, TG, TH, TNTC]. It refers to the contents both of what is preached and believed [TH]. It refers to both the activity and to the contents of what was preached [NIC2].

QUESTION—What words are emphasized in this verse?
Both occurrences of κενός 'in vain' are emphasized by occurring first in their clauses [ICC, Lns, NTC, TNTC]. In its first occurrence it is emphasized by being placed first [Alf].

QUESTION—Why would the preaching of Paul and others be in vain?
It would be in vain because the resurrection was central to what they preached [Gdt, HNTC, Ho, MNTC]. It would be in vain because Christ based the validity of his claims on his resurrection. In Romans 1:3 Paul says that Christ was shown to be the Son of God by his resurrection. And the apostles were chosen to be witnesses of Christ's resurrection (Acts 1:22) [Ho].

QUESTION—What did Paul and others preach?
The content of their preaching is seen in 15:3-4 [MNTC]: They preached that Christ died, was buried and rose on the third day. The contents of their preaching are seen in 15:3-7 [NIC2]: They preached that Christ died, was buried, rose on the third day and was seen by many witnesses.

and your faith[a] (is) in-vain;[b]

TEXT—Instead of ὑμῶν 'your', some manuscripts have ἡμῶν 'our'. GNT selects ὑμῶν 'your' with a B rating, indicating that the text is almost certain. Ὑμῶν 'your' is also taken by all the versions.

LEXICON—a. πίστις (LN 31.102) (BAGD 2.d.α. p. 663): 'faith' [AB, BAGD, Herm, HNTC, ICC, Lns, NIGTC, NTC; all versions except NLT, TEV], 'faith in it' [ICC], 'trust in God' [NLT], 'Christian faith'. This noun is also translated as a verb: 'to believe' [TEV]. This indicates believing in the good news about Jesus [BAGD, LN]. See this word also at 2:5 and 12:9.

b. κενός (See this word in the preceding clause): 'in vain' [NTC; NRSV], 'vain' [Herm; KJV], 'means nothing' [ISV], 'meaningless' [TNT], 'useless' [NLT], 'empty' [ICC; NAB, NET], 'worthless' [AB], 'empty' [Lns]. The phrase κενὴ καί 'and in vain' is translated 'and so' [CEV, NIV, NJB], 'and so too' [REB], 'also' [NIGTC]. This adjective is also translated as a verb: 'to have nothing (to believe)' [TEV], 'to go for nothing' [HNTC]. Their faith being in vain was first hinted at in 15:2 [NIC2].

15:15 Moreover[a] we-are-found[b] (to be) false-witnesses[c] of-God,

LEXICON—a. δέ καί (BAGD 4.a. p. 171): 'moreover' [Alf, HNTC, Lns], 'yes, and' [AB], 'yea, and' [KJV], 'and' [NLT, REB], 'also' [Herm; NET], 'more than that' [NIV, TEV], 'what is more' [NJB], 'and, what is more' [ICC], 'furthermore' [TNT], 'in addition' [NTC; ISV], 'indeed' [NAB], 'even' [NRSV], 'but also, but even' [BAGD], not explicit [NIGTC; CEV].

  b. pres. pass. indic. of εὑρίσκω (LN 13.7) (BAGD 2. p. 325): 'to be found (to be)' [BAGD, Herm, LN, Lns, NTC; ISV, KJV, NET, NIV, NRSV, TNT], 'to be found guilty of' [ICC], 'to be exposed as' [NIGTC; NAB], 'to be shown (to be)' [BAGD; TEV], 'to be discovered to be' [LN], 'to appear to be, to be shown to be' [BAGD], not explicit [CEV, NLT]. This passive is also translated actively: 'to prove (to be)' [HNTC; NJB], 'to turn out (to be)' [AB, LN; REB]. Εὑρίσκω here means to be in a state that has not been anticipated [LN]. See this word also at 4:2.

  c. ψευδόμαρτυς (LN 33.273) (BAGD p. 892): 'false witness' [AB, Herm, LN, Lns, NTC; ISV, KJV, NAB, NET, NIV, NJB], 'bearer of false testimony' [HNTC], 'liars in what we witness' [NIGTC], 'man who gives false testimony' [BAGD]. This noun is also translated as a verb phrase: 'to misrepresent (God)' [ICC; NRSV], 'to give false evidence' [REB, TNT], 'to lie' [NLT, TEV], 'to tell lies' [CEV].

QUESTION—What relationship is indicated by δὲ καί 'moreover'?

It emphatically indicates an additive and contrastive relationship [EGT]: but also. It indicates an additive relationship [ICC, TH]: and. The δέ adds a new point and the καί adds the point that this means being false witnesses [Lns]. It indicates an inference that is corollary to 15:13–14 but not coordinate with them [Ed].

QUESTION—How are the nouns related in the genitive construction ψευδομάρτυρες τοῦ θεοῦ 'false witnesses of God'?

  1. God is the object of the false witnessing [AB, Alf, Gdt, Herm, ICC, Lns, NIC, NIC2, NIGTC, NTC, Vn; CEV, ISV, NET, NIV, NJB, NLT, NRSV, REB, TEV, TNT]: false witnesses about God. It indicates that these witnesses were testifying falsely about what God had done [NTC].

  2. God is the one who sent the false witnesses [Ed, MNTC, NIC]: false witnesses whom God sent or who testify in God's name.

QUESTION—To whom does 'we' refer?

It refers to Paul and the other apostles [MNTC].

because we-testified[a] against/concerning[b] God that he-raised the Christ,
LEXICON—a. aorist act. indic. of μαρτυρέω (LN 33.262) (BAGD 1.a. p. 493): 'to testify' [AB, Herm, HNTC, NTC; ISV, KJV, NET, NIV, NJB, NRSV, TNT], 'to give testimony' [NIGTC], 'to bear witness' [Lns; NAB, REB], 'to say' [CEV, NLT, TEV], 'to bear witness (against God) by declaring that' [BAGD], 'to represent (someone) as' [ICC], 'to witness' [LN].
  b. κατά with genitive object (LN 89.4, 90.31) (BAGD I.2.b.β. p. 406): 'against' [AB, Ed, LN (90.31), Lns, NIGTC; NET, NJB], 'in contradiction to' [BAGD, NTC], 'before' [NAB], 'about' [CEV, NIV], 'on behalf of' [ISV], 'of' [Herm, HNTC; KJV, NRSV], 'in conflict with, in opposition to' [LN (90.31)], 'by' [LN (90.29)], 'in relation to, with regard to' [LN (89.4)], not explicit [ICC; NLT, REB, TEV]. The phrase κατὰ τοῦ θεοῦ ὅτι 'against God that' is translated 'that it was God who' [TNT].
QUESTION—What is meant by κατά 'against/concerning'?
  1. It means 'against' [AB, Ed, Gdt, Ho, Lns, NIC, NIC2, NTC, Rb, TH; NET, NJB]. It was to testify against what God did [NIC]. In effect it means that he would have made an accusation against God that he did what he really did not do [Ho, NIC2]. In legal terminology, this preposition is used with verbs of swearing and indicates that he was swearing by God [Lns, NTC].
  2. It means 'concerning' or 'in respect to' [Alf, ICC, MNTC, Vn; CEV, NIV].
QUESTION—What is implied by the inclusion of the article in τὸν Χριστόν 'the Christ'?
It indicates the title 'the Messiah' [EGT, NIC2]. God was bound by Scripture to raise 'the Messiah' from the dead (Luke 24:46, Acts 17:3, 26:22) [EGT]. It simply indicates *the* Christ about whom we have been speaking [ICC]. The article is included to match the formal argumentation [AB]. This is translated without the article, 'Christ' [all versions].

whom not he-raised if-indeed[a] (the) dead not are-raised.
LEXICON—a. εἴπερ ἄρα (LN **89.66**) (BAGD VI.11. p. 220): 'if indeed' [BAGD, Herm, LN; NET], 'if in fact' [NIC2; NIV, TNT], 'if, as a matter of fact' [AB, ICC], 'if in fact it's true' [ISV], 'if it is true that' [NJB, NRSV, TEV], 'if in reality, as they assert' [Alf], 'if really, as you say' [Ed], 'if' [NTC; NAB, NLT], 'whereas if' [REB], 'whereas, if, as they say' [HNTC], 'provided that' [BAGD], 'if so be that' [Lns; KJV], 'if, as they say, it were the case' [NIGTC], 'if after all' [**LN**]. This entire clause is translated 'when he really did not' [CEV].
QUESTION—What is the meaning of εἴπερ ἄρα 'if indeed'?
The suffix -περ functions to emphasize the εἰ 'if': 'if, indeed' [Alf, BAGD, Ed, Gdt, LN (89.66), Lns, NTC, Rb, TNTC]. Paul points out the evil hypothesis as though to say 'Yes—if!' [Lns]. The ἄρα indicates an opinion that is not Paul's own [Alf, Ed, Gdt, HNTC, ICC, NTC, TNTC]: if indeed, as they say. The ἄρα stresses the close connection between this if-clause, and

the main clause [Lns]. The ἄρα functions as an inferential particle 'therefore' [Rb]. The ἄρα functions to strengthen inference [NIC2]. Εἴπερ ἄρα means 'if that wrong assumption were really true' [NIC].

15:16 For if the-dead (are) not raised, not-even Christ is-raised;

QUESTION—What relationship is indicated by γάρ 'for'?

It functions to give the grounds for 15:15 [NIC]: we are found to be false witnesses of God...*since* if the dead are not raised.... It functions to introduce a second series of consequences which support the argument of the first series [Lns]. It functions to explain the reasoning of 15b by repeating it [Herm].

QUESTION—What is the function of this verse as a repetition of 15:13?

Paul repeats in order to keep his readers close to his argument [HNTC]. Paul repeats 15:13 to maintain precision [Alf]. By repeating their position, Paul seems to be pointing out, that ultimately the charge of false witness should be laid at the feet of those who deny the resurrection [NIC2]. It repeats 15:13 in order to take it to an even more hard to accept conclusion [EGT]. Paul repeats 15:13 because it is important. What is true of the dead must be true of Christ as well [NIC]. It functions to show the Corinthians the logical consequences of their position [TNTC]. It functions as the premise from which the inferences 15:17 and 18 are drawn [Gdt, ICC]. It functions to warn the Corinthians of the consequences of denying the resurrection. They were accusing God of lying and the apostles of being false witnesses [NTC].

QUESTION—Who is the actor of the passives ἐγείρονται 'are raised' and ἐγήγερται 'has been raised'?

The actor is God [NIC2, TH, TNTC]: God raised them.

15:17 And/but[a] if Christ not is-raised, your faith (is) futile[b],

LEXICON—a. δέ (See this word at 11:2): 'and' [HNTC, ICC, NTC; all versions except CEV, NRSV], 'but' [Herm, HNTC, Lns, NIGTC], not explicit [CEV, NRSV].

b. μάταιος (LN 65.37) (BAGD p. 495): 'futile' [ICC, LN; NIV, NRSV, TNT], 'useless' [LN, Lns; CEV, NET, NLT], 'worthless' [NTC; ISV, NAB], 'pointless' [NJB], 'vain' [HNTC; KJV], 'in vain' [Herm], 'a delusion' [TEV], 'empty' [BAGD, LN], 'has nothing to it' [REB], 'fruitless' [AB], 'without effect' [NIGTC]. Μάταιος has the meaning of being 'without result' [Ed, Gdt, Ho, ICC, Lns, Vn]. Μάταιος occurs in an emphatic initial position in its clause [TNTC]. See this word also at 3:20.

QUESTION—What relationship is indicated by δέ 'and/but'?

It explains 15:14 [Herm]: our preaching is in vain and your faith is in vain. *You see*, if Christ is not raised, your faith if futile. It repeats 15:14 [TNTC]. It is a repetition of 15:14 but elaborates on it [ICC, Lns, NIC2].

QUESTION—Are the words μάταιος 'futile' (here) and κενός 'in vain' (15:14) synonyms or do they contrast?

1. They are synonyms [AB, TG, TH].

2. They contrast [Ed, Gdt, Ho, ICC, Lns, NIC2, NIGTC, NTC, Rb]. Κενός indicates 'without reality', μάταιος indicates 'without future result' [Ed, Gdt, ICC]. Κενός indicates 'empty', μάταιος indicates 'without result' [Ho, Lns, NIC2, NIGTC]. Κενός indicates 'empty', μάταιος indicates 'aimlessness' [NTC]. Μάταιος, 'without truth' is stronger than κενός [Rb].

QUESTION—Why is their faith futile if Christ is not raised?

Their faith is futile if Christ is not raised because people are made right with God by the resurrection (see Romans 4:25, 5:10, 8:11, 10:9; Acts 13:32-38) [Alf, Ed, EGT, Ho, ICC, Lns, MNTC, NIC, NIC2, NTC]. If Christ did not rise, he was only a man like other men and did not die for our sins [NTC, Rb]. The resurrection of Christ is an essential part of setting people free from sin [AB]. Although Christ died for our sins, the forgiveness of sins is not effective if the victim does not survive [AB, EGT, Gdt]. The resurrection showed that God accepted Christ's sacrifice [EGT, Lns]. A dead Christ could not save others from sin's penalty [ICC].

you-are still[a] in your sins,[b]

LEXICON—a. ἔτι (BAGD 1.a.α. p. 315): 'still' [AB, BAGD, Herm, HNTC, ICC, NIGTC, NTC; all versions except KJV, NJB], 'yet' [BAGD, Lns; KJV]. The phrase ἔτι ἐστὲ ἐν 'you are still in' is translated 'you have not, after all, been released from' [NJB]. Ἔτι indicates the extension of time up to and beyond an expected point [LN]. See this word also at 12:31.

b. ἁμαρτία (LN 88.289, 88.310) (BAGD 1. p. 43): 'sin' [AB, BAGD, Herm, HNTC, ICC, LN (88.289, 88.310), Lns, NIGTC, NTC; all versions except REB], 'old state of sin' [REB], 'guilt' [LN (88.310)].

QUESTION—What is meant by ἔτι ἐστὲ ἐν ταῖς ἁμαρτίαις ὑμων 'you are still in your sins'?

It means that their sins are still unforgiven [EGT, Ho, Lns, NIC2, TG, TH]. It means that they are still in bondage to sin [Herm, TG, TH]. It means they are still like other unbelieving pagans (see John 8:21, Ephesians 2:1, Colossians 2:13) [Lns, MNTC, NIC, TNTC]. It means they are still under death's power [NIC]. It means that they are still liable to God's judgment since they have to relate to God in terms of their sin [HNTC]. It means that sin is still the sphere of their whole moral existence [Ed].

15:18 then[a] also the-ones having-fallen-asleep[b] in[c] Christ perished.[d]

LEXICON—a. ἄρα (BAGD 3. p. 104): 'then' [AB, BAGD, Herm, NIGTC, NTC; KJV, NIV, NRSV, TNT], 'as a result' [BAGD], 'it follows that' [REB], 'it would mean that' [TEV], 'in that case' [NLT], 'accordingly' [Lns], 'furthermore' [NET], 'yes' [HNTC; ISV], 'yes…it follows' [ICC], 'indeed' [NIC2], not explicit [CEV, NAB, NJB]. Here ἄρα emphasizes a further result [BAGD]. See this word also at 15:14.

b. aorist pass. (deponent = act.) participle of κοιμάω (See this word at 11:30): 'to fall asleep' [Herm, HNTC, Lns, NTC; KJV, NAB, NIV, NJB], 'to be laid to sleep' [NIGTC], 'to die' [AB; CEV, ISV, NLT, NRSV,

REB, TEV, TNT], 'to go to one's rest' [ICC]. This participle is also translated as a noun: 'the dead' [NET].

c. ἐν with dative object (LN 83.13, 89.119) (BAGD I.5.d. p. 259): 'in' [AB, Herm, HNTC, LN (83.13, 89.119), Lns, NIGTC, NTC; ISV, KJV, NAB, NET, NIV, NJB, NRSV, TNT], 'in union with, one with, joined closely to' [LN (89.119)]. The phrase ἐν Χριστῷ 'in Christ' is translated 'within Christ's fellowship' [REB], 'putting one's faith in him' [CEV], 'believing in Christ' [NLT], 'believers in Christ' [TEV], 'trusting in Christ' [ICC]. Ἐν indicates here a close personal relation [BAGD (2.a. p. 437)].

d. aorist mid. indic. of ἀπόλλυμι (LN 21.32): 'to perish' [AB, HNTC, LN, Lns, NTC; NET, NLT, NRSV], 'to be perished' [KJV], 'to be lost' [Herm, LN; ISV, NIV, TEV], 'to be completely lost' [CEV], 'to be utterly lost' [NJB, REB], 'to be lost for ever' [TNT], 'to be lost for good' [NIGTC] 'to be the deadest of the dead' [NAB], 'to be lost to Christ' [ICC]. Ἀπόλλυμι means to be lost in the spiritual sense of the word [LN]. The aorist of this verb and of the verb κοιμάομαι 'to fall asleep' indicates that the two events occurred simultaneously: as they were falling asleep they perished [Ed, NTC, TNTC]. See this word also at 10:9.

QUESTION—What relationship is indicated by ἄρα 'then'?

It indicates a further consequence of the position that Christ has not been raised [BAGD, EGT, Lns, NIC, NIC2, NIGTC, TG, TNTC]: if Christ has not been raised *then* those who died in Christ have perished. It indicates a further consequence to 15:16 [TH]. It emphasizes the consequence [BAGD, NIC2].

QUESTION—What is meant by οἱ κοιθέντες ἐν Χριστός 'the ones who have fallen asleep in Christ'?

It means those who died believing in Christ [AB, Ed, Ho, ICC, NIC2, NTC, TG, TH], hoping in Christ [NIC], in communion with Christ [Alf, Ho, ICC], in membership with Christ [Alf], in union with Christ by faith [Lns], in spiritual union with Christ in His death and resurrection [Vn]. For Christians, death is sleep. It is gain; it is to depart and be with Christ (see 1 Thessalonians 4:13, Philippians 1:13, 21, 23) [TNTC].

QUESTION—What is meant by ἀπώλοντο 'perished'?

It means they are in a state of being under the condemnation of God [Gdt]. They are in a state of eternal separation from God [Lns, NCBC]. They have entered the suffering of Hades [Alf]. They are under the rule of death's power [Herm]. They have entered the state of never-ending suffering [Ho, Lns, Rb], in Hell [Lns]. They are in a state of complete loss [ICC]. They have no future of any kind. They perished because they were still in their sins [NIC2]. It means eternal punishment [NTC]. It is the opposite of salvation [TH]. They are lost for good and will never awake from that sleep [NIGTC]. It means a loss of well being, a spiritual and everlasting disaster [Vn].

15:19 If in[a] this life in Christ we-have hoped[b] only,

LEXICON—a. ἐν with dative object (LN 67.136): 'in' [Herm, HNTC, ICC, Lns, NIGTC; ISV, KJV, NET], 'for' [AB, LN (67.136), NTC; NIV, NJB, NLT, NRSV, REB, TEV], 'during, in the course of, within' [LN (67.136)]. This preposition is also translated by a verb: 'to go beyond (this life)' [TNT], 'to be limited to (this life)' [NAB], 'to be good for (this life)' [CEV].

b. perf. act. participle of ἐλπίζω (BAGD 3. p. 252): 'to hope' [AB, HNTC, Lns, NTC; NRSV], 'to have hope' [Herm, ICC; KJV, NET, NIV, NLT], 'to set (one's) hope' [ISV], 'to place hope' [NIGTC], 'to put one's hope in' [BAGD]. This verb is also translated as a noun: 'hope' [CEV, NAB, NJB, REB, TEV, TNT]. The force of the perfect is that the action has been done and its effect continues in the present [Ed, Lns, NTC, TNTC]. See this word also at 13:7.

QUESTION—What part of the clause does μόνος 'only' modify?

1. It modifies the phrase 'in this life' [AB, Herm, Ho, NCBC, NIC, NIC2, NTC, TG; all versions]: if in this life *only* we have hoped in Christ. It modifies 'in this life' because it contrasts with those who have died in the previous verse—they died and perished and we, if our hopes in Christ are limited to this life, are the most miserable of men [Ho]. The word 'only' is emphatic and highlights the contrast between this life and the one to come [NIC].
2. It modifies the verb 'we have hoped' [EGT]: if in this life we have *only* hoped in Christ. The idea is that in this life *only* hope in Christ is all we have, that is, no rescue from sin and no inheritance in Heaven.
3. It modifies the whole clause [Alf, Ed, Gdt, HNTC, Lns, NIGTC, Rb, TNTC, Vn]: if in this life we have hoped in Christ, *and that is all we have done*. The position of μόνον 'only' at the end of the sentence seems to indicate that it modifies the whole clause rather than any one part of it [HNTC].

QUESTION—What is the meaning of the verb phrase ἠλπικότες ἐσμέν 'having hoped we are'?

1. It means the same as the perfect form ἠλπίκαμεν 'we have hoped (in Christ)' [AB, EGT, HNTC, NTC, Rb; ISV, NRSV].
2. The verb 'to be' should be taken as a *copula* with the resultant meaning '*we are* those who have hoped (in Christ)' [Ho, ICC, Lns, Vn]. The verb phrase expresses what we are more than what we do, we are hopers [Ho, Vn].

QUESTION—What words are emphasized in this verse?

The word μόνον 'only' is placed last in its clause for emphasis [ICC, Lns, NIC, TH, Vn]. Both the word μόνον 'only' and the phrase ἐν τῇ ζωῇ ταύτῃ 'in this life' are emphasized [ICC, TH, Vn].

we-are most-pitiable^a of-all people.^b

LEXICON—a. ἐλεεινότερος (LN **88.79**) (BAGD p. 249): 'most pitiable' [HNTC, **LN**, Lns; NAB, NJB, TNT], 'more pitiable' [Herm], 'most to be pitied' [NIGTC; REB], 'most miserable' [BAGD; KJV, NLT], 'worse off' [CEV]. This comparative adjective is also translated as a verb: 'more to be pitied' [AB; NET, NIV], 'more truly to be pitied' [ICC], 'most to be pitied' [NTC; NRSV]. The phrase ἐλεεινότεροι...ἐσμέν 'more pitiable...we are' is translated 'we deserve more pity' [**LN**; ISV, TEV]. The positive form of the adjective, ἐλεεινός, means 'pitiable, miserable' [BAGD, LN]. The adjective is comparative but the word πάντες 'all' causes the superlative meaning [AB].

b. ἄνθρωπος (See this word at 13:1): 'person' [AB; ISV, NJB, NRSV, REB], 'human being' [ICC, NIGTC], 'man' [Herm, HNTC, Lns; KJV, NAB, NIV, TNT]. The phrase πάντων ἀνθρώπων 'all people' is translated 'anyone' [NET], 'anyone else' [CEV], 'anyone else in all the world' [TEV], 'people in the world' [NLT].

QUESTION—Why would they be the most to be pitied of all persons?

They are most to be pitied because they have lived a life of hardship, self-denial, suffering, and possible martyrdom, but it was for no reason if Christ has not been raised [AB, Alf, EGT, Gdt, HNTC, Ho, ICC, Lns, MNTC, NCBC, NIC, Rb, TNTC]. They are most to be pitied because a person who has his hopes disappointed is worse off than a person who has no hope to start with [AB]. They are most to be pitied because the Christian would sacrifice present enjoyment and future eternal life [HNTC]. They are most to be pitied for the chain of consequences (15:13–18) that follow if there is no resurrection [NIGTC]. They are most to be pitied because there is no present forgiveness of sin and no inheritance in heaven [EGT, NIC]. They are most to be pitied because they hope for the restoration of all things in heaven and if Christ is not raised this is no longer true [NTC].

DISCOURSE UNIT: 15:20–34 [Ed]. The topic is the necessity of the resurrection of the dead.

DISCOURSE UNIT: 15:20–28 [AB, Alf, EGT, Gdt, ICC, MNTC, NCBC, NIC2, NTC, TNTC; NAB]. The topic is consequences of Christ's resurrection [AB, ICC, TNTC], restatement of Christ's resurrection [Alf], the resurrection plan [MNTC], firstfruits and harvest [NCBC], Christ being raised [NIC2], the reality of the resurrection [NTC], Christ, the firstfruit of the resurrection [EGT; NAB].

DISCOURSE UNIT: 15:20–22 [NTC]. The topic is existence in Adam and in Christ.

15:20 But-now^a Christ is-raised from (the) dead

LEXICON—a. νυνί δέ (See this phrase at 12:18): 'but now' [AB, Herm, Lns, NTC; KJV, NET], 'but now in fact' [HNTC], 'but at this moment' [ISV], 'but in fact' [NRSV, TNT], 'in fact, however' [NJB], 'in reality, however'

[NIGTC], 'but the fact is' [NLT], 'but the truth is' [REB, TEV], 'but as it is' [NAB], 'but…indeed' [NIV], 'but this dismal doctrine is not true' [ICC], 'but' [CEV]. Νυνί indicates 'as matters now stand' [Alf], 'now as things are' [Ed], 'now as matters actually stand' [Ho]. Νυνί δέ indicates something like 'but as it is, indeed' [NIC2].

QUESTION—What relationship is indicated by δέ 'but'?

It indicates contrast [AB, Ed, Gdt, HNTC, Ho, ICC, Lns, NIGTC, NTC, Rb, TH, TNTC, Vn; all versions]: if Christ is not raised, we are the most pitiable of all people, *but* Christ is raised from the dead. The contrast is with the preceding conditions [AB]. Νυνί δέ marks an emphatic transition from the negative hypothesis of no resurrection to the positive results of believing in the resurrection of Christ [TH]. The word *now* contrasts the truth of this fact and the emptiness resulting from its denial [Gdt]. The contrast is between the consequences of the denial of Christ's resurrection and the results of its affirmation [Ho].

QUESTION—What is indicated by νυνί 'now'?

The form is the emphatic form of νῦν 'now' [Rb]. It indicates the conclusion of Paul's long discussion of the Corinthian denial of the resurrection of the dead [EGT, NTC]. It functions to turn the discussion from a negative argument against an absurd idea to a positive treatment of facts [Vn]. It has a logical sense here [Lns]: at this point in the discussion. This introduces the real situation after having contemplated the unreal suppositions [NIGTC]. It has both a temporal and a logical sense here [NIC2, NTC].

QUESTION—Who is the agent of the passive verb ἐγήγερται 'has been raised'?

God is the agent [NIC, TH]: God raised Christ from the dead.

QUESTION—What is implied by the phrase ἐκ νεκρῶν 'from the dead'?

It implies bodily resurrection as it cannot mean that Christ was spiritually dead [Ed, Gdt].

(the) firstfruits[a] of-the-ones having-fallen-asleep.

LEXICON—a. ἀπαρχή (LN **61.8**, 53.23) (BAGD 1.b.α. p. 81): 'firstfruits' [AB, Herm, HNTC, Lns, NTC; KJV, NAB, NET, NIV, NJB, NRSV], 'firstfruits of the harvest' [NIGTC; REB], 'the first one offered in the harvest' [ISV], 'first' [BAGD, **LN** (61.8)], 'first portion, first offering' [LN (53.23)]. This whole phrase is translated 'as the guarantee that those who sleep in death will also be raised' [TEV], 'and he makes us certain that others will also be raised to life' [CEV], 'he has become the first of a great harvest' [NLT], 'this is the guarantee that those who have died will be raised also' [TNT], 'He is no solitary exception, but the first and foremost example of many that are to be awakened' [ICC]. Ἀπαρχή indicates the first of a set [LN]. It has almost the meaning of πρῶτος 'first' as the reference to 'first-fruits' here is greatly weakened [BAGD]. See Colossians 1:18 as a similar figure to "firstfruits" [Ed, Ho, Rb].

QUESTION—Does the word ἀπαρχή 'firstfruits' comprise a metaphor?

The word ἀπαρχή 'firstfruits' has lost its reference to the festival of firstfruits and means simply 'first' in a series [BAGD, Herm, LN]. It does not refer to Leviticus but may have meant that to the Jews [Alf]. (Note: other commentaries seemed to treat this as a metaphor.)

QUESTION—If the word ἀπαρχή 'firstfruits' is a metaphor, to what festival does it refer?

It refers to the Jewish festival of firstfruits described in Leviticus 23:10ff in which the people were to bring a sheaf of the newly ripened grain to the priest and he would offer it to God [AB, Ed, EGT, Gdt, HNTC, Ho, ICC, Lns, MNTC, NIC2, NTC, TNTC]. This was to be done on the day after the Sabbath of the Passover [Gdt, ICC, TH]. Jesus was crucified on the 14th of Nisan [Gdt], the festival of firstfruits took place on the 16th of Nisan, the day of Christ's resurrection [EGT, Gdt]. It refers to the earliest ripe portion of a crop or a tree [Vn].

QUESTION—If the image of this metaphor is the first sheaf of grain from the harvest, and the topic is Christ what is the point of similarity?

The point of similarity is a guarantee, pledge, promise, or down payment of future fulfillment [Ed, EGT, HNTC, Ho, Lns, MNTC, NCBC, NIC2, NTC, TG, TH, TNTC]: as the firstfruits guaranteed the full harvest, so the resurrection of Christ guaranteed the resurrection of those believers who had died. The point of similarity is certainty [Lns]: as the full harvest is certain to follow the offering of the firstfruits, so the resurrection of believers is certain to follow the resurrection of Christ. The point of similarity is identity of nature [ICC]: as the firstfruits are the same kind as the full harvest, so what happens to the first fruits happens to the whole. The point of similarity is membership in a whole [MNTC, NIC, TNTC]: as the firstfruits are part of the harvest, so what happens to one part happens to the whole. The metaphor indicates that the resurrection of believers is guaranteed by God himself [NIC2].

QUESTION—If others have also risen from the dead like Lazarus and those whom Elisha and Elijah raised, how is Jesus the firstfruits?

All others who were raised from the dead later died. Jesus' resurrection from the dead is unique in that he rose from the dead never to die again [AB, Ed, Lns, MNTC, NTC]. Jesus' resurrection was victory over death itself [NTC].

QUESTION—To whom does τῶν κεκοιμημένων 'of those who have fallen asleep' refer?

It refers to those who died believing in Christ [AB, Alf, NIC, NIC2, TG, TNTC].

15:21 For since[a] through[b] man (came) death,[c]

LEXICON—a. ἐπειδή (LN 89.32) (BAGD 2. p. 284): 'since' [AB, BAGD, Herm, HNTC, ICC, LN, Lns, NIGTC, NTC; ISV, KJV, NET, NIV, NRSV, REB, TNT], 'just as' [CEV, NLT, TEV], 'as it was' [NJB], 'because' [Ed, LN], 'inasmuch as' [LN], 'it is recognized' [Herm]. This conjunction is left implicit in the first clause but represented by its reciprocal in the second: 'hence (the resurrection of the dead comes...)' [NAB].

- b. διά with genitive object (See this word at 11:12): 'through' [AB, Herm, ICC, NIGTC; ISV, NAB, NET, NIV, NLT, NRSV], 'by' [HNTC, Lns, NTC; KJV, NJB], 'by means of' [Ho; TEV], 'because of' [CEV]. This preposition is also translated as a verb: 'to bring (death)' [REB], 'to cause (death)' [TNT]. Διά indicates that man is the agent by which death came about [NTC]. It indicates that man is the instrument by which death and resurrection came about [ICC]. It indicates that death and resurrection are caused by man [Gdt, Ho; TNT].
- c. θάνατος (LN 23.99) (BAGD 1.b.γ. p. 351): 'death' [AB, Herm, HNTC, ICC, Lns, NIGTC, NTC; all versions except CEV]. This noun is also translated as a verb: 'to die' [CEV]. This indicates physical death [Ho, TNTC].

QUESTION—What relationship is indicated by γάρ 'for'?

It explains 15:20 by showing how Christ's being the firstfruits necessarily implied the resurrection of the dead [Alf, EGT, Gdt, Lns, MNTC, NIC2]: Christ has become the firstfruits of them that sleep. *you see* since by man came death.... It indicates the reason for 15:20 [Ho, NIC]: Christ has become the firstfruits of them that sleep. *because* since by man came death.... The combination ἐπειδὴ γάρ 'for since' functions to explain how death came into the world [NTC].

QUESTION—What is the significance of the lack of articles before the nouns of this verse?

The lack of articles before the nouns functions to highlight the quality of the nouns man, death, resurrection, and dead [Lns, NTC]. The lack of article before 'resurrection' and 'death' focuses on the quality of each [NIC]. The repetition of the noun ἄνθρωπος 'man' and the lack of the article with it function to emphasize it.

QUESTION—To whom does ἄνθρωπος 'man' refer?

It refers to Adam [HNTC, Ho, MNTC, NIC2, NIGTC].

through man (came) also (the) resurrection of-(the)-dead.
QUESTION—To whom does ἄνθρωπος 'man' refer?
It refers to Christ [HNTC, Ho, MNTC, NIGTC, TH].

15:22 For as[a] in[b] Adam all die,[c]

LEXICON—a. ὥσπερ (See this word at 11:12): 'as' [Herm, HNTC, ICC, NTC; ISV, KJV, NIV, NRSV, REB], 'just as' [AB, NIGTC; NAB, NET, NJB, TEV, TNT], 'even as' [Lns], not explicit [CEV, NLT].

- b. ἐν with dative object (LN 89.119) (BAGD I.5.d. p. 260): 'in' [AB, Herm, HNTC, LN, Lns, NIGTC, NTC; all versions except CEV, NLT, TEV], 'because of (their) union with' [TEV], 'in virtue of (our) union with' [ICC], 'one with, in union with, joined closely to' [LN], 'because of a connection with' [BAGD]. This preposition is also translated by a verb phrase: '(Adam) brought (death)' [CEV], '(everyone dies, because all of us) are related to (Adam)' [NLT]. Ἐν indicates a close personal relation [BAGD].

c. pres. act. indic. of ἀποθνήσκω (See this word at 15:3): 'to die' [AB, Herm, HNTC, ICC, Lns, NIGTC, NTC; all versions except CEV]. This verb is also translated as a noun: 'death' [CEV]. The present tense indicates a continuous aspect [Lns, NIC]: all are dying.

QUESTION—What relationship is indicated by γάρ 'for'?

It indicates the reason supporting 15:21 [NIC]: by man came also the resurrection of the dead *because* as in Adam all die so also in Christ will all be made alive. It proves 15:21 [Gdt]. It explains why Adam is the source of death and Christ is the source of life [Ho]. It combines with 15:21 to further explain how Christ is the firstfruits of those who sleep [Alf, EGT, Lns, NIC2]. Verse 15:21 supports 15:20 by showing that Christ was man and only by being man could he have an influence on mankind. Verse 15:22 supports 15:20 by showing that Christ was the source of life as Adam was the source of death to men [Alf].

QUESTION—What is the meaning of ἐν 'in'?

It means to have a kinship relation with [TNTC]. It means to be in union with [Ed, Ho, TG; TEV], a union that is a representative and living union [Ho]. It means to be related to [TH, Vn; NLT]. It means to be connected with [BAGD, Lns, NIC]. It means to have a common nature with [Alf, ICC]. It means to have a natural relation to Adam but a spiritual relation to Christ [Vn]. It means on one had to be born from Adam and so share in his sin and death, but on the other hand to be part of a new humanity that Christ made available [NIC2]. It means to have one's origin in Adam but to be part of Christ through faith [NTC].

so^a also in^b Christ all will-be-made-alive.^c

LEXICON—a. οὕτως (See this word at 11:12): 'so' [AB, Herm, HNTC, ICC; ISV, KJV, NAB, NET, NIV, NJB, NRSV, REB, TNT], 'even so' [NIGTC], 'in the same way' [TEV], 'thus' [Lns, NTC], not explicit [CEV, NLT].

b. ἐν with dative object (See above in this verse): 'in' [AB, Herm, HNTC, Lns, NIGTC, NTC; all versions except CEV, NLT, TEV], 'because of (one's) union with' [TEV], 'in virtue of (our) union with' [ICC]. This preposition is also translated with verbal phrases such as: '(Christ) will bring (life)' [CEV], '(all who) are related to (Christ)' [NLT].

c. fut. pass. indic. of ζωοποιέω (LN **23.92**) (BAGD 1. p. 341): 'to be made alive' [AB, Herm, ICC, LN, Lns, NTC; ISV, KJV, NET, NIV, NRSV], 'to be raised to life' [**LN**; TEV], 'to be brought to life' [HNTC, NIGTC; NJB, REB, TNT], 'to be given new life' [NLT], 'to be given life' [BAGD]. This passive is also translated actively: 'to bring life to' [CEV], 'to come to life' [NAB]. The future tense refers to the resurrection on the last day [Lns, NIC, NTC].

QUESTION—How inclusive is the word 'all' in πάντες ζῳοποιηθήσονται 'all will be made alive'?
1. It is not universal, but includes only those who are ἐν τῷ Χριστῷ 'in Christ', that is, those who believe in Him [AB, Ed, Gdt, Herm, HNTC, Ho, Lns, MNTC, NIC, NIC2, NTC, Rb, TG, TNTC, Vn]. The reasons this 'all' is not inclusive of all mankind are as follows: (a) the word πάντες 'all' in both clauses is modified, in the first clause by the words 'in Adam', in the second by the words 'in Christ'; (b) the verb ζωοποιέω 'to make alive' is never used to describe those outside of Christ; (c) the context is only discussing the destiny of the righteous [Ho]. All men will not be raised to life in Christ (see Matthew 12:32, 25:46; Mk 9:48, 14:21; 2 Thessalonians 1:9; and Phil 3.19) [Gdt]. See 1 Thessalonians 4:16 [HNTC].
2. It is universal including all men [ICC, TH]. It may mean that all mankind will be raised but that not all will be saved [ICC]. It probably indicates that only because of Christ will there be a resurrection of the dead [TH].

QUESTION—Who is the actor of the passive ζῳοποιηθήσονται 'they will be made alive'?

Christ is the actor [NTC]: Christ will make them alive.

DISCOURSE UNIT: 15:23–28 [HNTC, NTC]. The topic is the Christian apocalypse [HNTC], the coming of the Lord [NTC].

15:23 But[a] each-one in his-own order;[b]

LEXICON—a. δέ (See this word at 11:2): 'but' [AB, Herm, ICC, NIGTC, NTC; all versions except ISV], 'however' [HNTC; ISV], 'yet' [Lns].
b. τάγμα (LN **62.7**) (BAGD 1.b. p. 803): 'order' [Herm, **LN**, Lns, NTC; KJV, NET, NLT, NRSV], 'proper order' [ICC; ISV, NAB, NJB, REB, TEV, TNT], 'particular order' [AB], 'proper arranged order'. [NIGTC], 'turn' [NIV], 'rank' [HNTC], 'class, group' [BAGD], 'right order, good order, in order, in an orderly manner' [LN]. This noun is also translated as a verb: 'to wait one's turn' [CEV].

QUESTION—What is implied in this phrase?

The words 'is made alive' are implied [HNTC, NIC, TH; CEV, ISV, NLT, TEV]: each *is made alive* in his own order.

QUESTION—What relationship is indicated by δέ 'for'?

It indicates contrast [NIC2, NTC, TH]: all will be made alive, *but* each one in his own order. It indicates a slight contrast with the statement that all will be made alive in 15:22 [NIC2]. The contrast is probably between 'all' of 15:22 and 'each' of this verse [TH]. It indicates a conjoining relationship [EGT, Lns], adding a new point to the explanation of all believers being made alive [Lns].

QUESTION—What is implied in the word τάγμα 'order'?
1. It implies order of sequence in which one thing follows another [AB, Gdt, Ho, ICC, MNTC, NIC2, Rb, TG, TH; CEV, NIV]: each following in its own turn. It refers to a place in a series allotted to a group or individual

[Gdt]. It is a military term referring to a company or troop and here indicates such a company marching up in its proper position and order [ICC]. It implies class, company, or group [ICC, NIC2, Rb]: each in his own company. The picture is of companies of soldiers moving along in their proper position and order [ICC].
2. It implies order of rank or status [Alf, EGT, NTC, Vn]: each in its own rank. It refers to rank in which Christ has supremacy [NTC, Vn].
3. It implies both a group and a position [HNTC]. It is best to keep the ambiguity of the Greek term which initially carried the meaning of a troop of soldiers and later was used to denote any group or position [HNTC].

(the) firstfruits[a] Christ, then[b] at[c] his coming[d] the-ones of-Christ,
LEXICON—a. ἀπαρχή (See this word at 15:20): 'firstfruits' [AB, Herm, HNTC, Lns, NIGTC, NTC; KJV, NAB, NET, NIV, NJB, NRSV, REB], 'first sheaf' [ICC], 'first' [ISV], 'first of all' [TEV], 'first as guarantee' [TNT]. This adverb is also translated as a clause: 'was raised first' [NLT], 'was the first to be raised to life' [CEV].
b. ἔπειτα (See this word at 12:28): 'then' [Herm, HNTC, Lns, NTC; ISV, NAB, NET, NIV, NLT, NRSV, TEV, TNT], 'afterward(s)' [ICC; KJV, REB], 'then afterward' [NIGTC], 'after this' [Ed], 'next' [AB], 'and next' [NJB], 'next in order' [NCBC], not explicit [CEV]. Ἔπειτα 'then' is more specifically defined by the words 'at his coming' [EGT, Lns, NIC2]: then—at his coming.
c. ἐν with dative object (LN 67.33) (BAGD II.2. p. 260): 'at' [Herm, HNTC, Lns, NIGTC, NTC; KJV, NAB, NJB, NRSV, REB], 'at the time of' [LN; TEV], 'when' [LN; CEV, ISV, NET, NIV, NLT, TNT], 'in' [AB, BAGD, ICC].
d. παρουσία (LN 15.86) (BAGD 2.b.α. p. 630): 'coming' [AB, BAGD, Herm, HNTC, LN, NIGTC, NTC; KJV, NAB, NJB, NRSV, REB, TEV], 'day of His Coming' [ICC], 'Parousia' [Lns], 'advent' [BAGD], 'arrival' [LN]. This noun is also translated as a verb: 'to come' [ISV, NET, NIV, TNT], 'to come back' [NLT], 'to return' [CEV]. Παρουσία refers to the Second Coming of Christ [Ed, EGT, Ho, ICC, NIC, NIC2, TNTC]. More specifically it indicates Christ's coming at the last day [Lns, TG].
QUESTION—How are the nouns related in the genitive construction οἱ τοῦ Χριστοῦ 'the ones of Christ' and to whom does it refer?

They are related in a possessive relationship [AB, HNTC, Lns, MNTC, NIC2, NIGTC, NTC, TG, TH, TNTC; all versions]: those who belong to Christ. This group refers to the dead in Christ (see 1 Thessalonians 4:16) [Alf]. It refers to those whom Christ rules [Ed]. It refers to believers in Christ [Herm, HNTC, Lns, MNTC, NTC, TG]. Paul had just been talking in 15:22 about 'those made alive in Christ'. Here this phrase refers to all the saved [ICC].

15:24 Then[a] the end,[b] when he-hands-over[c] the kingdom[d] to God and (the) Father,

LEXICON—a. εἶτα (See this word at 15:5): 'then' [AB, Herm, HNTC, Lns, NIGTC, NTC; all versions except NAB, NJB, NLT], 'after that' [ICC; NAB, NJB, NLT], 'after this' [Ed], 'next, after that' [NCBC].

b. τέλος (LN 61.17, 67.66) (BAGD 1.b. p. 811, 1.d.α. p. 812, 2. p. 812): 'end' [AB, BAGD (1.b.), Herm, LN (67.66), Lns, NTC; all versions], 'the End' [HNTC, ICC, NIGTC]. The phrase τὸ τέλος 'the end' also means 'finally' [BAGD (1.d.α.), LN (61.17)], 'in conclusion' [LN (61.17)], 'rest, remainder' [BAGD (2)]. See this word also at 1:8 and 10:11.

c. pres. act. subj. of παραδίδωμι (See this word at 11:2 and 13:3): 'to hand over' [Herm, HNTC, NIGTC; ISV, NAB, NET, NIV, NJB, NRSV, TEV], 'to turn over' [NLT], 'to give' [CEV], 'to give up into the hands of' [ICC], 'to deliver' [AB, Lns, NTC; TNT], 'to deliver up' [KJV, REB].

d. βασιλεία (LN 1.82, 37.64) (BAGD 1. p. 134): 'kingdom' [AB, BAGD, HNTC, LN (1.82), Lns, NTC; all versions except NLT, TEV, TNT], 'Kingdom' [NLT, TEV, TNT], 'sovereignty' [Herm], 'kingship' [BAGD, ICC], 'rule' [LN (37.64), NIGTC], 'reign' [LN (37.64)], 'royal power, royal rule' [BAGD]. This word can either refer to an area over which a king rules or the thing that a king does [LN (1.82, 37.64)]. See this word also at 4:20.

QUESTION—Does εἶτα 'then' imply an interval of time between the resurrection of believers and the end?

1. It may imply an interval of time [Gdt, MNTC, NCBC, TNTC, Vn]. It implies an interval of indeterminate length but the context indicates that the interval is short [NCBC]. Εἶτα does not indicate 'then immediately' as τότε would, but rather 'then' after an interval [Gdt, Vn] (see Mark 4:17, 28 and verses 5 and 7 of this chapter). The interval indicated here refers to Christ's Millennial reign [MNTC, Vn]. The interval between the resurrection of believers and the end will be filled with the action of Christ abolishing all rule, authority and power [Gdt]. The interval between Christ's coming and the establishment of his kingdom referred to here can be seen in Matthew 24 and 25. There the gathering of his elect is described as one of the signs that precede the establishment of his kingdom [MNTC]. The end will be separated from Christ's coming by the period in which Christ subdues his enemies [Gdt].

2. It does not imply an interval [EGT, HNTC, Ho, Lns, NIC2, NTC]. The brevity of the phrase εἶτα τὸ τέλος 'then the end' suggests that there is no interval between the resurrection of believers and the end [NTC]. The words ἀπαρχή 'firstfruits', ἔπειτα 'then' (of 15:23) and εἶτα 'then' (here) do not indicate three periods of time. There is a definite period between the first two (between Christ's resurrection and the resurrection of believers), but that is not signified by ἔπειτα 'then' but by the two phrases, ἔπειτα...ἐν τῇ παρουσίᾳ αὐτοῦ 'then...at his coming', since ἔπειτα can mean either 'immediately after' or 'at some time after'. Here

the εἶτα is defined by the two following 'when' clauses. The general resurrection of believers and unbelievers of John 5:29 is a single event and is what is signified here [Lns]. There are only two events in the resurrection referred to here: Christ's resurrection and the resurrection of believers [NIC2, TNTC]. The εἶτα indicates that following Christ's coming and the resurrection of believers, there will be the two events of handing over the kingdom and the abolishing of authority. These are two aspects of the end [NIC2]. It seems to imply that there is no time lapse between the resurrection of the believers and the end of the world [Ho].
3. It is impossible to say whether an interval is implied or not since εἶτα 'then' may either indicate something immediately following simply to something just following [ICC, NIGTC].

QUESTION—To what does βασιλεία 'kingdom' refer here?

It refers to *rule* rather than *realm* [NIC2, TNTC]. It refers to 'realm' or 'royal power' [TG]. It refers to Christ's rule, not to the church [Lns]. It refers to 'sovereignty' that was given to Christ by God for a definite purpose [ICC].

QUESTION—What is the function of the two when-clauses here?

The two when-clauses function to define the word εἶτα 'then' [EGT, Lns, NIC, NIC2]: then comes the end, that is, *when* he hands over the kingdom to God even the Father *and when* he abolishes all rule and all authority and power. The two when-clauses function to define the phrase τὸ τέλος 'the end' [Herm]. The when clauses indicate the time when the end will come. It will be at the same time Christ delivers the kingdom to the Father [Ed].

QUESTION—Does τὸ τέλος 'the end' mean 'the rest (of the dead)' here?

Τὸ τέλος does not mean 'the rest' referring to a third group to be raised [Herm, HNTC, Lns, NCBC, NIC, NIC2, NTC, TNTC]. This meaning is not supported anywhere else in the New Testament [Herm, HNTC, Lns]. This meaning is seldom and only debatably attested in Greek literature [NCBC, TNTC]. Such a meaning is not even in the dictionaries [Lns]. The context is not referring to unbelievers, but to believers [NIC, NIC2, TNTC]. Τέλος never indicates a group of people [TNTC].

QUESTION—To what does the τὸ τέλος 'the end' refer?

It refers to the end of the world [EGT, Ho, NCBC, NIC, Rb, TG]. 'The end' is defined by the two following when-clauses [EGT, Herm, HNTC, Lns, NCBC, NIC, NIC2]: then comes the end, that is, *when* he hands over the kingdom to God even the Father *and when* he abolishes all rule and all authority and power. It refers to the completion of the saving work of Christ [Alf, Gdt, NTC]. It refers to the end of the present age [Ed, Ho, NCBC]. It refers to the reaching of God's goal or final stage toward which all has been directed [AB, Gdt, Ho, TNTC]. It refers to the end in an absolute sense [Gdt, NIC]. Τό τέλος refers to the last event in a series which is given in 15:25–28 [Vn]. See Matthew 24:6, 14, Mark 13:7, Luke 21:9, and 1 Peter 4:7 [Ed, Ho].

QUESTION—In what sense will Christ hand over the kingdom to God?

God gave power to Christ for a specified purpose. When he fulfills that purpose he returns it back to God [ICC, Vn]. This does not refer to Christ's authority over all creatures which belongs to him as a divine person of the trinity nor his authority over his own people which belongs to him as the incarnate Son of God. After Christ's resurrection he was given all authority and power, which included authority over 'all rule, authority, and power'. It is this authority, to accomplish all that is involved in the work of redemption, that he will hand back to God and no longer rule as Mediator, but only as God [Ho, NIC]. God gave Christ power after his resurrection for the purpose of destroying hostile powers. It is this kingship that Christ gives back to the Father [Herm, NTC]. It does not mean that he will cease to rule, but rather that God's eternal kingdom will begin [EGT]. A difference in role and procedure are implied, but not a difference in status [HNTC]. It does not mean that Christ will lose anything but that he will bring a specified period to a victorious completion [ICC]. To the extent that the Father does not rule while Christ is ruling, to that extent Christ will not rule when he hands back the rule to the Father [Lns]. Christ began to establish the kingdom at the beginning of his ministry. At the end he will hand the kingdom over to God [NIC]. At the end Christ will have gained full authority over absolutely everything. He will give this authority to God [TNTC].

when he-abolishes[a] all rule[b] and all authority[c] and power.[d]

LEXICON—a. aorist act. subj. of καταργέω (LN 76.12): 'to abolish' [LN, Lns, NTC; NJB, TNT], 'to destroy' [CEV, NAB, NIV, NRSV], 'to do away with' [ISV], 'to bring to an end' [NET], 'to nullify' [AB], 'to bring to naught' [HNTC, ICC], 'to put down' [KJV, NLT], 'to depose' [REB], 'to overcome' [TEV], 'to annihilate' [Herm, NIGTC], 'to invalidate, to cause not to function' [LN]. Καταργέω indicates 'to make ineffective' [NTC, TH, TNTC]. It means to render null and void [TNTC], to reduce to inactivity [Vn], to reduce to impotence [Gdt, NIC], to render inoperative [NIGTC], to subdue, to deprive of power [Ho], to abolish so as not to exist [MNTC], to reduce to inactivity, to supersede, to subdue, to abolish, to destroy [ICC]. It does not mean 'to annihilate' [Ho, NIC]. See this word also at 13:8.

b. ἀρχή (LN 12.44, 37.56) (BAGD 3. p. 112): 'rule' [AB, Lns, NIGTC, NTC; KJV, NET, TNT], 'other rule' [ICC], 'ruler' [BAGD, LN (12.44, 37.56); ISV, NRSV], 'Ruler' [HNTC], 'spiritual ruler' [TEV], 'sovereignty' [NAB, REB], 'dominion' [NIV], 'power, lordship, wicked force' [LN (12.44)], 'authority' [BAGD, Herm, LN (12.44)], 'principality' [NJB]. The phrase πᾶσαν ἀρχὴν καὶ πᾶσαν ἐξουσίαν καὶ δύναμιν 'all rule and all authority and power' is translated 'all powers and forces' [CEV], 'all enemies of every kind' [NLT]. Ἀρχή here refers to angelic or demonic powers [BAGD].

c. ἐξουσία (LN 12.44, 37.35, 37.38, 76.12) (BAGD 4.c.β. p. 278): 'authority' [AB, LN (12.44), Lns, NIGTC, NTC; all versions except CEV, NJB, NLT], 'Authority' [HNTC], 'other authority' [ICC], 'ruling force' [NJB], 'supernatural power' [LN (12.44)], 'power' [Herm, LN (12.44, 76.12)], 'authority to rule, right to control' [LN (37.35)], 'an authority' [LN (37.38)], 'ruler' [LN (12.44, 37.38)], 'lordship, wicked force' [LN (12.44)], not explicit [CEV, NLT]. Ἐξουσία here refers to rulers and functionaries of the spirit world [BAGD]. See this word also at 11:10.

d. δύναμις (LN 12.44, 37.61, 76.1) (BAGD 6. p. 208): 'power' [AB, BAGD, LN (12.44, 76.1), Lns, NIGTC, NTC; all versions except CEV, NLT], 'force' [Herm], 'Power' [HNTC], 'other power' [ICC], 'ruler' [LN (12.44, 37.61)], 'authority, lordship, wicked force' [LN (12.44)], not explicit [CEV, NLT]. Δύναμις here refers to a personal supernatural spirit or angel [BAGD].

QUESTION—What is the time relationship between the two 'when' clauses?

The action of the second clause precedes the action of the first [Ed, EGT, Gdt, Herm, ICC, NIC, NIC2, NTC, TNTC; CEV, ISV, NAB, NIV, NJB, NLT, NRSV, REB, TEV, TNT]: he abolishes all rule and all authority and power, *and then* he hands over the kingdom to God even the Father. The aorist tense of καταργήσῃ 'he abolishes' indicates that this action precedes the action of the present subjunctive παραδιδῷ 'he gives over' [NIC, TNTC]. The aorist in the second clause does not necessarily indicate a prior action to the first, but the following context supports this position [NIC2].

QUESTION—To what do the words ἀρχή, ἐξουσία, and δύναμις 'rule, authority', and 'power' refer?

Here they refer collectively to all evil powers opposed to God [AB, EGT, Gdt, HNTC, Ho, ICC, Lns, MNTC, NIC, NIC2, NTC, Rb, TG, TH; NLT]. They refer to invisible opposing powers (see Romans 8:38; Colossians 1:13, 16, 2:15; Ephesians 2:2, 6:11, 12) [Gdt]. They refer not only to all hostile power, but to absolutely all power, kings, and kingdoms [Alf, TNTC]. They refer to different orders of angels: ἀρχή, the highest rank, ἐξουσία, a lower rank, and δύναμις, the lowest rank. Verse 15:25 indicates that Paul is referring to evil angels here (see Ephesians 6:12) [Ed]. They include angelic as well as earthly powers [EGT, ICC]. They refer to demonic powers [Herm]. They refer to angels or (evil) spirits [TG, TH] who have power over the universe [TG]. They control the area between heaven and earth [TH]. Ἀρχή refers to rule of any kind, ἐξουσία to the authority to exercise the rule, and δύναμις means the power to exercise the rule [Vn]. These terms may include every kind of structural power that opposes God and oppresses people [NIGTC].

15:25 For it-is-necessary[a] for-him to-rule[b]

LEXICON—a. pres. act. indic. of the impersonal verb δεῖ (See this word at 11:19): 'to be necessary' [LN (71.34)]. The phrase δεῖ αὐτόν 'it is necessary for him' is translated 'he must' [Herm, ICC, Lns, NIGTC,

NTC; ISV, KJV, NET, NIV, NRSV], 'Christ must continue' [HNTC], 'he has to' [AB], 'Christ must' [NAB, NLT, TEV, TNT], 'Christ will' [CEV], 'he is destined' [REB], 'he is' [NJB].
  b. pres. act. infin. of βασιλεύω (LN 37.64) (BAGD 1.b.β. p. 136): 'to rule' [BAGD, LN; CEV, ISV, TEV], 'to reign' [Herm, LN, NIGTC; KJV, NAB, NET, NIV, NLT, NRSV, REB, TNT], 'to be (a) king' [BAGD, LN; NJB]. The present infinitive indicates a continuative aspect [AB, HNTC, ICC, Lns, TH]: he must continue to reign.
QUESTION—What relationship is indicated by γάρ 'for'?
  It explains the preceding statement [ICC, Lns, NIC2, NTC]: when he abolishes all rule and authority and power. *You see*, it is necessary.... It explains why Christ continues to rule [ICC, Lns]. It explains the two events of 15:24, the abolishing and the handing over (based on Psalm 110:1 and 8:6) [NIC2]. It explains the importance and length of Christ's rule [NTC]. It indicates the reason why Christ cannot hand over his mediatorial rule until the end and then why he will hand it over [Ho]. It indicates the reason why Christ will hand over his rule to the Father: his rule must come to an end when he has subjected all his enemies [NIC].
QUESTION—What is implied by δεῖ αὐτὸν βασιλεύειν 'it is necessary for him to rule'?
  It indicates that this activity is part of God's plan and must be carried out [Ho, Lns, NTC, TH, TNTC, Vn]. He would not be really King if at the end one enemy were not subdued. It was imperative that he subdue all enemies [Lns].

until he-puts[a] all the enemies under his feet.
LEXICON—a. aorist act. subj. of τίθημι (LN **37.8, 67.119**, 85.32) (BAGD I.1.a.β. p. 816): 'to put' [BAGD, Herm, LN (85.32), NIGTC; ISV, KJV, NAB, NET, NIV, NRSV, REB], 'to set' [TNT], 'to humble' [NLT], 'to defeat and put' [TEV], 'to place' [BAGD, LN (85.32)], 'to lay' [BAGD]. The idiom, 'to put under one's feet' is translated 'to make (one's enemies one's) footstool' [NJB], 'to completely control (one's enemies), to defeat (one's enemies)' [**LN** (37.8)], 'to put under (one's) power' [CEV]. The aorist tense indicates completeness 'will have put' [Lns, NIGTC]. See this word also at 12:18 and 12:28.
QUESTION—Who is the subject of θῇ 'he puts'?
  1. The subject is Christ [Alf, Ed, EGT, Gdt, Herm, Ho, ICC, Lns, MNTC, NIC2, NIGTC, NTC; CEV, KJV, NET, NIV, NJB, NLT, NRSV]: Christ must reign until he puts all enemies under his own feet. The grammar supports this view since 'he (puts)' is the natural antecedent of 'he must reign' [Herm, NIC2]. Also this verse explains 15:24 where Christ is said to 'abolish all rule...' [ICC, NIC2]. In Scripture God does things, but he does them through his Son. Here the context requires that Christ is the subject even though Psalm 110 says that God will do this work [Ho]. This is an allusion to Psalm 110:1, not a quotation, and the grammar points to

298   1 CORINTHIANS 15:25

Christ [NIGTC]. This act of putting his enemies under his feet will be carried out during the millennial rule of Christ on earth [MNTC].
2. The subject is God [HNTC, LN (**67.119**), NCBC, NIC, TG, TH, Vn; ISV, NAB, REB, TEV, TNT]: Christ must reign until God puts all enemies under his feet. Paul loosely quotes Psalm 110:1 to refer to Christ in which God is the one who puts the Messiah's enemies at his feet. God is therefore the subject here [HNTC].

QUESTION—Who is the antecedent of αὐτοῦ 'his'?
1. The antecedent is Christ with Christ as actor [Alf, Ed, Gdt, Herm, Ho, Lns, MNTC, NIC2, NIGTC]: until Christ has put all enemies under his own feet.
2. The antecedent is Christ with God as actor [HNTC, NIC, TG, TH]: until God has put all enemies under Christ's feet.

QUESTION—What is implied by θῇ πάντας τοὺς ἐχθροὺς ὑπὸ τοὺς αὐτοῦ 'he puts all enemies under his feet'?

It alludes to an old custom in which kings would put their feet on the necks of their enemies to give a public display of victory over them [MNTC, TG, TH]. It signifies triumphant victory and shameful public defeat [TG]. It signifies complete subjection [NIC].

QUESTION—What is implied by 'ruling until one's enemies are subdued'?

It implies a time-consuming struggle to subdue one's enemies [Ed, Gdt, HNTC].

15:26 (The) last enemy death is-being-destroyed;^a

LEXICON—a. pres. pass. indic. of καταργέω (See this word at 13:8 and 15:24): 'to be destroyed' [KJV, NAB, NIV, NLT, NRSV], 'to be abolished' [TNT], 'to be annihilated' [Herm], 'to be done away with' [ISV, NJB], 'to be deposed' [REB], 'to be defeated' [TEV], 'to be eliminated' [NET], 'to be brought to nothing' [NIGTC]. This passive voice is translated actively: 'he destroys' [CEV].

QUESTION—What is the significance of the lack of a conjunction in this verse?

It functions to give the verse strong prominence between the two Scriptural references of 15:25 (Psalm 110:1) and 27 (Psalm 8:6) [NIC2].

QUESTION—What is the function of this verse?

This verse is the peak of Paul's argument. Some Corinthians had claimed that there was no resurrection, Paul says rather that there is no death [EGT].

QUESTION—What is the significance of the present tense of καταργεῖται 'is being destroyed'?

The present tense draws attention to the process: believers are dying and being raised to life while death is being abolished [AB]: death is being destroyed. The present tense refers to the process of destroying, which began in the past with Christ's death and resurrection [NIGTC]. The present tense views the process as a whole [HNTC, TH; ISV, NAB, NET, NIV, NJB, NLT, NRSV, REB, TEV, TNT]: the last enemy to be destroyed is death. The present tense has a future sense [NTC, Rb, TNTC; KJV]: death shall be

1 CORINTHIANS 15:26   299

destroyed. The present tense implies certainty [ICC, TNTC]. The present tense makes the action more vivid and certain [Lns, TNTC]. The present tense indicates what is true now from God's perspective [EGT]. Καταργέω may or may not indicate a ceasing to exist [Ed]. There will be no more death [Ho, TNTC]. It means to make inactive [Vn]. It seems to imply total destruction here [ICC, Lns]. See 2 Timothy 1:10 and Revelation 20:14 for similar expressions of the truth of this verse [ICC]. It does not mean to annihilate but to take away effectiveness [HNTC].

QUESTION—Who is the actor of καταργεῖται 'is being destroyed'?
1. The actor is Christ [Gdt, Lns, MNTC, NIC, NIC2; CEV, NLT]: Christ destroys the last enemy, death. Referring to 15:24, it is Christ who abolishes these powers [NIC2].
2. The actor is God [NTC; ISV, NAB, REB, TEV, TNT]: God destroys the last enemy, death.

15:27 For "he-put-in-subjection[a] all-things under his feet."

LEXICON—a. aorist act. indic. of ὑποτάσσω (BAGD 1.a. p. 848): 'to put in subjection' [Herm, ICC; NET, NRSV, REB], 'to place in subjection' [HNTC, NIGTC], 'to subject' [AB; TNT], 'to give authority over' [NLT], 'to put' [Lns, NTC; ISV, KJV, NIV, NJB, TEV], 'to place' [NAB], 'to put under the power of' [CEV], 'to bring to subjection' [BAGD]. This word denotes being subordinate to another power [TH]. See this word also at 14:32.

QUESTION—What relationship is indicated by γάρ 'for'?
It indicates the reason why death is also subject to Christ [Lns]: death is destroyed *because* he put all things in subjection under his feet. It explains 15:25–26 [NIC2]: *you see*. It gives Scriptural proof that death is destroyed [Alf, Ed, Ho, NIC].

QUESTION—What word is emphatic in this verse?
The word πάντα 'all things' is emphatic [ICC, TG, TH, TNTC; TEV]. The words 'all things' include death [ICC, Lns].

QUESTION—Who is the subject of ὑπέταξεν 'he has put in subjection'?
1. God is the subject [Alf, Ed, EGT, Gdt, HNTC, ICC, Lns, NCBC, NIC, NIC2, NIGTC, NTC, Rb, TH, TNTC; CEV, ISV, NAB, NLT, NRSV, TEV, TNT]: God has put all things in subjection under his feet. Verse 15:28 determines that the subject here must be God for there it is God who makes all things subject to Christ [HNTC].
2. Christ is the subject [Herm]: Christ has put all things in subjection under his feet. That Paul makes it clear that God is all in all in 15:28 argues for the interpretation of Christ being the subject here. His concern is that the Corinthians do not think that Christ is the supreme King [Herm].

QUESTION—What is the source of this quote?
It is a quote from Psalm 8:6 or 7 [AB, Alf, Ed, EGT, Gdt, Herm, HNTC, Ho, ICC, Lns, NCBC, NIC, NIC2, NTC, Rb, TH, TNTC, Vn]. It is a near quote from Psalm 110:1 [TG]. Although Psalm 8 refers to mankind, it is referred to

by the New Testament writers in several places where they apply the Psalm to Christ (Ephesians 1:22, Hebrews 2:8 and 1 Peter 3:22). This inspired use of the Psalm shows its deeper meaning [Ho].

But[a] when he/it-says that all-things have-been-subjected, (it is) clear[b] that (it is) except[c] the-(one) having-subjected everything to-him.

LEXICON—a. δέ (See this word at 11:2): 'but' [EGT, Herm, Lns, NIGTC; KJV, NAB, NET, NJB, NRSV, REB], 'now' [AB, HNTC, ICC; NIV, TNT], 'and' [NTC], 'of course' [NLT, TEV], not explicit [CEV, ISV, NLT].

b. δῆλος (LN **28.58**) (BAGD p. 178): '(it is) clear' [AB, BAGD, **LN**, NIGTC, NTC; NAB, NET, NIV, TEV], '(it is) plain' [Herm, HNTC, LN; NRSV], '(it is) manifest' [KJV], '(it is) obvious' [ICC], '(it is) evident' [LN, Lns], 'clearly known, easily known' [LN]. This adjective is also translated as an adverb: 'clearly' [ISV, REB, TNT], 'obviously' [NJB], not explicit [CEV, NLT].

c. ἐκτός (BAGD 2.b. p.246): 'except' [BAGD, Herm]. This adverb is also translated as a verb phrase: '(it) excepts' [AB], '(he) is excepted' [NTC; KJV], '(he) is excluded' [NAB], '(this) excludes' [NIGTC; ISV], '(it) means to exclude' [REB], '(this/it) does not include' [NET, NIV, NLT, NRSV, TNT], '(God) is not included' [AB], '(this) cannot include' [NJB], '(the words "all things") do not include' [TEV], '(they) don't include' [CEV], 'this is with the exception (of him)' [HNTC, Lns]. See this word also at 14:5.

QUESTION—What is the correct translation of the aorist subjunctive εἴπῃ 'he/it says'?

It should be rendered as a future perfect [Alf, Ed, Ho, ICC]: he will have said. This refers to what God will say at the time when all things have been subjected [Alf, Ed]. It should be rendered as a present [AB, HNTC, NTC, Rb; all versions except NJB]: he/it says. It should be rendered as past active [Lns]: he said. It should be rendered as a passive past [ICC; NJB]: it is said.

QUESTION—Who is the subject of εἴπῃ 'he/it says'?

1. The subject is Christ [EGT; NJB]: when Christ says. This is the happy declaration by the Son that the promise of the Psalm has been fulfilled. It is spoken at the time when he completes his work [EGT].
2. The subject is the Scripture [HNTC, NIC2, NTC, TH; CEV, NAB, NET, NIV, NLT, NRSV, REB, TEV, TNT]: when the Scripture says.
3. The subject is God [Alf, Ed, Gdt, Ho, ICC, Lns, NIC]: when God says. Grammar requires that the subject of 'says' be the same as the subject of 'he has put in subjection' [ICC]. The time of speaking is the time of the quotation in Psalm 8 [NIC]. The time of speaking will be when all things are finally subjected to Christ [Alf, Ed, Ho, ICC].
4. The subject is impersonal [AB, Herm; NJB]: when it says.

QUESTION—Who is the one who is excluded in the subjection of all things?
  God is excluded [Ed, Gdt, HNTC, Ho, ICC, Lns, MNTC, NCBC, NIC, NIC2, NTC, Rb, TG, TH, TNTC; CEV, ISV, NAB, NIV, NLT, NRSV, REB, TEV, TNT]: it is clear that God is not included.
QUESTION—To whom were all things subjected?
  They were subjected to Christ [Gdt, HNTC, Ho, ICC, NCBC, NIC, NIC2, NTC, Rb, TH, TNTC; CEV, NAB, NIV, NLT, TEV, TNT]: who subjected everything to Christ. The following context makes it clear that Christ is indicated for it speaks of God's making all things subject to Christ [HNTC, ICC].

15:28 But^a when all-things are-subjected to-him, then the Son himself [also] will-be-subjected^b to-the-one having-subjected all-things to-him,
TEXT—The word καί 'also' does not occur in some manuscripts. It is included by GNT in brackets indicating difficulty in deciding to include it in the text. This word is included by Gdt, Herm, HNTC, ICC, Lns, NTC; ISV, KJV, NRSV, REB, TNT. It is omitted by AB; CEV, NAB, NET, NIV, NJB, NLT and TEV, but it is not certain whether the omission is textually based or is merely stylistic.
LEXICON—a. δέ (See this word at 11:2): 'but' [AB, Herm, HNTC, ICC, NIGTC; ISV, TEV, TNT], 'and' [NTC; KJV, NET, REB], 'now' [Lns], 'then' [NLT], not explicit [CEV, NAB, NIV, NJB, NRSV].
  b. fut. pass. indic. of ὑποτάσσω (See this word at 14:32): 'to be subjected' [AB, BAGD, Herm, HNTC, NTC; NET, NJB, NRSV, TNT], 'to be made subject' [NIGTC; NIV, REB], 'to be subordinated, to obey' [BAGD]. It is also translated as a middle voice: 'to be subject' [KJV], 'to become subject' [ICC], 'to subject oneself' [BAGD, EGT, Lns; NAB], 'to present (oneself)' [NLT], 'to put (oneself) under the power of' [CEV], 'to place (oneself) under' [TEV], 'to become subject' [ISV].
QUESTION—Who is the agent of the passive ὑποταφῇ 'are subjected' and who is the antecedent of αὐτῷ 'to him'?
  The agent is God [TH; CEV, NIV, TEV, TNT]: God subjected all things. The antecedent is Christ [HNTC, ICC, Lns, TH; CEV, NAB, NIV, TEV, TNT]: when all things are subjected to Christ.
QUESTION—In what sense is Christ subjected to God?
  That Christ is in the end subordinated to God is clearly expressed in the three words αὐτὸς ὁ υἱός 'the Son, himself' [Alf]. Christ's subjection here is to be understood in terms of his work of subduing and handing over the kingdom to God. This he did as the God-man who is God incarnate. In terms of being the eternal Logos, he continues his dominion as God over all creation. As Son he may be officially subordinate while remaining coequal with the Father [Ho, NTC]. He is subordinate in relation to his work of redeeming man, not in his essential being [HNTC, Ho, NIC, NIC2, NTC, TNTC]. He is subordinate in regard to his rule that he hands over to the Father, but also in regard to his being a Son. The meaning of son implies the

potential of being subordinate. It is his joy to acknowledge the Father as supreme. This relationship still retains his underlying equality with God [Ed, Gdt]. The Son will subject himself as a son as he had throughout his ministry (see John 8:29, 12:27, 17:2, 5; Philippians 2:9; and Hebrews 10:7) [EGT]. As a word is subordinate to thought while remaining one with it, so the Son is subordinate to the Father while remaining one with him [Gdt]. The subordination of the Son is seen in Psalm 8 where man is seen as made 'a little lower than God'. Man lost his dominion when he tried to rise above God. Jesus, the Son, then regains man's dominion which is remains secure in the unchanging subordination of the Son to the Father [HNTC]. Christ, as Son, subjects himself to the triune God, Father, Son and Holy Spiri, so that God may be supreme [Lns, MNTC]. Christ will be subject to the Father from the point of view of government [Vn].

QUESTION—What is the sense of the passive ὑποταγήσεται 'he will be subjected'?

1. It is a normal passive [AB, BAGD, NTC; NET, NIV, NJB, NRSV, REB, TNT]: he will be subjected. If an agent is required, God would be the agent [TH].
2. It should be taken as a middle or reflexive [EGT, Gdt, HNTC, Lns; CEV, ISV, NAB, NLT, TEV]: he will subject himself. To take this verb as a passive is to imply that some force is used to subject the Son to God. This would not fit the context in which it has just been stated that God subjected all things to him. No, Christ, of his own free will subjects himself [Lns].

QUESTION—What words are emphatic in this verse?

The words αὐτὸς ὁ υἱός 'the son himself' are emphatic [Herm, TH].

so-that God may-be [the] all-things in[a] all.

TEXT—The definite article τά 'the' does not occur in some manuscripts. It is included by GNT in brackets indicating difficulty in deciding to include it in the text.

LEXICON—a. ἐν with dative object (LN 83.13): 'in' [AB, Herm, HNTC, ICC, LN, Lns, NIGTC, NTC; ISV, KJV, NAB, NET, NIV, NJB, NRSV, REB], 'to' [CEV]. The phrase ᾖ [τὰ] πάντα ἐν πᾶσιν 'may be [the] all things in all' is translated 'may rule over all' [TNT], 'will rule completely over all' [TEV], 'will be utterly supreme over everything everywhere' [NLT].

QUESTION—On what does this purpose clause marked with ἵνα, 'so that', depend?

It depends on the clause αὐτὸς ὁ υἱὸς ὑποταγήσεται 'the Son himself will be subjected' [EGT, Gdt, ICC]: the Son himself will be subjected *so that* God may be all in all. It depends on the complete sentence preceding it [Lns]: when all-things are subjected to him, then the Son himself [also] will be subjected to the one having subjected all things to him, *so that* God may be all things in all.

QUESTION—What is the meaning of ὁ θεὸς ᾗ [τὰ] πάντα ἐν πᾶσιν 'God may be all things in all'?

It probably means that God's will may be supreme everywhere and in every way [NIC2]. It means that God may be supreme in everything [Lns, NIC, TNTC, Vn] (see Colossians 3:11) [NIC, Rb]. It means that God may be acknowledged as only Lord and King [Alf, HNTC]. It means that God alone will rule [Ho, NTC]. It means that God will fulfill all relations in all creatures. This means that there will be an end to the need for a mediator since all relations between God and his children will be direct [ICC]. God here refers to the Triune God, Father, Son, and Holy Spirit [Gdt, TNTC, Vn].

DISCOURSE UNIT: 15:29–34 [AB, Alf, Ed, EGT, Gdt, HNTC, ICC, MNTC, NCBC, NIC, NIC2, NTC, TNTC; NAB]. The topic is implications of the resurrection [AB], arguments regarding the resurrection [Alf, NTC], the effect of unbelief in the resurrection [EGT], *ad hominem* arguments for resurrection [HNTC, NIC2], arguments from experience [ICC, TNTC], resurrection incentives [MNTC], practical arguments [NCBC], baptisms for the dead [NIC], practical faith [NAB].

15:29 Otherwise[a] what will-they-do[b] the-ones being-baptized[c] for[d] the dead?

LEXICON—a. ἐπεί (See this word at 14:16): 'otherwise' [AB, Ho, ICC, NIC2, NIGTC, NTC; ISV, NET, NJB, NRSV], 'for otherwise' [BAGD, Gdt], 'since otherwise' [EGT, HNTC], 'otherwise, if not true' [Rb], 'else' [EGT, Gdt, Lns; KJV], 'for' [Herm], 'then' [NLT], 'now' [NIV, TEV], 'again' [REB], not explicit [CEV, NAB, TNT]. This conjunction is also translated as a clause: 'if there is no resurrection' [HNTC], 'if it be as the adversaries suppose' [Alf]. The words 'if the dead do not rise' are implied [Ed, Gdt, Ho, ICC, Lns, NCBC, NIC, NTC].

b. pres. act. indic. of ποιέω (LN 90.45) (BAGD I.1.b.ε. p. 681): 'to do' [AB, Herm, HNTC, LN, Lns, NTC; CEV, ISV, KJV, NET, NIV, NRSV, REB]. The phrase τί ποιήσουσιν 'what will they do' is translated 'what are they to do' [BAGD], 'what are people up to' [NJB], 'what do those people think they are doing' [NIGTC], 'what good will those people do' [TNT], 'what about' [NAB, TEV], 'what point is there' [NLT].

c. pres. pass. participle of βαπτίζω (BAGD 2.b.γ. p. 132): 'to be baptized' [AB, BAGD, Herm, HNTC, ICC, Lns, NIGTC, NTC; all versions except NRSV, REB], 'to receive baptism' [NRSV, REB]. The present tense indicates that this was a regularly occurring practice and was known to the Corinthians [NIC]. See this word also at 10:2.

d. ὑπέρ with genitive object (BAGD 1.c. p. 839): 'for' [Herm, NTC; CEV, ISV, KJV, NET, NIV, NLT, TEV, TNT], 'on behalf of' [AB, BAGD, HNTC; NAB, NJB, NRSV, REB], 'out of consideration for' [ICC], 'with a view to' [Lns], 'for the sake of' [BAGD, NIGTC]. See this word also at 11:24.

QUESTION—What is the significance of referring to this group in the third person?
>It indicates that the whole group was not engaged in it but that probably they knew about and approved of it [NIC2]. It indicates that Paul was distancing himself from the group [Alf, TNTC].

QUESTION—What is implied by τί ποιήσουσιν 'what will they do'?
>It implies a question about the value of doing it [Gdt, ICC, Vn; TNT]. It implies a question about the purpose of doing it [Ed]. It inquires about the future of those doing it [ICC]. It inquires about what explanation they will give for doing it [Alf, Ho]. It implies that they will be in an absurd and pathetic position if there is no resurrection [ICC]. It implies that they will appear to be fools when the resurrection occurs [HNTC].

QUESTION—What is meant by βαπτιζόμενοι ὑπὲρ τῶν νεκρῶν 'baptizing for the dead'?
>1. It indicates substitutionary baptism for the unbaptized deceased.
>>1.1 The dead were believers before they died [HNTC, TNTC]. The words refer to people who undergo a substitutionary baptism for a fellow Christian who died without being baptized [HNTC]. The practice is not known in the first century and only among heretics in the second [TNTC].
>>1.2 The dead were not necessarily believers before they died [AB, Alf, Ed, Herm]. Those who died may or may not have been Christians [Alf]. It indicates substitutionary baptism for dead people [Herm].
>2. It indicates that the death of Christians results in the (baptism) conversion of survivors [EGT, Lns, MNTC, NIGTC]. These are baptized *for the sake of* their beloved dead ones and in hope of reunion [EGT]. Τῶν νεκρῶν 'the dead' in this case are believers who had been baptized but who have died. Their example prompts others to be baptized as they were. This interpretation requires the meaning 'with a view to' for the preposition ὑπέρ [Lns]. Baptism was merely the sign of their being saved and it may be that this is saying that people were being saved because of the lives and witness of Christians who had died. This view requires the meaning 'because of' for the preposition ὑπέρ [MNTC, NIGTC].
>3. It indicates a death by martyrdom [Gdt]. In Luke 12:50 and Mark 10:38 baptism refers to bloody deaths that the Lord and the disciples were to suffer. The Christian in being baptized for the dead would give his life in martyrdom to join the ranks of the dead [Gdt].
>4. It is uncertain what it means [Ho, ICC, NCBC, NIC, NIC2, NTC, Rb]. There is no other reference in the New Testament to such a practice. There are also no examples of it in pagan religions. It either means baptism for those who were in process of becoming believers but died unbaptized or baptism for acquaintances who died before becoming believers [NIC2]. It either means being baptized for believers who died before they were baptized or being baptized in order to be reunited with deceased Christian friends in the next life [NCBC]. Although the interpretation is uncertain,

the second alternative above is one of the best and if chosen would require the meaning 'out of consideration for' for the preposition ὑπέρ [ICC].
5. The verse should be punctuated differently [Vn]. The Greek text does not include punctuation marks. The best way to punctuate the text is: 'What will they do who are baptized? (It is) for the dead if the dead are not raised at all. Why then are they baptized for them?' This means that if the dead do not rise then baptism is not for life in the ordinary Christian understanding of the term, but for death [Vn].

QUESTION—What is the function of this rhetorical question?
It indicates that it was absurd to baptize for the dead if there was no resurrection of the dead [ICC, NIC2]. It indicates the inconsistency of baptizing for the dead if there was no resurrection of the dead [Ed, Herm]. It shows that baptism for the dead is pointless if there is no resurrection of the dead [NCBC, NTC, TG]. It shows that baptism for the dead is irreversibly contradictory if there is no resurrection from the dead [AB].

QUESTION—What is Paul's opinion of this practice?
He neither approves nor disapproves of it in this passage [AB, HNTC, NCBC, NIC2]. He probably did not approve of it [Ed, NIC, NTC]. Both the article, οἱ 'the ones (being baptized)' and the use of the third person indicate that Paul is distancing himself and his readers from this group [Alf, TNTC].

If (the) dead are-raised not at-all,[a]

LEXICON—a. ὅλως (LN 70.1) (BAGD p. 565): 'at all' [AB, Ed, Herm, Lns, NIC2, NTC; ISV, KJV, NET, NIV, NJB, NRSV, REB, TNT], 'it is true as, some claim' [TEV], 'actually' [BAGD, LN], 'really' [LN, NIGTC], 'absolutely' [EGT], not explicit [CEV, NLT]. This word is joined with οὐκ 'not' and translated 'never' [HNTC], 'never...at all' [ICC], '(the raising of the dead is) not a reality' [NAB]. This word functions to emphasize the condition [Ed]. See this word also at 5:1 and 6:7.

QUESTION—Does this condition go with the preceding or following question?
It goes with the following question [Ho, ICC; all versions except CEV, NLT]: If the dead are not raised at all, why indeed are they baptized for them? It goes with both questions [CEV, NLT]: If the dead are not raised at all what will they do who are baptized for them and why are they baptized for them?

why indeed[a] are-they-baptized for them?

TEXT—Instead of αὐτῶν 'them', some manuscripts have τῶν νεκρῶν 'the dead'. GNT does not deal with this variant. Τῶν νεκρῶν 'the dead' is read by KJV and TEV.

LEXICON—a. καί (LN 91.12) (BAGD II.5. p. 393): 'indeed' [EGT], 'then' [AB, Herm, NTC; KJV, NET, TNT], 'at all' [BAGD, Lns, NIC2], 'still' [BAGD], '(why) in the world' [ICC], 'why do they go so far as even' [Ed], 'what is the point of' [NIGTC], not explicit [CEV, ISV, NAB, NIV, NLT, NRSV, TEV]. Καί functions to emphasize the question [HNTC, ICC]. It means 'notwithstanding' [Gdt]. See this word also at 12:14.

QUESTION—What is the function of this rhetorical question?
It shows the unreasonableness of being baptized for the dead if the dead are not raised [TH]. It shows the inconsistency of being baptized for the dead if the dead are not raised [Ed].

15:30 Why also[a] we are-in-danger[b] every hour?[c]
LEXICON—a. καί (See this word at 15:29): 'also' [AB, Lns], 'and' [ICC, NTC; all versions except ISV, NET, TNT], 'too' [HNTC, NIGTC; NET, TNT], 'then' [Herm], 'indeed' [LN (21.2), NIC2], 'and in fact' [ISV].
  b. pres. act. indic. of κινδυνεύω (LN **21.2**, 21.6) (BAGD p. 432): 'to be in danger' [**LN** (21.2), NTC; NET], 'to be endangered' [ISV], 'to undergo danger' [AB], 'to go in danger' [HNTC], 'to be in peril' [BAGD], 'to stand in peril' [ICC], 'to stand in jeopardy' [Herm; KJV]. It is also translated as a middle voice: 'to endanger (oneself)' [NIV, NJB], 'to risk (one's) life' [CEV, NLT], 'to put (oneself) in danger' [NAB, NRSV], 'to face danger' [Lns; REB, TNT], 'to run the risk of danger' [TEV], 'to let yourself be put at risk' [NIGTC], 'to run a risk' [LN (21.6)].
  c. ὥρα (LN 67.199) (BAGD 2.b. p. 896): 'hour' [LN; ISV, KJV, NET, NIV, NJB, NRSV, TEV, TNT]. The phrase πᾶσαν ὥραν 'every hour' is translated 'every hour' [AB, BAGD, Herm, HNTC, ICC; KJV], 'hour after hour' [BAGD], 'hour by hour' [NTC; REB], 'every hour of the day' [NIGTC], 'constantly' [BAGD, NTC], 'continually' [NLT], 'always' [CEV], 'all the time' [Lns, NIC2]. The phrase πᾶσαν ὥραν is idiomatic for 'all the time' [NIC2, NTC].

QUESTION—What condition is implied to this question?
The implied condition is, 'If there is no resurrection of the dead, why…' [TH].

QUESTION—What is the function of καί 'and' in this verse?
  1. It functions as a conjoining conjunction between verses 29 and 30 [AB, ICC, Lns, NTC; CEV, ISV, KJV, NAB, NET, NIV, NJB, NLT, NRSV, REB, TEV]: *and* why…?
  2. It functions with ἡμεῖς 'we' to add them to the previous example [Ed, EGT, Gdt, HNTC, ICC, NIGTC]: we *also*. Here it adds Paul and others to those who in 15:29 acted as though the resurrection of the dead were true [EGT, ICC]. The phrase καί ἡμεῖς 'we also' implies that Paul and his colleagues are not among those who are baptized for the dead [ICC].
  3. It functions to emphasize the word τί 'why' [LN, Lns, NIC2; ISV]: why *indeed*.

QUESTION—What word is emphasized in this question and who is included?
The word ἡμεῖς 'we' is emphatic [Lns, NIC2, NTC; NIV, NJB, NLT, REB, TEV, TNT]. It may include other apostles but excludes the Corinthians [NIC2]. It includes Paul and those like him who risk their lives continually [Alf, Lns, NIC, NTC]. It includes Paul and all those who risk their lives for the Good News [ICC]. It includes Paul and other missionaries [EGT, Vn]. It

includes Paul, Silas, Timothy, and other apostles [Gdt]. It includes apostles and Christians in general [TNTC].

QUESTION—How was Paul's life in danger?

Some of the dangers include hunger, thirst, exposure, physical attack, verbal abuse, persecution, imprisonment, flogging, and stoning [NTC]. See the references 2 Corinthians 4:7-15, Philippians 3:10, Romans 8:36–39 and the book of Acts [AB]. See 2 Corinthians 11:23 [HNTC].

QUESTION—What is the function of this rhetorical question?

It functions to indicate that unless there was a resurrection Paul would be crazy to risk his life all the time [NIC2]. It indicates that risking one's life was meaningless unless there was a resurrection of the dead [AB, Lns, MNTC, NIC, TH]. It indicates that unless there was a resurrection it would be absurd to risk one's life all the time [Alf, NIC2, Vn]. It indicates that unless there is a resurrection it is inconsistent reasoning to risk one's life all the time [Alf].

15:31 I-die[a] daily,[b]

LEXICON—a. pres. act. indic. of ἀποθνῄσκω (LN **23.117**) (BAGD 2. p. 91): 'to die' [AB, Herm, HNTC, Lns, NTC; KJV, NIV, NRSV, REB, TNT], 'to face death' [BAGD, **LN** (23.117); CEV, ISV, NAB, NJB, NLT, TEV], 'to be in danger of death' [NET], 'to stand face to face with death' [ICC], 'to face the reality of death' [NIC2], 'to court fatality' [NIGTC], 'to be in danger of being killed' [**LN**], 'to be likely to die' [LN]. See this word also at 15:3.

b. καθ' ἡμέραν (LN 89.90) (BAGD II.2.c. p. 406): 'daily' [BAGD, HNTC; KJV, NLT, TNT], 'every day' [BAGD, NTC; CEV, ISV, NAB, NET, NIV, NJB, NRSV, REB, TEV], 'day by day' [AB, Herm], 'from day to day' [Lns, NIGTC], 'there is not a day that' [ICC]. The preposition κατά means, 'throughout, from…to, …after…' [LN].

QUESTION—What is meant by ἀποθνῄσκω 'I die'?

It does not mean a literal death, but the risk or danger of dying or being killed [Alf, Ed, EGT, Gdt, Ho, ICC, LN, Lns, NIGTC, NTC, Rb, TNTC, Vn; CEV, ISV, NAB, NET, NJB, NLT, TEV]. In addition to bodily dangers Paul is referring to the denial of self that being an apostle requires [Ed]. Paul was in actual danger of being killed (see 2 Corinthians 1:8, 4:10, 11:23 and Romans 8:36) [EGT]. It means that he is prepared to die every day [NIC].

QUESTION—What words are emphasized in this clause?

The words καθ' ἡμέραν 'daily' are placed first for emphasis [NIC2, TNTC].

by[a] your boasting,[b] [brothers,][c]

TEXT—Some manuscripts include ἀδελφοί 'brothers'. It is included by GNT with a C rating and enclosed in brackets, indicating difficulty in deciding to include it in the text. It is included by AB, Herm, HNTC, ICC, Lns, NTC; ISV, NAB, NET, NIV, NLT, NRSV, REB, TEV, and TNT. It is omitted by CEV, KJV, and NJB.

LEXICON—a. νή (LN **89.14**) (BAGD p. 537): 'by' [AB, BAGD, Herm, HNTC, NIGTC; KJV], 'I assure you by' [TNT], 'I swear by' [NIC2; NJB], 'I swear it by' [REB], 'I swear to you by' [NAB], 'I protest by' [Lns], 'I protest to (you)…as surely as' [ICC], 'yes, indeed' [NTC], 'by virtue of' [LN]. The phrase νὴ τὴν ὑμετέραν καύχησιν 'by your boasting' is translated '(I say this) on the basis of my pride in you' [**LN**], 'the pride I have in you…makes me declare this' [**LN**], '(yes, truly) by (my) pride in you' [BAGD]. Νή marks an oath or strong statement [LN]. It occurs only here in the New Testament and is followed by the accusative case of the thing or person by which one swears, here τὴν ὑπετέραν καύχησιν 'your boasting' [NTC]. See the next word for the other renderings.

b. καύχησις (LN 25.204, 33.368, 33.371) (BAGD 1. p. 426): 'boasting' [HNTC, LN (33.368), NTC], 'what one boasts about' [LN (33.371)], 'pride' [LN (25.204); NAB, NJB, REB, TNT], 'rejoicing' [KJV], 'glorying' [Herm, Lns]. The phrase νὴ τὴν ὑμετέραν καύχησιν 'by your boasting' is translated 'as surely as I may boast of you' [BAGD], 'this is as sure as my boasting in you' [NET], 'that is as certain…as my boasting of you' [NRSV], 'that is as certain as it is that I'm proud of you' [ISV], 'the pride that I have in you…is what makes me say this' [CEV], 'the pride I have in you…makes me declare this' [TEV], 'by all the pride in you…I so affirm' [NIGTC], 'I mean that…just as surely as I glory over you' [NIV], 'as surely as my boastings of you' [AB], 'I protest to you…as surely as I glory over you' [ICC]. This phrase and the following entire clause is translated 'I swear.…This is as certain as my pride in what the Lord Jesus Christ has done in you' [NLT]. See the verbal form of this noun at 13:3.

c. ἀδελφός (See this word at 10:1): 'brother' [AB, Herm, HNTC, ICC, Lns, NTC; ISV, NAB, NIV, TNT], 'brother and sister' [NET, NRSV], '(one's) friend' [REB, TEV], 'dear friend' [NLT], 'you that I hold dear' [NIGTC], not explicit [CEV, KJV, NJB]. Ἀδελφός includes 'sisters' as well [NTC]. Ἀδελφός refers to fellow Christians [TH].

QUESTION—How are the nouns related in the genitive construction ὑπετέραν καύχησιν 'your boasting'?

1. 'You' is the object of the 'boasting' [AB, Alf, BAGD, Ed, EGT, Gdt, HNTC, Ho, ICC, LN, Lns, NCBC, NIC, NIC2, NTC, Rb, TG, TH, TNTC, Vn; all versions except KJV, NAB]: I boast about you.
2. 'You' is the subject of 'boasting' [NAB]: you boast about me.

QUESTION—What does it mean 'to swear by one's boasting about someone'?

It means that the Corinthians as believers were so very dear to Paul that he based his oath on this fact [NIC2]. It means that his fatherly relationship to the Corinthians is as solemn to him as the risks of being an apostle [AB]. It means that he would not deceive anyone about whom he boasted in connection with Christ [Alf]. It means that the words 'I die daily' are just as true as the fact that he boasts about them is true [NTC]. It means that he swears by something that is dearest to him [EGT, NIGTC].

that I-have[a] in[b] Christ Jesus our Lord.
LEXICON—a. pres. act. indic. of ἔχω (LN 18.6): 'to have' [Herm, HNTC, Lns, NTC; KJV, NET, TEV, TNT], 'to cherish' [NAB], 'to maintain' [AB], 'to hold' [LN (18.6)]. The phrase ἣν ἔχω 'which I have' is translated 'a boast that I make' [NRSV], 'for…I am proud of you' [REB], not explicit [ICC, NIGTC; ISV, NIV, NJB, NLT]. The phrase ἣν ἔχω ἐν 'which I have in' is translated 'because of' [CEV]. See this word also at 11:22.
  b. ἐν with dative object (See this word at 15:22): 'in' [AB, Herm, HNTC, ICC, Lns, NIGTC, NTC; all versions except CEV, TEV], 'in our life in union with' [TEV], not explicit [CEV].
QUESTION—Is the word ἡμῶν 'our (Lord)' inclusive or exclusive?
  It is inclusive and refers to Paul and the believers in Corinth [TG].
QUESTION—What is the significance of ἣν ἔχω ἐν Χριστῷ Ἰησοῦ τῷ κυρίῳ ἡμῶν 'that I have in Christ Jesus our Lord'?
  It shows that Paul's pride was not his own but something he had because of Jesus Christ [Gdt, Herm, Lns, NIC2, TH, Vn]. It means that Paul's boasting is based on what Christ had accomplished through him [NIC2]. It refers to the conversion of the Corinthians [HNTC, NTC]. It means that Paul is boasting about the success of his work as an apostle, a work that Christ had effected [Lns, NIC]. It indicates that the Corinthians were the seals of his work [Ho].

15:32 **If according-to-man[a] I-fought-with-wild-animals[b] in Ephesus,[c]**
LEXICON—a. κατὰ ἄνθρωπος (BAGD 1.c. p. 68): 'according to man' [NTC], 'after the manner of men' [Herm, Lns; KJV], 'like an ordinary man' [BAGD], 'as a mere mortal' [TNT], 'from a human point of view' [NET], 'in a purely human perspective' [NJB], 'for merely human reasons' [NIV], 'from merely human motives' [ISV], 'simply from human motives' [TEV], 'for purely human motives' [NAB], 'with merely human hopes' [NRSV], 'with no more than human hopes' [REB], 'humanly speaking' [AB], 'on purely human terms' [HNTC], 'looking at it from a purely human point of view' [ICC], 'within human horizons' [NIGTC], not explicit [CEV, NLT].
  b. aorist act. indic. of θηριομαχέω (LN **39.28**) (BAGD p. 360): 'to fight with wild animals' [LN, NTC; CEV, ISV, NRSV], 'to fight wild animals' [NJB], 'to fight (with) wild beasts' [AB, HNTC; NET, NIV, NLT, REB], 'as it were, to fight wild beasts' [TEV], 'to fight with beasts' [Herm, Lns; KJV, TNT], 'to fight (those) beasts' [NAB], 'to fight "wild beasts," as it were' [**LN**], 'to battle with wild, bestial creatures' [NIGTC], 'to be in serious conflict' [**LN**], 'to be in a serious struggle with, to have to contend with' [**LN**], 'to be near being torn to pieces' [ICC]. Θηριομαχέω was something that one was forced to do as a punishment [BAGD].
  c. Ἔφεσος (LN 93.471) (BAGD p. 330): 'Ephesus' [AB, Herm, HNTC, ICC, Lns, NTC; all versions]. Ἔφεσος was a seaport on the western

shore of the Roman province of Asia [LN]. It was the capital of the Roman province of Achaia [TG].

QUESTION—What is the meaning of κατὰ ἄνθρωπον 'according to man'?

It means from the standpoint of one who looks for temporal rewards [EGT, Gdt, ICC, Lns, Rb, Vn]. It means from the standpoint of a natural man without the help of the Spirit of God [Ed, NIC2]. It means from the standpoint of one who has no hope in the resurrection from the dead [Alf, Vn]. It means from the human point of view [HNTC, ICC, NCBC, NIC]. The phrase seems to indicate that Paul was speaking figuratively of fighting with human beings rather than actual wild animals [AB, NCBC, NIC, NTC]. The phrase describes Paul's reason for fighting [MNTC; ISV, NAB, NJB, NRSV, REB, TEV]: if I fought with wild animals for human motives.

QUESTION—Should ἐθηριομάχησα 'I fought with wild animals' be taken literally or not?

1. It should be taken figuratively [AB, Alf, Ed, EGT, HNTC, Ho, ICC, LN, Lns, MNTC, NCBC, NIC, NIC2, NTC, TG, TH, TNTC, Vn; NLT, TEV]. It should be taken figuratively for these reasons: (a) the phrase 'according to man' may indicate that it is not meant literally [AB, NCBC, NIC, NTC], that is, these words would be unnecessary if Paul had actually fought with wild animals [NIC]; (b) it is not mentioned in Acts [AB, Alf, Ed, HNTC, Ho, ICC, NIC]; (c) it is not mentioned when he speaks of what happened in Ephesus in 2 Corinthians 1:8 [AB]; (d) Paul does not list it among other afflictions in 2 Corinthians 11:23ff. [BAGD, Ed, EGT, HNTC, Ho, ICC, Lns, NIC, NTC, Rb, TNTC]; (e) there is no historical record of such treatment of Christians in the first century, although there is evidence in the second and third centuries [AB]; (f) as a Roman citizen he could not have been compelled to do this [Alf, BAGD, Ho, ICC, Lns, NCBC, NIC, NIC2, NTC, Rb, TH, Vn]; (g) if it occurred he would have lost his Roman citizenship that he still had at a later date [BAGD, HNTC, NTC, TNTC], on the basis of which he appealed to Caesar [BAGD, NTC]; (h) the martyr Ignatius refers to his guards as wild animals [Ed, EGT, HNTC, NIC2, NTC, TNTC]; (i) it is unlikely that he would have survived a fight with wild animals [HNTC, NIC, NIC2, NTC, TNTC]; (j) the previous clause, 'I die daily', is figurative in meaning [Lns].

2. It should be taken literally [Gdt]. The literal sense is demanded by the context of Paul's claim in 15:31, 'I die daily'. This claim warrants a literal interpretation of Paul's actual fighting with wild animals in Ephesus. Also there are many facts mentioned in 2 Corinthians 11:23ff that are not mentioned in Acts.

QUESTION—If the reference to wild animals is figurative, to what is it compared?

It is compared with some encounter in Ephesus with infuriated men [Ho, ICC, Vn]. It is compared to dreadful experiences in Ephesus [AB]. It must have been compared to some experience involving the danger of death or else it loses its relevance in the context [HNTC]. It is compared with some life-threatening experience [HNTC, Lns, MNTC, NCBC]. It is compared with some kind of severe opposition [NIC, NIC2]. It is compared to the opposition of human beings [NTC, TH]. The opposition was physical as well as ideological [NIC2, NTC, TH]. This event was known to the Corinthians [NCBC, NIC, TNTC].

QUESTION—What words are emphasized in this verse?

The phrase κατα ἀνθρωπον 'according to man' is emphasized [EGT, HNTC, ICC, Lns], being placed forward in the clause [HNTC, ICC, Lns].

what (is) the benefit[a] to-me?

LEXICON—a. ὄφελος (LN 65.40) (BAGD p. 599): 'benefit' [AB, Herm, LN; TNT], 'advantage' [LN, NTC], 'profit' [NIGTC; NAB], 'value' [NLT], 'good' [BAGD]. This noun is also translated as a verb: 'to benefit' [NET], 'to advantage (it)' [KJV], 'to gain' [ICC; CEV, NIV, NJB, NRSV, TEV], 'to profit' [Lns]. The whole clause is translated 'what do I get out of it?' [ISV], 'what would have been the point of my (fighting)' [REB], 'what good does that do me' [HNTC].

QUESTION—What is the function of this rhetorical question?

It functions to indicate that it is meaningless to fight with wild animals if there is no resurrection of the dead [NIC2, TH]. It indicates that it is of no benefit [ICC, Lns, NCBC, NTC, TG], if there is no resurrection of the dead [ICC, Lns, NCBC, NTC]. It indicates that Paul's conduct is unexplainable if there is no resurrection [TNTC].

If (the) dead (are) not raised, "Let-us-eat and drink, for tomorrow[a] we-die."

LEXICON—a. αὔριον (LN **67.58**, 67.207) (BAGD 2. p. 122): 'tomorrow' [AB, Herm, HNTC, ICC, LN (67.207), Lns, NIGTC, NTC; all versions], 'soon' [BAGD, **LN** (67.58)], 'very soon' [LN], 'in a short time' [BAGD].

QUESTION—Does the conditional if-clause go with the following quotation or with the preceding sentence?

It functions as a condition to the following quotation [AB, Alf, Ed, EGT, Gdt, Ho, ICC, Lns, Vn]: If the dead are not raised, "then let us eat and drink, for tomorrow we die."

QUESTION—What is the meaning of this sentence?

It means that apart from the hope in life after death one should get all the enjoyment he/she can in this life [Gdt, Lns, MNTC, NCBC, NIC]. It means that apart from the hope in life after death, life is only meaningless activity and despair [NIC2]. Lack of hope in the resurrection leads to a life of sensuality [Vn].

QUESTION—From where is this quoted?

It is quoted from Isaiah 22:13 describing the Jews' reaction to the siege of the Assyrians on Jerusalem [Rb].

15:33 **(Do) not be-deceived;[a]**

LEXICON—a. pres. pass. impera. of πλανάω (LN 31.8) (BAGD 2.c.δ. p. 665): 'to be deceived' [Herm, LN, Lns; ISV, KJV, NET, NRSV], 'to be misled'

[HNTC, LN; NIV, TNT], 'to be led astray' [NAB], 'to be fooled' [NLT, TEV], 'to be seduced' [NIGTC]. It is also translated as a middle voice: 'to fool oneself' [CEV]. It is also translated actively: 'to make a mistake' [REB], 'to make a serious mistake' [ICC], 'to let (someone) lead (one) astray' [NJB], 'to deceive oneself' [AB, Gdt], 'to let (oneself) be deceived, to let (oneself) be misled' [BAGD]. See this word also at 6:9.

QUESTION—What is the significance of the present imperative?

It signifies that the action was already going on [AB, ICC, Lns, NIC, NIC2, NIGTC, NTC, Vn; ISV, NAB]: Stop being deceived!

QUESTION—About what are they to not be deceived?

They are not to be deceived that there is no resurrection of the dead [AB, EGT, NTC]. They are not to be deceived by men who among other errors deny the resurrection of the dead [Ho]. They are not to be deceived into leading a degenerate life of 'eating and drinking' like that described in 15:32 [NIC].

Bad[a] company[b] ruins[c] good[d] morals.[e]

LEXICON—a. κακός (BAGD 1.b. p. 397): 'bad' [AB, BAGD, HNTC, Lns, NIGTC; all versions except ISV, KJV], 'evil' [BAGD, Herm; KJV], 'wicked' [ISV]. This whole clause is translated 'there is risk in being friendly to these views and to those who advocate them' [ICC]. See this word also at 13:5.

b. ὁμιλία (LN **34.1**) (BAGD 1. p. 565): 'company' [AB, BAGD, Ed, Herm, HNTC, Lns; NAB, NET, NIV, NJB, NLT, NRSV, REB], 'companion' [TEV, TNT], 'friend' [CEV, ISV], 'gang' [NIGTC], 'communication' [KJV], 'association' [LN], not explicit [ICC]. This noun is also translated as a verb: 'to associate (with bad people)' [**LN**].

c. pres. act. indic. of φθείρω (LN 20.23, 20.39, 88.266) (BAGD 2.b. p. 857): 'to ruin' [BAGD, HNTC, LN (20.23, 88.266), NIGTC; NRSV, REB, TEV], 'to corrupt' [AB, BAGD, Herm, Lns; KJV, NAB, NET, NIV, NJB, NLT, TNT], 'to deprave, to pervert, to cause the moral ruin of' [LN (88.266)], 'to destroy' [LN (20.39); CEV], 'to cause harm' [LN (20.23)], not explicit [ICC]. The phrase φθείρουσιν ἤθη χρηστά 'ruins good morals' is translated 'to lead to evil ends' [ISV]. See this word also at 3:17.

d. χρηστός (LN **88.9**) (BAGD 1.a.β. p. 886): 'good' [AB, BAGD, Herm, HNTC, **LN**, Lns; all versions except CEV, ISV], 'useful, suitable' [LN], 'reputable' [BAGD, NIGTC], not explicit [ICC; CEV, ISV]. Χρηστός indicates 'morally good' [BAGD].

e. ἦθος (LN **41.25**) (BAGD p. 344): 'moral' [NAB, NET, NRSV], 'character' [NIV, NLT, REB, TEV], 'habit' [AB, BAGD, **LN**; TNT], 'lifestyle' [NIGTC], 'manner' [Herm, Lns; KJV], 'way' [HNTC; NJB], 'custom' [LN], not explicit [ICC; ISV]. The phrase χρηστὰ ὁμιλίαι 'good morals' is translated '(destroy) you' [CEV].

QUESTION—What is the significance of this saying?

It probably has reference to those people who do not believe in the resurrection of the dead and is warning the Corinthians about being influenced by them [Alf, Ed, NCBC, NIC2, NTC, TG, TNTC]. Association with those who deny Christian beliefs such as the resurrection may lead to adopting their way of life [AB, HNTC, MNTC, NIC]. Spiritual life is negatively affected by association with an ungodly society [Gdt, Ho, Vn].

15:34 Come-to-your-senses[a] as-you-ought[b] and (do) not sin,[c]

LEXICON—a. aorist act. impera. of ἐκνήφω (LN **30.26**) (BAGD p. 243): 'to come to (one's) senses' [BAGD, NTC; NLT], 'to come back to (one's) senses' [ISV, NIV], 'to return to reason' [NAB], 'to be sensible' [CEV], 'to wake up, to be sober' [REB], 'to wake up to a sober life' [HNTC], 'to awake' [KJV], 'to wake up from (one's) stupor' [NJB], 'to sober up' [AB, Lns; NET], 'to become sober' [BAGD], 'to rouse oneself from a paralyzing delusion' [ICC], 'to come to one's senses, wake up and sober up' [NIGTC], 'to change to a proper state of mind' [LN]. The phrase ἐκνήψατε δικαίως 'come to your senses as you ought' is translated 'to come to (one's) right senses' [LN; TNT], 'to be honestly sober' [Herm], 'to come back to (one's) right senses' [**LN**; TEV], 'to come to a sober and right mind' [NRSV]. Ἐκνήφω means to become sober as from a state of intoxication [AB, Alf, Ed, Gdt, Ho, Lns, NIC, NIC2, Rb]. The aorist indicates a single decisive act [Alf, Gdt, Ho, ICC, Lns, NTC, TH, Vn].

b. δικαίως (LN 88.15) (BAGD 1.b. p. 198); 'as one ought' [Alf, BAGD, NTC; NAB, NIV], 'as (one) should' [ISV, NET, NJB], 'as is fitting' [AB], 'honestly' [Herm], 'properly' [HNTC], 'in a right spirit' [ICC], 'in the right way' [Lns], 'in a righteous manner' [Ed], not explicit [NIGTC; CEV, NLT, REB]. This adverb is also translated as an adjective: 'right (senses)' [LN; NRSV, TEV, TNT]. It is also translated as a prepositional phrase: 'to righteousness' [KJV].

c. pres. act. impera. of ἁμαρτάνω (LN 88.289) (BAGD p. 42): 'to sin' [AB, Herm, HNTC, LN, Lns, NIGTC, NTC; all versions except NJB, TEV]. The phrase μὴ ἁμαρτάνετε 'do not sin' is translated 'to leave sin alone' [NJB], 'to stop (one's) sinful ways' [TEV], 'to persist in culpable error' [ICC]. The present imperative indicates that this was already going on [AB, Ed, EGT, HNTC, ICC, Lns, NCBC, NIC, NIC2, NTC, Rb, TH, Vn; CEV, TEV]: Stop sinning! See this word also at 6:18.

QUESTION—From what are the Corinthians to 'come to their senses and sin not'?

They are to come to their senses from spiritual intoxication that has resulted from a denial of the resurrection [Vn]. They are to come to their senses from thinking there is no resurrection or future to the kingdom of God [NIC2]. They are to come to their senses from hazy thinking about the resurrection [NTC]. Their sin was their incorrect idea about the resurrection of the dead [Ho, MNTC, NTC]. They are to come to their senses from their philosophy of drinking and enjoying life as stated in 15:33 [Herm]. They are to come to their senses from their conformity to the world's life style [AB]. They are to come to their senses from the attraction of physical pleasures and the numbing effect of intellectual superiority [EGT]. They are to come to their senses from the influence of decadent people around them [Alf].

QUESTION—What is meant by δικαίως 'as you ought'?

It refers to obligatory action [Alf, BAGD, NTC; ISV, NAB, NET, NIV, NJB], appropriate action [NIC2], proper action [Alf, Ho, NCBC], correct action [EGT, Lns, NIC2; NRSV, TEV, TNT], serious action [Gdt], action fitting to the faith [AB], action with a right attitude [ICC]. It means as from a correct perspective [NIC]. It means so as to recover one's righteousness [Alf].

for some have an-ignorance[a] of-God,

LEXICON—a. ἀγνωσία (LN **28.16**, **32.7**) (BAGD p. 12): 'ignorance' [AB, Herm, HNTC, LN, Lns], 'no knowledge' [BAGD, **LN** (28.16), NTC; NET, NRSV, REB, TNT], 'not the knowledge' [KJV], 'no understanding' [NJB], 'crass ignorance as to the very meaning (of God)' [ICC]. The phrase ἀγωσίαν...ἔχουσιν 'have no knowledge' is translated 'to not know' [NLT, TEV], 'to be without a true knowledge' [ISV], 'to have an utter lack of "knowledge"' [NIGTC], 'to not understand anything about' [**LN** (32.7)], 'to still not know about' [CEV], 'to be ignorant' [NIV], 'to be quite ignorant' [NAB].

QUESTION—What relationship is indicated by γάρ 'for'?

It indicates the grounds for the preceding exhortation [Gdt, Ho, NTC, TNTC]: wake up and do not sin *since* some have no knowledge of God. They must be called out of their stupor because those of them who deny the resurrection have no real knowledge of God [NTC]. It indicates that ignorance of God showed itself in denial of the resurrection [ICC, Lns, Vn]. This clause explains the words 'sin not'. Paul means that those who deny the resurrection in reality are ignorant of God [NIC2]. Paul was saying that their ignorance of God was to blame for their sinful behavior [AB, MNTC, TNTC]. This verse strongly implies that Paul was concerned that their ignorance of God would produce sinful behavior [HNTC].

QUESTION—To whom does τίνες 'some' refer?

It refers to some people among the Corinthians [Alf, Ed, EGT, Gdt, ICC, Lns, MNTC, NIC2, NTC, TH, Vn]. It refers to the 'some' mentioned in 15:12 who claimed that there was no resurrection of the dead [Alf, Lns].

QUESTION—What is the function of ἔχουσιν '(some) have'?

It indicates that they maintain an ignorance of God [AB, EGT]. It means that they actually possess an ignorance of God [Gdt].

QUESTION—What is the significance of ἀγνωσίαν γάρ θεοῦ τινες ἔχουσιν 'some have ignorance of God'?

Paul speaks of ἀγνωσία 'ignorance' as though it were a disease [ICC, Lns]. There are three other ways to say 'not to know' in Greek, but this is stronger than any of them [ICC]. It is not merely to lack something as it is to possess a real evil [Gdt, ICC]. Ἀγνωσία indicates a way of life that some were following [Herm]. Ἀγνωσία is not mere lack of knowledge, but blameworthy ignorance [Vn]. It indicates that some were ignorant of God like the heathen among whom they lived [Ed, EGT, NIC2, TG, TH]. In biblical terminology, 'to know' frequently means 'to have an intimate relationship with' [TG, TH]. Here then Paul was saying that some of them lacked a vital relationship with God [NTC, TG, TH].

I-speak (this) to[a] your shame.[b]

LEXICON—a. πρός with accusative object (LN 89.60, 90.25): 'to' [Herm, LN (90.25); all versions except CEV, NJB, TNT], 'for the purpose of' [LN (89.60)], 'about' [LN (90.25)], not explicit [AB, HNTC, ICC, Lns, NTC; CEV, NJB, TNT]. Πρός here indicates purpose [Lns].

b. ἐντροπή (LN **25.195**) (BAGD 1. p. 269): 'shame' [Herm, **LN**; all versions except CEV, NJB, TNT], 'embarrassment' [LN]. The phrase πρὸς ἐντροπήν 'for shame' is translated 'to put to shame' [BAGD]. The phrase πρὸς ἐντροπὴν ὑμῖν 'for the purpose of shame to you' is translated 'to shame you' [HNTC, NIGTC; TNT], 'to put you to shame' [NTC], 'in order to make you feel ashamed' [**LN**], 'to instill some shame in you' [NJB], 'to make you ashamed of yourselves' [ICC], 'to move you to shame' [Lns]. This entire clause is translated 'you should be embarrassed' [CEV], 'I say to you, "For shame!"' [AB].

DISCOURSE UNIT: 15:35-58 (Gdt, GNT, Ho, ICC, Lns, NIC2, NIGTC; CEV, ISV, NET, NIV, NLT, TEV). The topic is the mode of the resurrection of the body [Gdt], the nature of the resurrection body [Ho, ICC], the resurrection body [GNT, Lns, NIC2; ISV, NET, NIV, NLT, TEV], what our bodies will be like [CEV], the reasonableness of the resurrection [NIGTC].

DISCOURSE UNIT: 15:35-53 (NJB). The topic is the manner of the resurrection.

DISCOURSE UNIT: 15:35-50 (Alf, Vn). The topic is the nature of the resurrection of believers.

DISCOURSE UNIT: 15:35-49 (AB, HNTC, ICC, MNTC). The topic is the nature of the resurrection body [AB, MNTC], the old manhood and the new [HNTC], answers of nature and of Scripture [ICC].

DISCOURSE UNIT: 15:35-44 (Ed, NIC2). The topic is the proof confirmed by analogies [Ed], analogies of seeds and "bodies" [NIC2].

DISCOURSE UNIT: 15:35-44a (NAB). The topic is the manner of the resurrection.

DISCOURSE UNIT: 15:35-42a (EGT). The topic is the manner of the resurrection.

316   1 CORINTHIANS 15:35

DISCOURSE UNIT: 15:35–38 (NTC). The topic is life out of death.

15:35 But^a someone will-say, "How (are) the dead raised?"

LEXICON—a. ἀλλά (See this word at 10:5): 'but' [AB, Herm, HNTC, ICC, Lns, NTC; all versions except CEV, NAB, NJB, TEV], 'nevertheless' [NIGTC], not explicit [CEV, NAB, NJB, TEV].

QUESTION—What relationship is indicated by ἀλλά 'but'?

It indicates a strong contrast with the anticipated objection of some Corinthians to the resurrection and that Paul recognizes that he has yet to fully answer their objections [NIC2]. It indicates a contrast between those in 15:34 who had no knowledge of God and those who had serious questions about the resurrection. At the same time it signals a transition between the facts of the resurrection and the manner of its occurrence [TH]. It indicates a contrast between Paul's point of view and that of an objector [TNTC].

QUESTION—What is implied by these questions?

Skepticism is implied due to the questioner not believing that it is possible to raise the dead [EGT, ICC, MNTC, NIC2, NTC, Rb]. The questions imply doubt in regard to the resurrection with the further implication that it is absurd because it is inconceivable to think of the dead being given bodies [AB]. The questions imply derision [NTC]. The question implies 'how is it possible' [Ed, Ho, ICC, NTC]. 'How' refers to the power that will execute this and how it will work but the questioner believes that it is inconceivable [ICC]. 'How' inquires about how is it possible that they are raised rather than asking the manner in which they are raised [NIGTC]. These questions are not requesting information but expressing arguments against the resurrection of the dead [NCBC]. Paul is not expressing doubt about the resurrection but simply asking a hypothetical question about how it will happen [TH]. Πῶς 'how?' queries the manner of resurrection [TNTC].

QUESTION—Are these questions imaginary or real?

These questions were probably ones being asked by some in Corinth [AB, ICC, NIC, NIC2, NTC, Rb; CEV]: some of you are asking…. The following direct address (15:36), 'Foolish one!', indicates that Paul had a specific question in mind that had already been asked [NIC, NTC]. Τίς 'someone' refers back to the τίνες 'some' of 15:12 who were saying there was no resurrection [ICC]. Paul has no one in mind, he is merely asking a typical question [TH].

"And with-what-kind-of^a body do-they-come?"^b

LEXICON—a. ποῖος (LN **58.30**) (BAGD 1.a.β. p. 684): 'what kind of' [AB, BAGD, Herm, HNTC, LN, Lns, NIGTC, NTC; NET, NIV, NRSV, REB], 'what sort of' [**LN**], 'what manner of' [Lns], 'what' [KJV]. The dative phrase ποίῳ σώματι 'with what kind of body' is translated 'what kind of body/bodies (will they have)' [CEV, ISV, NAB, NLT, TEV, TNT], 'what sort of body (will they have)' [NJB].

   b. pres. pass. (deponent = act.) indic. of ἔρχομαι (LN 15.81, 13.50): 'to come' [AB, Herm, HNTC, LN, Lns (15.81), NIGTC, NTC; KJV, NET,

NIV, NRSV], 'to come back' [Lns], 'to have' [CEV, NAB, NLT, TEV, TNT], 'to have when (they) come (back)' [ISV, NJB], 'to become' [LN (13.50)], 'to be raised' [REB], 'to come forth' [Alf]. Ἔρχομαι here probably has reference to emerging from their graves [HNTC, ICC]. It refers to the resurrection [NIC]. It refers a return to the world of the living [TG].

QUESTION—What is the relationship between these two questions?

There is a generic-specific relationship, the first ('how?') being generic, the second ('with what kind of?') being specific [AB, Alf, NIC2, TH]. The second question further develops the first [Herm, NIC, NIGTC]. The second question rephrases the first [Lns]. The second question clarifies the difficulty of the first [Rb].

QUESTION—What does this question imply?

It implies incredulity and skepticism [EGT, NIC2, NIGTC]. It implies ridicule. How could a body rise from decayed remains [TNTC]? It implies that the questioner is mocking the idea of the resurrection of the dead [MNTC]. It implies that the manner of the resurrection of a corpse is inconceivable [EGT]. It implies that the real problem bothering the Corinthians had to do with bodies or corpses coming to life again [NIC, NIC2]. It implies that because of decay there will be no trace of the body remaining [Ed]. It queries whether it will be the same body that died or a different body. If the latter, can that be called a resurrection [ICC, NTC]?

15:36 Fool,[a]

LEXICON—a. ἄφρων (LN 32.52) (BAGD p.127): 'fool' [HNTC, Lns; KJV, NET, NRSV], 'you fool' [NTC; ISV, TEV], 'you foolish one' [Herm], 'foolish person' [AB], 'you nonsense person' [NIGTC]. This word is primarily an adjective 'foolish' [BAGD, LN], 'unwise, senseless' [LN], 'ignorant' [BAGD]. It is also translated as a clause: 'A nonsensical question!' [NAB], 'Don't be foolish' [CEV], 'What a foolish question!' [NLT, TNT], 'What stupid questions!' [REB], 'How foolish!' [NIV, NJB], 'The question may seem to be clever, but it is really very foolish' [ICC]. Ἄφρων means 'dull, senseless' [Ed].

QUESTION—What is implied by ἄφρων 'fool'?

It implies mental stupidity [EGT]. It implies disapproval and disdain [Ho]. It implies derision for someone who lacks understanding [MNTC]. It implies disgust [NTC]. To the Corinthians who prided themselves on their wisdom, this term would have been taken differently than a contemporary reader. It implies someone without wisdom. Paul uses it in the Old Testament sense as one who has rejected the notion of God [NIC2]. The vocative implies that the questioner is not willing to take a lesson from everyday life [AB].

not unless what you sow[a] **dies, is-it-made-alive;**[b]

LEXICON—a. pres. act. indic. of σπείρω (LN 43.6) (BAGD 1.a.β. p. 761): 'to sow' [AB, BAGD, Herm, HNTC, ICC, LN, Lns, NIGTC, NTC; KJV, NAB, NET, NIV, NJB, NRSV, REB, TNT], 'to plant' [ISV]. The phrase σὺ ὃ σπείρεις 'what you sow' is translated 'when you put a seed into the ground' [NLT], 'when you plant a seed in the ground' [TEV]. This entire phrase is translated 'a seed must die before it can sprout from the ground' [CEV].

b. pres. pass. indic. of ζωοποιέω (BAGD 2.c. p. 342): 'to be made alive' [BAGD], 'to be given (new) life' [BAGD, ICC; NJB], 'to be quickened' [Lns; KJV], 'to be brought to life' [HNTC, NIGTC]. It is also translated actively: 'to come to life' [AB, Herm, NTC; ISV, NET, NIV, NRSV, REB], 'to live again' [TNT], 'to sprout to life' [TEV], 'to sprout from the ground' [CEV], 'to germinate' [NAB], 'to grow into a plant' [NLT]. See this word also at 15:22.

QUESTION—What word is emphasized in this verse?

The word σύ 'you' is emphatic [AB, Alf, Ed, EGT, Gdt, HNTC, ICC, Lns, NIC2, NTC, Rb, TH, Vn; TNT]: you yourself. The pronoun emphasizes the clause 'what you sow' [EGT]: what you yourself sow. Paul is emphasizing that the person himself had the answer to his/her own question by observing common plant life [NIC2]. The pronoun stresses the foolishness of the person who should understand Paul's illustration [AB]. It may function to point out to the objector that this illustration is from his/her own experience [Alf]. The pronoun should be taken with the word ἄφρων 'fool' [Gdt]: Fool that you are! Paul is stressing the objector's *own* experience, saying that it contained the answer to his question [ICC, Vn].

QUESTION—What is Paul's point in this verse?

Paul is answering their question by saying that it is possible for the dead to rise as is seen in the common experience of sowing seed [Ed, EGT, NIC2]. Paul answers the first question, 'How are the dead raised?' [Ed, EGT, Gdt, ICC, Rb], with the reply, 'The dead are raised through death itself' [Gdt]. They were saying that a body cannot live again if it dies, Paul is saying that unless a seed dies it cannot live [Ho]. Paul is showing that the body can have more than one mode of existence [Lns].

QUESTION—If the image in this metaphor is a seed being put in the ground and sprouting with new life, and the topic is the resurrection of the dead, what is the point of similarity?

The point of similarity is that new life only comes after the death or disappearance of the seed [Alf, Rb, Vn]. The point of similarity is the necessity of death for transition to new life [Ed, EGT, Gdt, Herm, ICC, NTC]. Paul's point is not the necessity of death, but that death is the means of new life [HNTC]. Death and decay release the germ of life in the seed [Gdt, ICC, Lns]. The similarity is decomposition of an old form before coming to life in a new form [MNTC]. The point of similarity is the disappearance of the seed and body [AB]. Paul's point is the possibility of life from death [NIC2].

QUESTION—Who is the agent of the passive ζωοποιεῖται 'is made alive'?

The agent is God who creates life [NTC]: God makes it become alive.

15:37 And what you-sow, (it-is) not the body[a] that-will-be (that) you-sow but (a) bare[b] seed[c]

LEXICON—a. σῶμα (LN **8.1**) (BAGD 3. p. 799): 'body' [AB, BAGD, Herm, HNTC, ICC, LN, Lns, NIGTC, NTC; KJV, NET, NIV, NJB, NRSV, REB], 'body of the plant' [**LN**], 'form' [ISV], 'plant' [NAB, NLT], 'full-bodied plant' [TEV], 'full-formed plant' [TNT], not explicit [CEV]. Here the 'body' refers to the mature plant [HNTC, TH]. See this word also at 12:14.

b. γυμνός (LN 49.22) (BAGD 4. p. 168): 'bare' [AB, Herm, HNTC, Lns, NIGTC, NTC; ISV, KJV, NET, NJB, NRSV, REB, TEV, TNT], 'naked' [BAGD, LN], 'dry' [NLT], 'leafless' [ICC], 'just a' [NIV], not explicit [CEV, NAB]. Γυμνός here means 'just' or 'merely' [TH, TNTC; NIV]

c. κόκκος (LN **3.35**) (BAGD 1. p. 440): 'seed' [BAGD, **LN**; CEV, NET, NIV, NRSV, TEV, TNT], 'grain' [AB, BAGD, Herm, HNTC, ICC, Lns, NIGTC; KJV, NJB, REB], 'kernel' [NTC; ISV, NAB], 'little seed' [NLT].

QUESTION—What relationship is indicated by the καί 'and' that begins the verse?

It indicates an explanation of 15:36 [Lns]: what you sow does not come to life unless it dies. *You see* it is not…. It indicates a transition to the reply to the second question [Gdt, ICC]. It indicates that the theme will remain the same and something new will be added to it [TH].

perhaps[a] of-wheat or of some others;[b]

LEXICON—a. εἰ τύχοι (BAGD I.3. p. 219; 2.b. p. 829): 'perhaps' [BAGD (219, 829), Herm, NIGTC, NTC; NET, NIV, NRSV, REB, TEV, TNT], 'it may chance' [Lns; KJV], 'I dare say' [NJB], 'it may be' [BAGD (219), HNTC], 'for example' [BAGD (219)], 'whether' [AB; ISV], 'say (a grain of wheat or…)' [ICC], 'if so be' [Gdt], not explicit [CEV, NAB, NLT]. Εἰ τύχοι indicates indefiniteness which matters little; here the kind of grain is of little importance [ICC]. See this combination also at 14:10.

b. λοιπός (See this word at 11:34): 'other grain' [KJV, NAB, NRSV, TEV, TNT], 'other seeds' [CEV], 'other cereal' [HNTC], 'other variety' [AB], 'other kind' [Herm, Lns], 'something else' [NIGTC], 'any other plant' [ICC]. The phrase τινος τῶν λοιπῶν 'of some others' is translated 'something else' [NTC; ISV, NET, NIV, REB], 'some other kind' [NJB], 'whatever it is' [NLT]. Λοιπός here implies other grain or seed [Alf, EGT, HNTC, TH; CEV, KJV, NAB, NRSV, TEV, TNT].

QUESTION—If the image is a seed that becomes a plant, and the topic is the resurrection of the dead, what is the point of similarity?

The point of similarity is the difference between the seed and the plant that comes out of it [Alf, Ho, MNTC, NIC, NTC, Rb, TG, TH, Vn]. The point of similarity is the difference between the seed and the plant that comes out of it coupled with the identity of the two: wheat seed becomes a wheat plant

320   1 CORINTHIANS 15:37

[Gdt, NCBC, TNTC]. The point of similarity is the changed nature of the thing planted as well as the identity of the two [NIC2].

15:38 But/and[a] God gives to-it (a) body[b] just-as he-wanted,[c]

LEXICON—a. δέ (See this word at 11:2): 'but' [Herm, ICC, Lns, NIGTC, NTC; ISV, KJV, NET, NIV, NRSV], 'and' [REB], 'now' [AB], 'then' [NLT], not explicit [HNTC; CEV, NAB, NJB, TEV, TNT]. Δέ indicates a contrast between σύ σπείρεις 'you sow' of 15:36 and ὁ θεός 'God' here [EGT, Lns].

b. σῶμα (See this word at 15:37): 'body' [AB, Herm, HNTC, ICC, Lns, NIGTC, NTC; CEV, KJV, NAB, NET, NIV, NLT, NRSV, REB, TEV], 'the sort of body' [NJB], 'form' [ISV], 'own individual form' [TNT].

c. aorist act. indic. of θέλω (LN 25.1, 30.58) (BAGD 2. p. 355): 'to want' [BAGD, LN (25.1)], 'to want (it to have)' [CEV, ISV, NLT], 'to wish' [BAGD, LN (25.1), NTC; TEV], 'to please' [KJV, NAB], 'to choose' [Herm, HNTC; NJB, NRSV], 'to plan' [NET], 'to determine' [NIV], 'to ordain' [ICC], 'to will' [AB, BAGD, Lns], 'to purpose' [LN (30.58), NIGTC], 'to desire' [LN (25.1)]. This verb is also translated as a noun: '(according to his own) purpose' [TNT], '(of his) choice' [REB]. The aorist tense indicates a single act and points to the Creation (see Genesis 1:11) [AB, Alf, EGT, Gdt, Ho, ICC, NIC2, NTC]. See this word also at 10:27.

and to-each of-the seeds[a] its-own[b] body.

LEXICON—a. σπέρμα (LN 3.35) (BAGD 1.a. p. 761): 'seed' [AB, BAGD, Herm, HNTC, ICC, LN, Lns, NIGTC, NTC; KJV, NAB, NET, REB, TEV, TNT], 'kind of seed' [Alf, Ed; ISV, NIV, NJB, NLT, NRSV], not explicit [CEV].

b. ἴδιος (LN 57.4, 58.47): 'its own' [HNTC, LN (57.4), Lns, NIGTC, NTC; ISV, NAB, NET, NIV, NJB, NRSV], 'its own particular' [Herm; REB], 'a particular' [AB]. 'its own proper' [TEV], 'its own individual' [TNT], 'his own' [KJV], 'appropriate to it' [ICC], 'peculiar, distinctive' [LN (58.47)], not explicit [CEV, NLT]. See this word also at 11:21.

QUESTION—What is the point of what Paul is saying here?

Paul's point is that there is identity between seed and plant: wheat seeds produce wheat crops, acorns produce oak trees, and so on [Ed, MNTC, NCBC, NIC]. Paul's point is that there are many kinds of bodies and God decides what each will be [HNTC]. Paul's point is that God is the one who makes this happen and that there is variety of kinds of bodies [TNTC]. Paul's point is that what God did in creation he can do in the resurrection of the dead [Alf, EGT, Ho].

DISCOURSE UNIT: 15:39–41 (NTC). The topic is species, stars, and planets.

15:39 Not all flesh[a] (is) the same flesh

LEXICON—a. σάρξ (BAGD 1. p. 743): 'flesh' [AB, BAGD, Herm, HNTC, ICC, Lns, NIGTC, NTC; all versions except NAB], 'bodily nature'

[NAB]. Σάρξ here refers to the physical substance that covers the bones of living creatures [BAGD, NIGTC, NTC]. It refers to the material of bodies [NIC, TG]. See this word also at 10:18.

QUESTION—What is the function of this verse?

This verse functions to explain the phrase 'its own body' from 15:38 [NIC, NTC]. This is an elaboration of the preceding clause [MNTC, NIC2]. From grains and plants, Paul moves to flesh of animals and people [TNTC].

but (there is) on-one-hand one-kind[a] of-people,[b]

TEXT—Some manuscripts include σάρξ 'flesh' before ἀνθρώπων 'men'. It is omitted by GNT without mention. It is included by KJV.

LEXICON—a. ἄλλος (LN **58.36**, 58.37) (BAGD 1.e.α. p. 40): 'one kind' [AB, HNTC; ISV, KJV, NAB, NIV, TEV, TNT], 'one flesh' [NTC; NET, NRSV], 'one thing' [Herm], 'different' [LN (58.36)], 'other, another' [LN (58.37)], 'different in kind' [BAGD], not explicit [NIGTC; NJB]. The repeated words ἄλλη…ἄλλη…ἄλλη…ἄλλη… 'another…another… another…another…' are translated 'one type/kind… another…another… another' [AB, HNTC, **LN** (58.36), Lns; KJV, NIV, TEV, TNT], 'one kind…different kind…different kind…different kind' [**LN** (58.36)], 'all different' [ICC; REB], 'none of them alike' [CEV].

b. ἄνθρωπος (See this word at 13:1): 'person' [AB; CEV, NET], 'man' [HNTC, ICC, Lns, NTC; KJV, NAB, NIV, TNT], 'human being' [NRSV, TEV], 'human' [ISV, NLT]. This noun is also translated as an adjective: 'human (flesh)' [NIGTC; NJB, REB].

and another flesh of-animals,[a]

LEXICON—a. κτῆνος (LN **4.6**) (BAGD p. 455): 'animal' [BAGD, **LN**, NIGTC; all versions except ISV, KJV, REB], 'beast' [Herm, HNTC, ICC, Lns, NTC; KJV, REB], 'animals in general' [ISV], 'cattle' [AB, Ed, LN], 'beast of burden, riding animal' [LN]. It probably refers to large domesticated animals here [LN]. Κτῆνος here refers to all four-footed animals [Ed, EGT, Gdt, NCBC].

and another flesh of-birds,[a]

TEXT—Some manuscripts omit σάρξ 'flesh' before πτηνῶν 'birds'. GNT includes it and does not mention its omission. It is omitted by KJV. It is also omitted by NIGTC; NET, NIV, NJB, NRSV, REB, TEV, and TNT, but perhaps without accepting the textual variant.

TEXT—Some manuscripts place this phrase after the phrase ἄλλη δὲ ἰχθύων 'and another of fish'. GNT places it before this phrase and does not mention this variant. Only KJV transposes these phrases.

LEXICON—a. πτηνός (LN **4.38**) (BAGD p. 727): 'bird' [AB, BAGD, Herm, HNTC, ICC, **LN**, Lns, NIGTC, NTC; all versions]. It is also used as an adjective 'feathered, winged' [BAGD].

and another of-fish.^a

LEXICON—a. ἰχθύς (LN 4.59) (BAGD p. 384): 'fish' [AB, BAGD, Herm, HNTC, ICC, LN, Lns, NIGTC, NTC; all versions].

15:40 **And (there are) heavenly**^a **bodies, and earthly**^b **bodies;**

LEXICON—a. ἐπουράνιος (LN **1.8, 1.26**) (BAGD 1.b. p. 306): 'heavenly' [AB, Herm, HNTC, **LN** (1.26), NTC; all versions except CEV, KJV, NLT], 'celestial' [BAGD, **LN** (1.8), Lns; KJV], 'in the sky' [LN (1.8)], 'fitted for existence in heaven' [ICC], 'super-earthly' [NIGTC]. This plural is translated 'in the heavens' [CEV, NLT].

  b. ἐπίγειος (LN 1.41) (BAGD 1. p. 290): 'earthly' [AB, BAGD, Herm, HNTC, NTC; all versions except CEV, KJV, NLT], 'on (the) earth' [LN; CEV, NLT], 'in the world' [LN], 'terrestrial' [Lns; KJV], 'fitted for existence on earth' [ICC], 'for beings of earth' [NIGTC]. Earthly bodies would be bodies of living beings on earth [NIC, TG].

QUESTION—Does 'heavenly bodies' refer to stars and planets or to angels?

1. Here σῶμα 'body' refers to an inorganic entity such as a star or planet [AB, Ed, Gdt, Herm, HNTC, Ho, ICC, Lns, MNTC, NIC, NIC2, NIGTC, NTC, TG, TH]. The lack of a conjunction between this verse and 15:41 shows a close connection to the words 'sun, moon, and stars' in that verse. This is the correct interpretation of 'bodies' here [Ed]. The word 'body' can refer to objects as well as to flesh and blood. He compares the heavenly luminaries with the creatures that inhabit the earth [NIC, NTC, TG, TH]. The stars are here conceived as being living entities in contrast to the earthly bodies of living creatures [Herm,].

2. It refers to angels or heavenly beings [Alf, EGT, TNTC]. Σῶμα is not used elsewhere in Scripture to refer to inorganic entities. Also the context here calls for a contrast between bodies for inhabitants of the earth and bodies for inhabitants of Heaven, the angels [EGT]. The correct contrast to 'heavenly bodies', if these referred to stars, would be 'the earth', not 'earthly bodies'. Here the contrast is between the bodies of heavenly beings and the bodies of earthly beings [TNTC].

but on-one-hand the glory^a **of-the heavenly (is) different,**^b

LEXICON—a. δόξα (LN 79.18, 14.49) (BAGD 1.a. p. 203): 'glory' [AB, HNTC, LN (79.18), Lns, NTC; KJV, NET, NLT, NRSV, TNT], 'splendor' [AB, BAGD, LN (79.18), NIGTC; ISV, NAB, NIV, NJB, REB], 'beauty' [ICC; TEV], 'luster' [Herm], 'radiance, brightness' [BAGD, LN (14.49)], 'shining' [LN (14.49)], not explicit [CEV]. Δόξα here refers to the appearance of a thing [LN (79.18)]. It refers to the brightness that shines from an object [Gdt]. It refers to degree of brightness [NCBC]. See this word also at 10:31.

  b. ἕτερος (LN **58.36**): 'different' [**LN**; CEV, NLT, TEV], 'quite different' [ICC], 'one thing' [AB, Herm; NAB, NRSV, REB], 'one kind' [AB; NIV, TNT], 'of one kind' [ISV], 'one sort' [NET], 'of (one's) own' [NJB], 'one' [LN, NTC; KJV], 'particular' [NIGTC]. (There are two occurrences of ἕτερος in this verse. ICC, LN; CEV, NLT and TEV translate both with a single rendering.) See this word also at 14:21.

on-the-other-hand the (glory) of-the earthly (is) different[a].
LEXICON—a. ἕτερος (LN **58.36**): 'different' [NJB], 'different kind' [BAGD], 'different one' [Lns], 'another' [Herm, HNTC, NTC; KJV, NAB, NET, NIV, NRSV, REB, TNT], 'quite another' [NIGTC], 'another kind' [AB], 'of another (kind)' [ISV], not explicit [CEV, NLT, TEV]. See this word just above.
QUESTION—What is the meaning of δόξα 'glory'?
It refers to brilliance, radiance, light, or splendor [AB, BAGD, HNTC, LN, NCBC, NTC, TH; ISV, NAB, NIV, NJB, REB]. It refers to beauty [ICC, TH; TEV], or splendor [TH]. While earthly bodies have glory they do not display it like the heavenly bodies that emit light [HNTC]. It refers to how a thing appears in regard to its beauty of form and color [Ed]. The glory of the heavenly bodies consists of light and radiance while that of earthly bodies consists of color or attractive form [Lns]. He may mean that heavenly bodies shine with their own light but earthly bodies shine with reflected light [AB].

15:41 **(There is) one-kind-of**[a] **glory**[b] **of-(the)-sun,**[c]
LEXICON—a. ἄλλος (See this word at 15:39): 'one kind of' [ISV, NIV, NLT, TNT], 'one' [AB, HNTC, Lns, NTC; KJV, NRSV], 'of (one's) own' [ICC; NAB, NJB, REB, TEV], 'one thing' [Herm], 'one particular thing' [NIGTC], not explicit [NET]. This and the following clause are translated 'the sun isn't like the moon' [CEV].
  b. δόξα (See this word at 15:40): 'glory' [AB, HNTC, Lns, NTC; KJV, NET, NLT, NRSV, TNT], 'splendor' [ICC, NIGTC; ISV, NAB, NIV, NJB, REB], 'beauty' [TEV], 'luster' [Herm], 'radiance' [NIC2], not explicit [CEV].
  c. ἥλιος (LN 1.28) (BAGD p. 345): 'the sun' [AB, Herm, HNTC, ICC, Lns, NIGTC, NTC; all versions].

and another glory of-(the)-moon,[a] **and another glory of-(the)-stars;**[b]
LEXICON—a. σελήνη (LN 1.29) (BAGD p. 746): 'the moon' [AB, Herm, HNTC, ICC, Lns, NIGTC, NTC; all versions].
  b. ἀστήρ (LN 1.30) (BAGD p. 177): 'star' [AB, Herm, HNTC, ICC, LN, NIGTC, NTC; all versions].

for[a] **star differs-from**[b] **star in glory.**
LEXICON—a. γάρ (See this word at 10:1): 'for' [AB, Herm, ICC, Lns, NIGTC, NTC; KJV, NET], 'and' [CEV, NIV, REB], 'yes, and' [HNTC], 'indeed' [NRSV, TNT], 'and even' [TH; NLT, TEV], 'in fact' [ISV], not explicit [NAB].
  b. pres. act. indic. of διαφέρω (LN **58.41**) (BAGD 2.a. p. 190): 'to differ from' [AB, BAGD, Herm, HNTC, LN, Lns, NIGTC, NTC; ISV, KJV, NAB, NET, NIV, NLT, NRSV, REB], 'to differ among' [NJB], 'to be different (from)' [LN; CEV]. The phrase ἀστὴρ ἀστέρος διαφέρει 'star

differs from star' is translated 'one star excels another' [TNT]. This entire clause is translated 'and even among stars there are different kinds of beauty' [TEV], 'for no two stars are the same in splendor' [ICC]. The difference lies in the brightness or magnitude of each star [HNTC, Lns, NCBC, Rb, TG]. Each star has its own color. This is part of its glory [MNTC].

DISCOURSE UNIT: 15:42–44a [NTC]. The topic is sown and raised.

15:42a So[a] also (is) the resurrection of-the dead.

LEXICON—a. οὕτως (See this word at 11:12): 'so' [Herm, HNTC, ICC, Lns; KJV, NAB, NIV, NRSV, REB], 'thus' [NIGTC, NTC], 'that/this is how (it will be)' [CEV, ISV, TEV], '(it is) the same' [NET, NJB, NLT], '(is) like that' [TNT], 'this is the way (it is)' [AB]. Οὕτως signifies that Paul is now applying the figure [NIC, NIC2, TH]. It refers to 15:37 and to the seed and the plant that grows from it [TG].

QUESTION—To what question is this verse (and the following) the answer?
It begins to answer the question 'With what kind of body do they come?' [Gdt, ICC]. The reply Paul gives is that the body will be completely different from the body that is sown [Gdt].

QUESTION—To what is the resurrection of the dead being compared?
1. It is being compared to heavenly bodies [Ho, MNTC, TH]. The body that is raised will differ from the body that is sown to the same degree that heavenly bodies differ from earthly bodies [Ho, MNTC].
2. It is being compared to a seed sprouting into a plant [Ed, NCBC, NIC2, NTC, Rb, TG, TNTC, Vn]. In 15:42b-43 Paul compares the resurrection to a sprouting seed. In 15:44a Paul compares the natural and the spiritual body to earthly and heavenly bodies [NIC2, NTC]. The words σπείρεται 'is sown' indicates that Paul's primary focus is on the sowing of the seed and the sprouting of the plant [TNTC].

DISCOURSE UNIT: 15:42b–49 [EGT]. The topic is the first Adam and the last.

15:42b It-is-sown[a] in[b] corruption,[c]

LEXICON—a. pres. pass. indic. of σπείρω (BAGD 1.b.δ. p. 761): 'to be sown' [BAGD, Herm, NIGTC; KJV, NAB, NET, NIV, NJB, NRSV, REB], 'to be buried' [TEV, TNT], 'to be planted' [ISV], not explicit [CEV, NLT]. Σπείρω here is used figuratively of the body as though it were a seed [BAGD]. See this word also at 15:36.
  b. ἐν (LN **13.8**): 'in' [Herm, HNTC, Lns, NIGTC, NTC; KJV], 'in a state of being' [**LN**; TNT], 'in a state of' [Alf], not explicit [AB, ICC; all versions except KJV, TNT].
  c. φθορά (LN 23.205, 13.8, 20.38) (BAGD 1. p. 858): 'corruption' [BAGD; KJV], 'perishable' [NET, NIV, NJB, NRSV, TNT], 'perishable thing' [REB], 'perishability' [Herm], 'mortal' [LN (13.8); TEV], 'decay' [LN (23.205), NIGTC], 'ruin, destruction' [BAGD, LN (20.38)], 'dissolution,

deterioration, state of being perishable' [BAGD]. The phrase ἐν φθορᾷ 'in corruption' is translated 'subject to decay' [NAB], '(what is planted is) decaying' [ISV], '(these bodies) will die' [CEV], '(earthly bodies, which) die and decay' [NLT]. Φθορά implies disintegration [LN (20.38)].

QUESTION—To what is the figure of 'sowing' being compared?
1. It is being compared to the general condition of mankind in mortal bodies [AB, Ed, EGT, HNTC, MNTC, NCBC, NIC2]. This contrasts the present body with its resurrection state [NIC2]. Paul sees burial as only part of a process of decay [HNTC]. Here 'sown' corresponds with 'being born' [MNTC]. Verse 15:43 refers to ἀσθένια 'weakness'. This condition does not properly belong to a corpse [Ed, EGT]. Man is in this state from the time he begins to live [Ed].
2. It is being compared to the burial of a body [Gdt, Ho, ICC, Lns, NIC, NTC, Rb, TG, TH, TNTC, Vn; TEV, TNT]. The word φθορά 'corruption' requires the interpretation of burial in this verse [Gdt]. Two things validate this interpretation: (a) verse 15:44 speaks about the body that is sown being a natural body and (b) verse 15:36 speaks about the necessity of death to new life [NIC].

QUESTION—What is the implied subject of the passive σπείρεται 'it is sown'?
The implied subject is 'body' [AB, Ed, Ho, Lns, NIC2, TNTC; CEV, NIV, NLT, TEV, TNT]: the body is sown. It should be taken merely as an impersonal passive [EGT, HNTC, NIC].

it-is-raised in incorruption;[a]

LEXICON—a. ἀφθαρσία (LN **23.127**) (BAGD p. 125): 'incorruption' [HNTC, Lns, NTC; KJV], 'imperishability' [Herm], 'imperishable state' [TNT], 'incorruptibility' [BAGD], 'immortality' [BAGD, LN], 'decay's reversal' [NIGTC]. The phrase ἐν ἀφθαρσίᾳ 'in incorruption' is translated 'imperishable' [AB, ICC; NET, NIV, NJB, NRSV, REB], 'incorruptible' [NAB], 'immortal' [**LN**; TEV], 'will live forever' [CEV], 'will never die' [NLT], 'can't decay' [ISV]. The Greeks believed that the body was corruptible and looked forward to being released from it. Paul is saying that by the resurrection the new body will be incorruptible [TNTC].

QUESTION—If the image is the seed sprouting into a plant, and the topic is the resurrection of the dead, what is the point of similarity?
The point of similarity is the transformation between the sown form and the emerging form [HNTC, NCBC, Rb, TG]. The point of similarity is development through death [Ed]. There are two similarities: (a) the newness of the resurrected body and (b) its continuity with the former body [NIC]. The point of similarity is the intimate connection between the thing sown and the thing that is produced [Vn].

QUESTION—If the image is the difference between heavenly bodies and earthly bodies, and the topic is the resurrection of the dead, what is the point of similarity?

The point of similarity is the difference between the two kinds of bodies [Ho, MNTC].

15:43 **It-is-sown in dishonor,ᵃ it-is-raised in glory;ᵇ**

LEXICON—a. ἀτιμία (See this word at 11:14): 'dishonor' [AB, HNTC, LN, Lns, NTC; ISV, KJV, NET, NIV, NRSV], 'humiliation' [BAGD, NIGTC; REB, TNT], 'disgrace' [Herm], 'disability' [ICC]. This noun is also translated as an adjective: 'ugly' [CEV, TEV], 'ignoble' [NAB], 'contemptible' [NJB]. It is also translated as a verb: '(our bodies) disappoint (us)' [NLT].

b. δόξα (See this word at 15:40): 'glory' [KJV, NET, NIV, NRSV, REB, TNT], 'honor' [Herm], 'splendor' [NIGTC; ISV]. This noun is also translated as an adjective: 'beautiful' [CEV, TEV], 'glorious' [NAB, NJB], 'full of glory' [NLT].

QUESTION—In what way is the body sown in dishonor and raised in glory?

1. When sowing is compared to the general condition of mankind in their mortal bodies.

   Ἀτιμία 'dishonor' has to do with how people esteem an object, here with loss of dignity [Ed]. It does not indicate positive shame so much as the absence of glory [NCBC]. The corpse is hidden in the earth [NIC]. The body is in a state of imperfection and incompleteness. The resurrected body will be perfect in pleasing and enjoying God [MNTC].

2. When sowing is compared to the burial of a body.

   It indicates that the attractiveness of a living being is now absent [Ho]. A person is robbed of all dignity at death [NTC]. In this context it means 'ugliness' [TH]. The Jews viewed a corpse as being unclean [TNTC]. Its dishonor is seen in the fact that we rush to dispose of it [Lns]. At the resurrection we will receive glorified bodies [NTC]. It not only refers to beauty and radiance but to the fact that our bodies will be like Christ's resurrected body in his honored position (Philippians 3:21) [Ed, Rb]. It indicates that they will be honorable [MNTC, NIC2], beautiful [TH, TNTC], glorious [Lns, TG]. Glory indicates luminosity [Ho]. They will be like Christ's body at his transfiguration [Lns].

it-is-sown in weakness,ᵃ it-is-raised in power;ᵇ

LEXICON—a. ἀσθένεια (LN 74.23) (BAGD 1.b. p. 115): 'weakness' [AB, BAGD, Herm, HNTC, LN, Lns, NIGTC, NTC; ISV, KJV, NAB, NET, NIV, NRSV, REB], 'powerlessness' [ICC], 'incapacity, limitation' [LN]. This noun is also translated as an adjective: 'weak' [CEV, NJB, NLT, TEV, TNT]. See this word also at 2:3.

b. δύναμις (See this word at 15:24): 'power' [AB, HNTC, Lns, NIGTC, NTC; ISV, KJV, NET, NIV, NRSV, REB], 'strength' [Herm; NAB], 'full vigor' [ICC]. This noun is also translated as an adjective: 'strong' [CEV,

TEV], 'powerful' [NAB], 'full of power' [NLT, TNT]. Δύναμις here does not refer so much to the permanent state of the body as it does to how it is raised [NIC2]. It refers to the power that raised Jesus from the dead (Ephesians 1:19) [NCBC]. It refers to the incredible power that the body will display at the resurrection [NTC]. It refers to the ability to act in any way necessary [Lns]. It refers to energy [Alf, Ho].

QUESTION—In what way is the body sown in weakness and raised in power?

1. When sowing is being compared to the general condition of mankind in mortal bodies.

   We are weak in regard to physical strength and can be physically harmed or be subject to disease. Our heavenly bodies will have immeasurable power so that anything our heavenly spirit wants to do will be accomplished [MNTC].

2. When sowing is compared to the burial of a body.

   A corpse is powerless and unresisting [Alf, Ho, ICC, NIC, TNTC], a mere shell left by the departed soul [NTC]. The resurrection body will have powers that we cannot imagine [Ho, NTC].

15:44a It-is-sown (a) natural[a] body,

LEXICON—a. ψυχικός (LN **79.2**) (BAGD 1. p. 894): 'natural' [EGT, HNTC, LN, Lns, Rb; KJV, NAB, NET, NIV, NJB], 'physical' [BAGD, **LN**, NTC; CEV, ISV, NRSV, REB, TEV, TNT], 'natural human (bodies)' [NLT], 'ordinary human' [NIGTC], 'psychical' [Herm], 'animal' [Gdt, ICC]. This adjective is also translated as a noun phrase: '(sown in) natural life' [AB]. Ψυχικός is synonymous with 'earthly' [Ed]. It means 'congenial with' or 'formed to be the instrument of' the soul [ICC]. See this word also at 2:14.

QUESTION—What is meant by a σῶμα ψυχικόν 'natural body'?

It is a body that is animated by the ψυχή 'soul/life' as animal life [Ho], and is adapted to the conditions of existence on earth [Ho, ICC]. It does not mean a body that is composed of ψυχή 'soul/life' [Gdt, Herm, Ho, ICC]. It has reference to the natural world in contrast to the supernatural [AB, TNTC]. The ψυχή is the immaterial part of the body that gives it life [Lns]. A natural body is the one that is the instrument of the soul [Ed, Gdt, Lns]. It is suited for the physical world and limited to it [EGT, Herm, MNTC, TNTC]. It indicates a life that is earthly and belongs to this present age [NIC2]. It is body that is subject to hunger, thirst, and fatigue and is limited to time and space [NTC]. It indicates the animal body that is animated and informed by the soul [Alf, HNTC]. It is a body that is governed by the soul. Through the soul, the self expresses itself and relates to others [Vn].

it-is-raised (a) spiritual[a] body.

LEXICON—a. πνευματικός (LN **79.3**): 'spiritual' [Herm, HNTC, ICC, **LN**, Lns, NTC; all versions], 'constituted by the Spirit' [NIGTC], 'not physical' [**LN**], 'not material' [LN]. This adjective is also translated as a noun phrase: '(raised a body in) spiritual life' [AB]. Πνευματικός is synonymous with 'heavenly' [Ed]. It means 'congenial with' or 'formed to be the instrument of' the spirit [ICC]. See this word also at 10:3.

QUESTION—What is meant by a σῶμα πνευματικόν 'spiritual body'?

It means either it is composed of spirit or it is under the rule of the Spirit of God or both [AB]. It is a body controlled by the Spirit of God [AB, NIC, NIC2, NTC]. It is a body completely filled by the Spirit of God [NTC]. It is a body created new by the Spirit of God [NIC]. It is a body that is given life by the Spirit of God [HNTC, TH, Vn]. It is a body created by a life principle the function of which is to serve the spirit [Gdt]. It is a body that is adapted to heavenly existence [EGT, HNTC, Ho, MNTC]. It is a body that is controlled by the spirit and is in harmony with God's Spirit [ICC]. It is a body in which the spirit is predominant and is guided by the Spirit of God [Alf]. It does not mean a body that is composed of πνεῦμα 'soul/life' [Gdt, Ho, ICC, Lns, NIC2, TH, TNTC]. The πνεῦμα 'spirit' is the immaterial part of the body that is sensitive to the Spirit of God. A 'spiritual body' is one that is an instrument for the spirit and one which the spirit controls [Lns]. It does not indicate an immaterial body, but a supernatural one, one that belongs to the Spirit and the coming age. It is one that resembles Christ's resurrection body (see 15:49) [NIC2]. It is a body that is not limited by time and space, yet one that is material, a body that Jesus' disciples could recognize [NTC]. The spiritual body is one that is the appropriate instrument for the supernatural activity of the Holy Spirit [Ed]. A spiritual body is one that corresponds to the needs of a spirit [TNTC].

DISCOURSE UNIT: 15:44b–49 [Alf, NTC; NAB]. The topic is the existence of the spiritual body [Alf], physical and spiritual bodies [NTC; NAB].

15:44b **If there-is (a) natural body, there-is also (a) spiritual.**

TEXT—Some manuscripts omit εἰ 'if'. GNT includes it without comment. It is omitted by KJV, CEV, and TNT.

TEXT—Some manuscripts include σῶμα 'body' before πνευματικόν 'spiritual'. GNT does not include this word but does not discuss it. It seems to be included by CEV, ISV, KJV, NET, NIV, NJB, NLT, NRSV, REB, TEV, and TNT, though possibly only for stylistic reasons.

QUESTION—What words are emphasized in this clause?

The word ἔστιν 'there is' is emphasized by its two occurrences [EGT, ICC]: *there is* a natural body; *there is* also a spiritual body. Paul implies that no one can deny that there is a natural body [ICC, NIC2]. The Corinthians would have had no objection to σῶμα ψυχικός 'natural body' but a σῶμα πνευματικός 'spiritual body' would have troubled them. Paul therefore affirms that there is such a thing [NIC2]. The term 'spiritual body' is a contradictory expression. This statement is needed to support such a claim [Ho].

QUESTION—What is implied by this condition?

It is implied that this is a statement of fact [ICC, Rb, TH; CEV, KJV, NLT, TEV, TNT]: there is a natural body, so there is also a spiritual body.

DISCOURSE UNIT: 15:45–49 [Ed, NIC2]. The topic is the proof confirmed by Scripture [Ed], the analogy of Adam and Christ [NIC2].

15:45 So also it-is-written, "The first man Adam became into[a] (a) living soul,"[b]

LEXICON—a. εἰς with accusative object (LN 13.62): 'into' [LN]. The phrase ἐγένετο εἰς 'became into' is translated 'to become' [AB, Herm, HNTC, ICC, LN, Lns, NIGTC, NTC; all versions except CEV, KJV, TEV], 'to be' [CEV], 'to be made' [KJV], 'to be created' [TEV]. Εἰς adds the sense of 'resulting in' [NTC].

b. ψυχή (LN 9.20) (BAGD 2. p. 894): 'soul' [BAGD, HNTC, ICC, Lns, NTC; KJV, NAB, NJB], 'person' [LN, NIGTC; CEV, NET, NLT], 'being' [NTC; ISV, NIV, NRSV, TEV, TNT], 'living, natural being' [AB], 'living soul' [Herm], 'creature' [REB], 'living being' [NIC], 'that which possesses life, a living creature' [BAGD]. Ψυχή literally means 'inner self, mind' but it can be used figuratively of 'person' [LN].

QUESTION—What is the function of 15:45–47?

This section functions to explain how the body sown in death is ψυχικός 'natural' [NIC2].

QUESTION—What is the significance of the phrase οὕτως καὶ γέγραπται 'so also it is written'?

When Paul quotes Scripture he usually introduces it with καθὼς γέγραπται 'as it is written'. The phrase here may indicate that Paul is not quoting exactly [Gdt, TNTC]. Paul is confirming 15:44 by this quote from Scripture [Alf]. It functions to show that the Scriptures themselves support the use of the term σῶμα ψυχικόν 'natural body' [Lns].

QUESTION—Is this an exact quote of Genesis 2:7?

It is not exact, as the words πρῶτος 'first' and Ἀδάμ 'Adam' are added by Paul [Alf, Ed, EGT, GNT, Herm, HNTC, MNTC, NIC, NIC2, NTC, TH, TNTC].

QUESTION—Who is the 'the first Adam'?

He is the first man, Adam, as referred to in Genesis 2:7 [AB, Alf, Ed, EGT, Gdt, Herm, HNTC, Ho, ICC, Lns, MNTC, NCBC, NIC, NIC2, NTC, TG, TH, TNTC, Vn].

QUESTION—What is the meaning and significance of the term ψυχή 'soul' here?

It indicates more than a mere animating principle and should not be limited to the senses and inferior abilities, but includes the faculties of mind, will, and heart as well [Gdt]. It not only indicates common animal life but includes the rational, eternal principle of our being [Ho]. It refers back to 15:44, to the words σῶμα ψυχικόν 'natural body' [Alf, HNTC, Lns]. It functions to explain the term σῶμα ψυχικόν 'natural body' as being a body that is animated by the soul [Lns]. Paul's point is that man from his beginning is characterized by the term 'soul' [TNTC].

QUESTION—When did Adam become a ψυχὴν ζῶσαν 'living soul'?
He became a living soul at creation [Alf, Gdt, NIC, NTC].

the last Adam (became) into (a) life-giving[a] spirit.[b]

LEXICON—a. pres. act. participle of ζωοποιέω (See this word at 15:22): 'to give life' [Herm, HNTC, ICC, Lns, NIGTC, NTC; all versions except KJV], 'to make life' [AB], 'to quicken' [KJV].
  b. πνεῦμα (LN 12.33) (BAGD 5.f. p. 677): 'spirit' [AB, BAGD, Herm, HNTC, ICC, LN, Lns, NTC; all versions except NLT, TEV], 'Spirit' [HNTC, NIGTC; NLT, TEV]. Πνεῦμα refers to a supernatural non-material being [LN]. It refers to Christ here [BAGD]. See this word also at 14:2.

QUESTION—Is this part of the quote from Scripture?
These words are not a quote from Scripture but are Paul's words [Alf, Herm, ICC, Lns, NIC, NIC2, TNTC].

QUESTION—Who is 'the last Adam'?
It refers to Christ [AB, Alf, Ed, EGT, Gdt, HNTC, Ho, ICC, Lns, MNTC, NCBC, NIC, NIC2, NIGTC, NTC, Rb, TG, TH, TNTC, Vn; CEV, NLT]. The phrase was common among Jews as a reference to the Messiah [Alf, EGT, Ho]. Verses 15:21, 22 support this interpretation [TH].

QUESTION—What is the significance of the term ἔσχατος 'last' here?
It means that after Christ there are no other heads of the human race [ICC, NIC, NTC, TNTC, Vn]. It indicates that Christ is the highest in an ascending order of progression [ICC]. It indicates that Christ is the complete realization of the first Adam [NTC].

QUESTION—Why is the term 'Adam' used here?
Adam was the first human being and the source of the whole race of human beings. The name Adam therefore carries the sense of being the first of a race. Christ was the first of a new race of spiritual beings and is therefore also referred to as 'Adam' [Gdt, Lns, NIC, NIC2, NTC, TNTC]. The term signifies the humanity of Christ [EGT].

QUESTION—When did Christ become a 'life-giving spirit'?

1. He became a life-giving spirit at his incarnation [Ed, Gdt, Ho, NIC]. Adam became a living soul at his creation so Christ became a life-giving spirit at his incarnation when God entered the realm of humanity [Ed]. It began at his incarnation but became complete at his ascension into Heaven [Gdt]. Christ became a life-giving spirit in his work as Mediator [NIC].
2. He became a life-giving spirit at his resurrection [EGT, HNTC, ICC, Lns, NCBC, NIC2, NTC, TG]. Verse 15:22 indicates that Christ became a life-giving spirit at the resurrection [NIC2]. The context and especially 15:42 support this interpretation. Christ's body was a natural body before the resurrection [EGT]. It was at his resurrection that Christ became the Son of God in power (see Romans 1:4) [AB, HNTC]. He became a life-giving spirit at his resurrection and possibly more so at his ascension [ICC]. The

aorist ἐγένετο 'became' is historical and points to a specific time. This occurred at Christ's resurrection and glorification [Lns]. It was at his resurrection that Christ received the power to give life [NTC].
3. The exact time should not be a concern [Alf, TNTC]. It was during the period of Christ's suffering and victory that he became a life-giving spirit. It was in his work of saving the lost that he became a life-giving spirit [TNTC].

QUESTION—What is Paul teaching by this verse?

He is focusing on two kinds of bodies, natural and spiritual. Here 'living soul' corresponds to the natural body while 'life-giving spirit' corresponds to the spiritual body [HNTC]. Paul is teaching among other things that the only path to becoming 'spiritual', as the Corinthians were styling themselves, was through the resurrection, as Christ attained it [NIC2].

15:46 **But the spiritual (is) not first but the natural, then**[a] **the spiritual.**

LEXICON—a. ἔπειτα (See this word at 12:28): 'then' [AB, Herm, HNTC, ICC, Lns, NTC; ISV, NET, NRSV, REB, TEV, TNT], 'afterward' [KJV, NJB], 'after that' [NIGTC; NAB, NIV], 'after' [CEV], 'later' [NLT].

QUESTION—What relationship is indicated by ἀλλά 'but'?

It indicates an adversative relationship [AB, ICC, Lns, NIC2, NTC, TNTC; KJV, NET, NJB, NRSV]: the first man Adam became a living soul, the last Adam became a life-giving spirit *but* the spiritual is not first. The word should be translated as an imperative [NAB, REB, TNT]: Note, the spiritual is not first! The contrast indicates that although the spiritual is greater than the natural, still the natural comes first [NIC]. Paul is correcting the implication that the reference to the 'life-giving spirit' might have given—that it was first. The life-giving spirit had reference to Christ's resurrection both for Christ himself and for believers. So for both Adam and Christ and for believers, the natural comes first, then the spiritual. Further, Paul is countering the belief of some Corinthians that they had already entered a spiritual state by saying that the spiritual state only comes after the natural and like Christ, after the resurrection [NIC2].

QUESTION—To what does ἔπειτα 'then' refer?

It refers to a time after the death of the body [AB]. It refers to the resurrection [NIC2].

QUESTION—Is the word 'body' implied after 'spiritual' and 'natural'?
1. The word body is implied after 'spiritual' and 'natural' [AB, Ed, Gdt, HNTC, Ho, NIC, NIC2, NTC, Vn; CEV, NJB, NLT, REB]: spiritual body…natural body. Τὸ ψυχικόν 'the natural' and τὸ πνευματικόν 'the spiritual' are not general references, but refer to Adam and the natural body and Christ and the spiritual body [Ed].
2. This is a general reference to 'spiritual' and 'natural' and does not imply 'body' [Alf, EGT, ICC, Lns]. The principle is that the lower stage must precede the higher [ICC].

QUESTION—Why does Paul emphasize the order of 'natural' and 'spiritual'?

He is countering the belief of some Corinthians that there was no resurrection of the dead because it had in a spiritual sense already occurred [NIC2, NTC].

15:47 The first man (is) from earth made-of-dust,[a]

LEXICON—a. χοϊκός (LN **1.42, 2.16**) (BAGD p. 883): 'made of dust' [BAGD, HNTC, **LN** (1.42, 2.16); CEV, NET, NLT, REB, TNT], 'made from dust' [NIGTC], 'formed from dust' [NAB], 'came from the dust' [ISV], 'of (the) dust' [**LN** (2.16); NIV], 'from the dust' [ICC, NTC], 'earthy' [AB, BAGD, Herm, Lns; KJV], 'earthly' [**LN** (1.42); NJB], 'made of earth' [BAGD, **LN** (1.42); TEV], 'created out of earth' [**LN** (1.42)], 'comes from the earth' [**LN** (1.42)], 'of earth' [**LN** (1.42)], 'made of soil' [LN (2.16)], 'formed out of soil' [**LN** (2.16)], 'made from the ground' [**LN** (2.16)]. This word is also translated as a noun: 'a man of dust' [NRSV]. Χοϊκός here explains the term ψυχικός 'natural' while ἐξ οὐρανοῦ 'from heaven' explains πνευματικός 'spiritual' [Herm].

the second man (is) from heaven.

TEXT—Some manuscripts include ὁ κύριος 'the Lord' after ἄνθρωπος 'man'. It is omitted by GNT with an A decision, indicating that the text is certain. It is included only by KJV.

QUESTION—What verb should be supplied between 'man' and 'from earth' and 'man' and 'from heaven'?

The appropriate form of the verb 'come' should be supplied [HNTC, TH; ISV, TEV, TNT]: the first man *came* from the earth…the second man *came* from heaven. The verb 'to be' should be supplied [AB, ICC, Lns, NTC; KJV, NAB, NET, NIV, NJB, NRSV, REB]: the first man *is* from the earth…the second man *is* from heaven.

QUESTION—Does ἐξ οὐρανοῦ 'from heaven' refer to Christ's ultimate origin or to his resurrected body?

1. It refers to his ultimate origin as being 'from heaven' [AB, Alf, Ed, Ho, MNTC, NIC, NTC, TNTC, Vn]. Philippians 2:6–7 indicates that Christ's origin was in Heaven with God [AB]. He lived on earth in a natural body but he had existed eternally and came from heaven [MNTC]. It could either refer to Christ's glorified body at his Second Coming or to his eternal character as the God-man. John 3:13 indicates that the latter is more probable [Alf].

2. It refers to his resurrected form (that had its origin in Heaven), and/or to the Second Coming when he will descend 'from Heaven' [Gdt, HNTC, ICC, Lns, NCBC, NIC2, Rb]. The phrases 'from the earth' and 'from Heaven' are synonymous with the words ψυχικός 'natural' and πνευματικός 'spiritual' and do not refer to origin. Christ, who also had an earthly body, became the second man 'from Heaven' at His resurrection. Verse 15:48 also indicates that this refers to Christ's resurrected body and not to his incarnation [NIC2]. Philippians 3:20, 21,

1 Thessalonians 4:16, and 2 Thessalonians 1:7 indicate that the phrase 'from Heaven' refers to Christ's Second Coming [Gdt]. The context requires that the reference be to the Second Coming and not to Christ's heavenly origin [HNTC]. Paul is here answering the question, 'With what kind of body do they come?' Christ can be described as being 'from Heaven' from the time of his Ascension to his Second Coming [ICC]. 2 Corinthians 5:1ff support this interpretation [NCBC].

QUESTION—How is the term ἄνθρωπος 'man' used here?

It is used to refer to Adam and Christ as types of humanity rather than to man in general (see 15:21, 22, 45) [NIC, TH].

15:48 As[a] the earthy-man,[b] so[c] also (are) the earthy-persons,[d]

LEXICON—a. οἷος (LN 64.1) (BAGD p. 562): 'as' [BAGD, Herm, ICC, Lns, NTC; KJV, NIV, NRSV], 'just as' [AB], 'such as' [BAGD, LN], 'like' [LN; CEV, ISV, NAB, NET, TEV, TNT], 'just like' [NLT], 'corresponding to' [HNTC], 'of what sort' [BAGD], 'similar, likewise' [LN]. This adverb is also translated as a verb phrase: 'to be a pattern for' [NJB, REB], 'to be a model for' [NIGTC].

b. χοϊκός (See this word in 15:47): 'earthly man' [NIV, NJB], 'earthly one' [AB, ICC, Lns], 'man of earth' [NAB], 'one who was made of earth' [TEV], 'man of dust' [NRSV, TNT], 'one man made of dust' [HNTC], 'one from dust' [NIGTC], 'one made of dust' [NTC; NET], 'man from the dust' [ISV], 'Adam's (body)' [NLT], 'earthy' [Herm; KJV], 'made from the dust of the earth' [CEV], 'made of dust' [REB].

c. τοιοῦτος (BAGD 1. p. 821): 'so' [AB, Herm, NTC; NET, NIV, NRSV], 'such' [ICC, LN, Lns; KJV], 'like such, like that' [LN], 'such as this, of such a kind' [BAGD], not explicit [HNTC, NIGTC; CEV, ISV, NAB, NJB, NLT, REB, TEV, TNT]. See this word also at 11:16.

d. χοϊκός (See this word above): 'earthly person' [AB; NJB], 'earthly man' [NAB], 'earthly one' [Lns], 'one who belongs to the earth' [TEV], 'of the earth' [NIV], 'earthy' [KJV], 'one that is earthy' [Herm], 'everyone on earth' [CEV], 'man of dust' [TNT], 'person of dust' [NIGTC], 'man who is made of dust' [HNTC], 'one (who is) made of dust' [ISV, NET, REB], 'one who is of the dust' [NRSV], 'one who is dust' [NTC]. This adjective is also translated as a verb: 'to have an earthly body' [NLT]. Women are not excluded by this term [TH].

QUESTION—To whom does ὁ χοϊκός 'the earthly man' refer?

It refers to Adam, the first man [Alf, Ed, EGT, Gdt, HNTC, Ho, ICC, Lns, MNTC, NCBC, NIC2, Rb, TG, TH, TNTC, Vn]. There is no specific reference to Adam but only to a general condition of being 'earthly' [NIC]. The verse indicates that both Adam and all his descendants are from the dust of the earth [NTC].

QUESTION—What is the similarity between the earthly man and the earthly people?
The similarity is in the fact that both are subject to death and decay [Ed, EGT, ICC, NCBC, NIC2, TNTC, Vn]. There is also a similarity in the sinful condition of both (see Philippians 3:18ff, Colossians 3:1–4, and Romans 6:4) [Ed, EGT]. Both bodies come from and return to the earth [AB]. The similarities are that both are made of earth [AB, Lns, MNTC, NTC, TH, Vn], and are controlled by the soul [Lns]. The similarities are that they are both natural and are animated by the soul [HNTC].

and like the heavenly-man,[a] so also (are) the heavenly-ones;[b]
LEXICON—a. ἐπουράνιος (LN 1.12) (BAGD 1.a.β. p. 306): 'heavenly man' [NJB, TNT], 'heavenly Man' [HNTC], 'man of heaven' [NAB, NRSV], 'Heavenly One' [ICC], 'heavenly one' [AB, Lns, NTC], 'heavenly' [BAGD, Herm, LN; KJV, REB], 'one from heaven' [NET], 'one who came from heaven' [TEV], 'man from heaven' [NIV], 'Christ's (body)' [NLT], 'from heaven' [CEV, ISV], 'in heaven, pertaining to heaven' [LN]. See this word also at 15:40.

b. ἐπουράνιος (BAGD 1.a.γ. p. 306): 'heavenly one' [Lns; NJB], 'heavenly man' [BAGD, HNTC; NAB, TNT], 'heavenly person' [AB], 'the heavenly' [REB], 'one who is heavenly' [Herm, ICC, NTC; ISV, KJV, NET], 'one who is of heaven' [NIV, NRSV, TEV], 'one who pertains to heaven' [NIGTC], 'one's heavenly body' [NLT], 'the One from heaven' [NIGTC], 'everyone in heaven' [CEV].

QUESTION—To whom does ὁ ἐπουράνιος 'the heavenly man' refer?
It refers to Christ [Alf, Ed, EGT, Gdt, HNTC, Ho, ICC, Lns, MNTC, NCBC, NIC2, NTC, Rb, TG, TH, TNTC]. There is no specific reference to Christ but only to a general condition of being 'heavenly' [NIC].

QUESTION—What is the similarity between the heavenly man and the heavenly people?
The similarity is in the fact that both have, or will have, resurrected heavenly bodies (see 2 Corinthians 5:4 and Philippians 3:21) [AB, Ed, EGT, HNTC, Ho, ICC, Lns, NIC2, Rb, TH, TNTC]. Both will be risen from the dead and eternally glorified [ICC]. There is also a similarity in that they both now have similar characters [NIC2]. Both are now spiritual and heavenly (see Philippians 3:18ff, Colossians 3:1–4, Romans 6:4, Ephesians 2:6) [Ed, EGT, Vn]. Both bodies are ruled by the spirit [Lns]. At the resurrection both beings will be completely full of heavenly glory [NTC]. The focus is on the nature of both bodies, that they are heavenly [TNTC, Vn].

15:49 And as we-bore[a] the likeness[b] of-the earthly-man,[c]
LEXICON—a. aorist act. indic. of φορέω (LN **13.2**, 49.11) (BAGD 2. p. 865): 'to bear' [BAGD, **LN** (13. 2); ISV, KJV, NET, NIV, NJB, NRSV, TNT], 'to wear' [Herm, LN (49.11), NIGTC; REB, TEV], 'to be in' [**LN** (13.2)], 'to be' [LN (13. 2); CEV]. The phrase ἐφορέσαμεν τὴν εἰκόνα 'we have borne the image' is translated 'to resemble' [NAB], 'to be like' [NLT].

Φορέω here means to represent in one's own appearance [BAGD]. The aorist 'we bore' should be understood from the perspective of the resurrection [Alf, Lns]. The aorist can be either inceptive 'we began to bear' or 'we bore' from the perspective of the resurrection [TNTC].
  b. εἰκών (LN **58.35**): 'likeness' [**LN**; ISV, NIV, NJB, REB, TEV, TNT], 'image' [Herm, NIGTC; KJV, NET, NRSV], 'same form' [LN]. The phrase ἐφορέσαμεν τὴν εἰκόνα 'we bore the likeness' is translated 'we are like' [CEV, NLT], 'we resemble' [NAB]. See this word also at 11:7.

QUESTION—To whom does 'we' refer?
  It refers to all believers [NIC, TH].

we-will-bear also the likeness of-the heavenly.
TEXT—Instead of φορέσομεν 'we will bear', some manuscripts have φορέσωμεν 'let us bear'. GNT selects the reading φορέσομεν 'we will bear' with a B rating, indicating that the text is almost certain. This same reading is also taken by AB, Alf, Gdt, Herm, HNTC, Ho, ICC, Lns, NCBC, NTC, Rb, TH, Vn, and all versions except NET. The reading Φορέσωμεν 'let us bear' is taken by Ed, EGT, NIC, NIC2, and NET. The aorist subjunctive and the future in Koine Greek are quite close [NIC].

QUESTION—Is the focus of the resemblance on body alone, or on moral character as well?
  1. The focus of the resemblance is on body [AB, Gdt, HNTC, Ho, ICC, Lns, NIC, NTC]. This verse is part of the answer to the question of 15:35 "With what kind of body will they come?" [Gdt, Lns, NIC]. The body will be appropriate to a spiritual existence just as the physical body was appropriate to a natural existence [Gdt]. Paul's intent is to answer the objection to the resurrection that was based on the idea that resurrection bodies are the same kind as natural bodies [Ho]. The resemblance will not only be in appearance, but also in similar abilities and functions [Lns]. The similarity will not only be in appearance but also in manner of existence [NTC]. We will have a heavenly body like Christ's (see 2 Corinthians 5:4) [AB].
  2. The focus of resemblance is on body and moral character [Ed, EGT, NIC, NIC2, Vn; NET]. The subjunctive reading must be original and as such urges the Corinthians conform their behavior to be like the Heavenly Man's. Paul's point is both that they will be like Christ at the resurrection, but in their present existence they should also be like him in their daily living [NIC2]. Εἰκών 'image' includes the whole person, not just the body. Romans 13:14 and Galatians 3:27 indicate that we should be like Christ in our behavior [EGT]. Εἰκών includes resemblance both in spiritual body as well as moral character. God's purpose for us is that we be made into the image of his Son (see Romans 8:30) [Vn].

DISCOURSE UNIT: 15:50–58 [HNTC, ICC, MNTC, NIC, TNTC; NAB]. The topic is the Christian apocalypse [HNTC], victory over death [ICC, MNTC, TNTC], the assurance of victory [NIC], the glorification of the body [NAB].

336   1 CORINTHIANS 15:50

DISCOURSE UNIT: 15:50–57 [AB, ICC, NCBC, NTC]. The topic is the mystery of the end [AB], victory over death [ICC], a new revelation [NCBC], immortality and victory [NTC].

DISCOURSE UNIT: 15:50–54 [Alf, Ed]. The topic is the necessary change from psychical to spiritual [Ed].

DISCOURSE UNIT: 15:50–53 [NTC]. The topic is transformation.

15:50 Now this I-say, brothers, that flesh and blood not are-able to-inherit[a] (the) kingdom of-God

LEXICON—a. aorist act. infin. of κληρονομέω (LN 57.138, 57.131) (BAGD 2. p. 434): 'to inherit' [AB, Herm, HNTC, LN (57.138), Lns, NIGTC, NTC; ISV, KJV, NAB, NET, NIV, NJB, NLT, NRSV], 'to share' [CEV], 'to share in' [TEV], 'to have a share in' [ICC], 'to possess' [REB, TNT], 'to receive, to gain possession of, to be given' [LN (57.131)], 'to come into possession of, to obtain, to acquire' [BAGD], 'to receive as from a deceased parent' [LN (57.138)]. Κληρονομέω means to obtain in a secure manner [NIC, TNTC]. It means to take possession of something [TH]. Βασιλείαν θεοῦ κληρονομῆσαι 'to inherit the Kingdom of God' is synonymous with the resurrection of the dead [NTC]. See this word also at 6:9.

QUESTION—What is Paul's point in this verse?

Paul's is making the same point that he has been making since 15:37 that the resurrected body of a believer is a changed form of the body that was buried [NIC2].

QUESTION—What is the function of the statement τοῦτο δέ φημι ἀδελφοί 'now this I say, brothers'?

It functions to introduce a new turn of thought [Herm, NIC2, TH]. This is seen: (a) in the use of δέ 'now' (which should have been γάρ 'for' if the thought of 15:49 were continuing), (b) the vocative 'brothers', and (c) the words 'I say that'. At 7:29 the same statement is used and a new thought is introduced there [NIC2]. It functions to restate the idea of the previous paragraph concerning the contrast between Adam's natural body and Christ's spiritual body [EGT]. It functions to emphasize the statement of 15:50. The vocative, 'Brothers', indicates a new subject [Lns]. 'Now this I say' calls attention to something that might be overlooked [Alf]. It functions to call attention to an explanation of what Paul has just said [Gdt]. It functions to bring in a principle that will confirm 15:49 and prepare for 15:51 [ICC]. It indicates that a misconception will be corrected [Ed]. 'This I say' functions to emphasize the following [TNTC]. 'This' refers to 15:49 [NIC]. 'Brothers' includes sisters as well [NTC, TH].

QUESTION—To what does σάρξ καὶ αἷμα 'flesh and blood' refer?

It refers to the human body as being composed of flesh and blood [Gdt, Ho, Lns, NIC; CEV]. It refers to the physical body which is subject to death [NCBC, NTC, TNTC]. It does not refer to sinful nature [Ho, ICC, NIC]. It either refers to the composition of the human body or to humanity [AB]. It refers to our body without the soul [Alf]. It refers to our physical nature as being subject to death and decay [Ed, ICC]. Flesh is the material part of the body while blood is its life [EGT, Gdt]. While it refers to the body composed of flesh and blood, it also refers to the body as being weak and subject to decomposition and death [Ed, NIC2].

QUESTION—What is meant by βασιλείαν θεοῦ 'kingdom of God'?

It refers to heaven where God rules over everything and in the hearts of those present [MNTC]. It indicates being citizens in God's Kingdom [NIC]. It refers to eternal life with God after the resurrection [TG]. It indicates the final phase in which God's Kingdom is released from the powers of evil [NTC]. It indicates the believer's final existence in heaven where he/she receives the likeness of Christ (see 15:48–49) [NIC2].

nor (does) corruption^a inherit incorruption.^b

LEXICON—a. φθορά (See this word at 15:42): 'corruption' [Lns, NTC; KJV, NAB], 'the corruption of death' [HNTC], 'decay' [NIGTC], 'what decays' [ISV], 'what is perishable' [ICC; NJB, TNT], 'perishability' [Herm], 'perishable body' [NLT], 'what is mortal' [TEV], 'the perishable' [AB; NET, NIV, NRSV, REB], not explicit [CEV].

b. ἀφθαρσία (See this word at 15:42): 'incorruption' [HNTC, Lns, NTC; KJV, NAB], 'immortality' [TEV], 'the imperishable' [NET, NIV, NRSV, REB], 'imperishability' [AB, Herm]. This noun is also translated as a clause: 'what doesn't decay' [ISV], 'that which is free from decay' [NIGTC], 'what is imperishable' [ICC; NJB, TNT], 'which lasts forever' [CEV]. It is also translated as a verb: 'to live forever' [NLT].

QUESTION—What is the significance of the present tense κληρονομεῖ 'inherit'?

It functions to state a law or principle [Alf, Ed, Gdt].

QUESTION—Are the two parts of this verse synonymous or complementary?

1. They are complementary, the second giving information that completes the thought begun by the first [EGT, Gdt, HNTC, ICC, Lns, NCBC, TNTC]. The phrase 'flesh and blood' indicates living persons who need to undergo change at the resurrection to enter the Kingdom of God while 'corruption' refers to the dead who also need to undergo change at the resurrection to enter the Kingdom of God [HNTC, TNTC]. The verse indicates that our bodies, whether living or dead need to change to enter the Kingdom of God [ICC]. The second proposition functions to explain the first. That is, corruption further describes flesh and blood [EGT]. The second proposition functions to clarify the first [Lns].
2. They are synonymous parallelism in which the second restates the first [Herm, Ho, NIC2, NTC, Vn]. The second clause repeats the first in a generic way [Ho]. Flesh and blood are corruption and the Kingdom of God is incorruption [Lns, NTC, Vn]. Both propositions make the same

point, namely that in its present state the body cannot inherit God's Kingdom [NIC2]. The second proposition confirms the first [Vn].

DISCOURSE UNIT: 15:51-58 (Vn). The topic is the effects, future and present.

15:51 Look[a] I-tell you (a) mystery;[b]

LEXICON—a. ἰδού (LN 91.13, 91.10) (BAGD): 'look' [LN (91.13), NIGTC, NTC], 'see' [AB], 'behold' [Herm, HNTC, Lns; KJV], 'listen' [LN (91.13); NET, NIV, NRSV, REB, TEV, TNT], 'pay attention' [LN (91.13)], 'indeed' [LN (91.10)], not explicit [CEV, ISV, NAB, NJB, NLT]. Ἰδού indicates strong emphasis [LN (91.10)]. It functions here to emphasize or call attention to the following [Gdt, HNTC, Ho, ICC, Lns, TH, TNTC].

b. μυστήριον (See this word at 13:2): 'mystery' [AB, Herm, HNTC, Lns, NIGTC, NTC; CEV, KJV, NAB, NET, NIV, NJB, NRSV, REB], 'secret' [ISV, TNT], 'wonderful secret' [NLT], 'secret truth' [TEV], 'truth that has hitherto been kept secret' [ICC]. Μυστήριον refers to a truth that was secret but has now been revealed [AB, Ed, Gdt, Ho, Lns, MNTC, NCBC, NIC, NIC2, TH, TNTC]. It is revealed by God [AB]. It is revealed through Christ [NIC2]. In 1 Thessalonians 4:15, a similar context, Paul refers to his revelation as being 'a word of the Lord' [Ho, NTC].

(we will) not all sleep,[a]

LEXICON—a. fut. pass. (deponent = act.) indic. of κοιμάω (See this word at 11:30): 'to sleep' [KJV, NIV], 'to fall asleep' [Herm, HNTC, Lns, NTC; NAB, NJB], 'to sleep in death' [ICC], 'to fall asleep in death' [NIGTC], 'to die' [AB; CEV, ISV, NET, NLT, NRSV, REB, TEV, TNT].

QUESTION—What is meant by πάντες οὐ κοιμηθησόμεθα 'we will not all sleep'?

It means that 'not all of us will die', that is, 'some of us will not die' [all commentaries and versions]. The negative particle οὐ, while coming before the verb, negates the pronoun πάντες 'all' [NTC]. Believers who are alive when Christ returns will not have to die before their bodies are changed [MNTC].

but (we) all will-be-changed,[a]

LEXICON—a. fut. pass. indic. of ἀλλάσσω (LN 58.43) (BAGD 1. p. 39): 'to be changed' [AB, BAGD, Herm, HNTC, LN, Lns, NTC; all versions except NLT], 'to be transformed' [ICC; NLT], 'to undergo transformation' [NIGTC], 'to be made different' [LN], 'to be altered' [LN]. Ἀλλάσσω implies to receive eternity [NIC]. It implies to receive a resurrection body [Rb].

QUESTION—Who is meant by 'we' in ἀλλαγησόμεθα 'we will be changed'?

It refers to Paul [AB, Alf, Herm, ICC, NIC2, Rb, TH, Vn], Paul's readers [Ho, ICC, TH, Vn], and all believers [Ed, Herm, Lns, MNTC, NIC, NTC, TG, TNTC].

QUESTION—To whom does πάντες 'all' refer?

It refers to believers [Herm, Lns, NCBC, NIC, NTC, TNTC]. It refers to both the living and dead [Alf, Lns, NCBC, NIC, NIC2, Rb, TNTC].

QUESTION—Who is the agent of the passive ἀλλαγησόμεθα 'we will be changed'?

God is the agent [Lns]: God will change us.

15:52 in (a) moment,[a] in (the) blinking[b] of-(an)-eye,

LEXICON—a. ἄτομος (LN **67.149**) (BAGD p. 120): 'moment' [AB, BAGD, Herm, HNTC, ICC, LN, Lns, NTC; ISV, KJV, NET, NLT, NRSV], 'instant' [**LN**, NIGTC; NAB, TEV, TNT], 'flash' [LN; NIV, REB]. The phrase ἐν ἀτόμῳ 'in an instant' is translated 'suddenly' [CEV], 'instantly' [NJB]. Ἄτομος basically indicates something that is indivisible [Alf, Gdt, HNTC, Ho, Lns, MNTC, NIC2, NTC, Rb, TH, TNTC]. It here refers to a unit of time that cannot be further subdivided, that is, the shortest possible time [Lns, MNTC, NTC, TNTC]. It indicates instantaneity [Ed, EGT, HNTC, Ho, ICC, MNTC]. It could be expressed in English as a split second [NCBC, NIC2, NTC].

b. ῥιπή (LN **16.5, 67.114**) (BAGD p. 736): 'blinking' [**LN** (16.5), NIGTC; ISV, NLT, TEV], 'blink' [AB; CEV, TNT], 'twinkling' [BAGD, Herm, HNTC, ICC, Lns, NTC; KJV, NAB, NET, NIV, NJB, NRSV, REB]. The phrase ἐν ῥιπῇ ὀφθαλμοῦ 'in the blinking of an eye' is an idiom meaning 'suddenly, quickly' [**LN** (67.114)].

QUESTION—What is the significance of this double reference to time?

The double reference to time functions to emphasize the instantaneity of the change [Lns]. The two time references together indicate instantaneity [EGT]. The two references are saying the same thing, that the change will be instantaneous and complete [Ed].

QUESTION—Which actions do these two references to time modify?

They modify both the resurrection of the dead and the change [Herm, ICC, NTC]. It is as though both groups respond simultaneously to the same signal [ICC]. They modify the change that will occur to the living [TNTC].

at[a] the last trumpet;[b]

LEXICON—a. ἐν with dative object (LN 67.33, **67.114**) (BAGD II.2. p. 260): 'at' [AB, BAGD, Herm, HNTC, ICC, Lns, NIGTC, NTC; all versions except NJB, NLT, TEV], 'when' [**LN** (67.33, 67.114); NJB, NLT, TEV], 'at the time of' [LN (67.33)].

b. σάλπιγξ (LN **6.92, 6.93**) (BAGD 2. p. 741): 'trumpet' [AB, Herm, HNTC, Lns, NIGTC, NTC; NET, NIV, NJB, NLT, NRSV, TEV], 'trump' [**LN** (6.92, 6.93); KJV], 'trumpet-call' [ICC; REB, TNT], 'trumpet sound' [BAGD, LN (6.93); CEV, ISV, NAB], 'trumpet blast' [LN (6.93)]. See this word also at 14:8.

QUESTION—What is meant by ἐν τῇ ἐσχάτῃ σάλπιγγι 'at the last trumpet'?

It may be the same as the 'trumpet of God' referred to in 1 Thessalonians 4:16 (see also Matthew 24:31) [AB, EGT, HNTC, Ho, ICC, Lns, NTC]. It may also refer to the last of the seven trumpets described in Revelation 8:2 and 11:15 [ICC, NCBC]. The word ἔσχατος 'last' does not refer to a last in a series of trumpet sounds [Alf, Herm, HNTC, NIC2, NIGTC, TNTC]. It does not refer to the seven trumpet sounds of Revelation [Alf, Gdt, HNTC, Vn]. In 1 Thessalonians the trumpet is equated with the voice of an archangel [Ed, EGT, Gdt]. 'Last' indicates the End [Herm, NIC2]. 'Last' indicates the last trumpet sound in the events of the history of redemption [NTC]. 'Last' indicates the sound that will end the age of the church [MNTC]. 'Last' may indicate the trumpet sound that will bring in the end of the present world order (see Revelation 11:15) [NCBC]. 'Last' indicates the absolute end of time [Lns]. 'Last' indicates the last trumpet ever to sound, since it will sound on the last day [Ho]. 'Last' refers to the last event on earth [TNTC].

QUESTION—What did the sound of a trumpet indicate in Jewish culture and what may it indicate here?

It was used to signal a warning concerning the day of God's judgment in Joel 2:1, 3 [HNTC, NIC2]. It was used to signal the coming of the Lord in Zechariah 9:14 [Ed, NIC2]. It was used to summon God's people to come to Jerusalem (Isaiah 27:13) [Ho, MNTC, NIC2]. It was used to call men to battle in Jeremiah 51:27 [NIC2]. The war trumpet was used to give commands [EGT]. It was used in Exodus 19:16 to announce the coming of the Lord down on the mountain [Ed]. It was used in Leviticus 25:9 to proclaim the year of Jubilee, the Feast of Trumpets, and the Day of Atonement [NCBC]. In Matthew 24:31 Jesus said a trumpet call would call together his chosen from the ends of the earth. Aaron used the trumpet sound to summon people together, to get ready to move or to proclaim a feast (Numbers 10:2-10). Here it similarly calls people together, signals the last move and proclaims a feast [Gdt]. Here it may indicate the summoning of the dead from the grave [Ho, NIC2, TNTC], or to summon his people to himself [MNTC]. Here it signals the coming of the Lord [Ed].

for it-will-trumpet[a] and the dead will-be-raised incorruptible[b] and we will-be-changed.

LEXICON—a. fut. act. indic. of σαλπίζω (LN **6.92**) (BAGD p. 741): 'to trumpet' [Lns], '(a/the) trumpet sounds' [BAGD, HNTC, ICC, **LN** (6.92), NTC; all versions except CEV], 'to sound' [Herm], 'the trumpet blows' [AB], 'the trumpet will give its signal' [NIGTC], not explicit [CEV]. This verb is also translated 'people will hear the sound of the trumpet, the sound of the trumpet will be heard' [**LN** (6.92)].

b. ἄφθαρτος (LN **23.128**): 'incorruptible' [Lns, NTC; KJV, NAB], 'imperishable' [AB, Herm, LN; NET, NIV, NJB, NRSV, REB], 'immortal' [**LN**], 'state of incorruption' [HNTC]. This adjective is also translated as a phrase: 'never to decay' [ISV], 'never to die again' [TEV], 'never again to perish' [ICC], 'with transformed bodies' [NLT], 'without degenerating decay' [NIGTC], 'so that we will never die again' [CEV], 'and for ever freed from death' [TNT].

QUESTION—What relationship is indicated by γάρ 'for'?

It indicates that the following explains 15: 51–52a by describing how these things will be realized [Lns, NIC2].

QUESTION—To whom does ἡμεῖς 'we' refer?

1. It refers to those who are living at the time [AB, Ed, EGT, Gdt, HNTC, Ho, ICC, NCBC, NIC, NIC2, TG, TH; NLT]. 'We' refers to the living (see 2 Corinthians 5:2ff) [EGT]. The use of πάντες '(we) all' in 15:51 as the subject of 'will be changed' plus the contrast here in 15:52 with the dead who will be raised, supports the interpretation that Paul intends 'we' to refer to those still living [NIC2]. The word ἡμεῖς 'we' here is emphatic [AB, Lns, TH], suggesting a change of subject from 15:51. Here he means those who will be alive at Christ's return [TH]. The emphatic 'we' suggests that Paul expected to be in this group [AB]. Paul's main point in this verse is the contrasting of the two groups, the dead and living [NIC]. 'We' includes Paul [Gdt, HNTC, ICC, NCBC, NTC]. 'We' refers both to Christians as they were living at Paul's time and to Christians who will be living at the resurrection [NIC]. It indicates believers [NIC, NTC, Vn].

2. It refers to both the dead and the living [Herm, Lns, NTC, Vn]. 'We' here repeats the 'we all' of 15:51 and refers to all believers, those who were just raised as well as those who are still living [Lns]. Paul's intent is to bring out the basic equality of the destiny of the dead and the living [Herm]. Both this passage and 1 Thessalonians 4:15 teach that believers will comprise two classes, the living and the dead [Vn].

QUESTION—Who is the agent of the two passives ἐγερθήσονται 'will be raised' and ἀλλαγησόμεθα 'we will be changed'?

God is the agent [Ed, Lns, NTC]: God will raise the dead and will change us.

15:53 For it-is-necessary[a] (for) this perishable[b] (body) to-put-on[c] imperishability[d]

LEXICON—a. pres. act. indic. of the impersonal verb δεῖ (BAGD 1. p. 172): 'to be necessary' [AB, BAGD], '(one) must' [BAGD, Herm, HNTC, ICC, Lns, NTC; all versions except CEV], not explicit [NIGTC; CEV]. Δεῖ indicates necessity [Lns, NIC2, NTC, Vn]. See this word also at 11:19.

b. φθαρτός (LN 23.125) (BAGD p. 857): 'perishable' [Herm, LN; NLT], 'decaying' [CEV], 'mortal' [LN]. This adjective is also translated as a noun phrase: '(the) perishable' [NIV], 'perishable body' [NET, NRSV, REB], 'perishable (nature)' [BAGD, ICC; NJB], '(this) corruptible' [ICC, NTC; KJV], 'corruptible body' [HNTC; NAB]. The phrase τὸ φθαρτὸν τοῦτο 'this corruptible' is translated 'what is mortal' [TEV], 'what is decaying' [ISV], 'which is subject to decay' [NIGTC], 'what is liable to death' [TNT], 'this which is perishable' [AB]. See this word also at 9:25.

c. aorist mid. infin. of ἐνδύω (LN 49.1) (BAGD 2.b. p. 264): 'to put on' [BAGD, Herm, HNTC, ICC, LN, Lns, NTC; ISV, KJV, NET, NJB,

NRSV], 'to clothe oneself' [BAGD; NIV], 'to wear' [BAGD]. It is also translated as a passive: 'to be clothed (in/with)' [AB, BAGD, LN, NIGTC; NAB, REB], 'to be dressed' [BAGD, LN], 'to be transformed into' [NLT], 'to be changed into' [CEV, TEV]. The phrase ἐνδύσασθαι ἀφθαρσίαν 'to be clothed with incorruptibility' is translated 'to be for ever freed from death' [TNT]. The aorist tense indicates a momentary change rather than a slow process [Alf, ICC, Lns, Vn].

d. ἀφθαρσία (See this word at 15:42): 'imperishability' [AB, Herm; NJB, NRSV], 'the imperishable' [NET, NIV, REB], 'incorruptibility' [NAB], 'incorruption' [HNTC, Lns, NTC; KJV], 'heavenly body' [NLT], 'what is imperishable' [ICC], 'what can't decay' [ISV], 'what is immortal' [TEV], 'that which cannot wear out' [NIGTC], 'body that won't decay' [CEV]. This noun is also translated as a clause: 'for ever freed from death' [TNT].

QUESTION—What relationship is indicated by γάρ 'for'?

It indicates that this verse clarifies what is meant by change to the dead or the living in 15:52 [Lns]. It indicates the reason for the need for change [Herm, Ho]: we will be changed *because* it is necessary for this perishable body to put on imperishability.

and this mortal[a] (body) to-put-on immortality.[b]

LEXICON—a. θνητός (LN 23.124) (BAGD p. 362): 'mortal' [BAGD, Herm, LN; NET, NIV], 'earthly' [NLT], 'dead' [CEV]. This adjective is also translated as a noun phrase: 'mortal nature' [ICC; NJB], 'mortal body' [HNTC; NAB, NRSV], '(this) mortal' [Lns, NIGTC, NTC; KJV]. The phrase τὸ θνητὸν τοῦτο 'this mortal' is translated 'what is mortal' [REB, TNT], 'this which is mortal' [AB], 'what will die' [TEV], 'what is dying' [ISV].

b. ἀθανασία (LN 23.126) (BAGD p. 20): 'immortality' [AB, BAGD, Herm, HNTC, LN, Lns, NTC; KJV, NAB, NET, NIV, NJB, NRSV, REB], 'what is immortal' [ICC], 'what cannot die' [ISV, TEV], '(body) that won't die' [CEV], '(body) that will never die' [NLT] 'what is incapable of dying' [NIGTC]. This noun is also translated as an adjective: '(must become) immortal' [TNT].

QUESTION—To what does this twice repeated change apply?

1. It applies to both those dead and to those alive at Christ's Second Coming [Gdt, Herm, Ho, Lns, NIC]. The words apply primarily to those alive a Christ's coming but they are too general to restrict them to only the living [NIC]. The first word φθαρτός 'perishable' may apply to the dead, while θνητός 'mortal' applies to the living [Gdt]. Paul continues to point the equality of the two groups [Herm].

2. It applies only to those alive at Christ's Second Coming [Ed, EGT, HNTC, ICC, NIC2]. Τοῦτο 'this' cannot refer to someone already dead [NIC2]. The terms φθαρτός 'perishable' and θνητός 'mortal' refer to those then living and specifically to the ἡμεῖς 'we' of 15:52 [EGT]. That this refers to the living and not the dead is shown in 2 Corinthians 5:2-4

(see also 2 Peter 1:14) [Ed]. The word θνητός indicates 'subject to death' probably describing human nature and refers to the living not the dead [HNTC].

QUESTION—What is implied by τὸ φθαρτόν τοῦτο 'this perishable' and τὸ θντόν τοῦτο 'this mortal'?

The word 'body' is implied [Alf, Ed, EGT, Gdt, HNTC, ICC, Lns, NIC2, NTC; NAB, NET, NRSV, REB]: this perishable body, this mortal body. The demonstrative pronoun τοῦτο is neuter and could modify σῶμα 'body' [HNTC]. Paul is referring to his own body [Alf, Ed, ICC, Lns]. The word 'nature' is implied [BAGD, ICC, TH; NJB]: this perishable nature, this mortal nature. The word 'human being' is implied [TG]: this perishable human being, this mortal human being.

QUESTION—If the image is putting on of clothing and the topic is the putting on of immorality what is the point of similarity?

The point of similarity is the change from one condition to another [EGT; CEV, NLT, TEV]. The figure of putting on clothing indicates that something remains constant through the change in conditions. That something is the person him/herself [ICC]. The putting on of clothes does not indicate the of putting something new on over something old, but to a complete change from one to the other [Lns, NIC].

QUESTION—If ἐνδύσασθαι 'to put on' is taken as a passive 'to be clothed with', who is the agent?

The agent is God [NIC, NTC]: God will put imperishability on this perishable body. That the agent is God is seen from 15:57 [NIC].

QUESTION—What is the relationship between the adjectives and nouns of this verse?

The pairs are synonymous [Ed, Herm, ICC, NIC2, TG]: φθαρτός 'perishable' = θντός 'mortal', and ἀφθαρσία 'imperishability' = ἀθανασία 'immortality'. The repeated word τοῦτο referring to the same thing indicates that these two clauses are synonymous [NIC2]. In the pair of adjectives, the first is generic and the second is specific functioning to define the first [Lns]: perishable, that is, mortal; imperishable, that is, immortal.

QUESTION—What does this verse teach?

It teaches the continuity between the believer's present bodily existence and his/her future bodily existence [Gdt, NTC, Vn]. It teaches a continuity between the believer's present state and his future state [TNTC]. The repeated use of 'this body' and 'put on' indicates the continuity between the old and new bodies [Gdt]. In Greek thinking, immortality was a property of the soul. Here Paul is teaching that it a property gained at the resurrection [AB].

DISCOURSE UNIT: 15:54–58 [NJB]. The topic is a hymn of triumph: conclusion.

15:54 **And when this perishable (body) has-put-on imperishability and this mortal (body) has-put-on immortality,**

TEXT—Some manuscripts reverse the order of this and the following clause of this verse. Other manuscripts omit the first clause. Still others omit both clauses. GNT selects the text without these changes with a B rating, indicating that the text is almost certain. All versions concur with the text selected by GNT.

QUESTION—What is the function of repeating 15:53?

It functions to give solemnity to what Paul is saying and to build expectation [Lns]. It functions to strengthen the force of the argument [NIC2]. It functions to express Paul's feeling of triumph [Alf, Vn], and joyful self-assurance [Vn].

then will-come-to-pass the word which is-written, "Death was-swallowed-up[a] into[b] victory."[c]

LEXICON—a. aorist pass. indic. of καταπίνω (LN **13.43**, 20.52, 23.45) (BAGD 2. p. 416): 'to be swallowed up' [AB, BAGD, Herm, HNTC, ICC, **LN** (13.43), Lns, NIGTC, NTC; all versions except CEV, TEV], 'to be destroyed' [LN (20.52); TEV], 'to be swallowed' [LN (23.45)], 'to be completely ruined' [LN (20.52)], 'to be turned into' [**LN** (13.43)], 'to cause the end of' [LN (13.43)]. The phrase κατεπόθη...εἰς νῖκος 'was swallowed up in victory' is translated 'has lost the battle' [CEV]. The result is total extinction for what is swallowed [BAGD]. This word is used figuratively to mean to cause the complete cessation of a state [LN (13.43)], or to cause the complete and abrupt destruction of someone or something [LN (15.52)].

b. εἰς with accusative object (LN 13.62, 84.22): 'into' [ICC, LN (84.22)], 'in' [AB, Herm, HNTC, ICC, Lns, NIGTC, NTC; all versions except CEV, REB, TEV], 'by' [AB], 'so as to result in' [Alf, ICC], 'to' [LN (13.62)], not explicit [CEV]. The phrase εἰς νῖκος 'into victory' is translated 'victory is won!' [REB], 'victory is complete!' [TEV].

c. νῖκος (LN 39.57) (BAGD p. 539): 'victory' [AB, BAGD, Herm, HNTC, ICC, LN, Lns, NIGTC, NTC; all versions except CEV]. The phrase κατεπόθη...εἰς νῖκος 'was swallowed up in victory' is translated 'has lost the battle' [CEV].

QUESTION—In this metaphor, what is the point of similarity between swallowing and what is done to death?

The point of similarity is annihilation or abolition [Herm, ICC, NIC, NIC2, TG, Vn]. The point of similarity is absorption [Ed, Gdt]. The point of similarity is destruction [Lns, NTC, TG, TH, TNTC; TEV]. The point of similarity is defeat [AB, Ho, TNTC; CEV, REB]. The point of similarity is a change into something else [LN (13.43)]. There is also a reference to the change that will happen to the living at the resurrection (see 2 Corinthians 5:4). In this case the point of similarity is absorption by the law of life in Christ [Ed].

QUESTION—What is the meaning of εἰς νῖκος 'into victory'?
It indicates manner [Lns]: 'victoriously'. It indicates that the swallowing *results in* victory [Alf, ICC]. It refers to the conquering of death [NIC], with imperishable life [Gdt].

QUESTION—What Scripture is Paul citing?
He is probably citing Isaiah 25:8 and adapting the Hebrew translation of the verse which reads, "He will swallow up death forever." [AB, Ed, EGT, Herm, HNTC, ICC, Lns, MNTC, NCBC, NIC, NIC2, NTC, TG, TH, TNTC]. The antecedent of 'he' is God [Alf, Gdt, ICC, Lns, MNTC, NTC].

QUESTION—Who is the agent of the passive κατεπόθη 'was swallowed up'?
The agent is God as seen from the Isaiah prophecy [NIC2, NTC]: God will swallow up death.

15:55 "Where, O-death, (is) your victory?
TEXT—Instead of νῖκος 'victory', some manuscripts have κέντρον 'sting'. GNT selects the reading νῖκος 'victory' with a B decision, indicating that the text is almost certain. Κέντρον 'sting' is taken by Gdt, Ho, and KJV.

Where, O-death, (is) your sting?"[a]
TEXT—Instead of θάνατε 'death', some manuscripts have ᾅδη 'Hades'. GNT selects the reading θάνατε 'death' with a B decision, indicating that the text is almost certain. The reading ᾅδη 'Hades' (translated 'grave') is taken by Ho and KJV.

TEXT—Instead of κέντρον 'sting', some manuscripts have νῖκος 'victory'. GNT selects the reading κέντρον 'sting' with a B decision, indicating that the text is almost certain. Νῖκος 'victory' is taken by Gdt, Ho, and KJV.

LEXICON—a. κέντρον (LN 8.45, **20.69, 24.86**) (BAGD 1. p. 428): 'sting' [BAGD, Herm, LN (8.45), NIGTC; all versions except KJV, TEV], 'power to hurt' [**LN** (24.86); TEV], 'stinger' [LN (8.45)], 'means to hurt, power to cause suffering' [LN (24.86)], 'power to kill' [**LN** (20.69)], 'power to destroy' [LN (20.69)]. Paul uses this figure in the sense of the sting of insects (see Revelation 9:10) [Gdt, ICC, MNTC, NIC, NIC2, Rb, TNTC], scorpions (see Revelation 9:10) [Gdt, Herm, Ho, ICC, NIC2, NTC, Rb, TH, TNTC], a poisonous sting (of a serpent) [Alf, Ed, Lns, Rb, Vn], or a goad to drive oxen (see Acts 26:14) [Herm, ICC, NTC, Rb, TH].

QUESTION—What is the function of the rhetorical questions?
They function to taunt [AB, MNTC, NIC2, NTC], to deride [NIC2], to challenge defiantly [MNTC], or to mock death [HNTC, NTC]. This expresses a shout of triumph over death [Alf, Vn].

QUESTION—What are the implied answers to the rhetorical questions?
The answers are 'Nowhere!' [Lns, Vn]. The two question could be rendered as statements denying that death has either victory or ability to harm [TG, TH]. The answers are that Christ's victory has replaced death's [HNTC, Ho, Lns, NIC2, TNTC], and death's sting has been removed or replaced by the resurrection of Christ [AB, ICC, NIC, NIC2]. The answer to the first question is that death's victory will disappear [AB]. The victory of death is

gone [Alf, ICC], its sting is powerless [Alf, HNTC]. Death has lost its sting/goad [Gdt, ICC, NTC]. The answer to the second question is that its sting was left in Christ [MNTC].

QUESTION—What is the point of similarity between κέντρον 'sting' and death's ability?

The point of similarity is the ability to harm [LN (24.86), TG, TH], to cause pain [Ho, ICC, LN (24.86), NIC, Rb, TNTC], to punish [Herm], or to kill [Ed, Gdt, **LN** (20.69), Lns, NIC], or to dominate [Herm, NTC].

QUESTION—What is the Scripture that Paul cites?

The Scripture cited is Hosea 13:14 [AB, Ed, EGT, Gdt, Herm, HNTC, Ho, ICC, Lns, MNTC, NIC, NIC2, NTC, Rb, TG, TH, TNTC, Vn].

QUESTION—What is the function of forefronting the pronoun 'you' in the phrases, ποῦ σου, θάνατος, τὸ νῖκος 'where your, death, the victory?', and ποῦ σου, θάνατος, τὸ κέντρον 'where your, death, the sting?'

It functions to emphasize the word 'your' [Lns]. It functions to emphasize the personification of death [NIC2].

15:56 Now the sting of death (is) sin,

QUESTION—How are the nouns related in the genitive construction τὸ κέντρον τοῦ θανάτου 'the sting of death'?

'The sting of death' is the sting *that leads to* death [NIC2], the sting *that causes* death [Ed, Lns, MNTC, NTC, TG, TNTC].

QUESTION—In what sense is sin the sting (power to harm) of death?

Sin is the sting of death in the sense that apart from sin or where sin is forgiven, to die is gain (see Philippians 1:21, 23). So the sting is not in death, but in unforgiven sin [TNTC]. Sin is the sting of death in the sense that it causes death (see Romans 5:12 and 6:23) [Ed, Ho, Lns, MNTC, NTC, TG, TNTC]. It is the sting of death in the sense that sin gives death power. Genesis 2:17 reads, "In the day that you eat of it you will die" [Gdt].

and the power of sin (is) the law;[a]

LEXICON—a. νόμος (See this word at 14:21): 'law' [AB, HNTC, Lns, NIGTC, NTC; all versions except CEV, ISV, NJB, TEV], 'Law' [Herm, ICC; CEV, ISV, NJB, TEV].

QUESTION—In what sense is the law the power of sin?

The law is the power of sin in that without law there is no accountability for sin (see Romans 5:13, 7:7) [Gdt, HNTC, Ho, ICC, MNTC, NIC2].

QUESTION—Why does Paul bring this information in here?

Paul is celebrating the victory of Christ over death but remembers that sin is the cause of death and law is the cause of sin. But Christ's death has resulted in victory over death and sin [NIC2]. He does this to show the connection between the teaching about the resurrection and the teaching about salvation by the Cross. To him they are the same [EGT].

15:57 But↑a to-God the-one giving us victory through our Lord Jesus Christ (be) thanks.↑b

LEXICON—a. δέ (See this word at 11:2): 'but' [AB, HNTC, ICC, Lns, NIGTC, NTC; all versions except NJB, NLT], 'then' [NJB], not explicit [Herm; NLT]. Δέ signifies a significant contrast between this verse and the sin and death of 15:58 [HNTC, Lns, NTC].

b. χάρις (LN **33.350**): 'thanks' [AB, Herm, HNTC, ICC, **LN**, Lns, NIGTC, NTC; all versions except CEV, NJB, NLT]. This noun is also translated as a verb: 'to thank' [CEV, NJB, NLT]. See this word also at 10:30.

QUESTION—What words are emphasized in this verse?

The words τῷ θεῷ 'to God' are placed first for emphasis [Lns, NIC, NTC]: To God himself. The Triune God is the author of this victory [Lns].

QUESTION—What specific victory is referred to?

Victory over sin and death and law are referred to [EGT, Gdt, NIC2, TNTC]. The victory is over sin and the law which result in death [NIC2]. Victory over sin and death are referred to [HNTC, Rb]. The victory was over sin in that Christ died to sin (see Romans 7:39), and it was a victory over death in that Christ was raised from the dead [HNTC]. Victory over sin and law are referred to [AB]. Victory over death is referred to [Ed, Ho, TG]. The victory is over death and the grave [Ho].

QUESTION—What is the significance of the present tense in τῷ διδόντι 'the one giving'?

It implies that God continues to give us the victory [Gdt, ICC, Lns, Vn] as believers receive its benefits [ICC, Vn]. It implies that God is giving the victory even now [AB, NIC]. It implies that we have forgiveness now [Ed]. It may imply that it is characteristic of God to give victory [TNTC]. It implies that even though the victory is not finally won until the end, it is so sure that it can be spoken of as being already won [HNTC].

DISCOURSE UNIT: 15:58 [AB, ICC, NCBC, NTC]. The topic is exhortation [AB, NCBC, NTC], practical result [ICC].

15:58 Therefore↑a, my beloved brothers, be firm,↑b immovable,↑c

LEXICON—a. ὥστε (See this word at 10:12): 'therefore' [Herm, Lns, NIGTC; ISV, KJV, NIV, NRSV, REB, TNT], 'so then' [ICC, **LN** (89.52), NTC; NET, TEV], 'in consequence of this' [HNTC], 'so' [AB; NJB, NLT], not explicit [CEV, NAB].

b. ἑδραῖος (LN **31.92**) (BAGD p. 217): 'firm' [AB, BAGD, ICC, LN, NIGTC; CEV, NET, NIV, NJB, REB, TEV, TNT], 'steadfast' [Herm, HNTC, LN, Lns, NTC; ISV, KJV, NAB, NRSV], 'firmly established' [**LN**], 'unwavering' [LN], 'strong' [NLT]. They are to be firm in regard to their belief in the resurrection (see 15:12) [Ho, NIC, NIC2]. They are to be firm in regard to temptations to do evil [Vn].

c. ἀμετακίνητος (LN **31.81**) (BAGD p. 45): 'immovable' [AB, BAGD, Herm, HNTC, NIGTC, NTC; NJB, NRSV, REB, TNT], 'unmovable' [ICC, Lns; ISV, KJV], 'steady' [LN; NLT, TEV], 'persevering' [NAB], 'not wavering in belief' [**LN**], 'unshaken' [**LN**], 'firm' [LN]. This adjective is also translated as a verb clause: 'do not be moved' [NET], 'let nothing move you' [NIV], 'don't be shaken' [CEV]. The idea of immovability implies being moved from the hope of the resurrection of the dead [Ed, NIC2]. It implies being moved from Christian teaching and conduct [HNTC]. It implies being moved from God's will [MNTC]. It implies being moved from the gospel [NCBC, NIC2]. It implies being moved away from their faith [Vn].

QUESTION—What relationship is indicated by ὥστε 'therefore'?

It indicates a conclusion [Alf, Gdt, Ho, Lns, NIC, NIC2, NIGTC, NTC, TH; ISV, KJV, NET, NIV, NJB, NLT, NRSV, REB, TEV, TNT]: therefore. Since the resurrection is sure, this is how we should be [Gdt, Ho, MNTC, NIC]. The hope of the resurrection and of Christ's triumph over sin and law stand as the reason [NIC2]. Verse 15:57 stands as the reason for this conclusion [Alf]. Either the whole chapter or only 15:57 stands as the reason [Lns]. Chapter 15 stands as the reason [NIGTC, TH]. Either the whole chapter or the whole epistle stands as the reason [NTC].

QUESTION—What is the function of the vocative ἀδελφοί μου ἀγαπητοί 'my beloved brothers'?

It functions to draw close again to those he may have alienated by his sternness [Gdt]. It assures the Corinthians of his love even though he has used strong language with them [ICC]. The vocative ἀδελφοί 'brothers' calls special attention to the words that follow [TH].

QUESTION—What is the significance of the present imperative γίνεσθε 'be'?

1. The present imperative indicates that they were already doing this [AB, Lns, NIC, NTC, Rb; ISV]: Continue to be/become firm. By this period in the history of the Greek language, the meaning of 'become' had been lost from this verb and the meaning of 'be' remained. Here the imperative means 'continue to be' [Lns].
2. It functions to indicate that they should begin to do this [Gdt, ICC, TNTC, Vn]: Become firm!

always excelling[a] in the work of-the Lord,

LEXICON—a. pres. act. participle of περισσεύω (LN **59.52**) (BAGD 1.b.β. p. 651): 'to excel' [AB, BAGD; ISV, NRSV, TNT], 'to give (oneself) fully' [NIC2; NIV], 'to be outstanding' [BAGD; NET], 'to abound' [HNTC, ICC, LN, Lns, NIGTC, NTC; KJV], 'to abound in energy' [NJB], 'to be engaged' [NAB], 'to keep busy' [CEV, TEV], 'to grow' [Herm], 'to be very much occupied' [**LN**], 'to be always enthusiastic' [NLT]. The phrase περισσεύοντες ἐν τῷ ἔργῳ τοῦ κυρίου 'abounding in the work of the Lord' is translated 'to work for the Lord' [REB]. Περισσεύω means to exceed requirements [Lns, MNTC]. It indicates the idea of overflow [EGT, Gdt]. Here it indicates limitlessness in goal-setting [Ed]. See this word also at 14:12.

QUESTION—How are the nouns related in the genitive construction ἔργῳ τοῦ κυρίου 'work of the Lord'?

It indicates the work that the Lord gives us to do [Ed, EGT, Ho, ICC, Lns, Vn]. It is work done for the Lord [CEV, REB, TEV]. It indicates the work of spreading the gospel about the Lord [Gdt, HNTC, NIC2, NTC]. It indicates Christian character-building in reference to the fruit of the Spirit [Alf, Gdt, NTC]. It also indicates the building up of believers [HNTC, NTC]. It indicates work done in God's Kingdom but also good work in the broad sense [NIC].

knowing that your labor[a] is not in-vain[b] in (the) Lord.

LEXICON—a. κόπος (LN 42.47) (BAGD 2. p. 443): 'labor' [AB, BAGD, Herm, HNTC, Lns, NIGTC, NTC; KJV, NET, NIV, NRSV, REB, TNT], 'toil' [ICC, LN; NAB], 'work' [ISV], 'hard work' [LN]. This singular noun is also translated as a plural: 'labors' [NJB]. This noun is also translated as a verb: 'to do' [CEV, NLT, TEV]. See this word also at 3:8.

b. κενός (See this word at 15:10): 'in vain' [Herm, ICC, NTC; KJV, NAB, NET, NIV, NRSV, TNT], 'vain' [HNTC], 'useless' [NLT, TEV], 'wasted' [ISV, NJB], 'fruitless' [NIGTC], 'lost' [REB], 'void' [AB], 'empty' [Lns]. The phrase οὐκ ἔστιν κενός 'is not in vain' is translated 'is worthwhile' [CEV].

QUESTION—How is the participle εἰδότες 'knowing' used?

1. It expresses cause [AB, Ed, Gdt, HNTC, Ho, ICC, Lns, NIC; ISV, KJV, NIV, NLT, NRSV, REB, TEV]: because you know.
2. It expresses accompaniment [TNTC]: all the while knowing.

QUESTION—What is meant by ὁ κόπος ὑμῶν οὐκ ἔστιν κενὸς ἐν κυριῳ 'your labor is not in vain in the Lord'?

The phrase is a *litotes* (negation of a negative) and has the positive meaning of 'very productive of enduring results' [Lns]. The phrase indicates that their work would have good results [ICC]. It means that their work as Christians was not in vain [TH], their work was worthwhile [TG; CEV]. It means that the Lord would make sure they were rewarded [Ho, NTC, TH]. It means that their work under the Lord's direction and control was not in vain [EGT, Vn]. It means that their work was not without meaning because it was done with the Lord's strength [NIC]. Work done 'in the Lord' can no more fade away than He can [HNTC].

DISCOURSE UNIT: 16:1–24 [AB, Ed, EGT, Gdt, Herm, ICC, Lns, NIGTC, TNTC; NAB, NJB]. The topic is personal matters [AB, Ed, Lns], business, news, and greetings [EGT], further matters of concern [NIGTC], information and greetings [Herm; REB], conclusion [Gdt, ICC, TNTC; NAB], conclusion, commendations, and greetings [NJB].

DISCOURSE UNIT: 16:1–18 [Alf, NIC]. The topic is various directions and arrangements [Alf], final admonitions and communications [NIC].

DISCOURSE UNIT: 16:1–11 [NIC2]. The topic is the collection [NIC2].

350   1 CORINTHIANS 16:1

DISCOURSE UNIT: 16:1–9 [Ho]. The topic is the collection for the saints in Jerusalem.

DISCOURSE UNIT: 16:1–4 [AB, Alf, Ed, Gdt, GNT, HNTC, Ho, ICC, MNTC, NCBC, NIC2, NIGTC, NTC, TNTC; CEV, ISV, NAB, NET, NIV, NLT, TEV]. The topic is the collection [EGT, Gdt, HNTC, MNTC, NIC2, TNTC; NAB], the collection for the Jerusalem saints [AB, Alf, Ed, Ho, ICC, NCBC; ISV, NLT], the collection for God's people [GNT, NIGTC, NTC; CEV, NIV, TEV], a collection to aid Jewish Christians [NET].

16:1 Now concerning^a the collection^b for^c the saints^d

LEXICON—a. περί with genitive object (See this word at 12:1): 'concerning' [Herm, Lns, NIGTC, NTC; ISV, KJV, NRSV, TEV, TNT], 'about' [HNTC; NAB, NIV, NJB, NLT, REB], 'with regard to' [NET], 'with reference to' [AB], not explicit [CEV].

b. λογεία (LN 57.66) (BAGD p. 475): 'collection' [AB, BAGD, Herm, HNTC, LN, Lns, NIGTC, NTC; all versions except CEV, NLT, TEV], 'money being collected' [NLT], 'money being raised' [TEV]. This noun is also translated as a verb: 'to collect money' [CEV].

c. εἰς with accusative object (LN **90.41**) (BAGD 4.g. p. 229): 'for' [AB, BAGD, Herm, HNTC, LN, Lns, NIGTC, NTC; all versions except REB, TEV], 'on behalf of' [**LN**], 'in aid of' [REB]. This preposition is also translated as a verb: 'to help' [TEV].

d. οἱ ἅγιοι (See this word at 14:33): 'the saints' [AB, Herm, HNTC, Lns, NTC; ISV, KJV, NAB, NET, NRSV], 'God's holy people' [NJB], 'God's people' [NIGTC; CEV, NIV, REB, TNT], 'God's people in Judea' [TEV], 'Christians in Jerusalem' [NLT].

QUESTION—What is implied by the phrase περὶ δὲ τῆς λογείας 'now concerning the collection'?

It implies that Paul is turning to a new topic [Alf, Ed, EGT, Gdt, NIGTC, TNTC]. It probably implies that this was a matter about which the Corinthians had written and asked him [AB, Ed, EGT, Lns, NCBC, NIC2, NTC, TG, TNTC]. The definite article in τῆς λογείας 'the collection' indicates that the Corinthians already knew about this collection [Gdt, MNTC, NTC]. Since Paul does not mention to which collection he is referring or to which saints he is referring it indicates that these things were already known to the Corinthians [NIC]. We cannot be certain that the Corinthians had written him about it [Herm].

QUESTION—To whom does οἱ ἅγιοι 'the saints' refer?

It refers to the believers making up the church in Jerusalem [AB, Alf, Herm, HNTC, Ho, ICC, Lns, MNTC, NCBC, TH, TNTC, Vn]. See 16:33 [TNTC]. This term is applicable to all Christian believers and only the context determines its scope here [NIGTC]. The Corinthians knew to whom Paul was referring (see Romans 15:26) [Ho, Vn]. The definite article, '*the* saints', implies that the Corinthians already knew who these were [EGT, Gdt]. Οἱ ἅγιοι 'the saints' was a typical way to refer to the church at Jerusalem

[Herm]. The term refers to 'holy ones' but it does not mean that they were especially holy in contrast to other believers, but that they were fellow believers, a good reason to contribute to their welfare [ICC]. 'Saints' refers to the Christian community [TH]. It refers to the poor believers in Jerusalem [Ho, TNTC, Vn].

you do also, just-as I-directed[a] the churches of Galatia.
LEXICON—a. aorist act. indic. of διατάσσω (See this word at 11:34): 'to direct' [AB, NIC2, NIGTC, NTC], 'to give directions to' [ISV, NET, NRSV], 'to command' [TNT], 'to tell to do' [CEV, NIV, TEV], 'to instruct' [HNTC], 'to give instructions (to)' [NAB, REB], 'to give order to' [Lns; KJV], 'to prescribe for' [NJB], 'to give procedures to' [NLT], 'to appoint' [Herm]. The aorist indicates a definite time that Paul gave these directions [Ed, EGT]. It was either on his third missionary journey (Acts 28.23) or through a letter or messenger [EGT]. It was probably on his second missionary journey when he visited Galatia [Ed].
QUESTION—What is Γαλατία 'Galatia'?
Galatia is a district in the province of Asia [LN (93.442)]. It probably refers to a region in north central Asia Minor [HNTC]. It probably refers to the Roman province of Galatia [NCBC]. It is a Roman province in what is modern day Turkey [TG].
QUESTION—What word is emphasized in this verse?
The word ὑμεῖς 'you' is emphatic [ICC, TH]: you yourselves do. It contrasts with the churches in Galatia [TH].

16:2 **On[a] (the) first-(day) of-(the)-week[b]**
LEXICON—a. κατά with accusative object (LN 67.33) (BAGD II.2.c. p. 406): 'on' [BAGD, Herm, HNTC, Lns, NTC; ISV, NAB, NET, NIV, NJB, NLT, NRSV, TNT], 'at the time of' [LN (67.33)], 'upon' [KJV], not explicit [AB, NIGTC; CEV, REB, TEV].
b. σάββατον (LN 67.177) (BAGD 2.a. p. 739): 'week' [Herm, LN, Lns, NTC; ISV, KJV, NET, NJB], 'each week' [HNTC; NAB], 'every week' [AB; NIV, NRSV, TNT]. The phrase κατὰ μίαν σαββάτου 'on the first of the week' is translated 'every Lord's Day' [NLT], 'every Sunday' [BAGD, NIGTC; REB, TEV], 'each Sunday' [CEV].
QUESTION—What is the meaning of κατὰ μίαν σαββάτου 'on the first of the week'?
The word κατά is distributive meaning 'each' or 'every' [AB, BAGD, HNTC, Lns, NCBC, NIC, NIC2, NTC, Rb; CEV, NAB, NIV, NLT, NRSV, REB, TEV, TNT]: every week. The phrase μίαν σαββάτου 'one of the week' indicates 'the first day of the week' [AB, HNTC, Lns, NTC; ISV, KJV, NAB, NET, NIV, NJB, NRSV, TNT]. It indicates Sunday [AB, Herm, HNTC, Lns, MNTC, NCBC, NIC, NIC2, NTC, TH; CEV, NLT, REB, TEV]. This is the first evidence that believers observed the first day of every week [ICC, TNTC]. Early Christians met together on the first day of the week to mark Christ's resurrection, to worship and fellowship [NIC2, NTC].

QUESTION—What is the significance of doing this on the first day of the week?

Reference to the first day of the week shows us that this day was considered special and therefore a day for observing this religious obligation [Alf]. The day must have had significance otherwise Paul would have just instructed that they put money aside each week. Since it is similar to the Jewish tradition of counting days in reference to the Sabbath, it probably had religious significance. It was the day that Jesus rose from the dead. All of this points to the day that early believers met together for worship and celebration of the Lord's Supper. So it was an appropriate time for the believers of Corinth to do this [NIC2]. This was the day that Christians met regularly for worship (see Acts 20:7) [Gdt, Herm, Ho, ICC, Lns, MNTC, NIC2, NTC, TNT].

each of-you let-him-put-aside[a] **by-him**[b]

LEXICON—a. pres. act. impera. of τίθημι (LN **85.32**) (BAGD I.1.b.γ. p. 816): 'to put aside (some money)' [AB, BAGD, Herm, **LN**, NIGTC, NTC; CEV, NJB, NLT, NRSV, REB, TEV, TNT], 'to set aside (some money)' [HNTC; ISV, NAB, NET, NIV], 'to lay' [Lns; KJV], 'to put, to place' [LN]. The present imperative indicates a continuous or regular practice [Lns, Rb]. It may be that the word 'aside' is a translation for παρ' ἑαυτῷ 'by him' so that παρ' ἑαυτῷ τιθέτω 'to put by him' means 'to set aside' (see Gdt).

b. παρ' ἑαυτῷ (BAGD II.1.b.α. p. 610): 'by him' [Lns; KJV, REB], 'for himself' [HNTC], 'at home' [AB, BAGD, NIGTC], not explicit [Herm, NTC; all other versions].

QUESTION—What is meant by παρ' ἑαυτῷ 'by him'?

1. It means 'by himself' but does not imply a church collection [Herm, HNTC, NTC]. The literal meaning of παρ' ἑαυτῷ 'alongside himself' indicates that the believer kept his gift at home [NTC]. The believers will have already prepared a sum at home and will be ready to hand it over when Paul came [HNTC].
2. It implies that the collection is to be taken at church [Ho, MNTC, TNTC]. If the meaning 'at home' is taken, it would mean that a collection would need to be taken when Paul came and this was what Paul was trying to avoid [Ho, MNTC, TNTC]. 'By him' means on his own initiative [Ho, MNTC]. The time this was to be done was the first day of the week when the Christians came together for worship. At that time they would put their money into a common treasury [Ho].
3. It indicates 'at home', not at church [AB, Alf, BAGD, Ed, EGT, Gdt, ICC, Lns, NCBC, NIC, NIC2, NIGTC, NTC, Rb, TH, Vn]. The following verb θησαυρίζω 'to save up' implies that each person is to save up what he has set aside. Also there is linguistic evidence that παρ' ἑαυτῷ almost certainly means 'at home' [NIC2]. Perhaps this is to prevent comparisons with what others give [NIGTC].

saving[a] whatever he-may-prosper,[b] so-that when I-come no collections should-take-place then.

LEXICON—a. pres. act. participle of θησαυρίζω (LN 65.11) (BAGD 1. p. 361): 'to save' [BAGD; ISV, NET, NRSV], 'to save (for this offering)' [NLT], 'to save up' [HNTC; NIV, TEV, TNT], 'to keep' [REB], 'to reserve' [NJB], 'to store up' [BAGD, Herm, NTC], 'to keep safe, to treasure up' [LN]. This verb is also translated as: 'in store' [Lns; KJV], 'savings' [AB], 'an accumulation of savings' [NIGTC], not explicit [CEV, NAB].

b. pres. pass. (deponent = act.) subj. of εὐοδόω (LN **57.64**) (BAGD p. 323): 'to prosper' [BAGD, LN, Lns, NTC], 'to earn extra' [NRSV], 'to make profit' [HNTC], 'to earn' [**LN**; CEV, NLT, TEV], 'to spare' [Herm; NJB], 'to be able to save' [NAB], 'to afford' [REB], 'to gain in business, to gain by work' [LN]. The phrase ὅ τι ἐὰν εὐοδῶται 'whatever he may prosper' is translated 'as God hath prospered him' [KJV], 'to the extent that God has blessed you' [NET], 'appropriate to your prosperity' [AB], 'something from his profits' [TNT], 'as much as he gains' [BAGD], 'in keeping with his income' [NIV], 'in proportion to what you have' [ISV], 'in accordance with how you may fare' [NIGTC]. In our literature, only the passive form is used but not in its literal sense. It indicates 'get along well, prosper, succeed' [BAGD]. If it is taken as a passive, the agent is God [Vn; KJV, NET]: God has caused him to prosper.

QUESTION—How much was each person to give?

There is no specified amount, just the principle that their giving should be proportional to the amount that they had prospered [AB, Alf, Ed, EGT, Ho, ICC, NIC2, NTC, TG, TNTC].

16:3 And whenever I-arrive, whomever you-approve,[a] I-will-send these-ones with letters[b]

LEXICON—a. aorist act. subj. of δοκιμάζω (LN 30.114) (BAGD 2.b. p. 202): 'to approve' [LN, NIGTC; ISV, KJV, NET, NIV, NJB, NRSV, REB, TEV], 'to choose' [CEV, NAB, NLT, TNT], 'to consider qualified' [BAGD], 'to judge to be genuine, to judge as good' [LN]. Δοκιμάζω is also translated as a phrase: '(people) of your choice' [Herm]. See this word also at 11:28.

b. ἐπιστολή (LN 6.63, 33.48) (BAGD p. 301): 'letter' [BAGD, Herm, LN (6.63, 33.48); CEV, ISV, KJV, NRSV, TNT], 'letter of introduction' [NAB, NIV, NJB, REB, TEV], 'letter of explanation' [NET], 'letter of recommendation' [NLT], 'letter of authorization' [NIGTC]. The plural of ἐπιστολή may either refer to a single letter or to many letters [Ed, Gdt, NTC]. It may refer to a single letter [Gdt, NTC]. It probably is a plural as Paul would give them letters to several people in Jerusalem [AB, Herm]. The plural points to a number of individual messengers each needing a letter [TNTC]. The writing of such letters would set Paul free from

354

discharging his former promise to remember the poor (see Galatians 2:10) [NIC].

QUESTION—Do the words δι' ἐπιστολῶν 'with letters' connect with 'whomever you approve' or with 'I will send'?

1. They connect with the words 'I will send' [AB, Alf, Gdt, HNTC, Ho, ICC, Lns, MNTC, NIC, NIC2, NIGTC, NTC; CEV, ISV, NAB, NIV, NJB, NLT, REB, TEV, TNT]: I will send with letters. The words δι' ἐπιστολῶν 'with letters' are put forward in the clause for emphasis, not so that they will connect with 'approve' [Alf]. It is doubtful that δοκιμάζω 'to approve' can connect naturally with the words 'with letters'. Paul, having some relation to the church in Jerusalem, was the natural one to introduce the messengers to the church [Gdt]. The Corinthians were to select the men, but it was Paul's responsibility to send them and the gift to Jerusalem [Ho].
2. They connect with the words 'whomever you approve' [Ed, EGT, Rb; KJV]: whomever you approve with letters. It was important to Paul's integrity, as over against his enemies' accusations, that the church itself should accredit the messengers by letter [Ed]. Since the church has approved the messengers it is they who should write the letter of accreditation [EGT].

QUESTION—Who will write the letters?

1. Paul will write the letters [Gdt, HNTC, Ho, ICC, Lns, NIC, NIC2, NIGTC, NTC, TNTC; NAB, NIV, NJB, NLT, REB, TEV]. If the Corinthians wrote the letters they would be the natural ones to send the messengers, not Paul [Lns]. Paul's words, "I will send" and the uncertainty of his going with them argue for his being the author of the letters [NIC2].
2. The church at Corinth will write the letters [AB, Ed, EGT, TH; CEV, KJV, NRSV]. The letters were to be written by the Corinthian church or possibly by Paul [AB]. If Paul were to accompany them, there would be little point in his writing introductory letters [TH].

QUESTION—What words are emphasized in this verse?

The words δι' ἐπιστολῶν 'with letters' is forefronted for emphasis and contrasts with Paul's going to introduce them of 16:4 [Gdt, Vn]. The word τούτους 'these' is emphasized to indicate 'these men, and no other' [Ed].

to-take[a] your gift[b] to Jerusalem;

LEXICON—a. aorist act. infin. of ἀποφέρω (LN 15.202) (BAGD 1.b. p. 101): 'to take' [BAGD; CEV, ISV, NAB, NRSV, TEV, TNT], 'to carry' [NIGTC; NET, REB], 'to bring' [Herm; KJV], 'to deliver' [NJB, NLT], 'to take away, to carry away' [LN]. This verb is also translated as a preposition: 'with' [NIV].

b. χάρις (LN **57.103**) (BAGD 3.a. p. 878): 'gift' [BAGD, Herm, LN, NIGTC; all versions except CEV, KJV], 'liberality' [KJV], 'money' [CEV], 'gracious gift' [**LN**].

16:4 And if it-be fitting^a (for) me-also to-go, they-will-go with me.

LEXICON—a. ἄξιος (LN 66.6) (BAGD 1.c. p. 78): 'fitting' [BAGD, LN, NTC; NAB], 'advisable' [NET, NIV, NRSV], 'right' [HNTC, NIGTC, TG; REB, TNT], 'proper' [BAGD, LN], 'meet' [KJV], 'worthwhile' [BAGD, Lns; ISV, TEV], 'appropriate' [NLT], 'suitable' [AB], 'worthy of' [LN], 'sensible' [TG]. This adjective is also translated as a noun: 'worth (my going)' [NJB], '(your) mind' [Herm]. It is also translated as a verb: 'to think one should' [CEV].

QUESTION—What is meant by the phrase ἐὰν ἄξιον ᾖ 'if it be fitting'?
 1. It is a condition questioning the general appropriateness of Paul's going to Jerusalem [AB, Ed, Herm, NCBC, NIC, NIC2, NTC, Vn; CEV].
  1.1 From the perspective of the Corinthians [Ed, Herm, NTC; CEV]: if you think I should go. Paul was hesitant lest he be thought of as putting himself forward too much [Ed]. Paul himself wanted to go but he wanted the confirmation of the Corinthians (see Acts 19:21) [NTC].
  1.2 From Paul's own perspective [AB, NCBC, NIC, NIC2, NIGTC, Vn]. The reference of suitability is to Paul's schedule [AB]. Paul's concern is about circumstances in Jerusalem and elsewhere [NCBC, NIC, NIGTC].
 2. The word 'it' refers to the gift and the word 'fitting' implies 'large enough to warrant Paul's going' [Alf, EGT, Gdt, Ho, ICC, Lns, MNTC, Rb, TNTC]. It would not be appropriate for Paul to go if the amount were too small [Lns].

DISCOURSE UNIT: 16:5–24 [NCBC, NTC]. The topic is the conclusion.

DISCOURSE UNIT: 16:5–18 [NIV, NLT]. The topic is personal requests [NIV], Paul's final instructions [NLT].

DISCOURSE UNIT: 16:5–14 [NCBC]. The topic is plans and exhortations.

DISCOURSE UNIT: 16:5–12 [EGT, GNT, HNTC, MNTC, NIGTC, NTC; CEV, ISV, KJV, NET, TEV]. The topic is visits to Corinth [EGT], Paul's plans [HNTC; NAB, TEV], doing the Lord's work in the Lord's way [MNTC], Paul's requests [NTC], Paul's plans for travel [GNT, NIGTC; CEV, ISV, KJV], Paul's plans to visit [NET].

DISCOURSE UNIT: 16:5–11 [NIC2]. The topic is travel plans for Paul and Timothy.

DISCOURSE UNIT: 16:5-9 [AB, Alf, Ed, Gdt, ICC, NTC, TNTC]. The topic is Paul's travel plans [AB, NTC], a visit to Corinth [Alf, Ed, Gdt, ICC], Paul's plans [TNTC].

16:5 But I-will-come to you whenever I-go-through^a Macedonia;^b

LEXICON—a. aorist act. subj. of διέρχομαι (LN 15.10) (BAGD 1.a. p. 194): 'to go through' [BAGD, Lns, NTC; CEV, ISV, NET, NIV, TEV, TNT], 'to pass through' [AB, Herm, HNTC, NIGTC; KJV, NAB, NJB, NRSV, REB], 'to have been to (Macedonia)' [NLT], 'to travel around through, to journey all through' [LN]. Διέρχομαι is almost a technical term for an evangelistic tour (see Acts 13:6, 14:24, 15:3, 41, 18:23, 19:1, 21, 20:2) [ICC]. It implies a supervisory tour through the Macedonian churches in Philippi, Thessalonica, and Berea [NIC2]. See this word also at 10:1.

b. Μακεδονία (LN 93.527) (BAGD p. 487): 'Macedonia' [AB, Herm, HNTC, Lns, NIGTC, NTC; all versions]. Μακεδονία was a Roman province in Greece [LN]. It is now northern Greece, the capital of which is Thessalonica [TG].

for I-do-go-through Macedonia,
QUESTION—What relationship is indicated by γάρ 'for'?

It indicates the reason why Paul is going through Macedonia [TNTC]: I will come to you whenever I go through Macedonia, *because* I will go through Macedonia. It functions to explain [BAGD (2. p. 152), Lns]: *you see* I will go through Macedonia. It explains the contrast between what he will do in Macedonia and what he will do in Corinth; he will *only* go through Macedonia but he will *remain* with the Corinthians (see the next verse) [Lns]. Paul adds this since it was a change in what the Corinthians expected him to do. They knew he was coming but did not know of the plans to go through Macedonia [TNTC]. He repeats himself to emphasize his desire to return and to let the Corinthians know that his soon visit to them will be delayed (see 4:9) [NIC2].

QUESTION—What is the function of the present tense of διέρχομαι 'I go through'?

It functions to show Paul's intention or plan to do this [Alf, Gdt, HNTC, Ho, ICC, NIC2, NIGTC, Rb, TG, TH; ISV, NLT, NRSV, TNT]: I intend to go through Macedonia. It functions as a future tense [NIC, NIC2, TG; NET, NIV]: I will go through Macedonia. It indicates obligation [NJB, TEV]: I have to go through Macedonia.

QUESTION—From where is Paul writing this letter?

He is writing from the city of Ephesus (see 16:8) [ICC].

16:6 and/but[a] perhaps[b] I-will-stay[c] with you or even[d] spend-the-winter,[e]

LEXICON—a. δέ (See this word at 11:2): 'and' [AB, NTC; CEV, ISV, KJV, NET, NJB, NRSV, REB, TNT], 'but' [Herm, HNTC, Lns], not explicit [NIGTC; NAB, NET, NLT, TEV].

b. τυχόν (LN **71.10**) (BAGD 2.c. p. 829): 'perhaps' [BAGD, HNTC, **LN**, NTC; NET, NIV, NJB, NRSV, REB, TNT], 'probably' [ISV, TEV], 'possibly' [AB, **LN**], 'if possible' [BAGD, Herm], not explicit [CEV]. This adverb is also translated as a clause: 'if it is at all possible' [NAB], 'it may be (that)' [Lns, NIGTC; KJV], 'it could be that' [NLT], 'if it turns out that way' [BAGD]. See 14:10 and 15:37 for cognate constructions.

c. fut. act. indic. of παραμένω (LN **85.56**) (BAGD 1.b. p. 620): 'to stay with' [AB, BAGD, Herm, HNTC, LN; ISV, NET, NRSV, TNT], 'to stay some time with' [**LN**, NTC; NJB, REB], 'to stay for a time' [NIGTC], 'to stay awhile with' [NIV, NLT], 'to spend some time with' [TEV], 'to

remain with' [BAGD, LN, Lns], 'to remain for some time with' [NAB], 'to visit for a while with' [CEV], 'to abide with' [KJV].
- d. καί (LN 89.93): 'even' [AB, Herm, HNTC, LN, Lns, NIGTC, NTC; CEV, ISV, NAB, NET, NIV, NRSV, REB, TNT]. The phrase ἢ καί 'or even' is translated 'yea, and' [KJV], 'perhaps' [TEV], not explicit [NJB, NLT].
- e. fut. act. indic. of παραχειμάζω (LN 67.166) (BAGD p. 623): 'to spend the winter' [AB, BAGD, Herm, LN, NIGTC, NTC; ISV, NAB, NET, NIV, NRSV, TNT], 'to spend the whole winter' [TEV], 'to stay all winter' [CEV, NLT], 'to stay for the whole winter' [REB], 'to winter' [BAGD, HNTC, Lns; KJV, NJB], 'to be in a place during the winter' [LN]. Wintering in Corinth was advisable as it was dangerous after September 14 to travel on the ocean. After November 11 all sailing stopped [ICC].

QUESTION—What relationship is indicated by δέ 'and/but'?
1. It indicates a transition to 16:6 [AB, NTC; CEV, ISV, KJV, NET, NJB, NRSV, REB, TNT]: *now* perhaps I will stay with you.
2. It indicates a contrast between Paul's 'going through' Macedonia but his 'staying' in Corinth [EGT, Herm, HNTC, Ho, ICC, Lns, TNTC]: I intend to go through Macedonia, *but* perhaps I will stay with you. The words πρὸς ὑμᾶς δέ 'but with you' emphasizes 'you' and contrasts them with Macedonia [ICC, TNTC].

QUESTION—What is indicated by πρός in the phrase πρὸς ὑμᾶς 'with you'?
Πρός indicates active communication [Ed, EGT, ICC]. It indicates intimate communication [Vn].

so-that you may-send-(me)-on-my-way^a wherever I-may-go.

LEXICON—a. aorist act. subj. of προπέμπω (LN 15.72, 15.155) (BAGD 2. p. 709): 'to send someone on one's way' [AB, BAGD, Herm, HNTC, LN (15.72), NTC; ISV, NLT, NRSV], 'to help someone on one's way' [LN (15.72); CEV, REB], 'to send someone on one's journey' [NET], 'to start someone on one's journey' [NJB], 'to help someone on one's journey' [NIV], 'to send someone forward' [Lns], 'to help someone to continue one's trip' [TEV], 'to help someone forward on one's way' [TNT], 'to send someone with practical support' [NIGTC], 'to provide someone with what one needs' [NAB], 'to bring someone on one's journey' [KJV], 'to accompany, to escort' [LN (15.155)].

QUESTION—What word is emphasized in this clause?
The pronoun ἡμεῖς 'you' is emphatic [Alf, Ed, ICC, TNTC]: you yourselves. The emphatic 'you' expresses Paul's fond preference for them in his plans [Alf]. The emphatic 'you' implies 'you who now grieve me' [Ed].

QUESTION—What is meant by προπέμπω 'to send someone on one's way'?
It implies hospitality, including provision of food [Lns, NIC2, TNTC], of clothing [Lns], of lodging [TNTC], of money [NIC2, TG, TNTC], of traveling companions [NIC2, NTC], of arranging travel [Lns, NTC]. It does not necessarily imply more than good wishes and prayers [ICC].

16:7 For (I) do-not want to-see[a] you now[b] in passing,[e]
LEXICON—a. aorist act. infin. of ὁράω (LN 34.50) (BAGD 6. p. 221): 'to see' [AB, Herm, HNTC, Lns, NIGTC, NTC; ISV, KJV, NAB, NET, NIV, NRSV, TEV], 'to go to see' [LN], 'to visit' [BAGD, LN]. This verb is also translated as a noun: 'visit' [CEV, NJB, NLT, REB, TNT].
- b. ἄρτι (See this word at 15:6): 'now' [AB, HNTC, Lns, NTC; CEV, ISV, KJV, NET, NIV, NRSV, TNT], 'this time' [NLT], 'this (visit)' [REB], not explicit [NIGTC; NAB, NJB, TEV].
- c. πάροδος (LN **15.29**) (BAGD 2. p. 628): 'passing' [AB, BAGD, HNTC, NIGTC, NTC; ISV, NET], 'incidentally' [Rb]. This word is also translated as a verb phrase: 'to travel past' [**LN**], 'to pass by, to travel on through' [LN]. The phrase ἐν παρόδῳ 'in passing by' is translated 'in just passing' [Herm; NAB, NRSV], 'by the way' [Lns; KJV], '(make) only a passing (visit)' [NIV, NJB], '(pay you…) just a passing (visit)' [TNT], '(make) just a short (visit) and then go right on' [NLT], 'a flying (visit)' [REB], 'more than just briefly in passing' [TEV], 'only a short (visit)' [CEV].

QUESTION—What relationship is indicated by γάρ 'for'?
It explains why Paul wants to spend time with them [NIC2]: *you see* I don't want to see you now in passing. It explains why Paul is changing his original plan to come directly to Corinth instead of by way of Macedonia [Gdt].

QUESTION—What is meant by ἄρτι 'now'?
It means 'at the present time' as contrasted with a time after he had gone through Macedonia (see 16:5) [EGT, Gdt, HNTC, NCBC, NIC2]. It does not imply a contrast between now and a previous visit [ICC, NIC, NIC2, NTC]. Paul felt that a short visit would not be enough to accomplish all that he wanted to [MNTC].

for I-hope to-spend[a] some time with you if the Lord permits.[b]
LEXICON—a. aorist act. infin. of ἐπιμένω (LN 85.55) (BAGD 1. p. 296): 'to spend' [Herm, NIGTC; ISV, NAB, NET, NIV, NJB, NRSV, REB, TEV], 'to stay' [BAGD, HNTC, LN; TNT], 'to stay on' [AB], 'to remain' [BAGD, LN, Lns, NTC], 'to tarry' [KJV], not explicit [CEV]. The phrase χρόνον τινὰ ἐπιμεῖναι 'to remain some time' is translated 'to come and stay awhile' [NLT].
- b. aorist act. subj. of ἐπιτρέπω (See this word at 14:34): 'to permit' [AB, Herm, HNTC, Lns, NIGTC, NTC; ISV, KJV, NAB, NIV, NJB, NRSV, REB, TNT], 'to allow' [NET, TEV], 'to let' [CEV, NLT].

QUESTION—What word is emphasized in this clause?
The word ὑμᾶς 'you' is emphatic [ICC, TNTC, Vn]: with you yourselves. This functions to express Paul's affection for them [Vn].

QUESTION—To whom does ὁ κύριος 'the Lord' refer?
It refers to either God or Jesus Christ [ICC]. It refers to Jesus Christ [Ho, NIC2, TG].

QUESTION—Why does Paul want to stay longer at Corinth?
He wants to stay longer at Corinth probably because of the problems there that need his attention [AB, Gdt, HNTC, Ho, ICC, NTC, Vn]. He also wanted to stay longer because of his great affection for them [ICC, Vn].

16:8 But[a] I-will-remain in Ephesus until Pentecost;[b]
LEXICON—a. δέ (See this word at 11:2): 'but' [AB, HNTC, Lns, NIGTC, NTC; KJV, NET, NIV, NJB, NRSV, REB], 'however' [ISV], 'in the meantime' [NLT], not explicit [Herm; CEV, NAB, TEV, TNT].
  b. πεντηκοστή (LN 51.8) (BAGD p. 643): 'Pentecost' [AB, Herm, HNTC, Lns, NIGTC, NTC; all versions except NLT, TEV], 'Festival of Pentecost' [NLT], 'day of Pentecost' [TEV]. Πεντηκοστή was a Jewish festival celebrating harvest on the fiftieth day after Passover [LN]. Pentecost occurs on the sixth day of the month of Sivan (about May 20th) [TG]. This indicates that Paul was probably writing in the spring before Pentecost [NCBC, Rb]. 'Pentecost' can be translated either 'Festival of Pentecost' or 'Harvest Festival' [TH]. This occurred in the season that was favorable for traveling [NIGTC].
QUESTION—What is implied by ἐν Ἐφέσῳ 'in Ephesus'?
The word 'here' is implied [NIGTC, Rb, TH; ISV, NIV, NJB, NLT, REB, TEV]: here in Ephesus. Ephesus was the major city of western Asia Minor and therefore important in spreading the Good News [AB].

16:9 For (a) great[a] and effective[b] door[c] has-opened[d] to-me,
LEXICON—a. μέγας (LN 59.22, 87.22) (BAGD 1.b. p. 497): 'great' [AB, Herm, HNTC, LN (59.22, 87.22), Lns, NIGTC; KJV, NIV, REB, TEV, TNT], 'wide' [BAGD, NTC; NRSV], 'wide open' [NET, NJB, NLT], '(opened) wide' [ISV], 'extensive' [LN (59.22)], 'important' [LN (87.22)]. The phrase μεγάλη καὶ ἐνεργής 'great and effective' is translated 'wonderful (opportunity)' [CEV], 'great (opportunity)' [NET], '(opened) wide' [NAB].
  b. ἐνεργής (LN 13.124) (BAGD p. 265): 'effective' [BAGD, HNTC, LN, NIGTC], 'effectual' [Herm, Lns; KJV], 'active, powerful' [BAGD], 'very promising (door)' [NJB], 'great (opportunity)' [NET], 'productive' [AB], 'able to bring about' [LN], not explicit [CEV, NAB, NLT]. This adjective is also translated as a phrase: 'worthwhile work' [TEV], '(for) effective work' [NIV, NRSV, REB, TNT], '(for) effective service' [NTC], '(to do) effective work' [ISV]. The clause θύρα...μοι ἀνέῳγεν μεγάλη καὶ ἐνεργής 'a door to me has opened great and effective' is translated 'there is a wide-open door for a great work here, and many people are responding' [NLT]. It implies a potential rich field of labor [BAGD].
  c. θύρα (LN 7.39, 7.49) (BAGD 2.c. p. 366): 'door' [AB, Herm, HNTC, LN, Lns, NIGTC, NTC; all versions except CEV, REB, TEV], 'a door for a great work' [NLT], 'opportunity' [REB], 'real opportunity' [TEV], 'opportunity...to do some work here' [CEV], 'entrance, entrance-way,

portal' [LN (7.39)]. Θύρα is used figuratively here to indicate possibility or feasibility [BAGD].
  d. perf. act. indic. of ἀνοίγω (LN 71.9, 79.110) (BAGD 1.a., 2. p. 71): 'to open' [AB, BAGD, LN (79.110); NIV, NRSV, REB], 'to be open' [HNTC, Lns; TNT], 'to be opened' [Herm, NTC; ISV, KJV, NAB], 'to stand open' [NIGTC], 'to be' [CEV, TEV]. This verb is also translated as an adjective phrase: 'wide open (door)' [NLT]. It is also translated as an adverb: '(stands) open' [NET, NJB]. The phrase 'to open a door' indicates 'to be given an opportunity to work' [BAGD], 'to make it possible' [LN (71.9)]. The perfect tense indicates continuing opportunity [TNTC]: the door stands open.
QUESTION—What relationship is indicated by γάρ 'for'?
  It indicates the reason for Paul's staying in Ephesus until Pentecost [EGT, Ho, Lns, NIC2, NIGTC, Vn]: I will remain in Ephesus until Pentecost *because* a great and effective door has opened to me.
QUESTION—What does an 'open door' indicate?
  It indicates an opportunity to do something [Alf, BAGD, Ed, Gdt, Herm, HNTC, ICC, Lns, NCBC, NIGTC, NTC, TG, TH, TNTC, Vn]. The opportunity implied is to proclaim the Good News [Ed, Gdt, HNTC, Ho, ICC, Lns, NTC, Vn]. The opportunity is to teach new converts [Vn]. The opportunity is to do Christian work [TG].
QUESTION—What is meant by θύρα...μεγάλν 'a great door'?
  It indicates many opportunities [Ed, Gdt, NTC]. It indicates a good or great opportunity [Alf, Lns, TG]. It indicates a special or unusual opportunity [AB, Vn]. It indicates a wide open door [EGT, Rb, TG].
QUESTION—What is indicated by ἐνεργής 'effective'?
  It indicates an opportunity that will produce good results [Ed, Gdt, Ho, ICC, TG, TH, Vn]. It indicates an opportunity that will gain converts [NTC]. It indicates an opportunity to influence others [EGT, ICC]. It indicates an opportunity for much work [ICC, Rb, TH].

and[a] (there are) many adversaries.[b]
LEXICON—a. καί (LN 89.92, 91.12): 'and' [AB, Herm, HNTC, LN (89.92), Lns, NIGTC, NTC; KJV, NIV, NJB, NRSV, REB, TNT], 'but' [CEV, NAB, NET, NLT], 'although' [ISV], 'even though' [TEV], 'yet' [LN (91.12)].
  b. pres. mid. (deponent = act.) participle of ἀντίκειμαι (LN 39.1) (BAGD p. 74): 'adversary' [AB, Herm, Lns, NTC; KJV, NRSV], 'opponent' [NIGTC; NET, TEV, TNT], 'opposition' [REB]. Ἀντίκειμαι is a verb indicating 'to oppose' [LN; ISV, NIV, NLT], 'to be opposed' [BAGD; NAB], 'to be against' [CEV], 'to resist' [HNTC], 'to be hostile toward, to show hostility' [LN], 'to be in opposition to' [BAGD]. This is also translated as a phrase: '(many) against us' [NJB].

1 CORINTHIANS 16:9 361

QUESTION—What relationship is indicated by καί 'and'?
1. It indicates an additional reason why Paul will stay in Ephesus [AB, EGT, Gdt, HNTC, Ho, Rb, Vn]: because a door is open *and because* there are many adversaries. The work of evangelism increases under opposition [EGT]. Paul feels he must stay and confront those who oppose him [Gdt].
2. It indicates that what follows is in antithesis to his staying in Ephesus [TH; CEV, ISV, NAB, NET, NLT, TEV]: a door is open *but* there are many adversaries.

DISCOURSE UNIT: 16:10–14 [Ho]. The topic is a commendation of Timothy and Apollos.

DISCOURSE UNIT: 16:10-12 [Ed, Gdt, ICC, TNTC]. The topic is Timothy and Apollos [Ed, TNTC], Timothy's visit to Corinth, and Apollos [Gdt], Timothy and Apollos commended [ICC].

DISCOURSE UNIT: 16:10-11 [AB, Alf, ICC, NTC]. The topic is a recommendation of Timothy [AB, Alf], Timothy's arrival [NTC].

16:10 Now if Timothy should-come, see[a] that he-may-be with you without-fear;[b]

LEXICON—a. pres. act. impera. of βλέπω (LN **13.134**) (BAGD 4.d. p. 143): 'to see' [KJV, NET, NRSV, REB, TNT], 'to see to it' [Herm, **LN** (13.134); ISV, NIV], 'to be sure' [**LN** (13.134); NAB, TEV], 'to make sure' [NJB], 'to take care' [NIGTC], 'to direct (one's) attention to something, consider, note' [BAGD], 'to see to it that something happens, to arrange for something to happen' [LN (13.134)]. The phrase βλέπετε, ἵνα ἀφόβως γένηται πρὸς ὑμᾶς 'see, that without fear he may be with you' is translated 'give him a friendly welcome' [CEV], 'treat him with respect' [NLT].
b. ἀφόβως (LN 25.253) (BAGD 1. p. 127): 'without fear' [Herm, LN; KJV], 'without cause to be afraid' [BAGD], 'nothing to fear' [NET, NIV, NJB, NRSV, TNT], 'free from fear' [NIGTC], 'nothing to be afraid of' [ISV], 'fearlessly, not afraid' [LN]. The phrase ἵνα ἀφόβως γένηται 'that without fear he may be' is translated 'to put him at ease' [NAB, REB], 'to make him feel welcome' [TEV]. See the previous word for CEV and NLT.

QUESTION—How did the Corinthians know who Timothy was?
Timothy had been with Paul in Corinth [NIC, NIC2]. He had been there for over a year when the church was first founded [NIC2].

QUESTION—How did Paul know Timothy would come to the Corinthians?
Paul had sent Timothy and Erasmus from Ephesus to Corinth by way of Macedonia (see 4:17 and Acts 19:22) [Gdt, Ho, ICC, MNTC].

QUESTION—What is meant by ἐὰν… ἔλθῃ Τιμόθεος 'if Timothy comes'?
Ἐάν 'if' indicates uncertainty about Timothy's arrival [HNTC, NIC2, TH, Vn]: if Timothy comes. It expresses uncertainty about Timothy's arrival time [NIC2, NIGTC, NTC]. Travel in those days, being as it was, allowed for

doubt about arrival at one's destination [NIC2]. It means 'when' (see 4:17) [Lns, NCBC, TG, TNTC; CEV, NLT]: when Timothy comes. Here 'whenever' is probably a better translation [Herm, NIC2, NIGTC].

QUESTION—What are some reasons for Paul's instruction ἵνα ἀφόβως γένηται πρὸς ὑμᾶς 'that he be without fear with you'?

Timothy had no need to fear physical violence, but he might fear that he would not be regarded with respect or confidence [Ho]. Paul may have given this instruction because Timothy was young [Ed, EGT, Gdt, ICC, NCBC, NIC, NTC, TNTC, Vn]. Years later Paul writes that he was young (see 1 Timothy 4:12) [TNTC, Vn]. Timothy may have been of a shy disposition (see 2 Timothy 1:6, 7) [Alf, Ed, EGT, NCBC, NIC, NTC, TNTC]. The Corinthians had differences with Paul and might treat Timothy with hostility since he represented Paul (see 4:17–21) [MNTC, NIC, NIC2, Rb, TNTC]. Paul had sent Timothy to remind the Corinthians of Paul's ways (see 4:17) [NIC2]. Timothy was only a subordinate of Paul and already they had differences with Paul [Alf, NTC]. The Corinthians could be rude [HNTC, Ho, ICC, Vn].

for he-does the work of-(the)-Lord as I-also (do);

QUESTION—What relationship is indicated by γάρ 'for'?

It indicates the reason why the Corinthians should treat Timothy with respect [Lns]: see that he may be without fear *because* he does the work of the Lord as I also do.

QUESTION—How are the nouns related in the genitive construction ἔργον κυρίου 'work of (the) Lord'?

It means work done for the Lord [NTC, TH; TEV]. It means the work that the Lord has commanded him to do [ICC]. It can either mean the work the Lord does or the work he commands others to do [Ho]. The work of the Lord specifically was proclaiming the Good News and building up of the churches [HNTC]. The work of the Lord was the proclaiming of the Good News [Ho].

16:11 Therefore (let) not anyone despise^a him.

LEXICON—a. aorist act. subj. of ἐξουθενέω (LN 88.195) (BAGD 1. p. 277): 'to despise' [BAGD, Herm, HNTC, LN, Lns, NTC; KJV, NLT, NRSV, TNT], 'to treat with contempt' [NIC2; ISV, NET], 'to scorn' [AB], 'to treat disdainfully' [NAB], 'to disdain' [BAGD], 'to look down on' [TEV], 'to mistreat' [CEV], 'to refuse to accept' [NIV], 'to underrate' [NJB], 'to slight' [REB], 'to belittle as a nobody' [NIGTC]. Ἐξουθενέω means 'to treat as nothing' [ICC, TH, TNTC]. It is a stronger word than καταφρονέω 'to despise' occurring in 1 Timothy 4:12 [AB, ICC]. The aorist imperative indicates that one should not start to do what one had not yet begun [Lns].

QUESTION—What relationship is indicated by οὖν 'therefore'?

It indicates the conclusion to be drawn from the fact that Timothy is doing the work of the Lord as Paul did [Ho, NIC, TNTC]: he does the work of the Lord as I also do, *therefore*, let no one despise him.

QUESTION—Why would the Corinthians treat Timothy with disrespect?

Perhaps it would be because of Timothy's youth [Ho]. If Timothy carried out his mission of confrontation as seen in 4:17, he may have met with conflict [EGT]. Ἐξουθενέω 'to hold in contempt' is strong and reflects a serious difference between the Corinthians and Paul [NIC2]. Paul does not think that the whole congregation might despise Timothy in regards to what Timothy could fear, but certain individuals might [Lns].

But send-on-(his)-way[a] him in peace,[b]

LEXICON—a. aorist act. impera. of προπέμπω (See this word at 16:6): 'to send someone on one's way' [AB, Herm, HNTC, NTC; ISV, NAB, NET, NIV, NLT, NRSV], 'to send someone off' [CEV], 'to send someone on' [Lns], 'to speed someone on one's way' [REB], 'to start someone off' [NJB], 'to help someone forward on one's way' [TNT], 'to help someone continue one's trip' [TEV], 'to help on one's way with practical support' [NIGTC], 'to conduct someone forth' [KJV]. Προπέμπω indicates the supplying of basic needs of food, drink, lodging, and funds [NTC]. It indicates the supplying of whatever his needs may be on his journey [NIC, TNTC]. It indicates assistance on his journey [HNTC, TH].

b. εἰρήνη (LN **22.42**, 25.248) (BAGD 2. p. 227): 'peace' [AB, BAGD, Herm, HNTC, **LN** (22.42, 25.248), Lns, NIGTC, NTC; all versions except CEV, NLT, REB], 'tranquility' [LN (22.42)], 'freedom from worry' [LN (25.248)], '(one's) blessings' [CEV, NLT, REB]. Paul wants Timothy to leave Corinth with a feeling of good will [ICC, Vn]. See this word also at 14:33. Peace includes general well-being [NIGTC].

so-that he-may-come to me; for I-am-expecting[a] him with the brothers.[b]

LEXICON—a. pres. mid. (deponent = act.) indic. of ἐκδέχομαι (LN **30.53**): 'to expect' [AB, **LN**, Lns, NTC; ISV, NAB, NET, NIV, NRSV], 'to expect (one) back' [TEV], 'to look for' [CEV, KJV], 'to wait for' [Herm, NIGTC; NJB, REB, TNT], 'to await' [HNTC], 'to look forward to see' [NLT]. See this word also at 11:33.

b. ἀδελφός (See this word at 10:1): 'brother' [AB, Herm, HNTC, Lns, NTC; ISV, KJV, NAB, NET, NIV, NJB, NRSV], 'believer' [NLT, TEV], 'other follower' [CEV], '(one's) friend' [REB], 'brothers and sisters' [NIGTC]. In this case, 'brothers' probably refers to male traveling companions [TH; NET].

QUESTION—What is the significance of the clause ἵνα ἔλθῃ πρός με 'so that he may come to me'?

The repetition of the first person in the words 'to me' along with the verb 'I am expecting him' function to imply that Paul is significantly concerned about the mission he gave Timothy to carry out [NTC].

QUESTION—With what is the phrase μετὰ τῶν ἀδελφῶν 'with the brothers' connected?

1. It is connected with προπέμψατε 'I am expecting' [EGT, Gdt, ICC, NIC; NJB, TNT]: I and the brothers are expecting Timothy. These would be the

364   1 CORINTHIANS 16:11

Corinthian brothers who had brought the Corinthian letter to Paul and are waiting for Timothy's return before they themselves return home [EGT, ICC]. They would take back Paul's reply [ICC]. These would be fellow believers that the Corinthians knew about who were with Paul [NIC].
2. It is connected with αὐτόν 'him' [Alf, Ho, Lns, MNTC, NIC2; TEV]: I am expecting Timothy and the brothers. Paul had appointed others to travel with Timothy since it was not usual for anyone to travel alone [Ho].
3. It is difficult to decide for sure between these two [Herm, HNTC, NTC, TNT].

DISCOURSE UNIT: 16:12 [AB, Alf, NIC2, NTC]. The topic is the projected visit by Apollos, [AB, NIC2], Apollo's reluctance [NTC].

16:12 Now concerning^a Apollos the brother,^b

LEXICON—a. περί with genitive object (See this word at 12:1): 'concerning' [Lns, NIGTC, NTC; ISV, NRSV, TNT], 'with reference to' [AB], 'about' [HNTC; NIV, NLT, TEV], 'with regard to' [NET], 'as for' [NAB, NJB, REB], 'as touching' [KJV], 'as regards' [Herm], not explicit [CEV].
    b. ἀδελφός (See this word at 10:1): 'brother' [AB, Herm, HNTC, Lns, NIGTC, NTC; all versions except CEV, REB], 'friend' [CEV, REB].
QUESTION—What is meant by the phrase περὶ δὲ Ἀπολλῶ τοῦ ἀδελφοῦ 'now concerning the brother Apollos'?
    This may refer to a request from the Corinthians in their letter to Paul [AB, EGT, Gdt, HNTC, Ho, ICC, Lns, NIC, NIC2, NTC, TG, TNTC, Vn]. The phrase περὶ δέ 'now concerning' is used at 7:1, 25, 8:1 12:1, 16:1, and 16:12, each time indicating another matter about which the Corinthians had asked in their letter [Lns, NIC2, NTC, TG, TNTC].
QUESTION—What is the significance of the article in τοῦ ἀδελφοῦ 'the brother'?
    It probably indicates that Paul considered Apollos to be a co-worker. He used the same designation of Sosthenes in 1:1 [NIC2].

I-urged^a him strongly,^b that he-come to you with the brothers;

LEXICON—a. aorist act. indic. of παρακαλέω (LN 33.168) (BAGD 3. p. 617): 'to urge' [AB, Herm, Lns; ISV, NAB, NIV, NJB, NLT, NRSV, REB, TNT], 'to encourage' [NTC; NET, TEV], 'to beg' [BAGD], 'to beseech' [NIGTC], 'to desire' [KJV], 'to request, to ask for (earnestly), to plead for, to appeal to' [LN]. The phrase πολλὰ παρεκάλεσα 'I urged strongly' is translated 'I have tried hard' [CEV]. See this word also at 4:16.
    b. πολύς (BAGD I.2.b.β. p. 688): 'strongly' [AB; ISV, NAB, NET, NIV, NRSV, REB, TNT], 'earnestly' [BAGD, HNTC, NIGTC; NJB], 'greatly' [BAGD, NTC; KJV], 'often' [BAGD, Herm; TEV], '(tried) hard' [CEV], 'much' [HNTC], 'absolutely' [Gdt], not explicit [NLT]. See this word also at 12:22.

QUESTION—To whom does μετὰ τῶν ἀδελφῶν 'with the brothers' refer?

It may refer to the three men Stephanas, Fortunatus, and Achaicus mentioned in 16:17 [Gdt, Ho, NIC, NIC2, NTC]. It indicates the ones who would carry Paul's letter back to Corinth [Ed, Ho, ICC, MNTC, NIC]. It may refer either to Timothy's companions or to the ones of 16:17 who were to carry Paul's letter back to Corinth [Alf]. It may refer to Timothy and his companions [NCBC, TNTC]. It may refer to a group of brothers who would go to Corinth after Timothy's return [TNTC]. They were not the ones to carry Paul's letter to Corinth as it was supposed to arrive before Timothy went there and these three were to await Timothy's arrival from Corinth [Gdt].

but[a] it-was not at-all[b] (the) will that he-should-come now;

LEXICON—a. καί (LN 91.12): 'but' [Herm, HNTC, NIGTC, Rb; all versions except CEV, NIV, TNT], 'yet' [AB, LN], 'and' [Alf, Lns, NTC], 'and in spite of all I could say' [ICC], not explicit [CEV, NIV, TNT]. Καί is used to express contrast here [HNTC, Rb].

b. πάντως (LN 71.16, 91.10) (BAGD 5.a. p. 609): 'at all' [AB, Herm, Lns; KJV, NRSV], 'simply' [HNTC; NET], 'quite' [BAGD; NIV, TNT], 'certainly' [LN (71.16, 91.10)], 'really' [LN (71.16)], 'indeed' [LN (91.10), NTC], not explicit [CEV, ISV, NAB, NLT]. The phrase πάντως οὐκ ἦν θέλημα 'it was not at all the will' is translated 'he is not completely convinced' [TEV], 'he was quite determined not' [REB], 'he was fully determined not' [NIGTC], 'he was quite firm...not' [NJB]. Πάντως expresses strong refusal. The νῦν 'now' softens it [ICC].

QUESTION—What is implied by οὐκ ἦν θέλημα 'it was not (his) will'?

It implies that Apollos was not in Ephesus at the time Paul was writing this letter [NTC]. Taken together with the fact that Apollos is not mentioned in the greetings at the end of 1 Corinthians, it probably implies that Apollos was not in Ephesus at the time when Paul is writing this [NIC, TNTC].

QUESTION—Whose θέλημα 'will' is intended here?

1. It refers to the will of Apollos [AB, Alf, Ed, EGT, Gdt, Ho, ICC, Lns, MNTC, NIC, NIC2, NIGTC, NTC, TH, Vn; all versions]: it was not Apollos's will. Since the final clause of the verse has Apollos as its subject, it is better to take him as the one willing [NIC2]. The words παρεκάλεσα αὐτόν 'I urged him' indicates that it was Apollos's will that was against coming [ICC]. Since θέλημα stands without modifier, it is best to take it as referring to Apollos's will [NTC]. He did not want to go at that time because he did not want to encourage rivalry between him and Paul [Alf, Ed, Gdt, NIC2, NTC]. He did not want to go at that time because he was busy doing other things [Lns].
2. It refers to the will of God [HNTC, NCBC]: it was not God's will.
3. It is not possible to decide which is correct [Herm, TH, TNTC].

but he-will-come whenever he-has-(the)-opportunity.[a]

LEXICON—a. aorist act. subj. of εὐκαιρέω (LN **67.4**) (BAGD p. 321): 'to have an/the opportunity' [HNTC, **LN**, NTC; NET, NIV, NRSV], 'to find an opportunity' [AB, BAGD, Herm; NJB], 'to have convenient time' [KJV], 'to get the chance' [TEV], 'to have a chance' [**LN**], 'to have an appropriate time for, to have an occasion to' [**LN**], 'to be a favorable occasion' [**LN**]. This verb is also translated as a phrase: 'there is opportunity' [TNT], 'circumstances are more favorable' [NAB], 'the time is right' [NIGTC; ISV, NLT, REB], 'he can' [CEV], 'opportunity offers' [Lns].

DISCOURSE UNIT: 16:13–24 [GNT, HNTC, NIC2, NTC; CEV, KJV, NAB, NET, TEV]. The topic is concluding matters [NIC2; TEV], final greetings [KJV], final words and greetings [GNT, HNTC], directions and greetings [NIGTC, NTC; NAB], personal concerns and greetings [CEV], final challenge and blessing [NET].

DISCOURSE UNIT: 16:13–18 [EGT, Gdt, NIC2, NTC; ISV]. The topic is final instructions.

DISCOURSE UNIT: 16:13-14 [AB, Ed, ICC, MNTC]. The topic is exhortations [AB, ICC, TNTC], a summary of the practical lessons of the epistle [Ed], principles for powerful living [MNTC].

16:13 Be-alert,ª stand-firmᵇ in the faith,ᶜ

LEXICON—a. pres. act. impera. of γρηγορέω (LN **27.56**) (BAGD 2. p. 167): 'to be alert' [Herm, **LN**; TEV], 'to be on the alert' [BAGD, NTC; REB], 'to keep alert' [AB, NIGTC; CEV, NRSV], 'to remain alert' [ISV], 'to stay alert' [NET], 'to be watchful' [BAGD, LN, Lns; TNT], 'to watch' [HNTC; KJV], 'to be vigilant' [LN; NJB], 'to be on (one's) guard' [NAB, NIV, NLT].

b. pres. act. impera. of στήκω (LN 13.30, 17.1) (BAGD 2. p. 768): 'to stand firm' [BAGD, HNTC, NIGTC, NTC; ISV, NAB, NET, NIV, NRSV, REB, TEV, TNT], 'to stand fast' [AB, Herm; KJV], 'to stand true' [NLT], 'to stay firm' [NJB], 'to be firm' [Lns; CEV], 'to stand' [LN (13.30, 17.1)], 'to be steadfast' [BAGD]. The present imperative indicates a continued state [LN (13.30)].

c. πίστις (See this word at 15:14): 'faith' [AB, Herm, HNTC, Lns, NIGTC, NTC; KJV, NAB, NET, NIV, NJB, REB, TEV]. The phrase τῇ πίστει 'the faith' is translated 'faith' [TNT], 'your faith' [CEV, ISV, NRSV]. The phrase ἐν τῇ πίστει 'in the faith' is translated 'to what you believe' [NLT].

QUESTION—In what regard are they to 'keep alert'?

They are to keep alert in regard to watching for the Second Coming of the Lord (see Matthew 24:42, 25:13ff.) [Herm, HNTC, NIC, NTC, TH, TNTC]. They are to keep alert in regard to influences that would corrode the truth. This interpretation is more in keeping with the general tenor of the epistle [NIC2]. They are to keep alert in regard to hostile enemy influences [Gdt, Ho, ICC, Lns, NTC]. They are to keep alert in regard to dangers [ICC, NIC, Vn]. They are to be alert against the dangers from Satan, temptation,

1 CORINTHIANS 16:13

indifference, and false teachers [MNTC]. 'Alertness' is figurative here and refers to careful spiritual attention to the needs of the Christian assembly [TG].

QUESTION—What does 'standing firm' indicate?

It indicates immovability [NTC]. It indicates stability. Here it refers to a person's being firmly established in Christ [TNTC]. It indicates negatively that they should not fall into sin and should do this by the strength of faith [NIC].

QUESTION—What is meant by ἡ πίστις 'the faith'?

It means trusting or having confidence in God [HNTC, Lns, NCBC, NIC2, NTC]. It indicates the action of believing [NIC]. It means believing the Gospel or the truth of Christian teaching (see Jude 3) [Ho, Lns, MNTC, NIC, NIGTC, NTC, Vn]. It refers to belief in the atonement by Christ's death and in the resurrection [Gdt].

be-manly,[a] **be-strong.**[b]

LEXICON—a. pres. mid. (deponent = act.) impera. of ἀνδρίζομαι (LN **25.165**) (BAGD p. 64): 'to be manly' [Herm, Lns; TNT], 'to act like a man' [NAB], 'to play the man' [HNTC], 'to behave in manly fashion' [AB], 'to quit (oneself) like a man' [KJV], 'to conduct oneself in a manly way' [BAGD], 'to be a man of courage' [NTC; NIV], 'to be brave' [**LN**; NJB, TEV], 'to stay brave' [CEV], 'to be courageous' [LN; ISV, NLT, NRSV], 'to show courage' [NET], 'to show mature courage' [NIGTC], 'to conduct oneself in a courageous way' [BAGD], 'to be valiant' [REB], 'to increase in strength' [NIGTC]. Ἀνδρίζομαι has a non-figurative meaning of 'to be manly' but this meaning is not found in the New Testament [LN].

b. pres. pass. (deponent = act.) impera. of κραταιόομαι (LN **76.10**) (BAGD p. 448): 'to be strong' [AB, Herm, HNTC, LN, Lns, NTC; all versions except CEV], 'to become strong' [BAGD, LN], 'to stay strong' [CEV], 'to become powerful' [LN]. The reference is to spiritual strength sufficient to overcome any evil influence [LN].

QUESTION—To what attribute of 'manliness' does ἀνδρίζομαι 'to be manly' refer?

It refers to the attribute of courage or bravery [EGT, Gdt, Ho, LN, Lns, MNTC, NIC2, TH, TNTC; CEV, ISV, NET, NIV, NJB, NLT, NRSV, REB, TEV]. It refers to the mature qualities of self-control, confidence, and bravery [MNTC].

QUESTION—In regard to what are they to be manly?

They are to be brave in regard to the scorn of learned people and the persecution of influential people [Ho]. They are to be brave in regard to enemies [ICC]. They are to be brave in regard to dangers [ICC, NIC2]. They are to be courageous in regard to keeping true to the faith [Lns]. They are to be courageous in regard to error and loose moral living [NIC2]. They are to bravely pursue the Christian life [EGT].

QUESTION—In regard to what are they to be strong?
They are to be strong in regard to ethical living [EGT, ICC, Vn]. They are to be strong in keeping the faith [Lns, TH].
QUESTION—What is the significance of the present tense in all of these imperatives?
The present imperative indicates continuing activity [Lns, TNTC, Vn; ISV]: continue to be alert, continue standing firm in the faith, continue being brave, continue being strong.
QUESTION—What is the significance of the passive voice of κραταιοῦσθε 'be strong/be strengthened'?
It indicates that they are to be strong in the strength that the Lord gives them (see Ephesians 6:10) [Gdt, MNTC, NTC, TNTC]. They are to be made strong through the experiences that God prepares for them [NTC].

16:14 **Let-be-done[a] everything of-you in love.**
LEXICON—a. pres. mid. (deponent = act.) impera. of γίνομαι (LN 13.107, 13.48): 'to be done' [Herm, HNTC, Lns, NIGTC, NTC; ISV, KJV, NET, NJB, NLT, NRSV, REB, TNT], 'to be conducted' [AB], 'to be carried on' [EGT]. This verb is also translated actively: 'to do' [NAB, NIV, TEV], 'to happen' [LN (13.107)], 'to become' [LN (13.48)]. This entire clause is translated 'show love in everything you do' [CEV]. The present imperative indicates a continuing aspect [Lns]: keep letting everything you do be done in love.
QUESTION—What is the meaning of the phrase ἐν ἀγάπῃ 'in love'?
It indicates the way in which things should be done [TH]: lovingly, in a loving way, with a loving spirit. It indicates that one should *show* love in all one does [CEV]. Love should not merely accompany all one does, but should be the very atmosphere in which it is done [TNTC, Vn]. Ἐν indicates the sphere in which something takes place. Everything should be in the sphere of love—nothing outside of it [Lns].
QUESTION—Specifically, in regard to what are they to do things in love?
The Corinthians are to do things in love, specifically in regard to divisions among them [Ed, Gdt, Ho, NIC2, Vn], in the way they conduct the Lord's Supper [Ho, NIC2, Vn], in the attitude of the "haves" toward the "have-nots," in the attitude of those with knowledge toward the weak, in the attitude of some of them toward Paul, in their lawsuits, in husband-wife relationships [NIC2], in the need to build up others in their worship in place of selfish use of the spiritual gifts [Gdt, NIC2].

DISCOURSE UNIT: 16:15–20 [Ho]. The topic is exhortations and greetings.

DISCOURSE UNIT: 16:15-18 [AB, Alf, ICC, NCBC]. The topic is appreciation and commendation of Corinthian leaders [AB, Alf, NCBC], directions about Stephanas and others [ICC].

16:15 Now[a] I-urge[b] you, brothers;[c]

LEXICON—a. δέ (See this word at 11:2): 'now' [AB, Lns; ISV, NET, NRSV], 'one thing more' [REB], 'and' [NTC], not explicit [Herm, HNTC, NIGTC; all versions except ISV, NET, NRSV, REB].
- b. pres. act. indic. of παρακαλέω (BAGD 2. p. 617): 'to urge' [BAGD, Lns; all versions except CEV, KJV, TEV], 'to beseech' [KJV], 'to beg' [TEV], 'to ask' [NIGTC; CEV], 'to make a request of' [HNTC], 'to appeal to' [BAGD, NTC], 'to exhort' [BAGD, Herm], 'to encourage' [BAGD]. This verb is also translated as an interjection: 'please' [AB]. (Note that TNT, NAB, NRSV, and REB put the words 'I urge you' ahead in 16:16. However, CEV, NIV, NLT, and TEV keep the words 'I ask you' in this verse but make them a part of the sentence of 16:16.) See this word also at 16:12.
- c. ἀδελφός (See this word at 10:1): 'brother' [AB, Herm, HNTC, Lns, NTC; ISV, KJV, NIV, NJB, TNT], 'brother and sister' [NIC2, NIGTC; NET, NRSV], 'dear brother and sister' [NLT], 'friend' [CEV], '(one's) friend' [REB, TEV], not explicit [NAB]. Ἀδελφός includes sisters as well [NIC2, NTC, TG; NET, NLT, NRSV].

QUESTION—What is the function of the rest of this verse?
Since the object of παρακαλῶ 'I urge' begins with 16:16 this material functions to name and describe the family of Stephanas [Ed, EGT, Gdt, MNTC, NIC, NIC2, NTC, Rb, TG, TH; all versions]. It functions to give the reason why the Corinthians should be submissive to people like Stephanas and his family [Gdt, ICC].

you-know the family[a] of-Stephanas, that it-is (the) first-fruits[b] of Achaia[c]

LEXICON—a. οἰκία (LN 10.8) (BAGD 2. p. 557): 'family' [BAGD, LN, Lns; CEV, NJB, REB, TEV], 'members of the family' [ISV], 'household' [AB, Herm, HNTC, LN, NIGTC, NTC; NAB, NET, NIV, NLT, TNT], 'members of the household' [NRSV], 'house' [KJV]. The term οἰκία may include servants as well as family [MNTC, TH]. Since 'service' is mentioned, probably only the adults are indicated [AB, HNTC].
- b. ἀπαρχή (See this word at 15:20): 'firstfruits' [AB, Herm, Lns, NTC; KJV, NAB, NJB], 'first converts' [Alf, HNTC, NCBC, NIC, NIC2, Vn; ISV, NET, NIV, NRSV, REB, TNT], 'first of more converts' [NIGTC], 'first Christian converts' [TEV]. It is also translated as a phrase: 'first to have faith in the Lord' [CEV], 'first to become Christians' [NLT].
- c. Ἀχαΐα (LN 93.419) (BAGD p. 128): 'Achaia' [AB, Herm, HNTC, Lns, NIGTC, NTC; all versions except NLT], 'Greece' [NLT]. Ἀχαΐα was a Roman province consisting of the important parts of Greece: Attica, Boeotia, the Peloponneus and possibly Eprius [BAGD]. It refers to central and southern Greece [Herm]. Its capital was Corinth [Herm, NIC2, TG]. It refers specifically to the Peloponnesus [NIC2].

QUESTION—In view of the fact that there had been other converts from Achaia before the family of Stephanas, how are they called the 'firstfruits'?

The others mentioned in Acts 17:34 (Dionysius, Damaris, and others) were individuals, but the household of Stephanas was the first *family* to become Christians in Achaia [AB, EGT, ICC, NTC, TNTC]. They may be 'firstfruits' in the sense that they were a sign of a harvest to follow [Ed, EGT, MNTC, NIC2, NTC, TNTC]. It was with this family that the church came into being there [EGT, ICC]. It may have been that they were the first converts from Corinth [HNTC]. Epenetus, mentioned in Romans 16:5, was an early convert from Asia, not Achaia [Ho].

and-(that) they-devoted[a] themselves to[b] (the) service[c] (of) the saints;[d]

LEXICON—a. aorist act. indic. of τάσσω (LN **68.69**) (BAGD 1.b. p. 806): 'to devote (oneself)' [BAGD; ISV, NET, NIV, NJB, NRSV, REB], 'to be devoted' [NAB], 'to do with devotion' [LN], 'to give (oneself)' [LN, NTC; TEV], 'to spend (one's life)' [NLT], 'to exert (oneself)' [AB], 'to take on (oneself)' [HNTC], 'to set (oneself)' [Herm, Lns; TNT], 'to lay (oneself) out' [Ed], 'to appoint (oneself)' [ICC, TH], 'to assign (oneself)' [NIGTC], 'to addict (oneself)' [KJV]. The phrase καὶ εἰς διακονίαν... ἔταξαν ἑαυτούς 'and they gave themselves for service' is translated 'they have done all they can' [CEV].

b. εἰς with accusative object (LN 89.57): 'to' [Herm, NIGTC, NTC; all versions except CEV, NLT, TNT], 'for' [LN, Lns; CEV], 'for the purpose of' [LN], 'in' [AB; NLT], not explicit [HNTC; TNT].

c. διακονία (BAGD 1. p. 184): 'service' [AB, BAGD, Herm, HNTC, LN, Lns, NIGTC, NTC; NAB, NIV, NJB, NLT, NRSV, REB, TEV], 'ministry' [NTC; KJV, NET], 'help' [LN]. This noun is also translated as a verb: 'to serve' [TNT], 'to do all one can' [CEV]. It is also translated as a verbal noun: 'serving' [ISV]. See this word also at 12:5.

d. οἱ ἅγιοι (See this phrase at 14:33): 'the saints' [AB, Herm, HNTC, Lns, NTC; ISV, KJV, NAB, NET, NIV, NRSV], 'God's people' [TH, TNTC; CEV, REB, TEV, TNT], 'God's holy people' [NJB], 'other Christians' [NLT].

QUESTION—What kind of διακονία 'service' did the family of Stephanas render?

In view of the fact that Stephanas was then in Ephesus, one form of service was in missions and help on journeys [Alf, EGT, Gdt]. It may be the care of the poor [Gdt, Rb], the sick [Gdt, ICC, Lns], the needy [ICC, Lns, Rb], or travelers [ICC]. It may be hospitality in their home [Lns, NIC]. It may have been teaching and preaching as well as good deeds in general to believers [NIC2]. It may have been the business of the church [Gdt].

QUESTION—To which saints does this refer?

It refers to the Christians in Corinth [NCBC, NIC2]. It does not refer to 'the saints' in Jerusalem as noted in 16:1 [HNTC, ICC]. It refers to believers in general [ICC].

16:16 That you alsoᵃ be-subjectedᵇ to-the such-peopleᶜ

LEXICON—a. καί (See this word at 12:14): 'also' [NET], 'in turn' [AB, Alf, Ed, HNTC, ICC, Lns; NJB], not explicit [NIGTC; all versions except NET, NJB].

b. pres. pass. subj. of ὑποτάσσω (See this word at 14:34): 'to be subjected' [BAGD, LN]. This passive is also translated actively: 'to be subject' [Herm, NIGTC], 'to submit' [NTC; NET, NIV], 'to submit oneself' [Lns; ISV, KJV], 'to subordinate oneself' [HNTC], 'to serve under' [NAB], 'to put (oneself) at the service of' [NJB, NRSV], 'to accept the authority of' [TNT], 'to accept the leadership of' [REB], 'to follow the leadership of' [TEV], 'to obey' [CEV], 'to respect fully' [NLT], 'to yield' [AB].

c. τοιοῦτος (LN 92.31) (BAGD 3.a.α. p. 821): 'such a person' [AB, BAGD, Herm, Lns; NRSV], 'such' [KJV], 'of a kind such as this, of such a kind' [LN]. This plural noun is translated 'such men' [HNTC, NTC; NAB, TNT], 'such as these' [NIV], 'such people as these' [NIGTC; TEV], 'people like these' [ISV], 'people like them' [REB], 'people like this' [NET, NJB], 'leaders like them' [CEV], 'them' [NLT]. See this word also at 11:16 and 15:48.

QUESTION—What does καί 'also' indicate here?

The καί is reciprocal indicating that the family of Stephanas had done their part, now the Corinthians were to do theirs [AB, Alf, Ed, HNTC, ICC, Lns, NIC2, Rb, Vn; NJB]. Καί could either indicate that they are to be subjected to such people *in addition to* recognizing them, or it may be that they *in turn* (in addition to what the family of Stephanas does) are to do their part [NIC2]. It indicates that others have subjected themselves and the Corinthians are to subject themselves as well [NIC].

QUESTION—What is meant by ὑποτάσσω 'to be subject'?

It means that they should be willing to be directed by such people [AB, Lns, TH]. It means that they should respect them [Lns]. It means that they should voluntarily yield to them in love (see Ephesians 5:21) [NIC2]. It implies that those of the family of Stephanas were leaders in the congregation [NIGTC].

and to-everyone working-withᵃ and laboring.ᵇ

LEXICON—a. pres. act. participle of συνεργέω (LN 42.15) (BAGD p. 787): 'to work with' [LN, NTC; NRSV, TEV], 'to work together with, to be active together with' [LN], 'to help with' [KJV], 'to share in the work' [TNT], 'to join in the work' [HNTC; NIV], 'to cooperate in the work' [NET], 'to cooperate' [AB, Lns; NAB], 'to help in the work' [BAGD, Herm]. The phrase συνεργοῦντι καὶ κοπιῶντι 'working with and laboring' is translated 'who shares their labor and hard work' [ISV], 'who shares in hard toil in our common work' [NIGTC], 'who work hard with you' [CEV], 'that work with them in this arduous task' [NJB], 'who labors hard at our common task' [REB], 'who serve with such real devotion' [NLT].

b. pres. act. participle of κοπιάω (See this word at 15:10): 'to labor' [Herm; KJV, NIV], 'to labor hard' [NET], 'to labor as a Christian' [HNTC], 'to work hard' [AB], 'to toil' [Ed, Herm, Lns; NAB, NRSV], 'to toil hard' [TNT], 'to serve with' [TEV], not explicit [CEV, ISV, NJB, NLT, REB]. Κοπιάω indicates work carried out to the point of suffering [EGT, Gdt]. It indicates hard and long work towards a goal [NTC]. It indicates hard work [AB, TH; NET, TNT]. It indicates work to the point of weariness [TNTC].

QUESTION—Συνεργοῦντι 'working with' implies that someone else is working. Who are they?
  1. They are working with people like the family of Stephanas [Alf, BAGD, Gdt, Ho; NRSV, TEV]: be subject to those working with such people as the family of Stephanas.
  2. They are working with Paul and his co-workers [NIC, NTC; KJV]: be subject to those working with us.
  3. They are working with the Corinthians [CEV, NAB, NJB, NRSV]: be subject to those working with you.
  4. They are working in the general work of the Gospel or church [Ed, EGT, ICC, Lns, MNTC, TH]: be subject to those working in the work of the Gospel. It is best to leave this ambiguous indicating with fellow workers in general [TH].

16:17 And[a] I-am-glad[b] at the coming[c] of Stephanas and Fortunatus and Achaicus,

LEXICON—a. δέ (See this word at 11:2): 'and' [AB, Lns, NTC], not explicit [Herm, HNTC, NIGTC; all versions]. The δέ may be a bit adversative: they should be subject to these men when they return, *but* for now he is glad that they are with him [EGT, NIC2].
  b. pres. act. indic. of χαίρω (See this word at 13:6): 'to be glad' [CEV, ISV, KJV, NET, NIV], 'to be so glad' [NLT], 'to be happy' [AB; TEV], 'to be very happy' [NAB], 'to be delighted' [NIGTC; NJB], 'to be rejoicing' [HNTC], 'to rejoice' [BAGD, Herm, LN, Lns, NTC; NRSV, TNT], 'to be a pleasure to (someone)' [REB]. The present tense indicates that Paul is still happy about their coming [NIC2].
  c. παρουσία (LN 15.86, 85.25) (BAGD 1. p. 629): 'coming' [Herm, LN (15.86), Lns, NTC; KJV, NRSV, TEV], 'arrival' [NAB, NET, TNT], 'presence' [AB, BAGD, HNTC, LN (85.25)], 'being at hand, being in person' [LN (85.25)]. This noun is also translated as a verb: 'to arrive' [NIGTC; NIV, NJB, REB], 'to come here' [ISV, NLT], 'to see' [CEV]. This word denotes both arrival and presence [NIGTC]. See this word also at 15:23.

because[a] they made-up-for[b] your lack;[c]

LEXICON—a. ὅτι (See this word at 10:17): 'because' [AB, HNTC, Lns, NIGTC, NTC; ISV, NAB, NET, NIV, NRSV, REB, TNT], 'for' [Herm;

KJV], not explicit [CEV, NJB, NLT, TEV]. Ὅτι indicates that this is the reason for Paul's happiness [TH].
  b. aorist act. indic. of ἀναπληρόω (LN **57.79**) (BAGD 3. p. 59): 'to make up for' [AB, BAGD, **LN**, NIGTC; NAB, NJB, NLT, NRSV, TEV, TNT], 'to supply' [Herm, HNTC, NTC; KJV, NIV], 'to supply the fellowship' [NET], 'to provide what is lacking' [LN], 'to supply what was lacking' [ISV], 'to fill up' [Lns], 'to represent (one who is absent)' [BAGD], not explicit [CEV]. The phrase ὑστέρημα ἀνεπλήρωσαν 'they made up for (your) lack' is translated 'they have done what you had no chance to do' [REB]. See this word also at 14:16.
  c. ὑστέρημα (LN 57.38, **85.29**) (BAGD 1. p. 849): 'lack' [Lns], 'absence' [AB, BAGD, **LN** (85.29); ISV, NAB, NRSV, TEV, TNT]. This noun is also translated as a phrase or clause 'not being here' [LN (85.29); NJB], 'what was lacking' [Herm, LN (57.38), NTC; KJV, NIV], 'what is needed' [LN (57.38)], '(fellowship) that I lacked' [NET]. The phrase τὸ ὑμέτερον ὑστέρημα 'the your absence' is translated 'the help you weren't here to give me' [NLT], 'what you could not do for me' [HNTC], 'what you had no chance to do' [REB], 'my missing you here' [NIGTC]. This entire clause is translated 'having them here was like having you' [CEV].

QUESTION—How are the nouns related in the genitive construction τὸ ὑμέτερον ὑστέρημα 'your lack'?
  1. They are related in an objective manner (Paul lacked them) and this expresses Paul's affection for them and his joy in having at least some of them there with him [Alf, Ed, EGT, Gdt, Ho, Lns, NIC, NIC2, NIGTC, NTC, TNTC, Vn; CEV, NET]: they compensated for my lack of your presence. Paul's absence from Corinth left a void in his life. These three men filled it up as though they were the whole church visiting him [NIC2].
  2. They are related in a subjective manner (they lacked Paul) and this expresses Paul's gratitude in having some of them there to provide what the Corinthians wanted to do for him [HNTC, ICC; NLT, REB]: they compensated for your lack of my presence. The Corinthians could not all come to Paul, but the three came representing them and were a good substitute for them [ICC].

16:18 For they-have-refreshed[a] my spirit[b] and yours.
LEXICON—a. aorist act. indic. of ἀναπαύω (LN 23.84) (BAGD 1. p. 59): 'to refresh' [BAGD, HNTC, NTC; ISV, KJV, NAB, NET, NIV, NRSV], 'to set at rest' [NJB, TNT], 'to set at ease' [Herm], 'to ease' [Lns], 'to make (one) feel much better' [CEV], 'to be a wonderful encouragement to' [NLT], 'to cheer up' [TEV], 'to raise (one's spirits)' [NIGTC; REB], 'to give (someone) rest, to cause (someone) to rest' [BAGD, LN]. This whole clause is translated 'for they put my spirit and yours in a fresh relationship' [AB]. Ἀναπαύω means 'to set someone's mind at rest'

[TH]. It is the same verb Jesus used in Matthew 11:28 when he invited people to come to him and he would give them rest [TNTC]. It indicates that this delegation relieved some tension between Paul and the Corinthians [AB].

b. πνεῦμα (BAGD 3.b. p. 675): 'spirit' [AB, Herm, HNTC, Lns, NIGTC, NTC; ISV, KJV, NAB, NET, NIV, NRSV, REB], 'mind' [NJB, TNT]. The phrase τὸ ἐμὸν πνεῦμα καὶ τὸ ὑμῶν 'the my spirit and the of you' is translated 'both me and you' [BAGD], 'me as…to you' [NLT], 'me…, just as…you' [CEV, TEV]. Πνεῦμα 'spirit' here refers to the person him/herself [BAGD, Herm]. See this word also at 14:2 and 14:12.

QUESTION—What relationship is indicated by γάρ 'for'?

It explains how they made up for Paul's need to see the whole church [Gdt, Lns, NIC, NIC2]: they made up for your absence, *you see* they refreshed my spirit and yours.

QUESTION—In what sense had the three men refreshed the spirits of the Corinthians?

They did this by refreshing Paul and then upon learning that this had happened the Corinthians would also be refreshed [Ed, EGT, HNTC]. The three men had refreshed the spirits of the Corinthians in that a happy relationship between Paul and the Corinthians was established [AB]. Paul anticipates the return of the three to Corinth and the good results that their good report to the congregation there will have on it [Alf, Gdt, ICC, NTC, TH]. They did this by making it possible for the congregation in Corinth to communicate with Paul through them. This refreshed the spirits of the congregation [Lns]. As they refreshed Paul in Ephesus, they had done this same kind of thing when they were at home in Corinth [NCBC, NIC2, NIGTC]. They may have done this by carrying out the mission of the congregation in Corinth [NIC, TG, TNTC]. The Corinthians were apprehensive about being wrongly represented to Paul. They would be relieved that their own delegation had reported the truth to him [Vn].

Therefore give-recognition-to[a] such-people.

LEXICON—a. pres. act. impera. of ἐπιγινώσκω (LN **31.27**) (BAGD 1.c. p. 291): 'to give recognition to' [AB, BAGD; NRSV], 'to recognize' [Herm, HNTC; NET], 'to give proper honor to' [NLT], 'to recognize the worth of' [NAB, TNT], 'to appreciate' [CEV, ISV, NJB], 'to acknowledge' [BAGD, LN, Lns, NTC; KJV], 'to show due recognition' [NIGTC]. This verb is also translated by its reciprocal with τοὺς τοιούτους 'such people' as the subject: 'deserve recognition' [NIV, REB], 'deserve notice' [TEV]. Ἐπιγινώσκω indicates that they should know these men and their qualities and then credit them with their true value [TNTC].

QUESTION—What relationship is indicated by οὖν 'therefore'?
It indicates a command grounded on the fact of their having refreshed Paul and the Corinthians [NIC2]: they have refreshed my spirit and yours *therefore* respect such people.

DISCOURSE UNIT: 16:19–24 [EGT, Gdt, ICC, NCBC, NIC, NIC2, NTC, TNTC; ISV, NIV, NLT]. The topic is salutations [Gdt], salutations, warning, and benediction [ICC], final greetings and benediction [NCBC], final greetings [EGT, NIC, NIC2, NTC, TNTC; ISV, NIV, NLT].

DISCOURSE UNIT: 16:19–20 [AB, Alf, Ed]. The topic is greetings from Asian churches and leaders [AB], salutations [Alf, Ed].

16:19 **The churches of Asia^a send-greetings-to^b you.**

LEXICON—a. Ἀσία (LN 93.415) (BAGD p. 116): 'Asia' [AB, BAGD, Herm, HNTC, LN, Lns, NIGTC; all versions except NIV, NLT, TEV]. The phrase τῆς Ἀσίας 'of Asia' is translated 'in the province of Asia' [NTC; NIV, TEV], 'here in the province of Asia' [NLT]. It refers to the Roman province of Asia [AB, BAGD, Ed, Herm, Ho, ICC, LN, NIC, NTC, Rb, TG, TNTC]. It is located in the western part of Asia Minor [BAGD, Gdt, Herm, NTC, TNTC]. It is the western section of Anatolia [AB]. It is in present-day Turkey [LN, TG]. Ephesus was the capital of Asia [Ed, Ho, ICC, TG, Vn]. The Roman procurator lived in Ephesus but it was not the capital of Asia [Herm]. The Asian churches included the seven churches mentioned in Revelation [AB, Ho].

b. pres. mid. (deponent = act.) indic. of ἀσπάζομαι (LN 33.20) (BAGD 1.a. p. 116): 'to send greetings' [BAGD, LN, NIGTC; NAB, NET, NIV, NJB, NRSV, TEV], 'to greet' [AB, BAGD, Herm, HNTC, LN, NTC; ISV, NLT, TNT], 'to salute' [Lns; KJV], 'to wish to be remembered' [BAGD]. This verb is also translated as an interjection: 'Greetings!' [CEV, REB]. Ἀσπάζομαι indicates 'to wish safety to' [Ho]. It literally means 'to embrace' [Lns].

Aquila and Prisca^a with the church in^b their house greet you much^c in (the) Lord.

TEXT—Instead of Πρίσκα 'Prisca' some manuscripts have Πρισκίλλα 'Priscilla'. GNT has Πρίσκα 'Prisca' and does not mention the alternative. The reading Πρισκίλλα 'Priscilla' is either taken by or so rendered by NTC; CEV, KJV, NIV, NLT and TEV. All other versions and commentaries have Πρίσκα 'Prisca' with GNT.

LEXICON—a. Πρίσκα (LN 93.302) (BAGD p. 701): 'Prisca' [AB, BAGD, Herm, HNTC, LN, Lns, NIGTC; ISV, NAB, NET, NJB, NRSV, REB, TNT], 'Priscilla' [BAGD, LN, NTC; CEV, KJV, NIV, NLT, TEV]. Πρισκίλλα 'Priscilla' is the diminutive form of Πρίσκα 'Prisca' [AB, ICC, Lns, TH, Vn].

b. κατά with accusative object (BAGD II.1.c. p. 406): 'in' [BAGD, Herm, Lns; ISV, NRSV, TNT], 'at' [AB]. This preposition is also translated as a

clause: 'that is in' [KJV], 'that meets in/at' [HNTC, NIGTC, NTC; CEV, NAB, NET, NIV, NJB, REB, TEV]. The early church met in homes. There were no separate buildings for Christian worship before the 3rd Century [Ed].
c. πολύς (See this word at 10:33 and 16:12): 'much' [Lns; KJV], 'heartily' [NTC; NLT], 'warmly' [ISV, NET, NIV, NRSV], not explicit [CEV]. Πολύς is an adjective meaning 'many' [Herm; REB], 'cordial' [NAB], 'warm' [TEV, TNT], 'best (wishes)' [NJB], 'hearty' [HNTC], 'special' [AB]. The use of πολύς in greetings indicates frequency or intensity or both [EGT]. It indicates loving earnestness [ICC]. This adverb implies that there was a close relationship between Prisca and Aquila and the Corinthians [Lns].

QUESTION—Who were Aquila and Prisca?

They were Jews [Ed, NIC2]. They had left Rome and went to Corinth because all Jews were expelled from Rome by Emperor Claudius in 49 AD [Ed, NTC]. While in Corinth Paul had stayed with them (see Acts 18:1-3) [NTC, Rb]. They were tent makers like Paul [Ed, NIC2, NTC]. The had risked their lives for Paul (see Romans 16:4) [EGT, NCBC, TNTC]. They had helped Paul to found the churches in Corinth and Ephesus [Gdt].

QUESTION—What is meant by the phrase ἐν κυρίῳ 'in (the) Lord'?

It means 'Christian' [Ho, NIC, TH, Vn]: Christian greetings. It is more than mere friendship. It conveys the sense of love for and service to Christ [EGT]. It indicates that both parties are in fellowship with Christ [ICC].

QUESTION—What is Paul trying to do by extending these greetings?

He is trying to make the Corinthians feel they are a part of a larger community of Christian believers [EGT, NIC2, NTC].

16:20 All the brothers^a greet you.

LEXICON—a. ἀδελφός (See this word at 10:1): 'brother' [AB, Herm, HNTC, LN, Lns, NTC; ISV, KJV, NAB, NIV, NJB, TNT], 'brother and sister' [NET, NRSV], 'believer' [TEV], 'the Lord's follower' [CEV], 'other believer' [NLT], 'brotherhood' [REB], 'fellow Christian' [NIGTC]. Ἀδελφός 'brother' indicates both 'brothers and sisters' [NTC]. It indicates 'fellow Christians' [TH].

QUESTION—To whom does οἱ ἀδελφοὶ πάντες 'all the brothers' refer?

It refers to all believers in the church at Ephesus [Alf, Ed, EGT, Gdt, ICC, Lns]. It refers to a larger group than those who made up the churches in Asia and who met at the house of Aquila and Prisca [TH]. It refers to Paul's fellow missionaries there in Ephesus [NCBC]. It refers to Paul's co-workers and traveling companions [NIC2]. It refers to Paul's friends at Ephesus [NIC]. It may either refer to the part of the church in Ephesus that did not meet at Aquila and Prisca's house or to the Corinthian brothers who had traveled to Ephesus [HNTC].

Greet each-other with (a) holy[a] kiss.[b]

LEXICON—a. ἅγιος (LN 88.24): 'holy' [AB, Herm, HNTC, LN, Lns, NIGTC, NTC; ISV, KJV, NAB, NET, NIV, NJB, NRSV, TNT], 'of peace' [REB, TEV], 'pure, divine' [LN], not explicit [CEV, NLT].

b. φίλημα (LN 34.62) (BAGD p. 859): 'kiss' [AB, BAGD, HNTC, LN, Lns, NIGTC, NTC; all versions except CEV, NJB, NLT]. The phrase ἐν φιλήματι ἁγίῳ 'with a holy kiss' is translated 'with the holy kiss' [Herm; NJB], 'in Christian love' [NLT], '(give each other) a warm greeting' [CEV].

QUESTION—What is meant by φίλημα 'kiss' here?

The 'kiss' was an embrace accompanied by a touching of the cheeks on left and right and possibly a touching of the lips to cheek [NTC]. It was given on the cheek or forehead [Lns, MNTC]. It was a form of greeting [AB, Alf, Ed, NIC2, TH, TNTC, Vn]. It was common or customary [ICC, NIC, NIC2, NTC, TNTC]. It was a visible sign of affection [AB, Ho, ICC, Lns, MNTC]. It was a sign of peace [Ed], fellowship [NIC2], unity [Lns, NIC], honor [Lns], mutual forgiveness [Ho]. It was used between persons of the same sex [MNTC, Rb, Vn]. It is referred to five times in the NT, here, at 1 Thessalonians 5:26, 2 Corinth 13:12, Romans 16:16 and 1 Pet 5:14 [NIC2]. If a kiss has a wrong connotation it is better to translate a more general form of greeting [TH].

QUESTION—What is meant by ἅγιος 'holy' in this context?

It means that this was a kiss that belonged to the saints, God's holy people [NIC2]. It means 'Christian' [Alf, Ed, TG]: a Christian kiss. It means a beauty, purity, and meaningfulness in the expression of Christian love [MNTC]. It means that it is consistent with Christian purity [Vn]. It means that it is fitting for God's people [TH]. It means that it was not a romantic kiss [Lns, NTC]. It means that it was done in the name of the Lord and in public meetings [NIC]. It means that this kiss fulfilled a purpose in the fellowship of Christians [AB].

DISCOURSE UNIT: 16:21–24 [AB, Alf, Ed, EGT, Ho]. The topic is Paul's personal greeting, monition, and benediction [AB], autograph conclusion [Alf], concluding warning and prayer [Ed], salutation written with Paul's own hand [Ho].

16:21 **The greeting[a] with my-own Paul's hand.[b]**

LEXICON—a. ἀσπασμός (LN 33.20) (BAGD 2. p. 117): 'greeting' [AB, BAGD, Herm, HNTC, NIGTC, NTC; ISV, NAB, NET, NIV, NJB, NLT, NRSV, REB], 'greetings' [Herm; TEV, TNT], 'salutation' [Lns; KJV], not explicit [CEV]. Ἀσπασμός here indicates written greetings [BAGD]. (NTC, ISV, NIV, NLT, NRSV, and TEV include some form of the verb 'to write' in their translations. NAB, NET, and TNT include the verb 'to send' in their versions. CEV includes the verb 'to sign' in its version.)

b. χείρ (LN 8.30) (BAGD 1. p. 880): 'hand' [AB, Herm, HNTC, LN, Lns, NIGTC; all versions except CEV, TNT], 'finger' [LN], 'handwriting'

[BAGD; TNT], not explicit [CEV]. The Corinthians must have recognized his handwriting [NIC, NTC].
QUESTION—What is implied by this verse?
It implies that Paul used a secretary to write the rest of this letter [AB, Alf, Ed, EGT, HNTC, ICC, Lns, MNTC, NIC, NIC2, NIGTC, Rb, TG, TH, TNTC].
QUESTION—What is the purpose of this action?
It functions to authenticate that the letter was really from Paul [Ed, EGT, Gdt, HNTC, Lns, MNTC, NIC, NIC2, NTC, TH, Vn]. This was a necessary procedure as seen in 2 Thessalonians 2:2 where someone may have impersonated Paul [Gdt, NIC2]. The reason he did this was probably because of those in the church who questioned his authority [NIC2]. In 2 Thessalonians 3:17 Paul called this his distinguishing mark that he included in all of his letters [TNTC].
QUESTION—What is the relationship of the genitive Παύλου 'of Paul' in the phrase τῇ ἐμῇ χειρί Παύλου 'in my own hand, Paul's'?
It functions to modify the words 'my own' [Alf, Ed, EGT, ICC, NTC, Rb]: in my own, Paul's, hand.
QUESTION—How much of the closing is written by Paul?
All of 16:21–24 may have been written by Paul [EGT, HNTC, Ho, ICC, Lns, MNTC, NIC2, TH].

16:22 **If anyone (does) not love^a the Lord, let-him-be accursed.^a**

TEXT—Instead of τὸν κύριον 'the Lord' some manuscripts have τὸν κύριον Ἰησοῦν Χριστόν 'the Lord Jesus Christ'. GNT reads τὸν κύριον 'the Lord' and does not mention this variant. The alternate reading is only taken by KJV.
LEXICON—a. pres. act. indic. of φιλέω (LN 25.33) (BAGD 1.a. p. 859): 'to love' [AB, BAGD, Herm, HNTC, LN, Lns, NIGTC, NTC; all versions except NET, NRSV], 'to have love for' [NET, NRSV], 'to have affection for' [BAGD, LN]. Φιλέω indicates personal affection for someone [Alf]. It indicates personal loyalty and devotion to a person [HNTC]. Lack of love for the Lord in this context means lack of obedience to him in such things as exalting human wisdom over the wisdom of the cross, tolerating incest, and attending idol feasts [NIC2].
   b. ἀνάθεμα (LN 33.473): 'accursed' [BAGD, Herm, NTC; NET, NRSV], 'cursed' [ISV, NLT], 'damned' [AB], '(a) curse (be on him)' [LN; NAB, NIV, NJB, TEV, TNT], 'outcast' [REB], 'anathema' [HNTC, Lns, NIGTC; KJV]. This clause plus εἴ τις 'if anyone' from the preceding clause is translated 'I pray that God will put a curse on everyone who' [CEV]. Ἀνάθεμα implies God's judgment [Herm, Lns, NIC]. It implies separation from God [HNTC]. It implies exclusion from Christian fellowship and destruction by God at the Second Coming of Christ [TH]. See this word also at 12:3.

QUESTION—What is meant by φιλέω 'to love'?
1. It is synonymous with ἀγαπάω and means 'to love' [AB, TH, TNTC; all versions]. The reason Paul chose this word instead of ἀγαπάω may have been because he had just used the term φίλημα 'kiss' in 16:20 [EGT, ICC, TH].
2. It contrasts with ἀγαπάω and means a lesser kind of love [Ed, EGT, Gdt, ICC, Lns, MNTC, NTC]. Φιλέω means natural affection while ἀγαπάω means Christian love [Ed]. Φιλέω means more tenderness and familiarity, the love of friendship, while ἀγαπάω means a kind of respect or reverence [Gdt]. Φιλέω means affection, liking, and personal attachment while ἀγαπάω means a deeper kind of love. Paul only requires that someone *like* the Lord [Lns]. All Paul requires is just the love of affection for the Lord, nothing higher [ICC, MNTC]. Φιλέω means tender affection while ἀγαπάω means supreme love [MNTC]. Φιλέω means affection while ἀγαπάω means true authentic spiritual love [NTC]. 'Not to love' means to be heartless toward Him [ICC]. 'Not to love' here means 'to hate' [Ed, EGT].

QUESTION—To whom does κύριος 'Lord' refer?
It refers to Christ [AB, Ed, HNTC, Ho, ICC, NTC, TG, TH, TNTC; KJV].

QUESTION—Who is the actor of the passive ἤτω ἀνάθεμα 'let him be accursed'?
The actor is God [Herm, TG, TH]: Let him be accursed by God.

Our Lord[a] come.[b]

LEXICON—a. μαρανα (LN **12.11**) (BAGD p. 491): 'our Lord' [AB, BAGD, **LN**, NIGTC; ISV, NET, NLT, NRSV, TEV], 'Lord' [REB], 'O Lord' [NAB, NIV, TNT], 'the Lord' [CEV]. (Herm, HNTC, Lns, NTC; KJV and NJB only transliterate this word. TEV and TNT both translate and transliterate them.) Μαρανα is an Aramaic word [BAGD, LN].

b. θα (LN **15.82**) (BAGD p. 491): 'to come' [AB, BAGD, **LN**, NIGTC; all versions except KJV, NJB]. (Herm, HNTC, Lns, NTC, KJV and NJB only transliterate this word. TEV and TNT both translate it and transliterate it.) Θα is an Aramaic word [BAGD, LN].

QUESTION—How should the Aramaic word Μαραναθα be parsed?
1. It should be parsed as Μαρανα θα in which the second word is taken as an imperative or optative [AB, BAGD, Gdt, Herm, HNTC, LN, MNTC, NCBC, NIC, NIC2, NTC, TG, TH, TNTC; all versions except NJB]: Our Lord, come! This interpretation is rendered as follows: 'Our Lord, come!' [BAGD, Gdt, HNTC, LN, MNTC, NCBC, NIC2, NTC, TH; NET, NLT, NRSV], '*Marana tha*—Our Lord, come!' [TEV], 'O Lord, come!' [NAB], 'And may the Lord come soon' [CEV], 'May our Lord come!' [ISV], 'Marana tha—Come, Lord!' [REB], 'Come, our Lord' [AB], 'Come, O Lord' [NIC; NIV], '*Marana tha*—Come, O Lord!' [TNT]. This interpretation is supported by the similar words of Revelation 22:20, 'Come, Lord Jesus!' [Gdt, Herm, NCBC, NIC, NTC]. The word ἔρχου

'come' of Revelation 20:22 is clearly a translation of μαραναθα [Herm]. This interpretation makes better sense in this context where Paul expresses the common desire of believers to welcome the Lord [HNTC].
2. It should be parsed as Μαραν αθα in which the second word is taken as an indicative [Ed, EGT, Ho, ICC, Rb, Vn; NJB]: Our Lord has come. This interpretation is rendered as follows: 'Our Lord has come' [Rb], 'Our Lord is come' [Alf, Ed], 'Our Lord comes' [Alf, EGT, Ho, ICC, Rb], 'The Lord comes' [Alf, Ho], 'Our Lord will come' [Ed, EGT], 'Our Lord is at hand' [EGT], *'Maran atha'* [NJB]. If the past tense is chosen, it is referring to a future event as though it had already occurred [Rb].
3. It can be either 1 or 2 [Lns]. Either 'Our Lord is come' or 'Lord, come!' makes sense. If the past tense is chosen, it is referring to a future event as though it had already occurred [Lns].

QUESTION—To whom does κύριος 'Lord' refer?

It refers to Christ [Ed, Ho, NCBC, NIC2, TNTC]. It refers to God [MNTC].

QUESTION—Why would Paul use Aramaic while writing to a largely Gentile church?

Certain words of Aramaic origin were brought into usage without translation. Words like *abba, hallelujah, amen, hosanna* and *maranatha* came to be used as part of Christian vocabulary [Lns, NCBC, NIC, NTC, TH, TNTC]. For an Aramaic term to be adopted by the Greek-speaking Christians, it must have expressed a meaning that was especially important [TNTC]. The fact that he used this term shows that his readers would have understood them [Vn]. The word μαραναθα must have been in common use among Christians at that time [Gdt, ICC, NCBC].

QUESTION—What is the function of Μαραναθα 'Our Lord, come!/Our Lord comes'?

It functions as a plea to the Lord to come and be present among his people [AB, TNTC]. It functions as an appeal to the Lord to come and purify his church [Gdt]. It functions as an appeal to the Lord that he come and judge those who reject him [MNTC, NIC, NTC]; this is seen in the fact that it follows a curse on those who reject the Lord [NTC]. It functions as a solemn warning to those who reject him that he comes as judge [Ho, ICC, Vn]. It functions both as an appeal to the Lord to come and as a warning to those who reject him [NIC2]. It functions to express the active hope that the Lord would come [Rb].

16:23 The grace[a] of-the Lord Jesus (be) with you.

TEXT—Instead of Ἰησοῦ 'Jesus' some manuscripts have Ἰησοῦ Χριστοῦ 'Jesus Christ'. GNT has Ἰησοῦ 'Jesus' and does not mention this alternative. Only Lns and KJV read Ἰησοῦ Χριστοῦ 'Jesus Christ'.

LEXICON—a. χάρις (BAGD 2.c. p. 877): 'grace' [AB, BAGD, Herm, HNTC, Lns, NIGTC, NTC; all versions except CEV, NAB], 'favor' [BAGD; NAB]. This noun is also translated as a verb: 'to be kind to' [CEV]. Χάρις indicates favor [Ho; NAB]. It indicates unmerited favor [Lns]. It

1 CORINTHIANS 16:23

indicates God's favor made possible through Jesus Christ [NIC2]. It indicates forgiving grace and Jesus' presence [NTC]. See this word also at 15:10.

QUESTION—How are the nouns related in the genitive construction ἡ χάρις τοῦ κυρίου Ἰησοῦ 'the grace of the Lord Jesus'?

The genitive indicates that Jesus is the source of the grace [Lns, NTC, Vn; CEV]: the grace that Jesus gives. He either gives the grace himself or does so in cooperation with God the Father [Vn].

QUESTION—Should the verb εἰμί 'to be' that is implied, be in the optative or indicative mood?

It should be in the optative mood [AB, Gdt, Herm, HNTC, ICC, Lns, NIC2, NTC; all versions]: May the grace of the Lord Jesus be with you.

16:24 My love[a] (be/is) with you all in Christ Jesus.

TEXT—Some manuscripts include ἀμήν 'amen' at the end of this verse. It is omitted by GNT with a B rating, indicating that the text is almost certain. It is included by NTC, CEV, KJV and NIV.

LEXICON—a. ἀγάπη (BAGD I.1.b.β. p. 5): 'love' [BAGD; all versions except CEV]. Here ἀγάπη indicates 'love for someone' [BAGD]. This noun is also translated as a verb: 'to love' [CEV]. See this word also at 13:1.

QUESTION—How are the nouns related in the genitive construction ἡ ἀγάπη μου 'my love'?

Paul is the one who loves [CEV]: I love everyone who belongs to Christ Jesus.

QUESTION—What form of the verb εἰμί 'to be' is to be supplied in this clause?

This is translated 'my love is with you all' [Herm, Lns, NTC; ISV, NJB], 'my love to you all' [HNTC; NAB, NIV, NLT, REB, TNT], 'my love be with you all' [AB; KJV, NET, NRSV, TEV], 'I love everyone' [CEV]. Two take the optative mood 'my love be with you all' and argue that this is a wish not a fact, since Paul's love is not with those who reject his message [EGT, ICC].

QUESTION—What do the words ἐν Χριστῷ Ἰησοῦ 'in Christ Jesus' modify?

1. They modify πάντων ὑμῶν 'you all' [TG; CEV]: you all who are in Christ Jesus.
2. They modify ἡ ἀγάπη μου 'my love' [AB, EGT, Ho, ICC, Lns, NIC, TNTC, Vn]: my love that is in Christ Jesus. Paul's love was Christlike and not merely human [Vn]. The source of Paul's love was God's spirit and was given to him through Jesus Christ [AB]. It indicates Paul's Christian love [Ho]. Paul's love has its being in Christ Jesus [Lns].
3. They modify the whole sentence [HNTC, NIC2, NTC, TH]: In Christ Jesus may my love be with you all. While Paul writes to all who are in Christ, Paul wants to assure them that his love is genuinely spiritual in the Lord [NTC].

QUESTION—What is indicated by ἐν 'in'?

It indicates 'in union with' [TG]: all who live in union with Christ Jesus. It indicates 'belong to' [CEV]: all who belong to Christ Jesus.

www.ingramcontent.com/pod-product-compliance
Lightning Source LLC
Chambersburg PA
CBHW072119290426
44111CB00012B/1704